USHER iBT TOEFL
FINAL TEST
LISTENING

어셔 iBT 토플 파이널 테스트
리스닝

어셔 어학 연구소

USHER iBT TOEFL
FINAL TEST
LISTENING
어셔 iBT 토플 리스닝

초판 1쇄 발행· 2013년 9월 1일
개정증보판 1쇄 발행· 2019년 9월 1일
개정증보판 2쇄 발행· 2024년 11월 1일

지은이· 어셔토플연구소
펴낸곳· (주)어셔 어학연구소
펴낸이· 어셔 어학연구소
주 소· 서울시 서초구 잠원로 3길 40 태남빌딩 2층 어셔어학원
전 화· 02) 595-5679
홈페이지· www.usher.co.kr
ISBN· 979-11-85317-05-02

정 가· 25,000원

저작권자· ⓒ2016, 어셔 어학연구소

이 책 및 mp3 내용의 저작권은 저자에게 있습니다.
서면에 의한 저자와 출판사의 허락없이 내용의 일부 혹은 전부를 인용하거나, 발췌하는 것을 금합니다.
COPYRIGHT ⓒ 2016 by Usher Language Research Institute
All rights reserved including the rights of reproduction In whole or part in any form Printed in Korea

본 토플 교재는 iBT 토플 리스닝 영역에서 고득점을 얻길 원하는 학습자들을 위해 마무리 실전서로 출간된 책입니다.

■ 최신 iBT 토플 시험 경향 반영

과거 토플 형태인 PBT와 CBT를 거쳐 국내에서 2006년 9월 처음 시행된 iBT 형태의 토플 시험은 그동안 많은 변화를 보여왔습니다. 하지만 시중에는 여전히 iBT 토플 시험이 모습을 드러내기 전 시험 주관사인 ETS의 시험 방향 발표만을 듣고 만들거나 토플 시험 시행 후 어느정도 윤곽을 잡은 뒤 만들어낸 초기 형태의 문제지들을 세월이 지남에 따라 조금씩 개정하여 판매하는 경우가 많습니다. 그러나 안타깝게도 이 토플 책들은 최근 3년 사이에 크게 변화된 ETS의 출제 경향의 흐름을 읽지 못하고 그것을 반영하지 못한 부분이 많기에 최근 추세에 따른 문제지를 제작하게 되었습니다. 「USHER iBT TOEFL **FINAL TEST LISTENING**」의 문제들은 최신 토플 시험 경향이 반영되어 여러분은 실제와 동일한 수준의 문제들을 그대로 경험하며 실전 감각을 익힐 수 있을 것입니다.

■ 토플 리스닝 고득점 취득을 위한 최상의 난이도

iBT 토플 리스닝 시험의 최근 변화 중 가장 큰 부분은 들려주는 시험 내용의 수준과 문제 난이도의 향상입니다. 과거 iBT 토플 시험은 내용이 단순한 형태이었으나, 최근의 토플 리스닝의 주제 및 내용들은 대학에서 다뤄지는 여러 학문 분야의 전문적인 내용들을 포함하고 있기 때문에 대충 듣고 내용을 추측해서 접근하면 틀리게끔 구성되어 있습니다. 또한 문제 역시 과거의 문제들은 짧은 강의 내용을 듣고 핵심 내용만 이해하면, 문제의 답이 쉽게 구별되었습니다. 그러나 최근의 iBT 토플 시험은 답 중에서 본문에 분명 정확하게 나왔던 내용이더라도 질문이 원하는 답이 아니면 정답으로 처리되지 않고 있으며, 보기의 한 단어나 일부분을 틀리게 하고 나머지 부분을 정답과 유사하게 만들어 수험자에게 혼란을 주는 경우가 늘어났습니다. 또한 표면적인 내용이 아닌 말 속에 숨어 있는 의도나 뉘앙스를 파악 하는 추론 문제도 예전보다 많이 등장하고 있습니다. 본 토플 리스닝 교재에서는 이런 부분들을 포함하여 과거의 문 제들과는 다른 차이점들을 성실히 반영하였습니다. 토플 시험에서 고득점을 원하는 학생들은 실제 시험과 가장 유 사한 최상의 난이도를 가진 문제지를 원하는 경우가 많기에, 본 교재인 「USHER iBT TOEFL **FINAL TEST LISTENING**」은 그 요구에 걸맞는 난이도로 제작되었습니다. '해설지'에서는 그러한 지문과 문제 하나하나에 대해 학습자가 정답과 오답의 이유를 논리적으로 이해할 수 있게 풀어냈습니다. 따라서 수험생들은 본 토플 교재를 통해 최상위 난 이도에 맞는 영어 실력 향상을 꾀할 수 있으며 이는 토플 고득점이라는 결과로 이어질 것입니다.

■독학용으로도 유용한 교재(토플학원에 다니지 못하는 학생을 위한 추천 교재)

토플학원에 다니지 않고 혼자서 토플 리스닝 시험을 준비하는 학생들이 가장 힘들어 하는 부분이, 해설지에서 문제의 답에 대한 설명을 보통 정답만 표시해 놓았거나, 별로 도움이 되지 않는 정답 이유만을 간략히 적고 끝나는 경우가 많다는 것입니다. 이에, 본 교재는 토플 어학원에 다니지 않고 혼자 토플 공부하는 학생들을 위해, 정답이 되는 부분에 대한 설명은 물론이고 오답이 되는 이유까지 구체적으로 설명해 두었습니다. 먼저 학습자가 스스로 문제를 분석한 뒤, 이 부분을 참고하여 공부하면 문제의 출제의도와 정답을 유추하는 능력을 향상시키는데 더욱 효과적일 것입니다. 또한, 모든 시험 문제들이 그렇듯이 ETS가 낸 토플 문제에도 반드시 오답 패턴이 있기에 이런 부분을 집중 분석하였고, 수험자들이 자신의 취약점을 파악하고 정리하여 같은 실수를 반복하지 않게 문제해결력을 키울 수 있도록 하였습니다.

■2019년 8월 바뀐 뉴토플에서 리스닝 파트는 1회 테스트를 구성하는 두개의 셋

(* 1개 세트는 conversation 1개, Lecture 2개이므로,

뉴토플 이전 테스트 1회는

세트 1 conversation 1개, Lecture 2

세트 2 conversation 1개, Lecture 2 로 구성되어있었으나

2019년 8월에 새롭게 바뀐 뉴토플에서는,
문제 길이, 문제 구성, 문제 난이도 모두 동일하게 유지한채

두번째 세트에서 Lecture 1개만 나오는 형태로 바뀜으로서, 즉,

테스트 1회는

세트 1 conversation 1개, Lecture 2

세트 2 conversation 1개 만으로 바뀌었을 뿐입니다.

하지만, 본 교재는, 학생들이 리스닝 시험에서 가장 힘들어 하는 부분중 하나가, 리딩 시험 3지문을 풀고 집중력이 떨어진 상태에서, 리스닝 시험을 볼때도, 집중력 유지가 필수이므로, 사라진 두번째 세트의 두번째 렉처를 본 교재에 부록으로 수록해 둠으로서, 시험장에서의 집중력 유지를 강화 하고자 합니다.

「USHER iBT TOEFL **FINAL TEST LISTENING**」이 여러분의 꿈을 향한 과정 속에 함께하는 동반자가 될 수 있기를 바랍니다.

어셔 어학연구소

TABLE OF CONTENTS

USHER iBT TOEFL LISTENING
어셔 iBT 토플 리스닝

Introduction

	학생들이 자주하는 질문 Q&A	06
1	뉴 토플에 관하여	14
2	iBT TOEFL (iBT 토플) 시험 소개	15
3	iBT TOEFL Listening 소개	17
4	Listening Section 평가기준	21
5	본 iBT 토플 교재만의 특징	24
6	본 iBT 토플 교재의 구성	26
7	실력별 학습계획	30
8	Listening Strategies	
	1. 리스닝 학습 순서 및 방법	32
	2. 문제 분석 방법	38

문제 PART

TOEFL TEST 01
Set 1   50
Set 2   58

TOEFL TEST 02
Set 1   68
Set 2   76

TOEFL TEST 03
Set 1   86
Set 2   94

TOEFL TEST 04
Set 1   104
Set 2   112

답지   **121**
Note Taking   **139**
단어·구문   **189**
구문외우고·열번읽기   **239**
스터디 준비자료   **265**

해설 PART

TOEFL TEST 01
Set 1-1 Conversation   292
Implication of Bioluminescence
Set 1-2 Lecture 1   298
Type of Renaissance Gardens
Set 1-3 Lecture 2   304
Einstein's Theory of Relativity
Set 2-1 Conversation   310
Student's Opposition to Renovation
Set 2-2 Lecture 1   314
The Space Elevator Technology
***부록 Set 2-3 Lecture 2**   320
Investigation of Easter Island

TOEFL TEST 02
Set 1-1 Conversation   328
Biology Research Plan
Set 1-2 Lecture 1   332
Mysteries of the Egyptian Pyramid
Set 1-3 Lecture 2   338
Coral Reef Destructuion
Set 2-1 Conversation   344
Whale Breathing Patterns
Set 2-2 Lecture 1   348
Horse Domestication of Botai Peolple
***부록 Set 2-3 Lecture 2**   354
Biofuel Production Process

TOEFL TEST 03
Set 1-1 Conversation   362
Community Service at Museum
Set 1-2 Lecture 1   366
Architectural Acoustics
Set 1-3 Lecture 2   372
Disappearance of Anasazi People
Set 2-1 Conversation   378
Psychological Impact of Music
Set 2-2 Lecture 1   384
Invention of Electric Guitar
***부록 Set 2-3 Lecture 2**   392
Examination on Ball Lightning

TOEFL TEST 04
Set 1-1 Conversation   400
Tutoring
Set 1-2 Lecture 1   404
Global Temperatures
Set 1-3 Lecture 2   410
Monochromatic Sculptures
Set 2-1 Conversation   416
19th century Female artist
Set 2-2 Lecture 1   420
Light Energy
***부록 Set 2-3 Lecture 2**   426
Human Personality

별도 구매 서비스 소개   432

■ 학생들이 자주하는 질문 Q&A

1. 왜 청취 부분 점수가 잘 안 나오는 걸까요? LC 공부는 어떻게 해야 하는지 감이 잘 안 잡혀요.

TOEFL Listening Section에서 고득점을 받지 못하는 이유는 다음 6가지 경우에 해당됩니다. 학습자의 영어 실력에 따라 한 가지가 부족할 수도 있고, 여러 가지 이유가 복합적으로 섞여 있을 수도 있습니다.

    A) 단어를 모르는 경우,
    B) 영어 소리(발음)가 익숙치 않은 경우
    C) 문장이 잘 이해되지 않는 경우
    D) 논리적 사고력이 부족한 경우
    E) 문제스타일에 적응하지 못한 경우

이에 대한 청취 전략은 다음과 같습니다

(A) 단어를 모르는 경우

Spelling을 보았을 때는 아는 단어이지만 소리를 들었을 때 선뜻 의미가 생각나지 않는다면 리스닝에 있어서는 전혀 모르는 단어입니다. 이는 **머리 속에 단어의 글자와 의미만 있을 뿐 소리가 전혀 저장되어있지 않은 상태**이기 때문입니다. 많은 학생들이 딕테이션을 해보면 의외로 쉬운 단어들을 못 쓰곤 하는데, 그건 단어의 스펠링과 뜻은 머리속에 저장되어 있는데 발음 부분은 전혀 저장되어 있지 않거나 혹은 엉뚱한 소리로 저장되어 있어, native speaker의 발음을 들었을 때 빠르게 머리 속 에 떠오르지 않기 때문이죠. 따라서 기존의 아는 단어라도 원어민 발음이 전혀 다른 경우가 많으므로 본인의 기억하고 있는 한국식 소리를 수정해야 들립니다. 방법은 전자사전이나 인터넷 사전에서 단어를 찾아 발음을 듣고 여러 번 따라 말해보는 것인데, 새로운 단어를 암기할 때에도 꼭 발음을 함께 기억하는 것이 중요합니다. 이렇게 정확하게 소리를 저장하고 발음하면 Speaking 시험에서도 효과를 볼 수 있습니다.

(B) 영어 소리(발음) 자체에 익숙치 않은 경우

리듬 언어인 영어는 이어져서 나는 소리가 많고, 강세 단어들은 소리가 높고 길고 강하게, 약세단어들은 뭉치거나 축약되어 낮고 약하고 빠르게 발음됩니다. 그래서 모든 음절을 또박또박 발음하는 한국어에 익숙한 학생들은, 이러한 영어 소리의 특징을 알지 못하기 때문에, 청취가 잘 안되어 힘들어 하는 경우가 많죠. 해결책은 **못들은 부분을 중점적으로 Shadowing하면서 발음을 여러 번 듣고 따라 하면서 외우는 것입니다. 이때 강세와 연음 부분에 특히 신경을 쓰면서 말해봅니다.** 따라하기 어려운 소리나 문장은 따로 노트에 정리하여 틈나는 대로 연습하는 것도 도움이 됩니다. 중요한 건 **원어민의 실제 발음, 억양, 말하는 속도**에 익숙해지는 것이므로 Shadowing을 할 때 이 부분들을 똑같이 흉내 내면서 연습하셔야 합니다.

(C) 문장이 잘 이해되지 않는 경우

단어는 하나씩 잘 들리지만, 문장이나 단락의 내용 이해가 안되는 경우가 있습니다. 보통 학생들이 듣고 이해하지 못하는 것을 걱정하는데, 기초적인 독해조차 안되기 때문에 내용을 들어도 무슨 말인지 파악하지 못하는 경우를 의외로 많이 봅니다. 만약 Reading Section에서 20점대 점수가 나온다면, 청취훈련을 통해 영어소리의 특징에 익숙해지면 소리가 잘 들리게 되어 리스닝 점수도 곧 상승합니다. 하지만 독해 점수가 낮은 학생들은 청취 훈련과 더불어 문장을 글로 봤을 때 빠르고 정확하게 이해하는 훈련도 병행해야 빠른 효과를 볼 수 있습니다.
Native Speaker가 말하는 내용을 단어로만 이해하고 구나 문장의 의미를 통으로 이해하지 못하는 경우, 첫째는 영어와 우리말이 어순이 다르기 때문에 원어민이 말하는 속도에 비해 한국인이 들으며 바로 이해하는 속도가 늦어지게 되어 발생합니다. 이를 극복하기 위해서는 **문장을 의미단위로 끊어서 들으며 순차해석하는 연습**을 꾸준히 해야 합니다. 문장을 개별적인 단어가 아닌 의미를 이루는 덩어리로 이해하면, 머리 속에서 처리속도가 빨라지기 때문에 원어민이 말하는 속도가 부담스럽지 않습니다. 예를 들어, '아버지가 방에 들어가서 가방을 들고 나오신다' 라는 문장을 본 한국인들은 초등학교 저학년이 아닌 이상 단어를 하나씩 파악하지는 않습니다. 그보다는 '아버지가 방에 들어가서, '가방을 들고 나오신다' 처럼 2개의 의미 덩어리로 이해하죠. 이 문장을 소리로 들어도 처리방식은 같을 것입니다. 그렇기 때문에 뉴스나 강의 같은 긴 문장이나 여러 가지 내용을 한국어로 오래 들어도 뇌가 피곤하지 않은 것입니다. 이를 영어에 대입하면, 한국 학생들이 어느 정도 자신이 있는 부분이 독해이기 때문에, 리스닝 스크립트를 가지고 직독직해가 빠르게 안 되는 사람은 귀를 뚫겠다고 소리를 아무리 많이 들어도 효과를 보기 힘듭니다. 그냥 단어들만 하나씩 알아들을 뿐이죠. 여러 개의 단어가 모여 다른 의미를 이루는 구어체 표현이나 문장들은 전혀 이해되지 않습니다. 따라서 Reading 부분의 지문을 해석할 때나 Listening의 스크립트를 해석할 때 낱개의 단어가 아닌 의미덩어리로 묶은 뒤 영어어순에 맞춰 이해해나가는 습관을 기르셔야 합니다. 이 때 영어어순에 따라 이해한다 함은 영어문장을 읽을 때 우리말로 완전한 문장을 만들거나 뒤에서부터 해석해오지 않고, 순차적으로 뜻만 생각하면서 빠르게 읽는 훈련을 하는 것입니다. 즉, 한 나라의 말을 다른 나라 말로 매끄럽게 옮기는 Translation(번역)이 아닌 읽는 문장의 내용이 무슨 뜻인지만 알면 되는 Comprehension(이해)을 연습하는 것이지요.

둘째, 특정 문장 구조가 안 들리는 경우인데, 이것은 그 문장의 구조가 익숙히 않기 때문입니다. 따라서 **해당 문장 구조 (예: 가정법, 사역동사, 등..)를 가진 예문**을 3개 이상 찾아 말하면서 외우면, 틀은 똑같고 단어만 바뀌어 나오므로 나중에 그 문장을 들었을 때 한번에 이해할 수 있게 됩니다. 단, 단순히 글로 암기하면 전혀 소용이 없고, 꼭 소리로 원어민의 속도와 똑같이 따라 발음해 보아야 합니다.

(D) 논리적 사고력이 부족한 경우

모든 소리가 잘 들리고 내용도 정확하게 이해했는데 문제를 풀면 계속 틀리는 경우는, 청취력의 문제라기보다는 대화나 강의의 Topic이 익숙치 않아 핵심내용을 빠르게 파악하지 못하거나, 글의 전개방식을 논리적으로 따라잡지 못해 발생합니다. 낯설거나 어렵게 느껴지는 주제를 담고 있는 내용들은 문제를 풀고 스크립트를 통해 내용을 확인한 뒤, 안 들리는 부분들을 골라 딕테이션과 섀도잉을 활용해 다시 한번 내용을 듣고 이해하는 습관을 기르셔야 합니다. 이때 그 분야에서 필수적으로 알아두어야 할 단어(word)나 어구(phrase)들을 꾸준히 외우는 작업 또한 병행하셔야 합니다.

또한 자신이 취약한 분야의 토픽(Topic)과 핵심어(Keyword)에 대한 배경지식을 꾸준히 습득하는 것이 필요합니다. 관련지식을 많이 알고 있을수록 들리는 내용도 많아지고 문제에 대한 감을 잡기가 쉽기 때문이죠. 이런 식으로 본인이 약하다고 생각되는 분야에 관련된 어휘, 문장, 배경지식을 많이 쌓아나가면, 내용에 대한 이해가 많아지면서 청취력에 큰 도움이 됩니다.

이와 더불어, Lecture의 경우 흐름이나 전개방식을 이해하는 것도 도움이 됩니다. 하나의 주제를 설명하는 방식은 논리적인 순서가 있기 때문에 이 흐름을 파악하게 되면, 들으면서 중요한 부분을 골라낼 수 있고 문제가 나오는 부분까지 예측하게 되는 것이죠. 이것은 Summary 훈련을 통하여 향상시킬 수 있는데, 강의의 내용파악 및 문제분석을 다 끝내고 완벽히 이해 한 상태에서, 본인이 종이에 요약을 하는 것입니다. 마치 중고등학생 시절에 중간·기말 고사를 앞두고 시험범위에 해당하는 내용을 핵심내용만 간추려 간략하게 정리하는 것처럼요. 이렇게 하면, 내용에 대한 이해가 확실해지면서, 보이지 않는 전체 골격을 파악하게 되고, 각 단락의 핵심이 뭔지 강의 전체에서 교수가 전달하고자 주제가 뭔지 금방 알게 됩니다. 결국 이것들이 문제를 통해 물어보는 사항들이므로, 청취를 하면서도 어떤 부분이 중요하고 문제가 어떻게 나올지 미리 예상할 수 있게 되는 것이지요. 또한 Summary는 문제를 처음 풀 때 기록했던 Note-taking과 비교해 보면, 본인이 내용을 들으면서 어떤 부분을 놓쳤는지 쉽게 알 수 있어 청취력 향상에도 도움이 많이 됩니다. Summary 샘플은 뒷장 P.32를 참조하세요.

■ 학생들이 자주하는 질문 Q&A

(E) 문제스타일에 적응하지 못한 경우

청취력도 훌륭하고 대화나 강의의 내용도 정확하게 이해했는데 예상외로 고득점이 안 나오거나 만점을 받지 못하는 경우가 있습니다. 주로 외국에서 공부하는 학생들이 이에 해당되는데요. 특히 학생들이 많이 틀리는 Main Idea, Inference(다시 들려주고 푸는 문제, Purpose/Intention, Imply, Opinion/Attitude) 문제 등은, 단순히 들었던 내용을 제대로 기억하는지 묻는 차원이 아닌 들은 내용을 바탕으로 문제의 출제 알맞는 정답을 고르는 것이기 때문에 논리적 사고력과 추론 능력이 필요 합니다. 따라서, 이에 대한 처방은 본인이 **자주 틀리는 문제 유형과 출제의도를 정확히 분석한 후, 비슷한 문제를 반복하여 풀어봄으로써 정답을 골라내는 감을 기르는 것이 중요**합니다. **또한 LC 특유의 문제 풀이 유형을 충분히 숙지하고 있는지도 확인**해야 합니다. 모든 소리가 다 잘 들리고 내용도 정확하게 이해했는데 문제를 풀면 계속 틀리는 경우는, 청취력의 문제라기보다는 문제해결능력 부분을 향상시켜야 하는 경우가 대부분입니다. 이 때 **도움이 되는 것이 오답노트 정리**인데요. 틀린 문제를 계속 정리하다 보면, 문제를 낸 출제자의 의도, 문제에서 반복적으로 보이는 오답 패턴, 본인이 그 동안 잘 모르고 저질렀던 반복적인 실수 등이 파악되어 문제해결능력의 완성도를 높일 수 있는 길이 보일 것입니다. 본서에는 학습자들이 활용할 수 있도록 '오답정리표' 를 각 테스트마다 제공하고 있습니다.

2. 효과적인 점수대별 학습 방법은 뭔가요?

시험점수 : 25점 이상~

이 점수대를 받는 학습자는 리스닝 실력이 '상' 단계로서, 청취력이 웬만큼 갖춰져 있다고 판단됩니다. Listening Section에서 고득점을 쟁취할 수 있는 비결은 두 가지 입니다. 첫째, 본인의 청취력 중 부족한 부분을 지속적으로 보충해 주셔야 합니다. 아무리 일반적인 영어청취가 뛰어나다 하더라도, 토플은 학문적인 내용들을 담고 있기 때문에, 본인이 취약한 분야나 토픽(Topic)이 있기 마련입니다. 따라서 대화와 강의의 음성파일을 듣고 내용 이해가 얼마나 정확하게 되고 있는지를 판단하고, 본인의 단어 실력이나 문장 표현에 대한 이해 등 어휘력이 어느 정도인지를 꼼꼼히 따져, 부족한 부분을 지속적으로 채워야 시험에 맞는 청취 실력으로 발전될 수 있습니다. 안들리는 부분은 스크립트(script)에 표시한 후, MP3 파일을 이용하여 딕테이션(Dictation)과 새도잉(Shadowing)을 하면서 그 부분을 자신의 것으로 습득해 나가야 합니다. 또한 자신에게 낯선 토픽에 대한 배경지식을 인터넷을 통해 찾아보며 관련지식을 쌓아나가다 보면, 내용에 대한 이해가 많아지면서 청취력에 큰 도움이 됩니다. 둘째, 토플 LC 특유의 문제를 해결할 수 있는 문제풀이 능력을 향상시켜야 합니다. 오답노트 정리를 통하여 본인이 자주 틀리는 문제의 유형을 정확히 분석하고, 또한 비슷한 문제들을 계속 풀어봄으로써 토플 문제의 스타일에 익숙 해지는 것이 중요합니다.

시험점수 : 20~25점대

리스닝 실력이 '중상' 단계로써 대화 및 강의의 전반적인 내용이 어느 정도 들리는 상태입니다. 이 단계는 정확한 청취력을 위해 연음, 속도, 의미덩어리 등 소리를 좀더 정확하게 잡아내는 연습을 꾸준히 해야 합니다. 그리고 각 문제 유형을 정확히 파악한 후 본인이 취약한 부분을 꼼꼼히 분석함과 동시에 논리적 이해력을 지속적으로 키워나갈 필요가 있습니다. 또한 강 의를 들으며 세부사항을 명확하고 간략하게 효과적으로 Note-taking하는 훈련을 지속하여, 핵심 내용을 빠트리지 않고 잡아 내는 연습도 필요합니다. Inference 및 Purpose 와 같이 단순히 들은 내용을 기억하여 푸는 문제가 아닌, 추론을 통하여 답을 골라야 하는 난이도가 꽤 있는 문제유형들을 자주 다뤄보는 것도 도움이 됩니다. 특히 본인이 틀린 문제는 반드시 그 이유를 확인하고 실수를 줄여나가는 것이 중요합니다.

시험점수 : 15~19점대

'중' 단계의 리스닝 실력을 지닌 이 점수대의 학생들은 청취를 할 때 기본적인 맥락(outline)은 이해하나, 세부사항의 구체적인 내용을 놓치거나 잘못 이해하는 경향이 있습니다. 이때는 집중적인 영어 청취 및 문장 따라 하기를 통해 내용을 좀 더 명확하게 이해하는데 초점을 맞추는 청취력 향상에 주력하는 것이 좋습니다. 또한 리스닝의 각 문제 유형을 파악하여 ETS의 문제 스타일에 익숙해지는 것이 중요합니다. 문제를 분석할 때는 항상 스크립트에서 정답의 근거를 찾아 확인하는 습관을 가지고, 오답의 이유와 패턴을 파악하는 것도 많은 도움이 됩니다. 먼저 상대적으로 득점하기 쉬운 Conversation 먼저 공략하여 기본 점수를 획득하는 것이 좋으며, Lecture에서는 Main Idea 및 Detail 과 관련된 내용을 정확히 듣고 답을 골라 내는 것과 Purpose & Attitude(화자의 의도 및 태도)를 파악하는 훈련을 꾸준히 해 나갈 필요가 있습니다.

시험점수 : ~14점대

토플 시험을 전혀 접해보지 못했거나 영어 리스닝 자체가 잘 안되는 학생은 가장 우선적으로 청취력을 키워야 합니다. 토플리스닝 시험은 말그대로 Listening Comprehension을 측정하는 시험으로, 영어를 알아듣는 부분과 내용을 논리적으로 이해하는 사고력 부분을 동시에 평가합니다. 따라서 기본적인 영어 청취가 안된다면 토플 리스닝 시험에 접근 자체가 불가능하게 됩니다. 이 점수대의 학생은 LC에 자주 나오는 단어와 표현들, 영어 문장들을 들으며 지속적으로 청취력 향상에 힘을 쓰면서, 기본적인 유형의 토플 시험을 풀어보는것이 도움이 됩니다. 그리고 상대적으로 점수를 확보하기 쉬운 Conversation을 먼저 공략하시기를 추천하며, 자세한 청취력 향상 방법은 이 책의 뒷장에 있는 P.35 '청취력 향상 훈련 방법' 을 참고하시기 바랍니다.

3. 예전에 토플 시험을 본적이 있는데요. 요즘 시험은 Listening section이 훨씬 어려워진 것 같아요. 어떤 차이가 있는 건가요?

TOEFL(Test of English as a Foreign Language)이란 주로 영어권 국가에서 대학교 이상 수준의 학문을 공부하려는 외국인 학생의 영어실력을 평가하기 위하여 만들어진 시험입니다. 현재 TOEFL은 iBT(internet-Based Test) TOEFL이라 불 리며, PBT(Paper-based Test)와 CBT(Computer-Based Test)를 거쳐 채택된 3세대 방식으로 읽기, 듣기, 말하기, 쓰 기 등 다양한 분야의 영어실력을 평가하기 때문에 현재 세계적으로 가장 공신력있는 영어시험으로 자리 잡았죠. 현재 치뤄 지고 있는 iBT Test는 처음 시행된 2006년 9월 이후에, 많은 변화를 거쳐왔고, LC도 다른 영역과 마찬가지로 많은 진화를 거듭하여 현재에 이르렀는데요. 우선 눈에 띄는 점은 들려주는 내용의 길이가 전반적으로 길어졌고, Native speaker의 말하는 속도도 점점 빨라지고 어투나 표현도 실제상황처럼 자연스러워졌다는 것입니다. 또한 Listening 영역은 크게 대화 (Conversaton)와 강의(Lecture)로 구성되어 있는데, 이들의 주제가 예전에 비해 다양해지고 내용도 심화되고 있는 추세입니다. 문제도 예전과 달리 정답이 2개, 3개를 골라야 하는 문제도 자주 출제되고 있으며, 주제를 묻는 문제에 대한 정답을 고르는 문제가 어려워지고, 화자의 의도 및 태도를 묻는 등 추론형 문제 유형도 계속 증가하고 있습니다.

이처럼 청취력 위주의 영어 듣기 실력을 평가했던 과거의 시험 문제와 달리, 요즘은 내용을 정확하게 이해하는 고도의 청취력 뿐만 아니라, 내용 이면에 숨겨진 의도를 파악하는 분석력과 추론력, 흩어진 정보들을 모아 합성하는 통합적 사고력 등을 요구하는 문제들이 증가하고 있기 때문에 학생들이 예전에 비해 더 어렵다고 느끼고 있습니다.

■ 학생들이 자주하는 질문 Q&A

4. 효과적인 Note-taking 방법은 무엇인지 알려주세요.

리스닝을 하다 보면 짧지 않은 길이인 강의 내용을 모두 기억하기가 쉽지 않습니다. 이때는 청취를 하면서 도중에 중요하다고 판단되는 내용을 note-taking하면, 추후 문제를 풀 때 참고할 수 있으므로 도움이 됩니다. 그러나 대학교 수준의 전문적 인 내용을 모국어가 아닌 외국어로 들으며 동시에 글을 쓴다는 것은 생각보다 쉽지 않은 일인데다, 완전히 청취에만 의존해 서 듣게 되면 나중에 내용들이 혼란이 오기 때문에, 불안한 학생들은 어떻게 하면 노트테이킹을 잘 할 수 있는지 질문을 많이 합니다.

Note-taking은 말 그대로 '메모' 입니다. 한국어로 진행되는 강의를 교수님으로부터 들으며 메모를 한다고 생각해보세요. 여러분은 무엇을 적으려고 할까요? 당연히 중요하다고 판단되는 내용들을 간략하게 핵심단어 위주로 적을 것입니다. 손이 아무리 빨라도 말의 모든 내용을 다 적을 수 없기 때문에, 듣는 도중에 기억하기 힘든 용어(사람 이름, 지명, 전문 용어 등), 순서나 과정, 특징을 나타내는 단어 위주로 간략하게 적겠죠. 영어로 들으면서 하는 노트테이킹(Note-taking)도 이와 크게 다르지 않습니다. 핵심이 되는 내용을 본인이 알아보기 쉽게 간략하고 명료하게 적는 것이 효과적인 노트테이킹의 비결이죠. 이를 위해서는 평소에 자주 쓰이는 표현을 약자나 기호 등을 활용하여 받아쓰는 연습을 하는 것이 도움이 됩니다. 자세한 내용은 뒷장의 P.34 '효과적인 Note-taking방법' 을 참조하세요

5. 전 해외에서 유학하고 있는 학생인데요. 청취를 하면 내용은 이해가 잘 되는데, 문제를 풀면 많이 틀립니다. 뭐가 문제일까요?

첫째, 본인의 청취력 부분을 점검해 보셔야 합니다. 정말 내용이 완벽하게 이해가 되는 건지, 아니면 이해가 된다고 착각하 는 것인지 스스로 의문해 보세요. 후자의 경우라면 정확한 이해가 아닌 거죠. 아니면 단어는 들리지만, 단어로 구성되는 문 장이나, 그 문장들로 이뤄진 문단의 핵심내용이 이해가 안 되는 거죠. 들리는대로 다 이해하는데 문제가 풀리지 않는다는 건 상식적으로 말이 맞지 않는 부분이잖아요?^^ 대화내용에 대해서만 들릴 뿐, Lecture 부분에서 이해가 되지 않아 들리지 않 을 수도 있고, 아니면 Lecture 내용이 문장 하나씩은 들리지만, 전체 내용이 가리키는 핵심 내용이 뭔지 정확히 잡아내지 못할 수도 있죠. 해외에서 있었다고 해서 모든 영어를 다 잘 듣지는 않습니다. 한국 사람들이 한국의 모든 말들을 다 이해하 지 못하는 것과 마찬가지입니다. 한국어를 모국어로 쓰는 학생들 모두가 수능시험 언어영역에서 만점을 받지는 못하잖아요. 토플 Listening은 영어로 보는 언어영역 시험이라고 생각하시면 됩니다. 이런 수준의 시험에서는 단순히 청취력 뿐만이 아 닌 분석력, 논리력, 통합 이해력, 순간 판단력도 필요합니다.

둘째, 해외에서 살다 온 학생들이 약한 부분이 바로 문법과 어휘입니다. 단어를 강제로 외웠거나 했던 경험도 없을 뿐더러, 초등학교 때부터 유학한 게 아니라면 문법을 따로 공부하지 않았을 겁니다. 그래서 수업을 듣고 문제를 풀어도 그저 느낌상으로만 이해를 해왔기 때문에 정확한 내용 파악이 안되며, Listening을 들어도 그저 기본적인 내용만 들리는 수준이기 때문에, Conversation 문제는 어느 정도 풀 수 있으나, 전문적인 강의 내용인 Lecture는 이해하기 힘들죠. 이 부분은 또한 논리적 사고력이 큰 역할을 담당하는데, 이것은 단순히 언어능력을 떠나서 내용의 구조나 흐름을 파악하고, 그 내용을 바탕으로 주제를 도출할 수 있는 분석력과 추리력이 요구되기 때문입니다. 또한 내용은 알아들었지만 문제를 제대로 풀지 못하는 건, 각각의 문장을 하나씩 이해해도, 강의 전체의 내용 흐름이나 구조 파악이 논리적으로 분석되지 않기 때문에, 주제라든가 예시를 드는 목적, 교수의 의도 등 전체적인 틀이 머리 속에서 잡히지 않는 경우가 많습니다. 또한 본인이 접하지 못했던 Topic에 대한 설명이 중점적으로 나오는 경우, 배경지식이 전혀 없거나 부족하기 때문에 내용을 정확하게 파악하는데 어려움을 겪게 됩니다. 따라서 중고등학교 때 배운 배경지식이 중요하고 또한 문제를 빠르고 정확하게 해석하는 것도 중요합니다. 이해를 해야 문제를 풀 수 있으니까요. 이와 같은 문제풀이 능력은, 토플이 아무래도 시험문제이다 보니 시험의 성격에 맞는 문제 이해력과 해결능력을 갖춰야 좋은 점수를 얻을 수 있도록 초점이 맞춰져 있기 때

문이에요. 이를 위해서는 문제를 많이 풀어보고 자주 출제되는 유형을 알아가야 합니다. 하지만 단순히 문제만 많이 풀었다고 만족 해서는 안됩니다. 왜 답의 근거가 그 부분인지, 내가 틀린 답은 왜 오답이 될 수 밖에 없는지를 이해하지 못하면 나중에 똑같은 문제를 다시 풀었을 때 계속 틀릴 수 밖에 없고, 결국 점수는 제자리 걸음을 하게 될테니까요.

6. 저는 단기간에 토플을 끝내야 하는데, 고득점을 빠르게 올릴 수 있는 방법은 없나요?

학생들마다 개인차이가 있기 때문에, 토플 리스닝을 끝내는데 얼마의 시간이 걸린다고 단정적으로 말씀드리기는 어렵습니다. 하지만 학습자가 중고등학교 때 쌓은 기본 영어 실력이 탄탄하다면 단기간에 고득점을 얻는 것이 가능합니다. 반면, 영어와 별로 친하지 않았거나 영어 소리와는 완전히 담을 쌓고 지냈다면, 청취력 자체를 기초부터 쌓으셔야 하기 때문에 단기간에 고득점을 받기가 어려울 수도 있습니다. 원하는 점수를 얻는데 걸리는 시간은 현재 본인의 실력, 공부에 투자하는 시간, 공부 방법 그리고 학생 본인의 의지 등에 따라 다릅니다. **각자의 실력에 맞는 공부방법은 위의 '2. 효과적인 점수대별 학습 방법은 뭔가요?' 를 참조하시기 바랍니다.**

또한, 목표기간이 짧다고 해서 기본적인 영어 청취력을 갖추지 않은 학생이 어려운 내용을 아무리 여러 번 듣고 문제를 풀어도 실력이 금방 향상되지는 않습니다. 기초부터 차곡차곡 밟아가는 것보다 오히려 더 많은 시간이 흐를지도 모르죠. 영어 수준은 본인이 취약한 부분을 꾸준히 메꾸는게 우선이라고 봅니다. 이것은 토플 성적만을 취득하기 위해서뿐만 아니라 제대로 된 영어실력을 쌓는데도 도움이 됩니다. 특히, 토플 리스닝은 무조건 많이 듣는다고 해서 저절로 귀가 열리는게 아닙니다. 대학교 수준의 대화와 강의를 듣고 내용의 핵심을 파악해서 문제를 풀어야 하기 때문에, 총체적인 이해력과 내용의 포인트를 파악하는 분석력, 들은 정보를 바탕으로 문제가 요구하는 답을 골라내는 논리적 추론력 등, 단순한 청취 이외의 능력들도 함께 평가하고자 하는 시험입니다. **전반적인 토플 영어 청취실력 향상에 관한 방법은 앞장의 '1.왜 청취 부분 점수가 잘 안 나오는 걸까요? LC공부는 어떻게 해야 하는지 감이 잘 안 잡혀요.' 의 내용을 읽어보시기 바랍니다.**

7. 영어 공부를 한지 오래됐는데요. 리스닝을 따라갈 수 있을까요?

본인인 할 의지만 있다면 남들보다 시간이 조금 오래 걸릴지는 몰라도 다 따라오실 수 있습니다.^^ 다른 모든 section도 그렇지만, 단어는 리스닝의 첫 번째 기초이기 때문에, 뜻과 더불어 발음까지 정확하고 꼼꼼하게 외우면서 어휘의 양을 계속 누적시켜 나가야 합니다. 중고등 필수 영단어와 함께 토플단어를 외우면서 기초를 잡으시면 됩니다. 이때, 많은 학생들이 단순히 단어의 spelling과 뜻을 외우시는데, 영어는 한국어와 달리 글자와 소리가 일치하지 않는 부분이 많습니다. 따라서 각 단어의 소리를 하나씩 머리속에 입력하셔야 합니다. 이 작업은 그동안 영어공부를 글자 위주로 해온 한국 학생들이 가볍게 여기거나, 무시하는데 번거롭더라도 꼭 단어의 소리를 듣고 기억하셔야, 비단 리스닝 뿐만 아니라 speaking 에도 큰 도움이됩니다.

또한 문법과 독해 공부도 꾸준히 하셔야 합니다. 리스닝의 기초는 어휘도 중요하지만, 문법도 큰 역할을 하니까요. 문법을 통해 문장구조 파악을 빨리 할 수 있어야 들리는 문장의 내용이 머리 속에서 빠르고 정확하게 이해되거든요. 한국 학생들이 어느 정도 공부해온 독해실력으로 리스닝 스크립트를 쭉 읽어나가는데, 처음에 문장을 한번 보고 문장의 구조나 의미가 들어오지 않는다면, 리스닝은 무리가 따릅니다. 이런 식으로 기본 영어 실력을 꾸준히 쌓아가면서, 청취 훈련을 하고 문제를 풀어나간다면, 좋은 결과를 얻으실 수 있을 겁니다.

■ 학생들이 자주하는 질문 Q&A

8. 청취력을 키우려면 무엇부터 공부해야 하나요?

당연히 어휘부터입니다. 특히 단어는 영어의 기초입니다. 토플 네 과목인 Reading, Listening, Writing, Speaking 전 영역에 있어서 기본적으로 꼭 알고 있어야 하는 필수적인 부분이며, 가장 많은 효과를 볼 수 있는 부분입니다. 특히 리스닝은 대학교 교양과목 수준의 내용을 듣고 이해하여 문제를 푸는 것이기 때문에, 전문적인 어휘가 많이 등장합니다. 따라서, 차곡차곡 어휘를 쌓아간다는 건 본인이 전쟁에 나가기에 앞서 총알을 챙기는 것과 같죠. 군인이 전쟁에 나가는데 총알이 없거나 턱없이 부족하다면 어떻게 될까요? 반면에 넉넉히 준비하고 있다면, 일단 전투에 임하는 자세가 달라지고 자신감이 샘솟는 것뿐만 아니라 실제로 전투에서 이길 확률이 높아지겠죠.

주의하실 점은 단어 음원을 듣지 않은 상태에서 계속 외우기만 하면, 나중엔 쉬운 단어인데도 알아듣지 못하거나 엉뚱하게 다른 단어로 알아듣는 경우가 많다는 것입니다. 그러므로 스펠링과 함께 소리를 입력해주어야 하는데, 발음을 본인이 맘대로 창조하거나, 주변에서 한국인들끼리 통하는 소위 '된장' 발음은 지양하고, 정확한 소리를 기억해야 영어가 정확하게 들립니다. 또한 이런식으로 문장도 꾸준히 소리와 더불어 학습해 나간다면 얼마 안있어 청취력이 빠르게 향상되는 걸 느끼실 수 있습니다

9. 저는 Reading Section에서는 점수가 20점 이상 꾸준히 나오는데, Listening Section은 10점대 초반으로 점수차가 많이 납니다. 뭐가 문제일까요?

기본적인 영어실력은 어느 정도 머리 속에 있는데, 청취를 해본 적이 없거나 영어소리에 익숙하지 않은 경우 이런 현상이 나타납니다. 실제 수업에서, 학생들에게 영어문장을 들려주고 딕테이션(Dictation)을 시킨 다음, 스크립트를 보고 체크해 보라고 하면, 학생 스스로도 놀라는 경우가 많습니다. 어렵거나 이상한 단어를 못 적은 것이 아니라, 다 아는 단어인데 소리로 만 들었을 땐 안 들리거나 전혀 엉뚱한 단어로 들리기 때문에, 막상 적어보면 기본 어휘조차 잘 적지 못하는 것이지요. 또한 같은 문장을 글로 읽어보라고 하면, 쉽게 이해하고 해석합니다. 그러나 그 문장을 소리만 듣고 무슨 의미인지 얘기해 보라고 하면, 대답하지 못하는 경우를 많이 봅니다. 이것은 영어를 글자로만 공부했기 때문에 발생하는 문제인데요. 글자와 소리가 쉽게 매치되는 한국어와 달리, 영어는 특유의 강세와 리듬이 있으며, 철자를 보고 쉽게 발음이 판단이 안 되는 단어들도 많습니다. 그래서 한국인들이 느끼는 글자와 소리 사이의 괴리감이 발생하는 것이지요. 이것은 마치 한자를 보고 어떻게 발음 하냐고 물어보면 그 소리를 외우고 있지 않은 이상 선뜻 대답하지 못하는 것과 같습니다. 따라서 영어 소리 훈련을 통하여 머리 속에 저장된 글자 및 의미와 소리를 합치는 작업이 필요합니다. RC영역에서 성적이 어느 정도 나온다는 것은 어휘력, 문법, 문장력, 이해력 등 기본기가 갖춰져 있다는 뜻이기 때문에, 영어 소리의 특징에 익숙해지면 들은 내용이 머리 속에 이미 들어가 있는 정보들과 빠르게 매치되면서 이해가 잘 되고, 이에 따라 문제를 정확하게 풀게 되어 점수가 오르는 것입니다.

해결 방법으로는, 어떤 단어나 표현을 외울 때 전자사전이나 인터넷 사전에서 우선 찾아서, 그 단어의 글자와 의미를 확인한 뒤 발음을 들어보세요. 또한, 여러 번 들어보고 3번 정도 똑같이 따라 말해보세요. 이렇게 함으로써 한 단어의 spelling, 뜻, 발음 이렇게 3가지를 동시에 머리속에 넣어 기억하는 겁니다. 영어 리스닝은 글자가 보이는 것이 아닌 소리만으로 뜻을 이해해야 하기 때문에, 소리 자체를 기억해야 나중에 들었을때 뜻과 함께 떠오르게 되어 청취를 하는데 효과적입니다. 또한 청취력이 어느정도 뒷받침되어진다 하더라도, 리딩과는 다른 리스닝 문제 특유의 유형을 파악하지 못하면 정답이 아닌 오답을 고르기 쉽기 때문에 점수가 잘 나오지 않을 수도 있습니다. 때문에 문제를 정확하게 분석하는 스킬을 기를 필요가 있죠. 또한 Topic의 영향도 큰데, 자신이 취약한 주제가 나올 경우 친숙한 주제가 나올 때보다 난이도가 훨씬 어렵다고 느끼게 됩니다. 또한 내용을 들을때는 이해가 가지만 막상 문제를 풀 때 ETS가 출제하는 문제 유형이나 오답 방식에 익숙하지 않을 경우 정답이 아닌 오답을 고르게 됩니다. 이런 경우는 문제 해결력을 꾸준히 기르셔야 합니다.

10. 저는 학원을 다니지 않고 혼자 독학으로 토플 시험을 준비하고 있는데요. 어떻게 해야 효율적으로 공부 할 수 있나요?

학원에서 토플리스닝을 공부하는 경우에는 실제 문제 유형들을 접한 다음, 내용을 듣고 청취만을 바탕으로 본인이 알아들은 내용이 맞는지 파트너와 Discussion을 하고, 다시 선생님과의 내용 확인을 통해 단순히 내용만을 이해하는 것을 떠나 전반 적인 강의의 구조와 내용전개 방식 등을 파악하는 훈련에 집중하게 됩니다. 또한 딕테이션 방법과 노트테이킹 요령, 각 문제 별 유형과 대처법, 배경지식 쌓는 법 등 청취력을 향상시킬 수 있는 여러가지 팁들을 얻을 수 있죠.

반면에, 학생이 혼자서 토플 리스닝 시험을 준비하는 경우는 다음과 같은 순서로 공부하시면 효과를 보실 수 있습니다.

A) 실제시험과 비슷한 환경에서 긴장감있게 문제를 풀고 채점합니다. 그리고 나서 내용을 다시 들으면서 노트테이킹을 수정하세요. 이 때 처음에 놓쳤거나 잘못 들었던 내용을 정확히 잡으려고 노력합니다.
B) MP3를 전체적으로 다시 한 번 쭉 듣고나서, 안 들리는 부분을 한 문장씩 dictation합니다.
C) 스크립트 내용을 파악합니다. 이때 어휘나 표현, 문장을 정확히 해석하여 내용을 완벽하게 이해하기 위해, 이해가 안 가는 단어나 표현들은 사전이나 인터넷으로 확인합니다.
D) 문제를 분석합니다. 이때 틀린 문제 위주로 정답 근거를 스크립트에서 찾고, 본인이 선택한 오답의 이유를 분석해 봅니다.
E) 이제 완벽하게 이해한 강의의 내용을 summary해 봅니다. 핵심 내용 위주로 노트에 정리하면서 본인의 머리속에 배경지식으로 집어넣습니다.
F) Mp3를 다시 들으면서 내용을 다시 한번 정리하고, 딕테이션에서 수정한 부분이나 반복해서 들어도 잘 안들리는 문장은 소리를 그대로 따라하며 새도잉함으로써 귀를 열어줍니다.

☞ 자세한 학습 방법은 뒷장 P. 32 'Listening Strategies 1.리스닝 학습 순서 및 방법, 2. 문제 분석 방법' 을 참조하세요

11. 토플 리스닝 실력이 어느 정도 향상되었는지 한번 알아보고 싶은데, 어떻게 확인하죠?

본인이 공부를 잘 하고 있는지 혹은 내 실력이 어느정도 향상되었는지 알고 싶다면, 실제 시험을 보는 것도 좋지만 모의 토플을 추천해 드리고 싶습니다. 모의 토플은 실제 토플 시험을 출제하는 ETS에서 주관하기 때문에 현재 시험과 가장 유사한 형태의 문제들을 체험해 볼 수 있는 좋은 기회입니다. Reading과 Listening 2과목만 따로 보는 것도 가능하기 때문에 실제 시험과 달리 부담이 덜하다는 장점이 있죠. 그리고 꼭 내 점수에 대한 평가를 위해서 뿐만아니라, 실제 시험을 앞두고 있다면 모의 시험을 통해 시험방식과 시험장 환경에 미리 적응하는 것도 나쁘지 않습니다. 실제 토플은 컴퓨터로 시험을 보는 것이어서 종이로 문제를 푸는 것과는 많이 다르거든요. 모의고사를 통해 모니터 화면에 익숙해 질 수 있는 기회를 가질 수 있고, 실제 시험 과정이 어떻게 진행되는지 경험할 수 있습니다. 또한 시험과 같은 환경에서 긴장감을 느끼며 문제를 풀기 때문에 실제 시험장에서 빨리 적응하는데 훈련이 됩니다. 더불어 모의 토플에 나오는 문제들은 과거 ETS가 출제한 문제들 이므로 실제 문제에 대한 감을 익힐 수도 있죠. 다만, 종이로 풀 때와 컴퓨터로 풀 때 점수 차이가 나는 학생들이 많기 때문에, 실제 iBT시험과는 3~4점 정도 점수가 차이날 수도 있다는 가정하에 보셔야 합니다. 수능 전 모의고사를 여러 번 풀어 보듯이 실제 IBT문제를 접하기 전에 모의토플 시험을 신청하셔서 보시길 권해드립니다. 한 달에 1번씩 꾸준히 보고 본인만의 성적을 기록해 놓는 것도 좋은 방법입니다. 모의토플 응시는 www.toefltpo.com 또는 학원 (usherin.usher.co.kr)에 문의하시기 바랍니다.

2023년 7월 26일 바뀌는 뉴 토플에 관하여
ETS가 공식 배포한 모의토플 테스트를 기준으로 안내

전체적 변화

1. 스피킹 전에 주어졌던 쉬는 시간 10분이 없어졌습니다.
2. 평균 3시간 정도 걸렸던 토플 시험이 리딩 지문 갯수 축소 및 더미 문제 폐지로 인해 2시간 내외로 줄어들었습니다.

Writing

독립형 (independent) 대신에 academic discussion essay 로 변경되었습니다.
- academic discussion essay는 좌측에 있는 교수님의 지문을 읽고, 우측에 나오는 두학생의 상반되는 의견을 참고하여 본인의 의견을 제시하는 문제로, 10분동안 작성하는 시험입니다.

Reading

1. 지문의 수가 3지문에서 2지문으로 줄었습니다. (3지문 -> 2지문으로 감소)
2. 문제 풀이 시간은 지문당 17분 30초 정도로 줄어들었습니다.
   지문의 길이는 기존과 같이 800자 내외 입니다. (변화 없습니다)
3. 더미 문제가 삭제되었습니다.
   - 점수에 영향을 주지 않았지만, 시험시간을 늘렸었던 더미 문제가 없어졌습니다.

Listening

1. 문제 구성이나 시간적 변동은 없습니다.
2. 리딩과 마찬가지로 더미 문제가 삭제되었습니다.

Speaking

스피킹은 변동이 없는 유일한 파트입니다.

2 iBT TOEFL (iBT 토플) 시험 소개
USHER iBT TOEFL **FINAL TEST** LISTENING (어셔 iBT 토플 파이널 테스트 리스닝)

iBT TOEFL (iBT 토플)이란?

TOEFL(Test of English as a Foreign Language)이란 주로 영어권 국가의 대학교에 진학하는 외국인 학생의 영어실력을 평가하기 위하여 만들어진 시험입니다. 현재 TOEFL (토플)은 iBT(internet-Based Test) TOEFL이라 불리며, PBT(Paper-Based Test) 와 CBT(Computer-Based Test)를 거쳐 채택된 3세대 시험방식입니다. 읽기, 듣기, 말하기, 쓰기의 다양한 분야의 영어실력을 보기 때문에 현재 세계적으로 가장 공신력 있는 영어시험으로 자리잡았습니다.

iBT TOEFL (iBT 토플) 구성

시험순서	지문 개수	시간	세부사항	만점
Reading (상대평가)	Passage 2개 (700단어 X 2개)	35분	Passage 당 17분 30초 10문제	30점
Listening (상대평가)	Conversation 1개 Lecture 1개	36분	문제풀이시간 7분	30점
	Conversation 1개 Lecture 2개		문제풀이시간 10분	
Speaking (절대평가)	Independent 1개 Intergrated 3개	16분 내외	-	30점
Writing (절대평가)	Intergrated 1개 Independent 1개	29분	-	30점
총 약 2시간 (116분)				총점 120점

꼭 알아두세요!

접수	시험일정이 나오면 접수 가능 * Late fee(응시 7일 전 시험 신청 시) 40$추가
비용	시험 - 미화 $ 220 (원화결제 가능)
	취소한 성적 복원 - 미화 $ 20
	성적 전송 - 미화 $ 20 (1개 기관당)
	일자 변경 - 미화 $ 60
	재채점 - 미화 $ 80 (1개 section당: 성적 불신시 speaking, writing만 가능)

2 iBT TOEFL (iBT 토플) 시험 소개

꼭 알아두세요!

시험	3일에 1번 수/토/일 가능
시험장소	전국 27개 도시에 있는 Test Center 및 세계 각국의 ETS Test Center (안양, 아산, 부천, 부산, 천안, 청주, 춘천, 대구, 대전, 고성, 고양, 군포, 광주, 경기, 경주, 경산, 화성, 인천, 제주, 전주, 진주, 오산, 포천, 성남, 서울, 울산, 용인 등 27개 도시 - 토플 시험장에 대한 자세한 정보는 usherin.usher.co.kr 참조)
준비물	토플 web site에 등록되어 있는 신분증 지참
성적 발표일	리딩 리스닝은 시험 직후, 스피킹 라이팅은 최소 6일 ~ 최대 14일
성적 유효기간	2년
토플 시험 등록 취소	시험 등록 후 7일 까지 : 전액환불 시험 등록 후 8일 이후 : 금액의 50% 환불 시험보기 4일전 : 금액의 50% 환불 콜센터에 전화하거나 홈페이지에서 취소 (e-mail로는 불가능)

시험장에서!

1. 시험절차 시험장에 도착하면 여권 확인 후, 성적표에 나올 사진을 찍고 감독관의 안내에 따라 순서대로 시험을 시작한다.

2. 필기도구 연필과 종이는 감독관이 나누어주므로 따로 필요가 없고, 부족하면 얼마든지 더 달라고 할 수 있다. 다만, Section 시작 전에 종이에 필기할 경우, 부정행위로 간주될 수 있으므로 각별히 주의하자.

3. 헤드폰 음량 시험 도중 언제든지 조절할 수 있다.

4. 마이크 음량 시험 시작 직후와 Speaking Section 직전에 조절할 수 있다.

5. 휴식시간 없음

6. 주의사항 각 응시자마다 시험 진행 시간이 다르기 때문에, 내가 Listening이나 Writing Section을 풀고 있을 때, 다른 사람의 목소리가 방해가 되는 경우가 많으니 염두해 두자.

3 iBT TOEFL Listening 소개
USHER iBT TOEFL **FINAL TEST** LISTENING (어셔 iBT 토플 파이널 테스트 리스닝)

iBT TOEFL Listening이란?

　iBT TOEFL Listening 영역에서는 학생들이 미국 및 캐나다 등 영미권 국가에서 유학하는 동안, 학교 생활 및 강의의 내용을 이해하고 따라갈 수 있는 영어청취능력을 평가하고자 하는데 목적이 있습니다. 그러므로 리스닝 영역은 크게 2가지 종류의 테스트로 구성되어 있는데 바로 Conversation과 Lecture입니다. Conversation에서는 대학 캠퍼스에서 학생들이 겪을 수 있는 상황들(구내시설 이용, 교수와의 상담, 학생간의 토론)과 Lecture는 대학교 1, 2학년 학생들이 듣는 개론 수준의 교양과목 수업에 해당하는 다양한 강의들이 차지하고 있습니다. 특히 렉쳐는 다양한 Topics을 다루는 형태의 내용이 출제되지만 아주 전문적인 내용으로 구성되어 있지 않고, 국내 고등학교 수준까지의 학습내용과 겹치기 때문에 너무 겁먹을 필요는 없습니다. 하지만 대화와 강의 내용을 단 한번만 듣고 문제를 풀어야 하기 때문에, 고도의 집중력과 정확한 청취력이 필요합니다. 또한 녹음 내용을 다 듣고 난 뒤에 문제가 화면에 나타나므로, 청취 내용을 이해하는 동시에 논리적으로 핵심을 정리하며 기억하거나 메모하는 능력이 요구됩니다. 또한 제한된 시간내에 문제와 4개의 답들을 빠르고 정확하게 파악하는 독해능력 또한 중요합니다.

iBT Listening 구성

- 2개 대화(Conversation) : 각 지문당 길이 - 3~4분 / 각각 5문항 출제
- 3개 강의(Lecture) : 한 지문당 길이 - 5~7분 / 각각 5~6문항 출제
    → 기본 2개 Set (1번째 Set : conversation 1개+lecture 2개,
       2번째 Set : conversation 1개+lecture 1개)

    ☞ 시험문항수 : 28개 (1set(5+6) + 1set(5+6+6))
    ☞ 시험시간 : 36분 내외
    ☞ 점수범위 : 0~30점

iBT Listening 내용

A. 대화 (Conversation)
　캠퍼스에서 일어날 수 있는 상황(교무처, 기숙사, 도서관, 구내식당, 서점) + 교수연구실(강의내용 질문, 숙제 및 프로젝트 문의, 진로상담) + 학생간의 토론(강의내용 복습, 시험대비공부, 프로젝트 및 리서치 관련 대화)

B. 강의 (Lecture)
　대학교 1, 2학년 교양과목에서 다루는 개론 수준의 학문분야로 다양한 Topics 포함(생물학, 환경학, 천문학, 지구과학, 인류학, 고고학, 역사, 예술, 문학, 마케팅, 경제, 경영 등)

3 iBT TOEFL Listening 소개

iBTListening 특징

- Note-taking이 허용된다
- 대화와 강의 내용의 길이가 길어지고, 말의 속도(특히 conversation)가 빨라졌으며, 화자들의 어투가 자연스러워지고 실제 상황에서 쓰이는 표현들이 많이 등장하고 있다.
- 정답이 2개, 3개인 문제 형태가 출제된다. (Clik on 2 answers, Click on 3 answers)
- 들은 내용에 숨겨진 실질적인 의미나 화자의 의도, 다시 들려주는 부분을 듣고 화자의 의견이나 태도를 파악하는 문제유형이 증가하였다.
- 글의 구조 및 세부내용의 관계를 파악하는 순서 나열하기, 관련 내용 연결하기, OX맞추기 문제가 출제된다.

iBTListening 문제 유형 분석

난이도	기본문제유형	세부문제유형	문제유형 설명	지문당 문항수
상중하 (최근 어려워지는 추세임 - 약 20%차지)	Main Idea	Main Purpose Main Idea	방문목적 대화 및 강의 주제	1개
중하 (기본점수의 40% 이상 차지 - 청취력 확인)	Detail	Definition Example Characteristics Cause/Result Misunderstanding/ Correction Requirement Suggestion Future action	용어가 가리키는 내용 찾기 본문 내용 사실여부 파악하기 문제점에 대한 화자의 제안	2 ~ 4개
중상 (변별력 목적 - 약 20 - 40% 차지)	Inference	Purpose Imply Opinion Headset	제공된 정보로 화자의 의도 및 태도 파악하기 다시 들려주는 부분 듣고 화자의 의도 파악하기	1 ~ 3개
중상 (변별력 목적- 약 20% 차지, 항상 출제되는 것은 아님)	Category	Organize Click on 2, 3 answers Matching Ordering	내용의 전개구조 파악하기 동일 범주에 해당하는 내용 찾기 주어진 정보를 알맞게 정렬하기 정보들의 관계를 연결하기	1 ~ 2개

iBT Listening 화면 구성

문제를 풀 때 화면 상단에 진행과정을 도와주는 툴바(Tool Bar)가 나타난다. 이것을 통해 헤드셋의 볼륨을 조절하고, 현재 풀고 있는 문제의 번호와, 다음 문제로 넘어가기, 해당 Set의 종료시간까지 얼마 남았는지 알 수 있다.

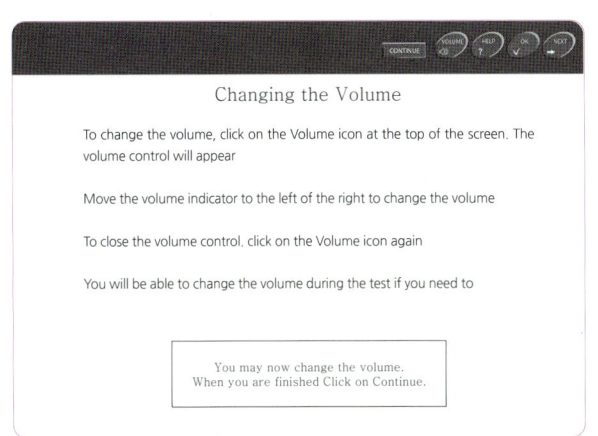

음량조절 화면

시험이 시작하기 전에 음량을 조절할 것인 묻는 화면으로 'VOLUME'을 클릭하면 음량을 조절할 수 있다.
시험을 보는 동안에도 음량 조절이 가능하다

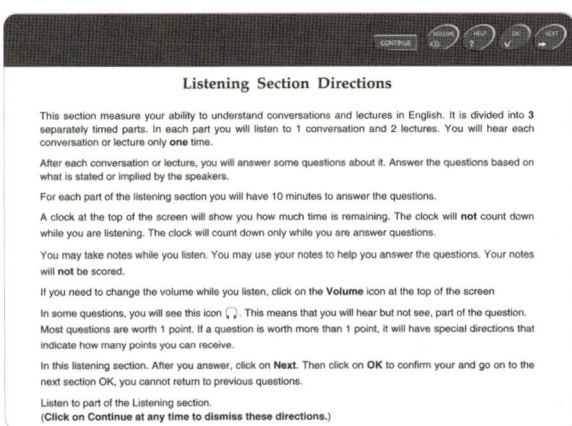

Listening Direction 화면

이 리스닝 시험 진행 방식에 대한 전반적인 설명이 나온다. 리스닝 파트에서는 17문제로 구성된 Part가 2r--3번 나오며, 각 Part는 Conversation 1개와 Lecture 2개로 이루어져 있다는 설명이다

대화 및 강의 내용을 들을 때 나오는 화면

대화가 나오는 동안 두 화자의 사진이 나오며 강의의 주제와 관련된 사진이 나오는 경우도 있다.
사진 아래의 바는 지문 분량의 진행정보를 알려준다.

iBT TOEFL Listening 소개

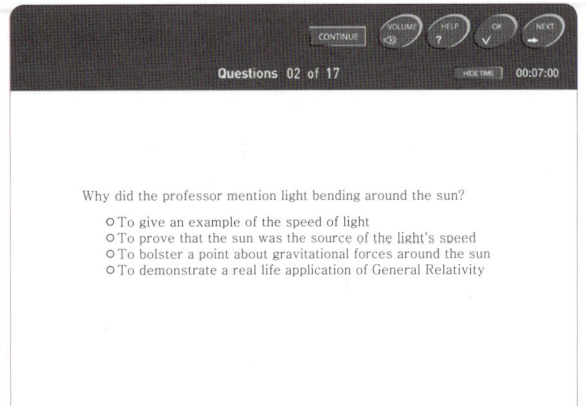

문제가 나오는 화면

문제가 나올 때 보이는 화면으로 문제를 들려주고 보기가 뜬다. 답을 클릭한 후 Next 버튼을 누르고 OK 버튼을 클릭하면 답이 확정되며 이전 화면으로 돌아갈 수 없으며, 답이 2개 이상인 문제는 반드시 모든 답을 클릭해야 다음 문제로 넘어갈 수 있다.

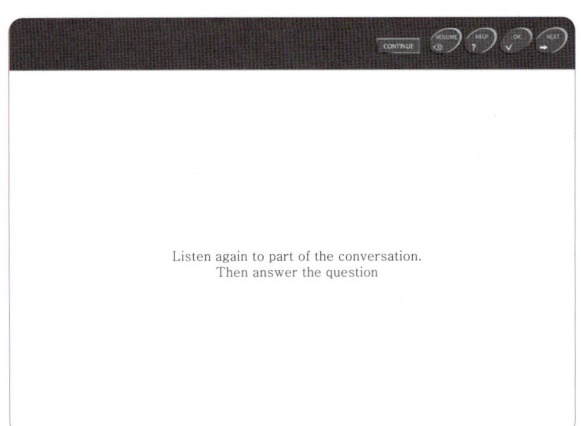

다시 들려주는 문제 유형의 Direction 화면

대화 및 강의의 일부를 다시 듣고 푸는 문제에서 주어지는 Direction화면이다. 이 화면이 나온 후 지문의 일부를 다시 들려준다.

4 Listening Section 평가기준 (ETS Scoring Criteria)
USHER iBT TOEFL **FINAL TEST LISTENING** (어셔 iBT 토플 파이널 테스트 리스닝)

리스닝 섹션의 문제를 통해 ETS가 평가하고자 하는 사항들을 설명한 것입니다. 학생들은 이 평가 기준을 통해 토플 리스닝 시험이 어떤 의도로 출제되는지 파악한 후, 이에 부합하는 어휘력, 청취력 및 논리적 사고력을 기르는데 힘쓴다면 고득점에 다가가기 훨씬 쉬울 것입니다.

High (22-30)

Test takers who receive a score at the HIGH level, as you did, typically understand conversations and lectures in English that present a wide range of listening demands. These demands can include **difficult vocabulary (uncommon terms, or colloquial or figurative language)**, complex grammatical structures, abstract or complex ideas and/or making sense of unexpected or seemingly contradictory information.

When listening to lectures and conversations like these, test takers at HIGH level typically can:

A. Understand **main idea** and **important details**, **whether they are stated or implied**;
B. **Distinguish more important ideas from less important ones**;
C. Understand how **information** is being **used** (for example, to provide **evidence** for a claim or describe **a step in a complex process**);
D. Recognize how pieces of information are **connected** (for example, in a **cause-and-effect relationship**);
E. Understand many different ways that speakers use language for **purpose other than to give information** (for example, to **emphasize a point**, express **agreement or disagreement**, or **convey intentions indirectly**); and
F. **Synthesize information, even when it is not presented in sequence**, and make **correct inferences** on the basis of that information.

Intermediate (15-21)

Test takers who receive a score at the INTERMEDIATE level, as you did, typically understand conversations and lectures in English that present a wide range of listening demands. These demands can include difficult vocabulary (uncommon terms, or colloquial or figurative language), complex grammatical structures and/or abstract or complex ideas. However, lectures and conversations that require the listener to make sense of unexpected or seemingly contradictory information may present some difficulty.

When listening to conversations and lectures like these, test takers at the INTERMEDIATE level typically can:

A. Understand explicitly stated main ideas and important details, especially if they are reinforced, but may have difficulty understanding main ideas that must be inferred or important details that are not reinforced.;
B. Understand how information is being used (for example, to provide support or describe a step in a complex process);
C. Recognize how pieces of information are connected (for example, in a cause-and-effect relationship);
D. Understand, though perhaps not consistently, ways that speakers use language for purposes other than to give information (for example, to emphasize a point, express agreement or disagreement, or convey intentions indirectly); and
E. Synthesize information from adjacent parts of a lecture or conversation and make correct inferences on the basis of that information, but may have difficulty synthesizing information from separate parts of a lecture or conversation.

4 Listening Section 평가기준 (ETS Criteria)

Low (0-14)

Test takers who receive a score at the **LOW** level, as you did, typically understand the main idea and some important details of conversations. However, test takers at the low level may have difficulty understanding lectures and conversations in English that involve abstract or complex ideas and recognizing the relationship between those ideas. Test takers at this level also may not understand sections of lectures and conversations that contain difficult vocabulary or complex grammatical structures.

Test takers at the **LOW** level typically can:

A. Understand main ideas when they are stated explicitly or marked as important, but may have difficulty understanding main ideas if they are not stated explicitly;

B. Understand important details when they are stated explicitly or marked as important, but may have difficulty understanding details if they are not repeated or clearly marked as important, or if they are conveyed over several exchanges among different speakers;

C. Understand ways that speakers use language to emphasize a point or to indicate agreement or disagreement, but generally only when the information is related to a central theme or is clearly marked as important; and

D. Make connections between the key ideas in a conversation, particularly if the ideas are related to a central theme or are repeated.

높음 (22-30)

높음(High) 수준의 점수를 받는 응시자는, 일반적으로 다양한 범위의 듣기 능력을 필요로 하는 영어 대화와 강의를 이해한다. 여기에서 요구되는 능력은 **어려운 어휘(자주 사용하지 않는 용어 또는 구어체 혹은 수사적 표현)**, 복잡한 문법구조, 추상적인 또는 복잡한 개념 그리고/또는 예상하지 못하거나 혹은 언뜻 보기에 모순적인 정보에 대한 이해를 포함한다.

이러한 강의와 대화를 들을 때, 높음 수준의 점수를 받는 응시자는 일반적으로 다음과 같은 것을 할 수 있다.

A. **제시되었든지 혹은 암시되었든지 간에 주제와 주요 세부사항**을 이해할 수 있다.

B. **더 중요한 개념과 덜 중요한 개념을 구분**할 수 있다.

C. **정보가 어떻게 사용**되고 있는지(예: 주장에 대한 **증거를 제공**하기 위함인지 또는 **복잡한 과정의 단계**를 설명하기 위함인지)이해 할 수 있다.

D. **정보 조각**들이 어떻게 **연결**되는지(예: **인과관계**)이해 할 수 있다.

E. **정보를 제공하는 것 이외의 목적**을 위해 **화자가 언어를 사용하는 다른 방식들**을 이해할 수 있다. (예: **핵심내용 강조**하기, **동의나 반대 표현하기, 간접적으로 의도 전달하기**) ; 그리고

F. **연속적으로 제시되어 있지 않더라도, 정보를 통합**할 수 있고 그 정보에 기초해서 **올바른 추론**을 할 수 있다.

중간 (15-21)

중간(Intermediate) 수준의 점수를 받은 응시자는, 일반적으로 다양한 범위의 듣기 능력을 필요로 하는 영어 대화와 강의를 이해한다. 여기서 요구되는 능력은 어려운 어휘(자주 사용하지 않는 용어 또는 구어체 혹은 수사적 표현), 복잡한 문법구조, 추상적이거나 또는 복잡한 개념들을 포함한다. 하지만, 강의와 대화에 있는 예상치 못하거나 혹은 언뜻 보기에 모순되게 제시 되는 정보를 청취자가 이해하는 것에 약간의 어려움을 느낀다.

이러한 강의와 대화를 들으면서, 중간 수준의 점수를 받는 응시자는 일반적으로 다음과 같은 것을 할 수 있다.

A. 명쾌하게 제시된 주제와 주요 세부사항을, 특히 이들이 강조되었을 때, 이해할 수 있다. 하지만 추론해야 하는 주제와 강조되지 않은 세부사항을 이해하는 데에는 어려움을 겪을 수 있다.
B. 정보가 어떻게 사용되고 있는지 이해할 수 있다. (예: 근거를 제공하거나 복잡한 절차의 단계를 묘사)
C. 정보 조각들이 어떻게 연결되어 있는지 파악할 수 있다. (예: 인과관계)
D. 지속적으로는 아닐지라도, 정보 제공 이외의 다른 목적을 위한 언어 사용 방법을 이해할 수 있다. (예: 강조하기, 동의 나 반대 표현하기, 간접적으로 의도 전달하기) ; 그리고,
E. 강의나 대화에서 서로 인접해 있는 부분의 정보들을 합치고 그 정보에 기초해서 올바른 추론은 할 수 있지만, 떨어져 있는 정보를 합치는 것에는 어려움을 겪을 수 있다.

낮음 (0-14)

낮음(Low) 수준의 점수를 받는 응시자들은 일반적으로 대화의 주제와 몇몇 중요한 세부사항을 이해할 수 있다. 하지만 이 수준의 응시자는 추상적이거나 복잡한 개념을 포함한 영어 강의나 대화를 이해하거나, 그 생각들의 관계를 파악하는데 어려움 을 겪을 수 있다. 이 수준의 응시자들은 또한 어려운 어휘나 복잡한 문법구조를 포함하는 강의와 대화의 부분들을 이해하지 못할 수 있다.

낮음 수준의 응시자들은 일반적으로 다음와 같은 것을 할 수 있다.

A. 명쾌하게 제시되거나 중요하다고 표시되어질 때 주제를 이해할 수 있지만, 만약 이들이 명쾌하게 제시되어 있지 않다면 주제를 이해하는데 어려움을 겪을 수 있다.
B. 명쾌하게 제시되거나 중요하다고 표시되어질 때 주요 세부사항을 이해할 수 있지만, 만약 그것이 반복되지 않거나 중 요하다고 명확하게 표시되어 있지 않다면, 혹은 이들이 서로 다른 화자들을 통해 몇 번의 대화를 거쳐 전달이 되면, 세부사항을 이해하는데 어려움을 겪을 수 있다.
C. 화자가 강조하기 위해 또는 동의나 반대를 나타내기 위해 언어를 사용하는 방식을 이해할 수 있지만, 일반적으로 정보 가 중심 주제와 연결되어 있을 때나 중요하다고 명확하게 표시되어 있을 때에만 이해한다.
D. 특히 개념들이 중심 생각과 관련되어 있거나 반복되었을 때만, 대화에서 핵심 생각들 사이를 연결할 수 있다.

본 iBT 토플 교재만의 특징
USHER iBT TOEFL **FINAL TEST LISTENING** (어셔 iBT 토플 파이널 테스트 리스닝)

1 실제 iBT 토플 시험과 가장 유사한 실전서

최신 출제 경향 반영
최신 토플 시험 출제 경향을 완벽히 반영한 지문과 문제로 구성되었으며, 학생들이 어려워하는 주제인 물리학, 고고학, 인류학, 역사, 생물학, 건축학 등 지문 내용의 다양화와 상향된 난이도를 반영하여 본 교재를 통해 iBT 토플 리스닝 영역을 효과적으로 학습할 수 있다.

토플 고득점 달성을 위한 최상의 난이도
기존의 타교재와 비교해 최고 난이도의 지문과 문제로 구성된 본 교재를 학습함으로써 iBT 토플 리스닝 시험에 대한 감각을 확실하게 터득할 수 있어, 실제 시험에 철저히 대비할 수 있다.

2 효과적인 iBT 토플 리스닝 공부 방법 제시

체계적인 공부방법 설명
대부분의 기존 토플 교재들이 소홀히 하고 있는 부분인, 해석에만 초점을 맞춘 것이 아니라 학생들이 리스닝 시험에 접근하기 위해 효과적으로 공부하는 방법 자체를 설명하고 있다. 책의 서문에 나와 있는 리스닝 학습 순서 및 방법, 문제분석방법, 문제유형별 세부전략 등을 읽고 활용할 수 있다.

문제 유형별 전략 제시
각 문제의 유형별 세부 전략을 통해 고득점 달성에 필수인 가장 빠르고 효과적인 문제 접근 능력을 키워 논리적인 해결 능력을 향상시킬 수 있다.

3 토플 독학하는 수험생에게도 유용한 추천 학습서

수준별 학습 플랜 제시

학습자 개개인의 수준에 맞게 제시된 최적의 학습 플랜을 통해 체계적인 시간 관리와 효과적인 학습 방법을 익힐 수 있다. 스스로의 실력과 여건에 맞는 일정표를 작성하여 목표를 갖고 공부에 임하여 더 좋은 결과를 가질 수 있다.

정확한 해석 및 상세한 해설, 문제오답패턴 제시

정확한 지문 해석은 물론, 정답만을 짚어주는 기존의 해설서의 방식을 탈피하여, 정답의 근거 표시와 오답이 왜 틀렸는지에 대한 이유가 자세히 설명되어 있어 토플 리스닝을 독학으로 공부하는 학생들에게 큰 도움이 될 수 있다. 또한 모든 ETS 문제는 정답과 오답을 만드는데 패턴이 있는 만큼, 이런 패턴들을 모아 정리하였다.

셀프 체크 시스템

교재 서문의 'Listening Strategies 2. 문제분석방법과 각 테스트마다 있는 'Self-Check List 및 '오답정리표'를 활용하여 정확한 문제 유형 파악과 본인이 반복적으로 실수하는 오답 패턴을 찾아 취약점을 집중적으로 공략할 수 있다.

6 본 iBT 토플 교재의 구성
USHER iBT TOEFL **FINAL TEST** LISTENING (어서 iBT 토플 파이널 테스트 리스닝)

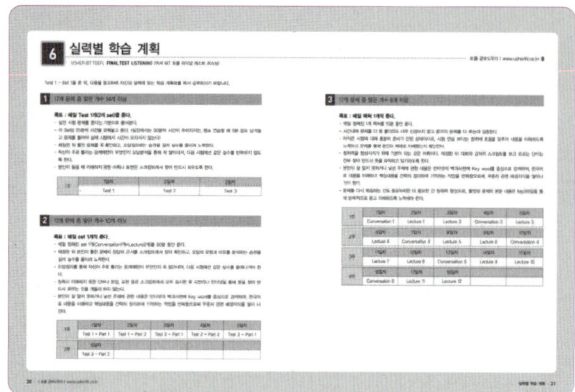

실력별 학습계획

각각 학생들의 실력 수준에 맞게 본 교재를 학습할 수 있는 학습플랜을 제시해 놓았습니다.

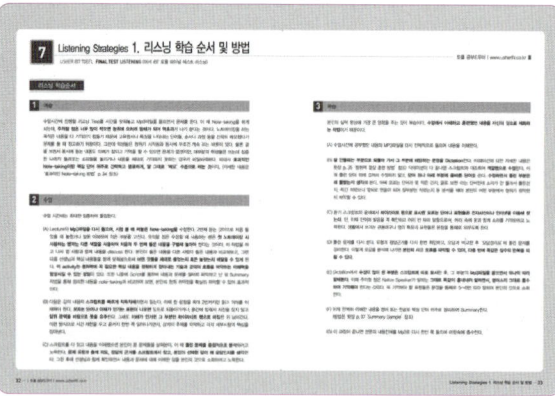

리스닝 학습순서 및 방법

학생들의 토플 리스닝 실력 향상을 위해 특별히 학습방법을 자세히 적어두었습니다. Listening Strategies 1. 리스닝 학습 순서 및 방법에서 '효과 적인 Note-taking 방법', '청취력 향상훈련', 'Direction Sample', 'Summary Sample'등을 자세히 읽고 활용하시기 바랍니다. 또한 토플 리스닝 문제 유형과 오답 패턴 및 그에 따른 전략을 정 리하였습니다. Listening Strategies 2. 문제분석방 법, '문제유형별 세부전략', '문제유형과 Signals'을 참고하시기 바랍니다.

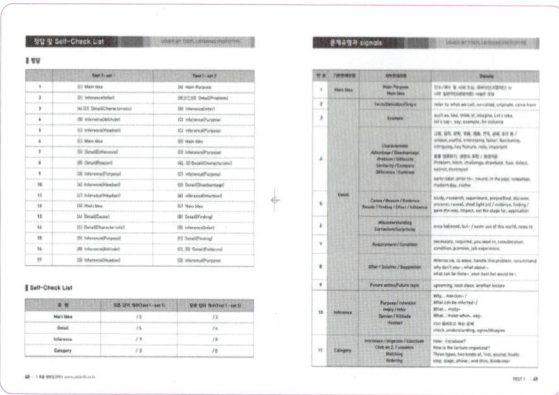

정답 및 Self-Check List

Test를 푼 후 정답을 맞출 때, 자신이 어떤 문제 유형을 틀렸는지 확인할 수 있도록 모든 문제의 정답 옆에 문제 유형을 표시하였습니다. 또한 자신의 문제 풀이 방식과 태도를 스스로 점검할 수 있도록 'Self-Check List'와 '오답정리표'를 제공하였습니다

| 토플 공부도우미 | usherin.usher.co.kr

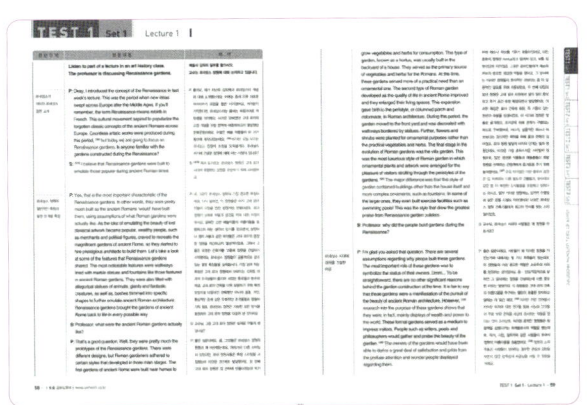

지문+해석, 해설

매회 테스트를 풀어본 후 심화학습을 할 수 있도록 해석과 자세한 해설, 정답의 근거를 제공하였습니다. 또한 토플을 혼자 공부하는 수험생들을 위해 본문에 정답의 단서가 되는 부분을 붉은색으로 표시하고, 각각 문제들의 유형 및 오답의 이유에 대한 상세한 설명을 넣어 공부의 편의성을 더하였습니다.

Vocabulary List

어휘 실력 향상을 위해 매 테스트에서 나온 어휘 중 필수 어휘만을 따로 선별하여 정리하였습니다. 이로 인해 번거롭게 사전을 찾을 필요없이 효율적으로 단어를 학습할 수 있습니다. 본문에 나온 토플 단어 정리를 해 두었습니다.

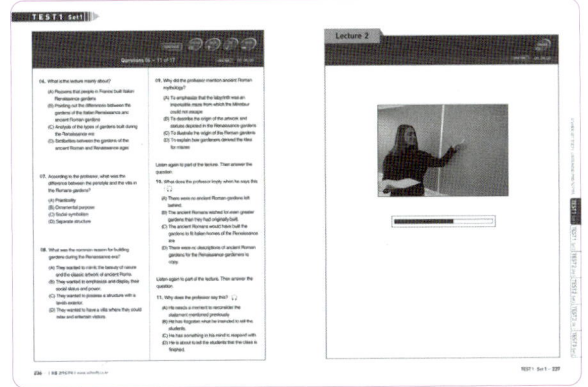

Test

실전 감각을 쌓을 수 있도록 총 3회분의 테스트를 수록하였고, 실제 시험 환경에 익숙해질 수 있도록 매 테스트를 실제 iBT 토플 시험과 동일한 형태의 화면으로 구성하였습니다. 시간을 맞춰 놓고 실전처럼 문제를 풀어 주시기 바랍니다.

6 본 iBT 토플 교재의 구성

지문+해석, 해설 추가설명

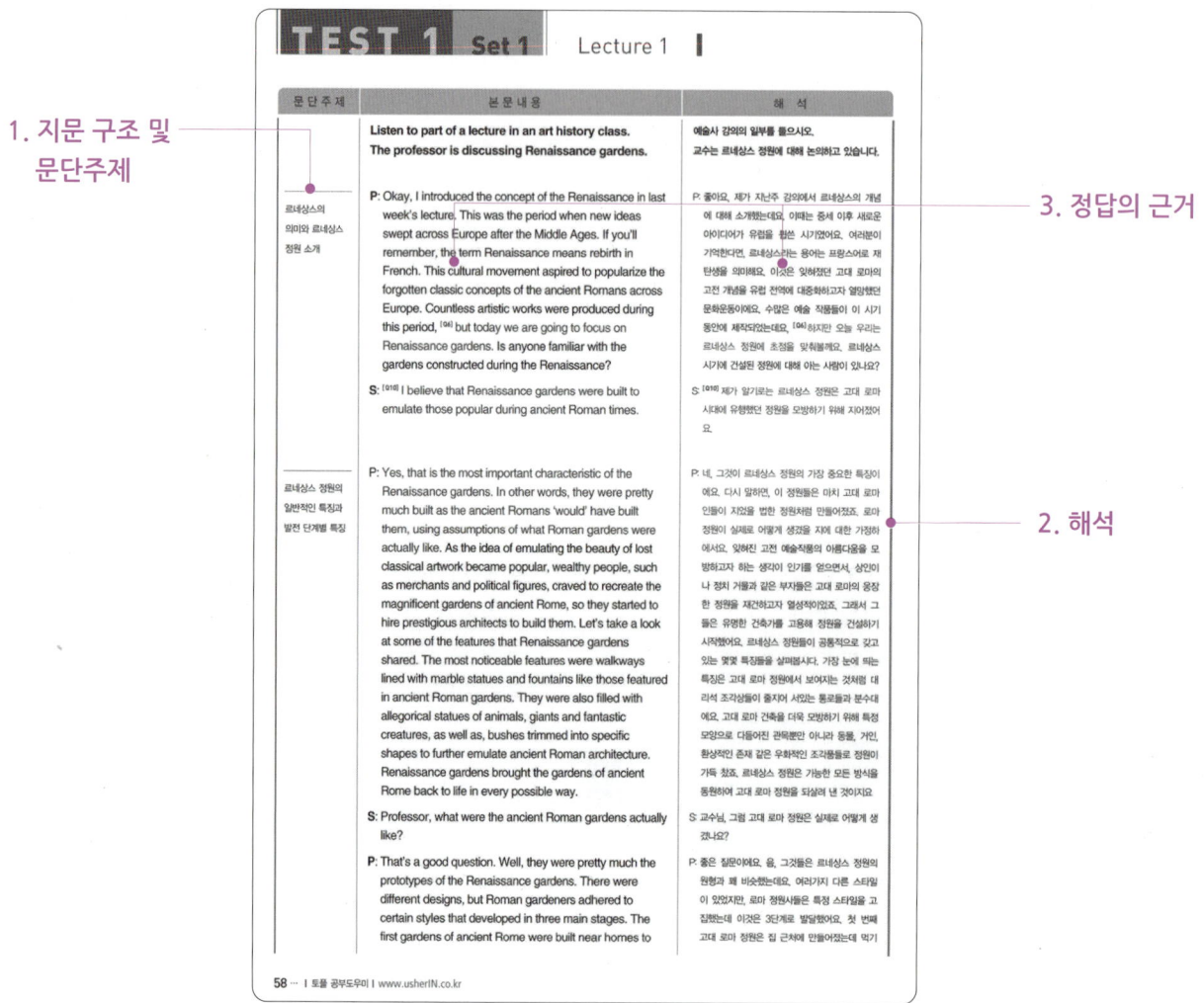

1. 지문 구조 및 문단주제
2. 해석
3. 정답의 근거

1. 지문구조 및 문단 주제
지문의 전체적인 흐름을 볼 수 있도록 지문의 핵심 내용을 요약하여 구조로 제시하였다.

2. 해석
지문 내용의 이해를 돕기 위해 정확한 해석을 제공하였다.

3. 정답의 근거
정답을 선택하는 데 단서가 되는 부분을 붉은 색으로 표시하여, 정답의 근거를 확실히 확인할 수 있도록 하였다.

4. TOEFL VOCABULARY
스크립트를 해석할 때 사전을 찾는 불편을 덜 수 있도록 지문에서 사용된 단어 중 꼭 알아야 할 필수 단어의 뜻과 발음을 정리하였다.

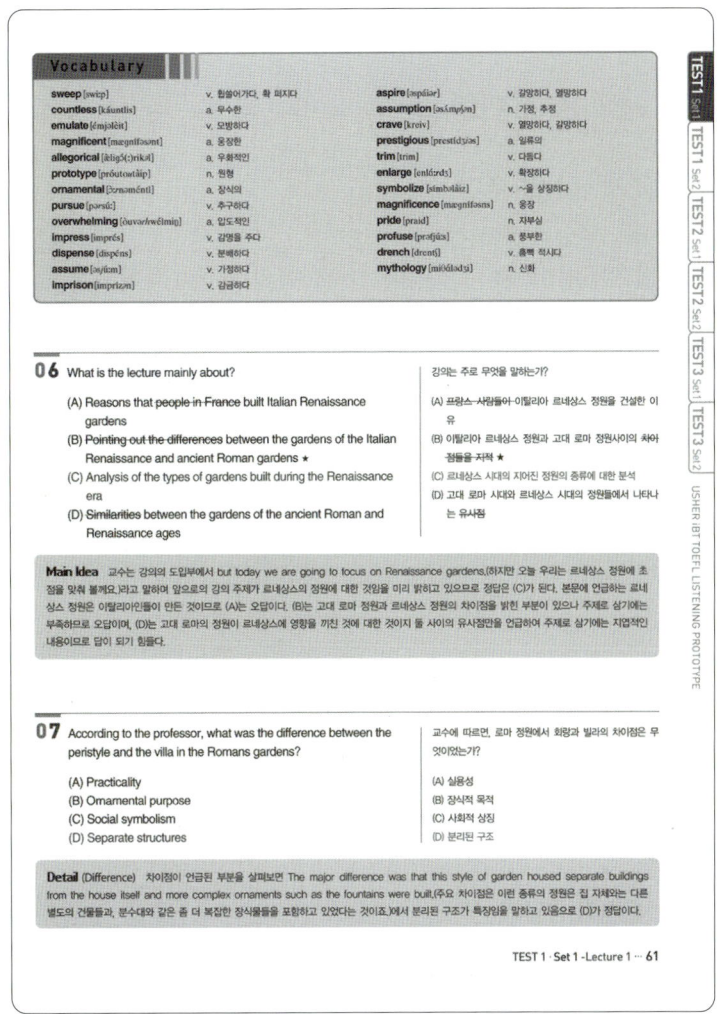

5. 문제의 정답

문제의 정답을 다른 색으로 표시하여 쉽게 알 수 있도록 했고, 찾기 쉽도록 옆의 해석 부분과 위치를 맞추었다.

6. 오답 이유

일반 문제들이 정답 근거만 제시하는 것에 반해, USHER iBT TOEFL FINAL TEST LISTENING (어셔 iBT 토플 파이널 테스트 리스닝)에서는, 오답의 이유도 밝혀 두어 혼자 공부하는 토플 독학생들에게 도움이 될 수 있도록 하였다.

7. 해설

각각의 문제 유형에 대한 표시, 정답이 되는 이유와 오답의 이유를 상세히 설명하여 혼자 공부하는 학생들에게 도움이 될 수 있도록 하였다.

7 실력별 학습 계획
USHER iBT TOEFL FINAL TEST LISTENING (어셔 iBT 토플 파이널 테스트 리스닝)

Test 1 - Set 1을 푼 뒤, 다음을 참고하여 자신의 실력에 맞는 학습 계획표를 짜서 공부하시기 바랍니다.

1 17개 문제 중 맞은 개수 14개 이상

목표 : 매일 Test 1개(2개 set)를 푼다.
- 실전 시험 문제를 푼다는 기분으로 풀어본다.
- 각 Set당 25분씩 시간을 맞춰놓고 푼다. (실전에서는 30분씩 시간이 주어지지만, 평소 연습할 때 5분 정도 남겨놓고 문제를 풀어야 실제 시험에서 시간이 모자라지 않는다)
- 채점한 뒤 틀린 문제를 꼭 확인하고, 오답정리하는 습관을 길러 실수를 줄이려 노력한다.
- 자신이 주로 틀리는 문제패턴이 무엇인지 오답분석을 통해 꼭 알아내서, 다음 시험에선 같은 실수를 반복하지 않도록 한다.
- 본인이 들을 때 이해하지 못한 어휘나 표현은 스크립트에서 찾아 반드시 외우도록 한다.

1주	1일차	2일차	3일차	4일차
	Test 1	Test 2	Test 3	Test 4

2 17개 문제 중 맞은 개수 10개 이상

목표 : 매일 set 1개씩 푼다.
- 매일 정해진 set 1개(Conversation1개+Lecture2개)를 30분 동안 푼다.
- 채점한 뒤 본인이 틀린 문제의 정답의 근거를 스크립트에서 찾아 확인하고, 오답의 유형과 이유를 분석하는 습관을 길러 실수를 줄이려 노력한다.
- 오답정리를 통해 자신이 주로 틀리는 문제패턴이 무엇인지 꼭 알아내어, 다음 시험에선 같은 실수를 줄여나가야 한다.
- 청취시 이해하지 못한 단어나 문장, 표현 등은 스크립트에서 모두 표시한 후 사전이나 인터넷을 통해 뜻을 찾아 반드시 외우는 것을 게을리 하지 않는다.
- 본인이 잘 알지 못하거나 낯선 주제에 관한 내용은 인터넷의 백과사전에 Key word를 중심으로 검색하여, 한국어로 내용을 이해하고 핵심내용을 간략히 정리하여 기억하는 작업을 반복함으로써 꾸준히 관련 배경지식을 쌓아 나간다.

1주	1일차	2일차	3일차	4일차	5일차
	Test 1 - Set 1	Test 1 - Set 2	Test 2 - Set 1	Test 2 - Set 2	Test 3 - Set 1
2주	6일차	7일차	8일차		
	Test 3 - Set 2	Test 4 - Set 1	Test 4 - Set 2		

3 17개 문제 중 맞은 개수 8개 이상

목표 : 매일 렉쳐 1개씩 푼다.
- 매일 정해진 1개 렉쳐를 10분 동안 푼다.
- 시간내에 문제를 다 못 풀더라도 너무 신경쓰지 말고 끝까지 문제를 다 푸는데 집중한다.
- 아직은 시험에 대해 충분히 준비가 안된 상태이므로, 시험 연습 보다는 청취에 초점을 맞추어 내용을 이해하도록 노력하고 문제를 통해 본인이 제대로 이해했는지 확인한다.
- 청취력을 향상시키기 위해 기본이 되는 것은 어휘이다. 채점한 뒤 대화와 강의의 스크립트를 보고 모르는 단어는 전부 찾아 반드시 뜻을 파악하고 암기하도록 한다.
- 본인이 잘 알지 못하거나 낯선 주제에 관한 내용은 인터넷의 백과사전에 Key word를 중심으로 검색하여, 한국어로 내용을 이해하고 핵심내용을 간략히 정리하여 기억하는 작업을 반복함으로써, 꾸준히 관련 배경지식을 쌓아나가야 한다.
- 문제를 다시 복습하는 것도 중요하지만 더 중요한 건 청취력 향상으로, 풀었던 문제의 본문 내용은 Mp3파일을 통해 반복적으로 듣고 이해하도록 노력해야 한다.

	1일차	2일차	3일차	4일차	5일차
1주	Conversation 1	Lecture 1	Lecture 2	Conversation 2	Lecture 3
	6일차	7일차	8일차	9일차	10일차
2주	Lecture 4	Conversation 3	Lecture 5	Lecture 6	Conversation 4
	11일차	12일차	13일차	14일차	15일차
3주	Lecture 7	Lecture 8	Conversation 5	Lecture 9	Lecture 10
	16일차	17일차	18일차	19일차	20일차
4주	Conversation 6	Lectuer 11	Lecture 12	Conversation 7	Lecture 13
	21일차	22일차	23일차	24일차	
5주	Lecture 14	Conversation 8	Lecture 15	Lecture 16	

8 Listening Strategies 1. 리스닝 학습 순서 및 방법

USHER iBT TOEFL **FINAL TEST LISTENING** (어셔 iBT 토플 파이널 테스트 리스닝)

리스닝 학습순서

1 예습

수업시간에 진행할 리스닝 Test를 시간을 맞춰놓고 Mp3파일을 들으면서 문제를 푼다. 이 때 Note-taking을 하게 되는데, **주의할 점은 너무 많이 적으면 청취에 오히려 방해가 되어 역효과**가 나기 쉽다는 것이다. 노트테이킹을 하는 목적은 내용을 다 기억하기 힘들기 때문에 고유명사나 특징을 나타내는 단어들, 순서나 과정 등을 간략히 메모했다가 문제를 풀 때 참고하기 위함이다. 그런데 학생들은 청취가 시작됨과 동시에 무조건 계속 쓰는 버릇이 있다. 물론 글을 쓰면서 동시에 듣는 내용도 이해가 잘되고 기억을 할 수 있으면 문제가 없겠지만, 대부분의 학생들은 쓰는데 집중한 나머지 들려오는 소리들을 놓치거나 내용을 제대로 기억하지 못하는 경우가 비일비재하다. 따라서 **효과적인 Note-taking이란 핵심 단어 위주로 간략하고 명료하게, 말 그대로 '메모' 수준으로 하는 것**이다. (자세한 내용은 p.34 '효과적인 Note-taking 방법' 참조)

2 수업

수업 시간에는 최대한 집중하여 몰입한다.

(A) Lecture의 **Mp3파일을 다시 들으며, 시험 볼 때 써놓은 Note-taking을** 수정한다. 2번째 듣는 것이므로 처음 들었을 때 놓쳤거나 잘못 이해하여 적은 부분을 고친다. 유의할 점은 수정할 때 사용하는 펜은 **첫 노트테이킹 시 사용하는 펜과는 다른 색깔을 사용하여 처음과 두 번째 들은 내용을 구별해 놓아야 한다**는 것이다. 이 작업을 하고 나서 옆 사람과 함께 내용을 discuss 한다. 본인이 들은 내용을 다른 사람이 들은 내용과 비교해보고, 그런 다음 선생님과 핵심 내용들을 함께 맞춰봄으로써 **어떤 것들을 제대로 들었는지 혹은 놓쳤는지 깨달을 수 있게** 된다. **이 activity는 청취력에 꼭 필요한 핵심 내용을 정확하게 잡아내는 기술과 강의의 흐름을 파악하는 이해력을 향상시킬 수 있는 장점**이 있다. 또한 나중에 Script를 통하여 내용과 문제를 철저히 파악하고 난 뒤 Summary 작업을 통해 정리한 내용을 note-taking과 비교하여 보면, 본인의 청취 취약점을 확실히 파악할 수 있어 효과적이다.

(B) 다음은 강의 내용의 **스크립트를 빠르게 직독직해**하면서 읽는다. 이때 한 문장을 최대 2번까지만 읽고 의미를 이해해야 한다. **모르는 단어나 이해가 안가는 표현이 나오면** 앞으로 되돌아가거나, 중간에 멈춰서 사전을 찾지 말고 **앞뒤 문맥을 바탕으로 뜻을 유추**한다. 그래도 **이해가 안가면 그 부분만 하이라이트 펜으로 마킹**한 뒤 넘어간다. 이런 방식으로 시간 제한을 두고 끝까지 한번 쭉 읽어나가면서, 강의의 주제를 파악하고 각각 세부사항의 핵심을잡아낸다.

(C) 스크립트를 다 읽고 내용을 이해했으면 본인이 푼 문제들을 살펴본다. 이때 **틀린 문제를 중점적으로 분석**하려고 노력한다. **문제 유형과 출제 의도, 정답의 근거를 스크립트에서 찾고, 본인이 선택한 답이 왜 오답인지를 생각**한다. 그런 후에 선생님과 함께 확인하면서 내용과 문제에 대해 이해한 점을 본인의 것으로 소화하려고 노력한다.

3 복습

본인의 실력 향상에 가장 큰 영향을 주는 것이 복습이다. **수업에서 이해하고 훈련했던 내용을 자신의 것으로 체화하는 작업**이기 때문이다.

(A) 수업시간에 공부했던 내용의 MP3파일을 다시 전체적으로 들으며 내용을 이해한다.

(B) **잘 안들리는 부분으로 되돌아 가서 그 부분에 해당하는 문장을 Dictation**한다. (딕테이션에 대한 자세한 내용은 뒷장 p.36 '청취력 향상 훈련 방법' 참조) 딕테이션이 다 끝나면 스크립트와 대조하며 **색깔펜으로 수정**한다. 이 때 틀린 단어 위에 겹쳐서 수정하지 말고, **단어 위나 아래 부분에 올바른 단어를 쓴다. 수정하면서 틀린 부분은 왜 틀렸는지 생각**해 본다. 아예 모르는 단어라 못 적은 건지, 글로 보면 아는 단어인데 소리가 안들려서 틀린건 지, 적긴 적었으나 앞뒤로 연음이 되어 일부분만 적었는지 등 분석을 해야 본인이 어떤 부분에서 청취가 취약한지 파악할 수 있다.

(C) 듣기 스크립트와 문제에서 **하이라이트 펜으로 표시한 모르는 단어나 표현들은 전자사전이나 인터넷을 이용해 찾는다.** 단, 이때 단어의 발음을 꼭 확인하고 여러 번 따라 말함으로써, 머리 속에 뜻과 함께 소리를 기억하려고 노력한다. 생활에서 쓰이는 관용어구나 영어 특유의 표현들은 문장을 통째로 외우도록 한다.

(D) 틀린 문제를 다시 본다. 유형과 정답근거를 다시 한번 확인하고, 오답과 비교한 후'청오답정리표'에 틀린 문제를 정리한다. 이렇게 오답을 분석해 나가면 **본인의 사고 오류를 파악할 수 있어, 다음 번에 똑같은 실수의 반복을 피할 수 있다.**

(E) Dictation에서 **수정이 많이 된 부분은 스크립트에 따로 표시**한 후, 그 부분의 **Mp3파일을 듣으면서 하나씩 따라 말해본다.** 이때 주의할 점은 Native Speaker가 말하는 **그대로 똑같이 흉내내어 말하면서, 영어소리 그대로 흡수 하여 기억해야** 한다는 것이다. 꼭 기억해야 할 표현들은 문장을 통째로 5, 6번 따라 말하며 본인의 것으로 소화한다.

(F) 이제 완벽히 이해한 내용을 영어 또는 한글로 핵심 단어 위주로 정리하여 Summary한다. (방법은 뒷장 p.37 'Summary Sample' 참조)

(G) 이 과정이 끝나면 본문의 내용전체를 Mp3로 다시 한번 쭉 들으며 머릿속에 흡수한다.

8 Listening Strategies 1. 리스닝 학습 순서 및 방법

리스닝 학습방법

1 효과적인 Note-taking 방법

1. Note-taking의 목적 및 효과

A) 목적

대화(Conversation)는 내용이 짧고(3분정도) 물어보는 질문이 거의 패턴화 되어 있기 때문에 노트테이킹이 큰 역할을 하지는 않는다. 그러나 강의(Lecture)의 경우 길기 때문에(5~6분), 내용을 모두 기억하기란 쉽지 않으므로, 청취 **중에 중요하다고 판단되는 내용**을 메모하면 **문제를 풀 때 참고할 수 있어 유용**하다. 들으면서 동시에 기록하는 것은 쉽지 않기 때문에, **평소에 들으면서 주요내용을 파악하며 기억하기 어려운 부분을 빠르고 명료하게 받아쓰는 연습이 필요**하다.

B) 효과

효과적인 Note-taking은 **강의의 전체적인 흐름을 파악**하는 것과, **세부 정보를 기억하는데 도움**을 주며, 들려주는 **내용이 서로 어떤 연관성을 지니는가를 쉽게 파악**할 수 있도록 해준다.

▶ 유의점 : 대화 및 강의의 내용에 대한 이해를 하면서 Note-taking을 해야 효과적이며 청취를 통한 기본적인 이해가 없는 상태에서는 오히려 Listening에 방해가 될 수 있다.

▶ 방　향 : 모든 내용을 다 기록하려고 하기보다는, **핵심내용**만을 **논리적으로 간략하게 정리**해야 효과적이다.

2. Note-taking 요령

A) 세부사항을 간략하게 메모하기

세부사항을 기록할 때는 **Key Words를 이용하여 중심내용을 간략하게 정리**한다. 표기하기 쉽고 나중에 읽을 때 눈에 빨리 들어올 수 있도록, 평소에 글을 요약할 때 기호화 및 도식화하는 훈련을 하는 것이 도움이 된다. 또한 **각 세부 화제별로 내용을 묶어서 정리**할 수 있으면 좋다. 화제가 전환되거나 화자가 잠깐 중심 내용을 벗어난 얘기를 할 때는 Signal Words(Now, First of all, Another, Finally, etc)를 파악하면 변화를 알 수 있다.

B) 기호 및 약어

Note-taking시에는 들리는 말을 모두 받아쓰는 것이 아니라(시간소요, 뒤에 따라오는 내용 청취 방해), **기호 및 약어를 이용해서 간략하게 본인이 알아볼 수 있도록** 쓰는 것이 좋다.

【기호】	x : no, not	+ : and, plus, addition
	e.g. : example, instance	∵ : because, since
	→ : lead to, cause, go to	← : come from, originate from
	↑ : increase, rise, grow	↓ : decrease, decline, reduce
	/h : per hour	>, < : more / less than
【약어】	pl : people	etc : and so on, and so forth
	info : information	c : century
	tech : technology	Q : question
	vs : versus, compare	ea. : each
	S : step	T : types

3. Note - taking의 예

MT : Develop. of Piano.

    1) likes & dislikes of patron

       - Dev. of tech — inf.

    2)

Harp	Piano
String Quill — pluck	Percu-Hammer Dynamic Convey emo.

    3) influence

       - mid class / mass pro — price ↓

       - lives of women ↑ : e.g. Clar Shu - pub recital

8 Listening Strategies 1. 리스닝 학습 순서 및 방법

Dictation Sample

문장의 의미상 꼭 필요한 핵심단어(강세단어)는 모두 적어야 합니다.

Listen to a conversation between a student and an employee in the university bookstore

S: Hi, bought this book beginning semester, but some things come up, like return

E: full refund, store policy have to return merchandise two weeks time purchased. but assigned textbooks, anything having to do with specific courses… wait, specific course?

S: Yeah, but actually…

E: for course books, deadline four weeks after beginning semester. So this fall semester, deadline October 1st.

S: Ouch, then missed ? But, why October 1st?

E: guess reasoning by October 1st, semester in full gear, everyone kind of knows what courses taking that semester.

딕테이션이 끝나면, **script와 비교하여, 색깔펜으로 틀린 단어를 수정**합니다.

B) 강의 내용의 **스크립트를 빠르게 직독직해** 합니다. 이때 한 문장을 최대 2번까지만 읽으면서 내용의 흐름을 따라 이해하고 해석해 나갑니다. 모르는 단어나 표현이 나와도 <u>중간에 멈춰서 사전을 찾지 말고 그 부분만 하이라이트 펜으로 마킹한 뒤, 앞뒤 문맥을 바탕으로 뜻을 유추하면서 끝까지 한번 쭉 읽어나갑니다</u>. 글의 마지막까지 다 읽 었으면 이제 표시해 두었던 단어나 표현을 사전에서 찾아 확인합니다.

C) 이제 새<u>도잉을 하시되 Dictation 단계에서 많이 틀린 곳을 script에 하이라이트 펜으로 표시한 후, 그 부분만 한 문장씩 끊어서 따라 말해보세요</u>. 긴 문장은 의미단위로 나누어 여러 번 따라 말해본 후에, 잘되면 붙여서 그 문장 전체를 한번에 따라 말합니다. 잘 안되는 문장(발음이 꼬이거나, 길어서 한번에 말하지 못하는 문장등…)은 좀 더 많이 따라해서 소리가 익숙해지도록 합니다. 특히 **통째로 외워야 하는 어휘나 생활표현 <u>(colloquial expression)</u>** 등은 소리와 뜻이 머리 속에 합쳐져 기억될 수 있도록 **문장자체를 소리로 암기**해 주셔야 합니다. 5번 정도 이상 Native speaker의 발음과 스피드를 똑같이 흉내내면서 연습하면 발음뿐만 아니라 그 문장 자체가 머리 속에 남 게 되며 이렇게 익힌 표현들은 speaking 및 Writing 시험에서도 큰 효과를 발휘하게 됩니다.

D) **script를 보지말고 mp3를 다시 들으며 전체 내용을 머리 속에 정리**합니다. 이미 해석한 내용이므로 소리 파일을 중간에 멈추지 말고 native speaker의 속도를 그대로 따라가면서 내용을 이해하려고 노력합니다.

이런 식으로 대화 및 강의를 훈련하다 보면, 일정한 양이 쌓이면서 영어 소리에 대한 귀가 점차 열리게 됩니다. 더불 어 본인의 발음까지 교정되기 때문에, Listeing 뿐만 아니라 speaking 시험에도 상당한 도움을 받을 수 있습니다. 명심할 것은 **"내가 말할 수 있는건 다~~ 들린다"**는 사실입니다. 리스닝은 입과 귀를 동시에 사용해서 뚫는 것이 가장 빠르고 효과적인 방법입니다.

2 Summary

▶ Summary를 하는 목적은?
1) 강의내용을 구조(structure) 및 흐름(flow)을 파악, 문제 예측 가능
2) 핵심내용만을 기억하여 추후 배경지식으로 활용
3) 리스닝과 동시에 진행되는 Note-taking의 기본골격 연습

Summary Sample

예1) 영어요약 - Conversation

1. **Purpose** : To find out about volunteering for archeology project
2. **Issue**
   A) **Need to have any experience with these kinds of projects?**
      → Not really. Most students have little or no experience with research
   B) **Specific contents on the project**
      1. Studying history of campus
      2. The site where they'll be studying :
         - The main lecture hall ; once farmhouse and barn
         - Excavating the site to see artifacts things
         - No travelling involved
3. **Suggestion:**
   A) **What the project offers for the student**
      - Any extra credit in class? —can arrange something
      - Professor thinks extra credit is always good incentive for students
   B) **Training schedule?**
      - Professor will schedule a training class when it's convenient for everyone

예2) 한글 요약 - Lecture

MI: 가장 오래된 동굴 미술 - 프랑스의 Chauvet cave

1. **Chauvet 동굴의 연대 측정**
   - 3만년 이상
   - 오래되었으나 원시적 X, 걸작품 O
   - Chauvet 동굴 연대측정에 대한 의심 : Altamira and Lasco 동굴보다 훨씬 오래됨
                                근거) 다른 실험실의 결과 확인 X

2. **동굴 그림들의 배경**
   1) 구석기 : 날씨가 현저히 다른 때보다 추웠음, 동굴에서 주거 → 동굴 벽에 그림 그렸음
   2) Chauvet : 사람이 살았던 흔적 없음
         - 인간 거주 흔적 없으나, 보러는 왔었음 → 증거) 숯의 흔적
         - 무엇이 그들로 하여금 그림 그리게 했나? : 알 수 없음

3. **Chauvet 동굴벽화가 말해주는 것**
   1) 구석기 : 초식동물
   2) Chauvet 초기벽화 : 크고 위험한 동물, But 인간은 그리지 않음 → 왜 특정 동물인가? : 알 수 없음

8 Listening Strategies 2.문제 분석 방법
USHER iBT TOEFL **FINAL TEST LISTENING** (어셔 iBT 토플 파이널 테스트 리스닝)

실전에서 문제를 풀때, 본인이 정답이라고 생각되는 보기가 빨리 눈에 띄었다 하더라도 침착하게 남은 보기 모두를 끝까지 확인하는 습관을 길러야 합니다. 최근 토플리스닝 문제의 경향은 정답과 흡사한 오답이 등장하는 경우가 예전에 비해 현저히 증가하여, 수험자들에게 혼란을 주는 경우가 많다는 것입니다. 따라서 문제와 답을 하나씩 끝까지 확인하여 실수의 가능성을 최소화함으로써, 내용을 정확하게 듣고도 문제의 의도에 맞는 정답을 고르지 못하거나, 출제자가 의도적으로 만들어 놓은 함정에 빠져 아까운 점수를 잃는 경우를 없애야 합니다. 이를 위해, 평소에 훈련할 때 정답의 근거 파악과 본인이 틀린 문제는 왜 틀렸는지를 꼼꼼히 분석하는 습관을 기르는 것이 도움이 됩니다.

정답과 오답을 분석하는 방법은 다음과 같습니다.

1. 문제에서 정답을 확인한 뒤 script에서 답의 근거가 해당되는 위치를 찾아 표시합니다.
2. 각각 오답의 유형을 분석한 뒤 표시합니다. (아래 Example1 참조)
3. 틀린문제와 답은 오답정리표에 따로 기록하여 다시 한번 정리한 뒤, 추후 복습용으로 활용합니다.
   (▶ 오답정리표는 각 테스트에 위치)

오답 유형

Type 1	선택하려는 답이 지문에서 **언급이 안된 경우** (not mentioned)
Type 2	선택하려는 답이 지문의 사실과 **반대되거나 잘못된 정보**를 주는 경우 (opposite / wrong fact)
Type 3	선택하려는 답이 **지문에서 정확히 언급이 되었지만 문제에서 요구하는 답이 아닌 경우** (fact, but not related to the question)
Type 4	선택하려는 답이 그럴싸하게 정답인 듯 보이지만 **한 단어 또는 일부 때문에 오답이 되는 경우** (one word or partial error)

Example 1 : 정답 및 오답 표시

6. What does the professor mainly discuss?

   (A) Some characteristics that are common in several languages : 정답
   (B) A way to represent languages that are genetically related : Type 1
   (C) Which languages probably evolved from Proto-Indo-European : Type 3
   (D) Linguists' opinions about why languages change over time : Type 1

문제 유형별 세부 전략

1 방문 목적 및 강의 주제

대화(conversation)나 강의(Lecture)의 중심내용을 찾는 문제 유형으로, Conversation은 찾아온 목적이나 대화의 중심내용, Lecture는 강의의 주제를 주로 물어본다.

【 질문형태 】
- Why does the student talk to the employee?
- Why does the student go to see his professor?
- Why does the professor ask to see the student?
- What is the conversation mainly about?
- What do the speakers mainly discuss?
- What is the lecture mainly about?
- What is the purpose of the lecture?

【 전   략 】

A) 처음에 나오는 Direction 및 내용의 도입부를 집중해서 듣는다.

앞부분을 놓치지 않는다. 대화 및 강의는 앞부분에서 중심내용이 무엇인지 파악할 수 있는 경우가 많으므로 앞부분 에 특별한 주의를 기울여 전체적인 내용이 무엇일지 예측하면서 들어야 한다. 대화 및 강의 내용이 나오기 전에 들 려주는 Direction에서 앞으로 설명될 분야가 언급되기 때문이다. 이를 통해 학생의 대화상대가 직원인지 혹은 교수 인지를 알 수 있고, 강의의 경우 해당 강의의 과목을 미리 파악할 수 있어 내용을 따라가는데 도움이 된다. 또한 대 화나 강의의 앞부분에 특별한 주의를 기울여 들으면, 주로 도입부에서 중심내용이 무엇인지 파악할 수 있는 실마리 나 힌트를 얻게 경우가 많으므로, 앞부분의 내용과 함께 전체적인 내용이 무엇일 것인지 예측하면서 들어야 한다.

- **Conversation** : 주로 화자들이 인사를 나눈 다음에 찾아온 목적이나 대화의 중심내용이 언급됨. 최근에는 도입 부 분에서 다른 얘기를 하다가, 중간 부분에서 찾아온 이유나 중심내용을 시작하는 경우도 증가하고 있음.
- **Lecture** : 지난 수업에서 다루었던 내용을 간략히 언급한 후에, 주로 강의의 주제나 방향에 대해 언급됨. 도입부 분 에서 주제가 뚜렷이 언급되지 않고 강의의 내용 전체를 끝까지 듣고 유추해야 하는 경우도 증가하고 있음.

B) 중심내용을 언급하는 표시어(signal words)에 집중하며 듣는다.

중심내용을 언급할 때 자주 쓰이는 표현이 있는데, 이 표시어 앞뒤로 중심내용이 등장하는 경우가 많으므로 집중 해서 들어야 한다.

- **Conversation** : I'm here because ~, That's why I came by. I want to(I'd like to) talk to you about ~. I was wondering If ~
- **Lecture** : Today, we will be discussing ~, Let's look at~, We'll be continuing ~ , Today, we're going to look at ~

▶ 주의 : 도입부에서 주제가 확실히 언급되지 않는 경우가 간혹 있는데, 이때는 지문 전체를 듣고 전반적인 내용을 파악한 후 문제에서 적합한 답을 찾아야 함.

8 Listening Strategies 2. 문제 분석 방법

2 세부사항

대화나 강의를 통해 알 수 있는 세부사항을 파악하는 문제로, 주로 화자가 언급한 내용 중 주제와 관련된 중요한 세부사항을 묻는 경우가 대부분이다.

【 질문형태 】

- What does the man / professor say about~ ?
- According to the conversation/professor, how does~ ?
- What are some reasons that~ ?
- What are two features/characteristics/ factors of~ ?
- What are the two examples the man gives facors of~ ?
- According to the conversation / lecture, what can be inferred from~ ?

【 전　　략 】

A) <u>주제와 관련하여 주요 세부 사항을 주의깊게 듣는다.</u>

　　화자는 중심내용과 밀접하게 관련된 세부사항을 언급하므로 이를 주의깊게 파악하여 들으며 기억하거나 메모한다.
　　- **Conversation** : 문제점, 예시, 제안, 충고, 필요요건, 반응 등
　　- **Lecture** : 이유, 특징, 부연설명, 방법, 결과, 질문, 질문에 대답하는 내용, 강조하고자 하는 내용 등

B) <u>새로이 소개되는 용어를 주의깊게 듣는다.</u>

　　강의에서 화자가 새로이 소개하는 용어가 있다면 그에 대한 정의 및 부가 설명이 뒤이어 오는 경우가 많고, 이 용어는 강의내용 상 반드시 이해해야 할 개념인 경우가 대부분이므로, 문제로 이어질 가능성 크다. 따라서 용어는 나오는대로 기억하거나 메모할 필요가 있다.

C) <u>예시를 사용하여 설명할 때 주의깊게 듣는다</u>

　　주제와 관련하여 예시를 사용해 내용을 설명하는 경우는 토플 리스닝 렉쳐에서 많이 사용하는 방법이다. 따라서 예시를 나타내는 표시어가 들리면 긴장하여 듣고, 특히 주제와 관련하여 어떤 부분을 설명하는지 연결하여 들을 필요가 있다.

D) <u>화제가 전환되는 부분을 파악하며 듣는다</u>

　　화자가 중간에 화제를 전환하거나 중심내용에서 잠깐 벗어나 다른 얘기를 할 때, 이를 파악하며 듣는 것은 전체적인 내용의 흐름과 화자의 목적, 세부 내용과 중심내용의 관계 등을 이해하는 데 필요하다.

E) <u>표시어(signal words)를 통해 내용들간의 관계를 파악하며 듣는다.</u>

　　용어, 예시, 특징, 비교/대조, 요건, 제안, 인과관계, 분류, 순차적인 관계 등을 나타내는 표시어를 주의깊게 들으면 내용들을 더 쉽게 파악할 수 있다.
　　- 용어 : It's called"'-, What we call"'-, so-called"'-, It's referred as"'-

- 예시 : For example, For instance, Let's say, say, take, such as, like, think of, imagine
- 특징 : It's interestingA., unique, fascinating, intriguing, important, useful, note, unusual, odd, weird, strange
- 비교/대조 : early, later, compare, contrast, analogy, evolve, develop, in the past, decades ago, in ancient times, today, nowadays, modern day
- 요건 : required, necessary, consider, condition, premise, experience, you need to~.
- 제안 : to solve/handle this problem, recommend, Why don't you~.?, What about~?, What can be done~., Your best bet would beA.
- 인과관계/증거/결과/발견/영향 : study, research, experiment, project, find, discover, uncover, reveal, evidence, impact, pave the way, application
- 순서/분류 : step, stage, phase, and then, divide intoA., three types, two kinds of, first, second, finally

3 내용의 암시 및 화자의 의도 파악

지문에서 들은 정보를 바탕으로 추론할 수 있는 사실을 묻는 문제이다. Purpose는 화자가 특정 내용을 언급한 목적이 무엇인지 문제로 지문에서 직접적으로 드러나지 않고, 간접적으로 알 수 있는 정보에 대해 묻는다. 세부사항에 해당하 는 내용을 물어보기도 하고 지문의 특정 부분 내용을 다시 들려준 후 문제를 푸는 형태로 출제되기도 한다. 겉으로 드 러나는 말 뒤에 숨어있는 내용이 암시하는 바와 이 말을 하는 화자의 의도를 묻는 문제이기 때문에, 화자가 특정한 언급을한 의도가 무엇인지 파악하고 화자의 의견이나 이 유형은 세부사항에 해당하는 내용을 물어보기도 하고 지문의 특 정 부분을 다시 들려 준 후 문제로 푸는 형태로 출제되기도 한다.

【 질문형태 】

- Why does the professor mention/ discuss / talk about~ ?
- What does the professor imply about ~?
- What can be inferred about ~?
- What is the professor's opinion/attitude/stance towards~?
- How does the professor feel about~?
- Why does the student say this :
- What does the man/ woman mean when he/she says this :
- What does the professor imply when he/she says this :
- What will the man/ woman probably do next?

8 Listening Strategies 2. 문제 분석 방법

【 전 략 】

A) 문제가 나올수 있는 부분을 예측하며 듣는다.
화자가 자신의 의도를 직접적으로 말하지 않고 간접적인 방식으로 돌려 말할 때, 자신의 의견이나 평가 또는 강조나 동의를 구할 때, 놓치지 않고 화자의 의도나 태도를 생각하며 듣는다.

B) 화자의 어조를 통해 태도를 파악하며 듣는다.
화자의 어조가 긍정적, 부정적, 비판적, 불확실인지 등을 판단하여, 화자의 의견이나 강의 대상에 대한 평가와 화자의 숨어있는 태도를 정확히 파악하며 듣는다.

C) 화자가 언급한 말의 이면적인 뜻을 생각하며 듣는다.
화자가 직접적으로 말하지는 않았으나 화자가 한말을 통해 간접적으로 알 수 있는 사실을 추론하며 듣는다.
제시된 사실을 단순히 그대로 받아들이지 말고 화자가 말하고자 하는 바가 무엇인지를 생각하며 듣는다.

D) 맥락을 파악하며 듣는다.
다시 들려주는 부분의 맥락을 통해 화자가 한말의 의도를 파악한다. 예전과 달리 최근에는 다시 들려주는 부분이 줄어들었기 때문에, 처음에 내용을 들을 때 흐름을 정확히 파악하며 들어야 문제가 물어보는 위치를 기억할 수 있다.

4 내용의 암시 및 화자의 의도 파악

화자가 어떤 방식으로 내용을 전개하여 정보를 전달하는지 묻는 문제이다. 지문에 언급된 여러가지 정보들 간의 연관성을 이해하는지를 묻는 문제유형으로, 정보들이 어떻게 조직되어 있는지를 확인하거나 흩어져 있는 정보들이 어떻게 서로 연결되는지 파악, 범주별로 알맞은 정보를 연결하거나 사건 및 절차를 순차적으로 나열하는 문제 등이 출제된다.

【 질문형태 】
- How does the professor introduce/ conclude ~?
- How is the lecture/discussion organized?
- How does the professor emphasize his point about~?
- What are the features/characteristics/ factors of~ ? Click on 2/3 answers
- In the lecture/conversation, ~. Indicate whether each of the following is a ~.

	Included	Not Included
Statement A		
Statement B		
Statement C		

• Match each of the following to types of ~.

	Type A	Type B	Type C
Example 1			
Example 2			

• The professor explains the steps in the process of ~. Put these steps in order.

Step 1	
Step 2	

【 전　　략 】

A) 나올 수 있는 가능성있는 문제를 예측하며 듣는다.

화자의 정보전달 방식을 파악하는 필요하다. 지문의 큰 구조를 이해하면서 화자가 어떤 방식으로 정보를 전달하는지 유의면서 듣는디. 화자가 정보를 전달하는 전개 방식에는 두 가지 사항의 비교 혹은 대조, 시간 흐름에 따른 나열, 구체적인 예 제시, 장단점 기술 등이 있으며, 이러한 형태의 문제는 대화보다 강의에서 등장하는 경우가 많다.

B) 하나 이상의 범주에 포함되는 정보들이 나열될 때, 주의깊게 듣거나 메모한다.

하나의 범주에 대한 정보들 (ex: conversation - 특정과목을 수강등록하기 위한 조건들/Lecture-성층화산의 특징 들), 두 개 이상의 범주에 관한 정보들 (ex: 비교/대조, 장점/단점)이나 정답을 2개 이상 고르는 문제 (Click on 2 answers, Click on 3 answers), 관련된 정보들을 연결하는 문제, 그리고 몇가지 정보들이 특정한 순서 및 전개 방식으로 전달될 때 (ex: 절차, 과정, 사건), Ordering 문제를 예상하며 듣는다.

C) 자주 쓰이는 표시어(signal words)를 주의 깊게 듣는다.

- 특징/요건 : requirement, condition, necessary, include, reasons, features
- Matching : types, features, characteristics, points
- Ordering : steps, stages, phase, divide into

8 Listening Strategies 2. 문제 분석 방법

5 문제 유형과 Signals

번호	기본문제유형	세부문제유형	Signals
1	Main Idea	Main Purpose / Main Idea	국부적인(지엽적인) or 너무 일반적인(광범위한) 사실은 오답, 시제 및 단수 / 복수 주의
2	Details	Term/Definition/Irigin	refer to, what we call, so-called, originate, come from
3		Example	such as, like, think of, imagine, Let's take, let's say~, say, example, for instance
4		Characteristic / Advantage / Disadvantage / Problem / Difficulty / Similarity / Compare / Difference / Contrast	그림, 음악, 문학, 무용, 영화, 연극, 공예, 조각 등 / unique, useful, interesting, faster, fascinating, intriguing, key feature, note, important 동물 멸종위기, 생명의 위협 / 환경적응 Problem, hitch, challenge, drawback, flaw, defect, extinct, destroyed early-later, prior to~, recent, in the past, nowadays, modern day, evolve
5		Cause / Reason / Evidence / Result / Finding / Effect / Influence	study, research, experiment, project(find, discover, uncover, reveal, shed light on) / evidence, finding / pave the way, impact, set the stage for, application
6		Misunderstanding / Correction/Surprising	once believed, but~ / seem out of this world, news to
7		Requirement / Condition	necessary, required, you need to, consideration, condition, premise, job experience,
8		Offer / Solution / Suggestion	Alternative, to solve, handle this problem, recommend, why don't you~, what about~, what can be done~, your best bet would be~,
9		Future action/Future topic	upcoming, next class, another lecture
10	Inference	Purpose / Intention / Imply / Infer / Opinion / Attitude / Headset	Why... mention~ / What can be inferred~/ What... imply~ What... mean when...say~ 다시 들려주고 푸는 문제 check ,understanding, agree/disagree
11	Category	Introduce / Organize / Conclude / Matching / Ordering	How~ introduce? How is the lecture organized? Three types, two kinds of, first, second, finally step, stage, phase , and then, divide into~

6 Listening Lecture 기출 Topic

아래는 과거 토플 리스닝 시험 Lecture에서 출제되었던 토픽(Topics)들을 모아놓은 것입니다. 쭉 살펴보고 본인이 익숙하지 않은 것들은 인터넷을 통해 검색해서 내용의 개요를 알아두면 도움이 될 것입니다. 리스닝에 나오는 토픽들은 또한 리딩과 라이팅에도 주제가 겹쳐 나오는 경우가 종종 있기 때문에, 배경지식으로 알아두면 여러모로 쓸모가 있습니다.

Social Science (사회과학)

Anthropology : calendar, Aztec, Maya, Egypt, Inuit People, Neolithic age, Inca, Artic pottery, Natufians, Fertile Crescent, etc.

Archaeology : GPR(Ground Penetrating Radar), Passage Grave, Stone Henge, Troy, hieroglyph, Anasazi, radiocarbon dating, etc.

Psychology / Child Development : memory, blind spot, imagination, hypersomnia, stress, Placebo effect, child attachment, Piaget, Montessori, Separation Anxiety disorder, reciprocal helping & altruistic helping, insight, social-evaluations, etc.

History / U.S. history : Gold Rush, eyeglasses, printing press, railroad, Tourism, U.S. President, Navajo, Clovis people, Iroquois People, Prehistoric Nevada, feudalism, Civil War, etc.

Linguistics : Grice's maxim, human language vs. animal communication, tree model, universal grammar, Webster, etc.

Business / Economics : AHP, famine, Sherman Act, boom & bust, function & project, Segmentation, etc.

Sociology : AMA, guilds, Labor Union, Zif's law, bureaucracy, etc.

Mass Communication : Newspaper, magazine, radio, etc.

Philosophy : Socrates, paradigm shift, Plato, etc.

Art (예술)

Painting : Cubism, Dadaism, Impressionism, Naturalism, fresco painting, Jackson Pollack, Picasso, etching, Paul Cezanne, Vincent Van Gogh, Johannes Jan Vermeer, Frida Kahlo, Andrew Warhol, Chauvet cave painting, Hudson River School, etc.

Literature : Book of Kells, detective novel, memoir vs. autobiography, Sherwood Anderson, Postmodernism, parchment & palimpsest, Mary Shelley's Frankenstein, etc.

Film / Theater : films in 1920s~30s, Nickelodeon, sound editing, well-made play, Method Acting, classical acting vs naturalism, structure of Greek theare, etc.

Music history : drum, opera, piano vs harpsichord, saxophone, records sale & radio in early 1900s, etc.

Architecture : roof style, Central Park, straw bale house, architect Frank, pedestrian mall, etc.

Crafts & Sculpture : stained glass, Navajo textile, Roman sculpture(polychrome), etc.

Photography : pin-hole camera, Camera obscura(Johannes Vermeer), etc.

8 Listening Strategies 2. 문제 분석 방법

Social Science (사회과학)

Biology

- **Botany** : maple syrup, pollination, rare tree, Mangrove, Venus flytrap, symbiosis(coral reefs), etc.

- **Zoology & Insectology** : bat, bird, snake, Polar bear, Humming bird, wolf, animal communication (dolphin, honey bee), habitat and the adaptation (bird migration, habitat selection, camouflage, hibernation, etc), cicada, dragonfly, spider's web, termite, etc.

- **Marine biology** : dolphin, whale, pearl, Spartina, squid, salmon, chemosynthesis, etc.

- **Taxonomy** : classification, binomial nomenclature, etc.

Environmental Science & Ecology : Eutrophication, phosphorous cycle, oil making, drying up lakes, greenhouse effect, glacier, alternative energy(ethanol), renewable energy, predation risk effects carbon capture(post combustion & pre combustion), etc.

Paleontology : Archaeopteryx, Amber, living fossil, dinosaur(cold blooded vs warm blooded), etc.

Physiology : lens of eyes, joints, sleep cycle, neuron, brain, etc.

Social Science (사회과학)

Astronomy : asteroid, comet, geocentric model, planet formation, star formation, stellar parallax, Supernova, Milky Way, Variables, Mercury, life on Mars, Venus, Saturn, Pluto, Protostar, albedo, Kuiper belt, Sagittarius galaxy, etc.

Geology : limestone cave, continental drift theory, rocks, Zircon, hoodoo, sand dune, seismic waves, volcanoes, Tundra, K-T boundary, etc.

Chemistry : charcoal, carbon & diamond, decaffeination, ice molecular structure, Leidenfrost Effect, Periodic Table, graphene, etc.

Physics : rainfall, standing waves, properties of light/sound (speed of light, resonance), Electromagnetic radiation (e.g. gamma ray), etc.

Earth Science : climate change, length of a day, ocean's salinity, Plate Tectonics, Flotsam Science, carbon sequestration, etc.

Engineering : airfoil, Bicycle Canada Bridge, Eiffel Tower, Hoover Dam, Shape Memory Alloy, semiconductor switch, etc.

Meteorology : hail, rain, snow, lightening, etc.

USHER iBT TOEFL
FINAL TEST
LISTENING | 문제집

(어셔 iBT 토플 파이널 테스트 리스닝 문제집)

어셔 어학 연구소

usherin.usher.co.kr

USHER iBT TOFLE
FINAL TEST
LISTENING
TEST 1

TEST 1   set 1

Listening Section Directions

This section measure your ability to understand conversations and lectures in English. It is divided into 3 separately timed parts. In the first part you will listen to 1 conversation and 2 lectures. In the second part you will listen to 1 conversation and 1 lecture. You will hear each conversation or lecture only one time.

After each conversation or lecture, you will answer some questions about it. Answer the questions based on what is stated or implied by the speakers.

For the first part of the listening section, you will have 10 minutes to answer the questions.
For the second part of the listening section, you will have 07 minutes to answer the questions.

A clock at the top of the screen will show you how much time is remaining. The clock will not count down while you are listening. The clock will count down only while you are answer questions.

You may take notes while you listen. You may use your notes to help you answer the questions. Your notes will not be scored.

If you need to change the volume while you listen, click on the Volume icon at the top of the screen

In some questions, you will see this icon 🎧. This means that you will hear but not see, part of the question. Most questions are worth 1 point. If a question is worth more than 1 point, it will have special directions that indicate how many points you can receive.

In this listening section. After you answer, click on Next. Then click on OK to confirm your and go on to the next section OK, you cannot return to previous questions.

Listen to part of the Listening section.
(Click on Continue at any time to dismiss these directions.)

> 리스닝 섹션은 PART 1, PART 2로 나누어져 있습니다.
> PART 1에서는 세 지문을 듣게 됩니다. 10분 동안 질문에 답하세요.
> 지문을 듣는 동안 시간이 줄어들지 않습니다.

Conversation

TEST 1   set 1

Question 01 ~ 05 of 17

01. What is the conversation mainly about?

(A) The student's thoughts about the conference in South Florida
(B) A new field of molecular biology that the student learned about during a conference from which he has just returned.
(C) The topic of the student's research paper
(D) The professor's research project on the bioluminescence of jellyfish

02. What can be inferred about the student?

(A) He met a lot of interesting people who research organisms that emit light.
(B) He is hardly surprised that some squid, shrimp, and fungi are bioluminescent.
(C) He attended a lecture about the molecular biological aspect of bioluminescence at the conference.
(D) He basically had no idea how some organisms produce light within themselves.

03. According to the conversation, what points were mentioned about the bioluminescence of organisms?

Click on 2 answers

(A) Some of them produce light in order to attract prey when they choose to.
(B) They utilize magnesium and other internal chemicals to produce light only when avoiding predators.
(C) The emission of light is an intermittent process with no specific purpose.
(D) The color of light emitted varies by organism.

04. What is the professor's attitude toward jellyfish as a topic of research for the student's paper?

(A) They are a radical topic that she has always expected students to write about.
(B) They can be an adequate topic of research only if the student manages to do it adeptly.
(C) They lack the scientific interest of other complex creatures.
(D) There has not been sufficient research in the field because getting into the details would take too much time.

Listen again to part of the conversation. Then answer the question.

05. What does the professor mean when she says this :

(A) She is asking the student if he understands what she is saying.
(B) She is asking the student to work harder than usual.
(C) She is asking the student if he thinks he can pull off this topic with success.
(D) She is asking the student if he agrees with everything she has just said.

Lecture 1

TEST 1   set 1

Question 06 ~ 11 of 17

06. What is the lecture mainly about?

(A) Reasons that people in France built Italian Renaissance gardens
(B) Pointing out the differences between the gardens of the Italian Renaissance and ancient Roman gardens
(C) Analysis of the types of gardens built during the Renaissance era
(D) Similarities between the gardens of the ancient Roman and Renaissance ages

07. According to the professor, what was the difference between the peristyle and the villa in the Romans gardens?

(A) Practicality
(B) Ornamental purpose
(C) Social symbolism
(D) Separate structure

08. What was the common reason for building gardens during the Renaissance era?

(A) They wanted to mimic the beauty of nature and the classic artwork of ancient Rome.
(B) They wanted to emphasize and display their social status and power.
(C) They wanted to possess a structure with a lavish exterior.
(D) They wanted to have a villa where they could relax and entertain visitors.

09. Why did the professor mention ancient Roman mythology?

(A) To emphasize that the labyrinth was an impossible maze from which the Minotaur could not escape
(B) To describe the origin of the artwork and statues depicted in the Renaissance gardens
(C) To illustrate the origin of the Roman gardens
(D) To explain how gardeners derived the idea for mazes

Listen again to part of the lecture. Then answer the question.

10. What does the professor imply when he says this :

(A) There were no ancient Roman gardens left behind.
(B) The ancient Romans wished for even greater gardens than they had originally built.
(C) The ancient Romans would have built the gardens to fit Italian homes of the Renaissance era
(D) There were no descriptions of ancient Roman gardens for the Renaissance gardeners to copy.

Listen again to part of the lecture. Then answer the question.

11. Why does the professor say this :

(A) He needs a moment to reconsider the statement mentioned previously.
(B) He has forgotten what he intended to tell the students.
(C) He has something in his mind to respond with.
(D) He is about to tell the students that the class is finished.

Lecture 2

TEST 1 set 1

Question 12 ~ 17 of 17

---

12. What is the lecture mainly about?

(A) The debate between Einstein and his opponents on the existence of relativity
(B) The struggles Einstein faced and validity of his bold theory
(C) The impact of the Theory of Relativity on modern physics
(D) Discussion of Einstein's Theory of Relativity and his recognition for it

13. According to the professor, what contributed to the foundation of Einstein's theory during his time at the patent office?

(A) The reverse engineering process of new inventions and ideas for patent approval
(B) Incorporation of various ideas and invention he designed
(C) Sources and methods of new discoveries and inventions
(D) His creativity assisted him in examining patent applications.

14. According to the professor, what is true about the Theory of Special Relativity?

(A) The theory used scientific evidence to explain the natural phenomenon of time dilation
(B) The theory explained how time is affected by gravity.
(C) The theory challenged the long established concept of time's progression being fixed.
(D) The theory supported the traditional idea that time flows at the same speed

15. Why did the professor mention light bending around the sun?

(A) To give an example of the speed of light
(B) To prove that the sun was the source of the light's speed
(C) To bolster a point about gravitational forces around the sun
(D) To demonstrate a real life example of General Relativity

16. According to the professor, what can be inferred about Einstein's attitude towards his own theory?

(A) He had unwavering faith in his theory and provided hard evidence for it.
(B) He thought that he could share Miller's fate and be proven wrong in the future
(C) He had a strong belief that no one could disprove his theory.
(D) He thought that his theory was not yet conclusive but he had enough evidence to prove his theory.

Listen again to part of the lecture. Then answer the question.

17. Why does the professor mention this :

(A) To indicate why Einstein's theory was wrong
(B) To prove that Einstein's theory was more satisfactory to the world
(C) To give additional information regarding the inferiority of Miller's theory
(D) To explain one reason Miller gained support he physics community

You have reached the end of this part of the test.

Click on **Continue** to go on.

Listening Directions

In this part you will listen to **1 conversation** and **1 lecture**.

You must answer each question. After you answer, click on **NEXT**. Then click on **OK** to confirm your answer and go on to the next question. After you click on **OK**, you cannot return to previous questions.

You will now begin part of the Listening section. You will have **7 minutes** to answer the questions.

Click on **Continue** to go on.

PART 2에서는 두 지문을 듣게 됩니다.
7분 동안 질문에 답하세요.
지문을 듣는 동안 시간이 줄어들지 않습니다.

Conversation

TEST 1   set 2

Question 01 ~ 05 of 17

01. Why does the student go to talk to the office clerk?

(A) To ask for proper approval for a protest she has been planning
(B) To ask for funding regarding a protest
(C) To make sure that she has taken the right steps in organizing a protest
(D) To make sure that a protest is not against school regulations

02. According to the student, what are the problems with the renovation?

Click on 3 answers

(A) The construction would cost way too much for the school to handle.
(B) The library seems to be in a condition that does not require renovation.
(C) The construction would lead to academic difficulties for students in terms of space.
(D) The information that the students need may not be accessible for a certain period of time.
(E) The school may not be able to provide scholarships to students

03. According to the speakers, what can be inferred about the current views on the renovation project?

(A) Rumors about the construction have just begun to spread and may or may not be valid.
(B) Some students of the school are against the possible reconstruction.
(C) The school has decided to push for the renovation after considering their monetary situation.
(D) The reasons why students are against it are nearly all academic.

04. Why does the student mention a new wing on the library building?

(A) To specify which area of the library is intact enough to avoid construction
(B) To show her concern about a new wing jeopardizing the current library
(C) To suggest an alternative plan to the renovation
(D) To show that there is a flaw in the blueprint that the school released

Listen again to part of the conversation. Then answer the question

05. Why does the student say this :

(A) She doesn't want to talk about other problems the students may possibly face
(B) She finds it too painful to even imagine the hardships the students may go through
(C) She believes the clerk has already been given enough information to understand
(D) She is asking the clerk if he needs additional reasons for the protest

Lecture 1

06. What is the author mainly discussing?

(A) How the invention of a space elevator would bring innovations in technology
(B) The innovations and setbacks involved in space elevator technology
(C) The opinions of scientists and other famous figures on the idea of a space elevator
(D) How the concept of a space elevator has affected popular culture

07. Why does the professor mention escape velocity?

(A) To give an example of natural phenomena caused by gravity
(B) To show that a rocket needs a lot of energy to leave Earth's gravitational pull
(C) To explain that building a ladder into space is impossible
(D) To correct an idea that is misunderstood by many people

08. What does the professor say about space elevators?

Click on 2 answers

(A) Carbon nanotubes are the best candidate for space elevator cables.
(B) The space elevator can only be built on Earth.
(C) The space elevator cannot function without a rocket.
(D) The idea of building space elevators was inspired by the Eiffel Tower.

09. Why does the professor mention geosynchronous orbit at the height of 36,000 km?

(A) To describe the model of a space elevator that was proposed by a science fiction author
(B) Because current technology allows the elevator to be built only up to 36,000 km
(C) Because the space elevator will remain in one location relative to earth if its center of mass is at that height
(D) To illustrate that more research is required before the construction of the space elevator becomes plausible

10. According to the professor, what is the disadvantage of using carbon nanotubes to construct the space elevator cable?

(A) It is too light to be used as a construction material for a space elevator
(B) It is difficult to make long carbon nanotube structures
(C) It will be hard to find enough carbon deposits to build a space elevator
(D) Nanotubes are undesired because carbon is more valuable when used in other products

Listen again to part of the lecture. Then answer the question.

11. What does the professor mean when he says this :

(A) He wants to emphasize that it would be impossible to climb such a ladder
(B) He realizes that the student overlooked an important detail
(C) He wants to clarify that the climber will get quite far up the ladder
(D) He wants to illustrate his explanation using another example

*부록 **Lecture 2**

12. What is the lecture mainly about?

(A) The gap between the past and present day conditions of Easter Island
(B) How to solve the puzzle of the demise of an island.
(C) Investigation of the disaster and chaos behind an island's modern conditions
(D) Two possible theories about what could have caused Easter Island's disaster

13. According to the professor, what did the Dutch explorer Roggeeveen find mysterious about Easter Island?

(A) The fact that the moai statues looked like animals
(B) The absence of the devices and labor force required for the construction of the impressive of moai
(C) The low grade craftsmanship and knowledge of the sea displayed in the poorly built canoes
(D) A lack of evidence of civil leadership and ongoing warfare

14. What can be inferred about the native people who once lived on Easter Island?

(A) They were most likely Polynesian seafarers from Europe.
(B) They are probably a mixed group of people who travelled from place to place.
(C) A series of DNA tests on the inhabitants confirmed that Polynesian sailors had settled on the island.
(D) Their origin is uncertain but theories suggest that they were either from Chile or Polynesia.

15. What is revealed about palm trees through pollen analysis?

(A) Palm trees could be used to measure the age of dead organisms in the sediment.
(B) The palm trees were necessary to supply food for the islanders.
(C) The palm trees were required to supply the basic necessities and tools for daily life once existed on the island.
(D) The palm trees were raw ingredients necessary for the production and transportation of moai.

16. According to the professor, what is the main piece of evidence that suggests that rats were the main reason for deforestation?

Click on 2 answers

(A) There was an excessive use of palm trees for fire and housing
(B) Chewed premature palm trees were discovered on the island
(C) There were no natural predators to control the growth of the rat population
(D) Rat-gnawed palm seeds were found throughout the island

Listen again to part of the lecture. Then answer the question.

17. Why does the student say this :

(A) He needs more information on the details of pollen analysis to understand the radiocarbon dating method.
(B) He thinks that pollen analysis and radiocarbon dating are the same.
(C) He is curious about the accuracy and validity of radiocarbon dating method.
(D) He needs clarification about the procedures used to determine the date of materials once found on the island.

You have finished this section and will now being the next one.

Click on **Continue** to go on.

usherin.usher.co.kr

USHER iBT TOFLE
FINAL TEST
LISTENING
TEST 2

TEST 2 set 1

Listening Section Directions

This section measure your ability to understand conversations and lectures in English. It is divided into **3** separately timed parts. In the first part you will listen to 1 conversation and 2 lectures. In the second part you will listen to 1 conversation and 1 lecture. You will hear each conversation or lecture only **one** time.

After each conversation or lecture, you will answer some questions about it. Answer the questions based on what is stated or implied by the speakers.

For the first part of the listening section, you will have 10 minutes to answer the questions.
For the second part of the listening section, you will have 07 minutes to answer the questions.

A clock at the top of the screen will show you how much time is remaining. The clock will **not** count down while you are listening. The clock will count down only while you are answer questions.

You may take notes while you listen. You may use your notes to help you answer the questions. Your notes will **not** be scored.

If you need to change the volume while you listen, click on the **Volume** icon at the top of the screen

In some questions, you will see this icon 🎧. This means that you will hear but not see, part of the question. Most questions are worth 1 point. If a question is worth more than 1 point, it will have special directions that indicate how many points you can receive.

In this listening section. After you answer, click on **Next**. Then click on **OK** to confirm your and go on to the next section OK, you cannot return to previous questions.

Listen to part of the Listening section.
(Click on Continue at any time to dismiss these directions.)

> 리스닝 섹션은 PART 1, PART 2로 나누어져 있습니다.
> PART 1에서는 세 지문을 듣게 됩니다. 10분 동안 질문에 답하세요.
> 지문을 듣는 동안 시간이 줄어들지 않습니다.

Conversation

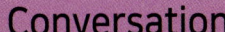

TEST 2 — set 1

Question 01 ~ 05 of 17

01. What is the conversation mainly about?

(A) The difficulties of purifying a certain protein from human tissue
(B) A step a student missed in a research project and a plan to make it up
(C) An experiment the professor performed during the biology lecture
(D) A topic in a research paper that the student will submit to the journal

02. What can be inferred about the student from the conversation?

(A) She had high hopes for her research on the protein.
(B) She has completed this experiment successfully before.
(C) She does not know exactly what she is supposed to do at each step of the experiment.
(D) She is not accustomed to working in the laboratory on the weekends.

03. Why is the professor worried about leaving town for a week?

(A) He does not want to work with the proteins unless they are freshly purified.
(B) He thinks that the proteins will return to their original state if they are left for a week.
(C) He is concerned that the temperature will fluctuate too much, affecting the functions of the proteins.
(D) He is afraid that the graduate student will not practice enough to reduce the margin of error while he is away.

04. Why does the professor mention spinach?

(A) To explain specifically what he was going to research with his protein
(B) To explain a breakthrough in a field regarding proteins
(C) To explain how unnoticed errors can go a long way in science
(D) To explain that some plants can be utilized in scientific experiments

Listen again to part of the conversation. Then answer the question.

05. What does the professor imply when he says this :

(A) To encourage the student to make fewer mistakes in the future
(B) To imply that the student's mistake did not cause permanent damage
(C) To imply that the foul odor of the protein means damage has been done to it
(D) To show his frustration with the current situation regarding his project

Lecture 1

06. What is the lecture mainly about?

(A) In-depth analysis of the structure and composition of the Great Pyramid of Giza
(B) A revolutionary idea suggested by Jean-Pierre Houdin using modern 3-D modeling
(C) Explanations behind the enigmatic construction techniques used for the Egyptian Pyramid
(D) Theories regarding the mysterious development of pyramid architecture

07. Why was the theory of ramps so popular amongst Egyptologists?

(A) In the ancient times, ramps were able to transport heavy objects efficiently.
(B) Ramps were the most common devices used to haul overwhelmingly large objects at the time.
(C) Evidence that pointed towards ramps was provided by renowned Egyptologists.
(D) Ramps were the only device of the ancient times for transportation of stone.

08. According to the lecture, why was the suggestion of spiral ramps flawed?

(A) Because they took longer to build and ruined the aesthetic aspect of the pyramids
(B) Because they lacked sturdiness and made it too challenging for the workers to transport stone
(C) Because they ruined the viewing angles and potentially risked brittle composition
(D) Because they ruined the builders' ability to utilize their measuring tools and made it too difficult to convey stone blocks

09. Why does the professor mention mountain roads in the lecture?

(A) To explain the vulnerability of using mountain roads
(B) To emphasize the great height of the external ramps used to construct the pyramids
(C) To correlate the similarity of mountain roads and spiral ramps
(D) To describe the differences between spiral ramps and roads

10. According to the lecture, what were the conveniences of internal ramps?

Click on 2 answers

(A) They did not require as much time to be built as straight ramps.
(B) They provided safety for the workers around the corners when transporting stone blocks.
(C) They could also serve as routes for the laborers when they were building pyramids from within.
(D) Their construction was more efficient because they eventually become a part of the pyramid.

Listen again to part of the lecture. Then answer the question.

11. What does the professor imply when he says this :

(A) He implies that a pharaoh's belongings were meant to make the afterlife even better.
(B) It was their belief that a pharaoh's belongings were to be reserved for him only.
(C) He is explaining that a pharaoh's treasures were sacred and they were to be used after death.
(D) It was only natural for a pharaoh's goods to be buried with him due to tradition.

Lecture 2

TEST 2　set 1

Question 12 ~ 17 of 17

12. What is the main topic of the lecture?

   (A) Suggested causes of crown-of-thorns starfish outbreaks
   (B) Problems caused by the increasing number of crown-of-thorns starfish
   (C) Hypotheses on how to protect coral on the Great Barrier Reef
   (D) Human influence on the ecosystems of the Great Barrier Reef

13. What does the professor imply about crown-of-thorns starfish outbreaks?

   (A) The outbreaks are triggered by increases in the coral population.
   (B) Researchers believe that outbreaks occurred even before the 1960s due to their occurrence recently.
   (C) Their reproduction rate is solely responsible for the starfish outbreaks.
   (D) The coral population has been threatened even without a starfish outbreak.

14. According to the lecture, why is the giant triton no longer a threat?

   (A) Because most of them get stung by the starfish's venomous spines
   (B) Because they were caught for aesthetic purposes
   (C) Because they are slow and cannot catch up with the crown-of-thorns starfish
   (D) Because a species of fish that preys on the starfish was introduced to the Great Barrier Reef

15. Why does the professor mention fertilizers with nitrogen and phosphorous?

   (A) To explain that starfish larvae feed on nutrients in the runoff sediment
   (B) To provide examples of chemicals that maintain ocean water salinity
   (C) To imply that human influence was a factor in starfish population increase
   (D) To suggest a possible solution to water contamination

16. What is one way the crown-of-thorns starfish benefit the coral?

   (A) They keep the coral from occupying too much of the ocean floor.
   (B) They release nutrients when they die which helps coral grow.
   (C) They protect uninfested coral patches from other coral predators.
   (D) They allow certain coral types to compete more effectively.

Listen again to part of the lecture. Then answer the question.

17. What does the professor mean when she says this:

   (A) The early misconception of coral was easy to understand.
   (B) Scientists were responsible for people thinking that coral is a form of rock.
   (C) Coral's strange appearance causes confusion for the professor.
   (D) Scientists proved that coral was made of living organisms.

You have reached the end of this part of the test.

Click on **Continue** to go on.

TEST 2　set 2

Listening Directions

In this part you will listen to **1 conversation** and **1 lecture**.

You must answer each question. After you answer, click on **NEXT**. Then click on **OK** to confirm your answer and go on to the next question. After you click on **OK**, you cannot return to previous questions.

You will now begin part of the Listening section. You will have **7 minutes** to answer the questions.

Click on **Continue** to go on.

PART 2에서는 두 지문을 듣게 됩니다.
7분 동안 질문에 답하세요.
지문을 듣는 동안 시간이 줄어들지 않습니다.

Conversation

01. Why does the student go to talk to his professor?

(A) To ask about different diving patterns of whales during migration
(B) To clear up some of the difficulties he was having regarding whales
(C) To ask for definitions of some of the names of different whale species
(D) To talk about why he got a low grade on the midterm exam about whales

02. Why does the professor mention differences in ethnicity, gender and age?

(A) To discuss that ethnicity, gender and age matter in deciding the diving time of whales.
(B) To show that gender and age play vital roles in determining the capacity of whale lungs.
(C) To show that even within a species there are various subtypes.
(D) To tell the student to pick whales of a specific age and gender to research further.

03. What can be inferred about the student?

(A) He already knows quite a bit about whales, but is still eager to learn more.
(B) He already knows that whales adjust their oxygen usage when they dive below the water.
(C) He already knows that whales take intermittent short breaths during their migrations.
(D) He already knows whales travel with other mammals of the opposite sex during their migration.

04. According to the professor, how do whales effectively use oxygen during their dives?

Click on 2 answers

(A) They intentionally release air from their lungs in order to allow themselves to dive deeper into the water.
(B) They make little use of the reserve oxygen in their muscles and blood to survive once they are in the water.
(C) They keep their muscles loosened to ensure sufficient oxygen.
(D) They keep their oxygen distributed evenly throughout their bodies.

Listen again to part of the conversation. Then answer the question

05. What does the student mean when he says this:

(A) To imply that the professor may have misunderstood the student's question
(B) To ask another question that wasn't his initial purpose
(C) To imply that the professor may have digressed a bit
(D) To show his amazement at the professor's knowledge

Lecture 1

06. What is the lecture mainly about?

(A) The ways that the domestication of horses influenced the Botai people
(B) Evidence that the Botai people had a cultural and economic relationship with horses
(C) A theory about horse domestication by the Botai people that is proven through skeletal structures
(D) The signs pointing to the domestication of horses that have been uncovered in the Botai region

07. What can be inferred about horses as livestock?

(A) Horses were not well suited as livestock since they grazed well year-round.
(B) The Botai were able to use them for sustenance through the harsh weather conditions.
(C) The Botai constructed pit houses that provided insulation to accommodate these animals.
(D) They were not stronger than sheep and cattle to survive year-round.

08. According to the professor, what are two effects of the 'equine revolution'?

Click on 2 answers

(A) By providing a stable source of food, it lowered the people's dependence on agriculture.
(B) It broadened the limits of the area people could cover due to the previous lack of an efficient means of travel.
(C) It brought about the advent of mounted troops which greatly changed the way wars were fought.
(D) It helped prove that the Botai people were the first to domesticate horses.

09. Why does the professor mention the presence of nitrogen in the soil samples?

(A) To further support the theory by proving that the phosphorus in the soil had ancient origins
(B) To explain the high concentration of nitrogen in soil containing horse manure
(C) To explain why the presence of nitrogen is not a possible cause of the high levels of the phosphorus in question
(D) To point out that the markings left in the horses' teeth were caused by consuming nitrogen from the soil while wearing a harness

10. What does the professor say about the skeletal structures of the remains?

(A) All animals undergo an alteration of physical traits.
(B) Bone shape is a good indicator of the time period the horse originated from.
(C) Milking mares may cause a change in the skeletal structure.
(D) Horses have not physically changed over time as a result of domestication.

Listen again to part of the lecture. Then answer the question

11. What does the professor mean when he says this :

(A) He believes milking wild horses is a valid alternative theory.
(B) He is skeptical about the possibility of milking a wild horse.
(C) He is unsure of whether the Botai took part in milking wild horses.
(D) He is opening up the possibility of another possible theory.

Lecture 1

12. What is the lecture mainly about?

(A) The characteristics of one particular biofuel production process
(B) The differences between cellulosic ethanol and corn ethanol
(C) The history of alternative energy source development
(D) The multiple aspects of cellulose in plant structures

13. According to the lecture, what are the advantages of cellulosic ethanol over corn ethanol?

Click on 2 answers

(A) It mainly uses resources that are denser than corn ethanol.
(B) Its production process releases no pollution into the environment.
(C) It can be converted from a wider variety of feedstock.
(D) It is drawn from an ingredient which is essential to humans.

14. Why does the professor mention baker's yeast?

(A) To point out that the biological approach costs more than the thermo-chemical approach
(B) To explain the need for suitable temperatures and pH levels for ethanol production
(C) To introduce the catalyst used in the fermentation process
(D) To give an example of one of the products of ethanol production process

15. In the Lecture, the professor explains two ethanol production methods. Indicate whether each of the following was a feature of celluloysis or gasification

	Celluloysis	Gasification
(A) Fermentantation is needed to produce ethanol		
(B) Gas compounds are fed to microorganisms		
(C) Cellulose molecules are combusted		
(D) Enzymes break down cellulose molecules		

16. Which of the following is NOT a drawback of cellulosic ethanol production?

(A) The conversion process is much more expensive.
(B) Very little financial support is directed towards alternative energy research.
(C) The public is against the idea of alternative energy.
(D) Few production plants exist where the production can be implemented.

Listen again to part of the lecture. Then answer the question.

17. Why does the professor say this :

(A) She does not think the students are paying attention.
(B) She wants to emphasize an important concept.
(C) She wants to correct the student's answer to her question.
(D) She thinks that the students didn't understand her explanation.

*부록 **Lecture 2**

usherin.usher.co.kr

USHER iBT TOFLE
FINAL TEST
LISTENING
TEST 3

TEST 3　set 1

Listening Section Directions

This section measure your ability to understand conversations and lectures in English. It is divided into **3** separately timed parts. In the first part you will listen to 1 conversation and 2 lectures. In the second part you will listen to 1 conversation and 1 lecture. You will hear each conversation or lecture only **one** time.

After each conversation or lecture, you will answer some questions about it. Answer the questions based on what is stated or implied by the speakers.

For the first part of the listening section, you will have 10 minutes to answer the questions.
For the second part of the listening section, you will have 07 minutes to answer the questions.

A clock at the top of the screen will show you how much time is remaining. The clock will **not** count down while you are listening. The clock will count down only while you are answer questions.

You may take notes while you listen. You may use your notes to help you answer the questions. Your notes will **not** be scored.

If you need to change the volume while you listen, click on the **Volume** icon at the top of the screen

In some questions, you will see this icon 🎧. This means that you will hear but not see, part of the question. Most questions are worth 1 point. If a question is worth more than 1 point, it will have special directions that indicate how many points you can receive.

In this listening section. After you answer, click on **Next**. Then click on **OK** to confirm your and go on to the next section OK, you cannot return to previous questions.

Listen to part of the Listening section.
(Click on Continue at any time to dismiss these directions.)

리스닝 섹션은 PART 1, PART 2로 나누어져 있습니다.
PART 1에서는 세 지문을 듣게 됩니다. 10분 동안 질문에 답하세요.
지문을 듣는 동안 시간이 줄어들지 않습니다.

Conversation

TEST 3   set 1

Question 01 ~ 05 of 17

01. Why does the student go to see the museum officer?

(A) To ask the officer whether her background knowledge of history may help in getting a job at the museum
(B) To decide how many working hours at the museum can be counted as community service hours
(C) To ask if her experiences at the museum will be of help in getting into graduate school to study education
(D) To inquire about the possibility of volunteering at the museum for community service hours

02. What can be inferred about the museum?

(A) It offers different types of art that interest children.
(B) The Egyptian room is off-limits due to problems with mummy preservation.
(C) It has a special course that involves a room of Picasso's works in it.
(D) The museum offers artwork that is too confusing for children.

03. What is the student's attitude towards the job at the museum?

(A) She doesn't necessarily need the community service hours.
(B) She is worried that she may not have enough background in the field.
(C) She has experience in dealing with children and is confident enough to do it well.
(D) She has her own set of rules that she would like to apply.

04. What will the museum officer do for the student?

(A) Provide a list of questions that the children may ask the student.
(B) Help the student fill out the parts of the application that the student finds confusing.
(C) Work together with the student to find the most appropriate work hours.
(D) Just pick a specific time for the student and notify her later.

Listen again to part of the conversation. Then answer the question.

05. Why does the student say this :

(A) To learn more about the museum and what it offer its visitors
(B) To ask the officer the exact times that the museum opens and closes
(C) Because she has not yet understood what she would be asked to do.
(D) Because she wants to explore the museum for own interests.

Lecture 1

TEST 3　set 1

Question 06 ~ 11 of 17

06. What is the lecture mainly about?

(A) The acoustical problems that some older structures had
(B) The importance of reverberation time in the field of architectural acoustics
(C) The scientific explanation behind how reverberation time affects the acoustics of a structure
(D) The factors that determine the acoustics of a sound related structure and how they can be adjusted

07. Why does the professor mention piano recitals?

(A) To further establish the relationship between acoustically live and dead environments
(B) To explain that the optimum reverberation time of a structure varies with its usage
(C) To point out the significance of reverberation time in the field of architectural acoustics
(D) To describe how correct acoustics can further enhance the quality of music

08. What can be inferred about Sabine's method being used mainly with older buildings?

(A) It did not require altering the fundamental dimensions of a structure.
(B) It was the most structurally dependent means of adjusting the acoustics of a building.
(C) It had already proved its effectiveness with the Fogg Art Museum at Harvard.
(D) It also helped improve the stability of the building.

09. What does the professor say about the acoustic problems that often occur in older structures?

(A) Acoustic echoes were created when the focus of the sound was confined to a limited of the audience.
(B) The diffraction of sound waves would consequently increase its intensity.
(C) Older materials in the structures would make the acoustics inaudible to certain sections of the audience.
(D) Acoustic flaws were created when the sole design emphasis was placed on constructing aesthetically pleasing structures.

10. What can be inferred about the problems presented by the varying number of people present in a structure?

(A) The total level of absorption caused by the audience can be accurately calculated prior to construction.
(B) Architects need to calculate not only the size of the audience but also the absorbency of their clothes.
(C) By designing space with optimal reverberation times at full occupancy, engineers make it easier for adjustments to be made after the space has been completed.
(D) Sabine's calculation of human to cushion absorption is one way engineers avoid the problem.

Listen again to part of the lecture. Then answer the question.

11. What does the professor imply when he says this :

(A) Acoustics cannot be changed to fit a concert hall or a theatre.
(B) Ensuring optimal acoustics is an ongoing process that must be performed throughout the life of a venue.
(C) The number of people in a structure is a variable that cannot be controlled.
(D) Engineers need to continue to calculate the number of audience members even after construction is finished.

Lecture 2

12. What is the lecture mainly about?

(A) Figuring out the reason for the disappearance of the Anasazi people using computer simulations
(B) Understanding the reasons for the failure of harvest in the Four Corners region
(C) How mistakes were found in previous research regarding the climate in the 1300s
(D) The reasons for fluctuation in the population of the Anasazi society

13. What does the professor imply about computer simulations?

(A) They offer speculative answers, not necessarily precise ones.
(B) Scientists have used them to accurately map the rise and fall of civilizations.
(C) They can always predict unexpected events.
(D) They are not accurate enough to support theories about the past.

14. According to the professor, which of the following is one of the characteristics of the Anasazi villages?

(A) They were built like ranches.
(B) Their structures resembled apartment complexes.
(C) The ladder was considered an important tool due to its use in hunting.
(D) They did not form a community since they were nomads who travelled often.

15. Why does the professor mention Jeffrey Dean?

(A) Dean was one of the people who challenged the idea that the Anasazi disappeared due to climate change.
(B) He supported Carla Van West's conclusion that a drought caused the Anasazi society to move away from the valley.
(C) Jeffrey Dean analyzed the rainfall that occurred during the 1300s that led to poor harvest.
(D) He pointed out that poor nutrition led to the disappearance of the Anasazi population.

16. According to the professor, which two of the following were the results of the computer model?

Click on 2 answers

(A) The population increased then decreased.
(B) It confirmed the location of settlements.
(C) The amount of harvest should have been enough to support a large population.
(D) The results illustrated the current locations of the descendants.

17. What does the professor conclude about the disappearance of the Anasazi?

(A) He states that the model does not give an exact answer.
(B) He thinks climate did not have any impact.
(C) He implies that using computer simulations was a waste of time and energy.
(D) He explains that some Anasazi people are still alive today.

You have reached the end of this part of the test.

Click on **Continue** to go on.

TEST 3 set 2

Listening Directions

In this part you will listen to **1 conversation** and **1 lecture**.

You must answer each question. After you answer, click on **NEXT**. Then click on **OK** to confirm your answer and go on to the next question. After you click on **OK**, you cannot return to previous questions.

You will now begin part of the Listening section. You will have **7 minutes** to answer the questions.

Click on **Continue** to go on.

PART 2에서는 두 지문을 듣게 됩니다.
7분 동안 질문에 답하세요.
지문을 듣는 동안 시간이 줄어들지 않습니다.

Conversation

TEST 3　set 2

Question 01 ~ 05 of 17

01. Why does the student go to see her professor?

(A) To ask for guidance so can get a proper start on his class assignment
(B) To ask if she can incorporate her major into the assignment
(C) To get approval for her choice of genres for her music project
(D) To get further information on a psychology symposium she needs for her report

02. What does the professor suggest the student do regarding the assignment?

(A) Use information from a psychology symposium and write on how classical music affects infants.
(B) Wait until the student feels an emotion that she feels comfortable enough with to link it to her favorite genre.
(C) Elaborate on the history of hip-hop and focus on how it succeeded in captivating the public.
(D) Utilize psychology in order to further study a certain type of music and its effect on infants.

03. Why does the professor mention music and its effect on infants?

(A) To let the student know about a symposium that can help her finish the assignment
(B) To indicate that behavioral psychology of infants is an area of study that will be covered in the professor's class
(C) To encourage the student to study a new topic that the professor is not familiar with
(D) To indicate that the professor is new to the field and would like some assistance

04. What can be inferred about the students of the psychology department?

(A) The accommodations may be too expensive for the students to handle.
(B) The students may be able to attend the symposium if the professor can get them excused from the project.
(C) The topic covered at the symposium may be too difficult for the students to fully understand.
(D) The students are not an important part of the psychology experiment, but are still reluctant to attend the symposium.

Listen again to part of the conversation. Then answer the question

05. What does the professor imply when he says this :

(A) His assignment included a specific set of instructions that stated the genre and topic.
(B) He assumes that the student hasn't even decided on a topic yet.
(C) It has been long enough since the assignment was given out for the students to choose a genre and topic
(D) He is asking if the student has chosen a proper genre and topic.

Lecture 1

TEST 3 set 2

Question 06 ~ 11 of 17

06. What is the lecture mainly discussing?

(A) The differences between a Hawaiian lap steel guitar and an electric Spanish guitar
(B) The series of events that occurred in the invention of the electric guitar
(C) The evolution and development of the guitar throughout history
(D) The ways popular guitarists influenced the designs of electric guitars

07. What does the professor say about the pickup that Beauchamp invented in 1931?

(A) The first pickup in history was mounted on 'the Frying Pan'.
(B) It was based on an electrical device in a Hawaiian lap steel guitar.
(C) It was invented by engineers who worked for a guitar company.
(D) It was invented to allow guitarists to produce more sounds with their instruments.

08. What can be inferred about the 'Frying Pan' from the lecture?

(A) It was not awarded a patent until several years later.
(B) It incited the invention of many new types of guitars.
(C) It could not entice Spanish-style guitarists to switch over to Hawaiian-style guitars.
(D) It was more popular than the guitars made by Beauchamp's rivals.

09. According to the lecture, what were two problems of ES-150?

Click on 2 answers

(A) The guitar could not digitize certain unique sound ranges.
(B) The guitar's amplifier rebooted the sounds it had already produced.
(C) It could not play higher notes without a pickup selector.
(D) It picked up any vibrations around it.

10. In the lecture, the professor identifies key events regarding the electric guitar. Arrange them in order from earliest to latest.

(A) Pickups were invented by Beauchamp and his partner.
(B) Popular musicians started using ES-150 guitars.
(C) Phonographs and radios created a need for louder guitars.
(D) Jimi Hendrix introduced a popular technique of guitar playing

Step 1	
Step 2	
Step 3	
Step 4	

Listen again to part of the lecture. Then answer the question

11. Why does the professor say this :

(A) To note that other musicians experimented with guitar effects
(B) To indicate that the student's remark is a matter of personal taste
(C) To imply that others share the student's opinion
(D) To acknowledge that other students have also listened to Jimi Hendrix

*부록 Lecture 2

12. What is the lecture mainly discussing?

(A) The different types of lightning and their characteristics
(B) Various scientists' explanations of a particular type of lightning
(C) A hypothesis on lightning that has replaced older ones
(D) The cause of the creation and destruction of ball lightning

13. According to the lecture, why does the professor mention black holes and extra-terrestrials?

(A) To describe the differences between ball lightning and the urban legends
(B) To compare ball lightning with other types of urban legends
(C) To show how unreliable the proof of ball lightning's existence is
(D) To explain the causes of some of types of lightning

14. What does the professor say about plasma and the plasmic cloud hypothesis?

(A) It is costly and difficult to contain and control plasmic clouds.
(B) The plasmic cloud hypothesis was disproved by the silicon hypothesis.
(C) The substance created by Fussmann was mistaken for plasma.
(D) Water is the only compound that can be used to create plasma.

15. According to the silicon hypothesis, why does ball lightning glow?

(A) Small lightning strikes are constantly created inside the silicon ball.
(B) Electrical attractions between the pure silicon molecules cause them to shine.
(C) Atmospheric water vapor becomes energized and burns brightly.
(D) Silicon and oxygen in the air react to produce light.

16. What does the professor imply about foo fighters?

(A) They prove that the silicon hypothesis is not very reliable.
(B) They helped fighter jets navigate to their bases at night.
(C) They were developed by nations that were not involved in the war.
(D) Ball lightning can be created at the same altitudes at which foo fighters were reported.

Listen again to part of the lecture. Then answer the question.

17. Why does the professor say this :

(A) To provide an example of the inconclusiveness of ball lightning's existence
(B) To introduce one of the most devastating disasters of ball lightning
(C) To show that there are exceptions to the characteristics of ball lightning
(D) To explain the need to study and understand lightning more clearly

You have reached the end of this part of the test.

Click on **Continue** to go on.

usherin.usher.co.kr

USHER iBT TOFLE
FINAL TEST
LISTENING
TEST 4

TEST 4　set 1

Listening Section Directions

This section measure your ability to understand conversations and lectures in English. It is divided into **3** separately timed parts. In the first part you will listen to 1 conversation and 2 lectures. In the second part you will listen to 1 conversation and 1 lecture. You will hear each conversation or lecture only **one** time.

After each conversation or lecture, you will answer some questions about it. Answer the questions based on what is stated or implied by the speakers.

For the first part of the listening section, you will have 10 minutes to answer the questions.
For the second part of the listening section, you will have 07 minutes to answer the questions.

A clock at the top of the screen will show you how much time is remaining. The clock will **not** count down while you are listening. The clock will count down only while you are answer questions.

You may take notes while you listen. You may use your notes to help you answer the questions. Your notes will **not** be scored.

If you need to change the volume while you listen, click on the **Volume** icon at the top of the screen

In some questions, you will see this icon 🎧. This means that you will hear but not see, part of the question. Most questions are worth 1 point. If a question is worth more than 1 point, it will have special directions that indicate how many points you can receive.

In this listening section. After you answer, click on **Next**. Then click on **OK** to confirm your and go on to the next section OK, you cannot return to previous questions.

Listen to part of the Listening section.
(Click on Continue at any time to dismiss these directions.)

리스닝 섹션은 PART 1, PART 2로 나누어져 있습니다.
PART 1에서는 세 지문을 듣게 됩니다. 10분 동안 질문에 답하세요.
지문을 듣는 동안 시간이 줄어들지 않습니다.

Conversation

TEST 4　set 1

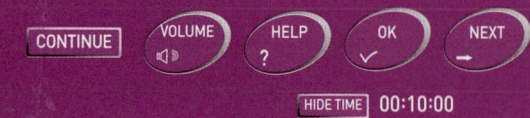

01. What does the professor want to discuss with the student?

   (A) He wants to give the student some advice about her term paper in his chemistry class.
   (B) He wants to know if the student is willing to take a job as a tutor.
   (C) He wants to introduce the tutoring system to the student and ask her to spread the word about it.
   (D) He wants to get the student's permission to use her papers as examples in his class.

02. Why does the professor need to recruit more people urgently?

   (A) Because he needs help with organizing the tutoring system that has yet to be established.
   (B) Because the student body is getting bigger, and he's expecting that more students will wish to be tutored.
   (C) Because the number of tutors will decrease in the near future.
   (D) Because he needs more people to tutor his literature-class students.

03. What do the literature class the student took last year and the training course have in common?

   (A) Both of them offer students an opportunity to fulfill their graduation requirements.
   (B) Both of them guarantee a certain number of community service hours.
   (C) Both of them are prerequisites for the tutoring job.
   (D) Both of them are required for a degree in the English field.

04. Which of the following is the first method the professor suggests for helping students who need to correct their unorganized papers?

   (A) To directly tell the students how to revise their papers.
   (B) To help the students research the information they lack in their papers.
   (C) To encourage the students to fix what they think is wrong by asking questions.
   (D) To suggest alternative sources that may help them improve their papers on their own.

Listen again to part of the conversation. Then answer the question.

05. Why does the professor say this :

   (A) To distinguish the training course from other regular classes the student has taken
   (B) To let the student know about the potential non-monetary compensation that the job provides
   (C) To tell the student that the training course is a way of giving back to the community
   (D) To inform the student that she will be receiving homework assignments in the training course, just like any other class

Lecture 1

TEST 4   set 1

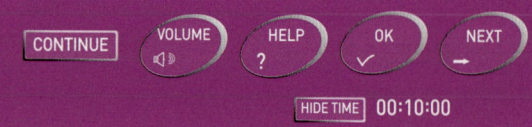

06. What is the main topic of the lecture?

(A) Solutions to the increase in global temperatures
(B) Detrimental effects of carbon dioxide and nitrous dioxide
(C) The factors contributing to the rise in global temperatures
(D) Comparison of oxy-fuel combustion and pre- and post-combustion capture

07. Which of the following is true about nitrous oxide?

(A) It plays a major role in pre- and post-combustion capture.
(B) It is a great solution to the increase in global temperatures.
(C) Along with other factors, it contributes to CO_2 emission.
(D) It is a greenhouse gas and contributes to the increase in global temperatures.

08. What are the disadvantages of post-combustion capture?

Click on 2 answers

(A) Construction of new power plants is required
(B) Excessive amounts of absorbent materials and chemicals are required
(C) It is not ready to be used right now and can't be implemented right away
(D) It is economically demanding and burdensome

09. How is pre-combustion capture different from post-combustion capture?

(A) After fossil fuels are burned, pre-combustion capture comes into play
(B) Pre-combustion capture is much more sophisticated and a more advanced form of technology
(C) Pre-combustion capture takes place before the fossil fuels are burned and CO_2 is released into the air
(D) Pre-combustion capture can be easily implemented to already existing power plants.

10. Why does the professor mention the 'climate deadline'?

(A) To imply that the issue of global climate change has been settled
(B) To emphasize that there is a plenty of time to decide which solution to focus on
(C) To give an opportunity for students to guess when the climate deadline is
(D) To alert the students to the urgency and danger of global climate change

11. What is the professor's opinion regarding pre- and post-combustion capture?

(A) She believes that awareness of the solutions is widespread.
(B) She thinks that employing one of the methods now and trying to handle the global climate issue immediately is an urgent matter.
(C) She believes both of them are insufficient, and other solutions are required.
(D) She feels that more research on both of the methods should be done before using either of them.

Lecture 2

TEST 4 set 1

12. What is the lecture mainly about?

(A) The historical backgrounds of the Greek and Roman empires
(B) A general exploration of the notable characteristics of Emperor Augustus' statue
(C) Technological advances that help archaeologists interpret ancient sculptures
(D) The evolution of our understanding of Greek and Roman sculptures

13. How did the Greek and Roman sculptures influence the Renaissance artists?

(A) They helped the artists to establish that form was the primary principle.
(B) They caused the artists to use color as a mechanism to highlight certain features of their sculptures
(C) They helped artists abandon the practice of sculpture and employ other methods of representation, such as painting.
(D) They motivated the artists to solely focus on applying various forms of paint to their sculptures.

14. According to the professor, how does ultraviolet light aid archaeologists studying polychromatic sculptures?

(A) It helps them discern the colored parts of statues by illuminating organic compounds.
(B) It enables them to figure out the time period in which they were made.
(C) It distinguishes the parts of sculptures with a dense concentration of organic compounds from those without.
(D) It works like an x-ray machine and locates sculptures during excavation.

15. Why does the professor mention the Roman Emperor Augustus?

(A) To illustrate that his sculpture represents his great authority
(B) To clarify the common misconception that his sculpture was originally monochromatic
(C) To explain how polychromatic sculptures are interpreted in regard to the artists' motive
(D) To begin a new discussion of the various pigments used in painting sculptures during the Roman era

16. What property or characteristic of the pigments in paints calls for an immediate investigation of the Greek and Roman sculptures?

(A) The value of the paint pigments used during Greek and Roman time was extremely high.
(B) Certain colors, such as red and blue, decompose due to factors, such as the wind.
(C) The pigments gradually change color depending on the amount of sunlight absorption.
(D) The pigments used on the sculptures deteriorate at quite a rapid rate.

Listen to part of the lecture again, then answer the question

17. What does the professor imply when he says this :

(A) Scrubbing is very damaging to paints, especially those used on sculptures
(B) The latter case is also one of the most compelling theories to explain the disappearance of the paints
(C) Keeping sculptures clean required strenuous work in the ancient times
(D) There are many possible reasons that the pigments disappeared from the statues

You have reached the end of this part of the test.

Click on **Continue** to go on.

TEST 4 set 2

Listening Directions

In this part you will listen to **1 conversation** and **1 lecture**.

You must answer each question. After you answer, click on **NEXT**. Then click on **OK** to confirm your answer and go on to the next question. After you click on **OK**, you cannot return to previous questions.

You will now begin part of the Listening section. You will have **7 minutes** to answer the questions.

Click on **Continue** to go on.

PART 2에서는 두 지문을 듣게 됩니다.
7분 동안 질문에 답하세요.
지문을 듣는 동안 시간이 줄어들지 않습니다.

Conversation

TEST 4 set 2

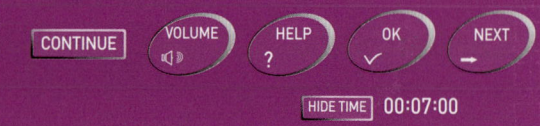

01. Why does the student go to see her professor?

(A) To get guidance on what references would be of help to her
(B) To get the professor's approval for her paper
(C) To get advice from the professor on how to approach her paper
(D) To ask her professor if extra points are available for the paper

02. What do the speakers say about Rosa Bonheur?

Click on 2 answers

(A) It has been argued that she was a pioneer in the feminist movement.
(B) Her artistic work portrayed women that wore men's clothing.
(C) She formed an organization of people who shared her artistic views.
(D) Her early life is not very significant when compared to other aspects of it.

03. What is the professor's attitude towards the student's completing her assignment?

(A) The professor thinks the student should disregard her personal preferences and view Rosa Bonheur objectively
(B) The professor suggests that the student can choose a harder approach to the assignment if she wants to
(C) The professor encourages the student to do what she has always been interested in.
(D) The professor believes the student should include some parts from the professor's book in her research paper

04. According to the professor, what should be included in the student's paper in order to receive extra points?

(A) Abstract information that is presented in an organized manner
(B) Indisputable information which proves that Bonheur was an actual feminist
(C) Persuasive information that argues for or against the validation of Bonheur's statement
(D) Insightful analysis of Bonheur's standing in the history of feminism

Listen again to part of the conversation. Then answer the question.

05. What does the student mean when she says this?:

(A) She is being pressured by two people that have different views.
(B) She is having a hard time deciding between Bonheur's legacy as a feminist and her life as an artist.
(C) She is considering choosing a different 19th century artist to write about.
(D) She is uncertain about whether she should focus on the 19th century or the 20th century.

Conversation

TEST 4   set 2

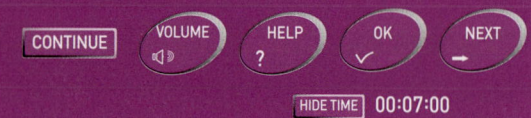

06. What is the main topic of the lecture?

(A) Technologies that generate electrical energy using other forms of energy
(B) Electromagnetic energy and its use in generating heat energy
(C) The evolutionary developments in light-generating technology
(D) Chemical reactions that significantly reduce the amount of heat generation

07. What is the major drawback of incandescent light bulbs?

(A) Toxic chemicals that are hard to dispose of
(B) Their heaviness makes them difficult to carry around
(C) Short duration of usefulness caused by the filament used in the process
(D) The excessive production of unwanted heat energy

08. How were scientists able to reduce the amount of heat production in fluorescent light bulbs?

(A) By using natural chemicals that prevent the reactions that create heat
(B) By filling light bulbs with a non-toxic gas
(C) By using mercury gas that glows when stimulated
(D) By inserting a gas into a bulb that has a special inner coating

09. How is chemiluminescence different from incandescent or fluorescent light bulbs?

(A) Genes for chemiluminescence extracted from human beings play a vital role in it.
(B) It uses a chemical to minimize the amount of heat production.
(C) A chemical reaction replaces the input of energy sources such as heat or electricity.
(D) It generates very low quantities of heat and high quantities of light.

10. According to the professor, what can be inferred about the chemiluminescent technology?

(A) Since the input of energy is not required, the brightness of the light is dim.
(B) The genes for chemiluminescence cannot be found in modern organisms.
(C) The technology has yet to become accessible to consumers.
(D) Chemiluminescence causes an increase in room temperature.

11. What does the professor imply when he says this : 🎧

(A) The method has a critical disadvantage.
(B) Today's environment needs to be improved as quickly as possible
(C) Developing a light-generating device is not a priority
(D) All light generating devices are harmful to the environment

*부록 Lecture 2

12. What is the topic of the lecture?

(A) Criticism of the theories that support the stability of personality
(B) General exploration of the functions of various highly technical tools.
(C) Current progress in personality psychology with supporting details
(D) The advantages that traditional research methods have over the new highly technical tools

13. According to the professor, for what is Electroencephalography or EEG insufficient?

(A) Substantiating the stability of the nature of personality
(B) Elucidating why human beings behave the way they do
(C) Analyzing the brain's activities and waves when stimuli are applied
(D) Enhancing our understanding of the nature of human personality

14. What makes FMRI more suitable for research purposes than MRI?

(A) FMRI captures the activities of the brain as well as its structures.
(B) FMRI enables researchers and scientists to detect tumorous cells in the body.
(C) FMRI helps scientists prove that the personality goes through a series of changes over time
(D) FMRI can detect changes in blood flow and oxygen levels throughout the body

15. What does the professor insinuate about the validity of the amygdala case study?

(A) It is revolutionary and refutes other conventional beliefs and theories
(B) Though it may seem credible to a certain degree, it's not a reliable means for proving the stability of the personality
(C) It also accounts for the behavior of human beings
(D) Its results prove that human personality does not change at all

16. Why does the professor mention traditional research methods?

(A) To start a new class discussion on how people behave when responding to lists of questions
(B) To give an example of a tool that can supplement the highly technical tools
(C) To criticize the people who question the validity of the results of tests performed with highly technical tools.
(D) To point out the incapability of highly technical tools

17. What does the professor imply when she says this :

(A) In her belief, it's unnecessary to spend so much money on fields in which it is difficult to conduct research
(B) The government should pay for the highly technical tools and labor required for the study of personality change
(C) Other areas of scientific study are unfairly treated compared to neuroscience and psychology
(D) Understanding the human personality is so important today that vast sums are being spent to further research in the field

You have reached the end of this part of the test.

Click on **Continue** to go on.

usherin.usher.co.kr

USHER iBT TOFLE
FINAL TEST
LISTENING

답지

정답 및 Self-check list
문제유형과 signals
오답 정리표

TEST 1 — 정답 및 Self-Check List

정답

	Test 1 - set 1	Test 1 - set 2
1	(C) Main Idea	(A) Main Purpose
2	(D) Inference(Infer)	(B),(C),(D) Detail(Problem)
3	(A),(D) Detail(Characteristic)	(B) Inference(Infer)
4	(B) Inference(Attitude)	(C) Inference(Purpose)
5	(C) Inference(Headset)	(C) Inference(Purpose)
6	(C) Main Idea	(B) Main Idea
7	(D) Detail(Difference)	(D) Inference(Purpose)
8	(B) Detail(Reason)	(A), [D] Detail(Characteristic)
9	(D) Inference(Purpose)	(C) Inference(Purpose)
10	(A) Inference(Headset)	(B) Detail(Disadvantage)
11	(C) Inference(Headset)	(A) Inference(Intention)
12	(D) Main Idea	(C) Main Idea
13	(A) Detail(Cause)	(B) Detail(Finding)
14	(C) Detail(Characteristic)	(D) Inference(Infer)
15	(D) Inference(Purpose)	(C) Detail(Finding)
16	(B) Inference(Attitude)	(C), (D) Detail(Evidence)
17	(D) Inference(Headset)	(D) Inference(Purpose)

Self-Check List

유 형	맞춘 답의 개수(Test 1 - set 1)	맞춘 답의 개수(Test 1 - set 2)
Main Idea	/ 3	/ 3
Detail	/ 5	/ 6
Inference	/ 9	/ 8
Category	/ 0	/ 0

문제유형과 Signals

번호	기본문제유형	세부문제유형	Signals
1	Main Idea	Main Purpose / Main Idea	국부적인(지엽적인) or 너무 일반적인(광범위한) 사실은 오답, 시제 및 단수 / 복수 주의
2	Details	Term/Definition/Irigin	refer to, what we call, so-called, originate, come from
3		Example	such as, like, think of, imagine, Let's take, let's say~, say, example, for instance
4		Characteristic / Advantage / Disadvantage / Problem / Difficulty / Similarity / Compare / Difference / Contrast	그림, 음악, 문학, 무용, 영화, 연극, 공예, 조각 등 / unique, useful, interesting, faster, fascinating, intriguing, key feature, note, important 동물 멸종위기, 생명의 위협 / 환경적응 Problem, hitch, challenge, drawback, flaw, defect, extinct, destroyed early-later, prior to~, recent, in the past, nowadays, modern day, evolve
5		Cause / Reason / Evidence / Result / Finding / Effect / Influence	study, research, experiment, project(find, discover, uncover, reveal, shed light on) / evidence, finding / pave the way, impact, set the stage for, application
6		Misunderstanding / Correction/Surprising	once believed, but~ / seem out of this world, news to
7		Requirement / Condition	necessary, required, you need to, consideration, condition, premise, job experience,
8		Offer / Solution / Suggestion	Alternative, to solve, handle this problem, recommend, why don't you~, what about~, what can be done~, your best bet would be~,
9		Future action/Future topic	upcoming, next class, another lecture
10	Inference	Purpose / Intention / Imply / Infer / Opinion / Attitude / Headset	Why... mention~ / What can be inferred~/ What... imply~ What... mean when...say~ 다시 들려주고 푸는 문제 check ,understanding, agree/disagree
11	Category	Introduce / Organize / Conclude / Matching / Ordering	How~ introduce? How is the lecture organized? Three types, two kinds of, first, second, finally step, stage, phase , and then, divide into~

오답정리표 : Test 1

번호	문제유형	틀린 답번호	오답유형	출제의도파악 (문제 및 정답 요약)
Sample	Purpose	Test 4-15	T1	교수가 Wood Thrush를 언급한 이유는 ➡ 동물의 Displacement activities가 주변 환경으로부터 어떤 영향을 받는지에 대한 예
1	Main Purpose Main Idea Introduce Organize Conclusion			
2	Term Definition Origin			
3	Example			
4	Characteristic Advantage Disadvantage Problem Difficulty Similarity Compare Difference Contrast			

5	Cause, Reason, Evidence Result, Finding, Effect, Influence			
6	Misunderstanging Correction Surprising			
7	Requirement Condition			
8	Offer Solution Suggestion			
9	Future action Future topic			
10	Purpose Intention Imply Infer Opinion Attitude Headset			
11	Introduce Organize Conclude Matching Ordering			

TEST 2 정답 및 Self-Check List

정답

	Test 1 - set 1	Test 1 - set 2
1	(C) Main Idea	(B) Main Purpose
2	(D) Inference(Infer)	(C) Inference(Purpose)
3	(A) Detail(Reason)	(A) Inference(infer)
4	(C) Inference(Purpose)	(A), (C) Detail(Characteristic))
5	(B) Inference(Headset)	(C) Inference(Headset)
6	(C) Main Idea	(D) Main Idea
7	(B) Detail(Reason)	(B) Inference(Infer)
8	(D) Detail(Problem)	(B), (C) Detail(Influence)
9	(C) Inference(Purpose)	(A) Inference(Purpose)
10	(B), (D) Detail(Advantage)	(D) Detail(Characteristic)
11	(A) Inference(Headset)	(B) Inference(Headset)
12	(A) Main Idea	(A) Main Idea
13	(B) Inference(Imply)	(A), (C) Detail(Adventage)
14	(B) Detail(Reason)	(D) Inference(Purpose)
15	(C) Inference(Purpose)	Celluloysis - (A),(D) / Gasification - (B), (C) Catergory (Matching)
16	(D) Detail(Adventage)	(D) Inference(Purpose)
17	(A) Inference(Headset)	(D) Inference(Headset)

Self-Check List

유 형	맞춘 답의 개수(Test 1 - set 1)	맞춘 답의 개수(Test 1 - set 2)
Main Idea	/ 3	/ 3
Detail	/ 5	/ 6
Inference	/ 9	/ 8
Category	/ 0	/ 0

문제유형과 Signals

번호	기본문제유형	세부문제유형	Signals
1	Main Idea	Main Purpose Main Idea	국부적인(지엽적인) or 너무 일반적인(광범위한) 사실은 오답, 시제 및 단수 / 복수 주의
2	Details	Term/Definition/Irigin	refer to, what we call, so-called, originate, come from
3		Example	such as, like, think of, imagine, Let's take, let's say~, say, example, for instance
4		Characteristic Advantage / Disadvantage Problem / Difficulty Similarity / Compare Difference / Contrast	그림, 음악, 문학, 무용, 영화, 연극, 공예, 조각 등 / unique, useful, interesting, faster, fascinating, intriguing, key feature, note, important 동물 멸종위기, 생명의 위협 / 환경적응 Problem, hitch, challenge, drawback, flaw, defect, extinct, destroyed early-later, prior to~, recent, in the past, nowadays, modern day, evolve
5		Cause / Reason / Evidence Result / Finding / Effect / Influence	study, research, experiment, project(find, discover, uncover, reveal, shed light on) / evidence, finding / pave the way, impact, set the stage for, application
6		Misunderstanding Correction/Surprising	once believed, but~ / seem out of this world, news to
7		Requirement / Condition	necessary, required, you need to, consideration, condition, premise, job experience,
8		Offer / Solution / Suggestion	Alternative, to solve, handle this problem, recommend, why don't you~, what about~, what can be done~, your best bet would be~,
9		Future action/Future topic	upcoming, next class, another lecture
10	Inference	Purpose / Intention Imply / Infer Opinion / Attitude Headset	Why... mention~ / What can be inferred~/ What... imply~ What... mean when...say~ 다시 들려주고 푸는 문제 check ,understanding, agree/disagree
11	Category	Introduce / Organize / Conclude Matching Ordering	How~ introduce? How is the lecture organized? Three types, two kinds of, first, second, finally step, stage, phase , and then, divide into~

오답정리표 : Test 2

번호	문제유형	틀린 답번호	오답유형	출제의도파악 (문제 및 정답 요약)
Sample	Purpose	Test 4-15	T1	교수가 Wood Thrush를 언급한 이유는 ➡ 동물의 Displacement activities가 주변 환경으로부터 어떤 영향을 받는지에 대한 예
1	Main Purpose Main Idea Introduce Organize Conclusion			
2	Term Definition Origin			
3	Example			
4	Characteristic Advantage Disadvantage Problem Difficulty Similarity Compare Difference Contrast			

5	Cause, Reason, Evidence Result, Finding, Effect, Influence			
6	Misunderstanging Correction Surprising			
7	Requirement Condition			
8	Offer Solution Suggestion			
9	Future action Future topic			
10	Purpose Intention Imply Infer Opinion Attitude Headset			
11	Introduce Organize Conclude Matching Ordering			

TEST 3 정답 및 Self-Check List

정답

	Test 1 - set 1	Test 1 - set 2
1	(D) Main Purpose	(A) Main Purpose
2	(A) Inference(Infer)	(B) Detail(Suggestion)
3	(C) Inference(Atitude)	(D) Inference(Purpose)
4	(D) Detail(Future Action)	(B) Inference(Infer)
5	(A) Inference(Headset)	(C) Inference(Headset)
6	(D) Main Idea	(B) Main Idea
7	(B) Inference(Purpose)	(A) Detail(Caracteristic)
8	(A) Inference(Infer)	(A) Inference(Infer)
9	(D) Detail(Problem)	(B),(D) Detail(Problem)
10	(C) Inference(Infer)	(C)-(A)-(B)-(D) Catergory(Ordering)
11	(B) Inference(Headset)	(C) Inference(Headset)
12	(A) Main Idea	(B) Main Idea
13	(A) Inference(Imply)	(C) Detail(Purpose)
14	(B) Detail(Characteristic)	(A) Detail(Characteristic)
15	(A) Inference(Purpose)	(C) Detail(Cause)
16	(A),(B) Detail(Result)	(A) Inference(Imply)
17	(D) Inference(Opinion)	(D) Inference(Headset)

Self-Check List

유 형	맞춘 답의 개수(Test 1 - set 1)	맞춘 답의 개수(Test 1 - set 2)
Main Idea	/ 3	/ 3
Detail	/ 4	/ 5
Inference	/ 10	/ 8
Category	/ 0	/ 1

문제유형과 Signals

USHER iBT TOEFL FINAL TEST LISTENING PROTOTYPE

번호	기본문제유형	세부문제유형	Signals
1	Main Idea	Main Purpose Main Idea	국부적인(지엽적인) or 너무 일반적인(광범위한) 사실은 오답, 시제 및 단수 / 복수 주의
2	Details	Term/Definition/Irigin	refer to, what we call, so-called, originate, come from
3		Example	such as, like, think of, imagine, Let's take, let's say~, say, example, for instance
4		Characteristic Advantage / Disadvantage Problem / Difficulty Similarity / Compare Difference / Contrast	그림, 음악, 문학, 무용, 영화, 연극, 공예, 조각 등 / unique, useful, interesting, faster, fascinating, intriguing, key feature, note, important 동물 멸종위기, 생명의 위협 / 환경적응 Problem, hitch, challenge, drawback, flaw, defect, extinct, destroyed early-later, prior to~, recent, in the past, nowadays, modern day, evolve
5		Cause / Reason / Evidence Result / Finding / Effect / Influence	study, research, experiment, project(find, discover, uncover, reveal, shed light on) / evidence, finding / pave the way, impact, set the stage for, application
6		Misunderstanding Correction/Surprising	once believed, but~ / seem out of this world, news to
7		Requirement / Condition	necessary, required, you need to, consideration, condition, premise, job experience,
8		Offer / Solution / Suggestion	Alternative, to solve, handle this problem, recommend, why don't you~, what about~, what can be done~, your best bet would be~,
9		Future action/Future topic	upcoming, next class, another lecture
10	Inference	Purpose / Intention Imply / Infer Opinion / Attitude Headset	Why... mention~ / What can be inferred~/ What... imply~ What... mean when...say~ 다시 들려주고 푸는 문제 check ,understanding, agree/disagree
11	Category	Introduce / Organize / Conclude Matching Ordering	How~ introduce? How is the lecture organized? Three types, two kinds of, first, second, finally step, stage, phase , and then, divide into~

오답정리표 : Test 3

번호	문제유형	틀린 답번호	오답유형	출제의도파악 (문제 및 정답 요약)
Sample	Purpose	Test 4-15	T1	교수가 Wood Thrush를 언급한 이유는 ➡ 동물의 Displacement activities가 주변 환경으로부터 어떤 영향을 받는지에 대한 예
1	Main Purpose Main Idea Introduce Organize Conclusion			
2	Term Definition Origin			
3	Example			
4	Characteristic Advantage Disadvantage Problem Difficulty Similarity Compare Difference Contrast			

5	Cause, Reason, Evidence Result, Finding, Effect, Influence			
6	Misunderstanging Correction Surprising			
7	Requirement Condition			
8	Offer Solution Suggestion			
9	Future action Future topic			
10	Purpose Intention Imply Infer Opinion Attitude Headset			
11	Introduce Organize Conclude Matching Ordering			

TEST 3 ···133

TEST 4

정답 및 Self-Check List

정답

	Test 4 - set 1	Test 4 - set 2
1	(B) Main Idea	(C) Detail
2	(C) Detail	(A), (D) Detail
3	(A) Detail	(B) Inference
4	(A) Detail	(C) Detail
5	(B) Inference	(B) Inference
6	(A) Main Idea	(C) Main Idea
7	(D) Detail	(D) Detail
8	(B), (D) Detail	(D) Detail
9	(C) Detail	(C) Detail
10	(D) Inference	(C) Inference
11	(B) Inference	(A) Inference
12	(D) Main Idea	(C) Main Idea
13	(A) Category	(A) Detail
14	(A) Detail	(A) Detail
15	(C) Inference	(B) Inference
16	(D) Detail	(B) Inference
17	(D) Inference	(D) Inference

Self-Check List

유 형	맞춘답의 개수(Test 4 - set 1)	맞춘답의 개수(Test 4 - set 2)
Main Idea	/ 3	/ 2
Detail	/ 8	/ 8
Inference	/ 5	/ 7
Category	/ 1	
전 체	/ 17	/ 17

문제유형과 signals

번 호	기본문제유형	세부문제유형	Signals
1	Main Idea	Main Purpose Main Idea	국부적(지엽적인) or 너무 일반적인(광범위한) 사실은 오답, 시제 및 단수 / 복수 주의
2	Detail	Term/Definition/Origin	refer to, what we call, so-called, originate, come from
3		Example	such as, like, think of, imagine, Let's take, let's say~, say, example, for instance
4		Characteristic Advantage / Disadvantage Problem / Difficulty Similarity / Compare Difference / Contrast	그림, 음악, 문학, 무용, 영화, 연극, 공예, 조각 등 / unique, useful, interesting, faster, fascinating, intriguing, key feature, note, important 동물 멸종위기, 생명의 위협 / 환경적응 Problem, hitch, challenge, drawback, flaw, defect, extinct, destroyed early-later, prior to~, recent, in the past, nowadays, modern day, evolve
5		Cause / Reason / Evidence Result / Finding / Effect / Influence	study, research, experiment, project(find, discover, uncover, reveal, shed light on) / evidence, finding / pave the way, impact, set the stage for, application
6		Misunderstanding Correction/Surprising	once believed, but~ / seem out of this world, news to
7		Requirement / Condition	necessary, required, you need to, consideration, condition, premise, job experience,
8		Offer / Solution / Suggestion	Alternative, to solve, handle this problem, recommend, why don't you~, what about~, what can be done~, your best bet would be~,
9		Future action/Future topic	upcoming, next class, another lecture
10	Inference	Purpose / Intention Imply / Infer Opinion / Attitude Headset	Why... mention~ / What can be inferred~/ What... imply~ What... mean when...say~ 다시 들려주고 푸는 문제 check ,understanding, agree/disagree
11	Category	Introduce / Organize / Conclude Matching Ordering	How~ introduce? How is the lecture organized? Three types, two kinds of, first, second, finally step, stage, phase , and then, divide into~

오답정리표 : Test 4

번호	문제유형	틀린 답번호	오답유형	출제의도파악 (문제 및 정답 요약)
Sample	Purpose	Test 4-15	T1	교수가 Wood Thrush를 언급한 이유는 ➡ 동물의 Displacement activities가 주변 환경으로부터 어떤 영향을 받는지에 대한 예
1	Main Purpose Main Idea Introduce Organize Conclusion			
2	Term Definition Origin			
3	Example			
4	Characteristic Advantage Disadvantage Problem Difficulty Similarity Compare Difference Contrast			

5	Cause, Reason, Evidence Result, Finding, Effect, Influence			
6	Misunderstanging Correction Surprising			
7	Requirement Condition			
8	Offer Solution Suggestion			
9	Future action Future topic			
10	Purpose Intention Imply Infer Opinion Attitude Headset			
11	Introduce Organize Conclude Matching Ordering			

usherin.usher.co.kr

USHER iBT TOFLE
FINAL TEST
LISTENING

Note Taking

Note taking Test 1 Set 1-Conversation

Student	Office Clerk
Rebuild Sc. Lib. AGANST Q1 Need sig. board to PROTEST St ID # 110-509	
Right now good . X Reno. Recently renovated Rely to study Q2 May lose scholarships Q5 Need to study (Reference)	Why prob.? Yes, see the point may move, provide study area
	X funds. Might not even.
250 ↑	How many sig? Q3 Sympathize!
Q4 Why not add a wing? Blueprint, close? Ridic. Others feel same. glad!	
When decision final?	Check the rumors Sometime this week

TEST1 Set1 -Conversation

St.	Prof.
Good - Met good ppl. - Make prof. network	Conf. in S. Florida?
Okay - Interesting theories - Met people (later future study) Q1	Lecture on molecular biology?
Seashore walking, (Jellyfish glowed)	Bioluminescence - prod. Light by living org. - Jellyfish, Fireflies, Glowworms, Certain squids, Shrimps, Fungi - Natural "Chemical reactions → energy as light'
Explain mechanism (for term paper)	
Why light?	Only certain times. Differs 1. Interspecies communication 2. Avoid predator - Jellyfish (3. Attract prey)
(Process? Biologically?) Q2 Q3	Jellyfish - Enough energy → oxidize magn. → light - Produce chem. needed itself - (Light differ)
Bioluminescence jellyfish for term paper?	(Interesting, but requires work) Q4 Q5 - Relatively new field - Radical in marine bio

Note taking — Test 1 Set1-Lecture1

Art History
Prof. R.g.
R. – New ideas (EU)
   – Rebirth in French
   – Pop. Classic C. of a.R.
R.g.
  ↳ Emulate pop. In a.R. → Most imp. Charac.
  ↳ (Built on assumptions) Q10
Idea 'lost classical arts' pop. ↑
  – Wealthy ppl. Recreate gardens
    ↳ Arch. Build
(Features)
  ↳ Walkways w/ marble statues
  ↳ Fountains   Q6
  ↳ Statues (animal, giants, creatures)
  ↳ Bushes
(What actually like?)
3 stages
  1. Near homes for veg. & herbs – back of house (practical)
  2. Quality, living space ↑ (Front yard) – statues, flowers (peristyle)
  3. Villa garden – Artworks, plants, (buildings (ex. Fountains, swimming pool)) Q7

Why build?
  ↳ Status symbol
  ↳ X reason
  ↳ Pursuit beauty   Q8
  ↳ Display wealth, power
  ↳ Impress guests

(Other unique?)
  ↳ (Coin operated fountains) Q11
  ↳ 'Water jokes' – entertain visitors   Q6

(Labyrinth to emulate)
  ↳ X clue
Why common in R.g.
  ↳ (Entertainment (myth)) Q9
  ↳ Outdoor playground
  ↳ Walls w/ herbs, flowers → enjoy walking

Art History – Renaissance Garden

Renaissance
- New ideas in EU
- 'Rebirth' in French
- Popularize classic concepts of ancient Romans

Rs. Gardens – to emulate those pop. In a.R. → Most imp. Characteristic
  └ Built as a.R. 'would have', using assumptions Q10
    ↳ Idea became popular
        - Wealthy ppl. (Merchants & political fig.) recreate gardens
          ↳ Hire architects to build

Features of Rs. Gardens
- Walkways w/ marble statues & fountains
- Statues (animals, giants, creatures)   Q6
- Bushes trimmed in shapes

What actually like?
3 stages.
  1. Near homes – vegetables & herbs to eat (backyard)
          Primary source (practical > ornamental)
  2. Quality, living space ↑ (Front yard) – Walkways w/ statues
                                          – Flowers & shrubs
                                          (Practical < Ornamental)
  3. Villa garden – Luxurious – Plants & Artworks for pleasure
        – Other buildings (ex. Fountains, swimming pool) Q7

Why build gardens? Q8
  ↳ Symbolize status
  ↳ X reason
    - Pursuit of beauty
    - Display wealth, power
    - Impress guests → pride

Contained labyrinth?
  ↳ To emulate?
    ↳ X evidence of laby. In a.R.
Why become common in R.g.?
  ↳ Imitate myth
  ↳ Entertainment   Q9
  ↳ Change meaning → Outdoor playground
  ↳ Love walk, enjoy nature (walls with herbs & shrubs)

Other unique features? Q11
  ↳ Coin operated fountains
    ↳ Called 'water jokes'
    ↳ Added to Italian R.g.

Note taking — Test 1 Set1-Lecture2

Physics - Relativity
Einstein
  └→ T. Relativity
      └→ What light is, how it works
      └→ Change mod. Phy.
      └→ (X recog. That time - X Nobel) Q12
          └→ Legitimacy, unorthodox method → Q.
  └→ Proper recog.? - Still
Where from?
  └→ Born in Ger, 1879
  └→ Love academics, X formal = drop → fail univ. 1st tttryyy
  └→ Return, grad., 1900
  └→ X employ → patent Swit., 1902 → Most prod., creativity!
Genius + Exp.

  [Approve patent
    └→ Break down invent. / idea
    └→ Study   Q13
    └→ Foundation]

(What?)
2 Parts
1. Special, 2. General
1. Has own time
      └→ Time dilation (time affected by velo.)
    Twin paradox
      └→ A → Space (speed light) → younger (travel faster)
      └→ B → Home
    Speed > Time
      └→ Time slows
          └→ (Revolution (to time same)) Q14
2. 1915, Previous + gravity
  └→ Light bends
      └→ Around sun! - can see stars behind   Q15
          └→ Only prove after (lack equi., tech.)
          (Try discredit (Miller))

Miller - Light's speed - Ether
  └→ # measure, data
  (X convincing, but data & position → O) Q17
  └→ Other exp. → Ether X
          └→ Lack equip. 1. Vacuum
                          2. X grav.
                          3. X press.

(Nobel = X Einstein) Q12
  └→ = R. Miller
      └→ Lack data, results
      └→ Shaky foundations
      └→ Need source & method, E ≠ trad. Sci.
  └→ Acted fair
  └→ (E accepted limits) Q16
How affect?
1. GPS
2. Quantum phy.
    └→ Microchips, elec. Microsc., MRI
3. Create new Sci.

TEST1 Set1-Lecture2

Physics – Relativity
Einstein – Greatest phy.
　└▸ T. of relativity
　　　└▸ What light is, how it works
　　　　　└▸ Reshape phy.
　　　└▸ X recog. That time – X Nobel prize
　　　　　Work's legitimacy, unorthodox method Q by contemporaries ⎫ Q12
　└▸ Whether Einstein received proper recog.? → still continues
Where he is from?
　└▸ Germany, 1879
　└▸ Love academics, hate formal edu. Sys. → Drop out → fail univ. entry 1st attempt
　└▸ Return formal school → graduate, 1900
　└▸ X employment in academia → patent office in Swiss, 1902
　　　└▸ Most productive time
　　　　　└▸ Creativity
　　　　　└▸ Productivity
　　　└▸ How help?
　　　　　└▸ Genius + Experience
　　　　　　└▸ To approve patent   ⎫ Q13
　　　　　　　└▸ Breakdown invent. / idea for validity
　　　　　　　└▸ Study ideas. / inven. → foundations for T. relativity
Q12
What the T is?
2 parts
1. T. special relativity 2. T. general relativity

1. Everything has own time
　└▸ Time dilation (Time affected y fast velo. Ex. Light)
　└▸ Twin paradox
　　┌ Jeff → spaceship speed of light → much younger when return
　　│ John → home
　　└▸ Traveled faster than John's time
　Speed > Time, time slowed
　　└▸ Revolutionary   ⎫ Q15
　　└▸ Traditional view (Time same for everyone)
2. 1915, 1+gravity
　└▸ Light travels straight
　　　└▸ But bends around heavy mass (ex. Stars)
　　　└▸ Common (ex. Light bend around sun)
　　　│　　　　　　See stars behind sun
　　　└▸ Validation later (lack of equip. & tech.)
　└▸ Miller, try discredit   Q12
　　└▸ Believed light's speed deter by Ether
　　　└▸ Produced # of measurements & data   Q17
　　　└▸ X convincing, but exp. Measure & position → support
　　　└▸ Other exp. (ex. Michelson – Morley) → Ether X
　　　　　　　　　　└▸ Due to lack of equip.
　　　　　　　　　　　└▸ Vacuum
　　　　　　　　　　　└▸ gravity
　　　　　　　　　　　└▸ pressure

Nobel comit. → X recog. Einstein   Q12
　└▸ Same reason as Miller
　└▸ Lacked data & results
　└▸ Shaky foundation (ingenuity & creativity)
　└▸ Einstein disregard trad. method, X evidence
　└▸ Phys. Comit. ← → Einstein
　└▸ Einstein accepted limit. of T.   Q16
How affect life?
　└▸ Gps
　└▸ Quantum Phy.
　　　└▸ Microchips, electron microscopes, MRI
　└▸ Create new sci.

Note taking Test 1 Set2-Conversation

Student	Office Clerk
Rebuild Sc. Lib. AGANST Q1 Need sig. board to PROTEST St ID # 110-509	
Right now good . X Reno. Recently renovated Rely to study Q2 May lose scholarships Q5 Need to study (Reference)	Why prob.? Yes, see the point may move, provide study area
250 ↑ Q4 Why not add a wing? Blueprint, close? Ridic. Others feel same. glad!	X funds. Might not even. How many sig? Q3 Sympathize!
When decision final?	Check the rumors Sometime this week

TEST1 Set2-Conversation

Student	Office Clerk
Re-build Science library (Against) Q1 Need board sig. to start protest	
ID# : 110509	Give name, Student ID
1. Like the way it is right now 2. X need renovation (Recently renovated) 3. Rely library to study Q2 Q5 4. EVEN MAY LOSE SCHOLARSHIPS 5. Source, reference need for study	Why Problem? Probably move & provide alternate study area
	X enough fund (may not even be able)
250 and ↑	How many signatures against? Office workers sympathize
Q4 Why not just add wing? (Blueprint looked ridiculous to close) Glad others feel the same	Q3
	Check if the rumors are true
When final decision?	Sometime this week

Note taking Test 1 Set2-Lecture1

Engineering Class

Barriers between Nations X = Barriers betw. Earth & Univ. X

Energy, Resource, Efficiency (method) - Expensive
- Fuel → 11km/s
- Tank = big, heavy

Misconceptions Q7
11km/s to escape ≠ only way
↳ Overcome Earth's pull = X lose velo.

1. Constant f. ↑
2. Holding one firmly in place
   ↳ Sci. try build

Ex. Huge ladder, slowly ↑ to space = Yes
  ↳ X 11km/s, but
  ↳ Improbable (exhausted, O2 tank & space suit) Q11

Q6 = Space elevator
  Rus. Sci. Eiffel tower, 1895 Q8
  S. f. author Arthur C Clarke 1979 Fountains of Paradise

How?

Base station - Pillar (elevator) = Cable
Strong, tall enough?
Centrifugal force
Elevator need counterweight
Cable = Hindrance
  ↳ Light, durable
Carbon made material Q8
  ↳ Carbon nanotube

How long?
Sat → How high above Earth their orbits
Mass center 36,000km (Geosync. Orbit)
  ↳ Orbit sync. Earth's rotation
Q9 = Appear same place

Q6
Problems
1. Nanotubes = few cm… impractical
2. Navigational Prob.
3. Exposed to radiation belt

TEST1 Set2-Lecture1

Engineering Class

Barriers between nations X = Barrier between Earth & Univ.

Method of space travel = (expensive)
  ↳ ↑Energy
  ↳ ↑Resources
  ↳ ↓Efficiency

○ Fuel required → Escape velocity (11km/s)
      ↳ Inefficient (Fuel tank big & heavy)

Misconceptions - to space
Traveling at 11km/s ≠ only way | Q7
      ↳ Speed to overcome gravity
  ↳ Constant force ↑
  ↳ Holding one firmly in place → scientists try to build

Ex) Build huge ladder, climb (?) = YES
  ↳ X reach 11km/s, but can go to space
  ↳ IMPROBABLE, can't climb (carrying oxygen tank, space suit)   Q11
→ X outrageous = Concept of Space elev. (transport materials. Earth ←→ Space)   Q6

Space Elev.
  - Russian Rocket Sci. - Inspired by Eiffel tower, 1895 > Q8
  - Arthur C. Clarke (S.f. author) → Fountains of paradise, 1979

How?
1. Base station - Attached to elev. Travel pillar (Flexible = Cable)
      Cable strong, tall enough   How? (원심력)

Q6 Cable = Hindrance (Light & Durable) Q8
  ↳ Carbon nanotube (Strong bond)
          ↳ Conduct electricity

2. How long the cable?
  - peed of satellites → How high above the Earth it orbits
  - Attached to the Earth
      ↳ Mass centered at 36,000km (Geosynchronous orbit)
              ↳ Orbital period = Earth's rotation   Q9
                = Object appear at same spot

↳ Problems...
  ↳ Longest = few cm… Impractical
  ↳ Navigational Hazzard   Q10
  ↳ Exposed to radiation belt (exposed)

Note taking Test 1 Set2-Lecture2

Archeology
　└→Easter Isl.
　　　└→Dutchman 1722
　　　　└→Cannibals
　　　　　└→Once advanced civil
What happened? Q12
　- Famous for m? statues
Back. Info.
　- 64miles²
　- S. Pacific 2,000 miles West of Chile
　- 1,400 miles neighbor
　- Subtropic, mild Wint., rainst. Sum. → good inhabit.
X connection outside
　　　2,000 barba.
　- Moai
　　└→ ◯ Statues
　　└→ 887
　　└→ 14.5 ft, 14 T (some 33 ft, 165 T)... 크다
　　└→ 2,000 ppl? How? X Trees... Q13

Q14
Who live there?
Past T.
　1. Nor. Expl. - Chile, Moai - Incan statues
　2. Modern Sci. - DNA (Skel.) - Polynesia (Aus.) - migrate by canoe
　　　X all from Poly.　　　　└→ from Easter closest

Now T.
　- from Easter closest - 11,000 ~ 15,000 - esti.
　　Labor, lands
Dispersion Moai = condition past diff.
　　　└→ True = pollen analysis
　　　　　　└→ Swamp, Pond collect
Q17　　　　└→ Diff. layers from time　　Q12
　　　　　　└→ Dated Radio - carbon
↘What?
　　Remaining carbon levels (dead)

Once Palm trees
　- Canoe, build Moai, Houses, Fire　Q15
Animals, Trees extinct
　　└→ 111 ppl, 1877
1. Ame. Sci. - dest. Over consmp. Deforest
　　　- Cut trees → Moai → X tree → Fire, House = luxury → Chaos
　= Only T.
2. Archeo. - Rats - bones (likely landing spot)
　　　└→ For food → X pred., popul. ↑　Q16
　　　└→ Ate palm seeds
　　　Rat popul. ↑ → X palm seeds → deforest.
　　　X canoe → X Fish → O animals → Cannibal
　　　1722 → X trace of civil.

Archeology
  Easter Island
    - Found by a Dutchman, 1722
    - Cannibalistic savages
    - Once occupied by an advanced civil
  (What happened? (To the prominent civil → demise)) Q12
Easter Island
    - Famous for ◯ statues
Background Info.
    - 64 miles²
    - Southern Pacific (2,000 miles west of Chile)
    - Closest inhabited island 1,400 miles away
    - Humid, subtropical, mild winter, rainstorm filled summer = ideal habitat
Found 2,000 people & Moai (X Trees & animals)
       ◯ Statues
    - 887 faces on stones
    - Average 14.5 ft, 14 T (some 33 ft, 165 T)
How could 2,000 people build Moai? Q13   Q14
  ↳ Even X trees

Who lived there? Why?
Past T.
    - Nor. Expl. -T.- Chile (closest land) - Moai ≒ Incan statues
    - Modern sci. -T.- DNA test (Skel.) - Polynesia (AUS) - Seafarers who migrate by canoe got
                                                                    lost → settle down
          ↳ but X all are from Poly.
Present T.
Estimate 11,000~15,000 few C. ago
    ↳ Based on labor required, habitable area

Dispersion of Moai → (Conditions in the past = diff.)
                = True - Pollen analysis
                        Sediment from swamp & pond   Q12
                        Different layers over time
        What?   Dated through radiocarbon
Measure ages of dead   Q17
    - Remaining carbon levels

Island once had ◯ palm trees   Q15
      ↳ Canoes, logs, ropes, houses, fire
Palm trees & Animals extinct
    ↳ Population of 111 in 1877
Traditional T.
    - Ame. Sci. - Destroyed through overconsumption & deforestation
                Cut trees → Moai → X trees → fire & house = luxury → chaos
  → Only Theory
Archeologist - Rats → demise
          ↳ Rat bones from beach soil (likely landing spot)
          ↳ Brought for food → X natural predators → population ↑   Q16
          ↳ Eat palm seeds
          = Rat population ↑ → X palm seeds → deforestation
          X canoe → X fishing → eat animals → X animals → cannibalism
          1722, X trace of civil.

Note taking Test 2 Set1-Conversation

G. St.	B. Prof
Why lab? Time in lab… X go smooth	How exp.? Many time!
Task – exp. Go well Cooling process prob. Q1	Why? X fully heat?
~heat process = perf., Overslept & forgot Q2	Know exact process X used lab Sat.
Sorry… submit journal (possi. Use)	Heated weekend, X purify… It can wait Function X change Q5
X long (few days)	When result?
Worry protein X condition?	Prob. Leave town for week (tmrw.) Yes. Work with good condi. Q3
Start again… Good practice, ↓error, my fault	Ask too much g. stu. Glad prof. att. ↓error = critical as Sci.
Guess X true. Supposed	Supposed spinach strengthen music? Ppl. Believe spinach ↑iron Ger. Sci mistake 10* Q4 - Everything right, misplace deci. - Continues to fool

TEST2 Set1 - Conversation

G. St.	B. Prof
Why come to lab today?	Check how exp. Heard a lot of time put
Put time in… as X go well	
	Why?
Task – purify protein RP73 – X go well Cooling process prob. Q1	Forgot to fully heat?
	Reversible (O / X), know exact process
~ heating process = perfect	When I grad. Stu. X used to lab on Sat.
Alarm Friday, come next day to cool. Forgot & overslept Q2	
	If heated all weekend, X purify…
Sorry… you hoped to submit to journal - (possible use)	It can wait Function X change Q5
Working on it. Couple of days	When result?
	Prob. : Leave town for a week (tmrw.)
Worried protein X be best condition?	Yes. Want to work - Freshly purified protein Q3
Should start again	

X worry
   1. Good practice
   2. ↓error margin
   3. My fault X result now
	Ask too much to grad. stu.

	Glad professional attitude ↓error margin = critical - Design & implement experiment
	Story abt spinach's supposed effect on strengthening muscles?

X but guess X true. "Supposed" Q4	Ppl. Believe spinach is rich in iron
	German chemist, 1870 made error
	    - 10* more iron
	    - Everything else right, misplace decimal
	    - Still fool ppl.

Note taking Test 2 Set1-Lecture1

History - Pyramids
Pyramid
- 756 ft ←→, 450 ft ↑
- 2,300,000 stones
How?
  ↳ X Evidence
  ↳ (Sci. Arch. - T.)
Why?
- Afterlife
- Tombs rest
- ◯ Chambers, only one   Q6
       ↳ Fool robbers
Why treasures?
- Afterlife eternal   Q11
- Precious belonging
X well
Advanced, structures remain
       T. How?
       Ancient Greek His. T.
         ↳ Wooden cranes - lift
         ↳ Prob. Giza - X wood, X space
         ↳ + Other source, (T. - ramps (main device)) Q7

Many T. shape
  ↳ Egyptologist - Straight ramps
         ↳ Massive, 1/2 mile slope
Too much work?
  ↳ Yes. Waste
Spiral ramp
  ↳ Complex
  ↳ Wrap around Py.
  ↳ ↓material & labor
  ↳ Prob. 1. Ruin external sight   Q8
           ↳ Rope measure, clear vision check
         2. Ramp corner
             Turn corner 2.5t stone
Both T. Prob.
  ↳ Destroy ramps
French arch. New T.
  ↳ Infrared cam → 3D model Py.
         ↳ Internal ramp
Begin - 141 ft ext. ramp, switch
  ↳ Wrap around inside (spiral)

Corners prob.   Q9
  ↳ Spiral ≅ winding roads, mount.
     Cars risk
  ↳ Workers easily stumble

Internal   Q10
  ↳ Space around corners
      ↳ Easier, safer
Ramps - ◯ labor & material?
  ↳ Internal = part of Py.
      ↳ Sealed off.

Revolu. T. - Likely accept

TEST2 Set1 -Lecture1

History - Pyramids
Pyramid at Giza
- 756 ft ←→, 450 ft ↑
- 2,300,000 stone blocks

How build 4,500 yrs ago?
　└▸ X direct evidence
　└▸ Sci. Arch. - come up with T.   Q6

Why Py. built?
- Tombs to rest during afterlife
- Had multiple chambers & passages
　　└▸ To fool grave robbers

Why treasures in tomb?
　└▸ Consider afterlife = Eternal   Q11
　　　└▸ Prepare
　└▸ Take most precious belonging

X work well
　└▸ Advanced arch. & craft. → Structures to remain

Many T. on possible shapes
　└▸ Straight ramps
　　　└▸ 1/2 mile slope to reach top
　　　　　└▸ Waste of labor & materials

Spiral ramp
　└▸ Complex - Wrap around Py.
　└▸ ↓materials & labor compared to other ramps
　└▸ Prob. 1. Ruin external sight (builders')
　　　　└▸ Use ropes to measure
　　　　　└▸ Need clear vision
　　　　2. Ramp corner   Q8
　　　　　　Turning 2.5t stone high in air

Both ramp T. Prob.
　└▸ Destroy ramps after

French arch. → New T.
　└▸ Surveyed with infrared cam
　　　└▸ Develop 3D model of Py.
　　Internal ramp
　　　└▸ External ramps of 141 ft in the beginning
　　　　└▸ Then internal ramps
　　　└▸ Wrap around inside pyramid (like spiral)

Internal ramps
　　└▸ Space around corners
　　　　└▸ Easier, safer   Q10
Ramps require too much labor & material
　└▸ Internal = diff. - become part of Py.
　　└▸ X taken down after construction
　　└▸ Sealed off after, save materials & labor

T. How Py. Built?
　└▸ Ancient Greek His. T.
　　　└▸ Wooden cranes on every level to lift stones
　　　└▸ Prob. = X wood for crane & X space
　　　└▸ + Other source, T. - ramps
　　　　　└▸ Ramps to transport stones   Q7
　　　　　　└▸ Main device atm.

Corners prob.   Q9
　└▸ Spiral ramps ≅ Winding roads on mount.
　　　└▸ Cars risk falling off
　└▸ Workers easily stumble

Revolu. T.
　└▸ Likely to be accepted
　　　└▸ Eliminates prob. of prev. T.

Note taking Test 2 Set1-Lecture2

Marine bio. - coral reef dest.
G.B. Reef
- 400 coral, 1500 fish, 200 bird
- Coral polyps.
    ↳ Attach to ocean floor

Before
- Sci.
    ↳ Coral - strong rock   Q17
        ↳ X move
        ↳ Fish home - tough cal.-carb. Skel.

Crown of thorns
↳ Popul. ↑, prey on coral
↳ Poison. Spine.
↳ 2nd largest
↳ Eat coral
    ↳ Liquefy coral
T. to Explain sudden ↑

(1st Expl.)
- Natural
    ↳ Species popul & temp. vari
        ↳ ↑starfish, ↓coral = natural
→ 1960, X scuba tech = diff. study
Q12 3 outbreaks last few dec.   Q13
    ↳ Think natural

Crown of thrones - billion eggs
    1% ↑survival → 10 mil. More → popul. ↑

(2nd hypo.)
- ↓predator
- Thorns, X many predator
    ↳ Giant triton
Smell → chase → attach → stab → paralyze → feed
Hunted for ornamental shells
    ↳ 1969, popul. ↓   Q14
    ↳ 40yrs, X enough

(Final hypo.) Q12
- Human act.
Deforestation → land vulnerable
Rainy season → fert. & org. mat. To Sea
Fertil. - Nit & Phosph.
    ↳ Algae & plankton   Q15
         ↓
      Copious nourishment
- ↓ salinity
Starfish larvae X osmore.
- Sea too salty
    ↳ Dilute → survival ↑

C. O. T. positive too   Q16
    1. Feed rapid ↑ coral
       - kept check, slow growing coral ↑
       - Diverse species
Natural part of ecosys.
    X giant influ.

TEST2 Set1-Lecture2

Marine bio. - Coral reef destruction
Great Barrier Reef
- Home to 400 coral, 1500 fish, 200 bird species
- Made of coral polyps.
  - Attach to ocean floor

Before research
- Sci.
  - Coral - strange shaped rock   Q17
    - X blame - X move
  - Provide homes for fish
    - tough calcium carbonate skeletons

Coral popul. ↓ recently
  - Crown of thorns popul. ↑, prey on coral
    - Poisonous spine
    - 2nd largest starfish
    - Eat coral (liquefy coral)
      - Liquefy coral
Sci. several T. explain sudden popul. ↑

1st Expl. Q12
- Natural phenomenon
  - ↑ starfish popul. & ↓coral ≒ species popul. ↑ & cyclical variation Earth temp.
  - Studying ocean floor diff. ← 1960, (X scuba tech.)
  - Last few dec, 3 outbreaks. Starfish   Q13
    - Think coral destruction natural

Crown of thrones produce billion eggs
  1% ↑ survival chance → 10 mil. More → domino → popul. ↑

2nd hypo.
- Predator decline
- X many predators due to thorns
- Predator - giant triton
  - Smell starfish → chase → attach → stab with radula → paralyze → feed
  - Hunted for ornamental shells
    - Popul. ↓ → unsustainable, 1969   Q14
    - 40 yrs of gov. protection, X enough

Q12

Final hypo.
- Human activities on land
  - Deforestation (80% land adjacent to G. B. R)
    - Vulnerable to sediment run off & flooding
- Rainy season
  - Fertilizers & organic matters → sea   Q15
    1. Fertilizers contain nitrogen & phosphorous
       - Algae & plankton ↑ → copious nourishment
    2. Dilutes water, ↓salinity
       - Larvae X osmoregulate
       - Sea = too salty
       - Dilute → survival chance ↑

C. O. T. useful function   Q16
1. Feed on rapidly growing coral
   - Kept check by starfish
     - Allow slow growing coral survive
   - Maintain species diversity
Starfish = Natural part of ecosys.
  - Better take care X influence on popul.

Note taking Test 2 Set2-Conversation

St.	Prof
Academ. Prob. Q1 Res. Whale breathe pattern… Baleen – 2 Toothed – 1 Q3	Diff whale, diff pattern
?	Whales – mammals, Some attrib. differ completely Human – mammal, Bio. Diff – Ethni. – Gender – Age Q2 Pick type
Bow head	Baleen
? Anatomy & breath patt. → migrate w/ X breath	40 mins per dive
Others? Q5	Depends Some – kilo ↓ water 90 ~ 120 mins
Originally, bio. Whale ↓ water long time?	Few things, some T. 1st obvious
Size?	◯ Oxygen in bloodstreams
Another?	↓ oxy. Need while dive ↓ oxy. delivered
X know	
	Expel air lung. (dive) X float Q4 Rest squeeze Lose oxy., release more from blood & muscl. Relax muscl. – thrust ↓ strokes. Glide ↓

TEST2 Set2-Conversation

St.	Prof
Academical Problem Q1 Researching whale breathing pattern during migration	Different whale = Different pattern
Baleen whales – 2 blow holes Toothed whales – 1 Q3	

?	Whales – mammals,
	Some attributes differ completely
	Humans – mammals,
	Biologically Diff
	  1. Ethnicity
	  2. Gender
	  3. Age Q2
	Pick specific type

Report on Bowhead	Baleen
? Anatomy & breathing patterns → migrate w/ X breathing	Bowhead 40 mins submerge per dive
Others whales?	Depends (species, reason) Some – kilo ↓ water for 90 ~ 120 mins
How stay ↓ water for a long time? (bio.) Q5	Few things, some theoretical 1st obvious
Size?	X. Phys. Hold oxygen in bloodstream
Another?	↓ oxy. Needed while submerged ↓ oxy. Deliv. To X use body (dive)
X know	
	Expel air from lungs (dive) – X float Q4 Rest = squeeze, ↑water p. Release more oxy. from blood & muscl. Relax muscl. – thrust ↓ w/ few strokes, glide ↓

Note taking Test 2 Set2-Lecture1

Anthrop.
Anthrop. - horse domes. (Bronze, Eurasia)
New evi. N. Kaza.
  ↳ Botai domes. ← 1,000
  ↳ Controversy
  ↳ Close w/ horse
  ↳ Domes.?
(Examine evi.) Q6
Botai?
  ↳ C. Asia
  ↳ Hunters?
  - Nomads
    ↳ Hunted game
    ↳ Horse meat imp. (90% remains)
    ↳ Shallow camp w/ 1~2 house
    ↳ Travel small, X stay
    ↳ Change → domes.
How?
  ↳ Horse = food
Botai
  ↳ Domes. Horse ← 6,000 → stable meat
     ↳ Popul. ↑, settle → pit house (insulation)
(N. Kaza. - Cold
  ↳ ↓0 T. 9 m. winter
Horse - useful   Q7
  ↳ Survive snowstorm
  ↳ Sheep & cattle X)
Revolution - ppl. Lives
Equine revol.
 - Agric. ~ war
Early
Stable meat & milk
Later → horse transp.
  ↳ ↑range, globaliz.
           Interaction & idea
  ↳ Revol. War   Q8
     ↳ Ground → mounted
        ↳ Quicken pace

How prove 1st?
Archeo.
  ↳ 3 Claims
     1. Soil sample
     2. Bit wear
     3. Markings & fat molecules
Soil sample?
  ↳ Around posts (horses tied)
  ↳ Phosph. 10X ↑(horse manure ↑phosph. & nit.)
  ↳ (↓Nit. - Volatile, easily washed) Q9
     ↳ X recent
Horse remains
  ↳ Skulls - teeth
       ↳ Indent - bridle
Lipid / Fat analysis
  ↳ Mare's milk - Botai pottery
1st 2 - Circumstantial
↳ Direct
  ↳ Milked mare, milk in pottery - 'smoking gun'
  ↳ (Unless milk wild horse) Q11
Why X skeletal struc.?
  ↳ Domes. X change phy.
     ↳ Certain do - domes. & selective
  ↳ (X horse - X tame/ wild/ era) Q10
Evi
  ↳ T. Probable
     ↳ New evi & pers. Archeo. → accept

TEST2 Set2-Lecture1

Anthrop.
Anthropologists - horse domes. (Bronze Age, Eurasian steppes)
New evi. - N. Kaza.
↳ Botai domes. 1,000 yrs earlier
↳ Ground breaking, controversy
↳ Close relat. w/ horse
↳ Q = Domes.?
(Examine evi. Proponents) Q6
Who are Botai?
↳ C. Asia
↳ Hunters?
↳ Nomads - hunted 1. Deer
                   2. Moose
                   3. Equus Ferus
↳ Horse meat imp. food
   (90% remains from horse)
↳ Shallow campsites w/ 1~2 house
↳ Traveled small, X stay long
↳ Change → domes.
How?
↳ Horse = food
Botai
↳ Domes. Horse ← 6,000yrs → stable meat
   → Popul. ↑, settle → pit house (X cold)
   Popul. ↑, settle → pit house (insulation)
↳ N. Kaza. - Cold (↓0 temp. 9 months winter)
Horse - useful
↳ Survive snowstorm & forage
   ↳ Sheep & cattle X   Q7
Equine revol. - agri. ~ war
 - Stable meat & milk (early)
 - Transport (later)
 - ↑society range → early form of globaliz.
   (interaction & spread idea)
 - Revol. War   Q8
   ↳ Ground troops → mounted soldiers
       ↳ Cover more ground (quicken pace)

How prove Botai 1st?
Archeologist
↳ 3 Claims
   1. Soil samples from Botai
   2. Bit wear
   3. Markings & fat molecules on pottery
Soil sample?
↳ From ground around posts (horse tied)
   ↳ Phosph. 10X ↑than others
   (Horse manure ↑phosph. & nit.)
↳ ↓Nit. - Volatile, easily washed & released
   ↳ Phosph. X recent manure   Q9
Horse remains
↳ Skulls - peculiarity teeth
  ↳ Indentation - only caused by bridle, bit (to ride)
Lipid / Fat analysis
↳ Fats from mare's milk on pottery
  1st 2 - Circumstantial
↳ Direct evi.
   ↳ Milked & preserved in pottery → 'smoking gun'
      ↳ (Unless milk wild horse) Q11
Why X examine skeletal struc.?
↳ Domes. X change phy. (part true)
   ↳ Certain ani. do - domes. & selective breeding
(X horse - ? (tame/ wild/ era)) Q10
Evi
↳ T. Probable
   ↳ New evi & persistency → accept

Note taking — Test 2 Set2-Lecture2

Bio. – Alter. E.
Ethanol from corn
　└▸ Beverage
　└▸ Sub. Fossil fuels (crude oil & coal)
　　Bio. ↔ Fossil
　　　Renewable　　long time (↑t. & p.)
　　Living org.
New way ethan. – cellulosic ≠ corn ethan.　Q12
　└▸ Carb. → ethan.

Cellulose?
　└▸ Rigid struc. Plant cell.
　└▸ Polymer of glucose　Q17
　　　└▸ Long sugar unit
　└▸ Most abundant, 33% Of plant
　　　　└▸ Comp. change corn → cellulosic

Other adv.
1. Corn ethan. – use plant starch (carb.)
　　　　　└▸ Humans
　Cellulose – X human
2. All plants supply　　　　　Q13
　└▸ ↑options & supplies
　　　└▸ Supplies & fuels industry
　Main – woody plants
　　└▸ ↑density than corn
　　　└▸ Transp. Efficient

Ex. Fill 2 boxes
1. Papers 2. Wrap
1. Heavier (carry more)
Transp. Raw mat. ◯ In busin.
Cellulosic. Plants cheaper & eco. > corn
　　　　└▸ ↓ gas 85%
Effici. Prod. E → future bright
　　└▸ Try ↑ effici. Cellulosic

Celluloysis → loosen. → glucose → fermented　Q15
　　　　　　　　　　　　　→ soup (ethanol, etc.)
Distillation – isolate ethanol
Yeast in fermenting
　└▸ Abundant　Q14
　└▸ ↑temp., pH
Resilient yeast – cellul. → ethanol
　└▸ Cellul. → glucose X
　└▸ ↑product. & ↓cost
Gasification (therm. – chem.)　Q15
　└▸ Cellul. Combusted (carbon atoms)
　　　└▸ Compounds → fed to micro org.
　　　　└▸ release wat. & ethanol → distilled

Prob. Switch
　└▸ Major – ↑ effici., + 120$ / barrel
　└▸ X funded, X research　Q16
　└▸ X plants (execute conver.)
Prob. Can O gov. support
Public attention & interest → ↑ support

TEST2 Set2-Lecture2

Biology – Alternative Energy
Produce ethanol from corn
  └→ In alcohol beverage
  └→ Candidate to sub. Fossil fuels (ex. crude oil & coal)
    Biofuels (ethan.) ↔ Fossil fuels
      └→ Renewable   └→ form after long time (↑t. & p.)
      └→ From living org.   Q12
New way ethan. – cellulosic. Ethan. Prod. ≒ corn ethan.
                        └─ Carb. Comp. → ethan. ─┘

Cellulose?
  └→ Support struc. (Plant cells)
  └→ Polymer of glucose / Long sugar unit   Q17
  └→ Most abundant, 33% of a plant
    └→ R. corn → cellulosic

Other adv.
1. Corn ethan. – use plant starch (carb.)
            └→ Human nutrient
   Cellulose – humans X digest
2. All plants can supply
   └→ ↑options & supplies of feed stock
  Q13   └→ Raw materials for machines & industry
   Woody plants (main)
      └→ ↑density than corn – transp. efficient

Ex. Fill 2 boxes
    1. Stacks of paper   2. Bubble wrap
       └→ Heavier (carry more subs.) └→ mostly air
   Density – transp. Raw materials ◯ role in busin.
   Cellulosic. Plants cheaper & eco-friend. > corn
              └→ ↓ greenhouse gas 85%
   Effici. Prod. E → future bright
        └→ R. ↑attempts to ↑ effici. Cellulosic
   ↑tech → new process → Celluloysis (bio. Approach)
              └→ Cellulose – loosen → break to glucose (smallest)
              → fermented   Q15
                └→ thick soup (ethanol & other chem.)

Distillation – boiling (compounds evap. separately) → isolate ethanol
Baker's yeast in fermenting   Q16
  └→ Abundant   Q14
  └→ Withstand ↑temp. & pH
Resilient yeast – cellulose – direct → ethanol
  └→ (Cellulose → glucose) X
  └→ ↑production process & ↓cost
Gasification (thermo – chemical)
  └→ X fermenting, cellulose combusted   Q15
      └→ separate carbon atoms
        └→ compounds → fed to Clostridium Ijungdahlii
          └→ release ethanol & water
            └→ distilled

Progress, prob. switching to cellulosic
  └→ Major – ↑ effici., cellulosic = + 120$ / barrel
  └→ X well funded, X much research
  └→ Lack commercial plants
  └→ Can be solved by gov. support
Gain public attention & interest
        → ↑ financial support

Note taking Test 3 Set1-Conversation

St.	M. O.
Q. commu. Serv. Q1	
Checked, can't submit work as commu. serv. How here?	Yes. X mind forms
History major, ◯ knowl., prepare?	6~7 yrs old
X know	History X imp. Supervising
Children activities? Typical day? Q5	Picasso. Explain shapes, colors, sizes ↳ More interested
Picasso - lots of colors, shapes, size	Q2
	Egyptian - mummies
	Hist. know?
Yes, review…	X, simple Q. Walk, brief expl., Q.
Easy, fun	Children… Hard
Part. T. job. Daycare. Q3	Help
Excited. (edu. After grad.)	
	Applic. & when. → How process. Q?
Working hours	Flexible (suit both) Me select? Q4
Yes. Open sched.	

TEST3 Set1 - Conversation

St.	M. O.
Q. on community service	
Work in Downtown Museum, submit X commu. Serv. How work here? Q1	Can submit. X mind filling forms
History major, ◯ background knowledge. Anything to prepare?	Visitors 6~7 years old
X aware	Dealing children > History Supervising kids
Children activities? Explain typical day. Q5	Picasso's paintings Explain (shapes, colors, sizes) > artistic techniques
Picasso perfect - lots of colors, shapes, size	Q2
	Egyptian room – mummies History major, know lot?
Yes, but review…	X need, simple Q. Walk, brief expl., answer Q.
Sounds easy & fun Part-time job in daycare center Q3 Excited! (want in edu. after grad.)	X underestimate. Harder Will help
	Fill out applic. & when start → How process. Q?
Working hours?	Flexible (suit both) Just select time? Q4
Yes. Open schedule	

Note taking — Test 3 Set1-Lecture1

Architech. - acoustics.
Features - opera h, concert h
  └→ Unique
Science - design
Sound building - why
Archi ←?→ sound
↑acoust. → ↑attention
(Factors defining struct. Acoustics) Q6
Reverberation t.
  └→ Sound wave
Listener - direct + reflection
↓60 deci - X human hear - rever. T.
  └→ Quanti. Indi. - room's acous.
↑rever. T. → ↑acous?
  └→ X
  └→ Opti rever t. - its use
↑rever. T. = live = ↓percept.
↓rever t = dead - lecture halls
Solo & piano - 'dead'
  1 inst.   Q7
  Clarity & precision
Symphony - 'live'
  └→ Blends notes
  └→ Harmony - 'body'

History - Harvard phys. Prof.
  └→ ↑acous. Lect. H → X train
    └→ Persistence - exp. Diff mat.
      └→ Cushions
        └→ Rugs
          └→ #ppl
  └→ Mat. In room → rever. T.
    └→ Absorb diff. sound, ↑ or ↓ t.
    └→ Ex. Foam insulation - completely absorb
       Paint concrete - mirror
  └→ (Thick drapes & cushions - ↓ rever. T.) Q8
    └→ Interior to change rever t.
    └→ Part. Effect. → adjust. Acous. Preexist & old. Build.

Old struc. Poor acous. Prob?
  └→ Imp. design & construc. Limit
  └→ (Archi. Acous X → only grandeur) Q9
  └→ Ex. Sound focused one section (domes & curved walls)
Other factors rever. T.
  └→ Size & shape
       ↓
↑ → longer - more space travel   # reflecting surface - rever t.
↓ → shorter - small size   ↑ walls = ↑ reflec. = ↑ rever t.
                                  Domes → ↑ rever. t. (high ceilings - ↑ size)

Acous perf struc. X - Audi. Affect.   How solve prob.?
  └→ Human = 6 seat cushions   └→ Edu. Esti.
    └→ Biggest dilem.   Q10
    └→ How many ppl? - uncontrollable variable   └→(Design opti rever t. - full occup. - imperfect.)
       └→ Weight, height, clothes (?)   Factors involved - diffi.
                                                  └→ Adjust acous. - (continuous) Q11

Architech. - acoustics.
Architech. Features - opera house, concert halls
  ↳ Unique & appeal.
Sci. involved in design & sound related build. - why
Archi ⟷ sound = X researched
↑imp. acous. → ↑attention
(Explore integral factors in structural acoustics) Q6
Reverberation time
Listener - direct source
           +
         reflection
           ↳ Rever. S.
              ↳ ↓60 deci - human X hear - rever. T.
                 ↳ Imp. quanti. Indi. - deter room's acous.

History of the field - Harvard phys. Prof.
  ↳ ↑acous. Of lect. Hall → Had X training
     ↳ Tackled with persistence - exp. Utilize diff. mat. → Cushions
                                                            ↳ Rugs
  ↳ Mat. In room → rever. T.   ↳ #ppl
     ↳ Absorb diff. sounds - absorbency - ↑ or ↓ t.
     ↳ Ex. Foam insulation - completely absorb - X reflect
        Paint concrete - mirror
     ↳ (Used thick drapes & absorbent cushions - ↓ room's rever. T.) Q8
        ↳ Success - switch interior to change rever t.
           ↳ Part. Effect. → adjust. Acous. Preexisting & old buildings

Why old struc. Poor acous.?
  ↳ Improper design & construc. Limit
  ↳ (Before archi. Acous. Studied, only emph. Grandeur - X acous.) Q9
     ↳ Ex. Sound focused one section (domes & curved walls)

Other factors rever. T.
  ↳ Size & shape
       ↓
↑ → longer t. - more space travel   # reflecting surface - rever. t.
↓ → shorter t.- small size   ↑ walls = ↑ reflec. = ↑ rever t.
                           Domes → ↑ rever. t. (high ceilings - ↑ size)

Acous perf struc. X - Audi. Affect.
  ↳ Human = 6 seat cushions
     ↳ Biggest dilemma
     ↳ How many ppl? - uncontrollable variable
        ↳ Weight, height, clothes (?)

↑rever. T. → ↑acous?
  ↳ X
  ↳ Opti rever t. → depends on its use
↑rever. T. = live = ↓percept.
↓rever t = dead - lecture halls
Music, Solo & piano
 - performed in 'dead'
   ↳ Only 1 instrument
   ↳ Clarity & precision most important
Symphony orche. - 'live'   Q7
   ↳ ↑rever. T. blends notes
   ↳ Harmony - 'body'

How solve prob.?
  ↳ Edu. Esti.   Q10
     ↳ (Design opti rever t. - at full occupancy
                              - still imperfect.)
Factors involved - diffi & imperfect
  ↳ (Adjust acous. - continuous   Q11
                 X end with construction)

Note taking — Test 3 Set1-Lecture2

Anthrop. - Anasazi
Adv. Tech. - fam., popul., soci.
Devel. V.S. → ancient civil.
  └→ Enter data
          └→ Envi
              └→ Rules
                  └→ Patterns
  └→ Find → what happened
          → Patterns in families
Ex. How popul. Density affected - life expect. ↑
      What happen, ppl spread
(Imp. models - T. answ) Q.13
Real - diff.
  └→ Popul - unique
  └→ Unexpect
Model - large patt. - relat. Correct.
(Simul. - cause of decline) Q.12
  └→ Ex) Anasazi
       └→ Lived 700 yrs ago
       └→ S.W. U.S (Utah, Arizo., Colo., New Mex.)
       └→ Mud villages
            └→ House 100 ppl. Each.
            └→ (Apartment (X stairs)) Q.14
       └→ Mat. - Bricks (Straw, clay, stones)
       └→ Excellent build.
       └→ Intricate tech.
       └→ Kiva - ask assist. Serpents, fire, sun → Agri.
       └→ Left engravings   Health
       └→ Artif. & knowledge X why disappear

Assume - Climate change
  └→ 50 yr - little rain 1200s
       └→ Farming X
Research - (Q. T. - Archeo.) Q.15
  └→ Study rings in logs (building)
       └→ Trees growth
            └→ Climate & nutrient avail.
  └→ X drought, shift precipi. Patt.
       └→ Summer rain X
            └→ X god & religious
- Other research - harvest & consump.
     └→ Drought - X leave land / enough harvest

Simul. Useful - location, what eat, envi.
   Put in data & where lived & water supply & character.
                         Ex) ↓child - X harvest,
                         Leave area

Recreate 800s - 1300 (When disappeared)
  └→ Program - hist. info. - (1st popul. ↑, ↓ over time
                  └→ ↑ - harvest good, ↓ - bad) Q.16
                  - (Confirm where lived)
Biggest inaccu. - comp. - (1300) few fam
                Real - X
Conclusion - envi. - popul., size, where lived
  └→ (X answer their disappear) Q.17
  └→ Show ↓popul. Kept living
  └→ Still wonder why

Anthropology - Anasazi
Adv. Tech. - fam., popul., soci.
Devel. V.S. → look into ancient civil.
  └→ Enter data
        └→ Envi
            └→ Society rules & patterns
  └→ Find what happened to civil.
        → Point patterns in fam.
  Ex. If life expect. ↑ → how popul. Density affected
       What happens ppl. Spread from dense.
Important - models
              └→ (Only t. answ. (results of change)) Q13
Real - diff.
  └→ Popul. - unique individuals
  └→ Unexpected events
Models - large popul. patt. - relatively Correct.
(Simulations - to find cause of decline of soci.) Q12
  └→ Anasazi   - ex. Anasazi
    └→ Lived 700 yrs ago
    └→ S.W. U.S. Four Corners (Arizo., Utah, Colo., New Mex.)
    └→ Known for mud villages
            └→ Buildings that can house 100 ppl. Each.
            └→ (Resemble apartment (X stairs)) Q14
    └→ Common mat. - Bricks (Straw, clay, stones)
    └→ Still standing - excellent builders
    └→ Intricate tech. used
    └→ Kiva - separate circular underground room
        └→ ask assistance to serpents, fire, sun
    └→ Left engravings - culture & belief   Agri.
    └→ Provide artif. & knowledge, X why disappear   Health

Assume
- Climate change
  └→ 50 year period - little rain (1200s)
        └→ Farming X - X sustain
In-depth research
- (Q. T. - Archeologist Jeffrey Dean) Q15
  └→ Study rings in logs used in buildings
        └→ Developed through trees growth patt.
            └→ Signs of climate & nutrient avail.
        └→ X drought, shift precipi. Patt.
            └→ Heavy summer rain X
                └→ Unsure of god & religious
- Other research
  - harvest & nutri. consump. Of indiv.
    └→ Drought - X popul. leave land / sustainable

Comp. Simul. Useful - Know location, what eat, envi.
  What happened, put in data & where lived & water supply & character.
                    Ex) ↓child - X harvest,
                        Leave area

Recreate period 800s - 1300 (When disappeared)
  └→ Program gave hist. info. Already have - (1st popul. ↑, then ↓ over time)
                    └→ ↑ harvest good, ↓ - bad   Q16
                    - (Also confirm where lived)

Biggest inaccuracy - comp. - (1300) few fam. left
                    Real - X
Conclusion - envi. Affect - popul., size, where lived
  └→ (Still X answ. their disappearance) Q17
    └→ Shows small popul. Could have lived
    └→ Still wonder why disappeared

Note taking Test 3 Set2-Conversation

St.	Prof.
Project…	O genre & topic, ? trouble Q5
Other class, X genre & topic Swamped & X idea Q1	Busy / Procrast.
?	Backwards. X worry Draft. Feeling at time → genre best Hip-hop? Q2
Random feeling - genre?	Yes. Capture feeling need to listen genre Ex. Feel rapid beat
	Hip-hop - Personal Short hist. & rapid spread & devel.
Anything else? ?	Technical, slang - oxymorons Oxy. → 2 ↔ words phrase Ex. Dark sun Note, write how
Psychology? (major) Yes Q3	Yes. Psy… help? Symposium - types music & effects infants Help psy… Music ~ pregnancy
Psy. change of mother - affect fetus Think - calm, classic → happy… Review specific. - old - might cover new	
	Friends. School - expenses
X know much help & ◯ project, students used X leave (?) Q4 Want to leave	Contact head of psy.

TEST3 Set2 -Conversation

St.	Prof.
In music appreciation Project…	Assume O genre & topic, Q5 What trouble?
Other classes, X genre & topic Swamped & X good idea Q1	Busy / Procrastinating
?	Think diff. backwards. X worry Rough draft - feeling at certain time - topic Q2 ↳ find best-fit genre Hip-hop?
Match Random feeling - genre?	Yes. Capture moment - feeling need to listen to genre Ex. Feel need rapid beat
	Hip-hop - Personal eager Short hist. & rapid spread, develop. fascinate
Anything else? ?	Technicality, slang - oxymorons Oxymoron → 2 ↔ words make phrase Ex. Dark sun, mandatory charity
	Note, write how
Incorporate psychology? (major) Yes Q3	Yes. Psy. Major, help? Symposium - certain types of music & their effect on infants O music, X psy… Heard of R. music ~ pregnancy
Psy. change of mother - affect fetus ↳ listen to calm, classic ↳ happier childhood Review specifics - old - might cover new	
X much help & depart. ◯ project, students used Leave town (?) Q4 Want to leave	Friends? School cover expense Contact psy. head

Note taking   Test 3   Set2-Lecture1

Music hist. - E. guitar
Devel. Mus. Inst. 20th C.
Jazz, R&R, Country, Blues
　　- e. guitar
　　　　↳ 1900, versatile, influ.
Harmony w/ other & own
(Changes e. guitar went through) Q6

What devel. E. guitar
　↳ Strange noise - acous. Guitar wider?
Wider sound X considered
Effects devel. - guitarists
→ 1. Amplify sound
　　　↳ X in concerts / ensembles
　　　　　↳ Brass, horn
　　→ Recordings & radio pop. 1920
　　　　↳ Big band pop. → guitar change. → louder
　　　　　　↳ Exp. Change - archtop shape, larger
Tinker elec. & guitar
　↳ Magn. - capture motion → elec. E.
　　　　　　　　　　　　↳ By vibra.
　　　　　　　　　　　　↳ Strength - Thickness
　　　　　　　　　　　　　　　　　　Rate
　　　　　　　　　　　　　　　　　　Distance
　　　↳ Unique sound
　　　　digitized & ampli.

Q10

1931 - horseshoe magn. - ('pickup') + Hawaii lap steel
　　　　　　　　　　　　　=
　　　　　　　　　　1st e. guitar. (Frying pan) - shape   Q7
Instant success - (others copied. Tech. (stop 6yrs later)) Q8
Now - Larger & curved (sideways & finger)
Gibson - Impl. & comm. Tech in Spanish guitar.
　1933 - 1st e. guitar (ES-150)
　　　(Guitarists) - innovative sounds
　　　　X perfect → (pickups X adv.)
　　　　　　　　↳ X isol. Vibra. - mic. (ampl. Everything)
Q10　　　　　　　　　Q9
　　　　　　　　　　　Fuzzy
　　　　↳ Audio feedback
　　　　　　↳ Strum, sound ampl. → strings, vibra. more → picked, ampl. Again → loop
Fix - 1940 - 'The Log' - solid wood. X hollow
　　　　　↳ X feed back
　　　　　↳ Notes last longer
Makers try ↓ e. guitar's effect
　↳ Sound cool - prefer - Jimi Hendrix   Q11
X incorp. e. effect until 1950
Hendrix - greatest - style
　　　　　　↳ X avoid feedback
↳ 3 pickups, switch to choose - X satis.
　　　　　　　　↳ Play w/ 2 pickups - strange new. - Pop.

e. guitar's evolution - music
guitar's ↑ → new music style

TEST3 SET2-Lecture1

Music hist. - E. guitar
Devel. Mus. Inst. 20th C.
Jazz, R&R, Country, Blues
  - common - e. guitar
1900s inst., e. guitar
  - most versatile & influential
  → Harmony w/ other inst.
  → Hold spotlight its own   Q6
Changes e. guitar went through - today

What motiv. devel. E. guitar
  → Can make strange noise - give acous. Guitar wider?
Effects X consi. Devel. - guitarists
  → 1. Amplify sound
      → Guitar X in concerts / ensembles
          → Brass & horn louder
      → Phonograph recordings & commercial radio pop. 1920
          → Big band music pop. → guitars need change. → louder necess.
          → Makers exp. Change - curved archtop, larger

Engineers & inventors tinker elec. & guitar
  → Magn. - capture motion (string) in mag. Field → elec. E.
      → Unique sound from string   → By vibra.
        digitized & ampli.   → Strength - Thickness
                                                       Rate
                                                       Distance
      ↓
      1931 - Horseshoe magn. 'pickup' + Hawaiian lap steel guitar
                              ||
                              1st e. guitar. - 'Frying pan' (shape)   Q7

Instant success - others copied. Tech. & produce e. guitars (stopped 6yrs later) Q8
X used. Now - Larger & curved - Spanish-style (sideways & finger-strummed)
Gibson - Impl. & comm. Tech in Spanish guitars
  → 1933 - produce 1st e. guitar (ES-150)
      → Guitarists switched - innovative sounds   Q9
          → X perfect → pickups X adv.
Q10   → X isolate Vibra. From string - mic. (amplify everything) (ex. Vibra. Guitar body)
                              → Fuzzy
                          → Audio feedback
                              → Strums guitar → sound amplified → reach strings → vibrate more → loop

Fix - 1940 - 'The Log' - solid wood. X hollow
  → X feed back
  → Notes last longer
Seems like makers try ↓ e. guitar's effect
  → Sound cool - prefer - Jimi Hendrix   Q11
X incorp. e. effect until 1950
Hendrix - greatest - innovative style
              → X avoid feedback, took advantage
  → 3 pickups, switch to choose - X satis. Only 3
              → Jam selector, play w/ 2 pickups - strange new sounds - Pop.

e. guitar's evolution - music
guitar's ↑ → new music style

Note taking Test 3 Set2-Lecture2

Phys. - Lightning
Lightning - dang. & short - X understood
　└→ 8 types - cloud-to-ground
　　　└→ Long last - X cloud - ball L.
　　　　　└→ ? true - X evi.
　　　　　　　└→ Descrip. Diff. - X credible
　　　　└→ Retell facts - X trust
　Sci. - X own intuition - only data.
　　└→ Lack cause - little ↑than legend (black holes, extra-terre.)　Q 13
　　　　└→ Only hypothetical

Ball lightning
　　Lumi., sphe., elec.
　　Golf ball
　　During storms
　　Red, orange, yellow
　　Horizontal move
　　Explodes - sulfur smell
　Property - X clear　Q 17
　　Ex. Church, Engl. - Hit by 2.4 dia.
　　　　　　└→ Knock walls
　　　　　　└→ Kill 4, injure 60
　　Exp. Try create.
　　　　2006, plasma 10~20cm dia.
　　　　　　└→ 4th state matter
　　　　　　└→ E. current - beaker (salt water) → heat until enough e. → plasma bubble (300 milisec)
　　　　　　└→ X ignite paper

Diff. prev. underst. - plasma - X shape
　Plasma in shape - ↑equip. & power (fraction of sec.)　Q 14
　X plasma hypo. - sci. plausible t.

t. - ball l. - sili. Parti. Burn in air.
　　　　└→ Make electronics & mirrors, ground
L. hit ground - heat & current turn sili. → vapor → pure sili. In air attracted (elec. Charge) - bind
Sili. - Oxy = glow　Q 15
　└→ Outside → in, until unreacted sili.
Prob.　　　　　　　　　　　　　　　　　　Q 16
WW2, 'ball of fire' - 'foo fighters' (thought secret weapon)
　Expl. 'foo fighters' & 'ball l.' - identical
　　└→ Another prob.
　　　　└→ Sili. Hypo. - X reach high.
X explain - unpredictable & infrequent
　Find famous for ball l. & wait

Phys. – Lightning

Lightning – dangerous & short-lived – X understood
  └→ 8 types – cloud-to-ground
      └→ Long last – X cloud – ball L.
          └→ X be true – X evi. (only witness)
              └→ Descriptions different – X credible
          └→ Sci. X trust – retell facts

(Sci. – X trust own intuition – only data.
    └→ Lack of cause – (blamed on black holes & extra-terrestrials)) Q.13
        └→ little ↑than legend, only hypothetical

Define ball l.   (Property – X clear) Q.17
  Lumi., sphe., elec.   Ex. Usual – tiny
  Size – Golf ball   Church, Engl. – Hit by 2.4 dia.
  During storms   └→ Knock walls
  Red, orange, yellow   └→ Kill 4, injure 60
  Move horizontally   Exp. Try create. – Promising
  Pass walls & approach, X harm   └→ 2006, produced plasma 10~20cm dia.
  Explodes – sulfur smell   └→ 4th state matter, energetic
                                   └→ Pass elec. current – beaker (salt water)
                                      → heat until enough e.
                                      → plasma bubble (300 milisec)
                                   └→ X even ignite paper

Cloud created – diff. prev. underst.
  plasma – ↑energetic, X shape
  (Plasma in shape, lots of equip. & power needed (even fraction of sec.)) Q.14
  X figure plasma hypo. – sci. plausible t.

Prof. J.A. – t. – ball l. – Chem. reaction sili. Parti. Burn in air.
  Sili. – chem – found in ground
              – Electronics & mirrors
L. hit ground – heat & current turns sili. → vapor, ↑to air → pure sili. Parti. attracted (elec. Charge)
                                                                    – bind ball shape
(Sili. React w/ oxy. = glows) Q.15
  └→ Outside → in, until unreacted sili. left

Prob.   Q.16
  └→ WW2, pilots 'balls of fire' – 'foo fighters' (thought secret weapon)
  └→ Descriptions of 'foo fighters' & 'ball l.' (color & speed) – identical
        └→ Another prob.
            └→ Sili. Hypo. – X reach altitudes

X explain – unpredictable & infrequent
  Study – Find loca. famous for ball l. & wait

Note taking Test 4 Set1-Conversation

calc prof

최근 : HW 多

Lit class에서 본게 마지막 → papers impressive

有 tutoring program . (tutors quitting.) Q2

(나 하라고? 응) Q1

writting skills & papers

나 chem major (biomed engineer)

→chem/sci-related papers 도와줘.

training 필요해?   weekly training courses

⊕ class credits   ⊕ service hours (grad req) Q3

observed? → ✓only 1st session   Q5

tips?   perseverance

unorganized paper ┌ 직접 tell them the flaws Q4
                  └ ask Qs to guide them .

할래

TEST4 Set1-Conversation

calculus professor "Lit prof가 너 찾더라"

최근 : 할 일 완전 많음.

쌤 마지막으로 본게 Lit class → papers impressive

tutoring program . but tutors quitting. Q2

나 하라고? 응 Q1

→ improve writting skills & papers 도와줘

나 chem major (biomed engineer). writting 이랑 노상관

→ chem/science-related papers 도와줘.

training 필요해? weekly training courses 듣고
                     ⊕ class credits / community service hours Q5
                         (graduation requirement) Q3

observed? → only during 1st session → 그 뒤로는 free

tips? perseverance

unorganized paper ┌ 직접 tell them the flaws Q4
                     └ ask Qs to guide them.

할래요

Note taking Test 4 Set1-Lecture 1

global climate △

recent tech

CO_2 emission ⊕ effect

global temp ↑ > 2℃ → 10yrs 안에 catastrophe

(solution?) Q1

① oxy fuel combustion
    air 대신 pure oxygen ··· nitrogen × heated
                      nitrous oxide prod ↓
                      (greenhouse gas) Q2

② carbon capture & storage
    collects / stores emission of combustion ┬ post -
                                               └ pre -

   post - after combustion CO_2/gas
                          ↳ chem solution

          saturates gas ··· releases gas
                         → underground

       ⊖ chem required 多
         economic burden] Q3
         equipments expensive

       ⊕ 비교적 developed
        → implemented rightaway
        working power plants
        reuse 가능

   pre - (before burning) Q4
    · efficient Fuel → hydrogen & CO2
                  → power
            × release of CO2 → underground

     ⊖ needs improvement
       less developed (15~20 yrs)
       construction work 많이 필요.
       new power plants needed

post가 better ·· (speed 敀 급해) Q5
   pre - development 필요.
   post - can start working immediately

   → 하나에 집중! 시간 낭비 하지말고 post Q6 awareness

TEST4 Set1-Lecture1

global climate change
recently developed technology
Last class : CO_2 emission & its effect
global temp increase > 2℃ (allowable maximum) ··· catastrophe in 10yrs
|solutions to global temparature rise| Q1

① oxy fuel combustion
    air 대신 pure oxygen 쓰임 ··· nitrogen x heated
                     (nitrous oxide) production ↓ Q2
                      (=greenhouse gas . global temp↑)

② carbon capture & storage
    collects & stores emission of conbustion   ⎡ post - combustion capture
                                              ⎣ pre - combustion capture

    i) post - combustion capture : after combustion   (separate)
                                                   CO_2 ↔ gas
                                                      chem solution

                                       saturates gas → releases gas
                                                         → underground

                                 ⊖ chem required ⎤ Q3
                                      economic burden ⎦
                                      equipments expensive

                                 ⊕ 비교적 developed
                                    → can be implemented
                                        right away
                                   working power plants: reuse 가능

    ii) pre - combustion capture : |before burning| Q4
          · efficient   ∵ Fuel → hydrogen & CO_2
                            → power
                            x release of CO_2 → underground

          ⊖ needs improvement
             less developed (15~20 yrs)
             construction work 많이 필요
             new power plants needed

⇒ post가 better ∵ |speed가 관건. 급함!| Q5
   pre - combustion capture : development
   post - combustion capture : can start working immediately
    → 하나에 집중! 시간 낭비 하지말고 post Q6 spread awareness도 중요ㅇ

Note taking — Test 4 Set1-Lecture2

art history

roots of greek & roman mythology ⊕ backgrounds
mere myths? (x) → 有 political & social parallels
→ tangible evidence = art sculptures (white)

15C Euroupe (Italy)

ancient G&R sculptures rediscovered
Apollo Bel~ white (aesthetic perfection)
Renaissance artists: emulate monochromatic coloration
　　　　　　　　　　　(uniformly white)
　↳ new set of standards: form > color

early 19c art historians traces of visible paint
　　　　　　　　　　　∴ statues = mono(X) poly(o)

color could have deteriorated　∵ wind, water, etc

new tech … in-depth research
　　　　　ex) ultraviolet light: colored vs X colored distinguish
　　　　　　　→ (organic compounds) fluoresce
　　　　　　　　　당시 paints

poly ~ sculptures: evidence
G&R sculptures → BCE ~ 4C CE ⊜ poly
multiple interpretations of art 가능
mono - emphasis on form
artist's intentions ✫ (esp poly)

① role & colors
　　↳ parts features acc
　　↳ colors symbolize facts
　ex) Augustins statues: 1963 / Apr / 20 prima porta
　　　= imperator commander military clothing baton
　　　most abundant color = red (E. war. passion. strength)

② kind of pigments
　quality of color ← q of pigment
　ex) Augustins
　　pigment used: $ $
　　→ importance. authority (as emperor. imperator)

⇒ colors … social / economic / political values
　　　有 tech for further investigation
　　얼른 조사! ∵ paint pigments 빨리 deteriorate
　　　⊕ knowledge of art & understanding of culture ↑

TEST4 Set1-Lecture2

Art history class

last class : roots of greek & roman mythology & backgrounds
　　　　　　mere myths? (x) → 有 political & social parallels
　　　　　　→ tangible evidence = art. [sculptures] → white

15C Euroupe (Italy)

ancient Greek & Roman sculptures rediscovered
Apollo Belvedere → white (aesthetic perfection)
Renaissance artists : emulated monochromatic coloration
　　　　　　　　　　　　　(uniformly white)
　↳ new set of standards : form > color

early 19c art historians : found traces of visible paint
　　　　　　　　　　　　∴ statues = monochromatic (x)
　　　　　　　　　　　　　　　　　polychromatic (o)
　　　　　　　　　　→ color could have deteriorated
　　　　　　　　　　　　　　∵ wind, water, etc.

new tech … in-depth research　distinguish between
　　　　　ex) ultraviolet light : colored vs none-colored
　　　　　　　　　　→ organic compounds fluoresce
　　　　　　　　　　　당시 paints 多함유

polychromatic sculptures : evidence
Greek & Roman sculptures → BCE ~ 4C CE ⊖ polychromatic

multiple interpretations of art 가능
monochromatic - emphasis on form
artist's intentions 중요 (especially for polychromatic)

① role & colors
　　↳ parts features accentuated
　　↳ colors symbolize facts
　　ex) Augustins statues : discovered in 1963 / Apr / 20 prima porta
　　　　=imperator commander military clothing baton
　　　　most abundant color = red (Energy. war. passion. strength)

② kind of pigments
　　quality of color ← depentent on quality of pigment
　　ex) Augustins
　　　　pigment used : expensive
　　　　→ importance. authority (as emperor. imperator) 상징

⇒ colors … social / economic / political values
　　　　　有 tech for further investigation
　　　　얼른 조사! ∵ paint pigments deteriorate rapidly
　　　　　　⊕ to enhance knowledge of art & understanding of
　　　　　　　　　　　　　　　　　Greek & Roman culture

Note taking Test 4 Set2-Conversation

paper due next week (19c female artist)

feminist era : Rosa B~

Q1 topic 정하기 힘듦 : legacy as pivotal fig. vs. life as artist?

Q5 so much info → 딴 사람 고를까 고민 but big fan of her work

Rosa B's early life : Q2 별로 쓸거 X. 학교생활 힘듦 & family : 끝

  그럼 life X? → 응.

role in feminist movement (남자 옷) vs. artwork
  ↳ controversial - "more comfortable. better suited for work"

그러면 her work에 대해서? 응. controversy 어려움.

  → 쓰면 extra credit 줌. Q3

  Q4 criterion? prove whether / X B's
              statement is true.

    abstract … find info to support opinion.
           Like persuasive essay.

  tempting. but sounds hard → 그니까 e.c. 준다고.

paper due next week (about 19th century female artist)

example from feminist era : Rosa Bonheur

Q1 (topic 정하기 힘듦): legacy as a pivotal figure in feminist movement vs. life as artist?

Q5 so much information → 다른 사람 고를까 고민 but big fan of her work

Rosa Bonheul's early life : Q2 별로 쓸거 없음. except 학교생활 힘듦 & family

그럼 life에 대해서 쓰지 마요? → 응.

(role) in feminist movement (by wearing 남자 옷) vs. artwork
　↳ controversial - "more comfortable. better suited for work (traveling)"

그럼 her work에 대해서 써요? 응. controversy 어려움.
　　　　　　　　　→ 쓰면 extra credit 줌. Q3

　　　　Q4 (criterion?) prove whether or not Bonheul's
　　　　　　　　　　　　statement is true.

　　　　　　abstract 해요! … find infomation to support opinion.
　　　　　　　　　　　　Like persuasive essay.

　　　　tempting. but sounds hard → 그니까 extra credit 준다고.

Physics
Energy: heat, light, electricity.
불 키면: electrical E → light E
Transformation of E
e- and atoms ☆
stimulated → e- collide, Δ orbital levels → release Ⓔ
　　　　　　　　　　　　　　　　　　↳ electromagnetic E
　　　　　　　　　　　　　　　　　　　ex) light, heat, X rays, microwaves.

Q1 Tech (Light E generation)

옛날에 campfire.
fire - not efficient.
　　　light E ← thermal E
　　　　　　　PE & KE of burning materials
≒ incandescent 전구
electrical E → light E (　major (-))
electricity $\xrightarrow{\text{(filament)}}$ heat
　　　　　　　　　　↳ 여기서 light 나옴, heat → light.
　　　　　　Q2 90%, electricity 낭비, not efficient enough, inconvenient (room temp ↑)

demand for better tech … fluorescent light tubes (filled w/ mercury gas)
e- in gaseous mercury → bounce off special coating inside → coating glows → light
　　　　　　　　　　　　　　　　　　　　　　　　Q3
(+) production of heat ↓
Q6 (-) det. effect on env. (gas mercury: toxic) ∴ safe disposal 불가능.
solving env. prob = priority　∴ not effective
→ incandescent & fluorescent 둘 다 별로
　　다른 기술들도 비슷한 drawbacks
　　X fully developed lighting devices
　　but　new form of tech : chemiluminescence.
　　　　　　　　　　　↳ result of exo chem rxn
　　　　　　　　　　Q4 ∴ X require E input
　e- stimulated → R breakdown → chem rxns → light emission
　(+) X produce sig q of heat, all natural chem sources, ∴ safe disposal 가능.
Q5 (-) not perfected tech yet, developmental stage.

source of E for C.L. → in nature
ex) fireflies & marine animals.
　　　extraction of genes → enhance brightness → apply to existing tech
→ need improvement but promising

TEST4 Set2-Lecture1

Physics

Energy: heat. light. electricity.

불 키면: electrical Energy → light Energy

Transformation of Energy

electrons and atoms 중요.

stimulated → electrons collide & Change orbital levels → release Energy
                                                   ↓
                              electromagnetic Energy

Q1 Technology of (Light Energy generation)   ex) light. heat. X rays. microwaves.

옛날에 campfire.

fire - not efficient.

    light Energy ← thermal Energy
                  Potential energy & Kinetic energy of burning materials

≒ incandescent 전구

electrical Energy → light Energy (major drawback 있음)

electricity $\xrightarrow{\text{(filament)}}$ heat
              └→ 여기서 light 나옴. heat → light.
          Q2 90%. electricity 낭비. not efficient enough. inconvenient
                게다가 room temperature↑

demand for better technology ··· fluorescent light tubes (filled with mercury gas)

electrons in gaseous mercury → bounce off special coating inside → coating glows → light
                                          Q3

(+) production of heat ↓

Q6 (-) detrimental effect on environment (gaseous mercury: toxic) ∴ safe disposal 불가능.

solving environmental problem = priority   ∴ not effective

→ incandescent & fluorescent 둘 다 별로

    다른 기술들도 비슷한 drawbacks 있음

    no fully developed lighting devices

    but new form of technology : chemiluminescence.
                          └→ result of exothermic chemical reaction
                   Q4 ∴ doesn't require Energy input
                       election stimulated → Reactants breakdown
                       → chemical reactions → light emission
                     (+) X produce sig q of heat. all natural chem sources.
                        ∴ safe disposal 가능.
                 Q5 (-) not perfected tech yet. developmental stage.

    source of Energy for Chemiluminescence → in nature

    ex) fireflies & marine animals.
        extraction of genes → enhance brightness → apply to existing technology

    → need improvement but promising

Note taking Test 4 Set2-Lecture2

Q1 personality psychology = branch of P. studies human personality.
　　　　　　　　　　　related to neuroscience

　ever since HGP: roots of personality & whether / X personality static

Q6 Obama → fund $100m to study brain.
　∵ discovery process complicated. Involved highly tech. tools.

　1900s: EEG - detect brain activities by measuring oscillations.
　　　　carry out tests on subjects & figure out Δ
　　　　brains experience

Q2 → now obsolete.
　　∵ shift in focus (stability of personality)
　→ new form of tech (FMRI)

　　　　　　　MRI vs. FMRI
≒ camera.　　　　　　　↳ Lab research tool
takes pics of brain structure.　↳ f(x) of brains ⊕ structures Q3
diagnostic purposes.
　　　　　　ex) stress → sudden urge to express
　　　　　　stimuli … brain activates diff parts
　　　　　　≒ command control center
　　　　　　detect Δ in blood flow, oxygen level in brain → using FMRI

emotions = output of brain activity
　express/restrain? ≡ personality → static? (논란　)
　FMRI 로 stable 하다고 과학자들 주장.
case studies: amygdala (process ext. stimuli)
subjects 한 줄로 sit → wartime 사진 보여줌.
some subjects' amygdala activated (FMRI)
→ brought back 2 years later. 같은 실험.
　　sig: brain responded the same way.
∴ response to stimuli X Δ → personality stable

contradictory arguments exist (but 너무 김)
FMRI studies = X perfect. = controversies Q4
neuroscientists exaggerate.
brain: perplexing. knowledge of brain: rudimentary.
FMRI: practical & efficient.
　but X account for why we behave the way we do
　　　X enough to determine personality X Δ
　∴ traditional research methods
　　　questionnaires ┌ = drawbacks (ex. respondents manipulating answers)
　　　　　　　　　　 └ but reliable way to inquire ppl's behavioral pref & personalities
　　　　　　　　Q5

TEST4 Set2-Lecture2

Q₁ personality psychology = branch of Psychology that studies human personality.
　　　　　　　　　　　　　　　　　related to neuroscience

　ever since advent of HGP: roots of personality & whether or not personality is static

Q₆ Obama → fund $100million to study brain.
　∵ discovery process complicated. Involved highly tech. tools.

　1900s: EEG - detect brain activities by measuring oscillations.
　　　　　　　carry out tests on subjects & figure out changes that brains experience

Q₂ → now obsolete.
　　　because shift in focus (stability of personality)
　　→ new form of technology : FMRI

MRI	FMRI
Like camera	Lab research tool
takes pictures of brain structure	function of brains & structures Q₃
Used for diagnostic purposes	ex) stress → sudden urge to express stimuli ⋯ brain activates different parts. like command control center. detect changes in blood flow & oxygen level in brain using FMRI

emotions = output of brain activity

whether express or restrain emotions ⋯ particular personality

∴ personality가 static한지 논란 많았음

FMR를 근거로 stable 하다고 과학자들 주장.

case studies: amygdala (process external stimuli)

subjects 한 줄로 앉혀두고 wartime 사진 보여줌.
　some subjects' amygdala activated (FMRI)

→ amygdala activated 됐던 subjects는 brought back 2years later. 그리고 같은 실험.
　　significance: brain responded the same way.

　∴ response to stimuli didn't change ⋯ 즉, personality stable

contradictory arguments exist (but 너무 김)

FMRI studies perfect 하지 않음. controversies 있음. Q₄

neuroscientists exaggerate.

brain: perplexing. knowledge of brain: rudimentary.

FMRI: practical & efficient.
　　but ┌ doesn't account for why we behave the way we do
　　　　 └ isn't enough to determine that personality doesn't change

　∴ traditional research methods
　　　　questionnaires ┌ have drawbacks (ex. respondents manipulating answers)
　　　　　　　　　　　　└ but reliable way to inquire ppl's behavioral preference & personalities
　　　　　　　　　Q₅

usherin.usher.co.kr

USHER iBT TOFLE
FINAL TEST
LISTENING
구문 · 단어

TEST 1 Set 1 Conversation

VOCABULARY

01	**conference** [ˈkɒnfərəns]	n. 학회, 회의
02	**opportunity** [ˌɒpəˈtjuːnəti]	n. 기회
03	**professional** [prəˈfeʃnl]	a. 직업의, 전문적인
04	**lecture** [léktʃər]	n. 강의, 강연
05	**molecular biology**	n. 분자 생물학
06	**theory** [ˈθɪəri]	n. 이론, 학설, 의견
07	**broad** [brɔːd]	a. (폭이) 넓은
08	**perspective** [pəˈspektɪv]	n. 관점, 시각
09	**field** [fiːld]	n. 분야
10	**useful** [ˈjuːsfl]	a. 유용한, 쓸모 있는
11	**decide** [dɪˈsaɪd]	v. 결정하다
12	**further** [ˈfɜːðə]	v. 발전시키다
13	**interest** [ˈɪntrəst]	n. 관심, 흥미, 호기심
14	**seashore** [ˈsiːʃɔː]	n. 해안
15	**jellyfish** [dʒelifɪʃ]	n. 해파리
16	**intrigue** [ɪnˈtriːg]	v. 강한 흥미를 불러일으키다
17	**witness** [ˈwɪtnəs]	v. 목격하다
18	**bioluminescence** [baɪəʊluːmɪˈnesns]	n. 생물 발광
19	**organism** [ˈɔːgənɪzəm]	n. 유기체, 생물
20	**mechanism** [ˈmekənɪzəm]	n. 방법, 기제
21	**firefly** [ˈfaɪəflaɪ]	n. 반딧불이, 개똥벌레
22	**glowworm** [glóuwèːrm]	n. 개똥벌레 유충
23	**squid** [skwɪd]	n. 오징어
24	**shrimp** [ʃrɪmp]	n. 새우
25	**fungi** [fʌndʒaɪ]	n. 곰팡이류
26	**time-consuming**	a. 시간이 많이 걸리는
27	**mysterious** [mɪˈstɪəriəs]	a. 이해하기 힘든, 기이한, 불가사의한
28	**emission** [iˈmɪʃn]	n. 배출
29	**differ** [ˈdɪfə(r)]	v. 다르다
30	**categorize** [ˈkætəgəraɪz]	v. 분류하다
31	**means** [miːnz]	n. 수단, 방법
32	**intraspecies** [ˌɪntrəspíːʃiːz]	a. 같은 생물종의 내의
33	**avoidance** [əˈvɔɪdəns]	n. 회피, 방지
34	**attract** [əˈtrækt]	v. 끌어들이다
35	**chemistry** [ˈkemɪstri]	n. 화학
36	**basically** [ˈbeɪsɪkli]	ad. 근본적으로, 기본적으로
37	**specifically** [spəˈsɪfɪkli]	ad. 분명히, 명확하게
38	**expose** [ɪkˈspoʊz]	v. 노출시키다, 드러내다, 폭로하다
39	**activation** [ˌæktəvéɪʃən]	n. 활성화
40	**oxidize** [ˈɒksɪdaɪz]	v. 산화시키다
41	**magnesium** [mægˈniːziəm]	n. 마그네슘
42	**emit** [iˈmɪt]	v. 내다, 내뿜다
43	**gist** [dʒɪst]	n. 요지
44	**illumination** [ɪˌluːmɪˈneɪʃn]	n. 빛, 조명
45	**consider** [kənˈsɪdə(r)]	v. 고려하다, 숙고하다
46	**term paper**	n. 학기말 리포트
47	**definitely** [ˈdefɪnətli]	ad. 분명히, 틀림없이, 절대
48	**relatively** [ˈrelətɪvli]	ad. 비교적
49	**radical** [ˈrædɪkl]	a. 근본적인, 급진적인, 과격한
50	**marine** [məˈriːn]	a. 해양의, 바다의
51	**organize** [ˈɔːgənaɪz]	v. 정리하다, 구조화하다, 조직하다
52	**scientific data** [ˌsaɪəntífɪk dèɪtə]	n. 과학 데이터
53	**complicated** [ˈkɒmplɪkeɪtɪd]	a. 복잡한
54	**guidance** [ˈgaɪdns]	n. 안내, 지도, 유도

TEST 1
SET1-C

구문정리 | 본문 중 중요 구문 정리한 내용입니다. 우선 암기하고 많이 읽으시길 바랍니다.

Implications of Bioluminescence

→ 정답

#	구문	뜻
01	opportunity to do	to do 할 기회
02	lecture on	-에 대한 강의
03	give A B	A에게 B를 주다
04	decide to do	to do 하는 것을 결정하다
05	those with interests	관심을 가진 사람들
06	ask A B	A에게 B를 묻다
07	on day	날에
08	walk along	-를 따라 걷다
09	step on	-를 밟다
10	start -ing	-ing하는 것을 시작하다
11	wonder if	-인지 아닌지 궁금하다
12	be interested in -ing	-ing하는 것에 흥미가 있다
13	use A as B	A를 B로서 사용하다
14	in the form of	-의 형태로
15	get into the details	자세한 내용까지 들어가다
16	at certain times	특정 시간에만
17	differ from	-와는 다르다
18	in ways	방법으로
19	as a means of	-의 수단으로
20	fall into	-로 나뉘다
21	use O to do	O를 to do 하는데 사용하다
22	avoid predator	포식자를 피하다
23	expose A to B	A를 B에 노출 시키다
24	emit a light	빛을 발산하다
25	necessary for	-에 필요한
26	consider -ing	-ing하는 것을 고려하다
27	want to do	to do 하는것을 원하다
28	be going to do	to do 할 예정이다
29	easy to do	to do 하기에 쉬운
30	a new field of study	새로운 연구 분야
31	find O OC	O를 OC로 간주하다
32	in the field of	-의 분야에서
33	up for~	(어떤 행동을) 기꺼이 하려고 하는
34	I'm a big fan of~	나는 ~의 팬이다
35	be excited to do	to do 하는것에 흥분되다
36	feel free to do	자유롭게 to do 하다
37	at any time	언제든지

TEST 1 Set 1 Lecture 1

VOCABULARY

01	**sweep** [swi:p]	v. 휩쓸어가다, 확 퍼지다
02	**aspire** [əspáiər]	v. 갈망하다, 열광하다
03	**popularize** [ˈpɒpjələraɪz]	v. 대중화하다, 보급하다
04	**countless** [káuntlis]	a. 무수한
05	**emulate** [èmjəlèit]	v. 모방하다
06	**assumption** [əsʌ́mpʃən]	n. 가정, 추정
07	**crave** [kreiv]	v. 열망하다, 갈망하다
08	**magnificent** [mæɡnífəsənt]	a. 웅장한
09	**prestigious** [prestídʒiəs]	a. 일류의
10	**architect** [ˈɑːkɪtekt]	n. 건축가
11	**feature** [ˈfiːtʃə(r)]	n. 특징, 특성
12	**noticeable** [ˈnəʊtɪsəbl]	n. 뚜렷한, 현저한, 분명한
13	**walkway** [ˈwɔːkweɪ]	n. 통로, 보도
14	**allegorical** [æ̀liɡə(ː)ríkəl]	a. 우회적인
15	**trim** [trim]	v. 다듬다
16	**prototype** [próutoutàip]	n. 원형
17	**consumption** [kənˈsʌmpʃn]	n. 소비, 소모
18	**hortus**	n. 정원, 공원
19	**primary** [ˈpraɪməri]	a. 주된, 주요한, 기본적인
20	**ornamental** [ˌɔːnəˈmentl]	a. 장식용의
21	**enlarge** [enláːrdʒ]	v. 확장하다
22	**stroll** [stroʊl]	v. 거닐다, 산책하다
23	**symbolize** [símbəlàiz]	v. ~을 상징하다
24	**pursue** [pərsùː]	v. 추구하다
25	**significant** [sɪɡˈnɪfɪkənt]	a. 중요한, 의미 있는
26	**manifestation** [ˌmænɪfeˈsteɪʃn]	n. 표현, 징후
27	**pursuit** [pərˈsuːt]	n. 추구
28	**architecture** [ˈɑːkɪtektʃə(r)]	n. 건축학
29	**formal** [ˈfɔːrml]	a. 공식적인
30	**medium** [ˈmiːdiəm]	n. 수단, 도구, 매개체
31	**impress** [imprés]	v. 감명을 주다
32	**derive** [diráiv]	v. 끌어내다, 얻다
33	**satisfaction** [ˌsætɪsˈfækʃn]	n. 만족
34	**profuse** [prəfjúːs]	a. 풍부한
35	**besides** [bɪˈsaɪdz]	prep. ~외에
36	**dispense** [dispéns]	v. 분배하다
37	**literally** [ˈlɪtərəli]	ad. 말 그대로, 정말로
38	**conceal** [kənˈsiːl]	v. 감추다, 숨기다
39	**drench** [drentʃ]	v. 흠뻑 적시다
40	**unsuspecting** [ˌʌnsəˈspektɪŋ]	a. 의심하지 않는
41	**labyrinth** [ˈlæbərɪnθ]	n. 미로
42	**ironically** [airánikəli]	ad. 반어적으로
43	**misconception** [ˌmɪskənˈsepʃn]	n. 오해
44	**mythology** [mɪˈθɒlədʒi]	n. 신화
45	**maze** [meɪz]	n. 미로
46	**imprison** [imprízən]	v. 감금하다
47	**imitate** [ˈɪmɪteɪt]	v. 모방하다, 본뜨다
48	**mythical** [ˈmɪθɪkl]	a. 신화 속에 나오는, 가공의
49	**venue** [ˈvenjuː]	n. 장소
50	**redefine** [ˌriːdɪˈfaɪn]	v. 재정립하다
51	**comprise** [kəmˈpraɪz]	v. 구성하다, 차지하다

TEST 1
SET1-L1 — Type of Renaissance Gardens

구문정리 | 본문 중 중요 구문 정리한 내용입니다. 우선 암기하고 많이 읽으시길 바랍니다.

→ 정답

#	구문	뜻
01	across Europe	유럽 전역에 걸쳐
02	in French	프랑스어로
03	aspire to do	to do 하는 것을 열망하다
04	be going to do	to do 할 예정이다
05	focus on	-에 집중하다
06	familiar with	-에 친숙한
07	in other words	다시 말하면
08	crave to do	to do 하기를 열망하다
09	start to do	to do 하기를 시작하다
10	take a look at	-를 살펴보다
11	line A with B	A를 B로 덧대다, 줄지어 세우다
12	fill A with B	A를 B로 채우다
13	as well as	-뿐만 아니라
14	trim A into B	A를 B로 다듬다
15	bring A back to life	A를 되살려내다
16	in way	-방식으로
17	adhere to	-를 고집하다
18	in stage	단계로
19	know A as B	A를 B로 알다
20	serve as	-로 역할을 하다
21	at the time	그 당시에
22	serve need	필요를 충족하다
23	the quality of life	삶의 질
24	give birth to	-을 낳다
25	decorate A with B	A를 B로 꾸미다
26	for purposes	목적으로
27	stroll through	정원을 산책하다
28	other than	…외에 ('=except)
29	to be straightforward	단도직입적으로
30	it is fair to say that	-라고 말하는 것이 맞다
31	research into	-에 대한 연구
32	in fact	사실상
33	would have done	done 했을 것이다
34	derive A from B	A를 B로부터 얻다
35	come from	-에서 나오다
36	come up with	-를 생각해내다
37	in the same way	같은 방법으로
38	add to	-에 더하다
39	for the purpose of	-의 목적으로
40	for this reason	이러한 이유로
41	lead A to B	A를 B로 이끌다
42	according to	-에 따르면
43	come to life	부활하다
44	use A as B	A를 B로 사용하다
45	comprise A of B	A를 B로 구성하다
46	love to do	to do 하는 것을 좋아하다
47	take a walk	산책하다

TEST 1 Set 1 Lecture 2

VOCABULARY

01	influential [ɪnfluˈenʃl]	a. 영향력 있는
02	figure [fíɡjər]	n. 인물
03	insight [ínsàit]	n. 이해
04	reshape [ˌriːˈʃeɪp]	v. 재구성하다
05	legitimacy [lidʒítəməsi]	n. 합리성, 타당성
06	unorthodox [ʌnɔ́ːrθədàks]	a. 비정통적인, 정통적이 아닌
07	contemporary [kənˈtemprəri]	a. 동시대인
08	recognition [rèkəɡníʃən]	n. 인정
09	signature [sígnətʃər]	a. 대표하는
10	impact [ímpækt]	n. 영향
11	formal [fɔ́ːrməl]	a. 정규적인
12	patent [pǽtənt]	a. 특허의
13	clerk [kləːrk]	n. 직원, 사무원
14	cite [saɪt]	v. 언급하다
15	application [æplikéiʃən]	n. 적용, 응용
16	validity [vəlídəti]	n. 유효함, 타당성
17	innumerable [injúːmərəbəl]	n. 무수한, 셀 수 없이 많은
18	foundation [faundéiʃən]	n. 기반, 근거
19	phenomenon [finámənàn]	n. 현상
20	time dilation	n. 시간 팽창, 시간 지체
21	velocity [vəˈlɒsəti]	n. 속도
22	paradox [pǽrədàks]	n. 역설
23	exceed [iksíːd]	v. 초과하다, 넘다
24	revolutionary [ˌrevəˈluːʃənəri]	a. 혁명의, 혁명적인
25	contradict [kàntrədíkt]	v. 반박하다, 모순되다
26	follow-up [fáloυʌp]	n. 후속
27	theorize [ˈθɪərɑɪz]	v. 이론을 제시하다
28	position [pəˈzɪʃn]	v. 배치하다, 두다
29	empirical [ɪmˈpɪrɪkl]	a. 경험의, 실증적인
30	discredit [diskrédit]	v. 신뢰를 떨어뜨리다, 믿을 수 없는 것으로 간주하다
31	regardless [riɡáːrdlis]	ad. 개의치 않고
32	convince [kənˈvɪns]	v. 납득시키다, 확신시키다
33	established [istǽbliʃt]	a. 자리를 잡은, 확고한
34	numerical [njuːmérikəl]	a. 수의, 수와 관련된
35	margin [máːrdʒin]	n. 차이
36	laboratory [lǽbərətɔ̀ːri]	n. 실험실
37	vacuum [vǽkjuəm]	n. 진공
38	variable [vɛ́əriəbəl]	n. 변수
39	committee [kəˈmɪti]	n. 위원회
40	initially [ɪˈnɪʃəli]	ad. 처음에
41	brilliance [bríljəns]	n. 탁월, 특출함
42	ridiculous [rɪˈdɪkjələs]	a. 웃기는, 터무니없는
43	ingenuity [ìndʒənjúːəti]	n. 독창성
44	conclusive [kənklúːsiv]	a. 결정적인, 확실한
45	reformulate [riːfɔ́ːrmjuːleit]	v. 새로 만들다
46	equation [i(ː)kwéiʒən]	n. 등식, 방정식
47	tremendous [trəˈmendəs]	a. 엄청난
48	evaluate [ɪˈvæljueɪt]	v. 평가하다
49	shaky [ʃéiki]	a. 불안정한, 불확실한
50	methodology [ˌmeθəˈdɒlədʒi]	n. 방법론
51	contribution [kàntrəbjúːʃən]	n. 기여, 이바지
52	disregard [ˌdɪsrɪˈɡɑːd]	v. 무시하다
53	hindsight [ˈhaɪndsaɪt]	n. 뒤늦게 깨달음
54	deserve [dɪˈzɜːrv]	v. ~을 받을 자격이 있다

TEST 1
SET1-L2

구문정리 | 본문 중 중요 구문 정리한 내용입니다. 우선 암기하고 많이 읽으시길 바랍니다.

Einstein's Theory of Relativity

→ 정답

01	have all heard of	모두 들어왔다		27	at the speed of	-의 속도로
02	one of the figures	인물중 하나		28	at the same rate	같은 속도로
03	come up with	생각해 내다		29	combine A with B	A를 B와 결합하다
04	give A B	A에게 B를 주다		30	due to	-때문에
05	insight into	-에 대한 통찰력		31	attempt to do	to do 하는 것을 시도하다
06	change the way	방식을 바꾸다		32	in opposition to	-와 반대로
07	award A a prize	A에게 상을 주다		33	belief that	-라는 믿음
08	this is because	이것은 ~ 때문이다		34	be able to do	to do 할 수 있다
09	debate over	-에 대한 논쟁		35	ability to do	to do 할 수 있는 능력
10	receive recognition for	-에 대해 인정받다		36	allow O to do	O가 to do 하는 것을 허락하다
11	to this day	오늘날까지		37	gain support	지지를 얻다
12	get into	~을 시작하게 되다,(특정한 전문직종에)들어가다		38	fall within	-에 포함되다
13	come from	-에서 나오다		39	margin of error	오차범위
14	so - that -	너무 -해서 -하다		40	perfom the experiment	실험을 수행하다
15	result in	~을 야기하다		41	could have done	-할수있었을지도 모른다 (추측)
16	failure to do	to do 하는 실패		42	at the time	그 당시에
17	enter university	대학에 입학하다		43	seem ridiculous	터무니없어 보이다
18	be unable to do	to do 할 수 없다		44	base A on B	A를 B에 기초하다
19	cite A as B	A를 B로 인용하다		45	think something up	~를 생각해 내다
20	have to do	to do 해야만 하다		46	use O to do	O를 to do 하는데 사용하다
21	in order to do	to do 하기 위해서		47	need to do	to do 할 필요가 있다
22	become the foundation of	-의 기초가 되다		48	opposition to	~에 대한 반대
23	divide A into B	A를 B로 나누다		49	show A B	A 에게 B를 보여주다
24	in other words	다른 말로 하면		50	accept the limit of	-의 한계를 받아들이다
25	call A B	A를 B라고 부르다		51	prove O O.C	O가 O.C임을 증명하다
26	take off	이륙하다		52	trace A back to B	A를 B까지 거슬러 올라가다

구문·단어 ···195

TEST 1 Set 2 Conversation

VOCABULARY

01	**rebuild** [ˌriːˈbɪld]	v. 다시 세우다		14	**rumor** [rúːmər]	n. 소문, 풍문
02	**against** [əˈgenst]	prep. ~에 반대하여		15	**raise** [reɪz]	v. (자금 사람 등을) 모으다
03	**signature** [ˈsɪgnətʃə(r)]	n. 서명		16	**fund** [fʌnd]	n. 기금
04	**officially** [əˈfɪʃəli]	ad. 공식적으로		17	**sympathize** [sìmpəθàiz]	v. 동정하다, 공감하다
05	**protest** [prəˈtest]	n. 항의, 반대, 시위		18	**appalled** [əpɔ́ːld]	a. 끔찍해 하는, 어이없어 하는
06	**authorize** [ɔ́ːθəràiz]	v. 권한을 부여하다		19	**blueprint** [blúːprìnt]	n. 청사진, 설계도
07	**renovation** [rènəvéiʃən]	n. 수리, 수선		20	**ridiculous** [ridìkjələd]	a. 웃기는, 말도 안되는, 터무니 없는
08	**authority** [ɔːˈθɒrəti]	n. 권한		21	**bet** [bet]	v. 틀림없다, 분명하다
09	**intact** [intǽkt]	a. 온전한, 전혀 다치지 않은		22	**ignore** [ɪgˈnɔː(r)]	v. 무시하다
10	**scholarship** [skálərʃip]	n. 장학금		23	**foul** [faul]	a. 불쾌한, 아주 안 좋은
11	**board** [bɔːrd]	n. 이사회, 위원회		24	**eager** [ˈiːgə(r)]	a. 열렬한, 간절히 바라는, 열심인
12	**place** [pleɪs]	v. 놓다, 설치하다		25	**hearing** [hìəriŋ]	n. 공청회
13	**alternative** [ɔːlˈtɜːnətɪv]	a. 대안적인, 대체 가능한		26	**faculty** [ˈfæklti]	n. 교수단

TEST 1
SET2-C

구문정리 | 본문 중 중요 구문 정리한 내용입니다. 우선 암기하고 많이 읽으시길 바랍니다.

Student's Opposition to Renovation

→ 정답

01	know if	~인지 아닌지를 알다		19	at first	처음에
02	be going to do	to do 할 예정이다		20	how many signatures	얼마나 많은 서명들
03	be against~	-에 반대하다		21	so far	지금까지
04	Long story short	간략하게 말하면		22	as well	마찬가지로
05	authorize o to do	o가 to do 할 권한 주다		23	add A to B	A를 B에 더하다
06	contact information	연락처		24	release A to B	A를 B에 공개하다
07	deliver a message	메시지를 전하다		25	look ridiculous	우스워 보이다
08	mind O ing	O가 ing하는 것을 꺼리다		26	deliver an idea	의견을 전달하다
09	as as possible	가능한 ~하게		27	enough to do	to do 할 만큼 충분한
10	not at all	전혀 ~아닌		28	make a difference	차이를 만들어내다
11	to be honest	솔직히		29	feel the same way	같이 느끼다
12	need to do	to do 할 필요가 있다		30	get O done	O를 done한 상태로 만들다
13	rely on	-에 의지하다		31	get excited over	~에 관해 흥분하다
14	need I say more?	제가뭘 더 말해야 하나요?		32	be in mood	-한 기분이다
15	cut out	삭제하다		33	eager to do	to do하기를 열망하다
16	place A in B	A를 B에 두다		34	leave A B	A에게 B를 남기다
17	fail to do	to do 하는 것을 실패하다		35	get back to~	(회답을 위해) ~에게 다시 연락하다;
18	raise funds	기금을 마련하다				

TEST 1 Set 2 Lecture 1

VOCABULARY

01	barrier [bǽriər]	n. 장애 장벽
02	foray [fɔ́:rei]	n. 진입, 진출
03	remarkable [rimá:rkəbəl]	a. 주목할 만한
04	inefficiency [ìnifíʃənsi]	n. 비효율성
05	proposition [ˌprɒpəˈzɪʃn]	n. 문제, 과제
06	enormous [inɔ́:rməs]	a. 거대한, 엄청난
07	velocity [vilásəti]	n. 속도
08	oddly [ádli]	ad. 이상하게도
09	external [ikstə́:rnəl]	a. 외부의
10	misconception [mískəsépʃən]	n. 잘못된 생각, 오해
11	atmosphere [ˈætməsfɪə(r)]	n. 대기
12	absolutely [ˈæbsəluːtli]	ad. 전적으로, 틀림없이
13	gravitational [grӕvətéiʃənəl]	a. 중력의
14	theoretically [θí:ərétikəli]	ad. 이론적으로, 이론상으로
15	constant [ˈkɒnstənt]	a. 끊임없는
16	firmly [fə́:rmli]	ad. 견고하게 단단하게
17	passenger [ˈpæsɪndʒə(r)]	n. 승객
18	payload [péilòd]	n. 탑재화물
19	somehow [sÁmhàu]	ad. 어쨌든, 어떻게든
20	gravity [grǽvəti]	n. 중력
21	conceptually [kənséptʃuəli]	ad. 개념상으로
22	improbable [imprábəbəl]	a. 일어날 것 같지 않은, 실현되기 힘든
23	outrageous [autréidʒəs]	a. 터무니 없는
24	transport [trænspɔ́:rt]	v. 수송하다
25	inspire [inspáiər]	v. 고무하다, 영감을 주다
26	propose [prəˈpoʊz]	v. 제안하다
27	immediately [ɪˈmiːdiətli]	ad. 즉시, 즉각
28	ridicule [rídikjù:l]	v. ~을 비웃다
29	fellow [félou]	n. 동료
30	enthusiastic [ɪnˌθjuːziˈæstɪk]	a. 열렬한, 열광적인
31	proponent [prəˈpoʊnənt]	n. 지지자
32	terraforming	n. 행성을 지구의 환경처럼 만드는 기술
33	pillar [pílər]	n. 기둥
34	flexible [fléksəbəl]	a. 유연한
35	centrifugal [centrífjəgəl]	a. 원심의
36	counterweight [káuntərwèit]	n. 평형추
37	circular [sə́:rkjələr]	a. 원의, 원형의
38	accomplish [əˈkʌmplɪʃ]	v. 완수하다, 성취하다
39	hindrance [ˈhɪndrəns]	n. 방해, 장애
40	durable [djúərəbəl]	a. 튼튼한, 내구력이 있는
41	promise [ˈprɒmɪs]	n. 가능성, 전망
42	satellite [sǽtəlàit]	n. 인공위성
43	orbit [ˈɔːrbɪt]	v. 궤도를 돌다
44	orbital [ɔ́:rbitl]	a. 궤도의
45	synchronize [ˈsɪŋkrənaɪz]	v. 동시에 움직이다
46	rotation [routéiʃən]	n. 자전
47	actualize [ˈæktʃuəlaɪz]	v. 현실로 만들다, 실현하다
48	navigational [nævəgèiʃənl]	a. 비행의, 항해의
49	hazard [hǽzərd]	n. 위험, 모험
50	radiation [rèidiéiʃən]	n. (빛) 방사, 복사
51	shield [ʃi:ld]	v 보호를 하다, 막다
52	feasible [fí:zəbəl]	a. 실현 가능한

TEST 1
SET2-L1
The Space Elevator Technology

본문 중 중요 구문 정리한 내용입니다. 우선 암기하고 많이 읽으시길 바랍니다.

→ 정답

번호	구문	뜻
01	break down	부수다; 고장나다
02	due to	-때문에
03	this is because	이것은 - 때문이다
04	require O to do	O가 to do할 필요가 있다
05	escape velocity	탈출속도
06	look at	-를 보다
07	seem to do	-하는 것처럼 보인다
08	have misconceptions about	-에 대해 오해하다
09	let O do	O가 do하게 하다
10	the idea that	-라는 생각
11	way to do	to do 하는 방법
12	at velocity	속도로
13	go further	깊이 들어가다
14	make sure	확실히 하다
15	be on the same page	잘 이해하고 있다
16	speed at which	-하는 속도
17	enough that	that할만큼 충분히
18	need to do	to do 할 필요가 있다
19	try to do	to do 하기를 시도하다
20	travel up and down	올라갔다 내려갔다 하다
21	climb a ladder	사다리를 타고 올라가다
22	anywher near	가까운 어딘가(=close to)
23	pull down	아래로 당기다
24	hold on to	-에 붙어있다
25	make sense	이해하다
26	let's not forget that	-라는 것을 잊지 말자
27	as outrageous as it sounds	들리는 것만큼 터무니 없는
28	do research	연구하다
29	be being done	되어지고 있는 중이다
30	research on	-에 대한 연구
31	design O to do	O를 to do 하기 위해 설계하다
32	tell A B	A에게 B를 말하다
33	charge A with B	A에게 B책임을 지우다, 맡기다
34	a means of	-하는 수단
35	let's talk about	-에 대해 이야기해보자
36	attach A to B	A를 B에 붙이다.
37	called A B	A를 B라고 부르다
38	enough to do	to do 하기에 충분한
39	stand up	서 있다
40	tie A to B	A를 B에 묶다
41	full of	-로 가득 찬
42	stay inside	안에 머무르다
43	known A as B	A를 B로서 알다
44	away from	-로부터 멀리
45	apply to	-에 적용하다
46	at its highest point	-의 꼭대기에
47	make O O.C	O가 O.C하게 만들다
48	hindrance to	-에 대한 장애
49	make A of B	A를 B로 만들다
50	as long as	-하는한
51	dream of	-를 꿈꾸다
52	one another	서로 서로
53	conduct electricity	전기를 전도하다, 전달하다
54	show promise	전망이 밝다, 가망이 있다
55	attach A to B	A를 B에 붙이다.
56	at height	-한 높이
57	lead to	야기하다; -로 이끌다
58	synchronize A with B	A를 B와 동기화 시키다
59	in other words	다른 말로 하면
60	on Earth	지상의
61	for one	(여러가지 이유들 중에서) 우선 한가지 이유는
62	few centimeters long	길이가 몇 cm인
63	link A to B	A를 B로 연결 시키다
64	feel that	-라고 느끼다
65	present A to B	A를 B에 주다
66	expose A to B	A를 B에 노출시키다
67	shield A from B	A를 B로부터 보호하다
68	in your lifetimes	네가 살아있는 동안; 평생동안

TEST 1 Set 2 Lecture 2
VOCABULARY

01	civilization [sìvəlizéiʃən]	n. 문명
02	mysterious [mɪˈstɪəriəs]	a. 기이한, 불가사의한
03	cannibalistic [kænəbəlìstik]	a. 식인의, 동족을 잡아먹는
04	savage [sǽvidʒ]	a. 잔인한, 야만의 / n. 야만인
05	orderly [ɔ́ːrdərli]	a. 정돈된, 질서있는
06	demise [dimáiz]	n. 사망, 소멸
07	prominent [prámənənt]	a. 눈에 띄는, 현저한
08	archaeologist [àːrkiálədʒist]	n. 고고학자
09	unravel [ʌnˈrævl]	v. 풀다
10	obscurity [əbskjúərəti]	n. 불명료함
11	renowned [rináund]	a. 명성있는, 잘 알려진
12	inhabit [ɪnˈhæbɪt]	v. 살다, 거주하다, 서식하다
13	humid [hjúːmid]	a. 습기찬, 눅눅한
14	subtropical [sʌ̀btrápikəl]	a. 아열대의
15	approximately [əpráksəmitli]	ad. 대략, 약
16	devoid [dɪˈvɔɪd]	a. ~이 전혀 없는
17	astonishing [əˈstɒnɪʃɪŋ]	a. 정말 놀라운, 믿기 힘든
18	carve [kɑːrv]	v. 조각하다
19	haul [hɔːl]	v. 잡아끌다
20	remote [rɪˈmoʊt]	a. 외진, 외딴
21	barren [bǽrən]	a. 불모의
22	definitive [difínətiv]	a. 최종적인, 가장 확실한
23	propose [prəˈpoʊz]	v. 제안하다
24	continental [kàntənéntl]	a. 대륙의
25	resemble [rɪˈzembl]	v. 닮다, 유사하다
26	skeleton [skélətn]	a. 해골, 유골
27	seafarer [sìːfɛ̀ərər]	n. 선원, 해상 여행자
28	migrate [ˈmaɪɡreɪt]	v. 이동하다, 이주하다
29	house [hauz]	v. 거처를 제공하다, 살 곳을 주다
30	estimate [éstəmèit]	v. 추정하다
31	habitable [ˈhæbɪtəbl]	a. 주거할 수 있는
32	dispersion [dispə́ːrʒən]	n. 분산, 흩어짐
33	assume [əsjúːm]	v. 가정하다
34	pollen analysis [pálənən ənǽləsis]	n. 꽃가루 분석
35	sediment [ˈsedɪmənt]	n. 침전물, 퇴적물
36	swamp [swamp]	n. 늪, 습지
37	radiocarbon dating	n. 방사성연대측정법
38	flourish [ˈflɜːrɪʃ]	v. 번성하다
39	horizontally [hɔ̀ːrəzántəli]	ad. 수평으로
40	spell [spel]	v. (보통 나쁜 결과) 가져오다
41	doom [duːm]	n. 운명
42	overconsumption [òuvərkəʌ̀mpʃən]	n. 과소비
43	deforestation [diːfɔ̀ːristéiʃən]	n. 산림벌채, 산림파괴
44	halt [hɔːlt]	v. 멈추다, 서다, 세우다
45	descend [dɪˈsend]	v. 내려가다, 내려오다
46	inflict [inflìkt]	v. 고통을 주다
47	corroborate [kəˈrɒbəreɪt]	v. 확증하다, 입증하다
48	culprit [kʌ́lprit]	n. 범인
49	plethora [pléθərə]	n. 과잉
50	deduce [didjúːs]	v. 추론하다
51	strew [struː]	v. 흩뿌리다
52	germinate [dʒə́ːrmənèit]	v. 발아하다
53	insult [insʌ́lt]	n. 모욕
54	terrestrial [təréstriəl]	a. 지구의, 육지의
55	warfare [ˈwɔːrfer]	n. 전투, 전쟁

TEST 1 SET2-L2 — Investigation of Easter Island

구문정리
본문 중 중요 구문 정리한 내용입니다. 우선 암기하고 많이 읽으시길 바랍니다.

→ 정답

#	구문	뜻
01	let's continue	계속하자
02	continue -ing	-ing하는 것을 계속하다
03	fill A with B	A를 B로 채우다
04	happen to	-에게 일어나다
05	work together	함께 작업하다
06	unravel a mystery	수수께끼를 풀다
07	look into	-를 알아보다
08	in detail	자세히
09	Does anyone know anything about	~에 대해 아는사람?
10	famous for	-로 유명한
11	background information	배경지식
12	be located in~	~에 위치하다
13	west of	-의 서쪽
14	make O O.C	O를 O.C하게 만들다
15	ideal for	-에 이상적인
16	there were no sign of~	~의 흔적이 없다
17	devoid of	-이 없는
18	draw attention	이목을 끌다
19	carve A into B	A를 B로깎다
20	find O O.C	O가 O.C인 것을 발견하다
21	could not have done	~할 수 있었을 것이다
22	choose to do	to do 하는것을 선택하다
23	perform test on	-에 대한 테스트를 수행하다
24	in canoe	카누를 타고
25	it is likely that	-할 가능성이 있다
26	get lost	길을 잃다
27	strangely though	이상하긴 하지만
28	be of origin	~ 출신이다
29	house a lot more peolple	훨씬 많은 사람을 수용하다
30	base A on B	A를 B에 기초하다
31	require O to do	o가 to do하는것을 요구하다
32	lead O to do	O가 to do 하도록 이끌다
33	prove O O.C	o가 oc로 밝혀지다
34	call A B	A를 B라고 부르다
35	over time	시간이 지나면서
36	I'm confused about~	나는 ~에 관해서 헷갈린다
37	use O to do	O를 to do 하는데 사용하다
38	ideal for~	~에 이상적인
39	according to	-에 따르면
40	long story short	간단히 말해서
41	go extinct	멸종하다
42	for some reason	어떠한 이유로, 왠지
43	spell doom for	엉망으로 만들다; 불운을 가져오다
44	lead to	야기하다; -로 이어지다
45	as - as -	-만큼 -한
46	let's look at	-을 살펴보자
47	cut down	자르다
48	descend into ~	~로 서서히 빠져들다
49	come up with	떠올리다, 고안하다
50	point to A as B	A를 B로 지목하다
51	a plethora of	많은
52	deduce that	-라고 추론하다
53	bring A with B	A를 B와 함께 데려 오다
54	keep O in check	O를 조절하다, 억제하다
55	combine with	-와 결합하다
56	across the island	섬 전역에 걸쳐
57	lead A to B	A를 B로 이끌다
58	as if	마치 -인 것처럼
59	add A to B	A에 B를 더하다
60	no longer	더 이상 -않다
61	need A for B	A를 B위해 필요하다
62	start to do	to do 하는 것을 시작하다
63	turn to	~에 의지하다

TEST 2　Set 1　Conversation
VOCABULARY

01　**assign** [əˈsaɪn]　v. (일, 책임 등을) 배정하다, 맡기다

02　**purification** [pjùərəfikéiʃən]　n. 정제

03　**occur** [əˈkɜː(r)]　v. 일어나다, 발생하다

04　**reversible** [rivə́ːrsəbəl]　a. 되돌릴 수 있는

05　**room temperature**　n. 상온, 실온

06　**precipitation** [prisípətéiʃən]　n. 침전

07　**oversleep** [òuvərslíːp]　v. 늦잠 자다

08　**graduate student**　n. 대학원생

09　**purify** [pjúərəfài]　v. 정제하다

10　**submit** [səbˈmɪt]　v. 제출하다

11　**journal** [ˈdʒɜːrnl]　n. 학술지

12　**tiptop** [típtàp]　a. 최고급, 우수한

13　**rid** [rɪd]　v. 없애다, 제거하다

14　**practice** [ˈpræktɪs]　v. 실습하다, 실행하다

15　**margin of error**　n. 오차

16　**professional** [prəˈfeʃnl]　a. 직업의, 전문적인

17　**attitude** [ˈætɪtuːd]　n. 자세, 태도

18　**design** [dɪˈzaɪn]　v. 설계하다, 고안하다

19　**implement** [ímpləmənt]　v. 시행하다

20　**spinach** [ˈspɪnɪtʃ; -ɪdʒ]　n. 시금치

21　**supplement** [ˈsʌplɪmənt]　n. 보충

22　**misplace** [ˌmɪsˈpleɪs]　v. 잘못 두다

23　**decimal** [ˈdesɪml]　n. 소수

24　**inaccurate** [ɪnækjərit]　a. 부정확한, 오류가 있는

TEST 2 SET1-C 구문정리
본문 중 중요 구문 정리한 내용입니다. 우선 암기하고 많이 읽으시길 바랍니다.

Biology Research Plan

→ 정답

01 want to do	to do 하기를 원하다	22 look for	-를 찾다
02 check on	확인하다	23 work on	-에 공을 들이다, 애쓰다
03 come along	(원하는 대로)되어 가다	24 take long	오래 걸리다
04 put in hours in	시간을 ~에 쓰다	25 for a week	한 주 동안
05 to be honest	솔직히	26 you're worried that~	너는 that절을 걱정한다
06 assign A B	A에게 B를 맡기다, 할당하다	27 be in condition	~한 상태이다
07 in process	과정에서	28 in a week	1주일 내에
08 forget to do	to do 할 것을 잊어버리다	29 would like to do	to do 하고 싶다
09 lower the temperature	온도를 낮추다	30 as soon as	-하자 마자
10 determine if	-인지 아닌지 확인하다	31 get rid of	-를 제거하다
11 process~ follow	과정을 밟다	32 make O do	O가 do 하게 하다
12 set an alarm	알람을 맞추다	33 keep -ing	계속 -ing하다
13 cool A to room temperature	A를 상온으로 낮추다	34 take an attitude	입장을 취하다
14 be used to ing	ing 하는것에 익숙하다	35 critical in	~에서 중요한
15 on a Saturday	토요일에	36 effect on	-에 대한 효과
16 hope to do	to do 하기를 바라다	37 rich in	-가 풍부한
17 for weeks	몇 주 동안	38 10 times more	10배 더
18 It's not like	~은 아닌것 같다	39 provide A with B	A에게 B를 제공하다
19 be going to do	to do 할 예정이다	40 continue to do	to do 하기를 계속하다
20 anytime soon	곧 조만간	41 place A in B	A를 B에 두다
21 expect to do	to do 하기를 기대하다		

TEST 2　Set 1　Lecture 1

VOCABULARY

01	switch [switʃ]	v. ~으로 방향을 바꾸다. 전환하다.
02	manmade	a. 사람에 의한, 인공의
03	wonder [wʌ́ndər]	n. 불가사의한 물건, 놀라운 물건
04	compose [kəmpóuz]	v. ~을 구성하다
05	mere [miər]	a. 단지
06	archaeologist [à:rkiálədʒist]	n. 고고학자
07	clueless [klu:les]	a. 전혀 짐작가지않는, 단서가 없는
08	process [práses]	n. 과정, 진행상태
09	commission [kəmíʃən]	v. 위임하다, 명령하다
10	labor [léibər]	n. 노역, 노동
11	material [mətíəriəl]	n. 재료
12	multiple [mʌ́ltəpəl]	a. 여러 개의
13	chamber [tʃéimbər]	n. 방
14	passage [pǽsidʒ]	n. 통로
15	fool [fu:l]	v. (남을)속이다
16	precious [préʃəs]	a. 값비싼, 귀중한
17	treasure ['treʒə(r)]	n. 보물
18	eternal [itə́:rnəl]	a. 영원한
19	belonging [bilɔ́(:)ŋiŋ]	n. 소유물
20	trickery ['trɪkəri]	n. 속임수
21	rob [rab]	v. 강탈하다. 빼앗다
22	loot [lu:t]	v. 약탈하다
23	craftsmanship [krǽftsmənʃip]	n.솜씨, 기능
24	overall [óuvərɔ̀:l]	a. 전반적인, 종합적인
25	intact [ɪnˈtækt]	a. 온전한, 전혀 다치지 않은
26	crane [krein]	n. 기중기
27	ramp [ræmp]	n. 경사로
28	massive [mǽsiv]	a. (규모나 양이)큰, 대량의
29	device [diváis]	n. (기계-,) 장치
30	egyptologist [í:dʒiptládʒist]	n. 이집트학자
31	slope [sloup]	n. 경사면, 비탈
32	task [tæsk]	n. 과제
33	spiral [spáiərəl]	a. 나선의
34	excavator [ékskəvèitər]	n. 발굴자
35	wrap [ræp]	v. 싸다, 포장하다
36	ruin [rú:in]	v. 파멸시키다
37	external [ikstə́:rnəl]	a. 외부의
38	sightline [saitlain]	n. 시야
39	precisely [prisáisli]	ad. 정확히, 정밀히
40	smooth [smu:θ]	a. 매끄러운, 반들반들한
41	specialize [spéʃəlàiz]	v. ~을 전문적으로 연구하다.
42	survey [sərˈveɪ]	v. 조사하다, 살피다
43	infrared [ìnfrəréd]	a. 적외선의
44	internal [intə́:rnl]	a. 내부의, 내부에 있는
45	apex [éipeks]	n. 정점, 절정
46	problematic [ˌprɒbləˈmætɪk]	n. 문제가 있는
47	wind [waind]	v. ~을 감다. 둘러싸다.
48	risk [risk]	v. 위험을 무릅쓰다
49	stumble [ˈstʌmbl]	v. 발을 헛디디다
50	haul [hɔ:l]	v. 끌다, 움직이다
51	speculate [spékjəlèit]	v. ~이라고 추측하다
52	indeed [indí:d]	ad. 참으로, 정말 확실히
53	seal [si:l]	v. ~으로 막다, 봉인하다.
54	significantly [signifikəntli]	ad. 현저하게
55	conserve [kənsə́:rv]	v. 보존하다 보호하다
56	revolutionary [rèvəlú:ʃənèri]	a. 혁명적인, 혁신의
57	eliminate [ilímənèit]	v. 없애다. ~을 고려에서 제외하다

TEST 2
SET1-L1

구문정리 | 본문 중 중요 구문 정리한 내용입니다. 우선 암기하고 많이 읽으시길 바랍니다.

Mysteries of the Egyptian Pyramid

→ 정답

#	구문	뜻
01	be going to do	to do 할 예정이다
02	756 feet wide	756 feet 넓이(폭)
03	450 feet high	450 feet 높이
04	be composed of	-로 구성되다
05	cause O to do	O가 to do 하는 것을 야기하다
06	how on earth	도대체 어떻게
07	due to	~ 때문에
08	no one knows how~	아무도 ~하는 방법을 모르다
09	come up with	고안하다, 생각해내다
10	look at	-를 보다
11	might have done	-했었을지도 모른다
12	get to	-를 닿다; 시작하다
13	use O to do	O를 to do 하는데 이용하다
14	does anyone know why	~의 이유를 아는 사람
15	serve as	-로서 역할을 하다
16	try to do	to do 하려고 애쓰다, 노력하다
17	consider O to be OC	O가 O.C인 것으로 간주하다
18	want to do	to do 하고 싶다, 하기를 원하다
19	take A with B	A를 B와 함께 가져가다
20	the icing on the cake	금상첨화
21	over time	시간이 지나면서
22	luckily for	-에게 행운이게도
23	allow O to do	O가 to do 하게 하다, 허락하다
24	let's move on to	-로 넘어가자
25	according to	-에 따르면
26	be located in~	~에 위치하다
27	have access to	~에게 접근 할 수 있다
28	enough to do	to do 할 만큼 충분한
29	at the time	그 때
30	there have been	있어 왔다(복수)
31	concentrate on	-에 집중하다
32	would have been	-이었을 지도 모른다(w)
33	require O to do	O가 to do하는것을 필요로 하다
34	have to do	to do 해야 한다
35	waste of	-의 낭비
36	bring A to B	A를 B로 인도하다, 데려가다
37	would have done	-했을지도 모른다(w)
38	compare A to B	A를 B와 비교하다
39	line of vision	시선(=line of sight)
40	high in the air	하늘높이
41	in the beginning	처음에
42	need to do	to do 할 필요가 있다
43	specialize in	-을 전문적으로 하다
44	switch to	-로 바꾸다
45	reach the apex	정점에 달하다
46	be about to do	막 to do 하려는 참이다
47	compare A to B	A를 B에 비교하다
48	risk -ing	-ing 할 위험을 감수하다
49	in the same way	같은 방법으로
50	on the other hand	반면에, 한편
51	make O O.C	O를 O.C 하게 만들다
52	for O to do	의미상 주어 (f)
53	become a part of	-의 부분이 되다
54	take down	분해하다
55	sound like	-처럼 들린다
56	be likely to do	to do 할 가능성이 있다
57	associate A with B	A를 B와 연관시키다

TEST 2 Set 1 Lecture 2
VOCABULARY

01	**marine** [məˈriːn]	a. 바다의, 해양의
02	**reef** [riːf]	n. 산호초
03	**coral** [kɔ́ːrəl]	n. 산호
04	**organism** [ɔ́ːrənìzəm]	n. 생물, 유기체
05	**colony** [káləni]	n. 집단, 무리
06	**blame** [bleim]	v. ~을 탓하다
07	**skeleton** [skélətn]	n. 골격, 뼈대
08	**alarming** [əláːrmiŋ]	a. 깜짝 놀랄만한, 급격한
09	**sudden** [sʌ́dn]	a. 갑작스러운
10	**explosion** [iksplóuʒən]	n. 폭발적인 증가
11	**threaten** [ˈθretn]	v. 위협하다, 협박하다
12	**poisonous** [pɔ́izənəs]	a. 독이 있는
13	**spine** [spain]	n. 가시, 등뼈
14	**atop** [əˈtɑːp]	prep. 맨 위에
15	**digestive** [didʒéstiv]	a. 소화의
16	**enzyme** [énzaim]	n. 효소
17	**liquefy** [líkwifài]	v. 액화시키다
18	**cyclical** [sáiklikəl]	a. 주기적인, 순환하는
19	**outbreak** [ˈaʊtbreɪk]	n. 발생, 급격한 증가
20	**incline** [inkláin]	v. ~쪽으로 기울다
21	**destruction** [distrʌ́kʃən]	n. 파괴, 말살
22	**slight** [slait]	a. 약간의, 미세한
23	**salinity** [səlínəti]	n. 염분, 염도
24	**generation** [dʒénərèiʃən]	n. 세대
25	**mate** [meit]	v. 짝짓기를 하다
26	**successive** [səksésiv]	a. 연속적인
27	**theoretically** [θìːərétikəli]	ad. 이론상으로
28	**fluctuation** [flʌ̀ktʃuèiʃən]	n. 변동
29	**hypothesis** [haipáθəsis]	n. 가설
30	**cite** [sait]	v. 예를 들다, 말하다
31	**stab** [stæb]	v. 찌르다
32	**radula** [rǽdʒulə]	n. 치설
33	**chitin** [káitin]	n. 키틴질
34	**toothed** [tuːθt]	a. 이빨이 달린
35	**saliva** [səˈlaivə]	n. 침, 타액
36	**paralyze** [pǽrəlàiz]	v. 마비시키다
37	**ornamental** [ɔ̀ːnəˈmentl]	a. 장식용의
38	**unsustainable** [ʌ̀nsəˈsteinəbl]	a. 지속 불가능한
39	**deforestation** [diːfɔ̀ːristéiʃən]	n. 삼림 벌채, 파괴
40	**adjacent** [ədʒéisənt]	a. 인접한, 가까운
41	**vulnerable** [vʌ́lnərəbəl]	a. 연약한, 취약한
42	**sediment** [sédəmənt]	n. 퇴적물
43	**runoff** [rʌnɔːf]	n. 유출 액체, 땅위를 흐르는 빗물
44	**fertilizer** [fɔ́ːrtəlàizər]	n. 비료
45	**discharge** [distʃáːrdʒ]	v. 흐르다, 방출되다
46	**phosphorous** [fásfərəs]	n. 인
47	**algae** [ǽldʒi]	n. 조류
48	**bloom** [bluːm]	v. 꽃이 피다 / n. 증가
49	**copious** [kóupiəs]	a. 풍부한
50	**nourishment** [ˈnʌriʃmənt]	n. 영양, 음식물
51	**dilute** [dilúːt]	v. 희석하다, 묽게 하다
52	**osmoregulate** [ázmourəgáleit]	v. 삼투압을 조절하다
53	**larvae** [láːrvə]	n. larva의 복수형, 유충, 애벌레
54	**salinity** [səlínəti]	n. 염분, 염도
55	**diversity** [divɔ́ːrsəti]	n. 다양성
56	**unpredictable** [ʌ̀npriˈdiktəbl]	a. 예측할 수 없는

TEST 2
SET1-L2
Coral Reef Destruction

구문정리 | 본문 중 중요 구문 정리한 내용입니다. 우선 암기하고 많이 읽으시길 바랍니다.

→ 정답

01	be home to	~의 서식지이다
02	make A of B	A를 B로 구성하다
03	call A B	A를 B라고 부르다
04	attach A to B	A를 B에 붙이다
05	I don't blame	그럴만도 하다
06	provide A for B	A를 B를 위해 제공하다
07	at rate	~의 속도로
08	turn out	밝혀지다
09	prey upon	~를 잡아먹다 (p)
10	get one's name from	~로부터 이름을 얻다
11	the second largest	두 번째로 가장 큰
12	grow up to a meter across	지름이 1미터까지 자라다
13	break down	부수다, 허물다
14	absorb A into B	A를 B로 흡수하다
15	come up with	~를 고안하다, 생각해내다
16	increase in	~라는 점에서 증가
17	decrease in	~라는 점에서의 감소
18	be part of	-의 일부가 되다
19	due to the lack of	-의 부족 때문에
20	in the last few decades	최근 수십년간
21	be inclined to do	to do 하는 경향이 있다
22	have ground	근거를 갖다
23	in one's lifetime	일생동안
24	let's say	~라고 해보자
25	change in	~라는 점에서의 변화
26	such as	~같은
27	result in	~라는 결과를 낳다
28	survival chance	생존율(a+b)
29	cause a domino effect	도미노 효과를 야기하다
30	as you can see	너도 알다시피
31	bring about	야기하다
32	chase after	뒤쫓다
33	stab A with B	A를 B로 찌르다
34	make an opening in	-에 구멍을 내다
35	feed on	-을 잡아먹다 (f)
36	fortunately for	-에게 다행이게도
37	hunt A for B	A를 B의 이유로 사냥하다
38	so- that-	매우 -하여 -하다
39	to the level(to a level)	-의 수준으로
40	bounce back	되돌아오다, 회복하다
41	enough to do	to do 할 만큼 충분한
42	pose a threat to	-에 위협을 가하다
43	bring A to B	A를 B로 데리고 가다
44	seem strange	이상하게 보이다
45	land adjacent to	-에 인접한 땅
46	make O O.C.	O가 O.C.하게 만들다
47	vulnerable to	-에 취약한
48	rainy season	우기
49	get washed into	-로 쓸려가다
50	make one's way to	-로 나아가다
51	flood the land	땅을 침수하다
52	be discharged into	-로 흘러들어가다
53	in ways	방법으로
54	with regards to	-와 관련하여
55	too- to do	너무 ~해서 to do 할수없다
56	for O to do	의미상 주어 (f)
57	chance of survival	생존율(n+of+n)
58	tend to do	to do 하는 경향이 있다
59	keep in check	통제하다
60	allow A B	A에게 B를 허락하다
61	help do	do 하는것을 돕다
62	have an effect on	-에 영향을 주다
63	It's better that	that절 하는것이 낫다
64	take care to do	to do 하는 것을 주의하다
65	have an influence over	-에 영향을 주다

TEST 2 Set 2 Ceonversation

VOCABULARY

01	insight [ínsàit]	n. 통찰력, 이해
02	breathing [ˈbriːðɪŋ]	n. 호흡
03	migration [maigréiʃən]	n. 이주, 이동
04	blowhole [blóuhòul]	n. 고래머리 위의 분수공
05	mammal [mǽməl]	n. 포유동물
06	fundamental [ˌfʌndəˈmentl]	a. 근본적인, 필수적인
07	attribute [ətríbjuːt]	n. 특성
08	differ [ˈdɪfə(r)]	v. 다르다
09	differentiate [ˌdɪfəˈrenʃieɪt]	v. 구별하다, 구분 짓다
10	ethnicity [eθˈnɪsəti]	n. 민족성
11	anatomy [əˈnætəmi]	n. 해부학
12	submerge [səbmə́ːrdʒ]	v. 잠수하다
13	fascinating [fǽsənèitiŋ]	a. 멋진, 매력적인
14	sidetrack [sáidtræk]	v. 곁길로 새게 하다
15	theoretical [ˌθɪəˈretɪkl]	a. 이론의, 이론적인
16	obvious [ˈɒbviəs]	a. 명백한, 분명한
17	bloodstream [blʌ́dstriːm]	n. 혈류
18	fit [fɪt]	v. 설치하다
19	expel [ikspél]	v. 배출하다
20	lung [lʌŋ]	n. 폐, 허파
21	float [floʊt]	v. (물에) 뜨다
22	squeeze [skwiːz]	v. 짜다, 짜내다
23	relaxation [rìːlækséiʃən]	n. 휴식, 이완
24	thrust [θrʌst]	v. 밀다, 추진하다
25	stroke [stroʊk]	n. (수영에서 노를) 젓기
26	glide [glaid]	v. 미끄러지듯 가다

TEST 2
SET2-C 구문정리 | Whale Breathing Patterns

본문 중 중요 구문 정리한 내용입니다. 우선 암기하고 많이 읽으시길 바랍니다.

→ 정답

01	come on in	-에 들어오다
02	have a seat	앉다
03	what's on your mind?	무슨생각 하니?
04	look for	-를 찾다
05	insight into	-에 대한 견해
06	let me stop you right there	잠깐 멈춰봐
07	even though	그럼에도 불구하고
08	according to	-에 따르면
09	I'm not following	이해하지 못하겠어요
10	let me put it this way	(다시 설명할 때) 이렇게 말해 볼게
11	be differentiated by	-에 의해 구분된다
12	try to do	to do 하려고 애쓰다
13	a type of	-의 종류의
14	report on	-에 대한 논문
15	allow O to do	O가 to do 하게 하다, 허락하다
16	over distances	거리에 걸쳐서
17	for up to 40 minutes	최대 40분 동안
18	depend on	-에 의지하다
19	reason for	-에 대한 이유
20	have no choice but to do	to do 할 수밖에 없다
21	for 90 to 120 minutes	90분에서 120분 동안
22	get sidetracked	벗어나다
23	biologically speaking	생물학적으로 말해서
24	enable O to do	O가 to do 할 수 있게 하다, 가능하게 하다
25	for a long time	오랜 시간 동안
26	there are few things	몇가지가 있다
27	enable O to do	O가 to do 하는것을 가능케하다
28	for long	오랫동안
29	ability to do	to do 할 수 있는 능력
30	amount of	많은
31	deliver A to B	A를 B로 전달하다
32	in order to do	to do 하기 위해서
33	be aware of	-를 알고 있다
34	a few years ago	몇 년 전에
35	at a university	대학에서
36	fit A to B	A에게 B를 장착시키다
37	stop doing	doing 하는것을 멈추다
38	the rest	나머지
39	the secret is in-	비밀은 -에 있다
40	continue to do	to do 하는것을 계속하다
41	along with	(=with)
42	I'm glad to hear that	그 말을 들으니 기쁘네요

TEST 2 Set 2 Lecture 1

VOCABULARY

01	**anthropologist** [ænərəpálədʒist] n. 인류학자	28	**represent** [rèprizént] v. ~을 나타내다
02	**speculate** [spékjəlèit] v. 사색하다, 심사숙고하다	29	**quicken** [ˈkwɪkən] v. 빨라지다
03	**domesticate** [douméstəkèit] v. 길들이다	30	**corroborate** [kərábərèit] v. 확증하다
04	**steppe** [step] n. 나무가 없는 초원, 스텝	31	**harness** [háːrnis] n. 마구
05	**previously** [príːviəsli] ad. 미리, 이전에	32	**pottery** [ˈpɒtəri] n. 도자기
06	**groundbreaking** [gráundbrèikiŋ] a. 획기적인	33	**shard** [ʃaːrd] n. 파편
07	**controversy** [kántrəvəˌrsi] n. 논쟁	34	**vertical** [vɜ́ːrtikəl] a. 수직의
08	**veracity** [vəræsəti] n. 정확도, 정확성	35	**confinement** [kənfáinmənt] n. 가둠, 갇힘
09	**undeniable** [ʌndináiəbəl] a. 부정하기 어려운, 명백한	36	**domestication** [douméstəkèiʃən] n. 길들이기
10	**proponent** [prəpóunənt] n. 지지자	37	**phosphorus** [fásfərəs] n. 인
11	**nomad** [nóumæd] n. 유목민	38	**manure** [mənjúər] n. 동물의 배설물
12	**excavation** [èkskəvéiʃən] n. 발굴	39	**volatile** [válətil] a. 휘발성의
13	**imply** [ɪmˈplaɪ] v. 암시하다	40	**peculiarity** [pikjùːliǽrəti] n. 특이함
14	**drastically** [drǽstikəli] ad. 급격하게	41	**indentation** [indentation] n. 새긴 자국
15	**breed** [briːd] v. 사육하다, 양육하다	42	**bridle** [ˈbraɪdl] n. (말에게 씌우는) 굴레
16	**permanent** [pɜ́ːrmənənt] a. 영구적인	43	**lipid** [lípid] n. 지질
17	**eliminate** [ilímənèit] v. 제거하다	44	**mare** [mer] n. 암말, 당나귀
18	**insulation** [ˌɪnsjuˈleɪʃn] n. 단열, 절연	45	**circumstantial** [sèːrkəmstǽnʃəl] a. 상황의, 상황으로부터
19	**exceptionally** [ikspéʃənəli] ad. 특히, 유난히	46	**inference** [ˈɪnfərəns] n. 추론
20	**forage** [fɔ́ːridʒ] v. 먹이를 찾아 다니다	47	**smoking gun** n. 명백한 증거
21	**revolutionize** [ˌrevəˈluːʃənaɪz] v. 획기적으로 변화시키다	48	**skeletal** [skélətl] a. 해골의, 골격의
22	**equine** [íːkwain] a. 말의	49	**undergo** [ˌʌndərˈgoʊ] v. 겪다
23	**warfare** [wɔ́ːrfɛər] n. 전쟁	50	**morphological** [mɔːrfəládʒicəl] a. 형태학적인, 형태의
24	**transportation** [trænspərtéiʃən] n. 운송, 수송	51	**discern** [dɪˈsɜːn] v. 파악하다, 알아차리다
25	**range** [reindʒ] n. 범위	52	**tame** [teim] a. 길들여진
26	**globalization** [ˌgloʊbəlaɪˈzeɪʃn] n. 세계화	53	**precise** [prɪˈsaɪs] a. 정확한, 정밀한
27	**mount** [maunt] v. 오르다	54	**persistence** [pəˈsɪstəns] n. 지속됨

TEST 2 구문정리
SET2-L1 Horse Domestication of Botai People

본문 중 중요 구문 정리한 내용입니다. 우선 암기하고 많이 읽으시길 바랍니다.

→ 정답

#	구문	뜻
01	for decades	수 십 년 동안
02	begin to do	to do 하는 것을 시작하다
03	there is controversy	논쟁이 있다
04	the fact that	that절 이라는 사실
05	have a relationship with	-와 관계를 맺다
06	I would like to do	to do 하고 싶다
07	put forth	제시하다, 제안하다
08	jump right in	들어가다, 시작하다
09	originate in	-에서 기원하다
10	hunt game	사냥감을 사냥하다
11	such~ that~	너무 ~해서 ~하다
12	suited to	-에 적합한
13	travel in band	무리로 이동하다
14	stay in	-에 머무르다
15	for long	오랫동안
16	way of life	삶의 방식
17	provide A for B	A를 B에게 제공하다
18	around 6,000 years ago	약 6,000년 전에
19	gain access to	-에 접근하다
20	lead to	-를 야기하다
21	shift from A to B	A에서 B로의 변화, 이동
22	need to do	to do할 필요가 있다
23	sink into	-로 가라앉다
24	prove useful	유용한 것으로 밝혀지다
25	survive snowstorm	눈보라에서 살아남다
26	such as	- 같은
27	so called	소위, 이른바
28	from A to B	A로부터 B에 이르기까지
29	in the stage	단계에서
30	as time progresses	시간이 지날수록
31	begin ing	ing 하기 시작하다
32	allow O to do	O가 to do 하는것을 허락하다
33	due to	- 때문에
34	value in	-라는 점에서의 가치
35	quicken the pace of	-의 속도를 증가시키다
36	military campaign	군사활동
37	be the first to do	to do를 한 처음이 되다
38	gather A in B	A를 B에서 모으다
39	caused by the use of	-의 쓰임에 의해 야기된
40	have to do	to do 해야 한다
41	take A from B	A를 B로 부터 가져오다
42	would have done	~했었을 것이다
43	be ten times greater than that of	-의 그것보다 10 배 많다
44	from outside of	~의 바깥으로 부터
45	wash away	쓸어내다
46	release A into B	A를 B로 방출 시키다
47	come from	-에서 나오다
48	use O to do	O를 to do하는데 사용하다
49	rely on	-에 의지하다
50	direct evidence	직접적 근거
51	be able to do	to do 할 수 있다
52	over generations	수세대에 걸쳐
53	hold true for	-에 유효하다
54	it is impossible to do	to do 하는 것이 불가능하다
55	live in	-에 살다
56	it's safe to say	~라고 말할 수 있다, ~라는것은 과언이 아니다
57	in fact	사실상
58	start to do	to do하는 것을 시작하다

TEST 2 Set 2 Lecture 2

VOCABULARY

01	**beverage** [ˈbevərɪdʒ]	n. 음료
02	**candidate** [kǽndədeit]	n. 후보
03	**substitute** [sʌ́bstitjùːt]	v. 대체하다
04	**fossil fuel**	n. 화석 연료
05	**crude oil**	n. 원유
06	**ethanol** [éθənɔ̀(ː)l]	n. 에탄올
07	**biofuel** [ˈbaɪoʊ-]	n. 바이오 연료
08	**renewable** [rinjúːwəbəl]	a. 재생가능한
09	**derive** [diráiv]	v. 유래하다
10	**convert** [kənvə́ːrt]	v. 변환하다, 전환시키다
11	**carbohydrate** [kàːrbouháidreit]	n. 탄수화물
12	**compound** [kámpaund]	n. 혼합물, 화합물
13	**rigid** [ˈrɪdʒɪd]	a. 단단한, 뻣뻣한
14	**polymer** [pálimər]	n. 중합체
15	**molecule** [máləkjùːl]	n. 분자
16	**abundant** [əˈbʌndənt]	a. 풍부한
17	**typical** [ˈtɪpɪkl]	a. 보통의, 전형적인
18	**switch** [swɪtʃ]	v. 전환하다, 바뀌다
19	**advantage** [ədˈvɑːntɪdʒ]	n. 이점, 장점
20	**conversion** [kənvə́ːrʒn]	n. 전환, 변환
21	**starch** [stɑːrtʃ]	n. 녹말
22	**essential** [ɪˈsenʃl]	a. 필수적인, 본질적인
23	**digestible** [daɪˈdʒestəbl; dɪ-]	a. 소화하기 쉬운
24	**beneficial** [ˌbenɪˈfɪʃl]	a. 이로운, 유리한
25	**feedstock**	n. 공급원료
26	**raw** [rɔː]	a. 원자재의
27	**industrial** [ɪnˈdʌstriəl]	a. 산업의, 공업용의
28	**analogy** [əˈnælədʒi]	n. 비유
29	**substance** [ˈsʌbstəns]	n. 물질
30	**transportation** [ˌtrænspɔːˈteɪʃn]	n. 운송, 수송
31	**eco-friendly**	a. 친환경적인
32	**greenhouse gas**	n. 온실가스
33	**alternative** [ɔːltə́ːrnətiv]	n. 대안, 대체 /a. 대신의, 대체의
34	**loosen** [ˈluːsn]	v. 느슨하게 하다
35	**enzyme** [énzaim]	n. 효소
36	**ferment** [fə́ːrment]	v. 발효시키다
37	**distillation** [dístəléiʃən]	n. 증류, 정수
38	**evaporate** [ɪˈvæpəreɪt]	v. 증발하다
39	**yeast** [jiːst]	n. 효모균
40	**withstand** [wɪðˈstænd]	v. 견디다
41	**engineer** [ˌendʒɪˈnɪə(r)]	v. 제작하다
42	**resilient** [rizíljənt]	a. 회복력이 강한, 탄력이 있는
43	**forgo** [fɔːrgóu]	v. ~없이 지내다, 버리다
44	**gasification** [gæ̀səfikéiʃən]	n. 가스화
45	**approach** [əˈproutʃ]	n. 접근법
46	**combust** [kəmbʌ́st]	v. 연료를 태우다, 연소시키다
47	**atom** [ˈætəm]	n. 원자
48	**microorganism**	n. 미생물
49	**barrel** [ˈbærəl]	n. 배럴(석유 단위)
50	**execute** [ˈeksɪkjuːt]	v. 실행하다

TEST 2
SET2-L2
Biofuel Production Process

본문 중 중요 구문 정리한 내용입니다. 우선 암기하고 많이 읽으시길 바랍니다.

→ 정답

#	구문	뜻
01	talk about	~에 대해 이야기 하다
02	produce A from B	A를 B로부터 만들다
03	one of the NS	~중 하나
04	substitute for	~을 대신하다
05	such as	~와 같은
06	derive A from B	A가 B로부터 얻다
07	after long periods of time	긴 시간 이후에
08	under the condition	~환경에서, 조건에서
09	way of -ing	-ing 하는 방법
10	be going to do	~할 예정이다
11	similar to	~와 유사한
12	convert A into B	A를 B로 변환시키다
13	let's talk about	~에 대해 이야기 해보자
14	make up	구성하다
15	call A B	A를 B라 부르다
16	let's try that again	다시 시도해보자
17	in other words	다른말로 하면
18	make up A of B	A를 B로 구성하다
19	switch from A to B	A에서 B로 바꾸다
20	for one	우선, 첫째로
21	cut into	~을 줄이다
22	make O O.C	O를 O.C로 만들다
23	lead A to B	A를 B로 이끌다
24	with an analogy	비유와 함께
25	try to do	~하는 것을 시도하다
26	stack of	산더미 같은, 많은
27	fill A with B	A를 B로 채우다
28	in the process or in a process	이 과정에서
29	seem like	~처럼 보이다
30	big deal	중요한 것, 큰 거래;
31	play a role in	~한 점에서 역할을 하다
32	other than	=exept
33	use O to do	O를 to do 하는데 사용하다
34	be cheap to do	to do 하기에 싸다
35	by 숫자	~까지
36	attempt to do	to do하려는 시도
37	know A as B	A를 B로 알다
38	break A down into B	A를 B로 분해하다
39	compose A of B	A를 B로 구성하다
40	so that	그래서 그결과
41	each other	서로서로
42	speed up	속도를 높이다
43	reduce cost	비용을 줄이다
44	instead of	~대신에
45	blow up	부풀어지다, 폭발하다
46	feed A to B	A를 B에게 먹이다
47	in the same way	~와 같은 방법으로
48	in approach	~ 접근법으로
49	difficulty in ~ing	ing하는있어 어려움
50	for a few reasons	몇 몇 이유로
51	carry out research	연구하다
52	as much as they need	필요한 만큼 많은
53	suffer from	~로 부터 고통받다, 겪다
54	a lack of	~의 부족
55	to some extent	어느정도까지는
56	resolve A through B	A를 B를 통해 해결하다

TEST 3　Set 1　Conversation
VOCABULARY

01　**regarding** [rɪˈɡɑːdɪŋ]　　prep. ~에 관하여

02　**community service**　　n. 사회 봉사 활동

03　**submit** [səbmít]　　v. 제출하다

04　**complete** [kəmˈpliːt]　　v. 작성하다

05　**curious** [ˈkjʊəriəs]　　a. 호기심이 많은

06　**supervise** [súːpərvàɪz]　　v. 감독하다, 관리하다, 감시하다

07　**typical** [típikəl]　　a. 전형적인, 보통의

08　**exhibition** [ˌeksɪˈbɪʃn]　　n. 전시회

09　**stuff** [stʌf]　　n. 것, 것들

10　**technicality** [tèknəkǽləti]　　n. 전문적인 측면, 전문적인 방법의 사용

11　**remind** [rɪˈmaɪnd]　　v. 상기시키다

12　**awfully** [ɔ́ːfəli]　　ad. 아주, 매우, 몹시

13　**mummy** [mʌ́mi]　　n. 미이라

14　**grasp** [ɡræsp]　　v. 파악하다, 이해하다

15　**briefly** [bríːfli]　　ad. 간단히

16　**underestimate** [ʌ̀ndəréstəméɪt]　　v. 과소평가하다

17　**hectic** [héktɪk]　　a. 정신없이 바쁜

18　**definitely** [ˈdefɪnətli]　　ad. 분명히, 틀림없이

19　**application** [ˌæplɪkéɪʃən]　　n. 지원서, 신청서

20　**flexible** [fléksəbəl]　　a. 융통성 있는

21　**appropriate** [əˈproʊpriət]　　a. 적절한

TEST 3
SET 1-C

구문정리 | 본문 중 중요 구문 정리한 내용입니다. 우선 암기하고 많이 읽으시길 바랍니다.

Community Service at Museum

→ 정답

#	구문	뜻	#	구문	뜻
01	excuse me	실례합니다	31	have a grasp of	~을 이해하다
02	how may I help you?	어떻게 도와드릴까요?	32	have to do	to do 해야만 한다
03	have question regarding	~에 관한 질문이 있다	33	need to do	to do 할 필요가 있다
04	go ahead	계속 하세요	34	all you have to do	너가 해야하는 모든것
05	check with	~에게 문의하다	35	walk around	돌아다니다
06	communoth service	지역 봉사활동	36	answer question	질문에 답하다
07	mind ~ing	~하는 것을 꺼려하다	37	seem easy	쉽게 보이다
08	would like to do	~하고싶다, to do 하는 것을 바라다	38	according to	~에 따르면
09	a great deal of	다량의	39	so far	지금까지
10	background knowledge	배경지식	40	seem like	~처럼 보이다
11	prepare for	~를 준비하다	41	take care of	~을 돌보다 (t)
12	I don't know if~	~인지 아닌지 모르겠다	42	look after	~을 살피다, 돌보다(L)
13	be aware of	~을 알다	43	part time job	시간제 일
14	go on	계속하다	44	daycare center	탁아소
15	know about	~에 대해 알다	45	be glad that	~을 기뻐하다
16	as as	B만큼 A한	46	be help	~에 도움이 되다
17	be familiar with	~와 익숙하다	47	later on	나중에
18	deal with	대처하다	48	want to do	to do 하기를 원하다
19	anything else	그밖에 또 다른	49	get into	(특정한 전문직종에) 들어가다
20	walk A through B	A에게 B를 보여주다	50	fill out application	지원서를 작성하다
21	rather than	~라기 보다는	51	let O do	O를 do 하게 허락하다
22	such as	~와 같은	52	let you know how~	네게 ~하는 방법을 알려주가
23	each other	서로서로	53	as soon as possible	가능한 빨리
24	be interested in	~에 관심이 있다	54	wonder about	~에 대해 궁금해하다
25	stuff like that	그런것들	55	be going to do	to do 할 예정이다
26	I see	알겠다	56	working hours	근무시간
27	be perfect for	~에 안성맞춤이다	57	work out	해결하다;계획해 내다; 운동 하다
28	consist of	~로 구성되다	58	figure out	~을 계산하다
29	remind O that	O에게 that절을 기억나게 하다	59	would like for O to do	O가 to do 하도록 하시겠요?
30	popular with	~에게 인기있는			

VOCABULARY

TEST 3 Set 1 Lecture 1

VOCABULARY

01 **architectural** [àːrkətéktʃərəl] a. 건축의, 건축상의
02 **unique** [juːˈniːk] a. 독특한, 특별한
03 **aesthetically** [esθétikəli] ad. 미적으로, 심미적으로
04 **correlation** [kɔ̀ːrəléiʃən] n. 상호관계, 상관관계
05 **thoroughly** [ˈθʌrəli] ad. 완전히, 철저히
06 **acoustic** [əkúːstiks] n. 음향학, 음향 효과
07 **integral** [íntigrəl] a. 완전한, 필수의
08 **reverberation** [rivə̀ːrbəréiʃən] n. 잔향, 반사
09 **confined** [kənˈfaɪnd] a. 사방이 막힌
10 **interval** [íntərvəl] n. 간격, 기간
11 **quantitative** [kwántətèitiv] a. 양의, 수량적인
12 **indicator** [índikèitər] n. 지표, 지침
13 **suitability** [suːtəbíləti] n. 적합, 적당
14 **optimum** [áptiməm] n. 최적 조건, 최적
15 **maximize** [ˈmæksɪmaɪz] v. 극대화하다
16 **clarity** [klǽrəti] n. 명확함, 분명함
17 **intelligibility** [intèlədʒəbíləti] n. 명료함, 이해할 수 있음
18 **syllable** [síləbəl] n. 음절
19 **audible** [ɔ́ːdəbl] a. 들리는, 들을 수 있는
20 **perceptibility** [pə́ːrseptíbíləti] n. 이해력, 지각
21 **mumble** [mʌ́mbəl] v. 중얼거리다
22 **struggle** [ˈstrʌgl] v (~하기 위해) 싸우다, 분투하다
23 **recital** [rɪˈsaɪtl] n. 발표회, 연주회
24 **precision** [prɪˈsɪʒn] n. 정확성, 정밀성
25 **note** [noʊt] n. 음, 음표
26 **conversely** [kənvə́ːrsli] ad. 거꾸로, 반대로
27 **harmonious** [haːrmóuniəs] a. 조화로운, 화합한

28 **tackle** [ˈtækl] v. (힘든 문제 상황과) 씨름하다
29 **conduct** [kənˈdʌkt] v. (특정한 활동을) 하다
30 **persistence** [pəːrsístəns] n. 고집, 지속
31 **oriental** [ɔ̀ːriéntl] a. 동양의, 동방의
32 **absorbency** [əbsɔ́ːrbensí] n. 흡수력, 흡수성
33 **foam insulation** [foum ìnsəléiʃən] n. 발포단열재
34 **equivalent** [ikwívələnt] a. 동등한
35 **convert** [kənvə́ːrt] v. 전환하다, 바꾸다
36 **acceptable** [əkˈseptəbl] a. 받아들일 수 있는
37 **drape** [dreip] n. 천, 커튼
38 **absorbent** [əbsɔ́ːrbənt] a. 흡수성의
39 **particularly** [pərˈtɪkjələrli] ad. 특히, 특별히
40 **adjust** [əˈdʒʌst] v. 조절하다
41 **preexisting** [prìːigzístiŋ] a. 이전부터 존재하는
42 **limitation** [lìmətéiʃən] n. 한계, 제한
43 **emphasize** [ˈemfəsaɪz] v. (중요성을) 강조하다
44 **grandeur** [grǽndʒər] n. 웅장함, 위엄
45 **dictating** [díkteitiŋ] a. 좌우하는
46 **uninterrupte** [ˌʌnˌɪntəˈrʌptɪd] a. 중단되지 않는, 연속된
47 **available** [əˈveɪləbl] a. 이용할 수 있는, 유효한
48 **ultimately** [ˈʌltɪmətli] ad. 궁극적으로, 결국
49 **dilemma** [dilémə] n. 딜레마, 어려운 문제
50 **attendee** [ˌæten'diː] n. 참석자
51 **uncontrollable** [ˌʌnkənˈtroʊləbl] a. 통제할 수 없는
52 **beforehand** [bɪˈfɔːhænd] ad. 사전에, 미리
53 **occupancy** [ˈɒkjəpənsi] n. 사용
54 **imperfection** [ìmpərfékʃən] n. 결함, 결점

TEST 3

SET 1-L1 구문정리

본문 중 중요 구문 정리한 내용입니다. 우선 읽기하고 많이 읽으시길 바랍니다.

Architectural Acoustics

→ 정답

01	focus on	~에 집중하다
02	make O O.C	O를 O.C로 만들다
03	look at	~을 살피다
04	involve A in B	A를 B에 포함시키다
05	the way it is	그런 방식으로
06	correlation between A and B	A와 B 사이의 관계
07	until recently	최근까지
08	with the importance of	~의 중요성과 함께
09	the field of	~의 분야
10	gain attention	주의를 끌다
11	let's do	~을 하자
12	play a role in	~라는 점에서 역할을 하다
13	not only A but also B	A뿐만 아니라 B도
14	require O to do	O가 to do 하는것을 필요로 하다
15	drop by~	~까지의 감소
16	no longer	더 이상 ~이 아닌
17	define A as B	A를 B로 정의하다
18	not necessarily~	반드시 ~은 아닌
19	depend on	~에 의존하다
20	cause O to do	o가 to do하는 것을 야기하다
21	typically speaking	일반적으로 말해서
22	such as	~와 같은
23	in order to do	to do 하기 위해서
24	result in~	결국 ~이 되다
25	end up ~ing	결국 ing 하게 되다
26	on the other hand	반면에
27	struggle to do	to do 하려고 노력하다
28	enough to do	to do 하기에 충분히
29	let's take a look at	~을 한 번 보자
30	one of the NS	~중 하나
31	consider O to be O.C	O를 O.C라고 간주하다
32	ask O to do	O에게 to do하는 것을 요구하다
33	with persistence	끈질기게
34	for several years	몇 년 동안
35	conduct experiment	실험을 하다
36	after years of	~한 상태의 몇 년 후에
37	present in	~에 존재하는
38	at rate	비율로
39	either A or B	A 또는 B
40	for example	예를 들어
41	equivalent of	~에 상응하는
42	use O to do	O를 to do 하기 위해 사용하다
43	convert A into B	A를 B로 변환하다
44	lecture hall	강당
45	prove to be	to be로 밝혀지다
46	effective in	~라는 점에 있어서 효과적인
47	a lot of	많은
48	result from	~이 원인이다
49	apply A to B	A를 B에 적용하다
50	think about	~에 대해 생각하다
51	in case	경우에
52	suffer from	~로부터 고통 받다
53	focus A on B	A를 B에 집중시키다
54	factor in	~점에서의 요인
55	in general	일반적으로
56	I want something for him to read	의미상 주어(for)
57	travel across	횡단하다
58	die out	자취를 감추다; 멸종하다
59	due to	~때문에
60	the number of	~의 숫자
61	correlate to	~와 관계가 있다
62	with O in mind	O를 염두애 두고
63	it is impossible to do	to do 하는 것은 불가능하다
64	the amount of	~의 양
65	as you can see	보이는 바와 같이
66	show up	나타나다
67	even if	비록 ~일지라도
68	there is no way of	~할 방법이 없다
69	solve a problem	문제를 해결하다
70	at occupancy	사용하여
71	leave room for	~의 여지가 있다
72	many factors involved	관련된 많은 요소들
73	end with	~과 더불어 끝나다

TEST 3 Set 1 Lecture 2

VOCABULARY

01	computer model [kəmpjútər mádl]	n. 컴퓨터 모형
02	simulation [sìmjəléiʃən]	n. 모의실험, 시뮬레이션
03	virtual [vɔ́ːrtʃuəl]	a. 가상의
04	civilization [sìvəlizéiʃən]	n. 문명
05	regarding [rɪˈgɑːdɪŋ]	prep. ~에 관하여
06	life expectancy	n. 기대수명
07	theoretical [θìːərétikəl]	a. 이론상의
08	unexpected [ʌ̀nikspéktid]	a. 예기치않은, 뜻밖의
09	situation [ˌsɪtʃuˈeɪʃn]	n. 상황, 환경
10	decline [dikláin]	v. 감소하다, 쇠퇴하다
11	gathering [gǽðəriŋ]	n. 모임, 뿌리
12	strategically [strətíːdʒikəli]	ad. 전략적으로, 효과적으로
13	cliff [klɪf]	n. 절벽
14	house [hauz]	v. 거처를 제공하다
15	ranch [ræntʃ]	n. 목장
16	resemble [rizémbəl]	v. 유사하다, 닮다
17	straw [strɔː]	n. 밀짚
18	intact [ɪnˈtækt]	a. 온전한, 손상되지 않은
19	complexity [kəmˈpleksəti]	n. 복잡성
20	intricate [íntrəkit]	a. 정교한, 복잡한
21	serpent [sə́ːrpənt]	n. 뱀
22	petroglyph [pétrəglìf]	n. 암각화
23	engraving [ingréiviŋ]	n. 조각
24	peek [piːk]	n. 엿봄
25	artifact [áːrtəfækt]	n. 공예품, 인공물
26	thrive [θraɪv]	v. 번창하다
27	prolong [prouló:ŋ]	v. 장기화하다, 연장하다
28	availability [əvèiləbíləti]	n. 이용 가능성
29	harvest [háːrvist]	n. 추수, 수확
30	sustain [səˈsteɪn]	v. 지탱하다
31	question [ˈkwestʃən]	v. 의문을 갖다
32	archaeologist [àːrkiálədʒist]	n. 고고학자
33	log [lɔːg]	n. 통나무
34	tree ring	n. 나이테
35	inaccuracy [inǽkjurəsi]	n. 부정확, 잘못
36	drought [draut]	n. 가뭄
37	undergo [ˌʌndərˈgoʊ]	v. 겪다
38	shift [ʃɪft]	v. 변화
39	precipitation [prɪˌsɪpɪˈteɪʃn]	n. 강우, 강수량
40	unsure [ˌʌnˈʃʊə(r)]	a. 확신하지 못하는
41	religious [rɪˈlɪdʒəs]	a. 종교의
42	oppose [əˈpoʊz]	v. 반대하다
43	conduct [kənˈdʌkt]	v. (특정한 활동을) 하다
44	consumption [kənˈsʌmpʃn]	n. 소비, 소모
45	settlement [ˈsetlmənt]	n. 정착지
46	correspond [ˌkɔːrəˈspɑːnd]	v. 일치하다, 부합하다
47	plentiful [ˈplentɪfl]	a. 풍부한
48	shrink [ʃrɪŋk]	v. 줄어들다
49	confirm [kənˈfɜːm]	v. 확정하다
50	aspect [ǽspekt]	n. 측면, 양상, 모습

TEST 3
SET1-L2 — Disappearance of Anasazi People

구문정리 | 본문 중 중요 구문 정리한 내용입니다. 우선 암기하고 많이 읽으시길 바랍니다.

→ 정답

No	구문	뜻
01	have you heared of~?	~에 대해 들어본 적 있니?
02	not A but B	A가 아니라 B
03	allow O to do	O가 to do 하는 것을 가능케하다
04	one one's own	스스로
05	look deep into	깊이 살펴보다, 고찰하다
06	enter data	자료를 입력하다
07	what happens to	~에게 무슨일이 일어나다
08	over a certain amount of time	특정 시간 동안
09	point out	지적하다
10	from the past	과거로부터, 과거의
11	for instance	예를 들어
12	start ~ing	~ing 하는 것을 시작하다
13	spread out	퍼지다
14	it is important to do	to do 하는 것은 중요하다
15	change in	~라는 점에서의 변화
16	make A of B	A를 B로 구성하다
17	give A B	A에게 B를 주다
18	use O to do	O를 to do 하기 위해 사용하다
19	such as	~와 같은
20	around seven hundred years ago	대략 700년 전에
21	in the area of	~의 지역에서
22	know A as B	A를 B로 알다
23	be well-known for	~로 잘 알려져 있다
24	look like	~할 것 같다, ~인 것 처럼 보이다
25	place A above B	A를 B위에 두다
26	consist of	~로 구성되다
27	climb a ladder	사다리를 올라가다
28	appear to be	-인것처럼 보이다
29	a mixture of	~의 혼합물
30	for sure	확실히
31	look at	~를 보다, 살피다
32	be able to do	to do 할 수 있다
33	ask for	~을 구하다, 찾다
34	leave behind	남겨두다
35	because of	~때문에
36	during the period	기간 동안
37	decrease in	~점에서의 감소
38	seem like	~처럼 보이다
39	continue to do	to do 하는 것을 계속하다
40	sufficient for	~에 충분한
41	begin to do	to do 하는 것을 시작하다
42	as you know	너가 알다시피
43	cut down	베다, 쓰러뜨리다
44	see A as B	A를 B로 간주하다, 보다
45	instead of	~대신에
46	shift in	~라는 점에서의 변화
47	help do	do 하는 것을 돕다
48	as expected	예상된대로
49	may have done	~했을지도 모른다
50	lead O to do	O가 to do 하도록 이끌다
51	cause O to do	O가 to do하는것을 야기하다
52	leave O O.C	O를 O.C인 상태로 남기다
53	enough to do	to do 할만큼 충분히
54	base A on B	A를 B에 근거하다
55	could have been	~이었을지도 모른다 (추측)
56	figure out	~을 이해하다
57	put in	~을 집어넣다
58	know A about B	B에 대한 A를 알다
59	correspond to	~에 일치하다, 들어맞다
60	correlate with	~와 관련이 있다
61	grow in size	크기가 커지다
62	over time	시간이 지날수록
63	decrease to	~로 감소하다
64	in reality	사실은
65	answer the question	질문에 답하다
66	show A B	A에게 B를 보여주다
67	keep ~ing	~ing 하는것을 계속 하다
68	leave O to do	O가 to do 하도록 남겨두다
69	disappear from	~에서 사라지다

TEST 3 Set 2 Conversation

VOCABULARY

01	**appreciation** [əpriːʃiéiʃən]	n. 감상		15	**contradictory** [kàntrədíktəri]	a. 모순되는
02	**genre** [ʒáːnrə]	n. 장르		16	**mandatory** [mǽndətɔ̀ːri]	a. 의무적인, 강제적인
03	**frankly** [frǽŋkli]	ad. 솔직히 말하면, 솔직히		17	**charity** [tʃǽrəti]	n. 자선, 자애, 구호
04	**procrastinate** [proukrǽstənèit]	v. 꾸물거리다		18	**incorporate** [inkɔ́ːrpərèit]	v. 결합하다, 통합하다
05	**swamped** [swamp]	a. 일이 많은, 압도하는		19	**psychology** [saikálədʒi]	n. 심리학
06	**rough-draft**	n. 초안		20	**symposium** [simpóuziəm]	n. 심포지엄
07	**capture** [kǽptʃər]	v. 정확히 포착하다, 담아내다		21	**infant** [ˈɪnfənt]	n. 유아
08	**tempo** [témpou]	n. 박자		22	**aspect** [ǽspekt]	n. 측면
09	**wording** [wə́ːrdiŋ]	n. 가사		23	**pregnancy** [prégnənsi]	v. 임신
10	**spread** [spred]	n. 확산, 전파		24	**affect** [əfékt]	v. 영향을 미치다
11	**fascinate** [fǽsənèit]	v. 매료시키다		25	**fetus** [fíːtəs]	n. 태아
12	**technicality** [tèknəkǽləti]	n. 전문어, 전문적 성질		26	**cover** [ˈkʌvə(r)]	v. 돈을 대다
13	**slang** [slæŋ]	n. 속어, 은어		27	**accommodation** [əkámədèiʃən]	n. 숙박 시설, 숙소
14	**oxymoron** [àksimɔ́ːran]	n. 모순어법		28	**control group**	n. 제어집단, 대조군

TEST 3
SET2-C

구문정리 | 본문 중 중요 구문 정리한 내용입니다. 우선 암기하고 많이 읽으시길 바랍니다.

Psycological Impact of Music

→ 정답

#	구문	뜻
01	be in a class	수업듣다
02	I am here about	~에 관해서 말하러 왔다 (= I am here to talk about)
03	by now	지금쯤; 지금까지
04	have trouble with	~과 더불어 어려움이 겪다
05	be caught up with	~에 휩쓸리다, 열중하다
06	decide on	~에 대해 결정하다
07	let alone	말할 필요도 없이
08	must have been	~이어왔음이 틀림없다
09	be swamped	격무에 시달리다; 잠기다
10	why don't you~	~하는게 어때
11	try to do	to do 하는 것을 시도하다
12	think about	~에 대해 생각하다
13	think backwards	반대로 생각해보다
14	instead of	~대신에
15	I don't follow	이해하지 못하다
16	make a draft	얼추 잡다; 기안작성하다
17	at a certain time	특정한 시간에
18	best fit	가장 적합하다
19	be into	~에 관심이 많다, 푹 빠지다
20	need to do	to do 할 필요가 있다
21	listen to	~을 듣다
22	for example	예를 들어
23	need for	~에 대한 요구
24	be eager to do	to do 하기를 열망하다
25	read about	~에 대해 읽다
26	for a while	한동안; 잠시동안
27	keep in mind	명심하다
28	releate A to B	A를 B와 연관시키다
29	make up	구성하다
30	such as	예를 들어, ~와 같은
31	write about	~에 대해 쓰다
32	come into being	존재하기 시작하다
33	get it	이해하다
34	incorporate A into B	A를 B에 통합시키다
35	say...	예를들면..(구어체, 라이팅에선금지)
36	mind ~ing	~를 꺼리다
37	help A out with B	A를 B와 함께 도와주다
38	be up for	참여하다, 참가하다
39	effect on	~에 대한 효과
40	be okay with	~에 대해 괜찮다
41	research on	~에 대한 조사
42	want to do	to do 하고 싶다
43	be a part of	참가하다, 일원이 되다
44	listen to	~을 듣다(무조건 자동사)
45	lead to	야기하다, ~로 이어지다
46	have to do	to do 해야 한다
47	how about	~는 어때?
48	a couple of	몇몇의
49	bring O along	O를 데리고 오다
50	cover expense for	~에 대한 비용을 지불하다
51	talk to	~에게 말하다
52	I don't know if	~ 인지 아닌지 모르다
53	be of help	도움이 되다
54	conduct project	프로젝트를 실행하다, 이끌다
55	use A as B	A를 B로서 사용하다
56	control group	대조군(對照群) (동일 실험에서 실험 요건을 가하지 않은 그룹)
57	be able to do	to do 할 수 있다
58	the head of	~의 장
59	that'd be great	좋을거야
60	for a nice break	좋은 휴식을 위해

TEST 3 Set 2 Lecture 1

VOCABULARY

01 **instrument** [ínstrəmənt] n. 악기
02 **genre** ['ʒɑːnrə] n. 장르
03 **connection** [kənékʃən] n. 연결, 관련
04 **versatile** [vɔ́ːrsətl] a. 만능의, 다재다능한
05 **influential** [ìnfluénʃəl] a. 영향력 있는, 영향을 미치는
06 **harmony** ['hɑːməni] n. 조화
07 **motivate** [móutəvèit] v. 자극하다, 동기 부여하다
08 **belove** [bilʌv] v. ~을 사랑하다
09 **acoustic** [əˈkuːstɪk] a. 음향의
10 **incentive** [inséntiv] n. (~하는 것에 대한) 이점
11 **amplify** [ǽmpləfài] v. 증폭하다, 확대하다
12 **ensemble** [ɑːnsɑ́ːmbəl] n. 앙상블, 합주
13 **amidst** [əmìdst] prep. 중에
14 **brass** [bræs] n. 금관악기
15 **phonograph** [fóunəgræf] n. 축음기
16 **disappear** [dìsəpíər] v. 사라지다
17 **innovative** [ínouvèitiv] a. 혁신적인
18 **tinker** [tíŋkər] v. 만지작거리다
19 **magnet** ['mægnət] n. 자석
20 **string** [striŋ] n. 줄
21 **strength** [streŋθ] n. 힘
22 **vibration** [vaibréiʃən] n. 진동
23 **digitize** [dídʒitàiz] v. 디지털화하다
24 **device** [diváis] n. 장치, 도구
25 **horseshoe** [ˈhɔːrʃ] n. 말발굽 모양, 편자

26 **incorporate** [inkɔ́ːrpərèit] v. 통합하다
27 **instant** [ˈɪnstənt] a. 즉각적인
28 **strum** [strʌm] v. (악기를) 퉁기다
29 **sideway** [sáidwèi] n. 옆길, 샛길
30 **implement** [ímpləmənt] v. 시행하다
31 **commercialize** [kəmɔ́ːrʃəlàiz] v. 상업화하다
32 **innovative** [ínouvèitiv] a. 혁신적인
33 **switch** [swɪtʃ] v. 전환하다, 바뀌다
34 **isolate** [ˈaɪsəleɪt] v. 격리하다, 고립시키다
35 **fuzzy** [fʌ́zi] a. 흐릿한, 명확하지 않은
36 **crisp** [krisp] a. 선명한
37 **loop** [luːp] n. 고리
38 **prominent** [prámənənt] a. 저명한, 눈에 띄는
39 **hollow** [hálou] a. 텅 빈
40 **diminish** [dəmíniʃ] v. 줄이다
41 **resistant** [rɪˈzɪstənt] a. 저항력 있는, ~에 잘 견디는
42 **maintain** [meɪnˈteɪn] v. 유지하다
43 **note** [nout] n. 음조
44 **dissipate** [dísəpèit] v. 분산시키다
45 **distortion** [distɔ́ːrʃən] n. 왜곡, 찌그러짐
46 **satisfy** [ˈsætɪsfaɪ] v. 만족시키다
47 **jam** [dʒæm] v. 밀어 넣다
48 **evolution** [èvəlúːʃən] n. 진화, 발전
49 **adaptation** [ædæptéiʃən] n. 적응
50 **manufacturer** [ˌmænjuˈfæktʃərə(r)] n. 제조, 생산

TEST 3
SET2-L1
Invention of Electric Guitar

구문정리 | 본문 중 중요 구문 정리한 내용입니다. 우선 암기하고 많이 읽으시길 바랍니다.

→ 정답

01	move on to	~로 이동하다
02	have in common	공통으로 가지다
03	in harmony with	~와 조화롭게
04	on one's own	혼자서, 단독적으로
05	look at	~을 보다
06	go through	겪다
07	a lot of	많은
08	give A B	A에게 B를 주다
09	a range of	~범위의
10	experiment with	~을 실험하다
11	in the 1920s	1920s 시대에 (in 시간)
12	along with	~와 함께
13	need to do	~할 필요가 있다
14	such as	~와 같은
15	around this time	그 시간 쯔음에
16	begin ~ing	~하는것을 시작하다 (B)
17	tinker with	서투르게 손대다
18	as well	또한
19	of the time	당시의
20	convert A to B	A를 B로 변환시키다
21	depend on	~에 의존하다
22	call A B	A를 B로 부르다
23	incorporate A into B	A를 B에 통합시키다
24	start ~ing	~하는 것을 시작하다 (S)
25	get praise from	~로부터 찬사를 얻다
26	six years later	6년 뒤
27	use O to do	O를 ~하는데 사용하다
28	the first to do	~하는데 첫번째
29	as well as	~뿐만 아니라
30	switch over to	~로 바꾸다, 돌리다
31	for that matter	그 점에 대해서는
32	far from	~로부터 먼
33	at the time	당시에
34	rather than	~보다는, ~대신에
35	isolate A from B	A를 B로부터 떼어두다
36	act as	~로서 역할을 하다
37	sort of	일종의 ;어느정도
38	get done	~되어가다
39	cause O to do	O가 to do 하는것을 야기하다
40	fix problem	문제들을 고치다; 해결하다
41	go to work	착수하다, 일하기 시작하다
42	construct A of B	A를 B로 구성하다
43	have an advantage over~	~이상의 장점을 가지다
34	resistant to	~에 대해 저항하는
35	last long	오래 지속하다
36	the rest of	~의 나머지
37	seem like	~처럼 보이다
38	try to do	~하는것을 시도하다
39	open up	열다, 마음을 트다
40	until after	~한 후까지
41	due to	~때문에
42	take advantage of	이용하다
43	for example	예를 들어
44	select which to use	어떤것을 쓸지 선택하다
45	at the same time	동시에
46	become popular	유명해지다
47	tie A with B	A를 b로 묶다
48	experiment with	~을 가지고하는 실험
49	lead to	~를 야기하다

TEST 3 Set 2 Lecture 2

VOCABULARY

01 **phenomenon** [finámənàn] n. 현상
02 **renowned** [rináund] a. 명성 있는, 유명한
03 **atypically** [eitípikəly] ad. 비전형적으로, 대표적 예가 아닌
04 **eyewitness** [áiwìtnis] n. 목격자, 증인
05 **account** [əkáunt] n. 설명, 증언
06 **description** [dɪˈskrɪpʃn] n. 기술, 묘사
07 **credible** [krédəbəl] a. 신용할 수 있는
08 **retell** [ri:tél] v. 내용을 다시 말하다
09 **intuition** [ìntjuíʃən] n. 직관, 통찰
10 **reproducible** [rì:prədjú:səbəl] a. 재생할 수 있는
11 **experimental** [ikspèrəméntl] a. 실험의, 시험적인
12 **verifiable** [vérəfàiəbəl] a. 입증할 수 있는
13 **extra-terrestrials** [ékstrə-təréstriəl] n. 지구 밖의 생물, 우주인(ET)
14 **hypothetical** [hàipəθétikəl] a. 가설상의, 가설의
15 **luminous** [lú:mənəs] a. 야광의, 어둠에서 빛나는
16 **spherical** [sférikəl] a. 둥근, 구체의
17 **electrical** [iléktrikəl] a. 전기의
18 **horizontally** [hɔ̀:rəzántəli] ad. 수평으로
19 **explode** [ɪkˈsploud] v. 폭발하다
20 **sulfurous** [sʌ́lfərəs] a. 유황의, 노란
21 **property** [prápərti] n. (사물의) 특성
22 **clear-cut** [klíərkʌ́t] a. 명쾌한, 딱 떨어지는
23 **diameter** [daiǽmitər] n. 지름
24 **define** [dɪˈfaɪn] v. 정의하다
25 **promising** [prámisiŋ] a. 가망 있는, 기대할 수 있는
26 **recreate** [rékrièit] v. 재생하다, 재창조하다
27 **plasma** [plǽzmə] n. 플라스마(고도로 이온화된 기체)
28 **resemble** [rɪˈzembl] v. 닮다, 비슷하다

29 **stable** [stéibl] a. 안정된
30 **current** [kə́:rənt] n. 전류
31 **electrode** [iléktroud] n. 전극
32 **evaporate** [ivǽpərèit] v. 증발하다
33 **oval** [óuvəl] a. 타원형의
34 **previous** [ˈpriːviəs] a. 이전의
35 **ignite** [ignáit] v. 불을 붙이다
36 **characteristically** [kæ̀riktərístikəli] ad. 특징적으로
37 **fraction** [frǽkʃən] n. 아주 소량, 단편
38 **hypothesis** [haipáθəsis] n. 가설, 가정
39 **plausible** [plɔ́:zəbəl] a. 그럴듯한
40 **particle** [pá:rtikl] n. 입자, 소립자
41 **element** [ˈeləmənt] n. 요소, 성분
42 **electronics** [ilèktrániks] n. 전자기기
43 **vapor** [véipər] n. 증기
44 **electrical charge** [ɪlektrɪkəl tʃɑːrd] n. 전하
45 **glow** [glou] v. 빛을 내다
46 **allied** [əlaɪd] a. 동맹한, 연합한
47 **trail** [treil] v. 추적하다, 따라가다
48 **assume** [əˈsuːm] v. 추정하다
49 **identical** [aidéntikəl] a. 동일한
50 **molecule** [máləkjùːl] n. 분자
51 **hypothesize** [haipáθəsàiz] v. 가설을 세우다
52 **altitude** [ǽltətjùːd] n. 고도, 높이
53 **spot** [spat] v. ~을 발견하다
54 **unpredictable** [ʌ̀nprɪdíktəbəl] a. 예측할 수 없는
55 **infrequent** [infríːkwənt] a. 드물게 일어나는, 많지 않은

TEST 3
SET2-L2
Examination on Ball Lightning

본문 중 중요 구문 정리한 내용입니다. 우선 암기하고 많이 읽으시길 바랍니다.

→ 정답

01	tell A B	A에게 B를 말하다
02	not at all	전혀 ~아니다
03	call A B	A를 B라고 부르다
04	there is no evidence of	~의 증거가 없다
05	except for	~을 제외하고
06	eyewitness account	목격담, 목격자의 증언
07	what is more is that	더한것은 that절이다
08	claim to do	to do라는것을 주장하다
09	be different from	~로부터 다르다
10	one another	서로서로
11	trust O to do	O가 to do하다는것을 믿다, 신뢰하다
12	the lack of	~의 부족
13	blame A on B	B를 A의 탓으로 돌리다
14	consider A B	A를 B라고 여기다
15	go further	더 나아가다
16	according to	~에 따르면
17	be reported to do	to do 하다고 전해지다
18	pass through	통과하다
19	at the end of	~의 말기에
20	His dress is that of a gentleman, but his manners are those of a clown	That those 문장
21	for example	예를 들어
22	in diameter	지름이 (~인)
23	knock down	부수다
24	difficulty in ~ing	~ing 하는데 있어서의 어려움
25	result in	~(결과)을 야기하다
26	try to do	to do 하려고 시도하다
27	one of the first	처음중 하나
28	carry out experiment	실험을 수행하다
29	in 2016	2016년에
30	team led by	~에 의해 이끌어진 팀
31	for those of you who don't know	~를 모르는 사람들을 위해서
32	be familiar with	~와 친숙하다
33	come after	~를 뒤쫓다
34	fill A with B	A를 B로 채우다
35	gain energy	에너지를 얻다
36	enough to do	to do 할만큼 충분한
37	in shape	~한 모양으로
38	what is interesting is that	흥미로운 점은 that절이다
39	a piece of paper	종이 한 장
40	rise into the sky	하늘로 솟아 오르다
41	want to do	to do 하는 것을 원하다
42	lots of	많은
43	require O to do	O가 to do 하는 것을 요구하다
44	figure out	알아내다, 밝혀내다
45	come up with	생각해내다
46	at the university of~	~의 대학에서
47	in the sky	하늘에서
48	use A for B	A를 B때문에 사용하다
49	turn into	~으로 변하다
50	attract A to B	A를 B로 이끌다
51	each other	서로서로
52	bind together into shape~	~한 모양으로 묶다
53	react with	~에 반응하다
54	take place	일어나다, 발생하다
55	as long as	~하는 한; 동안
56	There is a problem with	~와 관련된 문제가있다
57	as well	또한
58	seem to do	to do 하는 것처럼 보이다
59	at night	밤에
60	lead to the conclusion that	~라는 결론으로 이끌다
61	give rise to	~이 생기게 하다, 발생하다
62	hypothesize O to do	O가 to do하다고 가설하다
63	it is hard to do	to do 하는 것은 어렵다
64	famous for	~로 유명한
65	wait for O to do	O가 to do 하기를 기다리다

TEST 4 Set 1 Conversation

VOCABULARY

01	**tutor** [tjú:tər]	n. 지도교사, 강사		14	**graduate** [grǽdʒuət]	v. 졸업하다
02	**pursue** [pərsú:]	v. 추구하다, 추진하다		15	**improve** [imprú:v]	v. 개선하다, 향상시키다
03	**portion** [pɔ́:rʃən]	n. 부분, 일부		16	**requirement** [rikwáiərmənt]	n. 조건
04	**reasonable** [rí:zənəbl]	a. 타당한, 합리적인		17	**reasonable** [rí:zənəbl]	a. 합리적인
05	**strenuous** [strénjuəs]	a. 격렬한, 힘든		18	**formal** [fɔ́:rməl]	a. 공식적인, 정식의
06	**perseverance** [pə̀:rsəvíərəns]	n. 인내심		19	**training** [tréiniŋ]	n. 훈련
07	**ultimately** [Λltəmətli]	ad. 궁극적으로, 최종적으로		20	**attention** [əténʃən]	n. 관심
08	**calculus** [kǽlkjuləs]	n. 미적분		21	**advice** [ædváis]	n. 조언, 충고
09	**assignment** [əsáinmənt]	n. 연구 과제, 숙제		22	**enhance** [inhǽns]	v. 향상하다, 개선시키다
10	**literature** [lítərətʃər]	n. 문학		23	**unorganized** [Λnɔ́:rgənàizd]	a. 체계적이지 않은
11	**organize** [ɔ́:rgənàiz]	v. 정리하다		24	**flaw** [flɔ:]	n. 결점
12	**impressed** [im|prest]	a. 감명받은, 인상받은		25	**guide** [gaid]	v. 지도하다
13	**recruit** [rikrú:t]	v. 채용하다, 모집하다		26	**appreciate** [əprí:ʃièit]	v. 감사하다, 고마워하다

TEST 4
SET 1-C
Tutoring

본문 중 중요 구문 정리한 내용입니다. 우선 암기하고 많이 읽으시길 바랍니다.

→ 정답

#	구문	뜻	#	구문	뜻
01	listen to	~을 듣다	29	I want to be	나는 ~이길 바란다
02	tell A B	A에게 B를 말하다	30	work in a lab	연구실에서 일하다
03	look for	찾다	31	save life	생명을 구하다
04	this morning	오늘 아침	32	sound like	~처럼 들리다
05	how have you been?	어떻게 지냈니?	33	formal training	정규(정식) 교육
06	come in	들어오다	34	take a course	강의를 듣다
07	take a seat	앉다	35	work with	~와 함께 일하다
08	be swamped with	~로 바쁘다	36	for a while	잠시
09	quite a while	꽤 오랫동안	37	start ~ing	~ing 하는것을 시작하다
10	go through	검토하다, 살펴보다	38	on one's own	혼자, 스스로
11	be impressed by	~에 의해 감명받다	39	get credit	학점을 취득하다(따다)
12	set up A for B	A를 B를 위해 세우다	40	count toward	포함되다
13	need help with	~와 더불어 도움이 필요하다	41	grab attention	주의를 끌다
14	half of	~의 절반	42	give A B	A에게 B를 주다
15	need to do	to do 할 필요가 있다	43	accept offer	제안을 받아들이다
16	as quickly as possible	가능한 빨리	44	when it comes to	~에 관한
17	want O to do	O가 to do 하기를 원하다	45	take perseverance	인내심을 갖다
18	take a spot	자리를 차지하다	46	keep in mind	명심하다
19	what would I do?	제가 무엇을 해야 할까요?	47	way to do	to do 하는 방법
20	as simple as it sounds	들리는 것만큼 단순한	48	most of the time	대부분의 시간
21	teach A B	A에게 B를 가르치다	49	what do you do	무엇을 하겠습니까?; 직업이 무엇 입니까?
22	writing skill	문장력, 글솜씨	50	need to fix	고칠 필요가 있다
23	help A with B	A를 B와 관련된 일로 돕다	51	ask A B	A에게 B를 요구하다
24	take a class	수업을 듣다	52	help O do	O가 do 하는 것을 돕다
25	meet the requirement	요건을 충족하다	53	put A down on the list	명단에 A를 적다
26	graduation requirement	졸업요건	54	convince O to do	O 가 to do 할 것을 설득하다, 납득 시키다
27	want to do	to do 하기를 원하다	55	take a job	직업을 갖다
28	different from	~와 다른	56	thank A for B	A에게 B에 대해 감사해 하다

TEST 4 Set 1 Lecture 1

VOCABULARY

01	**feasible** [fíːzəbl]	a. 실현 가능한		38	**consider** [kənsídər]	v. 여기다, 간주하다
02	**detrimental** [dètrəméntl]	a. 해로운		39	**allowable** [əláuəbl]	a. 허락할 수 있는
03	**catastrophic** [kætəstráfik]	a. 재앙적인		40	**maximum** [mǽksəməm]	n. 최대
04	**emission** [imíʃən]	n. 배출, 방출		41	**occur** [əkɔ́ːr]	v. 발생하다, 일어나다
05	**numerous** [njúːmərəs]	a. 무수한		42	**prevent** [privént]	v. 막다, 방지하다
06	**stride** [straid]	n. 진전, 보폭		43	**continually** [kəntínjuəli]	ad. 계속해서, 지속적으로
07	**enormous** [inɔ́ːrməs]	a. 거대한		44	**limit** [límit]	n. 제한, 한도
08	**combustion** [kəmbʌ́stʃən]	n. 연소		45	**suitable** [súːtəbl]	a. 적합한, 적절한
09	**nitrogen** [náitrədʒən]	n. 질소		46	**solution** [səlúːʃən]	n. 해결책
10	**component** [kəmpóunənt]	n. 구성물질, 요소		47	**production** [prədʌ́kʃən]	n. 생산
11	**contribute** [kəntríbjuːt]	v. 기여하다, 일조하다		48	**reduced** [ridjúːst]	a. 축소된, 절감된
12	**isolate** [áisəlèit]	v. 분리시키다, 단절시키다		49	**major** [méidʒər]	a. 주요한
13	**generate** [dʒénərèit]	v. 생성하다		50	**focus** [fóukəs]	v. 집중하다
14	**drawback** [drɔ'bæˌk]	n. 단점, 결점		51	**advanced** [ædvǽnst]	a. 선진의, 진보한
15	**aspect** [ǽspekt]	n. 국면, 양상		52	**storage** [stɔ́ːridʒ]	n. 저장, 보관, 비축
16	**speculate** [spékjulèit]	v. 추측하다		53	**imply** [implái]	v. 암시하다, 함축하다
17	**flue** [fluː]	n. 연통, 관		54	**collect** [kəlékt]	v. 모으다, 수집하다
18	**saturate** [sǽtʃərèit]	v. 포화시키다, 채우다		55	**technical** [téknikəl]	a. 기술의, 전문의
19	**subsequently** [sʌ́bsikwəntli]	ad. 이어서		56	**advantage** [ædvǽntidʒ]	n. 이점
20	**transport** [trænspɔ́ːrt]	v. 운반하다, 이송하다		57	**separate** [sépərèit]	v. 분리하다
21	**dispose** [dispóuz]	v. 처리하다, 버리다		58	**bind** [baind]	v. 결합하다
22	**emerge** [imɔ́ːrdʒ]	v. 나오다, 떠오르다		59	**trap** [træp]	v. 가두다
23	**absorbent** [æbsɔ́ːrbənt]	a. 흡수하는, 흡착의		60	**underground** [ə'ndərgrauˌnd]	a. 지하의
24	**implement** [ímpləmənt]	v. 수행하다, 실현시키다		61	**equipment** [ikwípmənt]	n. 장비, 기기
25	**retrofit** [re'troufiˌt]	v. 장치, 장비들을 개량하다, 개선하다		62	**machinery** [məʃíːnəri]	n. 기계
26	**convert** [kənvɔ́ːrt]	v. 전환하다		63	**efficient** [ifíʃənt]	a. 효율적인, 효과적
27	**hydrogen** [háidrədʒən]	n. 수소		64	**securely** [sikjúərli]	ad. 확실하게, 안정적으로
28	**leakage** [líːkidʒ]	n. 유출, 누출		65	**remain** [riméin]	v. 남다, 머무르다
29	**enhance** [inhǽns]	v. 강화시키다, 향상시키다		66	**construction** [kənstrʌ́kʃən]	n. 건설, 공사
30	**specifically** [spisífikəli]	ad. 특별히, 구체적으로		67	**completion** [kəmplíːʃən]	n. 완성, 완공
31	**approach** [əpróutʃ]	v. 접근하다		68	**deadline** [de'dlaiˌn]	n. 마감일, 최종기한
32	**irrefutable** [irifjúːtəbl]	ad. 반박할 수 없는		69	**effectiveness** [iféktivnis]	n. 효율성
33	**awareness** [əwéərnis]	n. 인식, 자각		70	**split** [split]	v. 나누다, 쪼개다
34	**discussion** [diskʌ́ʃən]	n. 논의, 토론		71	**waste** [weist]	v. 낭비하다
35	**remarkable** [rimɑ́ːrkəbl]	ad. 놀라운, 주목할 만한		72	**primarily** [praimérəli]	ad. 우선
36	**developed** [divéləpt]	a. 선진의		73	**encourage** [inkɔ́ːridʒ]	v. 격려하다, 장려하다
37	**mention** [ménʃən]	v. 언급하다, 이야기하다		74	**urgent** [ɔ́ːrdʒənt]	a. 긴급한, 긴박한

TEST 4
SET1-L1
구문정리 | 본문 중 중요 구문 정리한 내용입니다. 우선 암기하고 많이 읽으시길 바랍니다.

Global Temperatures

→ 정답

01	listen to	~을 들어보자		43	far more developed	훨씬 더 발전된
02	earth science	지구과학		44	ready to do	to do할 준비가된
03	discussion on	~에 대한 논의 (토론)		45	put A into use	A를 사용하다
04	I'd like to do	to do 하고 싶다		46	right away	곧바로, 즉시
05	last time	지난 시간에		47	take a look at	~을 보다
06	effect on	~에 대한 효과		48	take place	발생하다
07	at a rate	~의 속도로		49	convert A into B	A를 B로 변환하다
08	go beyond	~을 넘어서다		50	allow O to do	O가 to do 하는 것을 허락하다
09	consider A (to be) B	A를 B로 간주하다		51	release of A into B	A의 B로의 방출
10	within around 10 years	약 10년 이내에		52	the same as	~와 같은
11	be about to do	막 to do 하려는 참이다		53	transport A to B	A를 B로 수송하다
12	solution to	~에 대한 해결책		54	for thousands of years	수천년 동안
13	prevent O from ~ing	O가 ~ing 하는 것을 막다		55	leakage problem	유출 문제
14	past the limit	한계를 넘어		56	fit for~	~에 알맞은; 적임인
15	keep O O.C	O를 O.C상태로 유지하다		57	at present	현재
16	under control	~의 통제 하에		58	suffer from	~로 고통받다
17	there has been	~이 있어왔다		59	make O do	O가 do 하게 하다
18	an enormous amount of	엄청 많은 양의		60	need to do	to do 할 필요가 있다
19	solution to the problem	문제에 대한 해결		61	in many ways	다양한 방법으로
20	make a stride	진전을 만들다		62	far less	훨씬 덜
21	instead of ~ing	~하는것 대신에		63	take O to do	O가 ~하는데 시간이 걸리다
22	in the process	~의 과정에서		64	prior to	~ 이전에
23	by doing so	~함으로서		65	in your opinion	너의 의견은
24	contribute to	~에 기여하다		66	prefer A to B	A를 B보다 선호하다
25	increase in	~라는 점에서의 증가		67	key factor	주요 요소
26	focus on	~에 집중하다		68	make a move	시작하다
27	power plant	발전소		69	the 비교급, the 비교급	~할수록 ~하다
28	come into play	작동하기 시작하다		70	regardless of	~와 관계없이
29	separate A from B	A를 B로부터 분리하다		71	as of now	현재로서는
30	pass through	빠져 나가다, 지나가다		72	on the other hand	다른 한편으로는
31	go through	겪다		73	add A to B	A를 B에 추가하다
32	chemical solution	화학 용액		74	start ~ing	~하는 것을 시작하다
33	bind A with B	A를 B와 묶다		75	both of them	둘 다
34	out of	from		76	be going to do	to do 할 예정이다
35	go deep into	~에 깊이 파고들다		77	risk ~ing	~ing 하는 위험을 무릅쓰다
36	along with	~와 함께, 따라		78	miss the deadline	마감일을 못 맞추다
37	not only A (but) also B	A뿐 아니라 B 또한		79	won't do any good	도움이 되지 않다
38	huge amount of	많은 양의		80	waste time ~ing	~ing 하는데 시간을 소비하다
39	economic burden	경제적 부담		81	encourage O to do	O가 to do 하도록 장려하다
40	necessary for	~을 위해 필요한		82	look into	~을 살피다
41	first of all	첫번째로, 무엇보다		83	as ~ as possible	가능한 ~하게
42	compare A to B	A와 B를 비교하다				

TEST 4 Set 1 Lecture 2
VOCABULARY

01	fundamental [fʌndəméntl]	a. 기본적인, 근본적인
02	root [ru:t]	n. 뿌리
03	mythology [miθάlədʒi]	n. 신화
04	parallel [pǽrəlèl]	n. 유사점, 유사물
05	convincing [kənvínsiŋ]	a. 믿을 수 있는, 설득력 있는
06	tangible [tǽndʒəbl]	a. 명백한, 실재하는
07	evidence [évədəns]	n. 증거, 근거
08	belief [bilí:f]	n. 믿음, 신념
09	era [íərə, érə]	n. 시대
10	sculpture [skʌ́lptʃər]	n. 조각품
11	statue [stǽtʃu:]	n. 동상, 조각상
12	compatible [kəmpǽtəbl]	a. 적합한, 양립할 수 있는
13	the latter [lǽtər]	n. 후자, 마지막
14	monochromatic [mὰnəkroumǽtik]	adj. 단색의
15	impact [ímpækt]	n. 영향
16	rediscover [rì:diskʌ́vər]	v. 다시 발견하다,
17	depict [dipíkt]	v. 표현하다, 묘사하다, 그리다
18	aesthetic [esθétik]	a. 미학의, 미(美)의
19	perfection [pərfékʃən]	n. 완벽, 완전
20	ancient [éinʃənt]	a. 고대의, 오래된
21	strive [straiv]	v. 노력하다
22	emulate [émjulèit]	v. 모방하다
23	distinctive [distíŋktiv]	a. 독특한, 특유의
24	characteristic [kæriktərístik]	n. 특성
25	coloration [kʌ̀ləréiʃən]	n. 채색
26	influence [ínfluəns]	v. ~에 영향을 주다
27	significant [signífikənt]	a. 중요한, 상당한
28	uniformly [jú:nəfɔ̀:rmli]	ad. 한결같이, 균일하게
29	contravene [kὰntrəví:n]	v. 위반하다
30	perspective [pərspéktiv]	n. 관점, 시각
31	standard [stǽndərd]	n. 기준, 표준
32	contemporary [kəntémpərèri]	a. 동시대의
33	belief [bilí:f]	n. 신념, 믿음
34	inaccurate [inǽkjərit]	a. 정확하지 않은, 틀린
35	archaeologist [ὰ:rkiάlədʒist]	n. 고고학자
36	subtle [sʌ́tl]	a. 미묘한, 미세한
37	polychromatic [pὰlikroumǽtik]	a. 다색의
38	deteriorate	v. 악화되다
39	vigorously [vígərəsli]	ad. 정력적으로, 강하게
40	scrub [skrʌb]	v. 문지르다
41	advent [ǽdvent]	n. 출현, 등장
42	execute [éksikjù:t]	v. 집행하다
43	formerly [fɔ́:rmərli]	ad. 이전에, 원래는
44	efficient [ifíʃənt]	a. 효율적인
45	particular [pərtíkjulər]	a. 특정한
46	fluoresce [fluərés]	v. 형광을 발하다
47	principle [prínsəpl]	n. 원칙, 원리
48	interpretation [intə̀:rprətéiʃən]	n. 해석, 이해
49	intention [inténʃən]	n. 의도, 의향
50	accentuate [ækséntʃuèit]	v. 강조하다
51	compelling [kəmpéliŋ]	a. 설득력있는, 강제적인
52	symbolize [símbəlàiz]	v. 상징하다, 나타내다
53	invincibility [invìnsəbíləti]	n. 무적, 불패
54	patriotism [péitriətìzm]	n. 애국심, 애국
55	honor [άnər]	n. 경의, 명예, 영광
56	heroism [hérouìzm]	n. 영웅주의, 영웅심
57	founder [fáundər]	n. 창시자, 설립자
58	clarify [klǽrəfài]	v. 명백히하다, 명확히하다
59	imperator [ìmpərά:tər]	n. 황제
60	commander [kəmǽndər]	n. 사령관, 지휘관
61	observe [əbzɔ́:rv]	v. 관찰하다, (법을)준수하다
62	military [mílitèri]	a. 군대의, 군의
63	victorious [viktɔ́:riəs]	a. 승리의, 승리를 거둔
64	thoroughly [θə́:rouli]	ad. 완벽하게, 철저하게, 세세히
65	abundant [əbʌ́ndənt]	a. 풍부한, 많은
66	associate [əsóuʃièit]	v. 연상하다, 관계시키다
67	pigment [pígmənt]	n. 안료, 색소
68	expensive [ikspénsiv]	a. 비싼, 고가의, 사치스러운
69	importance [impɔ́:rtəns]	n. 중요성, 소중함
70	authority [əθɔ́:rəti]	n. 권위, 권한, 당국
71	explanation [èksplənéiʃən]	n. 설명, 해명, 해석
72	particular [pərtíkjulər]	a. 특별한, 특이한
73	decipher [disáifər]	v. 해독하다, 판독하다
74	pursue [pərsú:]	v. 추진하다, 추구하다
75	investigation [invèstəgéiʃən]	n. 조사, 연구
76	urgent [ɔ́:rdʒənt]	a. 긴급한, 급박한
77	enhance [inhǽns]	v. 향상하다, 강화하다

TEST 4 — SET1-L2 — 구문정리

Monochromatic sculptures

→ 정답

#	구문	뜻
01	in chapter	~장에서 (책의 장)
02	look at	~을 살피다
03	regard A as B	A 를 B로 여기다
04	there were	~가 있었다 (복수)
05	parallel in	~점에서 공통점
06	to be specific	구체적으로 말하자면
07	a variety of	다양한
08	compatible with	~와 잘맞는, 양립할수 있는 =consistent with)
09	the latter case	후자의 경우에는
10	from the head to the toes	머리에서 발끝까지
11	date back to	~로 거슬러 올라가다
12	in many parts	많은 부분에서
13	refer to	~을 참조하다
14	during this period	이 기간동안에는
15	in one color	하나의 색상으로
16	strive to do	to do 하려고 시도하다
17	so to speak	말하자면
18	in a way	~한 방식으로
19	think about	~에 대해 생각하다
20	this way	이 방법으로
21	at the time	그 당시에
22	in accordance with	~에 따라서, ~에 부합되게
23	instill A in B	A 에게 B를 심어주다 (주입하다)
24	a set of	일련의
25	not until ~ that	~가 되어서야 비로소 that절 이 하하다
26	belief that	~라는 믿음
27	arrive at	(논의, 생각 끝에)~에 이르다
28	believe O to do	O가 to do 하다고 믿다
29	could have done	~할 수 있었을지도 모른다(추측)(C)
30	due to the effect of	~의 효과 덕분에
31	over thousand of years	수천년동안
32	try to do	to do 하려고 시도하다
33	with the advent of	~의 출현과 더불어
34	be able to do	to do 할 수 있다
35	do research	연구하다 (d)
36	research into	~에 대한 연구
37	distinguish A from B	A를 B로부터 구분하다
38	efficient for	~에 효율적인
39	cause O to do	O가 to do 하는것을 야기하다
40	sort of	뭐랄까 ; 어느정도(다소); 일종의
41	compose A of B	A를 B로 구성하다
42	in the next lesson	다음 수업에서
43	let's get back on topic	다시 본론으로 돌아오자
44	talk about	~에 대해 얘기하다
45	it is unfortunate that	~하는것이 안타깝다
46	base A on B	A를 B에 기반하다
47	prove O OC	O가 OC라고 증명하다
48	to a certain extent	어느 정도까지
49	as I mentioned	말한것 처럼
50	with a heavy emphasis on	~에 크게 강조하며
51	in this sense	이런 의미에서
52	take an approach to -ing	-ing 하는 방법을 취하다, 다루다; 다가가다
53	when it comes to	~에 관한 한
54	the first thing to consider is~	첫번째로 고려해야할 것은 ~이다
55	accentuate A with B	A를 B로 강조하다.
56	relate A to B	A와 B를 관련 시키다.
57	and so on	기타 등등
58	take A into consideration	A 를 고려하다
59	clarify the point	요점을 명확히 하다
60	on date	~날짜에
61	in addition to	~에 더하여, ~뿐만이 아니라
62	in military clothing	군복차림의
63	pose as if	마치 ~인 것 처럼 포즈하다
64	victorious in	~에서 승리한
65	associate A with B	A를 B와 연관짓다
66	play a role in	~점에 역할을 하다
67	use O to do	O를 ~하는데 사용하다
68	be dependent upon	~에 의존하다
69	keep that in mind	그것을 명심해라.
70	let's take a look at	~을 보겠습니다
71	use A for B	A를 B를 위해 사용하다
72	at the time	그 당시에
73	associate A with B	A를 B와 연관짓다
74	have yet to do	아직까지 to do 않다
75	the way that	그런 방식으로
76	require O to do	O가 ~하는것을 요구하다
77	it is urgent that	~하는것이 긴급하다
78	carry out research	연구하다
79	I'm certain that	나는 ~라고 확신한다
80	along with	~와 함께

TEST 4 Set 2 Conversation

VOCABULARY

01	legacy [légəsi]	n. 업적		10	criterion [kraitíəriən]	n. [판단/평가를 위한] 기준
02	pivotal [pívətl]	a. 중추의, 중요한		11	conclusive [kənklú:siv]	a. 결정적인
03	initiation [inìʃiéiʃən]	n. 시작, 개시		12	approve [əprú:v]	v. 승인하다
04	adapt [ədǽpt]	v. 적응하다		13	abstract [ǽbstrækt]	a. 추상적인
05	background [bæˈkgrauˌnd]	n. 배경		14	objective [əbdʒéktiv]	a. 객관적인
06	controversial [kɑ̀ntrəvə́:rʃəl]	a. 논란의, 논쟁의		15	persuasive [pərswéisiv]	aj. 설득력 있는
07	comfortable [kʌ́mfərtəbl]	a. 편한		16	opportunity [ɑ̀pərtjú:nəti]	n. 기회
08	validate [vǽlədèit]	v. 입증하다		17	expand [ikspǽnd]	v. 확장하다, 넓히다
09	debate [dibéit]	v. 논하다		18	intriguing [intrí:giŋ]	a. 흥미를 자아내는

TEST 4 SET2-C 구문정리
19th century female artist

→ 정답

#	표현	뜻
01	ask O to do	O가 to do하는 것을 요구하다
02	turn in	제출하다
03	paper on	~에 관한 리포트, 문서
04	look for	~를 찾다
05	come across	우연히 만나다
06	name A B	A를 B라고 이름 짓다
07	come along	진행하다
08	have a hard time ing	ing 하는데 어려움을 겪다
09	write about	~에 대해 쓰다
10	in the initiation of	~의 초기에 (i)
11	focus on	~에 집중하다
12	do research	연구하다
13	so ~ that	너무 ~해서 그 결과 ~하다
14	make O do	O가 do 하게 하다(만들다)
15	I am a big fan of~	~의 팬이다, ~을 매우 좋아하다
16	be of two minds in this	이것에 대해 결정 내리지 못했다
17	adapt to	~에 익숙해지다
18	rule out	배제하다
19	that is	즉
20	decide to do	to do 하는 것을 결정하다
21	stick with	고수하다
22	play a role	역할을 하다
23	in the beginning of	~의 초기에 (b)
24	have to do	to do 해야만 한다
25	tell A B	A에게 B를 말하다
26	insist that	that절을 주장하다
27	suited for	~에 적합한
28	be able to do	to do 하는 것을 가능하게 하다
29	validate a theory	이론을 입증하다
30	be willing to do	기꺼이 to do 하다
31	go deeper into	더 깊이 들어가다
32	book on	~에 관한 책
33	go on	이어지다, 계속되다
34	go for it	계속하다
35	give A B	A에게 B를 주다
36	pull A off	A를 (힘든 것을) 해결하다
37	in a manner	방법으로
38	approve of	~을 승인하다
39	worry about	~에 대해 걱정하다
40	agree with	에 동의하다
41	use O to do	O를 to do 하기 위해 사용하다
42	sort of	뭐랄까; 어느 정도, 일종의
43	I want something for him to read	의미상 주어(f)
44	knowledge on	~에 관한 지식
45	sound easy	쉽게 들린다
46	that's why	그것이 ~한 이유이다.
47	manage to do	가까스로 to do 하다
48	make a decision	결정하다
49	as difficult as it is intriguing	흥미로운 만큼 어려운

TEST 4 Set 2 Lecture 1

VOCABULARY

01	**witness** [wítnis]	v. 보다
02	**encounter** [inkáuntər]	v. 마주치다, 직면하다
03	**transform** [trænsfɔ́ːrm]	v. 변형시키다
04	**phenomenon** [finάmənὰn]	n. 현상
05	**occur** [əkə́ːr]	v. 발생하다, 일어나다
06	**complicated** [kάmpləkèitid]	a. 복잡한
07	**electron** [iléktran]	n. 전자
08	**atom** [ǽtəm]	n. 원자
09	**vital** [váitl]	a. 중요한
10	**stimulate** [stímjulèit]	v. 자극하다, 촉진시키다
11	**collide** [kəláid]	v. 충돌하다, 부딪히다
12	**collectively** [kəléktivli]	ad. 전체적으로
13	**various** [véəriəs]	a. 다양한, 여러가지의
14	**generate** [dʒénərèit]	v. 생성하다, 발생시키다
15	**ancestor** [ǽnsestər, -tris]	n. 조상, 선조
16	**capable** [kéipəbl]	a. 가능한, 할 수 있는
17	**tremendous** [triméndəs]	a. 엄청난, 거대한
18	**incandescent** [ìnkəndésnt]	a. 백열의
19	**painful** [péinfəl]	a. 고통스러운, 아픈
20	**utilize** [júːtəlàiz]	v. 활용하다, 이용하다
21	**practical** [prǽktikəl]	a. 실용적인, 실제적인
22	**inconvenient** [ìnkənvíːnjənt]	a. 불편한
23	**fluorescent** [fluərésnt]	a. 형광성의, 형광을 내는
24	**sophisticated** [səfístəkèitid]	a. 복잡한
25	**substantially** [səbstǽnʃəli]	ad. 상당히
26	**detrimental** [dètrəméntl]	a. 해로운, 유해한
27	**priority** [praiɔ́ːrəti]	n. 우선, 중요
28	**contaminate** [kəntǽmənèit]	v. 오염시키다
29	**propose** [prəpóuz]	v. 제안하다, 제의하다
30	**feasible** [fíːzəbl]	a. 실현 가능한
31	**exception** [iksépʃən]	n. 예외
32	**exothermic** [èksouθə́ːrmik]	a. 발열의
33	**ultimately** [ʌ́ltəmətli]	adv. 결국
34	**disposal** [dispóuzəl]	n. 폐기, 처분
35	**unnecessary** [ʌnNeˈsəseˌri]	a. 불필요한
36	**pragmatic** [prægmǽtik]	a. 실용적인
37	**extract** [ikstrǽkt]	v. 추출하다
38	**strive** [straiv]	v. 노력하다, 애쓰다
39	**enhance** [inhǽns]	v. 향상하다, 개선시키다
40	**promising** [prάmisiŋ]	a. 유망한, 촉망되는

TEST 4
SET2-L1 — Light energy

구문정리 | 본문 중 중요 구문 정리한 내용입니다. 우선 암기하고 많이 읽으시길 바랍니다.

→ 정답

#	구문	뜻
01	such as	~와 같은
02	on a daily basis	매일
03	turn on	켜다
04	transform A into B	A를 B로 바꾸다 (t)
05	in daily life	일상생활에서
06	play a role in	~라는 점에서 역할을 하다
07	in the process	과정에서
08	release energy	에너지를 방출하다
09	call A B	A를 B라고 부르다
10	be aware of	~을 알다
11	focus on	집중하다
12	enable O to do	O가 to do하는 것을 가능하게 하다
13	Imagine what it would have been like	상상해봐라 무엇 같을 수 있을지
14	be capable of ing	ing 할 수 있다
15	result from	~로부터 비롯되다
16	give A B	A에게 B를 주다
17	ask O to do	O가 to do 하는 것을 요구하다
18	try to do	to do 하는 것을 시도하다
19	not long after	오래지 않아
20	turn off	끄다
21	pull A off of B	A를 B로부터 떼다
22	have experience	경험하다
23	utilize O to do	O를 to do 하는데 사용하다
24	go deeper into	더 깊이 들어가다
25	go through	통과하다
26	convert A into B	A를 B로 바꾸다©
27	result in	그 결과 ~가 되다
28	a great deal of	다량의
29	the same as	~와 마찬가지로
30	release A from B	A를 B로 부터 방출 시키다
31	satisfy desire	욕구를 충족하다
32	fill A with B	A를 B로 가득 채우다
33	keep in mind that	that절을 명심하다
34	a bit	약간
35	differently than	~와는 다르게(t)
36	stay with	~와 함께 머무르다
37	start ~ing	ing하는것을 시작하다
38	bouncing off of	=rebound from
39	that's how	그게 ~하는 방법이다.
40	hard to do	to do 하기 어려운
41	at this time	이때
42	effect on	~에 대한 영향
43	as well	또한, 역시
44	used in	~에 사용 된
45	as far as	~하는한
46	in a generation	~한 세대에서
47	solve a problem	문제를 해결하다
48	be a prioroty	최우선 순위 이다
49	see A as B	A를 B로 간주하다
50	neither A nor B	A도 B도 아니다
51	the latter	후자
52	drawback to	~에 대한 단점
53	those of	명사 반복 피하기(복수)
54	make O O.C	O를 O.C로 만들다
55	a lot of	많은
56	for now	당분간
57	at least	적어도
58	work on	~에 공들이다, 애쓰다
59	make O O.C	O를 O.C로 만들다
60	I want something for him to read	의미상 주어(f)
61	in the near future	가까운 미래에
62	hear of	~에 대해 듣다
63	be different from	~와 다르다 (f)
64	you bet	물론이지, 바로 그거야
65	the way it works is	이것이 작동되는 방법은 ~이다
66	a little	약간의, 거의 없는(L)
67	different from	~와 다른
68	and so on	기타 등등
69	this case is an exception	이 사례는 예외이다
70	instead of	~대신에
71	a series of	일련의
72	suffer from	~로부터 고통 받다
73	be composed of	~로 구성되다
74	sound like	~처럼 들리다
75	with respect to	~에 대하여, 관하여
76	in stage	단계에서
77	let O do	O가 do 하게 하다
78	give A B	A에게 B를 주다
79	help O do	O가 do 하게 도와주다
80	responsible for	~에 원인이 있는
81	strive to do	to do 하는 것을 노력하다
82	apply A to B	A를 B에 적용하다.
83	at this point	이시점에서
84	come up with	~을 생각해내다
85	so far	현재까지

TEST 4　Set 2　Lecture 2

VOCABULARY

01	**devoted** [divóutid]	a. 전념하는
02	**neuroscience** [njùərousáiəns]	n. 신경과학
03	**advent** [ǽdvent]	n. 출현, 등장
04	**tremendous** [triméndəs]	a. 엄청난, 많은
05	**identify** [aidéntəfài]	v. 밝히다
06	**fundamental** [fʌndəméntl]	a. 근본적인
07	**static** [stǽtik]	a. 정적인
08	**announce** [ənáuns]	v. 발표하다, 알리다
09	**intricate** [íntrikət]	a. 복잡한, 미묘한
10	**enhance** [inhǽns]	v. 향상하다
11	**apparent** [əpǽrənt]	a. 분명한, 명백한
12	**discovery** [diskʌ́vəri]	n. 발견
13	**complicated** [kǽmpləkèitid]	a. 복잡한, 어려운
14	**detect** [ditékt]	v. 발견하다, 탐지하다
15	**oscillation** [àsəléiʃən]	n. 진동
16	**enlightenment** [inláitnmənt]	n. 개몽, 개화
17	**obsolete** [àbsəlíːt]	a. 시대에 뒤진, 구식의
18	**stability** [stəbíləti]	n. 안정
19	**revolutionary** [rèvəlúːʃənèri]	a. 혁명의, 혁신적인
20	**distinction** [distíŋkʃən]	n. 구별, 차이
21	**originate** [ərídʒənèit]	v. 유래하다
22	**command** [kəmǽnd]	v. 명령하다, 지휘하다
23	**theorize** [θíːəràiz]	v. 이론을 세우다
24	**amygdala** [əmígdələ]	n. 편도선
25	**responsible** [rispánsəbl]	a. 담당의
26	**exaggerate** [igzǽdʒərèit]	v. 과장하다
27	**significance** [signífikəns]	n. 의의
28	**comprise** [kəmpráiz]	v. ~을 구성하다
29	**perplexing** [pərpléksiŋ]	a. 알기 어려운
30	**element** [éləmənt]	n. 요소
31	**rudimentary** [rùːdəméntəri]	a. 미발달의
32	**questionnaire** [kwèstʃənέər]	n. 설문지
33	**respondent** [rispándənt]	n. 응답자
34	**manipulate** [mənípjulèit]	v. 조작하다
35	**portray** [pɔːrtréi]	v. 묘사하다
36	**reliable** [riláiəbl]	a. 신뢰할 만한
37	**inquire** [inkwáiər]	v. 문의하다
38	**behavioral** [bihéivjərəl]	a. 행동의, 행동에 관한
39	**preference** [préfərəns]	n. 선호

TEST 4
SET2-L2
Psychology

본문 중 중요 구문 정리한 내용입니다. 우선 암기하고 많이 읽으시길 바랍니다.

→ 정답

#	구문	뜻	#	구문	뜻
01	in the last class	지난 수업에서	50	originate from	~에서 비롯되다
02	for those who were absent	결석한 사람들을 위해서	51	in response to	~에 반응하여
03	a branch of	~의 한 분야	52	work as	~로서 일하다, 활동하다
04	devote A to B	A를 B에 헌신하다	53	tell A which action to take	A에게 어떤 행동을 취할지 말하다
05	relate A to B	A와 B를 관련 시키다	54	take action	~에 대해 조치를 취하다
06	in particular	특히	55	change in	~라는 점에서의 변화
07	since the advent of	~의 출현 이래로	56	a lot of	많은, 다량의
08	a tremendous amount of	엄청난 양의	57	take in	받아들이다
09	do research	연구하다	58	at once	즉시, 당장
10	plan to do	~하려는 계획	59	let me help you	내가 널 도와줄게
11	unlock mystery	미스터리를 풀다	60	help A with B	A를 B와 관련하여 돕다
12	enhance understanding of	~에 대한 이해를 높이다, 강화하다	61	restrain O from ~ing	O가 ing 하는것을 막다
13	not only A but also B	A뿐 아니라 B 또한	62	because of	~때문에
14	look back to	되돌아보다	63	numerous times	수 차례
15	not long ago	오래전이 아닌; 얼마전에	64	in fact	사실상
16	begin to do	to do 하는것을 시작하다	65	do study	연구하다 (S)
17	refer to	~을 참고하다	66	responsible for	~에 책임이 있는
18	in that	~라는 점에서	67	have O do	O가 do 하도록 시키다
19	be able to do	~할 수 있다	68	in a straight line	직선으로
20	carry out test on	~에 테스트를 수행하다(c)	69	show A B	A에게 B를 보여주다
21	a series of	일련의	70	take a photograph	사진 찍다(ph)
22	perform experiments on	~에 실험하다	71	be able to do	to do 할 수 있다
23	figure out	~을 알아내다	72	in front of	~dml 앞에
24	over time	시간이 경과하면서, 지나면서	73	two years later	2년 후에
25	praise A as B	A를 B로서 칭찬하다	74	undergo process	과정을 겪다
26	a bit	다소, 약간	75	respond to	~에 대응하다
27	in the field of	~분야에서	76	in the same way as	~와 같은 방법으로
28	it seems that	~처럼 보이다	77	response to	~에 대한 답
29	shift in A to B	A라는 점에서 B로의 변화	78	over the course of	~동안에
30	seem to do	~할 것처럼 보이다	79	go into	~에 들어가다
31	take over	인수하다	80	try to do	to do 하려고 시도하다
32	sound familiar	익숙하게 들리다	81	keep in mind that	~을 명심하다
33	deal with	처리하다, 다루다	82	tend to do	to do 하는 경향이 있다
34	try to do	to do 하는것을 노력하다	83	comprise A of B	A를 B로 구성하다
35	get O done	o를 done되어지게 하다	84	come to the final stage	마지막 단계로 도달하다
36	use A as B	A를 B로서 사용하다	85	solve mystery	미스터리를 풀다
37	help O do	O가 ~하는것을 돕다	86	as of now	지금 현재는
38	draw a distinction	구별하다	87	account for	~을 설명하다
39	between the two	두가지 사이에서	88	tell A B	A에게 B를 말하다
40	take a picture of	사진을 찍다	89	enough to do	~하기에 충분한
41	I want something for him to read	의미상 주어(f)	90	for this reason	이러한 이유로
42	for a purpose	~목적으로	91	be familiar with	~와 친숙하다, 익숙하다
43	as the name suggests	이름이 암시하듯이	92	enjoy ~ing	ing 하는것을 즐기다
44	in addition to	~ 뿐만 아니라, 게다가	93	socialize A with B	A를 B와 교제시키다
45	in other words	다른 말로하면	94	get disappointed	실망하다
46	let's say	예를 들면 (=for example)	95	portray oneself differently	스스로를 다르게 묘사하다
47	be under stress	스트레스 받다	96	inquire about	~에 관하여 묻다
48	urge to do	~하려는 충동	89	at the present time	현재 로서는
49	express anger	분노를 표현하다, 나타내다			

usherin.usher.co.kr

USHER iBT TOFLE
FINAL TEST LISTENING
구문 외우고/열번읽기

정답 및 Self-check List

문제유형과 Signals

오답정리표

Implications of Bioluminescence

Listen to a conversation between a student and a professor.

S: Hello, Professor.

P: Good morning, Brian. How was the conference in South Florida?

S: It was a good experience. I met a lot of new people. I think it was a good [01)]**opportunity** for me **to create** a good professional network.

P: That's what conferences are for. How did you feel about the [02)]**lecture on** molecular biology?

S: It was okay. It provided a lot of interesting theories that [03)]**gave me a broader perspective** on the field. Like I said, I met a lot of interesting people. I think they'll be very useful if I [04)]**decide to further** my research.

P: Conferences are always a good place to meet [05)]**those with** similar professional **interests**.

S: I wanted to [06)]**ask you something**. [07)]**On** my third **day**, I think, I was [08)]**walking along** the seashore and almost [09)]**stepped on** a jellyfish. I didn't notice it was there, until it [10)]**started glowing**. I was quite intrigued.

P: I think you witnessed bioluminescence, the production of light by a living organism.

S: And… I was [11)]**wondering if** you could explain the mechanism a little bit. I'[12)]**m interested in** [13)]**using** it **as** a topic for my term paper.

P: Jellyfish, like the one you saw, are the most commonly known bioluminescent animals, but there are other organisms that do the same. Some others, like fireflies or glowworms, are quite common, but there are also some lesser known bioluminescent organisms, such as certain squid, shrimp and fungi.

S: Wow! Fireflies and glowworms were no surprise, but I didn't realize that there were so many others.

P: Bioluminescence is basically a naturally occurring process in which energy is released through a chemical reaction [14)]**in the form of** light. [15)]**Getting into the details** would be way too time-consuming right now.

S: As mysterious as this is, do you know why certain animals produce light? I mean, is it just a random… emission of energy?

P: Well… they only produce light [16)]**at certain times**, so the purpose [17)]**differs from** animal to animal, but it can generally be categorized [18)]**in three ways**: [19)]**as a means of** intraspecies communication, for predator avoidance, or to attract prey.

S: Ah… Do you know which category jellyfish [20)]**fall into**?

P: Jellyfish, I believe, [21)]**use** bioluminescence **to** [22)]**avoid** predators.

S: What I'm most intrigued by is the actual process of light production. I mean, how is that even possible, biologically speaking?

P: Well, I don't know how strong your knowledge of chemistry is, but it's basically a chemical reaction. More specifically, the jellyfish can, after [23)]**being exposed to** the necessary energy for activation, rapidly oxidize magnesium and [24)]**emit a** bright **light**. That's the gist of it.

S: So, the jellyfish produce the chemicals [25)]**necessary for** illumination within their bodies?

P: Exactly. The jellyfish you saw was probably an Aequorea Victoria. It produces a blue light, which is different from other jellyfish.

S: Yes, yes, it was producing a bluish light.

P: Then that's the most likely species. Are you [26)]**considering writing** about bioluminescent jellyfish for your term paper?

S: Well, I [27)]**wanted to ask** you what you thought about it. I mean, is it an interesting enough topic?

P: It's definitely interesting, but [28)]**it's going to require** a lot of work. Jellyfish aren't [29)]**easy to understand** because they are [30)]**a** relatively **new field of study** and scientists [31)]**find them radical** [32)]**in the field of** marine biology. Are you still [33)]**up for** it?

S: I am. I think it will be very fun.

P: Well, [34)]**I'm** also **a big fan of** jellyfish. I'[35)]**m excited to see** how you're going to organize the scientific data that may be…rather complicated. [36)]**Feel free to ask** me for guidance [37)]**at any time**.

Type of Renaissance Gardens

Listen to part of a lecture in an art history class. The professor is discussing Renaissance gardens.

P: Okay, I introduced the concept of the Renaissance in last week's lecture. This was the period when new ideas swept [01]**across Europe** after the Middle Ages. If you'll remember, the term Renaissance means rebirth [02]**in French**. This cultural movement [03]**aspired to popularize** the forgotten classic concepts of the ancient Romans across Europe. Countless artistic works were produced during this period, but today we [04]**are going to** [05]**focus on** Renaissance gardens. Is anyone [06]**familiar with** the gardens constructed during the Renaissance?

S: I believe that Renaissance gardens were built to emulate those popular during ancient Roman times.

P: Yes, that is the most important characteristic of the Renaissance gardens. [07]**In other words**, they were pretty much built as the ancient Romans 'would' have built them, using assumptions of what Roman gardens were actually like. As the idea of emulating the beauty of lost classical artwork became popular, wealthy people, such as merchants and political figures, [08]**craved to recreate** the magnificent gardens of ancient Rome, so they [09]**started to hire** prestigious architects to build them. Let's [10]**take a look at** some of the features that Renaissance gardens shared. The most noticeable features were walkways [11]**lined with** marble statues and fountains like those featured in ancient Roman gardens. They were also [12]**filled with** allegorical statues of animals, giants and fantastic creatures, [13]**as well as** bushes [14]**trimmed into** specific shapes to further emulate ancient Roman architecture. Renaissance gardens [15]**brought** the gardens of ancient Rome **back to life** [16]**in** every possible **way**.

S: Professor, what were the ancient Roman gardens actually like?

P: That's a good question. Well, they were pretty much the prototypes of the Renaissance gardens. There were different designs, but Roman gardeners [17]**adhered to** certain styles that developed [18]**in three main stages**. The first gardens of ancient Rome were built near homes to grow vegetables and herbs for consumption. This type of garden, [19]**known as** a hortus, was usually built in the backyard of a house. They [20]**served as** the primary source of vegetables and herbs for the Romans. [21]**At the time**, these gardens [22]**served** more of a practical **need** than an ornamental one. The second type of Roman garden developed as [23]**the quality of life** in ancient Rome improved and they enlarged their living spaces. This expansion [24]**gave birth to** the peristyle, or columned porch and colonnade, in Roman architecture. During this period, the garden moved to the front yard and [25]**was decorated with** walkways bordered by statues. Further, flowers and shrubs were planted [26]**for** ornamental **purposes** rather than the practical vegetables and herbs. The final stage in the evolution of Roman gardens was the villa garden. This was the most luxurious style of Roman garden in which ornamental plants and artwork were arranged for the pleasure of visitors [27]**strolling through** the peristyles of the gardens. The major difference was that this style of garden contained buildings [28]**other than** the house itself and more complex ornaments, such as fountains. In some of the larger ones, they even built exercise facilities such as swimming pools! This was the style that drew the greatest praise from Renaissance garden builders.

S: Professor, why did the people build gardens during the Renaissance?

P: I'm glad you asked that question. There are several assumptions regarding why people built these gardens. The most important role of these gardens was to symbolize the status of their owners. Umm... [29]**To be straightforward**, there are no other significant reasons behind the garden construction at the time. [30]**It is fair to say that** these gardens were a manifestation of the pursuit of the beauty of ancient Roman architecture. However, [31]**research into** the purpose of these gardens shows that they were, [32]**in fact**, mainly displays of wealth and power to the world. These formal gardens served as a medium to impress visitors. People such as writers, poets and philosophers would gather and praise the beauty of the garden. The owners of the gardens [33]**would have been** able to [34]**derive** a great deal of satisfaction and pride **from** the profuse attention and wonder people displayed regarding them.

S: Professor, were there any other unique features of these gardens, besides their beauty?

P: Hmm... Were there any other features? Umm... well, I do remember one thing that might interest you... Oh yes, there was another major interesting feature of the gardens: coin operated fountains. The idea behind these [35]**came from** the Greek mathematician "Heron of Alexandria". He [36]**came up with** a device that dispensed water when a coin was inserted. The fountains were set up to release water [37]**in the same way** as a coin operated vending machine. The official term for these was "giochi d'aqua", which literally means "water jokes," since they were concealed to drench unsuspecting visitors. These were one of the most famous features [38]**added to** Italian Renaissance Gardens [39]**for the purpose of** entertaining visitors.

S: Professor, I recall there being another interesting feature of Renaissance gardens. I believe that they contained labyrinths to emulate those of ancient Rome, right?

P: Well, ironically, they did build labyrinths [40]**for this reason**, but there is no evidence of ancient Roman gardens containing labyrinths. The fact that Renaissance gardeners included them has [41]**led** many **to** the misconception that they existed in ancient Rome. Why, then, did labyrinths become a common feature of Renaissance gardens? Well, [42]**according to** Roman mythology, the labyrinth was an impossible maze where the Minotaur was imprisoned. Later, Italians built labyrinths in their gardens to imitate the mythical maze, so the legendary labyrinth [43]**came to life** as an entertainment venue. The Italians redefined the meaning of the word to mean an outdoor playground for guests. Whenever there was a large group of guests, labyrinths [44]**were** not only **used as** multipurpose grounds for dancing and games, but they also offered a pleasant atmosphere for visitors, as their walls [45]**were comprised of** herbs and shrub plants. People [46]**loved to** [47]**take walks** and enjoy nature within the labyrinths.

Einstein's Theory of Relativity

Listen to part of a lecture in a physics class. The professor is discussing Relativity.

P: I'm sure you [01]**have all heard of** Albert Einstein, [02]**one of the** most influential **figures** of the past century and the greatest physicist of the modern era. You may wonder what he did to become so famous. Well, he [03]**came up with** the most significant discovery of modern physics: the Theory of Relativity. This theory [04]**gave us new** [05]**insight into** what light is and how it works, [06]**changing the way** physicists think and reshaping modern physics. Ironically, however, the greatness of this work wasn't fully recognized at the time and he was never [07]**awarded a** Nobel **Prize** for his Theory of Relativity. [08]**This is because** his work's legitimacy and his unorthodox methods were questioned by his contemporaries. The [09]**debate over** whether Einstein [10]**received** proper **recognition for** his signature work continues [11]**to this day**.

Before I [12]**get into** his work's impact, we should understand where Einstein [13]**came from**. He was born in Germany in 1879, and although he loved academics, he hated the formal education system [14]**so** much **that** he eventually dropped out, [15]**resulting in** his [16]**failure to** [17]**enter university** on his first attempt. He returned to formal schooling and eventually graduated from Zurich's Federal Polytechnic in 1900. After graduation, he [18]**was unable to find** employment in academia, so he became a patent office clerk in Switzerland in 1902. Although many have argued that he wasted his time there, Einstein disagreed, [19]**citing** this **as** the most productive time of his life and crediting it with his later creativity and productivity. How, then, did examining patent applications help reshape modern physics? Well, it was clearly a combination of genius and experience. In order for him to approve a patent, Einstein [20]**had to work** backwards, meaning he had to breakdown an invention or an idea himself [21]**in order to determine** the patent claim's validity. He studied innumerable ideas and inventions during those years. All the information, ideas, and experience he gained [22]**became the foundations of** his most famous work, the Theory of Relativity.

So, [23]**let's get into** what the theory actually is. First off, the Theory of Relativity can be [24]**divided into** two parts: the Theory of Special Relativity and the Theory of General Relativity. The Theory of Special Relativity states that everything has its own time. [25]**In other words**, each object or person has its own clock. Einstein claims that this is due to a phenomenon [26]**called** time dilation, under which time is affected by very fast velocities, like the speed of light. Ever heard of the twin paradox? The twin paradox is a good example of how time is affected by speed. Imagine that there are twins; let's call them Jeff and John. Say Jeff [27]**takes off** in a spaceship travelling [28]**at the speed of** light to a distant planet and John stays home. When Jeff returns, he will be much younger than his brother. This happens because he travels faster than time has passed for John. When speed exceeds time, time is slowed for quickly travelling objects. This revolutionary idea contradicted the traditional view that time flows for everyone [29]**at the same rate**.

In 1915, Einstein shocked the world again with his follow-up theory, known as General Relativity, which [30]**combined** the previous theory **with** gravity. He theorized that light usually travels straight, but when it hits heavy masses, such as planets and stars, it bends around them. We can't see the bending light, but the phenomenon clearly exists throughout nature. One example of this is light bending around the sun. This is how we see the light of stars that are positioned behind the sun. Validation of these theories only became possible after Einstein's time, [31]**due to** the lack of equipment and technology. Due to this lack of empirical data, physicists such as Dayton Miller spent decades [32]**attempting to discredit** Einstein's theory. [33]**In opposition to** Einstein's [34]**belief that** light travelled independently, regardless of its source's speed, Miller believed that light's speed was determined by an invisible matter surrounding it called ether. Unlike Einstein, he [35]**was able to produce** numerous measurements and data sets to support his argument. Even though Miller's data was less than convincing, his ability to experimentally measure ether over a course of decades and his established position in the physics community [36]**allowed** his theory **to** [38]**gain** widespread **support**. Eventually, review of other experiments such as the Michelson-Morley experiment showed that Miller's numerical measurements of ether [39]**fell within** the [40]**margin of error** and had most likely occurred due to the lack of laboratory equipment needed to [41]**perform the experiment** in a vacuum, or an area without pressure and gravity. These variables [42]**could have** easily **altered** his results.

Even the Nobel Prize Committee didn't initially recognize the brilliance of Einstein's theory [43]**at the time**. This may [44]**seem ridiculous** now, but at the time they had the same issues with it as Miller. The theory was [45]**based on** Einstein's ingenuity and creative mind, but lacked any conclusive data or experimental results to support it; he had simply [46]**thought it up** one day! The idea that a 26-year-old patent office clerk had simply [47]**used** reason **to come up** with ideas that reformulated the equations of physics was too shocking. While we can recognize the tremendous discovery he made today, Einstein's contemporaries and the Nobel Prize Committee could not accept concepts with such shaky foundations. They [48]**needed to** be able to evaluate the source and methodology of a contribution in order to recognize it, but due to Einstein's disregard of the traditional scientific method, the lack of empirical evidence and the physics community's [49]**opposition to** his ideas, the Nobel Committee could not award the prize for the theory. While hindsight [50]**shows** us that Einstein's theory was deserving of recognition, the committee acted fairly. Even Einstein [51]**accepted the limits of** his theories and once said that they were just his imaginings and could be [55]**proven** wrong by future experiments. After all this talk of the greatness of Einstein's theory, you may be wondering how it affects your daily life. Well, the GPS system in your car or mobile phone can be [53]**traced back to** Einstein's theory. His work also opened up new fields in physics, such as quantum physics, which has yielded numerous inventions like microchips, electron microscopes, and MRI. Einstein's work not only has changed physics, but created new previously unimaginable areas of science.

Student's Opposition to Renovation

Listen to a conversation between a student and an office clerk.

S: Excuse me, sir.

O: Yes, ma'am.

S: Well, I don't 01)**know if** you heard, but they'02)**re going to rebuild** the science library... and well, I'm here because I 03)**'m against** it, and... 04)**long story short**, I need a signature from the board so I can officially start a protest against it.

O: Well... I 05)'m not officially **authorized to give** out any names, but if I could get your name and 06)**contact information**, I would be happy to 07)**deliver a message**.

S: My name is Meghan Young, and my student ID number is 110509.

O: Got it. Do you 08)**mind me asking** why you have a problem with the renovations? I just want to deliver my message to the higher authorities 09)**as accurately as possible**.

S: 10)**Not at all**... 11)**To be honest**, I really like the way it is right now. I don't even think it 12)**needs to be renovated** at all! I think the glass walls are all still intact. Wasn't it recently renovated anyway?

O: I guess I see your point. It hasn't been that long.

S: Also... I mean... A lot of students 13)**rely on** the library to study... Some people may even lose their scholarships.

O: Uh-huh. Anything else?

S: Well, the source materials and reference materials that we require for our studies... 14)**need I say more?**

O: I understand... I'm pretty sure that the board won't just 15)**cut out** the reference sources; they'll probably 16)**place** the materials **in** another location, and even provide an alternative study area. But then again... there have been rumors that the school 17)**failed to** 18)**raise** enough **funds** and that there may not be any renovations at all.

S: Really?

O: Yeah... I mean... 19)**at first** I thought it was just a rumor too. But false rumors don't last this long... You know what I mean?

S: I guess so...

O: 20)**How many signatures** opposing the renovations do you have 21)**so far**? Do you mind me asking?

S: Not at all. There are currently about 250 people and the number is growing as we speak.

O: I can sympathize; we office workers were actually appalled 22)**as well**.

S: Yeah... I mean, why not just 23)**add a new wing to the library**? They 24)**released a possible blueprint to the students**, and it 25)**looked ridiculous** to close the whole place. I just want to 26)**deliver our new ideas**, and maybe even possibly shut down the whole project.

O: Even if the rumors aren't true, I bet you have 27)**enough people to** 28)**make a difference**. I mean 250 and growing... that's not a number the school can ignore.

S: I'm just glad there are others that 29)**feel the same way** that I do...

O: You know... If I were you... I would wait to find out if the rumors are true or not. I mean... I wouldn't want to 30)**get people excited** 31)**over something** that isn't even happening... you know how rough these things can get, don't you?

S: You're right... I thought everything was set. I 32)**was in** such a foul **mood** because of this... Thank you for the helpful information.

O: No problem.

S: Do you know when the decision is final though? I'm 33)**eager to find out**.

O: Well, there's a hearing sometime this week between the faculty and the board members.

S: That's great. Should I come back when it's over? Do you know when it starts?

O: Tell you what. If you 34)**leave me your number**, I'll 35)**get back to** you as soon as I can.

S: OK. Sounds great. Thank you!

The Space Elevator Technology

Listen to part of a lecture in an engineering class.

P: In our globalized world, barriers between nations are [01]**breaking down**, as is the barrier between Earth and the universe. Since its first foray into space, mankind has achieved remarkable things. However, [02]**due to** the energy and resource inefficiencies of the current methods of space travel, even a short trip into space remains an expensive proposition. [03]**This is because** an enormous amount of fuel [04]**is required to reach** Earth's [05]**escape velocity** of 11 kilometers per second. The inefficiency of this method is evident when you [06]**look at** the external fuel tanks of the space shuttle. They are the biggest, and heaviest, parts of the shuttles. Oddly, however, a lot of people still [07]**seem to** [08]**have misconceptions about** going to space. Um, [09]**let me give** you an example. [10]**The idea that** the only [11]**way to escape** Earth's atmosphere is by travelling [12]**at Earth's escape velocity** is not absolutely true. Um... before I [13]**go any further**, let's [14]**make sure** we[15]**'re on the same page** about the concept of escape velocity. Escape velocity is the [16]**speed at which** an object must move to overcome Earth's gravitational pull. Objects that reach their escape velocity are fast [17]**enough that** they won't lose their velocity before leaving Earth's gravitational influence. Theoretically though, all one really [18]**needs to enter** space is a constant force pushing upwards or holding one firmly in place. Scientists are, therefore, [19]**trying to build** that force: a sturdy human construction on which passengers or payloads could [20]**travel up and down**.

S: So... what you are saying is that if we could somehow build something like a huge ladder, then we could slowly climb our way up into space, right?

P: Exactly. You understand that a person [21]**climbing a ladder** wouldn't reach speeds that are [22]**anywhere near** the escape velocity, but that person wouldn't [23]**be pulled down** by gravity, because they would be [24]**holding on to** the ladder, right? There is a problem, however... although the ladder idea [25]**makes sense** mathematically and conceptually, it is very improbable. Nobody could climb thousands of kilometers before being exhausted. [26]**Let's not forget** that you would also need to be carrying a heavy oxygen tank and space suit. The ladder example is not [27]**as outrageous as it sounds**, though. [28]**Research** [29]**is being done** [30]**on** the construction of a very similar concept: a space elevator. The space elevator is a proposed structure [31]**designed to transport** material from Earth to space. A Russian rocket scientist, Konstantin Tsiolkovsky, who was inspired by the Eiffel Tower, first proposed this idea in 1895. His theory was immediately ridiculed and his fellow scientists [32]**told him that** it would never be possible. His idea wasn't totally forgotten though. One of the early, and most enthusiastic, proponents of the idea of a space elevator was the science-fiction author Arthur C. Clark, and it appears repeatedly in his works. One example was the 1979 novel 'The Fountains of Paradise'. In this novel, a 22nd century engineer [33]**is charged with** creating [34]**a means of** moving people and supplies to a 'terraforming' project in outer space. To do this, he develops a space elevator linking Earth to the 'circumterran' (Earth encircling) space station.

So... [35]**Let's talk about** how a space elevator would work. Hmm... The first part of the project would be a base station on Earth that would [36]**be attached to** a pillar upon which an elevator car could travel. This structure would be flexible, and would be [37]**called the cable**. You may be wondering how we could construct a cable that is strong [38]**enough to** [39]**stand up** straight, yet [40]**tall enough to** reach space. Well... Remember when you were kids, you would [41]**tie** a rope **to** a bucket [42]**full of** water, and swing it over your head? How did the water [43]**stay inside** the bucket while gravity pulled it downwards? A natural force, [44]**known as** centrifugal force, pushed the water into the bucket, [45]**away from** the center of the circular motion, which was the hand holding the rope. The same principle would [46]**apply to** the space elevator: when the cable is long enough, the spinning of the Earth will create a centrifugal force on the space elevator. To accomplish this, the space elevator would need a heavy weight, called a counterweight, [47]**at its highest** point to [48]**make it more stable**.

The cable itself is probably the biggest [49]**hindrance to** a space elevator's construction, as it would need to be [50]**made of an extremely light**, durable material, but [51]**as long as** people have been [52]**dreaming of** building a space elevator, no material strong enough has existed...until the recent discovery of a new material made purely of carbon, that is. Due to the extremely strong chemical bonds that carbon atoms form with [53]**one another**, scientists have discovered a way to form tiny tubes called 'carbon nanotubes,'which are stronger and lighter than steel, and able to [54]**conduct electricity**. These tubes of pure carbon have [55]**shown** great **promise**: they can be used in everything, from electronics to airplanes, as well as space elevator cables.

The next question about a space elevator is 'how long would the cable have to be'? Well, there are several factors that must be considered when determining this length. If you think about satellites orbiting Earth you'll recognize that their speed is actually determined by how high above Earth their orbits are. As the space elevator would [56]**be attached to** the Earth's surface, its mass would have to be centered at 36,000 km, which is the [57]**height at which** it would achieve geosynchronous orbit. That [58]**leads us to** the question 'What is geosynchronous orbit'? This is when an object's orbital period [59]**is synchronized with** the Earth's rotation. [60]**In other words**, the orbiting object will always appear at the same spot in the sky to an observer [61]**on Earth**.

P: Despite these high hopes and technological advances, there are still many hurdles to actualizing this dream. [62]**For one**, as a space elevator cable, carbon nanotubes, have a major problem. The longest nanotubes ever created were only a [63]**few centimeters long**, and [64]**linking** them together **to** a length of 36,000 km would be impractical. In addition, some [65]**feel that** a space elevator would [66]**present** a navigational hazard, both **to** aircraft and spacecraft, as well as space objects. Further, it would [67]**be exposed to** the radiation belts to [68]**be shielded from** them. You can see that a lot more work is necessary before construction of a space elevator is feasible. If technology advances enough, though, it may be built [69]**in your lifetimes**.

Investigation of Easter Island

Listen to part of a lecture in an archaeology class. The professor is discussing Easter Island.

P: ⁰¹⁾Let's ⁰²⁾continue researching lost civilizations with Easter Island; the mysterious island discovered by Dutchman Jacob Roggeveen in 1722. Roggeveen discovered an island ⁰³⁾filled with cannibalistic savages, but later found evidence suggesting that it was once occupied by an advanced, orderly civilization. If this was true, what ⁰⁴⁾happened to it? What could have caused the demise and destruction of this prominent civilization? Archaeologists and scientists are ⁰⁵⁾working together to ⁰⁶⁾unravel this mystery. And today, we'll ⁰⁷⁾look into this obscurity ⁰⁸⁾in detail.

P: ⁰⁹⁾Does anyone know anything about Easter Island?

S: Isn't it ¹⁰⁾famous for gigantic statues?

P: Ah, yes, Jonathan, Those are the island's most renowned features, but let's get some ¹¹⁾background information. Easter Island, measuring only 64 square miles, ¹²⁾is located in the southern Pacific about 2,000 miles ¹³⁾west of Chile, with its closest inhabited island neighbor being 1,400 miles away. Despite its isolation, the humid, subtropical climates with its mild winters and hot, rainstorm-filled summers ¹⁴⁾make it ¹⁵⁾ideal for inhabitation. When Roggeveen landed, however, ¹⁶⁾there were no signs of outside connections. He found approximately 2,000 barbarians on an island wasteland ¹⁷⁾devoid of trees and animals. On an island-wide search for usable resources, however, he discovered the astonishing moai.

S: What are the moai?

P: They're the gigantic statues that Jonathan mentioned. Anyway, this shocking discovery ¹⁸⁾drew a lot of worldwide attention. These 887 giant faces ¹⁹⁾were carved into giant stones, which averaged 14.5 feet tall and 14 tons, with some reaching 33 feet and ²⁰⁾weighing 165 tons! Roggeveen ²¹⁾found these strange because 2,000 people ²²⁾couldn't have possibly carved and hauled these statues, especially without the tools to perform such tasks! They didn't even have trees which are a basic component of construction tools.

S: Professor, who would have ²³⁾chosen to live in such a remote, barren place...and why?

P: There's no definitive proof of where the people came from, only competing theories. Norwegian explorer Thor Heyerdahl originally proposed that they were from Chile, the closest continental land. He also claimed that the moai resembled Incan statues found throughout present-day Chile. His theory was widely accepted until modern science proposed another explanation. Modern scientists ²⁴⁾performed a series of DNA tests on skeletons found on the island and discovered that they were from Polynesia, the area of islands near Australia in the southern Pacific Ocean inhabited by a population of seafarers who migrated over great oceanic routes ²⁵⁾in canoes. ²⁶⁾It is likely that they sailed from Marquesas or the Society islands, Easter Island's closest island neighbors, but ²⁷⁾got lost and settled on Easter Island. ²⁸⁾Strangely though, not all islanders ²⁹⁾are of Polynesian origin.

P: It's now believed that until a couple centuries ago, the island ³⁰⁾housed a lot more people: probably around 11,000 to 15,000, ³¹⁾based on estimates of the labor ³²⁾required to build the moai, and the habitable areas of the island. The dispersion of the moai around the island also ³³⁾leads archaeologists to assume that the conditions on the island in the past were quite different. This was ³⁴⁾proven true by ³⁵⁾a test called pollen analysis. The process involves a column of sediment collected from a swamp or pond, showing the different layers of sediment ³⁶⁾over time. Each of these layers is then dated through radiocarbon dating.

S: Professor, ³⁷⁾I'm confused about the procedure. What exactly is radiocarbon dating?

P: It's a process ³⁸⁾used to measure the age of dead organisms by measuring the remaining carbon levels.
These two tests proved that the island once supported flourishing gigantic palm trees, which were ³⁹⁾ideal for making canoes, logs, and ropes to transport the moai. They were also required for everyday things such as building houses and fires. ⁴⁰⁾According to scientists, the natives cut down these palm trees and rolled them horizontally to transport the moai.
Anyway, ⁴¹⁾long story short, the palm trees and animals ⁴²⁾went extinct ⁴³⁾for some reason, ⁴⁴⁾spelling doom for the islanders. This ⁴⁵⁾led to a dramatic population decrease; falling ⁴⁶⁾as low as 111 in 1877. ⁴⁷⁾Let's look at possible explanations behind the downfall of the civilization. The traditional theory, suggested by American scientist Jared Diamond, was that the civilization destroyed itself through overconsumption and deforestation. He claimed that native people ⁴⁸⁾cut down all of the trees to transport the moai. The lack of trees then halted the production of the moai. Soon, necessities such as fire and housing became luxuries. Eventually, the island ⁴⁹⁾descended into a self-inflicted chaos. This is, however, only a theory and there is no corroborating data.
Archaeologist Terry Hunt has ⁵⁰⁾come up with a theory that ⁵¹⁾points to rats as the main culprits behind the demise. He found ⁵²⁾a plethora of rat bones when sampling the soil from Anakena beach, the most likely landing spot for the first settlers. He ⁵³⁾deduced that the Polynesians ⁵⁴⁾brought rats with them for food, but there were no natural predators to ⁵⁵⁾keep the rat population in check. This ⁵⁶⁾combined with the tons of rat-chewed palm seeds strewn ⁵⁷⁾across the island ⁵⁸⁾led him to this new theory. He theorized that the rat population exploded and consumed all the palm seeds on the island. With no seeds to germinate and the natives still cutting down trees, deforestation occurred. It was ⁵⁹⁾as if they were ⁶⁰⁾adding insult to injury. Soon, all of the trees were extinct and the islanders could ⁶¹⁾no longer produce the canoes ⁶²⁾needed for fishing, so they ⁶³⁾started to consume the terrestrial animals. After these died out, they ⁶⁴⁾turned to warfare and cannibalism. By 1722, he says, no trace of the great civilization that once ruled the island existed.

Biology Research Plan

Listen to part of a conversation between a graduate student and her biology professor.

S: Hi, professor. What brings you by the lab today?

P: Hi Janet. I just 01)**wanted to** 02)**check on** how the experiments were 03)**coming along**. I heard you've 04)**put in** a lot of **hours in** the lab recently.

S: Well, 05)**to be honest**, I have been putting in more time at the lab because things haven't been going all that... smoothly.

P: May I ask why?

S: Well, **the task** that you 06)**assigned me**. The... uh... purification of protein RP73 from human tissue? Well, the experiment was going really well... until... a problem 07)**in** the cooling **process** occurred.

P: Oh. Did you 08)**forget to** fully **heat** it before you 09)**lowered the temperature**? If we're going to 10)**determine if** the problem is still reversible, we have to know the exact 11)**process** that you **followed**.

S: Not quite. Everything up to the heating process was perfect, I actually 12)**set an alarm** on Friday night to come back the next morning and 13)**cool** it **to room temperature**... and then do the precipitation process, hopefully. Well, anyway, I overslept and forgot to come back to the lab.

P: I've been there. Back when I was a graduate student like you, I 14)**was**n't **used to going** to a boring laboratory 15)**on a Saturday**, either. Well, if it was heated all weekend, there's no way we can still purify the protein.

S: I'm so sorry, professor. I know you were 16)**hoping to submit** a paper to the journal about its possible uses.

P: It can wait 17)**for** a couple of **weeks**. I mean... 18)**it's not like** the function of the protein 19)**is going to change** 20)**anytime soon**. So, no harm, no foul. Now the important question is 'When can I 21)**expect to see** the results that I'm 22)**looking for**?'

S: Well, I've been 23)**working on** it, even right before you arrived. So it shouldn't 24)**take** much **longer** than a couple days.

P: Well, the problem is, I leave town 25)**for a week** tomorrow... and...

S: Oh, 26)**you're worried that** the protein won't 27)**be in** tiptop **condition** when you come back 28)**in a week**.

P: Yes, I 29)**would like to work** with the material 30)**as soon as** it's successfully purified.

S: Okay... then I should probably 31)**get rid of** what I've been working on and start again sometime this week?

P: Oh, that would 32)**make me feel** like one of those professors who asks too much of their graduate students.

S: Don't worry. I think it's better if I 33)**keep practicing** the process. You know... to reduce the margin of error. Plus, it was my fault that you're not getting the results right now.

P: Well, I'm glad to see you have 34)**taken a** rather professional **attitude** about your job. You know, reducing the margin of error is quite 35)**critical in** designing and implementing an experiment as a scientist. You know the story about spinach and its supposed 36)**effects on** strengthening muscles, don't you?

S: No, but I'm guessing it's not true because you used the word 'supposed'... hahaha.

P: Hahaha... True. People believe that spinach is 37)**rich in** iron, a muscle supplement, but, in fact, a German chemist, in 1870, made an error in his experiments; making people think that spinach has 38)**10 times more** iron than it actually does! He did everything else right in his experiments, but a simple misplaced decimal 39)**provided** the public **with** inaccurate information that 40)**continues to fool** a lot of people.

S: Wow, I did not know that. I guess I get what you're trying to say. I'll have the protein ready and in perfect condition for your research when you return. And... 41)**place** all my decimal points **in** the right place!

P: Thanks, Janet. I'll be back in a week and we'll talk more then.

Mysteries of the Egyptian Pyramid

Listen to part of a lecture in a history class. The professor is discussing pyramids.

P: Today we'[01]**re going to switch** to manmade wonders and talk about the Great Pyramid at Giza! At [02]**756 feet wide** and [03]**450 feet high**, this massive ancient structure [04]**is composed of** 2,300,000 stone blocks. The mere sight of this giant, ancient structure [05]**causes many people to wonder**, '[06]**How on Earth** did the ancient Egyptians build this 4,500 years ago?' [07]**Due to the lack of** direct evidence, though, [08]**no one knows** exactly **how** the Great Pyramid was constructed. Scientists and archaeologists aren't clueless though; they have [09]**come up with** theories explaining the construction process. Let's [10]**look at** how the pyramid [11]**might have been built**.

P: Before we [12]**get to** the construction methods [13]**used to build** the Great Pyramid, [14]**does anyone know why** the pyramids were constructed?

S: Didn't they build pyramids for the afterlife?

P: Exactly. Pharaohs **commissioned** pyramids to [15]**serve as** tombs for them to rest in during the afterlife. All of the labor and construction materials consumed were for just one man! Anyhow, pyramids had multiple chambers and passages within them, but only one was the true resting place of the pharaoh. The others were made to fool grave robbers who may [16]**try to steal** the pharaoh's precious treasures.

S: Why would there be treasures in the pharaohs' tombs? Wouldn't that be kind of a waste?

P: Well, yes, but the ancient Egyptians [17]**considered** the afterlife **to be** eternal, so they [18]**wanted to be prepared** for it. To do this, they [19]**took** their most precious belongings **with** them. After living a life of luxury, they were [20]**the icing on the cake**. Unfortunately, their trickery didn't work that well. [21]**Over time**, most of the pyramids were robbed and looted. [22]**Luckily for** us, though, the advanced architecture and craftsmanship of the ancient Egyptians [23]**allowed** the overall structures **to remain** intact.

[24]**Let's move on to** theories explaining how the Great Pyramid was built. [25]**According to** the ancient Greek historian Herodotus, the ancient Egyptians used wooden cranes located on every level of the pyramid to lift the stones. There is a major problem with this theory though, because Giza [26]**is located in** a desert they wouldn't have [27]**had access to** [28]**enough** wood **to construct** cranes. Further, they would have also lacked space for the cranes.

Using Herodotus' records, and other sources, Egyptologists came up with the theory that the ancient Egyptians used ramps to transport the massive stone blocks, as they were the main devices for lifting heavy materials [29]**at the time**. [30]**There have been** many theories about possible ramp shapes, but I'm just going to [31]**concentrate on** the most common ones. Egyptologist Jean-Philippe Lauer suggested that straight ramps, reaching the top of the pyramid, were used. These simplest of ramps [32]**would have been** massive! They would [33]**require a slope** of about a half mile **to reach** the top of the Great Pyramid.

S: But professor, you said the ramp would [34]**have to be** about a half mile. Wouldn't this task be too much for the laborers? I mean, didn't they already have enough work?

P: Exactly! Constructing a ramp of that size would have been a massive [35]**waste of** labor and materials. This [36]**brings us to another style** of ramp, the spiral ramp, which was suggested by tomb excavator Mark Lehner. A spiral ramp is a more complex design that [37]**would have wrapped** around the pyramid until it reached the top. [38]**Compared to other ramps**, it would've required much less material and labor. However, this type of ramp also has problems.

First, it would have ruined the builders' external sightlines. Because they used ropes to measure, the ancient Egyptians needed clear [39]**lines of vision** [40]**to check** how precisely the blocks were layered. Another design problem is the ramp's corner... Imagine turning a corner [41]**high in the air** with a 2.5 ton stone block! Both ramp theories also share the problem of [42]**needing to destroy** the ramps to ensure a clean, smooth exterior surface for the pyramid.

P: Recently, a French architect who [43]**specializes in** 3D designs, Jean-Pierre Houdin, suggested a new theory. He surveyed the pyramid with infrared cameras and developed a 3-D model of the Great Pyramid to support his new theory that the Great Pyramid was built using internal ramps. He felt that the Egyptians built external ramps to reach about 141 feet in the beginning, and then [44]**switched to** using internal ramps. These ramps would wrap around the inside of the pyramid and [45]**reach the apex** like spiral ramps.

S: But professor, wouldn't corners still be problematic?

P: I [46]**was** just **about to explain** that. Spiral ramps can [47]**be compared to** the winding roads built on the sides of mountains. You know that cars driving along these roads [48]**risk falling** off. [49]**In** much **the same way**, workers could have easily stumbled off the side of an external spiral ramp. Internal ramps, [50]**on the other hand**, have space around the corners thus [51]**making it easier**, and safer, [52]**for laborers to haul** stones up the ramps.

S: Ah, so the internal ramps provided safety for the workers!

P: Exactly.

S: But, didn't you say that ramps require too much labor and material?

P: Yes, they do indeed, but internal ramps are different. They would basically [53]**become a part of** the pyramid. Since they weren't going to be [54]**taken down** after construction, they could simply be sealed off after use, significantly conserving materials and labor.

S: It [55]**sounds like** Houdin's theory is the best explanation.

P: Yes, his story is a revolutionary explanation regarding the construction of the pyramids and [56]**is likely to be accepted** by the community since it eliminates the problems [57]**associated with** the previous theories.

Coral Reef Destruction

Listen to part of a lecture in a marine biology class. The professor is discussing coral reef destruction by crown-of-thorns starfish.

The Great Barrier Reef, the world's largest reef system, **01) is home to** more than 400 coral, 1,500 fish, and 200 bird species. The reefs **02) are made of** living things **03) called** coral polyps... which are organisms that **04) attach** themselves **to** the ocean floor in large colonies. Before it was fully researched, scientists thought that coral was, uh, strangely shaped rock, and **05) I don't blame** them. Coral doesn't move and, therefore, **06) provides** homes **for** the local fish species among their tough calcium-carbonate skeletons. Recently, the coral population of the Great Barrier Reef has been decreasing **07) at** an alarming **rate**. It **08) turns out** that a species of starfish, the crown-of-thorns, has had a sudden population increase and is **09) preying upon** the coral, threatening the reef population. This species **10) got its name from** the poisonous spines that cover its body. As **11) the second largest** starfish in the world, they can **12) grow up to a meter across**, and eat coral by climbing atop the polyps and releasing digestive enzymes. These **13) break down** and liquefy the coral, which the starfish can then **14) absorb into** its stomach. Scientists have **15) come up with** several theories to explain the sudden explosion of the starfish population.

Their first explanation is that the **16) increase in** the starfish population doesn't really have a specific reason, but is a natural phenomenon. Like many species' populations and the cyclical variations in the Earth's temperature, the increase in the starfish population and **17) decrease in** the coral population may simply **18) be part of** a natural cycle that occurs in the ecosystem. Um... **19) Due to the lack of** scuba technology before the 1960s, studying organisms on the ocean floor was difficult, but **20) in the last few decades** we've already seen three major outbreaks of the crown-of-thorns starfish. This is one of the reasons why scientists **21) are inclined to think** that coral destruction is mostly natural... This claim also **22) has** more scientific **grounds**. We know that a crown-of-thorns starfish produces around a billion eggs **23) in its lifetime**. So **24) let's say** there is an extremely slight **25) change in** the conditions, **26) such as** water temperature or salinity, which **27) results in** a 1% increase in the **28) survival chances** of the starfish... That yields 10 million more starfish! With 10 million more individuals than the previous generation, the starfish will mate and reproduce even more, **29) causing a domino effect**, with the population increasing in each successive generation. **30) As you can see**, even the slightest change can theoretically **31) bring about** a huge increase in starfish population, so natural fluctuations seem a pretty believable cause.

The second hypothesis cites predator decline. Due to their thorns, crown-of-thorns starfish actually don't have many predators. One of the few is the giant triton. When these snails smell a starfish, they **32) chase after** it and attach themselves to the starfish, **33) stabbing** it **with** their radula. Um... this is kind of like a tongue, but **is** actually **34) made of** chitin, and is toothed, like a saw. So once the triton has **35) made an opening in** the starfish, it produces saliva that paralyzes the starfish, and it slowly **36) feeds on** its victim. **37) Fortunately for** the starfish, these snails **38) were hunted for** their ornamental shells **39) so greatly that** their population decreased **40) to** unsustainable **levels** around 1969. Even after 40 years of government protection, the population hasn't **41) bounced back 42) enough to 43) pose a threat to** the crown-of-thorns starfish.

Okay, that **44) brings** us **to** the final hypothesis. This one may **45) seem strange**, but it suggests that human activities on land, such as deforestation, are affecting starfish populations. Deforestation for farmland, which occurs on 80% of the **46) land adjacent to** the Great Barrier Reef, **47) makes** the land **48) vulnerable to** sediment runoff and flooding, so during the **49) rainy season** fertilizers and organic materials **50) get washed into** rivers and **51) make their way to** the Great Barrier Reef. When rivers **52) flood the land**, even more sediment-filled freshwater **53) is discharged into** the sea. This affects the starfish population **54) in** a number of **ways**. First, fertilizers contain nitrogen and phosphorous, which cause massive algae and plankton blooms, providing copious nourishment for the crown-of-thorns starfish larvae. It also dilutes the coastal water, lowering its salinity. Since starfish larvae cannot osmoregulate, ummm... regulate their salinity **55) with regards to** the environment, sea water is normally **56) too** salty **57) for many** of them **to survive**. When river water dilutes the ocean water, however, their **58) chances of survival** increase. Scientists believe that the combination of these two effects may explain the starfish population explosions.

So... today we've talked about how crown-of-thorns starfish affect the Great Barrier Reef negatively, but I should also mention that they have useful functions, too. First, they **59) tend to feed** on rapidly growing coral species. These coral species **60) are kept in check by** the starfish, which **61) allows** slower-growing coral a better chance of survival. This **62) helps maintain** species diversity on the reef. Further, we also know that the starfish is a natural part of the ecosystem, and is preyed upon by other species, such as the giant triton. Knowing that some species **63) have** unpredictable **effects on** their ecosystems, perhaps **64) it's better that** we **65) take care not to have** too great an **67) influence over** the starfish populations.

Whale Breathing Patterns

Listen to a conversation between a student and a professor.

S: Hello, Professor McGee.

P: Oh. Hello, Kevin. 01)**Come on in** and 02)**have a seat**. 03)**What's on your mind**?

S: Well, I was 04)**looking for** your 05)**insight into** a problem I've been having... I mean... academically.

P: Oh, Okay. Shoot.

S: Well, I was researching whale breathing patterns during migration... and...

P: 06)**Let me stop you right there**. You do know that different whales have different breathing patterns, right?

S: I know that baleen whales have two blowholes while toothed whales only have one.

P: 07)**Even though** all whales are mammals and have the fundamental characteristics of mammals, certain attributes differ completely 08)**according to** their specific species.

S: Uh... 09)**I'm not following**.

P: 10)**Let me put it this way**. Although humans are all mammals, we can 11)**be** biologically **differentiated by** ethnicity, gender, and even age. What I'm 12)**trying to say** is... you should pick 13)**a** specific **type of** whale.

S: I've already done that. I started my 14)**report on** the bowhead whale.

P: Ah, the bowhead whale. I believe they're baleen whales. Correct?

S: Of course. Well... I was wondering what about the anatomy and breathing patterns of whales 15)**allows** them **to migrate** 16)**over** such great **distances** without taking short breaths.

P: Well... what's interesting about bowhead whales is that unlike other whales, they can only stay submerged 17)**for up to 40 minutes** per dive.

S: 40 minutes? Isn't that a really long time? What about other whales?

P: Well... again, it 18)**depends on** the whale species, and their 19)**reason for** submerging. How long whales remain underwater when they are feeding or when they 20)**have no** other **choice but to remain** underwater differs completely. Certain species can stay a kilometer underwater 21)**for 90 to 120 minutes**.

S: That is so fascinating. Well... I think we 22)**got sidetracked**... What I was originally wondering was, 23)**biologically speaking**, what 24)**enables** whales **to stay** underwater 25)**for** such **a long time**?

P: Well... 26)**There are a few things** that 27)**enable** them **to stay** underwater 28)**for so long**, but some of them are highly theoretical. The first is the most obvious. Can you guess what it is?

S: Uh... their size?

P: Close. It's actually their 29)**ability to** physically **hold** large 30)**amounts of** oxygen, in their bloodstreams.

S: Aha, I see. What's another factor?

P: Well, another factor is a very unique ability that whales possess. They actually have the ability to reduce the amount of oxygen they need while they are submerged. They can reduce the amount of oxygen 31)**delivered to** the body parts they aren't using during their dives 32)**in order to use** it more efficiently.

S: Wow, I 33)**wasn't aware of** that.

P: Actually 34)**a few years ago**, a group of biologists 35)**at a university** 36)**fitted** cameras **to** whales, including a 100 ton blue whale. According to them, whales expel air from their lungs shortly after diving so they can 37)**stop floating**. 38)**The rest is** squeezed out by increasing water pressure. Although they lose oxygen, they are able to remain underwater by releasing more oxygen from their blood and their muscles. 39)**The secret is in** the relaxation of their muscles by simply thrusting themselves down with a few powerful strokes, and then 40)**continuing to glide down**...

S: Ok. I think that's the kind of information that can help me 41)**along with** my research...

P: 42)**I'm glad to hear that**. I'm always happy to help.

Horse Domestication of Botai People

Listen to part of a lecture in an anthropology class.

P: **01)For decades** anthropologists speculated that horses were domesticated during the Bronze Age in the Eurasian steppes. However, new evidence found in Northern Kazakhstan suggests that the Botai people **02)began to domesticate** horses there nearly 1,000 years earlier than previously thought. Because this idea is so groundbreaking, **03)there is some controversy** surrounding its veracity. **04)The fact that** the Botai people **05)had a close relationship with** horses is undeniable; the question is whether these animals were domesticated. Today **06)'d like to examine** some of the evidence **07)put forth** by the proponents of this theory.

P: Now before I **08)jump right in**, does anyone know who the Botai people were?

S: Well, you mentioned they **09)originated in** central Asia. Umm... weren't they also hunters?

P: Yes, the Botai were nomads who **10)hunted game** like red deer, moose, and Equus Ferus, an early cousin of the modern horse, in the steppes of modern day Kazakhstan. Horse meat was **11)such** an important food source **that** 90% of the remains found in excavation sites were from horses. For shelter, the Botai would build shallow campsites with one or two small mobile houses **12)suited to** their nomadic ways. This implies that they **13)traveled in small bands** and did not **14)stay in** a single area **15)for long**. This whole **16)way of life** changed drastically with the domestication of the horse. Does anyone know how?

S: If they bred horses as livestock, then wouldn't that **17)provide** food **for** more people?

P: Exactly. The Botai domesticated horses **18)around 6,000 years ago** and **19)gained access to** a stable source of meat year-round. This **20)led to** explosive population growth and a **21)shift from** a nomadic lifestyle **to** a more permanent, settled one. After eliminating the **22)need to follow** the wild horses, the Botai started to build pit houses **23)sunk into** the ground to provide insulation against the cold. You see... what I didn't mention is the weather in Northern Kazakhstan is frigidly cold, with subzero temperatures throughout the nine- month winter. Horses **24)proved** exceptionally **useful** since they could **25)survive snowstorms** and forage through snow unlike most animals domesticated later, **26)such as** sheep and cattle. The domestication of horses eventually revolutionized many aspects of people's lives worldwide.

P: The effects of the **27)so called** 'equine revolution' affected everything **28)from** agriculture **to** warfare. **29)In** the early **stages**, these animals provided a stable and reliable source of both meat and milk. **30)As time progressed**, humans **31)began using** horses for other tasks, such as transportation. This **32)allowed** societies **to** greatly **increase** their ranges and brought an early form of globalization **33)due to** cultural interaction and the spread of ideas. The domestication of horses even revolutionized warfare. War shifted from ground troops to mounted soldiers who represented a greater **34)value in** battle since they could cover much more ground and, thereby, **35)quicken the pace of 36)military campaigns**.

S: Umm... But how can we prove the Botai people **37)were the first to domesticate** horses?

P: Well, archeologist Sandra Olsen, one of the leading proponents of the theory, has been gathering evidence to corroborate these claims. The three most credible and positively reviewed of her claims are from soil samples **38)gathered in** the Botai region, the presence of 'bit wear,' or markings **39)caused by the use of** man-made bits or harnesses, on the horses' teeth, and compounds of fat molecules found on pottery shards.

S: Umm.. what do soil samples **40)have to do with** evidence of horse domestication?

P: That's a very good question. Scientists examining sites in Northern Kazakhstan **41)took** soil samples **from** the ground around ancient vertical posts where horses **42)would have been tied**, and found a phosphorus concentration that **43)was ten times greater than that of** soil **44)from outside of** them. How is this all related? Well, horse manure has higher phosphorus and nitrogen concentrations than normal soil, so high levels of phosphorus inside the large confinements would imply the presence of horses... Additionally, the soil samples had low nitrogen levels. Nitrogen, as we all know, is very volatile and is easily **45)washed away** or **46)released into** the atmosphere. The minute nitrogen traces eliminate the possibility that the phosphorus **47)came from** more recent manure. There's also proof to be found in the horses' remains. Examining the skulls from horse remains found in the region, researchers found a peculiarity in their teeth. Careful observation revealed indentations in the large hind teeth which could have only been caused by a bridle, or a man made bit, **48)used to mount and ride** a horse. And finally, by utilizing a method of lipid, or fat analysis, scientists found traces of fats from mare's milk on shards of Botai pottery. While the first two points were circumstantial evidence that **49)relied** heavily **on** inferences, this information was the first piece of **50)direct evidence** that proved the Botai domesticated horses. By proving they milked mares and preserved the milk in their pottery, researchers **51)were able to provide** the 'smoking gun.' I mean, unless you're suggesting the Botai were milking wild horses.

S: Umm... why didn't the researchers just examine the skeletal structures of the remains?

P: Well, I think you're assuming that all animals change physically due to domestication. This is only partly true. Certain animals, such as dogs, cattle or pigs, do develop different physical structures as they undergo morphological changes **52)over generations** of domestication and selective breeding. This does not **53)hold true for** horses, though. **54)It is** nearly **impossible to discern** whether a horse was tame or wild or even the precise era it **55)lived in** judging solely by the skeletal evidence.

P: Judging by the evidence presented by the researchers, I think **56)it's safe to say** the theory is probable. **57)In fact**, with the constant flow archeologist Sandra Olsen, more and more people have finally **58)started to accept** that the domesticated horses almost 1000 years earlier than previously thought.

Biofuel Production Process

Listen to part of a lecture in a biology class. The professor is discussing alternative energy.

P: So, last time we ⁰¹⁾**talked about** ⁰²⁾**producing** ethanol **from** corn. If you'll remember, ethanol is the same type of alcohol found in alcoholic beverages, and ⁰³⁾**one of the main candidates** to ⁰⁴⁾**substitute for** fossil fuels, ⁰⁵⁾**such as** crude oil and coal. The most important difference between biofuels, like ethanol, and fossil fuels is that biofuels are renewable. They ⁰⁶⁾**are derived** directly **from** living organisms, while fossil fuels can only be formed ⁰⁷⁾**after long periods of time** ⁰⁸⁾**under** specific **conditions**, like high temperature and pressure. But, guess what? Scientists have found a new process of making ethanol, which many believe is a more efficient ⁰⁹⁾**way of making** biofuel! It's called cellulosic ethanol production... which is what we'¹⁰⁾**re going to talk** about today. It's actually very ¹¹⁾**similar to** corn ethanol production because both ¹²⁾**convert** carbohydrate compounds **into ethanol**. First, ¹³⁾**let's talk about** what cellulose is. Does anyone remember? John?

S: Isn't cellulose a type of carbohydrate that ¹⁴⁾**makes up** the rigid support structures of plant cells?

P: Very good! Cellulose is a polymer of simple sugar molecules ¹⁵⁾**called** glucose. Uh... ¹⁶⁾**let's try that again**. Hmm... ¹⁷⁾**In other words**, cellulose is a long sugar unit ¹⁸⁾**made up of** smaller units called glucose. It is the most abundant organic compound on Earth, and makes up about 33 percent of a typical plant. This huge abundance is probably the biggest reason that biofuel companies are ¹⁹⁾**switching from** corn **to** cellulosic ethanol, but there are also other advantages.

P: ²⁰⁾**For one**, corn ethanol conversion uses plant starch. Starch is a carbohydrate, just like cellulose, but it is an essential nutrient for humans, so using it ²¹⁾**cuts into** our food supply. However, cellulose, is not digestible by humans, which ²²⁾**makes its use more beneficial**. Another reason why cellulosic ethanol is better is that all plants can supply cellulose for the process. This means that there are increased options and supplies of feedstock, which is the raw material that supplies or fuels machines or industrial processes. Feedstock ²³⁾**leads us to another advantage**. The main feedstock for cellulosic ethanol, woody plants, has much higher density than corn, which makes transporting it more efficient. Hmmm... let me explain ²⁴⁾**with an analogy**. Um... say you're ²⁵⁾**trying to fill** two boxes, one with ²⁶⁾**stacks of** paper and the other with bubble wrap. Obviously, the box filled with paper will be heavier, meaning you're carrying more... substance... whereas the box ²⁷⁾**filled with** bubble wrap will be mostly air, which is useless ²⁸⁾**in this process**. Although density doesn't ²⁹⁾**seem like a** ³⁰⁾**big deal**, transportation of raw material ³¹⁾**plays a** huge **role in** business. ³²⁾**Other than** that, plants ³³⁾**used to produce** cellulosic ethanol ³⁴⁾**are cheaper to grow** and more eco-friendly than corn, which could reduce greenhouse gas production ³⁵⁾**by 85 percent**! So... if we efficiently produce energy from this source, the future of alternative energy sources will be much brighter. This is why there have been so many ³⁶⁾**attempts to increase** the efficiency of cellulosic ethanol production.

P: As technology has progressed, a new process ³⁷⁾**known as cellulolysis**, or the 'biological approach' has been developed. In this method, the cellulose is um... loosened. After it's loosened, enzymes ³⁸⁾**break it down into** glucose, its smallest units. The glucose is then fermented. The fermentation process produces a... uh... thick soup ³⁹⁾**composed of** ethanol and other chemicals. A process called distillation, which is boiling the soup ⁴⁰⁾**so that** the compounds evaporate separately from ⁴¹⁾**each other**, isolates the ethanol. This approach normally uses baker's yeast in the fermenting process, which is a good choice since it's abundant and can withstand extreme temperature and pH levels. Recently, scientists have engineered special resilient yeasts that can convert cellulose directly into ethanol. This means that the process of breaking down cellulose into glucose can be entirely forgone, which ⁴²⁾**speeds up** the production process and ⁴³⁾**reduces costs** further!

P: Okay... So... The second major method used today is called gasification, or the thermo-chemical approach. In this process, ⁴⁴⁾**instead of** fermenting glucose, selected cellulose particles are... combusted, or ⁴⁵⁾**blown up**, to separate their carbon atoms. These atoms are then converted into compounds and ⁴⁶⁾**fed to** microorganisms called Clostridium ljungdahlii. The organisms eat the carbon compounds and release ethanol and water. This ethanol is then distilled ⁴⁷⁾**in the same way** as ⁴⁸⁾**in** the biological **approach**.

P: Even with recent progress, there are some ⁴⁹⁾**difficulties in making** the switch to cellulosic ethanol ⁵⁰⁾**for a few reasons**. A major one is that even with high efficiency, cellulosic ethanol costs an additional 120 dollars to convert per barrel. Moreover, alternative energy projects are not well-funded, so companies that make biofuel can't ⁵¹⁾**carry out** ⁵²⁾**as much research as they need**. They also ⁵³⁾**suffer from** ⁵⁴⁾**a lack of** commercial plants in which to execute conversion. The interesting part is that all of these problems could ⁵⁵⁾**be**, ⁵⁶⁾**to some extent, resolved through** government support. Once cellulosic ethanol production gains public attention and interest, hopefully the industry will acquire more financial support.

Community Service at Museum

Listen to a conversation between a student and a museum officer.

S: 01)**Excuse me**, sir.
M: Yes, ma'am. 02)**How may I help you**?
S: I 03)**have** some **questions regarding** community service.
M: Uh huh? 04)**Go ahead**.
S: Well, I already 05)**checked with** the Downtown Museum, and I can't submit the hours I worked there as 06)**community service**... so I was wondering how community service works here.
M: You can submit your hours here as community service. We don't 07)**mind completing** all of the necessary forms. Anything else you'08)**d like to know**?
S: Well, I am a history major, and I do have 09)**a great deal of** 10)**background knowledge** of world history, but I was just curious if there was anything... I... uh... should 11)**prepare for**.
M: Well... 12)**I don't know if** you already know or not, but younger children are our main customers. We mostly get visitors that are 6 or 7 years old.
S: I 13)**wasn't aware of** that... anyway, 14)**go on**.
M: So 15)**knowing** a lot **about** history isn't 16)**as** important **as** 17)**being familiar with** 18)**dealing with** children.
S: I see... Is there 19)**anything else** I should know?
M: Well the job is basically supervising kids.
S: (laughs) OK. What kinds of, uh... activities can children do around here? Can you 20)**walk me through** a typical day in the museum?
M: Well, right now, we have an exhibition of Picasso's paintings. With children, 21)**rather than** explaining the hidden meanings in the paintings, community service workers, 22)**such as** you, would explain the shapes, colors and sizes and how they suit 23)**each other**. The children seem more 24)**interested in** 25)**stuff like that** than the actual... artistic technicalities.
S: 26)**I see**. I guess Picasso's paintings would 27)**be perfect for** children since they 28)**consist of** a lot of different colors, shapes and sizes.
M: Exactly. It's a big hit right now, which 29)**reminds me**, the Egyptian Room is also 30)**popular with** children, especially the mummies. Children 31)**are** awfully **interested in** mummies.
S: I can totally see children being interested in mummies.
M: Since you're a history major you probably know a lot about Egyptian history, right?
S: I 32)**have a** good **grasp of** most of the concepts, although I would 33)**have to review**.
M: You probably don't 34)**need to do** that. Children usually have only simple questions about different Egyptian pharaohs and mummies and pyramids. 35)**All you have to do** is 36)**walk around** with the children, and briefly explain some of the pieces to them, and 37)**answer** any **questions** they might have.
S: That 38)**seems** pretty **easy**. I mean, 39)**according to** everything I've heard 40)**so far**, it 41)**seems like** a lot of fun.
M: Don't underestimate how hard 42)**taking care of** children is. I mean, 43)**looking after** children is a lot harder than it sounds.
S: I know... I had a 44)**part time job** before in a 45)**daycare center**... and it was... hectic.
M: I'46)**m glad that** you have some experience. It'll definitely 47)**be** a lot of **help** 48)**later on** when you actually start.
S: I can't say that I'm not excited; since I 49)**want to** 50)**get into** education once I graduate.
M: If you would just 51)**fill out this application**, and 52)**let me know** when you can start, I will 53)**let you know how** the process goes, 54)**as soon as possible**.
S: OK.
M: Do you have any questions?
S: I was just 55)**wondering about** the 56)**working hours**?
M: Well, since you'57)**re** just **going to be** a community service worker, hours will be flexible. We can 58)**work out** some kind of schedule and 59)**figure** something **out** that will suit both you and the museum. 60)**Would you like for me to** just **go** ahead and select an appropriate time?
S: Yeah, that shouldn't be a problem, I have a pretty open schedule.
M: Let me know when you're done filling out the application.

Architectural Acoustics

Listen to part of a lecture in an architecture class. The professor is discussing architectural acoustics.

P: We've been **01)focusing on** the architectural features of opera houses and concert halls that **02)make them so unique** and aesthetically **appealing**. Today, we'll **03)look at** the science **04)involved in these designs** and why sound related buildings are built **05)the way they are**. This **06)correlation between architecture and sound** has not been thoroughly researched **07)until recently**, but **08)with the** rising **importance of** acoustics when building concert halls or theatres, **09)the field of** architectural acoustics has been **10)gaining** much **attention**. **11)Let's explore** some of the integral factors that **12)play a role in** defining structural acoustics.

P: One of the most important concepts in architectural acoustics is called 'reverberation time.' When a sound wave is created in a confined space, the listener **13)not only** hears the sound wave directly from the source **but also** its reflections from the surrounding walls, floor, and ceiling. These reflected waves are called reverberant sound, and the time **14)required** for them **to 15)drop by** 60 decibels, when they can **16)no longer** be heard by humans after the original sound ceases, **17)is defined as** reverberation time. This interval is the most important quantitative indicator in determining a room's acoustic suitability.

S: Does longer reverberation time mean better acoustics?

P: **18)Not necessarily**. The optimum reverberation time of a space **19)depends** largely **on** its use. A space with a long reverberation time is called 'live,' whereas an acoustically 'dead' environment is one that **20)causes** sound **to fade** quickly. **21)Typically speaking**, facilities **22)such as** lecture halls require a shorter reverberation time **23)in order to maximize** the clarity and intelligibility of the words spoken. If the reverberation time is too long, the reflected sound from one syllable will still be audible while the next is spoken **24)resulting in** poor perceptibility and may **25)end up sounding** mumbled. **26)On the other hand**, if the reverberation time is too short, then the speaker or the performers will **27)struggle to be** loud **28)enough to fill** the room. In music, solos or piano recitals are often performed in a 'dead' environment because there is only one instrument playing and thus clarity and precision are the most important factors. Conversely, symphony orchestras require a 'live' space because the longer reverberation time blends the notes for a more harmonious sound that gives the music 'body'.

P: Now, **29)let's take a look at** the history of the field beginning with Harvard physics professor Wallace Sabine, **30)one of the first to study** the science behind acoustics and widely **31)considered to be** the father of modern architectural acoustics. Sabine had no acoustics training when Charles William Eliot, the president of Harvard, **32)asked** him **to improve** the acoustics of a lecture hall in the university's newly built Fogg Art Museum. Sabine tackled this seemingly impossible problem **33)with great persistence**. **34)For several years**, he **35)conducted experiments** utilizing different materials, such as cushions, oriental rugs and even different numbers of people, to see how they affected the acoustics of a space. **36)After years of** hard work, Sabine discovered that the materials **37)present in** a room could affect the reverberation time. Since various materials absorb different sounds **38)at** unique **rates**, depending on the absorbency of the material, they can **39)either increase or decrease** the reverberation time. Foam insulation, **40)for example**, almost completely absorbs sound and reflects little to none, while a thick, smooth painted concrete wall would be the acoustic **41)equivalent of** a mirror.

P: Wallace Sabine **42)used his findings to 43)convert** the Fogg Art Museum space **into** an acoustically acceptable **44)lecture hall** by using thick drapes and sound absorbent cushions to shorten the room's reverberation time. After the success of this project, switching up interior features to change reverberation time became widely used and **45)proved to be** particularly **46)effective in** adjusting the acoustics of preexisting and older buildings.

S: Umm... why do older structures have such poor acoustics? I mean, what were some of the problems?

P: Well, **47)a lot of** the times acoustic problems **48)result from** improper design or construction limitations. Before the field of architectural acoustics was widely studied and **49)applied to** real life designs, architects often only emphasized the grandeur of the structure without **50)thinking about** the acoustics. **51)In some extreme cases**, these non-acoustically engineered buildings **52)suffered from** sound being **53)focused on** only one section of the audience, especially in domes or structures with smooth curved walls.

S: You've mentioned materials, but what other factors determine the reverberation time of a room?

P: There are two other important ones: the room's size and the shape of the room. The size of a room is an important dictating **54)factor in** reverberation times. **55)In general**, larger rooms have longer reverberation times because there is more uninterrupted space **56)for the sound waves** to **57)travel across** and reverberate. On the other hand, smaller rooms have shorter reverberation times since sound waves are reflected, but quickly **58)die out 59)due to** the small size of the space. Shape also plays a critical role. Since reverberation time measures the reflected sound waves, **60)the number of** reflecting surfaces available directly **61)correlates to** the reverberation time. Therefore, more walls mean more reflection, which ultimately means longer reverberation times. Domes increase the reverberation time because their high ceilings increase the overall size of the space.

P: Even **62)with these factors in mind**, **63)it is nearly impossible to construct** an acoustically perfect structure, as even the audience will affect the acoustics. The average human, as Sabine roughly calculated, absorbs **64)the same amount of** sound as six seat cushions. **65)As you can see**, this is one of the biggest acoustical dilemmas faced by architects when designing such structures. I mean... How do you know how many people will **66)show up**? No one can accurately predict the effect of the attendees since this is an uncontrollable variable. **67)Even if** attendance is confirmed beforehand, **68)there is no way of** knowing the audience members' exact weight, height, or clothing type, all of which would affect the space's reverberation time.

S: Really? How do engineers **69)solve** this **problem**? Do they just guess?

P: Well, they make educated estimates. One way engineers and architects handle this problem is by designing the room to produce optimum reverberation **70)at** full **occupancy**, but this still **71)leaves room for** imperfections. The **72)many factors involved** make acoustics a difficult and calculations cannot create a perfect acoustical environment. This is also why adjusting the acoustics of a concert hall or a theater is a continuous task that doesn't **73)end with** construction completion.

Disappearance of Anasazi People

Listen to part of a lecture in an anthropology class. The professor is discussing Anasazi.

⁰¹⁾**Has anyone here** ever **heard of** computer models? ⁰²⁾**Not** models of computers, **but** rather, simulation models for would-be situations. Today's advanced technology ⁰³⁾**allows** researchers **to find** data about families, populations, or even entire societies using computer simulations they basically create ⁰⁴⁾**on their own**. Fortunately, the development of these virtual situations, has allowed us to ⁰⁵⁾**look deeper into** ancient civilizations. By ⁰⁶⁾**entering data** about the environment and societal rules and patterns, researchers can find answers regarding ⁰⁷⁾**what happened to** historical human civilizations ⁰⁸⁾**over a certain amount of time** and even ⁰⁹⁾**point out** patterns in specific families ¹⁰⁾**from the past**. ¹¹⁾**For instance**... they might use a model to see how population density is affected if life expectancy increases... or... what happens if people ¹²⁾**start** ¹³⁾**spreading out** from a densely populated area. ¹⁴⁾**It's important**, however, **to remember** that these models only give theoretical answers about the results of ¹⁵⁾**changes in** a population. Real life situations are obviously a little different since the population is ¹⁶⁾**made of unique individuals**, and, well, unexpected events can occur. Still, these computer models ¹⁷⁾**give us relatively correct answers** when researching large patterns in a population.

These computer simulations have ¹⁸⁾**been used to find** the likely causes of the declines of past societies, ¹⁹⁾**such as** the Anasazi. As we discussed last week, the Anasazi lived ²⁰⁾**around seven hundred years ago** ²¹⁾**in the area of** the southwestern United States now ²²⁾**known as** the Four Corners, present day Arizona, Utah, Colorado, and New Mexico. The Anasazi ²³⁾**are** probably most **well-known for** their mud villages that ²⁴⁾**look like** gatherings of boxes strategically ²⁵⁾**placed above** cliffs and along rivers. These villages ²⁶⁾**consist of** buildings that could house about a hundred people each. You would think they would have been spread out over the land, like ranches; however, they more closely resemble apartment buildings, but lack stairs to enter the higher levels, so you couldn't even enter most of them without ²⁷⁾**climbing a ladder**. Their most common building material ²⁸⁾**appears to have been** bricks which they made using ²⁹⁾**a mixture of** straw, natural clay, and stones. Because entire Anasazi villages are still standing intact in the region today, we know ³⁰⁾**for sure** that they were excellent builders. By simply ³¹⁾**looking at** the complexity of these buildings, we ³²⁾**are able to** see the intricate techniques that these people used. One of the unique buildings found there is the kiva, a separate circular underground room where they ³³⁾**asked for** assistance in agriculture and health from the serpents, fire, and sun. We know this because they also ³⁴⁾**left behind** petroglyphs, engravings in stone, that give us a peek inside their culture and beliefs. These historical sites have provided abundant historical artifacts and knowledge, but they haven't been able to explain exactly why the Anasazi suddenly disappeared after thriving for a thousand years.

Most people assumed that it was ³⁵⁾**because of** changes in the climate ³⁶⁾**during the period**. By studying their environment, we can see that there was a 50 year period with very little rain during the 1200s. Such a prolonged ³⁷⁾**decrease in** water availability ³⁸⁾**seems like** clear evidence that the farming Anasazi culture couldn't have ³⁹⁾**continued to produce** harvests ⁴⁰⁾**sufficient for** sustaining the population of the region. After more in-depth research, however, some scientists ⁴¹⁾**began to question** this theory. One of them was archaeologist Jeffrey Dean. He studied the rings in the logs used in the Anasazi buildings which are still standing today. Tree rings, ⁴²⁾**as you know**, are the circles found when you ⁴³⁾**cut down** a tree. Because they are developed through a trees growth pattern, they can be ⁴⁴⁾**seen as signs** of the climate and nutrients available during the time. Dean discovered possible inaccuracies in the drought theory by studying these rings from the 14th century. He found that ⁴⁵⁾**instead of** undergoing a true drought, the area may have experienced a ⁴⁶⁾**shift in** the typical precipitation patterns in which the heavy summer rains that ⁴⁷⁾**helped bring** late spring crops to harvest did not occur ⁴⁸⁾**as expected**. This ⁴⁹⁾**may have caused** the Anasazi to became unsure of their gods and religious practices. Other research opposing the theory was conducted by Carla Van West who studied the harvest and nutrition consumption of individuals during normal circumstances. Her data ⁵⁰⁾**led her to believe** that a drought wouldn't have ⁵¹⁾**caused** the entire population **to leave** the land or ⁵²⁾**leave them unable** to grow ⁵³⁾**enough** harvest **to sustain** themselves. ⁵⁴⁾**Based on** the data these two scientists developed, it began to look like drought ⁵⁵⁾**couldn't have been** the only reason the Anasazi civilization disappeared.

This is where computer simulations became useful. We already knew the location of their settlements, what they ate... even what the environment was like every year. So, to ⁵⁶⁾**figure out** what happened to the Anasazi, we ⁵⁷⁾**put in** all the data we ⁵⁸⁾**knew about** them and the valley in which they lived. We also entered facts about the water supply and gave people characteristics that ⁵⁹⁾**corresponded to** the environment. Say, like, they might have had fewer children if the harvest wasn't good enough that year, since not all of the families could survive, or... perhaps they left the area to find a place with better weather.

Basically we used the program to recreate a period of time from, uh... about the 800s to like, 1300, which is when they disappeared. Then do you know what happened? The program gave us results that ⁶⁰⁾**correlated with** the historical information that we already have. The first fact that the simulation supported was that the population ⁶¹⁾**grew in size**, then declined ⁶²⁾**over time**, which probably means that the population increased when the harvest was plentiful, then shrunk when the harvest wasn't as good. The results also confirmed where the people lived within the valley. The biggest inaccuracy in the conclusions was that the computer simulation showed that by 1300, the population had ⁶³⁾**decreased to** only a few families, but ⁶⁴⁾**in reality** the population had disappeared completely.

So what are some of the final conclusions that the computer simulation gave about the Anasazi people? Well, first, it shows that the environment really affects every aspect of a population, its size, where they lived... However, it still doesn't ⁶⁵⁾**answer** all of **the questions** about their disappearance. It ⁶⁶⁾**shows us that** a small population could have ⁶⁷⁾**kept living** there. We're still ⁶⁸⁾**left to wonder** why they all ⁶⁹⁾**disappeared from** the area if the land could still support some people.

Psycological Impact of Music

Listen to a conversation between a student and a professor.

S: Hi, Professor Wilkins. ⁰¹⁾**I'm in** your music appreciation **class**... ⁰²⁾**I'm here about** the project...

P: Well, I assume you've chosen the genre and topic of the music, ⁰³⁾**by now**. What are you ⁰⁴⁾**having trouble with**?

S: I've just ⁰⁵⁾**been** so **caught up with** other classes...and frankly, I haven't even ⁰⁶⁾**decided on** the genre, ⁰⁷⁾**let alone** the topic.

P: Oh, not even the genre? Wow, you ⁰⁸⁾**must have been** either really busy or procrastinating.

S: I've ⁰⁹⁾**been swamped** lately, and plus, I've had no good ideas regarding the genre of music.

P: Oh, ¹⁰⁾**why don't you** ¹¹⁾**try to** ¹²⁾**think about** it differently... ¹³⁾**think backwards**? I mean, ¹⁴⁾**instead of** worrying that you haven't chosen the genre yet.

S: ¹⁵⁾**I don't follow**.

P: ¹⁶⁾**Make a**... a rough-**draft** in your head; how you're feeling ¹⁷⁾**at a certain time** of day, this could be your topic. And then find a genre that ¹⁸⁾**best fits** those feelings. ¹⁹⁾**Are you into** hip-hop?

S: Huh? Are you saying that I should match a random feeling to a specific genre?

P: I sure am, but it sure would be helpful if you could actually capture the moment when you're feeling the ²⁰⁾**need to** ²¹⁾**listen to** a genre like hip-hop. Take, ²²⁾**for example**, when you feel the ²³⁾**need for** something with a rapid beat, tempo, and fast wording.

S: Oh, I certainly know that feeling.

P: The hip-hop genre ²⁴⁾**is** one that I'm personally **eager to** ²⁵⁾**read about**. Its relatively short history and rapid spread and development have fascinated me ²⁶⁾**for** quite **a while**.

S: Anything else I should ²⁷⁾**keep in mind**?

P: Technicality. The usage of slang, I believe some words in hip-hop ²⁸⁾**are related to** the concept of oxymorons.

S: What was that?

P: An oxymoron... It's when two contradictory words ²⁹⁾**make up** a phrase, ³⁰⁾**such as** 'dark sun', or 'mandatory charity'. I'm sure you've heard some of them in hip-hop. You can note them and ³¹⁾**write about** how they ³²⁾**came into being**.

S: I think I ³³⁾**get it**. Well, can I also ³⁴⁾**incorporate** some psychology **into** it; since it's my major?

P: Sure, whatever you can do. ³⁵⁾**Say**... if you're a psychology major, ³⁶⁾**would you mind** ³⁷⁾**helping me out** with something? There's not much glory in it, but if ³⁸⁾**you're up for** it.

S: Sure! What is it?

P: Well, I'm attending a symposium about certain types of music and their ³⁹⁾**effect on** infants. ⁴⁰⁾**I'm okay with** all the musical aspects, but the psychology part... I need someone to help me out. I'm sure you've heard of the ⁴¹⁾**research on** music during pregnancy...

S: Oh! I've actually ⁴²⁾**wanted to** ⁴³⁾**be a part of** that. I've read about it. They mentioned the psychological change of mothers and... surprisingly it affects the fetus. Many pregnant women ⁴⁴⁾**listen to** calm, classical music, which they feel ⁴⁵⁾**leads to** happier childhoods for their children. I'll ⁴⁶⁾**have to review** it to remember the specifics, though, the research was quite old... maybe the symposium will cover new details that I haven't read about yet.

P: ⁴⁷⁾**How about** you gather ⁴⁸⁾**a couple of** your friends from your department and ⁴⁹⁾**bring** them **along**? The school will ⁵⁰⁾**cover expenses for** accommodations.

S: I'll have to ⁵¹⁾**talk to** them, ⁵²⁾**I don't know if** we can ⁵³⁾**be of** much help with this sort of information... and plus, our department is ⁵⁴⁾**conducting a** huge research **project** and most of the students are ⁵⁵⁾**being used as** the ⁵⁶⁾**control group**. I don't know if we will ⁵⁷⁾**be able to leave** town during the project.

P: Well, I will contact ⁵⁸⁾**the head of** the psychology department and see what I can do.

S: ⁵⁹⁾**That'd be great**. We've all been wanting to leave town ⁶⁰⁾**for a nice break**.

Invention of Electric Guitar

Listen to part of a lecture on music history. The professor is discussing electric guitar.

P: We've been studying the development of 18th and 19th century musical instruments, but today we'll [01]**move on to** the 20th century... Okay... so what do jazz, rock'n' roll, country, and blues [02]**have in common**? Well, one major connection is the important role of the electric guitar in these genres. Of all the musical instruments used during the 1900s, the electric guitar is probably the most versatile and influential. It can be played [03]**in harmony with** almost any other instrument or hold the spotlight [04]**on its own**. Let's [05]**look at** the changes the electric guitar [06]**went through** to become the instrument that we know today.

P: Can anyone tell me what motivated the development of electric guitars?

S: Um... They can make [07]**a lot of** strange noises... Was it to [08]**give** the acoustic guitar [09]**a** wider **range of** sounds?

P: Close. An electric guitar does have a wider range of sounds, or effects, but they were not considered when designing the electric guitar. Effects were developed by guitarists [10]**experimenting with** fully constructed guitars, after the design was finished. One of the biggest incentives for developing an electric guitar was amplifying the guitar's sound. Already beloved by both artists and audiences alike, guitars couldn't be used in concerts or ensembles because they were buried and lost amidst the louder brass and horn instruments. Also, if you remember, phonograph recordings and commercial radio became popular music media [11]**in the 1920s**. [12]**Along with** big band music popularity, this meant that guitars [13]**needed to change**, or live guitar performances would disappear. This is why louder guitars became even more necessary, and guitar makers experimented with many innovative changes [14]**such as** the curved archtop shape and larger bodies.

P: [15]**Around this time**, engineers and inventors [16]**began** [17]**tinkering with** electricity and the guitar [18]**as well**; one of them was George Beauchamp. Beauchamp, co-founder of the biggest guitar maker [19]**of the time**, figured that a magnet could capture the motion of a steel string within its magnetic field and [20]**convert** it **to** electrical energy. The electrical energy created by the strings' vibrations' strength [21]**depended on** a combination of factors, such as the string's thickness, the rate of vibration, and the strings' distance from the magnet. Since the motion could be captured as electrical energy, each unique sound from the string could be digitized and amplified through a speaker or a similar device. In 1931, Beauchamp and his partner used horseshoe magnets to design a device [22]**called** a 'pickup' , that did exactly that. They [23]**incorporated** it **into** a Hawaiian lap steel guitar creating the first electric guitar in history, the 'Frying Pan'. If you think that name is funny, you should see its shape; you'd understand.

P: Beauchamp believed that the future of guitars was electric and [24]**started selling** electric guitars like the 'Frying Pan.' They were an instant success, [25]**getting praise from** the most popular guitarists of the time. Unfortunately, for Beauchamp, other manufacturers had copied his technology and began producing electric guitars before he could stop them [26]**six years later**.

P: Lap steel guitars like Beauchamp's are not really widely used today. We're more [27]**used to** the larger, curved bodies of Spanish- style guitars, which are held sideways and finger-strummed. A company called Gibson Guitars was [28]**the first to** successfully **implement and commercialize** Beauchamp's technology in Spanish guitars. By 1933, they'd produced their first electric guitar, the extremely popular ES-150. Country and blues guitarists, [29]**as well as** skilled jazz guitarists [30]**switched over to** this electric guitar and produced innovative sounds that were never before heard in guitars, or in any other instrument [31]**for that matter**.

P: The ES-150 was, however, [32]**far from** perfect. Since the pickups [33]**at the time** were not very advanced, [34]**rather than** [35]**isolating** the vibrations **from** the strings, they [36]**acted as** [37]**sort of** a microphone, amplifying everything, like the vibration of the guitar body. This caused a lot of fuzzy background noises, not the clean, crisp sound guitarists sought. Another problem was audio feedback. This occurs when a guitarist strums a guitar and the sound [38]**gets amplified** by a loudspeaker. If this amplified sound reaches the guitar strings, it [39]**causes** them **to** vibrate more. These vibrations are picked up and amplified again and again; creating a loop of loud, digitized noise.

P: To [40]**fix** those **problems**, a prominent jazz musician [41]**went to work** at a local guitar workshop. In 1940, he produced 'The Log,' a guitar whose body [42]**was constructed of** a long piece of solid wood instead of a hollow body. 'The Log' [43]**had** two major **advantages over** hollow bodies. The first is that feedback was diminished because the body was more [44]**resistant to** vibrations. Second, its notes [45]**lasted longer** because the strings maintained vibrations, rather than dissipating them to [46]**the rest of** the guitar.

S: Hmm... It [47]**seems like** all the guitar makers were [48]**trying to reduce** the electric guitar's effects. I always thought they sounded really cool, and actually prefer the effects, like in Jimi Hendrix's music.

P: You're not alone, but musicians didn't [49]**open up** to the idea of incorporating electric effects into their music [50]**until after** the 1950s, and largely [51]**due to** Jimi Hendrix. Hendrix is considered one of the greatest guitarists ever, due to his innovative style. Rather than avoiding feedback and distortion, he [52]**took advantage of** them. [53]**For example**, his Fender Stratocaster, had three pickups and a switch for [54]**selecting which to use**, but Hendrix wasn't satisfied with only three choices, so he jammed the pickup selector on his guitar so that he could play using two pickups [55]**at the same time** and create some strange new sounds. This technique has [56]**become** extremely **popular** since then.

P: Now you can see that the electric guitar's evolution is [57]**tied** very closely **with** that of music itself. As guitars improve, they introduce new musical styles and as musicians [58]**experiment with** new guitars, they [59]**lead to** adaptation by manufacturers.

Examination on Ball Lightning

Listen to part of a lecture in a physics class. The professor is discussing lightning.

P: We all think we know what lightning is, right? Well, scientists will [01]**tell you that** you actually don't. Because it's extremely dangerous and short-lived, it's a phenomenon that isn't understood very well, even by the most renowned scientists. Scientists have currently identified eight different types of lightning, with cloud-to-ground lightning being the best known and most common type. However, there's another atypically long-lasting type of lightning that does[02]**n't** even involve clouds **at all**. This type, [03]**called ball lightning**, may not even be true lightning at all, because [04]**there is no evidence of** its existence [05]**except for** [06]**eyewitness accounts**. [07]**What's more is that** descriptions from those who [08]**claim to have seen** ball lightning [09]**are** wildly **different from** [10]**one another**, meaning they're not very credible. If there's one thing scientists know, it is that people can't [11]**be trusted to accurately retell** facts. Scientists don't even trust their own intuition, only hard, reproducible, experimental data. [12]**The lack of** a verifiable cause for ball lightning - it's [13]**been blamed on** black holes and even extraterrestrials - means it [14]**is considered** little more than an urban legend and scientists consider it only a hypothetical phenomenon.

P: Before we [15]**go any further**, let's define ball lightning... OK... well... [16]**According to** witnesses, ball lightning is a luminous, spherical, and electrical object. It is around the size of a golf ball and is usually observed during thunderstorms. It's most often red, orange, or yellow, and moves horizontally. It has also [17]**been reported to** [18]**pass through** walls and approach people without harming them, and, usually explodes leaving a sulfurous smell [19]**at the end of** its life. The properties of ball lightning are not as clear-cut as [20]**those of** other lightning forms, though. [21]**For example**, despite the tiny size usually reported, a church in Widencombe-in-the-Moor, England was reported to have been hit by a ball lightning of 2.4 meters [22]**in diameter**, [23]**knocking down** the walls, killing four people and injuring 60. Despite these [24]**difficulties in defining** ball lightning, recent experiments have shown very promising [25]**results in** [26]**trying to recreate** it.

P: [27]**One of the first** of those experiments [28]**was carried out** [29]**in 2006** by a [30]**team led by** Professor Gerd Fussmann. His team produced clouds of plasma 10-20 centimeters in diameter that resembled ball lightning. [31]**For those of you who don't know what** plasma is, I'll explain. You'[32]**re all familiar with** the three states of matter: solid, liquid, and gas, and that matter is most stable during its solid state, and most active as a gas. Well... there is actually a fourth state of matter, called plasma that [33]**comes after** gas and is even more energetic. Now back to Fussmann's experiment... it worked by passing a huge electrical current through a beaker [34]**filled with** salt water using electrodes. The water was electrically heated until it [35]**gained** [36]**enough** energy **to become** plasma. This plasma bubble evaporated and left the beaker, burning brightly [37]**in an oval shape** above the water for about 300 milliseconds. [38]**What's interesting is that** this cloud couldn't even ignite [39]**a piece of paper**. It was a great discovery because the plasmic cloud created in the labs was different from our previous understanding of plasma. Plasma is actually a highly energetic form of matter that characteristically [40]**rises into the sky**, but does not have a defined shape. If scientists [41]**want to contain** plasma in a specific shape, [42]**lots of** equipment and power [43]**are required to keep** it in that shape for even a fraction of a second.

P: So instead of trying to [44]**figure out** the issues with the plasma hypothesis, scientists [45]**came up with** a more plausible theory. Professor John Abrahamson [46]**at the University of** Canterbury introduced a theory which suggested that ball lightning was a result of a chemical reaction of silicon particles that burn [47]**in the air**. Uh... silicon is a chemical element that is found naturally in the ground, and [48]**is** widely **used for** making electronics and mirrors. When a lightning bolt hits the ground, the heat and current cause a chemical reaction where silicon in the soil [49]**turns into** vapor and rises into the air. The pure silicon particles in the air [50]**are attracted to** [51]**each other** by the electrical charge created by the lightning strike, [52]**binding together into** a ball **shape**. The silicon [53]**reacts with** atmospheric oxygen and glows brightly. This chemical reaction between silicon and oxygen [54]**takes place** from the outside in, burning for [55]**as long as** there is unreacted silicon left.

P: [56]**There is a problem** with this theory [57]**as well**. During World War II, Allied pilots often noticed 'balls of fire' which [58]**seemed to trail** fighter jets [59]**at night**. These balls were later called 'foo fighters' and pilots assumed that they were secret weapons developed by Germany and Japan, but the Axis forces also reported them. Interestingly, the descriptions of foo fighters and ball lightning, like their color and speed, were almost identical, [60]**leading to the conclusion that** they were the same thing. But this conclusion [61]**gives rise to** another problem: the silicon molecules [62]**hypothesized to create** ball lightning cannot reach the altitudes where the foo fighters were spotted.

P: So... there is still no theory that can fully explain what ball lightning is, or what causes it. You can see that [63]**it is hard to study** these phenomena too, because they are so unpredictable and infrequent. The only way I can think of studying them is to find a location [64]**famous for** ball lightning sightings and basically [65]**wait for** something **to** happen.

Tutoring

S: Good afternoon, Dr. Lawlor. The, um…, calculus professor [01] **told me that** you were [02] **looking for** me earlier [03] **this morning**.

P: Yes, Sarah, [04] **how have you been**? Please [05] **come in** and [06] **take a seat**.

S: I've been great…just [07] **swamped with** all these assignments and papers… I haven't seen you since I was in your literature class.

P: Yes, it has been [08] **quite a while**, hasn't it? Well, when I was [09] **going through** my old files, you know, just to organize them, I remembered how [10] **impressed I was by** the papers you wrote for my class last year. And… You see, our school has a tutoring program [11] **set up for** students who [12] **need help with** writing. But since about [13] **half of** our tutors are quitting soon or graduating this July, we [14] **need to recruit** more tutors [15] **as quickly as possible**.

S: And, you [16] **want me to** [19] **take** one of their **spots**?

P: Exactly!

S: Hmm… [18] **What would I be doing**?

P: It's [19] **as simple as it sounds**! You'd just need to [20] **teach the students how to improve** their [21] **writing skills** and [22] **help** them **with** their papers.

S: But… I only [23] **took your class** to [24] **meet the** [25] **graduation requirement**. I'm a chemistry major. What I [26] **want to pursue** is completely [27] **different from** what I would be doing as a writing tutor… You know, someday [28] **I want to be** a biomedical engineer and [29] **work in a lab** to [30] **save** people's **lives**.

P: I understand that. I figured you could work with the students who [31] **need help with** their chemistry or science-related papers.

S: Oh, Okay. That [32] **sounds like** a reasonable plan, but wouldn't I need [33] **formal training** before I start tutoring since I'm not an English major? I mean, I don't want to do too much strenuous work just to tutor people in writing…

P: Well, not exactly. I mean, it's true you would be35 [34] **taking** one of our weekly training **courses** and [35] **work with** a mentor who has been tutoring [36] **for a while**, but once you complete the training sessions, you will be good to go and can [37] **start tutoring** [38] **on your own**. It's not just about tutoring people, though. You will also [39] **get** class **credits** and community service hours, which will [40] **count towards** your graduation requirements.

S: Oh, that certainly [41] **grabs my attention**! Also, would I be observed by anyone?

P: Just for your first session! The professor whose course you'd be taking for tutoring will be present and [42] **give you feedback and advice** for your next sessions.

S: Hmm… before I [43] **accept this offer**, do you have any tips, professor?

P: (laughs)Of course, Sarah. [44] **When it comes to** tutoring someone, it sometimes [45] **takes** a lot of **perseverance**. You should [46] **keep in mind** that there are two [47] **ways to teach** students how to enhance their papers. [48] **Most of the time**, their papers are unorganized, yet they don't see it. So, [49] **what do you do**? The simplest thing to do would be to directly [50] **tell them the flaws** they [51] **need to fix** to organize their papers. And…

S: …And the other way would be [52] **asking them questions** that would ultimately guide them and [53] **help them organize** their papers on their own, right?

P: Excellent!

S: Well, I think you should [54] **put me down on the list**. I'[55]**m** pretty much [56] **convinced to take the job**.

P: That's perfect. [57] **Thank you for** coming in today, Sarah. I really appreciate it!

Global temperatures

01)Listen to part of a lecture in an 02)earth science class

P: Continuing our 03)**discussion on** global climate change, 04)**I'd like to address** a remarkable and feasible technology that's been recently developed. 05)**Last time**, we talked about the current level of carbon dioxide, CO_2 emission, and its detrimental 06)**effect on** the global climate. I've mentioned that the 07)**rate at which** global temperatures are rising has 08)**gone beyond the** 2 degree centigrade limit that scientists 09)**consider to be** the allowable maximum. At the current rate of increase, catastrophic events could occur 10)**within around 10 years**.

S1: Yes, and… Last class, the bell rang right when you 11)**were about to introduce** some kind of solution, right?

P: Yes, that's exactly what we'll be talking about today: 12)**solutions to** the rising global temperatures. So, how can we 13)**prevent** the temperatures **from** continually **increasing** 14)**past the limit** and 15)**keep** our CO_2 emissions 16)**under control**? Well, 17)**there has been** 18)**an enormous amount of** research to find a suitable 19)**solution to the problem** and numerous 20)**strides** have **been made**.

S2: I think I remember something about oxy-fuel combustion in yesterday's reading. Is that one of the solutions?

P: That is certainly one of the solutions, yes. 21)**Instead of using** air 22)**in the** combustion **process**, it uses pure oxygen. 23)**By doing so**, nitrogen, which is the main component of air, is not heated, and therefore, nitrous oxide production is reduced. Remember, nitrous oxide is also a major greenhouse gas that 24)**contributes to** the global 25)**increase in** temperatures, just like carbon dioxide.

Today we will 26)**focus on** an advanced form of oxy-fuel combustion: Carbon capture and storage! As the name implies, it is a process that collects, isolates, and safely stores the emissions generated during fossil fuel combustion in 27) **power plants**. There are two types: post-combustion and pre-combustion capture.

Even though they're highly technical, both processes have advantages and drawbacks. I'd like to have a class discussion with you guys regarding these.

As you may already be speculating, post-combustion capture 28)**comes into play** after fossil fuels are burned and CO_2 29)**is separated from** the gas stream in the 'flue.' While the emitted CO_2 is 30)**passing through** the flue, it 31)**goes through** a 32)**chemical solution** that 33)**binds with** and saturates the gas, like smoke coming 34)**out of** the chimney. Well, the chemical itself is not very important for this lecture, so let's not 35)**go** too **deep into** that.

As the saturated solution leaves the flue, it releases the gas. Subsequently, the gas is collected, transported and trapped underground 36)**along with** the chemicals used in the process, and… that's where the problem with post-combustion capture emerges. 37)**Not only** are really, really 38)**huge amounts of** these absorbent materials and chemicals required, they are **also** an 39)**economic burden**. Additionally, the equipment and machinery 40)**necessary for** the process are extremely large, and of course, expensive. However, there are some positive aspects of post combustion capture. 41)**First of all, when** 42)**compared to** other solutions, it's a 43)**far more developed** form of technology and 44)**ready to be** 45)**put into use**, which means it can be implemented 46)**right away**. Also, working power plants that have already been built can be easily retrofitted, so it does not require the construction of new plants.

Okay, now let's 47)**take a look at** pre-combustion capture.

S3: Let me guess. It captures CO_2 emissions before the fossil fuels are burned, right?

P: Yes, you're right. Unlike post-combustion capture, pre-combustion capture 48)**takes place** before CO_2 is released. It is considered a very efficient method because… it first 49)**converts** the fuels **into** hydrogen and CO_2. By isolating CO_2, it only 50)**allows** hydrogen **to be combusted** to produce power, effectively preventing any 51)**release** of CO_2 **into the air**. The storage process of CO_2 works 52)**the same way as** in post-combustion capture: CO_2 53)**is securely transported to** underground storage sites, where it will remain 54)**for thousands of years** without any 55)**leakage problems**.

Anyway… Although some people believe that it is a better 56)**fit for** the future, 57)**at present** it 58)**suffers from** numerous drawbacks, which 59)**make me believe** that it 60)**needs to be improved** 61)**in many ways** before it can be considered the ideal method. The first is that it's a 62)**far less** developed form of technology than post-combustion capture, so 63)**it will take** another 15 to **20 years** until it's ready to be implemented. Another drawback is that it requires an enormous amount of construction work. I mean, unlike post-combustion capture, new power plants need to be built so that the equipment and machinery necessary can be installed 64)**prior to** completion.

S4: So, Professor, which is a better method 65)**in your opinion**?

P: Well, I can't really say one is better than the other. Many scientists and researchers 66)**prefer** post-combustion capture to pre-combustion because they believe that speed is the 67)**key factor**. We are currently living in a generation where the so-called 'climate deadline' is approaching, and we need to 68)**make a move** as quickly as possible. 69)**The longer** we wait, **the worse** the situation gets, so speed is the key here. Like I said, pre-combustion capture still needs to be developed and enhanced in many ways. 70)**Regardless of** its effectiveness, it's an irrefutable fact that it cannot be employed 71)**as of now**, and maybe not for another 15 to 20 years. Post-combustion capture methods, 72)**on the other hand**, can 73)**be added to** working power plants globally right now and immediately 74)**start reducing** CO_2 emissions, right? If we focus on 75)**both of them**, 76)**it's only going to split** our resources and 77)**risk** 78)**making us** 79)**miss the deadline** that we have set, so that 80)**won't do any good**. So my point is… Instead of 81)**wasting our time debating** which to use, we should primarily focus on 82)**encouraging** people **to start** 83)**looking into using** post-combustion capture, because if this trend continues, the next generations won't exist. It's a very urgent matter, and awareness of it should be spread 84)**as quickly and as widely as possible**.

Monochromatic sculptures

P: Okay… 01) **in** the last **chapter**, we 02) **looked at** the fundamental roots of Greek and Roman mythology and their historical backgrounds. Even though they 03) **are** mistakenly **regarded as** mere myths by some, we've learned that 04) **there were** once political and social 05) **parallels in** the stories, correct? Um, the most convincing tangible evidence of such a belief is, perhaps, the art made during these eras… sculptures, 06) **to be specific**. I'm sure you've all seen 07) **a variety of** statues, whether vibrantly colored or plain white. Our understanding of Greek and Roman statues is usually most 08) **compatible with** 09) **the latter case**, though, right? Everything is usually white 10) **from the head to the toes**…

Now, the history of these monochromatic sculptures 11) **dates back to** 15th century Europe… especially Italy, where the impact of the Renaissance was greatest. During this era, some ancient Greek and Roman sculptures were rediscovered 12) **in many parts** of the world. Umm… If you guys 13) **refer back to** the previous chapter, the Apollo Belvedere was one of the sculptures that was rediscovered 14) **during this period**. It depicts the Greek god, Apollo, 15) **in one color** - white… a symbol of aesthetic perfection. Anyway, what the Renaissance artists did when they rediscovered such ancient statues was that they 16) **strove to emulate** their most distinctive characteristic - the monochromatic coloration. This "trend," 17) **so to speak**, influenced the society 18) **in a significant way**… I mean, 19) **think about** 20) **it this way**. Let's just say that you were one of the people living 21) **at the time**, and all of the statues you saw were uniformly white. They were certainly beautiful, but they had no color. Contravening the earlier perspectives on sculpture, Renaissance era white marble statues, created 22) **in accordance with** these ancient sculptures, 23) **instilled** 24) **a** new **set of** standards **in** contemporary artists that suggested that form was more important than color. It was 25) **not until** the early 19th century **that** the art historians realized that their 26) **belief that** the ancient marble statues were originally white was inaccurate.

In the early 19th century, archaeologists found subtle traces of visible paint on the statue and, after further research, 27) **arrived at** the conclusion that the statues that 28) **were once believed to be** monochromatic were originally polychromatic. You see, the current absence of visible coloration doesn't necessarily mean that it never existed. The color 29) **could have** either simply **deteriorated** 30) **due to the effect of** wind, water, and other such factors 31) **over thousands of years**… or someone could have vigorously scrubbed the paint off while 32) **trying to clean** the statues… Anyway, today, 33) **with the advent of** new technology, archaeologists 34) **are able to** 35) **execute** more in-depth 36) **research into** these sculptures. For instance, they can use ultraviolet light on the statues and 37) **distinguish** formerly colored parts **from** the non-colored ones. Umm… UV light is very useful and 38) **efficient for** this particular task because it 39) **causes** organic compounds **to**, 40) **sort of, fluoresce**. You see, unlike modern paints, the paints that the Greek and Roman artists used 41) **were** mainly **composed of** organic compounds… Anyway, we'll be re-visiting this matter 42) **in the next lesson**, so 43) **let's get back on topic**.

We were 44) **talking about**… Oh, yeah. Right. The evidence they found proved that the statues were originally polychromatic. Today, it's generally accepted by art historians and researchers that the Greek and Roman sculptures from the 7th century B.C.E through 4th century C.E were all polychromatic. Some believe that 45) **it's unfortunate** that Renaissance art standards were established 46) **based on** the "supposed" Roman and Greek principle that has now 47) **been proven wrong**. I agree 48) **to a certain extent**, but I don't think that the principle was entirely wrong. I mean, there can certainly be multiple interpretations of one piece of art. 49) **As I mentioned** previously, monochromatic sculptures were interpreted 50) **with a heavy emphasis on** the form. 51) **In this sense**, we must first 52) **take a** careful **approach to understanding** the artists' intentions, particularly 53) **when it comes to** interpreting polychromatic sculptures.

54) **The first thing to consider is** the role of the colors. Some parts or features of the statues 55) **were accentuated with** different colors. How, you may wonder, could that 56) **be related to** the artists' intentions? Well, one compelling explanation is that a color may have symbolized many facets… things such as invincibility, patriotism, honor, heroism, 57) **and so on**. Let's 58) **take** the statue of Augustus, the founder and first emperor of the Roman Empire, **into consideration** to 59) **clarify the point**. It was discovered 60) **on April 20**, 1863 in the Villa of Livia at Prima Porta. 61) **In addition to** founding the Roman Empire, Augustus was also the imperator, or commander, of the great Roman army. Observing his statue, we can see that he's 62) **in military clothing**, holding a baton and 63) **posing as if** he'd been 64) **victorious in** battle. When the statue was examined thoroughly, it was revealed that its most abundant color was red, which 65) **is** generally **associated with** energy, war, passion, and strength. You see the connection now, right? The sculptures weren't just randomly polychromatic; the colors actually 66) **played a** symbolic **role in** highlighting certain features or characteristics of the subjects.

The next aspect we should study is the kind of pigments 67) **used to produce** the colors. As you may already know, the quality of paint color 68) **is dependent upon** the quality of the pigments used. 69) **Keeping that in mind**, 70) **let's take a look at** the statue of Augustus once again. The pigments 71) **used for** his statue weren't just… normal pigments. They were very expensive 72) **at the time**. The use of these particular pigments shows his importance and authority as the emperor, in addition to his importance as the imperator.

Okay. I think that was enough explanation of these statues, right? I'm sure you can see how the colors of the sculptures 73) **were associated with** social, economic, and political values. You see, there're still a great number of sculptures that 74) **have yet to be deciphered** 75) **the way that the** statue of Augustus has been. We have the technology 76) **required to pursue** further investigation, and 77) **it's urgent that** we 78) **carry out** more **research** and studies immediately, because the paint pigments deteriorate very rapidly. Through this, 79) **I'm certain that** our knowledge of the art of the Greek and Roman empires will be greatly enhanced, 80) **along with** our understanding of the culture that created the statues.

19th century female artist

S: Professor? Um… about the paper you 01) **asked** us **to** 02) **turn in** next week?

P: Ah… yes, the 03) **paper on** a 19th century female artist.

S: Yes, while I was 04) **looking for** a good example from the feminist era, I 05) **came across** an artist 06) **named** Rosa Bonheur.

P: Yes, the French proto-feminist. How's your research 07) **coming along**?

S: Um… I'm 08) **having a hard time choosing** what to 09) **write about**. I mean, should I just write about her legacy as one of the pivotal figures 10) **in the initiation of** the feminist movement? Or should I 11) **focus more on** her life as an artist?

P: I can definitely see that you've been 12) **doing** some **research**. Well, of course, you can't write a single paper on all of the topics, right?

S: There is 13) **so** much information about her **that** it 14) **made me think about** choosing someone else to write about, but 15) **I'm a** really **big fan of** her work personally… 16) **I'm of two minds on this**…

P: When researching the personal aspects of Rosa Bonheur's early life, there isn't really much to write about other than the fact that she had a hard time 17) **adapting to** school, I guess, and maybe her family's background.

S: So I should probably 18) **rule out** writing about her early life?

P: Exactly. There isn't much to write about. 19) **That is**, if you 20) **decide to** 21) **stick with** Bonheur…

S: Then I should choose between 22) **the role she played** 23) **in the beginning of** the feminist movement by wearing men's clothes and her artwork?

P: Yes. But I 24) **have to** 25) **tell you that** her role in the feminist movement is highly controversial. She 26) **insisted that** the only reason she wore men's clothing was because they were more comfortable and better 27) **suited for** her type of work, which involved a lot of traveling to farms for research. Nobody has 28) **been able to** 29) **validate this theory**, however.

S: I see. I should probably write about her work then, huh?

P: I would recommend that you do, unless you'30) **re willing to push** yourself to 31) **go deeper into** the controversy I just mentioned.

S: It would certainly be a challenge.

P: I actually have some 32) **books on** the topic, but the ones that debate the controversy 33) **go on** for nearly a thousand pages. I'll tell you what. If you decide to 34) **go for it**, I'm willing to 35) **give you extra credit**, if, and only if, you 36) **pull it off** 37) **in a manner** that I 38) **approve of**.

S: Any hints about the criterion on which I'll be graded?

P: Hmm… If you can prove whether or not Bonheur's statement was true, using conclusive proof and statements, I will approve it. You don't have to 39) **worry about** whether I 40) **agree with** your stance or not.

S: Isn't that… a bit abstract? I mean, "conclusive" is a rather objective term.

P: Yes, what I meant was, find information that can 41) **be used to support** your opinion on Bonheur's statement, 42) **sort of** like a persuasive essay. I think this assignment would be a great opportunity 43) **for you to expand** your 44) **knowledge on** the feminist era and your understanding of the artist.

S: Wow, as tempting as it sounds, it doesn't 45) **sound easy**.

P: That's true. 46) **That's why** I will **give you extra points** if you 47) **manage to do** it. Well, I hope you 48) **make the** right **decision**… Remember, this topic will be 49) **as difficult as it is intriguing**.

Light energy

P: We witness and encounter many different forms of energy, **01) such as** heat, light, and electricity, **02) on a daily basis**. When you **03) turn on the lights** in your room, what do you think you have just done? Well, you have simply **04) transformed** electrical energy **into** light energy. The same phenomenon occurs everywhere **05) in our daily lives**. So, how does the transformation of energy work exactly? Well, the way it works is a little complicated, so listen carefully. You guys remember electrons in atoms, right? They **06) play a** very vital **07) role in the process**. When stimulated, the electrons collide and change orbital levels, they **08) release energy** that we experience as light or heat. We collectively **09) call these forms** of energy emitted electromagnetic **energy**. **10) Is** anybody **aware of** this?

S: Of course, light, heat, x-rays, microwaves, and electricity are great examples of it.

P: Perfect! Today, we'll be **11) focusing** primarily on exploring various aspects of the technology that **12) enable us to generate** light energy. Hmm… **13) Imagine what it would have been like** back in our ancestors' times. There was almost total darkness because no electricity existed. Their solution was to use a campfire. Very simple, right? In today's society, where people demand more advanced forms of technology, a fire is not efficient enough. Why? Well… while fires **14) are capable of generating** light energy, they also produce tremendous thermal energy, which is the heat that **15) results from** the potential and kinetic energy of the burning materials. The problem with fires is that the amount of heat being produced is much higher than the amount of light they produce. A similar phenomenon happens with incandescent light bulbs… the light bulbs you probably have in your homes. Well… to **16) give you a clearer vision of it**, think about umm… your house! Has your mom ever **17) asked you to replace** a light bulb in the house? I'm sure some of you have accidently **18) tried to unscrew** a light bulb **19) not long after** it was **20) turned off**. You probably quickly **21) pulled** your fingers **off of** it because the light bulb was still hot.

S: Yes! I almost burned my finger when I was very young.. Why is it still hot even when it's turned off?

P: Yes, we've all **22) had** that kind of painful **experience**… Although they **23) utilize** electrical energy **to generate** light energy, the process of creating light itself creates a major practical drawback. **24) Going** a little **deeper into** the process, light is produced when electricity **25) goes through** a filament and **26) becomes converted to** heat. So, simply, electricity **27) results in** both heat and light. The problem with the process is that the amount of heat energy generated is much greater than the amount of light energy produced - about 90% of the output is heat, so **28) a great deal of** electricity is wasted. It's **29) the same** problem **as** the campfire… It's not effective enough, right? I mean, it's also quite inconvenient, because when heat **30) is released from** the bulbs it simultaneously increases the room temperature. Consumers demand better and more effective technologies. So, to **31) satisfy** their **desires**, fluorescent light tubes **32) filled with** mercury gas were developed.

Now, **33) keep in mind that** this light generating device works quite **34) a bit 35) differently than** incandescent bulbs. Okay, **36) stay with me**. First, when the electrons in the gaseous mercury are stimulated, they **37) start 38) bouncing off of** a special coating on the inside of the tube. The coating glows, and **39) that's how** we get light energy using fluorescent light bulbs. They're a little more sophisticated and **40) harder to understand** than incandescent bulbs, but their production of heat is substantially lower, so they sure are a better option **41) at this time**. Unfortunately, however, this method has detrimental **42) effects on** the environment **43) as well**. Since the gaseous mercury **44) used in** the tube is highly toxic, safe disposal of the tubes is nearly impossible. **45) As far as** we are concerned, we are living **46) in a generation where 47) solving** environmental **problems 48) is a priority**. Therefore, this method **49) isn't seen as** very effective. So, now, we can conclude that **50) neither** incandescent **nor** fluorescent light bulbs are good solutions because the former do not significantly reduce the amount of heat production, whereas **51) the latter** contaminate the environment. Although there are other light generating devices that have been developed, similar **52) drawbacks to 53) those of** incandescent and fluorescent bulbs have **54) made them less than ideal**.

S: Then, there's no way we can generate light energy without producing **55) a lot of** heat energy or contaminating the environment?

P: Well… **56) for now 57) at least**, we don't have any other fully developed lighting devices, but scientists and researchers have recently proposed a new form of technology, and they're currently **58) working on 59) making it feasible 60) for everyone to utilize 61) in the near future**. It's called chemiluminescence.

S: Chemiluminescence… I think I've **62) heard of** it before. Its mechanism **63) is** a little **different from** the other two methods, right?

P: **64) You bet! 65) The way it works is 66) a little 67) different from** the other two methods we've discussed! Okay, uh, I've mentioned that the other two methods require some kind of transformation of energy, right? Like… converting electrical energy to light energy **68) and so on**. Well, **69) this case is an exception**. **70) Instead of** providing some source of energy to generate another, chemiluminescence is a result of an exothermic chemical reaction, and thus, does not require any energy input, such as electricity or heat energy. When electrons are stimulated, they cause the breakdown of reactants, which go through **71) a series of** chemical reactions that ultimately result in a light emission, which is what chemiluminescence is. Furthermore, it does not produce significant quantities of heat, so that it doesn't **72) suffer from** the same drawbacks as incandescent light bulbs. Further, unlike fluorescent light bulbs, **73) it's composed of** all natural non-toxic chemical energy sources, so safe disposal of chemiluminescent bulbs would certainly not be a big concern. No unnecessary production of heat and no environmental contamination… It sure **74) sounds like** a great idea, doesn't it? Well… **75) with respect to** its pragmatic use, chemiluminescence is not a perfected technology yet, because it remains **76) in** the developmental **stage**. **77) Let me 78) give you a little background knowledge** about the mechanism to **79) help you understand** how it occurs. Okay, the source of energy for chemiluminescence is found in nature. It's what allows fireflies and marine animals to glow and light up in the darkness. Scientists have successfully extracted the genes **80) responsible for** the production of chemiluminescence, and they're now **81) striving to enhance** the brightness of the light generated by the chemical and to **82) apply** it **to** existing technologies. Although it does have a few aspects that need improvement **83) at this point**, it might be the most promising method we have **84) come up with**, **85) so far**.

Psychology

P: If I remember correctly, I briefly introduced the concept of personality psychology 01)**in the last class**, right? 02)**For those who were absent**, personality psychology is basically 03)**a branch of** psychology 04)**devoted to studying** the human personality. 05)**It's very closely related to** neuroscience, you know, the study of the nervous system and the brain 06)**in particular**. Umm… I also mentioned that ever 07)**since the advent of** the Human Genome Project, or the HGP, 08)**a tremendous amount of** 09)**research has been done** to identify the fundamental roots of personality and whether or not personality is static. President Barack Obama has even recently announced his 10)**plan to fund** a $100 million project to 11)**unlock** the incredibly intricate **mysteries** of the brain and to 12)**enhance our understanding of** its functions. Why so much money? Well… one of the most apparent reasons is that the discovery process is not 13)**only very** complicated **but also** involves the use of highly technical tools.

If we 14)**look back to** the beginning of the study of the human personality back in the 1990's, which is 15)**not that long ago**, we will find that researchers and neuroscientists 16)**began to use** Electroencephalography, or EEG… Umm… If you 17)**refer back to** the beginning of our textbook, you will see that EEG machines detect brain activity by directly measuring the oscillations caused by the neurons in the brain. Well, it was a fairly good start for neuroscientists 18)**in that** they 19)**were able to** 20)**carry out** 21)**a series of tests on** their subjects…you know, the people 22)**on whom** experiments are performed, and 23)**figure out** what changes their brains were experiencing 24)**over time**. Umm… It 25)**was** once **praised as** one of the most effective methods of promoting the enlightenment of the personality, but now it's 26)**a bit** obsolete 27)**in the field of** personality psychology. 28)**It seems that** 29)**with the shift in** focus **to** a new topic, the stability of personality, a new form of technology, called Functional Magnetic Resonance Imaging or FMRI, 30)**seems to have** 31)**taken over** as the new revolutionary invention in the field.

It sure 32)**sounds familiar**, doesn't it? Right! Our previous chapter 33)**dealt with** MRI and its medical uses. 34)**Try not to** 35)**get the similar names mixed up**, though. The new technology 36)**is used** almost exclusively **as** a laboratory research tool. Umm… 37)**To help you** 38)**draw a clear distinction** 39)**between the two**, MRI is almost like a camera; it 40)**takes pictures of** the brain structures 41)**for scientists to use** 42)**for** diagnostic **purposes**, while FMRI, 43)**as the name suggests**, depicts the functions of the brain 44)**in addition to** the structures… 45)**In other words**… Umm… Okay. 46)**Let's say** 47)**you're under stress** because of homework assignments and whatnot, and you feel the sudden 48)**urge to** 49)**express** your **anger**. Well, your emotions 50)**originate from** your brain's activities. 51)**In response to** stimuli, your brain activates its different parts and sort of 52)**works as** a command control center and 53)**tells your body which** 54)**action to take**. During this process, neuroscientists can detect 55)**changes in** blood flow and oxygen levels in the brain that occur in response to external stimuli using FMRI.

Okay… Now that's 56)**a lot of** information for you to 57)**take in** all 58)**at once**, so 59)**let me** 60)**help you with** it. I've mentioned that your emotions are the output of the brain activities that occur when your brain processes certain stimuli in the environment, correct? Whether you let yourself express those emotions or 61)**restrain yourself from doing** so is your particular personality. 62)**Because of** this property of the brain, or I should say nature, whether or not personality is static has been questioned 63)**numerous times** over the years. FMRI has become a very useful tool for scientists who argue that it is 64)**in fact** a stable aspect of the brain.

Those scientists, who theorize that personality does not change, have 65)**done** some case **studies**, and one of them involved the amygdala, the section of the temporal lobe 66)**responsible for** processing external stimuli, such as emotional reactions. To stimulate this part of the brain, the scientists 67)**had** all of the subjects **sit** 68)**in a straight line** and 69)**showed them** 70)**photographs taken** during wartime… angry, scared, horrified, and fearful faces. Using the FMRIs, the scientists 71)**were able to detect** that the amygdala was activated in some of the subjects when the pictures were displayed 72)**in front of** them. To ensure the validity of the experiment, the subjects, whose amygdalae were stimulated in the experiment, were brought back 73)**two years later** and 74)**underwent** the same **process**. The significance of this study was that when they were brought back, their brains 75)**responded to** the photos 76)**in the same way as** they had in the initial experiment. The scientists, therefore, claimed that since the 77)**response to** such stimuli didn't change 78)**over the course of two years**, it partially proved that personality was also stable… Well, a contradictory argument does exist, but it involves another long, boring experiment, so we won't 79)**go into** it in this class.

You should also 80)**try to** 81)**keep in mind that** FMRI studies aren't perfect yet… a lot of controversies concerning them still exist, and neuroscientists in the field 82)**tend to exaggerate** the significance of their findings. I mean, the brain is, 83)**after all, comprised of** the most perplexing elements… Although some scientists say we have 84)**come to the final stage of** 85)**solving** the brain's **mysteries**, truthfully, our knowledge of the brain is still rudimentary… You see, FMRI is certainly one of the most practical and efficient tools we have 86)**as of now**, but it still doesn't 87)**account for** why we behave the way we do. Yes, it 88)**tells us which** part of the brain is activated when certain stimuli are applied, but that's not 89)**enough to determine** that personality of human beings never changes.

90)**For this reason**, we shouldn't overlook our good, old traditional research methods. I'm sure most of you 91)**are familiar with** this concept. You know, using questionnaires… such as "Do you 92)**enjoy meeting** new people and 93)**socializing with** them?" or "Are you the type of person who 94)**gets disappointed** or sad easily?" Although using questionnaires has some drawbacks, like the respondents manipulating their answers to 95)**portray themselves differently**, it's perhaps the most reliable way we have to 96)**inquire about** people's behavioral preferences and personalities 97)**at the present time**.

usherin.usher.co.kr

USHER iBT TOFLE
FINAL TEST
LISTENING
스터디 준비자료

Implications of Bioluminescence

Listen to a conversation between a student and a professor.

S: Hello, Professor.

P: Good morning, Brian. How was the conference in South Florida?

S: It was a good experience. I met a lot of new people. I think it was a good opportunity for me to create a good professional network.

P: That's what conferences are for. How did you feel about the lecture on molecular biology?

S: It was okay. It provided a lot of interesting theories that gave me a broader perspective on the field. Like I said, I met a lot of interesting people. I think they'll be very useful if I decide to further my research.

P: Conferences are always a good place to meet those with similar professional interests.

S: I wanted to ask you something. On my third day, I think, I was walking along the seashore and almost stepped on a jellyfish. I didn't notice it was there, until it started glowing. I was quite intrigued.

P: I think you witnessed bioluminescence, the production of light by a living organism.

S: And… I was wondering if you could explain the mechanism a little bit. I'm interested in using it as a topic for my term paper.

P: Jellyfish, like the one you saw, are the most commonly known bioluminescent animals, but there are other organisms that do the same. Some others, like fireflies or glowworms, are quite common, but there are also some lesser known bioluminescent organisms, such as certain squid, shrimp and fungi.

S: Wow! Fireflies and glowworms were no surprise, but I didn't realize that there were so many others.

P: Bioluminescence is basically a naturally occurring process in which energy is released through a chemical reaction in the form of light. Getting into the details would be way too time-consuming right now.

S: As mysterious as this is, do you know why certain animals produce light? I mean, is it just a random… emission of energy?

P: Well… they only produce light at certain times, so the purpose differs from animal to animal, but it can generally be categorized in three ways: as a means of intraspecies communication, for predator avoidance, or to attract prey.

S: Ah... Do you know which category jellyfish fall into?

P: Jellyfish, I believe, use bioluminescence to avoid predators.

S: What I'm most intrigued by is the actual process of light production. I mean, how is that even possible, biologically speaking?

P: Well, I don't know how strong your knowledge of chemistry is, but it's basically a chemical reaction. More specifically, the jellyfish can, after being exposed to the necessary energy for activation, rapidly oxidize magnesium and emit a bright light. That's the gist of it.

S: So, the jellyfish produce the chemicals necessary for illumination within their bodies?

P: Exactly. The jellyfish you saw was probably an Aequorea Victoria. It produces a blue light, which is different from other jellyfish.

S: Yes, yes, it was producing a bluish light.

P: Then that's the most likely species. Are you considering writing about bioluminescent jellyfish for your term paper?

S: Well, I wanted to ask you what you thought about it. I mean, is it an interesting enough topic?

P: It's definitely interesting, but it's going to require a lot of work. Jellyfish aren't easy to understand because they are a relatively new field of study and scientists find them radical in the field of marine biology. Are you still up for it?

S: I am. I think it will be very fun.

P: Well, I'm also a big fan of jellyfish. I'm excited to see how you're going to organize the scientific data that may be…rather complicated. Feel free to ask me for guidance at any time.

Type of Renaissance Gardens

Listen to part of a lecture in an art history class. The professor is discussing Renaissance gardens.

P: Okay, I introduced the concept of the Renaissance in last week's lecture. This was the period when new ideas swept across Europe after the Middle Ages. If you'll remember, the term Renaissance means rebirth in French. This cultural movement aspired to popularize the forgotten classic concepts of the ancient Romans across Europe. Countless artistic works were produced during this period, but today we are going to focus on Renaissance gardens. Is anyone familiar with the gardens constructed during the Renaissance?

S: I believe that Renaissance gardens were built to emulate those popular during ancient Roman times.

P: Yes, that is the most important characteristic of the Renaissance gardens. In other words, they were pretty much built as the ancient Romans 'would' have built them, using assumptions of what Roman gardens were actually like. As the idea of emulating the beauty of lost classical artwork became popular, wealthy people, such as merchants and political figures, craved to recreate the magnificent gardens of ancient Rome, so they started to hire prestigious architects to build them. Let's take a look at some of the features that Renaissance gardens shared. The most noticeable features were walkways lined with marble statues and fountains like those featured in ancient Roman gardens. They were also filled with allegorical statues of animals, giants and fantastic creatures, as well as bushes trimmed into specific shapes to further emulate ancient Roman architecture. Renaissance gardens brought the gardens of ancient Rome back to life in every possible way.

S: Professor, what were the ancient Roman gardens actually like?

P: That's a good question. Well, they were pretty much the prototypes of the Renaissance gardens. There were different designs, but Roman gardeners adhered to certain styles that developed in three main stages. The first gardens of ancient Rome were built near homes to grow vegetables and herbs for consumption. This type of garden, known as a hortus, was usually built in the backyard of a house. They served as the primary source of vegetables and herbs for the Romans. At the time, these gardens served more of a practical need than an ornamental one. The second type of Roman garden developed as the quality of life in ancient Rome improved and they enlarged their living spaces. This expansion gave birth to the peristyle, or columned porch and colonnade, in Roman architecture. During this period, the garden moved to the front yard and was decorated with walkways bordered by statues. Further, flowers and shrubs were planted for ornamental purposes rather than the practical vegetables and herbs. The final stage in the evolution of Roman gardens was the villa garden. This was the most luxurious style of Roman garden in which ornamental plants and artwork were arranged for the pleasure of visitors strolling through the peristyles of the gardens. The major difference was that this style of garden contained buildings other than the house itself and more complex ornaments, such as fountains. In some of the larger ones, they even built exercise facilities such as swimming pools! This was the style that drew the greatest praise from Renaissance garden builders.

S: Professor, why did the people build gardens during the Renaissance?

P: I'm glad you asked that question. There are several assumptions regarding why people built these gardens. The most important role of these gardens was to symbolize the status of their owners. Umm… To be straightforward, there are no other significant reasons behind the garden construction at the time. It is fair to say that these gardens were a manifestation of the pursuit of the beauty of ancient Roman architecture. However, research into the purpose of these gardens shows that they were, in fact, mainly displays of wealth and power to the world. These formal gardens served as a medium to impress visitors. People such as writers, poets and philosophers would gather and praise the beauty of the garden. The owners of the gardens would have been able to derive a great deal of satisfaction and pride from the profuse attention and wonder people displayed regarding them.

S: Professor, were there any other unique features of these gardens, besides their beauty?

P: Hmm… Were there any other features? Umm… well, I do remember one thing that might interest you… Oh yes, there was another major interesting feature of the gardens: coin operated fountains. The idea behind these came from the Greek mathematician "Heron of Alexandria". He came up with a device that dispensed water when a coin was inserted. The fountains were set up to release water in the same way as a coin operated vending machine. The official term for these was "giochi d'aqua", which literally means "water jokes," since they were concealed to drench unsuspecting visitors. These were one of the most famous features added to Italian Renaissance Gardens for the purpose of entertaining visitors.

S: Professor, I recall there being another interesting feature of Renaissance gardens. I believe that they contained labyrinths to emulate those of ancient Rome, right?

P: Well, ironically, they did build labyrinths for this reason, but there is no evidence of ancient Roman gardens containing labyrinths. The fact that Renaissance gardeners included them has led many to the misconception that they existed in ancient Rome. Why, then, did labyrinths become a common feature of Renaissance gardens? Well, according to Roman mythology, the labyrinth was an impossible maze where the Minotaur was imprisoned. Later, Italians built labyrinths in their gardens to imitate the mythical maze, so the legendary labyrinth came to life as an entertainment venue. The Italians redefined the meaning of the word to mean an outdoor playground for guests. Whenever there was a large group of guests, labyrinths were not only used as multipurpose grounds for dancing and games, but they also offered a pleasant atmosphere visitors, as their walls were comprised of herbs and shrub plants. People loved to take walks and enjoy nature within the byrinths.

Einstein's Theory of Relativity

Listen to part of a lecture in a physics class. The professor is discussing Relativity.

P: I'm sure you have all heard of Albert Einstein, one of the most influential figures of the past century and the greatest physicist of the modern era. You may wonder what he did to become so famous. Well, he came up with the most significant discovery of modern physics: the Theory of Relativity. This theory gave us new insight into what light is and how it works, changing the way physicists think and reshaping modern physics. Ironically, however, the greatness of this work wasn't fully recognized at the time and he was never awarded a Nobel Prize for his Theory of Relativity. This is because his work's legitimacy and his unorthodox methods were questioned by his contemporaries. The debate over whether Einstein received proper recognition for his signature work continues to this day.

Before I get into his work's impact, we should understand where Einstein came from. He was born in Germany in 1879, and although he loved academics, he hated the formal education system so much that he eventually dropped out, resulting in his failure to enter university on his first attempt. He returned to formal schooling and eventually graduated from Zurich's Federal Polytechnic in 1900. After graduation, he was unable to find employment in academia, so he became a patent office clerk in Switzerland in 1902. Although many have argued that he wasted his time there, Einstein disagreed, citing this as the most productive time of his life and crediting it with his later creativity and productivity. How, then, did examining patent applications help reshape modern physics? Well, it was clearly a combination of genius and experience. In order for him to approve a patent, Einstein had to work backwards, meaning he had to breakdown an invention or an idea himself in order to determine the patent claim's validity. He studied innumerable ideas and inventions during those years. All the information, ideas, and experience he gained became the foundations of his most famous work, the Theory of Relativity.

So, let's get into what the theory actually is. First off, the Theory of Relativity can be divided into two parts: the Theory of Special Relativity and the Theory of General Relativity. The Theory of Special Relativity states that everything has its own time. In other words, each object or person has its own clock. Einstein claims that this is due to a phenomenon called time dilation, under which time is affected by very fast velocities, like the speed of light. Ever heard of the twin paradox? The twin paradox is a good example of how time is affected by speed. Imagine that there are twins; let's call them Jeff and John. Say Jeff takes off in a spaceship travelling at the speed of light to a distant planet and John stays home. When Jeff returns, he will be much younger than his brother. This happens because he travels faster than time has passed for John. When speed exceeds time, time is slowed for quickly travelling objects. This revolutionary idea contradicted the traditional view that time flows for everyone at the same rate.

In 1915, Einstein shocked the world again with his follow-up theory, known as General Relativity, which combined the previous theory with gravity. He theorized that light usually travels straight, but when it hits heavy masses, such as planets and stars, it bends around them. We can't see the bending light, but the phenomenon clearly exists throughout nature. One example of this is light bending around the sun. This is how we see the light of stars that are positioned behind the sun. Validation of these theories only became possible after Einstein's time, due to the lack of equipment and technology. Due to this lack of empirical data, physicists such as Dayton Miller spent decades attempting to discredit Einstein's theory. In opposition to Einstein's belief that light travelled independently, regardless of its source's speed, Miller believed that light's speed was determined by an invisible matter surrounding it called ether. Unlike Einstein, he was able to produce numerous measurements and data sets to support his argument. Even though Miller's data was less than convincing, his ability to experimentally measure ether over a course of decades and his established position in the physics community allowed his theory to gain widespread support. Eventually, review of other experiments such as the Michelson-Morley experiment showed that Miller's numerical measurements of ether fell within the margin of error and had most likely occurred due to the lack of laboratory equipment needed to perform the experiment in a vacuum, or an area without pressure and gravity. These variables could have easily altered his results.

Even the Nobel Prize Committee didn't initially recognize the brilliance of Einstein's theory at the time. This may seem ridiculous now, but at the time they had the same issues with it as Miller. The theory was based on Einstein's ingenuity and creative mind, but lacked any conclusive data or experimental results to support it; he had simply thought it up one day! The idea that a 26-year-old patent office clerk had simply used reason to come up with ideas that reformulated the equations of physics was too shocking. While we can recognize the tremendous discovery he made today, Einstein's contemporaries and the Nobel Prize Committee could not accept concepts with such shaky foundations. They needed to be able to evaluate the source and methodology of a contribution in order to recognize it, but due to Einstein's disregard of the traditional scientific method, the lack of empirical evidence and the physics community's opposition to his ideas, the Nobel Committee could not award the prize for the theory. While hindsight shows us that Einstein's theory was deserving of recognition, the committee acted fairly. Even Einstein accepted the limits of his theories and once said that they were just his imaginings and could be proven wrong by future experiments. After all this talk of the greatness of Einstein's theory, you may be wondering how it affects your daily life. Well, the GPS system in your car or mobile phone can be traced back to Einstein's theory. His work also opened up new fields in physics, such as quantum physics, which has yielded numerous inventions like microchips, electron microscopes and MRI. Einstein's work not only has changed physics, but created new previously unimaginable areas of science.

Student's Opposition to Renovation

Listen to a conversation between a student and an office clerk.

S: Excuse me, sir.

O: Yes, ma'am.

S: Well, I don't know if you heard, but they're going to rebuild the science library... and well, I'm here because I'm against it, and... long story short, I need a signature from the board so I can officially start a protest against it.

O: Well... I'm not officially authorized to give out any names, but if I could get your name and contact information, I would be happy to deliver a message.

S: My name is Meghan Young, and my student ID number is 110509.

O: Got it. Do you mind me asking why you have a problem with the renovations? I just want to deliver my message to the higher authorities as accurately as possible.

S: Not at all... To be honest, I really like the way it is right now. I don't even think it needs to be renovated at all! I think the glass walls are all still intact. Wasn't it recently renovated anyway?

O: I guess I see your point. It hasn't been that long.

S: Also... I mean... A lot of students rely on the library to study... Some people may even lose their scholarships.

O: Uh-huh. Anything else?

S: Well, the source materials and reference materials that we require for our studies... need I say more?

O: I understand... I'm pretty sure that the board won't just cut out the reference sources; they'll probably place the materials in another location, and even provide an alternative study area. But then again... there have been rumors that the school failed to raise enough funds and that there may not be any renovations at all.

S: Really?

O: Yeah... I mean... at first I thought it was just a rumor too. But false rumors don't last this long... You know what I mean?

S: I guess so...

O: How many signatures opposing the renovations do you have so far? Do you mind me asking?

S: Not at all. There are currently about 250 people and the number is growing as we speak.

O: I can sympathize; we office workers were actually appalled as well.

S: Yeah... I mean, why not just add a new wing to the library? They released a possible blueprint to the students, and it looked ridiculous to close the whole place. I just want to deliver our new ideas, and maybe even possibly shut down the whole project.

O: Even if the rumors aren't true, I bet you have enough people to make a difference. I mean 250 and growing... that's not a number the school can ignore.

S: I'm just glad there are others that feel the same way that I do...

O: You know... If I were you... I would wait to find out if the rumors are true or not. I mean... I wouldn't want to get people excited over something that isn't even happening... you know how rough these things can get, don't you?

S: You're right... I thought everything was set. I was in such a foul mood because of this... Thank you for the helpful information.

O: No problem.

S: Do you know when the decision is final though? I'm eager to find out.

O: Well, there's a hearing sometime this week between the faculty and the board members.

S: That's great. Should I come back when it's over? Do you know when it starts?

O: Tell you what. If you leave me your number, I'll get back to you as soon as I can.

S: OK. Sounds great. Thank you!

The Space Elevator Technology

Listen to part of a lecture in an engineering class.

P: In our globalized world, barriers between nations are breaking down, as is the barrier between Earth and the universe. Since its first foray into space, mankind has achieved remarkable things. However, due to the energy and resource inefficiencies of the current methods of space travel, even a short trip into space remains an expensive proposition. This is because an enormous amount of fuel is required to reach Earth's escape velocity of 11 kilometers per second. The inefficiency of this method is evident when you look at the external fuel tanks of the space shuttle. They are the biggest, and heaviest, parts of the shuttles.

Oddly, however, a lot of people still seem to have misconceptions about going to space. Um, let me give you an example. The idea that the only way to escape Earth's atmosphere is by travelling at Earth's escape velocity is not absolutely true. Um... before I go any further, let's make sure we're on the same page about the concept of escape velocity. Escape velocity is the speed at which an object must move to overcome Earth's gravitational pull. Objects that reach their escape velocity are fast enough that they won't lose their velocity before leaving Earth's gravitational influence. Theoretically though, all one really needs to enter space is a constant force pushing upwards or holding one firmly in place. Scientists are, therefore, trying to build that force: a sturdy human construction on which passengers or payloads could travel up and down.

S: So... what you are saying is that if we could somehow build something like a huge ladder, then we could slowly climb our way up into space, right?

P: Exactly. You understand that a person climbing a ladder wouldn't reach speeds that are anywhere near the escape velocity, but that person wouldn't be pulled down by gravity, because they would be holding on to the ladder, right? There is a problem, however... although the ladder idea makes sense mathematically and conceptually, it is very improbable. Nobody could climb thousands of kilometers before being exhausted. Let's not forget that you would also need to be carrying a heavy oxygen tank and space suit.

The ladder example is not as outrageous as it sounds, though. Research is being done on the construction of a very similar concept: a space elevator. The space elevator is a proposed structure designed to transport material from Earth to space. A Russian rocket scientist, Konstantin Tsiolkovsky, who was inspired by the Eiffel Tower, first proposed this idea in 1895. His theory was immediately ridiculed and his fellow scientists told him that it would never be possible. His idea wasn't totally forgotten though. One of the early, and most enthusiastic, proponents of the idea of a space elevator was the science-fiction author Arthur C. Clark, and it appears repeatedly in his works. One example was the 1979 novel 'The Fountains of Paradise'. In this novel, a 22nd century engineer is charged with creating a means of moving people and supplies to a 'terraforming' project in outer space. To do this, he develops a space elevator linking Earth to the 'circumterran' (Earth encircling) space station.

So... Let's talk about how a space elevator would work. Hmm... The first part of the project would be a base station on Earth that would be attached to a pillar upon which an elevator car could travel. This structure would be flexible, and would be called the cable. You may be wondering how we could construct a cable that is strong enough to stand up straight, yet tall enough to reach space. Well... Remember when you were kids, you would tie a rope to a bucket full of water, and swing it over your head? How did the water stay inside the bucket while gravity pulled it downwards? A natural force, known as centrifugal force, pushed the water into the bucket, away from the center of the circular motion, which was the hand holding the rope. The same principle would apply to the space elevator: when the cable is long enough, the spinning of the Earth will create a centrifugal force on the space elevator. To accomplish this, the space elevator would need a heavy weight, called a counterweight, at its highest point to make it more stable.

The cable itself is probably the biggest hindrance to a space elevator's construction, as it would need to be made of an extremely light, durable material, but as long as people have been dreaming of building a space elevator, no material strong enough has existed...until the recent discovery of a new material made purely of carbon, that is. Due to the extremely strong chemical bonds that carbon atoms form with one another, scientists have discovered a way to form tiny tubes called 'carbon nanotubes,' which are stronger and lighter than steel, and able to conduct electricity. These tubes of pure carbon have shown great promise: they can be used in everything, from electronics to airplanes, as well as space elevator cables.

The next question about a space elevator is 'how long would the cable have to be'? Well, there are several factors that must be considered when determining this length. If you think about satellites orbiting Earth you'll recognize that their speed is actually determined by how high above Earth their orbits are. As the space elevator would be attached to the Earth's surface, its mass would have to be centered at 36,000 km, which is the height at which it would achieve geosynchronous orbit. That leads us to the question 'What is geosynchronous orbit'? This is when an object's orbital period is synchronized with the Earth's rotation. In other words, the orbiting object will always appear at the same spot in the sky to an observer on Earth.

P: Despite these high hopes and technological advances, there are still many hurdles to actualizing this dream. For one, as a space elevator cable, carbon nanotubes, have a major problem. The longest nanotubes ever created were only a few centimeters long, and linking them together to a length of 36,000 km would be impractical. In addition, some feel that a space elevator would present a navigational hazard, both to aircraft and spacecraft, as well as space objects. Further, it would be exposed to the radiation belts to be shielded from them. You can see that a lot more work is necessary before construction of a space elevator is feasible. If technology advances enough, though, it may be built in your lifetimes.

Investigation of Easter Island

Listen to part of a lecture in an archaeology class. The professor is discussing Easter Island.

P: Let's continue researching lost civilizations with Easter Island; the mysterious island discovered by Dutchman Jacob Roggeveen in 1722. Roggeveen discovered an island filled with cannibalistic savages, but later found evidence suggesting that it was once occupied by an advanced, orderly civilization. If this was true, what happened to it? What could have caused the demise and destruction of this prominent civilization? Archaeologists and scientists are working together to unravel this mystery. And today, we'll look into this obscurity in detail.

P: Does anyone know anything about Easter Island?

S: Isn't it famous for gigantic statues?

P: Ah, yes, Jonathan, Those are the island's most renowned features, but let's get some background information. Easter Island, measuring only 64 square miles, is located in the southern Pacific about 2,000 miles west of Chile, with its closest inhabited island neighbor being 1,400 miles away. Despite its isolation, the humid, subtropical climates with its mild winters and hot, rainstorm-filled summers make it ideal for inhabitation. When Roggeveen landed, however, there were no signs of outside connections. He found approximately 2,000 barbarians on an island wasteland devoid of trees and animals. On an island-wide search for usable resources, however, he discovered the astonishing moai.

S: What are the moai?

P: They're the gigantic statues that Jonathan mentioned. Anyway, this shocking discovery drew a lot of worldwide attention. These 887 giant faces were carved into giant stones, which averaged 14.5 feet tall and 14 tons, with some reaching 33 feet and weighing 165 tons! Roggeveen found these strange because 2,000 people couldn't have possibly carved and hauled these statues, especially without the tools to perform such tasks! They didn't even have trees which are a basic component of construction tools.

S: Professor, who would have chosen to live in such a remote, barren place...and why?

P: There's no definitive proof of where the people came from, only competing theories. Norwegian explorer Thor Heyerdahl originally proposed that they were from Chile, the closest continental land. He also claimed that the moai resembled Incan statues found throughout present-day Chile. His theory was widely accepted until modern science proposed another explanation. Modern scientists performed a series of DNA tests on skeletons found on the island and discovered that they were from Polynesia, the area of islands near Australia in the southern Pacific Ocean inhabited by a population of seafarers who migrated over great oceanic routes in canoes. It is likely that they sailed from Marquesas or the Society islands, Easter Island's closest island neighbors, but got lost and settled on Easter Island. Strangely though, not all islanders are of Polynesian origin.

P: It's now believed that until a couple centuries ago, the island housed a lot more people: probably around 11,000 to 15,000, based on estimates of the labor required to build the moai, and the habitable areas of the island. The dispersion of the moai around the island also leads archaeologists to assume that the conditions on the island in the past were quite different. This was proven true by a test called pollen analysis. The process involves a column of sediment collected from a swamp or pond, showing the different layers of sediment over time. Each of these layers is then dated through radiocarbon dating.

S: Professor, I'm confused about the procedure. What exactly is radiocarbon dating?

P: It's a process used to measure the age of dead organisms by measuring the remaining carbon levels.
These two tests proved that the island once supported flourishing gigantic palm trees, which were ideal for making canoes, logs, and ropes to transport the moai. They were also required for everyday things such as building houses and fires. According to scientists, the natives cut down these palm trees and rolled them horizontally to transport the moai.
Anyway, long story short, the palm trees and animals went extinct for some reason, spelling doom for the islanders. This led to a dramatic population decrease; falling as low as 111 in 1877. Let's look at possible explanations behind the downfall of the civilization. The traditional theory, suggested by American scientist Jared Diamond, was that the civilization destroyed itself through overconsumption and deforestation. He claimed that native people cut down all of the trees to transport the moai. The lack of trees then halted the production of the moai. Soon, necessities such as fire and housing became luxuries. Eventually, the island descended into a self-inflicted chaos. This is, however, only a theory and there is no corroborating data.
Archaeologist Terry Hunt has come up with a theory that points to rats as the main culprits behind the demise. He found a plethora of rat bones when sampling the soil from Anakena beach, the most likely landing spot for the first settlers. He deduced that the Polynesians brought rats with them for food, but there were no natural predators to keep the rat population in check. This combined with the tons of rat-chewed palm seeds strewn across the island led him to this new theory. He theorized that the rat population exploded and consumed all the palm seeds on the island. With no seeds to germinate and the natives still cutting down trees, deforestation occurred. It was as if they were adding insult to injury. Soon, all of the trees were extinct and the islanders could no longer produce the canoes needed for fishing, so they started to consume the terrestrial animals. After these out, they turned to warfare and cannibalism. By 1722, he says, no trace of the great civilization that once ruled the island existed.

Biology Research Plan

Listen to part of a conversation between a graduate student and her biology professor.

S: Hi, professor. What brings you by the lab today?

P: Hi Janet. I just wanted to check on how the experiments were coming along. I heard you've put in a lot of hours in the lab recently.

S: Well, to be honest, I have been putting in more time at the lab because things haven't been going all that... smoothly.

P: May I ask why?

S: Well, the task that you assigned me. The... uh... purification of protein RP73 from human tissue? Well, the experiment was going really well... until... a problem in the cooling process occurred.

P: Oh. Did you forget to fully heat it before you lowered the temperature? If we're going to determine if the problem is still reversible, we have to know the exact process that you followed.

S: Not quite. Everything up to the heating process was perfect, I actually set an alarm on Friday night to come back the next morning and cool it to room temperature... and then do the precipitation process, hopefully. Well, anyway, I overslept and forgot to come back to the lab.

P: I've been there. Back when I was a graduate student like you, I wasn't used to going to a boring laboratory on a Saturday, either. Well, if it was heated all weekend, there's no way we can still purify the protein.

S: I'm so sorry, professor. I know you were hoping to submit a paper to the journal about its possible uses.

P: It can wait for a couple of weeks. I mean... it's not like the function of the protein is going to change anytime soon. So, no harm, no foul. Now the important question is 'When can I expect to see the results that I'm looking for?'

S: Well, I've been working on it, even right before you arrived. So it shouldn't take much longer than a couple days.

P: Well, the problem is, I leave town for a week tomorrow... and...

S: Oh, you're worried that the protein won't be in tiptop condition when you come back in a week.

P: Yes, I would like to work with the material as soon as it's successfully purified.

S: Okay... then I should probably get rid of what I've been working on and start again sometime this week?

P: Oh, that would make me feel like one of those professors who asks too much of their graduate students.

S: Don't worry. I think it's better if I keep practicing the process. You know... to reduce the margin of error. Plus, it was my fault that you're not getting the results right now.

P: Well, I'm glad to see you have taken a rather professional attitude about your job. You know, reducing the margin of error is quite critical in designing and implementing an experiment as a scientist. You know the story about spinach and its supposed effects on strengthening muscles, don't you?

S: No, but I'm guessing it's not true because you used the word 'supposed'... hahaha.

P: Hahaha... True. People believe that spinach is rich in iron, a muscle supplement, but, in fact, a German chemist, in 1870, made an error in his experiments, making people think that spinach has 10 times more iron than it actually does! He did everything else right in his experiments, but a simple misplaced decimal provided the public with inaccurate information that continues to fool a lot of people.

S: Wow, I did not know that. I guess I get what you're trying to say. I'll have the protein ready and in perfect condition for your research when you return. And... place all my decimal points in the right place!

P: Thanks, Janet. I'll be back in a week and we'll talk more then.

Mysteries of the Egyptian Pyramid

Listen to part of a lecture in a history class. The professor is discussing pyramids.

P: Today we're going to switch to manmade wonders and talk about the Great Pyramid at Giza! At 756 feet wide and 450 feet high, this massive ancient structure is composed of 2,300,000 stone blocks. The mere sight of this giant, ancient structure causes many people to wonder, 'How on Earth did the ancient Egyptians build this 4,500 years ago?' Due to the lack of direct evidence, though, no one knows exactly how the Great Pyramid was constructed. Scientists and archaeologists aren't clueless though; they have come up with theories explaining the construction process. Let's look at how the pyramid might have been built.

P: Before we get to the construction methods used to build the Great Pyramid, does anyone know why the pyramids were constructed?

S: Didn't they build pyramids for the afterlife?

P: Exactly. Pharaohs commissioned pyramids to serve as tombs for them to rest in during the afterlife. All of the labor and construction materials consumed were for just one man! Anyhow, pyramids had multiple chambers and passages within them, but only one was the true resting place of the pharaoh. The others were made to fool grave robbers who may try to steal the pharaoh's precious treasures.

S: Why would there be treasures in the pharaohs' tombs? Wouldn't that be kind of a waste?

P: Well, yes, but the ancient Egyptians considered the afterlife to be eternal, so they wanted to be prepared for it. To do this, they took their most precious belongings with them. After living a life of luxury, they were the icing on the cake. Unfortunately, their trickery didn't work that well. Over time, most of the pyramids were robbed and looted. Luckily for us, though, the advanced architecture and craftsmanship of the ancient Egyptians allowed the overall structures to remain intact.

Let's move on to theories explaining how the Great Pyramid was built. According to the ancient Greek historian Herodotus, the ancient Egyptians used wooden cranes located on every level of the pyramid to lift the stones. There is a major problem with this theory though, because Giza is located in a desert they wouldn't have had access to enough wood to construct cranes. Further, they would have also lacked space for the cranes.

Using Herodotus' records, and other sources, Egyptologists came up with the theory that the ancient Egyptians used ramps to transport the massive stone blocks, as they were the main devices for lifting heavy materials at the time. There have been many theories about possible ramp shapes, but I'm just going to concentrate on the most common ones. Egyptologist Jean-Philippe Lauer suggested that straight ramps, reaching the top of the pyramid, were used. These simplest of ramps would have been massive! They would require a slope of about a half mile to reach the top of the Great Pyramid.

S: But professor, you said the ramp would have to be about a half mile. Wouldn't this task be too much for the laborers? I mean, didn't they already have enough work?

P: Exactly! Constructing a ramp of that size would have been a massive waste of labor and materials. This brings us to another style of ramp, the spiral ramp, which was suggested by tomb excavator Mark Lehner. A spiral ramp is a more complex design that would have wrapped around the pyramid until it reached the top. Compared to other ramps, it would've required much less material and labor. However, this type of ramp also has problems.

First, it would have ruined the builders' external sightlines. Because they used ropes to measure, the ancient Egyptians needed clear lines of vision to check how precisely the blocks were layered. Another design problem is the ramp's corner... Imagine turning a corner high in the air with a 2.5 ton stone block! Both ramp theories also share the problem of needing to destroy the ramps to ensure a clean, smooth exterior surface for the pyramid.

P: Recently, a French architect who specializes in 3D designs, Jean-Pierre Houdin, suggested a new theory. He surveyed the pyramid with infrared cameras and developed a 3-D model of the Great Pyramid to support his new theory that the Great Pyramid was built using internal ramps. He felt that the Egyptians built external ramps to reach about 141 feet in the beginning, and then switched to using internal ramps. These ramps would wrap around the inside of the pyramid and reach the apex like spiral ramps.

S: But professor, wouldn't corners still be problematic?

P: I was just about to explain that. Spiral ramps can be compared to the winding roads built on the sides of mountains. You know that cars driving along these roads risk falling off. In much the same way, workers could have easily stumbled off the side of an external spiral ramp. Internal ramps, on the other hand, have space around the corners thus making it easier, and safer, for laborers to haul stones up the ramps.

S: Ah, so the internal ramps provided safety for the workers!

P: Exactly.

S: But, didn't you say that ramps require too much labor and material?

P: Yes, they do indeed, but internal ramps are different. They would basically become a part of the pyramid. Since they weren't going to be taken down after construction, they could simply be sealed off after use, significantly conserving materials and labor.

S: It sounds like Houdin's theory is the best explanation.

P: Yes, his story is a revolutionary explanation regarding the construction of the pyramids and is likely to be accepted by the community since it eliminates the problems associated with the previous theories.

Coral Reef Destruction

Listen to part of a lecture in a marine biology class. The professor is discussing coral reef destruction by crown-of-thorns starfish.

The Great Barrier Reef, the world's largest reef system, is home to more than 400 coral, 1,500 fish, and 200 bird species. The reefs are made of living things called coral polyps... which are organisms that attach themselves to the ocean floor in large colonies. Before it was fully researched, scientists thought that coral was, uh, strangely shaped rock, and I don't blame them. Coral doesn't move and, therefore, provides homes for the local fish species among their tough calcium-carbonate skeletons. Recently, the coral population of the Great Barrier Reef has been decreasing at an alarming rate. It turns out that a species of starfish, the crown-of-thorns, has had a sudden population increase and is preying upon the coral, threatening the reef population. This species got its name from the poisonous spines that cover its body. As the second largest starfish in the world, they can grow up to a meter across, and eat coral by climbing atop the polyps and releasing digestive enzymes. These break down and liquefy the coral, which the starfish can then absorb into its stomach. Scientists have come up with several theories to explain the sudden explosion of the starfish population.

Their first explanation is that the increase in the starfish population doesn't really have a specific reason, but is a natural phenomenon. Like many species' populations and the cyclical variations in the Earth's temperature, the increase in the starfish population and decrease in the coral population may simply be part of a natural cycle that occurs in the ecosystem. Um... Due to the lack of scuba technology before the 1960s, studying organisms on the ocean floor was difficult, but in the last few decades we've already seen three major outbreaks of the crown-of-thorns starfish. This is one of the reasons why scientists are inclined to think that coral destruction is mostly natural... This claim also has more scientific grounds. We know that a crown-of-thorns starfish produces around a billion eggs in its lifetime. So let's say there is an extremely slight change in the conditions, such as water temperature or salinity, which results in a 1% increase in the survival chances of the starfish... That yields 10 million more starfish! With 10 million more individuals than the previous generation, the starfish will mate and reproduce even more, causing a domino effect, with the population increasing in each successive generation. As you can see, even the slightest change can theoretically bring about a huge increase in starfish population, so natural fluctuations seem a pretty believable cause.

The second hypothesis cites predator decline. Due to their thorns, crown-of-thorns starfish actually don't have many predators. One of the few is the giant triton. When these snails smell a starfish, they chase after it and attach themselves to the starfish, stabbing it with their radula. Um... this is kind of like a tongue, but is actually made of chitin, and is toothed, like a saw. So once the triton has made an opening in the starfish, it produces saliva that paralyzes the starfish, and it slowly feeds on its victim. Fortunately for the starfish, these snails were hunted for their ornamental shells so greatly that their population decreased to unsustainable levels around 1969. Even after 40 years of government protection, the population hasn't bounced back enough to pose a threat to the crown-of-thorns starfish.

Okay, that brings us to the final hypothesis. This one may seem strange, but it suggests that human activities on land, such as deforestation, are affecting starfish populations. Deforestation for farmland, which occurs on 80% of the land adjacent to the Great Barrier Reef, makes the land vulnerable to sediment runoff and flooding, so during the rainy season fertilizers and organic materials get washed into rivers and make their way to the Great Barrier Reef. When rivers flood the land, even more sediment-filled freshwater is discharged into the sea. This affects the starfish population in a number of ways. First, fertilizers contain nitrogen and phosphorous, which cause massive algae and plankton blooms, providing copious nourishment for the crown-of-thorns starfish larvae. It also dilutes the coastal water, lowering its salinity. Since starfish larvae cannot osmoregulate, ummm... regulate their salinity with regards to the environment, sea water is normally too salty for many of them to survive. When river water dilutes the ocean water, however, their chances of survival increase. Scientists believe that the combination of these two effects may explain the starfish population explosions.

So... today we've talked about how crown-of-thorns starfish affect the Great Barrier Reef negatively, but I should also mention that they have useful functions, too. First, they tend to feed on rapidly growing coral species. These coral species are kept in check by the starfish, which allows slower-growing coral a better chance of survival. This helps maintain species diversity on the reef. Further, we also know that the starfish is a natural part of the ecosystem, and is preyed upon by other species, such as the giant triton. Knowing that some species have unpredictable effects on their ecosystems, perhaps it's better that we take care not to have too great an influence over the starfish populations.

Whale Breathing Patterns

Listen to a conversation between a student and a professor.

S: Hello, Professor McGee.

P: Oh. Hello, Kevin. Come on in and have a seat. What's on your mind?

S: Well, I was looking for your insight into a problem I've been having... I mean... academically.

P: Oh, Okay. Shoot.

S: Well, I was researching whale breathing patterns during migration... and...

P: Let me stop you right there. You do know that different whales have different breathing patterns, right?

S: I know that baleen whales have two blowholes while toothed whales only have one.

P: Even though all whales are mammals and have the fundamental characteristics of mammals, certain attributes differ completely according to their specific species.

S: Uh... I'm not following.

P: Let me put it this way. Although humans are all mammals, we can be biologically differentiated by ethnicity, gender, and even age. What I'm trying to say is... you should pick a specific type of whale.

S: I've already done that. I started my report on the bowhead whale.

P: Ah, the bowhead whale. I believe they're baleen whales. Correct?

S: Of course. Well... I was wondering what about the anatomy and breathing patterns of whales allows them to migrate over such great distances without taking short breaths.

P: Well... what's interesting about bowhead whales is that unlike other whales, they can only stay submerged for up to 40 minutes per dive.

S: 40 minutes? Isn't that a really long time? What about other whales?

P: Well... again, it depends on the whale species, and their reason for submerging. How long whales remain underwater when they are feeding or when they have no other choice but to remain underwater differs completely. Certain species can stay a kilometer underwater for 90 to 120 minutes.

S: That is so fascinating. Well... I think we got sidetracked... What I was originally wondering was, biologically speaking, what enables whales to stay underwater for such a long time?

P: Well... There are a few things that enable them to stay underwater for so long, but some of them are highly theoretical. The first is the most obvious. Can you guess what it is?

S: Uh... their size?

P: Close. It's actually their ability to physically hold large amounts of oxygen, in their bloodstreams.

S: Aha, I see. What's another factor?

P: Well, another factor is a very unique ability that whales possess. They actually have the ability to reduce the amount of oxygen they need while they are submerged. They can reduce the amount of oxygen delivered to the body parts they aren't using during their dives in order to use it more efficiently.

S: Wow, I wasn't aware of that.

P: Actually a few years ago, a group of biologists at a university fitted cameras to whales, including a 100 ton blue whale. According to them, whales expel air from their lungs shortly after diving so they can stop floating. The rest is squeezed out by increasing water pressure. Although they lose oxygen, they are able to remain underwater by releasing more oxygen from their blood and their muscles. The secret is in the relaxation of their muscles by simply thrusting themselves down with a few powerful strokes, and then continuing to glide down...

S: Ok. I think that's the kind of information that can help me along with my research...

P: I'm glad to hear that. I'm always happy to help.

Horse Domestication of Botai People

Listen to part of a lecture in an anthropology class.

P: For decades anthropologists speculated that horses were domesticated during the Bronze Age in the Eurasian steppes. However, new evidence found in Northern Kazakhstan suggests that the Botai people began to domesticate horses there nearly 1,000 years earlier than previously thought. Because this idea is so groundbreaking, there is some controversy surrounding its veracity. The fact that the Botai people had a close relationship with horses is undeniable; the question is whether these animals were domesticated. Today I'd like to examine some of the evidence put forth by the proponents of this theory.

P: Now before I jump right in, does anyone know who the Botai people were?

S: Well, you mentioned they originated in central Asia. Umm... weren't they also hunters?

P: Yes, the Botai were nomads who hunted game like red deer, moose, and Equus Ferus, an early cousin of the modern horse, in the steppes of modern day Kazakhstan. Horse meat was such an important food source that 90% of the remains found in excavation sites were from horses. For shelter, the Botai would build shallow campsites with one or two small mobile houses suited to their nomadic ways. This implies that they traveled in small bands and did not stay in a single area for long. This whole way of life changed drastically with the domestication of the horse. Does anyone know how?

S: If they bred horses as livestock, then wouldn't that provide food for more people?

P: Exactly. The Botai domesticated horses around 6,000 years ago and gained access to a stable source of meat year-round. This led to explosive population growth and a shift from a nomadic lifestyle to a more permanent, settled one. After eliminating the need to follow the wild horses, the Botai started to build pit houses sunk into the ground to provide insulation against the cold. You see... what I didn't mention is the weather in Northern Kazakhstan is frigidly cold, with subzero temperatures throughout the nine-month winter. Horses proved exceptionally useful since they could survive snowstorms and forage through snow unlike most animals domesticated later, such as sheep and cattle. The domestication of horses eventually revolutionized many aspects of people's lives worldwide.

P: The effects of the so called 'equine revolution' affected everything from agriculture to warfare. In the early stages, these animals provided a stable and reliable source of both meat and milk. As time progressed, humans began using horses for other tasks, such as transportation. This allowed societies to greatly increase their ranges and brought an early form of globalization due to cultural interaction and the spread of ideas. The domestication of horses even revolutionized warfare. War shifted from ground troops to mounted soldiers who represented a greater value in battle since they could cover much more ground and, thereby, quicken the pace of military campaigns.

S: Umm... But how can we prove the Botai people were the first to domesticate horses?

P: Well, archeologist Sandra Olsen, one of the leading proponents of the theory, has been gathering evidence to corroborate these claims. The three most credible and positively reviewed of her claims are from soil samples gathered in the Botai region, the presence of 'bit wear,' or markings caused by the use of man-made bits or harnesses, on the horses' teeth, and compounds of fat molecules found on pottery shards.

S: Umm.. what do soil samples have to do with evidence of horse domestication?

P: That's a very good question. Scientists examining sites in Northern Kazakhstan took soil samples from the ground around ancient vertical posts where horses would have been tied, and found a phosphorus concentration that was ten times greater than that of soil from outside of them. How is this all related? Well, horse manure has higher phosphorus and nitrogen concentrations than normal soil, so high levels of phosphorus inside the large confinements would imply the presence of horses... Additionally, the soil samples had low nitrogen levels. Nitrogen, as we all know, is very volatile and is easily washed away or released into the atmosphere. The minute nitrogen traces eliminate the possibility that the phosphorus came from more recent manure. There's also proof to be found in the horses' remains. Examining the skulls from horse remains found in the region, researchers found a peculiarity in their teeth. Careful observation revealed indentations in the large hind teeth which could have only been caused by a bridle, or a man made bit, used to mount and ride a horse. And finally, by utilizing a method of lipid, or fat analysis, scientists found traces of fats from mare's milk on shards of Botai pottery. While the first two points were circumstantial evidence that relied heavily on inferences, this information was the first piece of direct evidence that proved the Botai domesticated horses. By proving they milked mares and preserved the milk in their pottery, researchers were able to provide the 'smoking gun.' I mean, unless you're suggesting the Botai were milking wild horses.

S: Umm... why didn't the researchers just examine the skeletal structures of the remains?

P: Well, I think you're assuming that all animals change physically due to domestication. This is only partly true. Certain animals, such as dogs, cattle or pigs, do develop different physical structures as they undergo morphological changes over generations of domestication and selective breeding. This does not hold true for horses, though. It is nearly impossible to discern whether a horse was tame or wild or even the precise era it lived in judging solely by the skeletal evidence.

P: Judging by the evidence presented by the researchers, I think it's safe to say the theory is probable. In fact, with the constant flow archeologist Sandra Olsen, more and more people have finally started to accept that the domesticated horses almost 1000 years earlier than previously thought.

Biofuel Production Process

Listen to part of a lecture in a biology class. The professor is discussing alternative energy.

P: So, last time we talked about producing ethanol from corn. If you'll remember, ethanol is the same type of alcohol found in alcoholic beverages, and one of the main candidates to substitute for fossil fuels, such as crude oil and coal. The most important difference between biofuels, like ethanol, and fossil fuels is that biofuels are renewable. They are derived directly from living organisms, while fossil fuels can only be formed after long periods of time under specific conditions, like high temperature and pressure. But, guess what? Scientists have found a new process of making ethanol, which many believe is a more efficient way of making biofuel! It's called cellulosic ethanol production... which is what we're going to talk about today. It's actually very similar to corn ethanol production because both convert carbohydrate compounds into ethanol. First, let's talk about what cellulose is. Does anyone remember? John?

S: Isn't cellulose a type of carbohydrate that makes up the rigid support structures of plant cells?

P: Very good! Cellulose is a polymer of simple sugar molecules called glucose. Uh... let's try that again. Hmm... In other words, cellulose is a long sugar unit made up of smaller units called glucose. It is the most abundant organic compound on Earth, and makes up about 33 percent of a typical plant. This huge abundance is probably the biggest reason that biofuel companies are switching from corn to cellulosic ethanol, but there are also other advantages.

P: For one, corn ethanol conversion uses plant starch. Starch is a carbohydrate, just like cellulose, but it is an essential nutrient for humans, so using it cuts into our food supply. However, cellulose, is not digestible by humans, which makes its use more beneficial. Another reason why cellulosic ethanol is better is that all plants can supply cellulose for the process. This means that there are increased options and supplies of feedstock, which is the raw material that supplies or fuels machines or industrial processes. Feedstock leads us to another advantage. The main feedstock for cellulosic ethanol, woody plants, has much higher density than corn, which makes transporting it more efficient. Hmmm... let me explain with an analogy. Um... say you're trying to fill two boxes, one with stacks of paper and the other with bubble wrap. Obviously, the box filled with paper will be heavier, meaning you're carrying more... substance... whereas the box filled with bubble wrap will be mostly air, which is useless in this process. Although density doesn't seem like a big deal, transportation of raw material plays a huge role in business. Other than that, plants used to produce cellulosic ethanol are cheaper to grow and more eco-friendly than corn, which could reduce greenhouse gas production by 85 percent! So... if we efficiently produce energy from this source, the future of alternative energy sources will be much brighter. This is why there have been so many attempts to increase the efficiency of cellulosic ethanol production.

P: As technology has progressed, a new process known as cellulolysis, or the 'biological approach' has been developed. In this method, the cellulose is um... loosened. After it's loosened, enzymes break it down into glucose, its smallest units. The glucose is then fermented. The fermentation process produces a... uh... thick soup composed of ethanol and other chemicals. A process called distillation, which is boiling the soup so that the compounds evaporate separately from each other, isolates the ethanol. This approach normally uses baker's yeast in the fermenting process, which is a good choice since it's abundant and can withstand extreme temperature and pH levels. Recently, scientists have engineered special resilient yeasts that can convert cellulose directly into ethanol. This means that the process of breaking down cellulose into glucose can be entirely forgone, which speeds up the production process and reduces costs further!

P: Okay... So... The second major method used today is called gasification, or the thermo-chemical approach. In this process, instead of fermenting glucose, selected cellulose particles are... combusted, or blown up, to separate their carbon atoms. These atoms are then converted into compounds and fed to microorganisms called Clostridium Ijungdahlii. The organisms eat the carbon compounds and release ethanol and water. This ethanol is then distilled in the same way as in the biological approach.

P: Even with recent progress, there are some difficulties in making the switch to cellulosic ethanol for a few reasons. A major one is that even with high efficiency, cellulosic ethanol costs an additional 120 dollars to convert per barrel. Moreover, alternative energy projects are not well-funded, so companies that make biofuel can't carry out as much research as they need. They also suffer from a lack of commercial plants in which to execute conversion. The interesting part is that all of these problems would be, to some extent, resolved through government support. Once cellulosic ethanol production gains public attention and interest, hopefully the industry will acquire more financial support.

Community Service at Museum

Listen to a conversation between a student and a museum officer.

S: Excuse me, sir.

M: Yes, ma'am. How may I help you?

S: I have some questions regarding community service.

M: Uh huh? Go ahead.

S: Well, I already checked with the Downtown Museum, and I can't submit the hours I worked there as community service... so I was wondering how community service works here.

M: You can submit your hours here as community service. We don't mind completing all of the necessary forms. Anything else you'd like to know?

S: Well, I am a history major, and I do have a great deal of background knowledge of world history, but I was just curious if there was anything... I... uh... should prepare for.

M: Well... I don't know if you already know or not, but younger children are our main customers. We mostly get visitors that are 6 or 7 years old.

S: I wasn't aware of that... anyway, go on

M: So knowing a lot about history isn't as important as being familiar with dealing with children.

S: I see... Is there anything else I should know?

M: Well the job is basically supervising kids.

S: (laughs) OK. What kinds of, uh... activities can children do around here? Can you walk me through a typical day in the museum?

M: Well, right now, we have an exhibition of Picasso's paintings. With children, rather than explaining the hidden meanings in the paintings, community service workers, such as you, would explain the shapes, colors and sizes and how they suit each other. The children seem more interested in stuff like that than the actual... artistic technicalities.

S: I see. I guess Picasso's paintings would be perfect for children since they consist of a lot of different colors, shapes and sizes.

M: Exactly. It's a big hit right now, which reminds me, the Egyptian Room is also popular with children, especially the mummies. Children are awfully interested in mummies.

S: I can totally see children being interested in mummies.

M: Since you're a history major you probably know a lot about Egyptian history, right?

S: I have a good grasp of most of the concepts, although I would have to review.

M: You probably don't need to do that. Children usually have only simple questions about different Egyptian pharaohs and mummies and pyramids. All you have to do is walk around with the children, and briefly explain some of the pieces to them, and answer any questions they might have.

S: That seems pretty easy. I mean, according to everything I've heard so far, it seems like a lot of fun.

M: Don't underestimate how hard taking care of children is. I mean, looking after children is a lot harder than it sounds.

S: I know... I had a part time job before in a daycare center... and it was... hectic.

M: I'm glad that you have some experience. It'll definitely be a lot of help later on when you actually start.

S: I can't say that I'm not excited; since I want to get into education once I graduate.

M: If you would just fill out this application, and let me know when you can start, I will let you know how the process goes as soon as possible.

S: OK.

M: Do you have any questions?

S: I was just wondering about the working hours?

M: Well, since you're just going to be a community service worker, hours will be flexible. We can work out some kind of schedule and figure something out that will suit both you and the museum. Would you like for me to just go ahead and select an appropriate time?

S: Yeah, that shouldn't be a problem, I have a pretty open schedule.

M: Let me know when you're done filling out the application.

Architectural Acoustics

Listen to part of a lecture in an architecture class. The professor is discussing architectural acoustics.

P: We've been focusing on the architectural features of opera houses and concert halls that make them so unique and aesthetically appealing. Today, we'll look at the science involved in these designs and why sound related buildings are built the way they are. This correlation between architecture and sound has not been thoroughly researched until recently, but with the rising importance of acoustics when building concert halls or theatres, the field of architectural acoustics has been gaining much attention. Let's explore some of the integral factors that play a role in defining structural acoustics.

P: One of the most important concepts in architectural acoustics is called 'reverberation time.' When a sound wave is created in a confined space, the listener not only hears the sound wave directly from the source but also its reflections from the surrounding walls, floor, and ceiling. These reflected waves are called reverberant sound, and the time required for them to drop by 60 decibels, when they can no longer be heard by humans after the original sound ceases, is defined as reverberation time. This interval is the most important quantitative indicator in determining a room's acoustic suitability.

S: Does longer reverberation time mean better acoustics?

P: Not necessarily. The optimum reverberation time of a space depends largely on its use. A space with a long reverberation time is called 'live,' whereas an acoustically 'dead' environment is one that causes sound to fade quickly. Typically speaking, facilities such as lecture halls require a shorter reverberation time in order to maximize the clarity and intelligibility of the words spoken. If the reverberation time is too long, the reflected sound from one syllable will still be audible while the next is spoken resulting in poor perceptibility and may end up sounding mumbled. On the other hand, if the reverberation time is too short, then the speaker or the performers will struggle to be loud enough to fill the room. In music, solos or piano recitals are often performed in a 'dead' environment because there is only one instrument playing and thus clarity and precision are the most important factors. Conversely, symphony orchestras require a 'live' space because the longer reverberation time blends the notes for a more harmonious sound that gives the music 'body'.

P: Now, let's take a look at the history of the field beginning with Harvard physics professor Wallace Sabine, one of the first to study the science behind acoustics and widely considered to be the father of modern architectural acoustics. Sabine had no acoustics training when Charles William Eliot, the president of Harvard, asked him to improve the acoustics of a lecture hall in the university's newly built Fogg Art Museum. Sabine tackled this seemingly impossible problem with great persistence. For several years, he conducted experiments utilizing different materials, such as cushions, oriental rugs and even different numbers of people, to see how they affected the acoustics of a space. After years of hard work, Sabine discovered that the materials present in a room could affect the reverberation time. Since various materials absorb different sounds at unique rates, depending on the absorbency of the material, they can either increase or decrease the reverberation time. Foam insulation, for example, almost completely absorbs sound and reflects little to none, while a thick, smooth painted concrete wall would be the acoustic equivalent of a mirror.

P: Wallace Sabine used his findings to convert the Fogg Art Museum space into an acoustically acceptable lecture hall by using thick drapes and sound absorbent cushions to shorten the room's reverberation time. After the success of this project, switching up interior features to change reverberation time became widely used and proved to be particularly effective in adjusting the acoustics of preexisting and older buildings.

S: Umm... why do older structures have such poor acoustics? I mean, what were some of the problems?

P: Well, a lot of the times acoustic problems result from improper design or construction limitations. Before the field of architectural acoustics was widely studied and applied to real life designs, architects often only emphasized the grandeur of the structure without thinking about the acoustics. In some extreme cases, these non-acoustically engineered buildings suffered from sound being focused on only one section of the audience, especially in domes or structures with smooth curved walls.

S: You've mentioned materials, but what other factors determine the reverberation time of a room?

P: There are two other important ones: the room's size and the shape of the room. The size of a room is an important dictating factor in reverberation times. In general, larger rooms have longer reverberation times because there is more uninterrupted space for the sound waves to travel across and reverberate. On the other hand, smaller rooms have shorter reverberation times since sound waves are reflected, but quickly die out due to the small size of the space. Shape also plays a critical role. Since reverberation time measures the reflected sound waves, the number of reflecting surfaces available directly correlates to the reverberation time. Therefore, more walls mean more reflection, which ultimately means longer reverberation times. Domes increase the reverberation time because their high ceilings increase the overall size of the space.

P: Even with these factors in mind, it is nearly impossible to construct an acoustically perfect structure, as even the audience will affect the acoustics. The average human, as Sabine roughly calculated, absorbs the same amount of sound as six seat cushions. As you can see, this is one of the biggest acoustical dilemmas faced by architects when designing such structures. I mean... How do you know how many people will show up? No one can accurately predict the effect of the attendees since this is an uncontrollable variable. Even if attendance is confirmed beforehand, there is no way of knowing the audience members' exact weight, height, or clothing type, all of which would affect the space's reverberation time.

S: Really? How do engineers solve this problem? Do they just guess?

P: Well, they make educated estimates. One way engineers and architects handle this problem is by designing the room to produce optimum reverberation at full occupancy, but this still leaves room for imperfections. The many factors involved make acoustics a difficult and calculations cannot create a perfect acoustical environment. This is also why acoustic of a concert hall or a theater is a continuous task that doesn't end with construction completion.

Disappearance of Anasazi People

Listen to part of a lecture in an anthropology class. The professor is discussing Anasazi.

Has anyone here ever heard of computer models? Not models of computers, but rather, simulation models for would-be situations. Today's advanced technology allows researchers to find data about families, populations, or even entire societies using computer simulations they basically create on their own. Fortunately, the development of these virtual situations, has allowed us to look deeper into ancient civilizations. By entering data about the environment and societal rules and patterns, researchers can find answers regarding what happened to historical human civilizations over a certain amount of time and even point out patterns in specific families from the past. For instance... they might use a model to see how population density is affected if life expectancy increases... or... what happens if people start spreading out from a densely populated area. It's important, however, to remember that these models only give theoretical answers about the results of changes in a population. Real life situations are obviously a little different since the population is made of unique individuals, and, well, unexpected events can occur. Still, these computer models give us relatively correct answers when researching large patterns in a population.

These computer simulations have been used to find the likely causes of the declines of past societies, such as the Anasazi. As we discussed last week, the Anasazi lived around seven hundred years ago in the area of the southwestern United States now known as the Four Corners, present day Arizona, Utah, Colorado, and New Mexico. The Anasazi are probably most well-known for their mud villages that look like gatherings of boxes strategically placed above cliffs and along rivers. These villages consist of buildings that could house about a hundred people each. You would think they would have been spread out over the land, like ranches; however, they more closely resemble apartment buildings, but lack stairs to enter the higher levels, so you couldn't even enter most of them without climbing a ladder. Their most common building material appears to have been bricks which they made using a mixture of straw, natural clay, and stones. Because entire Anasazi villages are still standing intact in the region today, we know for sure that they were excellent builders. By simply looking at the complexity of these buildings, we are able to see the intricate techniques that these people used. One of the unique buildings found there is the kiva, a separate circular underground room where they asked for assistance in agriculture and health from the serpents, fire, and sun. We know this because they also left behind petroglyphs, engravings in stone, that give us a peek inside their culture and beliefs. These historical sites have provided abundant historical artifacts and knowledge, but they haven't been able to explain exactly why the Anasazi suddenly disappeared after thriving for a thousand years.

Most people assumed that it was because of changes in the climate during the period. By studying their environment, we can see that there was a 50 year period with very little rain during the 1200s. Such a prolonged decrease in water availability seems like clear evidence that the farming Anasazi culture couldn't have continued to produce harvests sufficient for sustaining the population of the region. After more in-depth research, however, some scientists began to question this theory. One of them was archaeologist Jeffrey Dean. He studied the rings in the logs used in the Anasazi buildings which are still standing today. Tree rings, as you know, are the circles found when you cut down a tree. Because they are developed through a trees growth pattern, they can be seen as signs of the climate and nutrients available during the time. Dean discovered possible inaccuracies in the drought theory by studying these rings from the 14th century. He found that instead of undergoing a true drought, the area may have experienced a shift in the typical precipitation patterns in which the heavy summer rains that helped bring late spring crops to harvest did not occur as expected. This may have caused the Anasazi to became unsure of their gods and religious practices. Other research opposing the theory was conducted by Carla Van West who studied the harvest and nutrition consumption of individuals during normal circumstances. Her data led her to believe that a drought wouldn't have caused the entire population to leave the land or leave them unable to grow enough harvest to sustain themselves. Based on the data these two scientists developed, it began to look like drought couldn't have been the only reason the Anasazi civilization disappeared.

This is where computer simulations became useful. We already knew the location of their settlements, what they ate... even what the environment was like every year. So, to figure out what happened to the Anasazi, we put in all the data we knew about them and the valley in which they lived. We also entered facts about the water supply and gave people characteristics that corresponded to the environment. Say, like, they might have had fewer children if the harvest wasn't good enough that year, since not all of the families could survive, or... perhaps they left the area to find a place with better weather.

Basically we used the program to recreate a period of time from, uh... about the 800s to like, 1300, which is when they disappeared. Then do you know what happened? The program gave us results that correlated with the historical information that we already have. The first fact that the simulation supported was that the population grew in size, then declined over time, which probably means that the population increased when the harvest was plentiful, then shrunk when the harvest wasn't as good. The results also confirmed where the people lived within the valley. The biggest inaccuracy in the conclusions was that the computer simulation showed that by 1300, the population had decreased to only a few families, but in reality the population had disappeared completely.

So what are some of the final conclusions that the computer simulation gave about the Anasazi people? Well, first, it shows that the environment really affects every aspect of a population, its size, where they lived... However, it still doesn't answer all of the questions about their disappearance. It shows us that a small population could have kept living there. We're still left to wonder why they all disappeared from the area if the land could still support some people.

Psycological Impact of Music

Listen to a conversation between a student and a professor.

S: Hi, Professor Wilkins. I'm in your music appreciation class… I'm here about the project…

P: Well, I assume you've chosen the genre and topic of the music, by now. What are you having trouble with?

S: I've just been so caught up with other classes…and frankly, I haven't even decided on the genre, let alone the topic.

P: Oh, not even the genre? Wow, you must have been either really busy or procrastinating.

S: I've been swamped lately, and plus, I've had no good ideas regarding the genre of music.

P: Oh, why don't you try to think about it differently… think backwards? I mean, instead of worrying that you haven't chosen the genre yet.

S: I don't follow.

P: Make a… a rough-draft in your head; how you're feeling at a certain time of day, this could be your topic. And then find a genre that best fits those feelings. Are you into hip-hop?

S: Huh? Are you saying that I should match a random feeling to a specific genre?

P: I sure am, but it sure would be helpful if you could actually capture the moment when you're feeling the need to listen to a genre like hip-hop. Take, for example, when you feel the need for something with a rapid beat, tempo, and fast wording.

S: Oh, I certainly know that feeling.

P: The hip-hop genre is one that I'm personally eager to read about. Its relatively short history and rapid spread and development have fascinated me for quite a while.

S: Anything else I should keep in mind?

P: Technicality. The usage of slang, I believe some words in hip-hop are related to the concept of oxymorons.

S: What was that?

P: An oxymoron… It's when two contradictory words make up a phrase, such as 'dark sun', or 'mandatory charity'. I'm sure you've heard some of them in hip-hop. You can note them and write about how they came into being.

S: I think I get it. Well, can I also incorporate some psychology into it; since it's my major?

P: Sure, whatever you can do. Say… if you're a psychology major, would you mind helping me out with something? There's not much glory in it, but if you're up for it.

S: Sure! What is it?

P: Well, I'm attending a symposium about certain types of music and their effect on infants. I'm okay with all the musical aspects, but the psychology part… I need someone to help me out. I'm sure you've heard of the research on music during pregnancy…

S: Oh! I've actually wanted to be a part of that. I've read about it. They mentioned the psychological change of mothers and… surprisingly it affects the fetus. Many pregnant women listen to calm, classical music, which they feel leads to happier childhoods for their children. I'll have to review it to remember the specifics, though, the research was quite old… maybe the symposium will cover new details that I haven't read about yet.

P: How about you gather a couple of your friends from your department and bring them along? The school will cover expenses for accommodations.

S: I'll have to talk to them, I don't know if we can be of much help with this sort of information… and plus, our department is conducting a huge research project and most of the students are being used as the control group. I don't know if we will be able to leave town during the project.

P: Well, I will contact the head of the psychology department and see what I can do.

S: That'd be great. We've all been wanting to leave town for a nice break.

Invention of Electric Guitar

Listen to part of a lecture on music history. The professor is discussing electric guitar.

P: We've been studying the development of 18th and 19th century musical instruments, but today we'll move on to the 20th century... Okay... so what do jazz, rock'n' roll, country, and blues have in common? Well, one major connection is the important role of the electric guitar in these genres. Of all the musical instruments used during the 1900s, the electric guitar is probably the most versatile and influential. It can be played in harmony with almost any other instrument or hold the spotlight on its own. Let's look at the changes the electric guitar went through to become the instrument that we know today.

P: Can anyone tell me what motivated the development of electric guitars?

S: Um... They can make a lot of strange noises... Was it to give the acoustic guitar a wider range of sounds?

P: Close. An electric guitar does have a wider range of sounds, or effects, but they were not considered when designing the electric guitar. Effects were developed by guitarists experimenting with fully constructed guitars, after the design was finished. One of the biggest incentives for developing an electric guitar was amplifying the guitar's sound. Already beloved by both artists and audiences alike, guitars couldn't be used in concerts or ensembles because they were buried and lost amidst the louder brass and horn instruments. Also, if you remember, phonograph recordings and commercial radio became popular music media in the 1920s. Along with big band music popularity, this meant that guitars needed to change, or live guitar performances would disappear. This is why louder guitars became even more necessary, and guitar makers experimented with many innovative changes such as the curved archtop shape and larger bodies.

P: Around this time, engineers and inventors began tinkering with electricity and the guitar as well; one of them was George Beauchamp. Beauchamp, co-founder of the biggest guitar maker of the time, figured that a magnet could capture the motion of a steel string within its magnetic field and convert it to electrical energy. The electrical energy created by the strings' vibrations' strength depended on a combination of factors, such as the string's thickness, the rate of vibration, and the strings' distance from the magnet. Since the motion could be captured as electrical energy, each unique sound from the string could be digitized and amplified through a speaker or a similar device. In 1931, Beauchamp and his partner used horseshoe magnets to design a device called a 'pickup', that did exactly that. They incorporated it into a Hawaiian lap steel guitar creating the first electric guitar in history, the 'Frying Pan'. If you think that name is funny, you should see its shape; you'd understand.

P: Beauchamp believed that the future of guitars was electric and started selling electric guitars like the 'Frying Pan.' They were an instant success, getting praise from the most popular guitarists of the time. Unfortunately, for Beauchamp, other manufacturers had copied his technology and began producing electric guitars before he could stop them six years later.

P: Lap steel guitars like Beauchamp's are not really widely used today. We're more used to the larger, curved bodies of Spanish-style guitars, which are held sideways and finger-strummed. A company called Gibson Guitars was the first to successfully implement and commercialize Beauchamp's technology in Spanish guitars. By 1933, they'd produced their first electric guitar, the extremely popular ES-150. Country and blues guitarists, as well as skilled jazz guitarists switched over to this electric guitar and produced innovative sounds that were never before heard in guitars, or in any other instrument for that matter.

P: The ES-150 was, however, far from perfect. Since the pickups at the time were not very advanced, rather than isolating the vibrations from the strings, they acted as sort of a microphone, amplifying everything, like the vibration of the guitar body. This caused a lot of fuzzy background noises, not the clean, crisp sound guitarists sought. Another problem was audio feedback. This occurs when a guitarist strums a guitar and the sound gets amplified by a loudspeaker. If this amplified sound reaches the guitar strings, it causes them to vibrate more. These vibrations are picked up and amplified again and again; creating a loop of loud, digitized noise.

P: To fix those problems, a prominent jazz musician went to work at a local guitar workshop. In 1940, he produced 'The Log,' a guitar whose body was constructed of a long piece of solid wood instead of a hollow body. 'The Log' had two major advantages over hollow bodies. The first is that feedback was diminished because the body was more resistant to vibrations. Second, its notes lasted longer because the strings maintained vibrations, rather than dissipating them to the rest of the guitar.

S: Hmm... It seems like all the guitar makers were trying to reduce the electric guitar's effects. I always thought they sounded really cool, and actually prefer the effects, like in Jimi Hendrix's music.

P: You're not alone, but musicians didn't open up to the idea of incorporating electric effects into their music until after the 1950s, and largely due to Jimi Hendrix. Hendrix is considered one of the greatest guitarists ever, due to his innovative style. Rather than avoiding feedback and distortion, he took advantage of them. For example, his Fender Stratocaster, had three pickups and a switch for selecting which to use, but Hendrix wasn't satisfied with only three choices, so he jammed the pickup selector on his guitar so that he could play using two pickups at the same time and create some strange new sounds. This technique has become extremely popular since then.

P: Now you can see that the electric guitar's evolution is tied very closely with that of music itself. As guitars improve, they introduce new musical styles and as musicians experiment with new guitars, they lead to adaptation by manufacturers.

Examination on Ball Lightning

Listen to part of a lecture in a physics class. The professor is discussing lightning.

P: We all think we know what lightning is, right? Well, scientists will tell you that you actually don't. Because it's extremely dangerous and short-lived, it's a phenomenon that isn't understood very well, even by the most renowned scientists. Scientists have currently identified eight different types of lightning, with cloud-to-ground lightning being the best known and most common type. However, there's another atypically long-lasting type of lightning that doesn't even involve clouds at all. This type, called ball lightning, may not even be true lightning at all, because there is no evidence of its existence except for eyewitness accounts. What's more is that descriptions from those who claim to have seen ball lightning are wildly different from one another, meaning they're not very credible. If there's one thing scientists know, it is that people can't be trusted to accurately retell facts. Scientists don't even trust their own intuition, only hard, reproducible, experimental data. The lack of a verifiable cause for ball lightning - it's been blamed on black holes and even extraterrestrials - means it is considered little more than an urban legend and scientists consider it only a hypothetical phenomenon.

P: Before we go any further, let's define ball lightning... OK... well... According to witnesses, ball lightning is a luminous, spherical, and electrical object. It is around the size of a golf ball and is usually observed during thunderstorms. It's most often red, orange, or yellow, and moves horizontally. It has also been reported to pass through walls and approach people without harming them, and, usually explodes leaving a sulfurous smell at the end of its life. The properties of ball lightning are not as clear-cut as those of other lightning forms, though. For example, despite the tiny size usually reported, a church in Widencombe-in-the-Moor, England was reported to have been hit by a ball lightning of 2.4 meters in diameter, knocking down the walls, killing four people and injuring 60. Despite these difficulties in defining ball lightning, recent experiments have shown very promising results in trying to recreate it.

P: One of the first of those experiments was carried out in 2006 by a team led by Professor Gerd Fussmann. His team produced clouds of plasma 10-20 centimeters in diameter that resembled ball lightning. For those of you who don't know what plasma is, I'll explain. You're all familiar with the three states of matter: solid, liquid, and gas, and that matter is most stable during its solid state, and most active as a gas. Well... there is actually a fourth state of matter, called plasma that comes after gas and is even more energetic. Now back to Fussmann's experiment... it worked by passing a huge electrical current through a beaker filled with salt water using electrodes. The water was electrically heated until it gained enough energy to become plasma. This plasma bubble evaporated and left the beaker, burning brightly in an oval shape above the water for about 300 milliseconds. What's interesting is that this cloud couldn't even ignite a piece of paper. It was a great discovery because the plasmic cloud created in the labs was different from our previous understanding of plasma. Plasma is actually a highly energetic form of matter that characteristically rises into the sky, but does not have a defined shape. If scientists want to contain plasma in a specific shape, lots of equipment and power are required to keep it in that shape for even a fraction of a second.

P: So instead of trying to figure out the issues with the plasma hypothesis, scientists came up with a more plausible theory. Professor John Abrahamson at the University of Canterbury introduced a theory which suggested that ball lightning was a result of a chemical reaction of silicon particles that burn in the air. Uh... silicon is a chemical element that is found naturally in the ground, and is widely used for making electronics and mirrors. When a lightning bolt hits the ground, the heat and current cause a chemical reaction where silicon in the soil turns into vapor and rises into the air. The pure silicon particles in the air are attracted to each other by the electrical charge created by the lightning strike, binding together into a ball shape. The silicon reacts with atmospheric oxygen and glows brightly. This chemical reaction between silicon and oxygen takes place from the outside in, burning for as long as there is unreacted silicon left.

P: There is a problem with this theory as well. During World War II, Allied pilots often noticed 'balls of fire' which seemed to trail fighter jets at night. These balls were later called 'foo fighters' and pilots assumed that they were secret weapons developed by Germany and Japan, but the Axis forces also reported them. Interestingly, the descriptions of foo fighters and ball lightning, like their color and speed, were almost identical, leading to the conclusion that they were the same thing. But this conclusion gives rise to another problem: the silicon molecules hypothesized to create ball lightning cannot reach the altitudes where the foo fighters were spotted.

P: So... there is still no theory that can fully explain what ball lightning is, or what causes it. You can see that it is hard to study these phenomena too, because they are so unpredictable and infrequent. The only way I can think of studying them is to find a location famous for ball lightning sightings and basically wait for something to happen.

Tutoring

Listen to a conversation between a student and an English professor

S: Good afternoon, Dr. Lawlor. The, um…, calculus professor told me that you were looking for me earlier this morning.

P: Yes, Sarah, how have you been? Please come in and take a seat.

S: I've been great…just swamped with all these assignments and papers… I haven't seen you since I was in your literature class.

P: Yes, it has been quite a while, hasn't it? Well, when I was going through my old files, you know, just to organize them, I remembered how impressed I was by the papers you wrote for my class last year. And… You see, our school has a tutoring program set up for students who need help with writing. But since about half of our tutors are quitting soon or graduating this July, we need to recruit more tutors as quickly as possible.

S: And, you want me to take one of their spots?

P: Exactly!

S: Hmm… What would I be doing?

P: It's as simple as it sounds! You'd just need to teach the students how to improve their writing skills and help them with their papers.

S: But… I only took your class to meet the graduation requirement. I'm a chemistry major. What I want to pursue is completely different from what I would be doing as a writing tutor… You know, someday I want to be a biomedical engineer and work in a lab to save people's lives.

P: I understand that. I figured you could work with the students who need help with their chemistry or science-related papers.

S: Oh, Okay. That sounds like a reasonable plan, but wouldn't I need formal training before I start tutoring since I'm not an English major? I mean, I don't want to do too much strenuous work just to tutor people in writing…

P: Well, not exactly. I mean, it's true you would be taking one of our weekly training courses and work with a mentor who has been tutoring for a while, but once you complete the training sessions, you will be good to go and can start tutoring on your own. It's not just about tutoring people, though. You will also get class credits and community service hours, which will count towards your graduation requirements.

S: Oh, that certainly grabs my attention! Also, would I be observed by anyone?

P: Just for your first session! The professor whose course you'd be taking for tutoring will be present and give you feedback and advice for your next sessions.

S: Hmm… before I accept this offer, do you have any tips, professor?

P: Of course, Sarah. When it comes to tutoring someone, it sometimes takes a lot of perseverance. You should keep in mind that there are two ways to teach students how to enhance their papers. Most of the time, their papers are unorganized, yet they don't see it. So, what do you do? The simplest thing to do would be to directly tell them the flaws they need to fix to organize their papers. And…

S: …And the other way would be asking them questions that would ultimately guide them and help them organize their papers on their own, right?

P: Excellent!

S: Well, I think you should put me down on the list. I'm pretty much convinced to take the job.

P: That's perfect. Thank you for coming in today, Sarah. I really appreciate it!

Global Temperature

Listen to part of a lecture in an earth science class

P: Continuing our discussion on global climate change, I'd like to address a remarkable and feasible technology that's been recently developed. Last time, we talked about the current level of carbon dioxide, CO_2 emission, and its detrimental effect on the global climate. I've mentioned that the rate at which global temperatures are rising has gone beyond the 2 degree centigrade limit that scientists consider to be the allowable maximum. At the current rate of increase, catastrophic events could occur within around 10 years.

S1: Yes, and⋯ Last class, the bell rang right when you were about to introduce some kind of solution, right?

P: Yes, that's exactly what we'll be talking about today: solutions to the rising global temperatures. So, how can we prevent the temperatures from continually increasing past the limit and keep our CO_2 emissions under control? Well, there has been an enormous amount of research to find a suitable solution to the problem and numerous strides have been made.

S2: I think I remember something about oxy-fuel combustion in yesterday's reading. Is that one of the solutions?

P: That is certainly one of the solutions, yes. Instead of using air in the combustion process, it uses pure oxygen. By doing so, nitrogen, which is the main component of air, is not heated, and therefore, nitrous oxide production is reduced. Remember, nitrous oxide is also a major greenhouse gas that contributes to the global increase in temperatures, just like carbon dioxide.

Today we will focus on an advanced form of oxy-fuel combustion: Carbon capture and storage! As the name implies, it is a process that collects, isolates, and safely stores the emissions generated during fossil fuel combustion in power plants. There are two types: post-combustion and pre-combustion capture.

Even though they're highly technical, both processes have advantages and drawbacks. I'd like to have a class discussion with you guys regarding these.

As you may already be speculating, post-combustion capture comes into play after fossil fuels are burned and CO_2 is separated from the gas stream in the 'flue.' While the emitted CO_2 is passing through the flue, it goes through a chemical solution that binds with and saturates the gas, like smoke coming out of the chimney. Well, the chemical itself is not very important for this lecture, so let's not go too deep into that.

As the saturated solution leaves the flue, it releases the gas. Subsequently, the gas is collected, transported and trapped underground along with the chemicals used in the process, and⋯ that's where the problem with post-combustion capture emerges. Not only are really, really huge amounts of these absorbent materials and chemicals required, they are also an economic burden. Additionally, the equipment and machinery necessary for the process are extremely large, and of course, expensive. However, there are some positive aspects of post combustion capture. First of all, when compared to other solutions, it's a far more developed form of technology and ready to be put into use, which means it can be implemented right away. Also, working power plants that have already been built can be easily retrofitted, so it does not require the construction of new plants.

Okay, now let's take a look at pre-combustion capture.

S3: Let me guess. It captures CO_2 emissions before the fossil fuels are burned, right?

P: Yes, you're right. Unlike post-combustion capture, pre-combustion capture takes place before CO_2 is released. It is considered a very efficient method because⋯ it first converts the fuels into hydrogen and CO_2. By isolating CO_2, it only allows hydrogen to be combusted to produce power, effectively preventing any release of CO_2 into the air. The storage process of CO_2 works the same way as in post-combustion capture; CO_2 is securely transported to underground storage sites, where it will remain for thousands of years without any leakage problems.

Anyway⋯ Although some people believe that it is a better fit for the future, at present it suffers from numerous drawbacks, which make me believe that it needs to be improved in many ways before it can be considered the ideal method. The first is that it's a far less developed form of technology than post-combustion capture, so it will take another 15 to 20 years until it's ready to be implemented. Another drawback is that it requires an enormous amount of construction work. I mean, unlike post-combustion capture, new power plants need to be built so that the equipment and machinery necessary can be installed prior to completion.

S4: So, Professor, which is a better method in your opinion?

P: Well, I can't really say one is better than the other. Many scientists and researchers prefer post-combustion capture to pre-combustion because they believe that speed is the key factor. We are currently living in a generation where the so-called 'climate deadline' is approaching, and we need to make a move as quickly as possible. The longer we wait, the worse the situation gets, so speed is the key here. Like I said, pre-combustion capture still needs to be developed and enhanced in many ways. Regardless of its effectiveness, it's an irrefutable fact that it cannot be employed as of now, and maybe not for another 15 to 20 years. Post-combustion capture methods, on the other hand, can be added to working power plants globally right now and immediately start reducing CO_2 emissions, right? If we focus on both of them, it's only going to split our resources and risk making us miss the deadline that we have set, so that won't do any good. So my point is⋯ Instead of wasting our time debating which to use, we should primarily focus on encouraging people to start looking into using post-combustion capture, because if this trend continues, the next generations won't exist. It's a very urgent matter, and awareness of it should be spread as quickly and as widely as possible.

Monochromatic sculptures

Listen to a part of lecture in an art history class

P: Okay… in the last chapter, we looked at the fundamental roots of Greek and Roman mythology and their historical backgrounds. Even though they are mistakenly regarded as mere myths by some, we've learned that there were once political and social parallels in the stories, correct? Um, the most convincing tangible evidence of such a belief is, perhaps, the art made during these eras… sculptures, to be specific. I'm sure you've all seen a variety of statues, whether vibrantly colored or plain white. Our understanding of Greek and Roman statues is usually most compatible with the latter case, though, right? Everything is usually white from the head to the toes…

Now, the history of these monochromatic sculptures dates back to 15th century Europe… especially Italy, where the impact of the Renaissance was greatest. During this era, some ancient Greek and Roman sculptures were rediscovered in many parts of the world. Umm… If you guys refer back to the previous chapter, the Apollo Belvedere was one of the sculptures that was rediscovered during this period. It depicts the Greek god, Apollo, in one color - white… a symbol of aesthetic perfection. Anyway, what the Renaissance artists did when they rediscovered such ancient statues was that they strove to emulate their most distinctive characteristic - the monochromatic coloration. This "trend," so to speak, influenced the society in a significant way… I mean, think about it this way. Let's just say that you were one of the people living at the time, and all of the statues you saw were uniformly white. They were certainly beautiful, but they had no color. Contravening the earlier perspectives on sculpture, Renaissance era white marble statues, created in accordance with these ancient sculptures, instilled a new set of standards in contemporary artists that suggested that form was more important than color. It was not until the early 19th century that the art historians realized that their belief that the ancient marble statues were originally white was inaccurate.

In the early 19th century, archaeologists found subtle traces of visible paint on the statue and, after further research, arrived at the conclusion that the statues that were once believed to be monochromatic were originally polychromatic. You see, the current absence of visible coloration doesn't necessarily mean that it never existed. The color could have either simply deteriorated due to the effect of wind, water, and other such factors over thousands of years… or someone could have vigorously scrubbed the paint off while trying to clean the statues… Anyway, today, with the advent of new technology, archaeologists are able to execute more in-depth research into these sculptures. For instance, they can use ultraviolet light on the statues and distinguish formerly colored parts from the non-colored ones. Umm… UV light is very useful and efficient for this particular task because it causes organic compounds to, sort of, fluoresce. You see, unlike modern paints, the paints that the Greek and Roman artists used were mainly composed of organic compounds… Anyway, we'll be re-visiting this matter in the next lesson, so let's get back on topic.

We were talking about… Oh, yeah. Right. The evidence they found proved that the statues were originally polychromatic. Today, it's generally accepted by art historians and researchers that the Greek and Roman sculptures from the 7th century B.C.E through 4th century C.E were all polychromatic. Some believe that it's unfortunate that Renaissance art standards were established based on the "supposed" Roman and Greek principle that has now been proven wrong. I agree to a certain extent, but I don't think that the principle was entirely wrong. I mean, there can certainly be multiple interpretations of one piece of art. As I mentioned previously, monochromatic sculptures were interpreted with a heavy emphasis on the form. In this sense, we must first take a careful approach to understanding the artists' intentions, particularly when it comes to interpreting polychromatic sculptures.

The first thing to consider is the role of the colors. Some parts or features of the statues were accentuated with different colors. How, you may wonder, could that be related to the artists' intentions? Well, one compelling explanation is that a color may have symbolized many facets… things such as invincibility, patriotism, honor, heroism, and so on. Let's take the statue of Augustus, the founder and first emperor of the Roman Empire, into consideration to clarify the point. It was discovered on April 20, 1863 in the Villa of Livia at Prima Porta. In addition to founding the Roman Empire, Augustus was also the imperator, or commander, of the great Roman army. Observing his statue, we can see that he's in military clothing, holding a baton and posing as if he'd been victorious in battle. When the statue was examined thoroughly, it was revealed that its most abundant color was red, which is generally associated with energy, war, passion, and strength. You see the connection now, right? The sculptures weren't just randomly polychromatic; the colors actually played a symbolic role in highlighting certain features or characteristics of the subjects.

The next aspect we should study is the kind of pigments used to produce the colors. As you may already know, the quality of paint color is dependent upon the quality of the pigments used. Keeping that in mind, let's take a look at the statue of Augustus once again. The pigments used for his statue weren't just… normal pigments. They were very expensive at the time. The use of these particular pigments shows his importance and authority as the emperor, in addition to his importance as the imperator.

Okay. I think that was enough explanation of these statues, right? I'm sure you can see how the colors of the sculptures were associated with social, economic, and political values. You see, there're still a great number of sculptures that have yet to be deciphered the way that the statue of Augustus has been. We have the technology required to pursue further investigation, and it's urgent that we carry out more research and studies immediately, because the paint pigments deteriorate very rapidly. Through this, I'm certain that our knowledge of the art of the Greek and Roman empires will be greatly enhanced, along with our understanding of the culture that created the statues.

19th century female artist

Listen to a conversation between a student and a professor

S: Professor? Um… about the paper you asked us to turn in next week?

P: Ah… yes, the paper on a 19th century female artist.

S: Yes, while I was looking for a good example from the feminist era, I came across an artist named Rosa Bonheur.

P: Yes, the French proto-feminist. How's your research coming along?

S: Um… I'm having a hard time choosing what to write about. I mean, should I just write about her legacy as one of the pivotal figures in the initiation of the feminist movement? Or should I focus more on her life as an artist?

P: I can definitely see that you've been doing some research. Well, of course, you can't write a single paper on all of the topics, right?

S: There is so much information about her that it made me think about choosing someone else to write about, but I'm a really big fan of her work personally… I'm of two minds on this…

P: When researching the personal aspects of Rosa Bonheur's early life, there isn't really much to write about other than the fact that she had a hard time adapting to school, I guess, and maybe her family's background.

S: So I should probably rule out writing about her early life?

P: Exactly. There isn't much to write about. That is, if you decide to stick with Bonheur…

S: Then I should choose between the role she played in the beginning of the feminist movement by wearing men's clothes and her artwork?

P: Yes. But I have to tell you that her role in the feminist movement is highly controversial. She insisted that the only reason she wore men's clothing was because they were more comfortable and better suited for her type of work, which involved a lot of traveling to farms for research. Nobody has been able to validate this theory, however.

S: I see. I should probably write about her work then, huh?

P: I would recommend that you do, unless you're willing to push yourself to go deeper into the controversy I just mentioned.

S: It would certainly be a challenge.

P: I actually have some books on the topic, but the ones that debate the controversy go on for nearly a thousand pages. I'll tell you what. If you decide to go for it, I'm willing to give you extra credit, if, and only if, you pull it off in a manner that I approve of.

S: Any hints about the criterion on which I'll be graded?

P: Hmm… If you can prove whether or not Bonheur's statement was true, using conclusive proof and statements, I will approve it. You don't have to worry about whether I agree with your stance or not.

S: Isn't that… a bit abstract? I mean, "conclusive" is a rather objective term.

P: Yes, what I meant was, find information that can be used to support your opinion on Bonheur's statement, sort of like a persuasive essay. I think this assignment would be a great opportunity for you to expand your knowledge on the feminist era and your understanding of the artist.

S: Wow, as tempting as it sounds, it doesn't sound easy.

P: That's true. That's why I will give you extra points if you manage to do it. Well, I hope you make the right decision… Remember, this topic will be as difficult as it is intriguing.

Light energy

Listen to part of a lecture in a physics class

P: We witness and encounter many different forms of energy, such as heat, light, and electricity, on a daily basis. When you turn on the lights in your room, what do you think you have just done? Well, you have simply transformed electrical energy into light energy. The same phenomenon occurs everywhere in our daily lives. So, how does the transformation of energy work exactly? Well, the way it works is a little complicated, so listen carefully. You guys remember electrons in atoms, right? They play a very vital role in the process. When stimulated, the electrons collide and change orbital levels, they release energy that we experience as light or heat. We collectively call these forms of energy emitted electromagnetic energy. Is anybody aware of this?

S: Of course, light, heat, x-rays, microwaves, and electricity are great examples of it.

P: Perfect! Today, we'll be focusing primarily on exploring various aspects of the technology that enable us to generate light energy.

Hmm… Imagine what it would have been like back in our ancestors' times. There was almost total darkness because no electricity existed. Their solution was to use a campfire. Very simple, right? In today's society, where people demand more advanced forms of technology, a fire is not efficient enough. Why? Well… while fires are capable of generating light energy, they also produce tremendous thermal energy, which is the heat that results from the potential and kinetic energy of the burning materials. The problem with fires is that the amount of heat being produced is much higher than the amount of light they produce. A similar phenomenon happens with incandescent light bulbs… the light bulbs you probably have in your homes. Well… to give you a clearer vision of it, think about umm… your house! Has your mom ever asked you to replace a light bulb in the house? I'm sure some of you have accidently tried to unscrew a light bulb not long after it was turned off. You probably quickly pulled your fingers off of it because the light bulb was still hot.

S: Yes! I almost burned my finger when I was very young.. Why is it still hot even when it's turned off?

P: Yes, we've all had that kind of painful experience… Although they utilize electrical energy to generate light energy, the process of creating light itself creates a major practical drawback. Going a little deeper into the process, light is produced when electricity goes through a filament and becomes converted to heat. So, simply, electricity results in both heat and light. The problem with the process is that the amount of heat energy generated is much greater than the amount of light energy produced - about 90% of the output is heat, so a great deal of electricity is wasted. It's the same problem as the campfire… It's not effective enough, right? I mean, it's also quite inconvenient, because when heat is released from the bulbs it simultaneously increases the room temperature. Consumers demand better and more effective technologies. So, to satisfy their desires, fluorescent light tubes filled with mercury gas were developed.

Now, keep in mind that this light generating device works quite a bit differently than incandescent bulbs. Okay, stay with me. First, when the electrons in the gaseous mercury are stimulated, they start bouncing off of a special coating on the inside of the tube. The coating glows, and that's how we get light energy using fluorescent light bulbs. They're a little more sophisticated and harder to understand than incandescent bulbs, but their production of heat is substantially lower, so they sure are a better option at this time. Unfortunately, however, this method has detrimental effects on the environment as well. Since the gaseous mercury used in the tube is highly toxic, safe disposal of the tubes is nearly impossible. As far as we are concerned, we are living in a generation where solving environmental problems is a priority. Therefore, this method isn't seen as very effective. So, now, we can conclude that neither incandescent nor fluorescent light bulbs are good solutions because the former do not significantly reduce the amount of heat production, whereas the latter contaminate the environment. Although there are other light generating devices that have been developed, similar drawbacks to those of incandescent and fluorescent bulbs have made them less than ideal.

S: Then, there's no way we can generate light energy without producing a lot of heat energy or contaminating the environment?

P: Well… for now at least, we don't have any other fully developed lighting devices, but scientists and researchers have recently proposed a new form of technology, and they're currently working on making it feasible for everyone to utilize in the near future. It's called chemiluminescence.

S: Chemiluminescence… I think I've heard of it before. Its mechanism is a little different from the other two methods, right?

P: You bet! The way it works is a little different from the other two methods we've discussed! Okay, uh, I've mentioned that the other two methods require some kind of transformation of energy, right? Like… converting electrical energy to light energy and so on. Well, this case is an exception. Instead of providing some source of energy to generate another, chemiluminescence is a result of an exothermic chemical reaction, and thus, does not require any energy input, such as electricity or heat energy. When electrons are stimulated, they cause the breakdown of reactants, which go through a series of chemical reactions that ultimately result in a light emission, which is what chemiluminescence is. Furthermore, it does not produce significant quantities of heat, so that it doesn't suffer from the same drawbacks as incandescent light bulbs. Further, unlike fluorescent light bulbs, it's composed of all natural non-toxic chemical energy sources, so safe disposal of chemiluminescent bulbs would certainly not be a big concern. No unnecessary production of heat and no environmental contamination… It sure sounds like a great idea, doesn't it? Well… with respect to its pragmatic use, chemiluminescence is not a perfected technology yet, because it remains in the developmental stage. Let me give you a little background knowledge about the mechanism to help you understand how it occurs. Okay, the source of energy for chemiluminescence is found in nature. It's what allows fireflies and marine animals to glow and light up in the darkness. Scientists have successfully extracted the genes responsible for the production of chemiluminescence, and they're now striving to enhance the brightness of the light generated by the chemical and to apply it to existing technologies. Although it does have a few aspects that need improvement at this point, it might be the most promising method we have come up with, so far.

Human personality

Listen to part of a lecture in a psychology class

P: If I remember correctly, I briefly introduced the concept of personality psychology in the last class, right? For those who were absent, personality psychology is basically a branch of psychology devoted to studying the human personality. It's very closely related to neuroscience, you know, the study of the nervous system and the brain in particular. Umm… I also mentioned that ever since the advent of the Human Genome Project, or the HGP, a tremendous amount of research has been done to identify the fundamental roots of personality and whether or not personality is static. President Barack Obama has even recently announced his plan to fund a $100 million project to unlock the incredibly intricate mysteries of the brain and to enhance our understanding of its functions. Why so much money? Well… one of the most apparent reasons is that the discovery process is not only very complicated but also involves the use of highly technical tools.

If we look back to the beginning of the study of the human personality back in the 1990's, which is not that long ago, we will find that researchers and neuroscientists began to use Electroencephalography, or EEG… Umm… If you refer back to the beginning of our textbook, you will see that EEG machines detect brain activity by directly measuring the oscillations caused by the neurons in the brain. Well, it was a fairly good start for neuroscientists in that they were able to carry out a series of tests on their subjects…you know, the people on whom experiments are performed, and figure out what changes their brains were experiencing over time. Umm… It was once praised as one of the most effective methods of promoting the enlightenment of the personality, but now it's a bit obsolete in the field of personality psychology. It seems that with the shift in focus to a new topic, the stability of personality, a new form of technology, called Functional Magnetic Resonance Imaging or FMRI, seems to have taken over as the new revolutionary invention in the field.

It sure sounds familiar, doesn't it? Right! Our previous chapter dealt with MRI and its medical uses. Try not to get the similar names mixed up, though. The new technology is used almost exclusively as a laboratory research tool. Umm… To help you draw a clear distinction between the two, MRI is almost like a camera; it takes pictures of the brain structures for scientists to use for diagnostic purposes, while FMRI, as the name suggests, depicts the functions of the brain in addition to the structures… In other words… Umm… Okay. Let's say you're under stress because of homework assignments and whatnot, and you feel the sudden urge to express your anger. Well, your emotions originate from your brain's activities. In response to stimuli, your brain activates its different parts and sort of works as a command control center and tells your body which action to take. During this process, neuroscientists can detect changes in blood flow and oxygen levels in the brain that occur in response to external stimuli using FMRI.

Okay… Now that's a lot of information for you to take in all at once, so let me help you with it. I've mentioned that your emotions are the output of the brain activities that occur when your brain processes certain stimuli in the environment, correct? Whether you let yourself express those emotions or restrain yourself from doing so is your particular personality. Because of this property of the brain, or I should say nature, whether or not personality is static has been questioned numerous times over the years. FMRI has become a very useful tool for scientists who argue that it is in fact a stable aspect of the brain.

Those scientists, who theorize that personality does not change, have done some case studies, and one of them involved the amygdala, the section of the temporal lobe responsible for processing external stimuli, such as emotional reactions. To stimulate this part of the brain, the scientists had all of the subjects sit in a straight line and showed them photographs taken during wartime… angry, scared, horrified, and fearful faces. Using the FMRIs, the scientists were able to detect that the amygdala was activated in some of the subjects when the pictures were displayed in front of them. To ensure the validity of the experiment, the subjects, whose amygdalae were stimulated in the experiment, were brought back two years later and underwent the same process. The significance of this study was that when they were brought back, their brains responded to the photos in the same way as they had in the initial experiment. The scientists, therefore, claimed that since the response to such stimuli didn't change over the course of two years, it partially proved that personality was also stable… Well, a contradictory argument does exist, but it involves another long, boring experiment, so we won't go into it in this class.

You should also try to keep in mind that FMRI studies aren't perfect yet… a lot of controversies concerning them still exist, and neuroscientists in the field tend to exaggerate the significance of their findings. I mean, the brain is, after all, comprised of the most perplexing elements… Although some scientists say we have come to the final stage of solving the brain's mysteries, truthfully, our knowledge of the brain is still rudimentary… You see, FMRI is certainly one of the most practical and efficient tools we have as of now, but it still doesn't account for why we behave the way we do. Yes, it tells us which part of the brain is activated when certain stimuli are applied, but that's not enough to determine that personality of human beings never changes.

For this reason, we shouldn't overlook our good, old traditional research methods. I'm sure most of you are familiar with this concept. You know, using questionnaires… such as "Do you enjoy meeting new people and socializing with them?" or "Are you the type of person who gets disappointed or sad easily?" Although using questionnaires has some drawbacks, like the respondents manipulating their answers to portray themselves differently, it's perhaps the most reliable way we have to inquire about people's behavioral preferences and personalities at the present time.

usherin.usher.co.kr

USHER iBT TOFLE
FINAL TEST LISTENING
TEST 1/해설

TEST 1 — Set 1-1

Conversation: Implications of Bioluminescence

문단주제	본문내용	해석
	Listen to a conversation between a student and a professor.	교수와 학생간의 대화를 들으시오.
	S: Hello, Professor.	S: 안녕하세요, 교수님.
	P: Good morning, Brian. How was the conference in South Florida?	P: 좋은 아침이야, Brian. south Florida에서의 학회는 어땠니?
	S: It was a good experience. I met a lot of new people. I think it was a good opportunity for me to create a good professional network.	S: 좋은 경험이었어요. 새로운 사람들도 많이 만났구요. 전문가 집단과 네트워크를 구축할 수 있는 좋은 기회였다고 생각해요.
	P: That's what conferences are for. How did you feel about the lecture on molecular biology?	P: 그게 바로 학회가 있는 이유란다. 분자 생물학 강의는 어땠니?
	S: It was okay. It provided a lot of interesting theories that gave me a broader perspective on the field. Like I said, I met a lot of interesting people. I think they'll be very useful if I decide to further my research.	S: 괜찮았어요. 확실히 흥미로운 이론들을 많이 알게 되었는데 그 분야에 대해 더 넓은 시야를 갖게 해줬어요. 아까 말씀드린 것처럼, 흥미로운 사람들을 많이 만났거든요. 만약 제가 연구조사를 좀더 심도있게 하게 되면, 그 사람들이 많은 도움이 될것 같아요.
	P: Conferences are always a good place to meet those with similar professional interests.	P: 학회는 비슷한 전문가적 관심을 가진 사람들을 만날 수 있는 좋은 장소이지
	S: I wanted to ask you something. On my third day, I think, I was walking along the seashore and almost stepped on a jellyfish. I didn't notice it was there, until it started glowing. I was quite intrigued.	S: 여쭤볼게 있었는데요. 3일차 정도였던 것 같은데, 제가 해변가를 걷고 있다가 해파리를 거의 밟을뻔 했거든요. 그게 빛을 내기 시작할 때까지, 거기있는지 몰랐어요. 꽤 호기심이 생겼어요.
	P: I think you witnessed bioluminescence, the production of light by a living organism.	P: 내 생각엔 네가 생물발광을 목격한 것 같은데, 생물체로부터 빛이 생산되는 것 말야.
	S: [Q1]And… I was wondering if you could explain the mechanism a little bit. I'm interested in using it as a topic for my term paper.	S: [Q1]그래서… 그것의 원리를 약간 설명해 주실 수 있나해서요. 제 학기말 리포트 주제로 삼으면 흥미로울 것 같아요.
	P: Jellyfish, like the one you saw, are the most commonly known bioluminescent animals, but there are other organisms that do the same. Some others, like fireflies or glowworms, are quite common, but there are also some lesser known bioluminescent organisms, such as certain squid, shrimp and fungi.	P: 네가 본 것처럼 해파리는 가장 널리 알려진 발광동물이지. 하지만, 그런 생물들이 더 있단다. 다른 것들로는… 반딧불이나 개똥벌레의 유충 또한 잘 알려져 있어. 하지만 잘 알려져 있지 않은 발광동물들도 있는데, 몇몇 오징어나 새우, 그리고 곰팡이류들이야.
	S: Wow! Fireflies and glowworms were no surprise, but I didn't realize that there were so many others.	S: 와우! 반딧불이나 개똥벌레 유충은 놀랍지 않은데, 다른 생물들이 그렇게 많다는 건 몰랐어요.

P: Bioluminescence is basically a naturally occurring process in which energy is released through a chemical reaction in the form of light. Getting into the details would be way too time-consuming right now.

S: [Q2]As mysterious as this is, do you know why certain animals produce light? I mean, is it just a random… emission of energy?

P: Well… [Q3]they only produce light at certain times, so the purpose differs from animal to animal, but it can generally be categorized in three ways: as a means of intraspecies communication, for predator avoidance, or to attract prey.

S: Ah… Do you know which category jellyfish fall into?

P: Jellyfish, I believe, use bioluminescence to avoid predators.

S: What I'm most intrigued by is the actual process of light production. I mean, how is that even possible, biologically speaking?

P: Well, I don't know how strong your knowledge of chemistry is, but it's basically a chemical reaction. More specifically, the jellyfish can, after being exposed to the necessary energy for activation, rapidly oxidize magnesium and emit a bright light. That's the gist of it.

S: So, the jellyfish produce the chemicals necessary for illumination within their bodies?

P: Exactly. The jellyfish you saw was probably an Aequorea Victoria. [Q3] It produces a blue light, which is different from other jellyfish.

S: Yes, yes, it was producing a bluish light.

P: Then that's the most likely species. Are you considering writing about bioluminescent jellyfish for your term paper?

S: Well, I wanted to ask you what you thought about it. I mean, is it an interesting enough topic?

P: 생물 발광이란 기본적으로 자연적으로 발생하는 과정으로써, 에너지가 화학반응을 통해 빛의 형태로 방출되는 거지. 지금 내용을 자세하게 들어가면 시간이 너무 많이 소비될 것 같구나

S: [Q2]이게 참 신비로운데요, 교수님은 혹시 특정 동물들이 왜 빛을 발산하는지 아세요? 그러니까… 그냥 무작위로… 에너지를 방출하는 건가요?

P: 음… [Q3]그것들은 특정한 경우에만 빛을 발산한단다. 그래서 동물마다 목적이 다르지만 일반적으로 3가지로 분류될 수 있지: 종들간의 의사소통을 위한 것, 포식자를 피하기 위한 것, 혹은 먹이를 유인하기 위한 것이야.

S: 아…해파리가 그중 어떤 분류에 속하는지 아시나요?

P: 해파리는 포식자를 피하기 위해서 생물발광을 하는 걸로 알고 있는데.

S: 제가 가장 호기심을 갖는 부분은 빛을 생산하는 실제 과정이에요. 제 말은… 그게 어떻게 생물학적으로 가능한 거죠?

P: 음… 네 화학 지식이 얼마나 강한진 모르겠다만, 사실 그건 기본적으로 화학 반응이야. 좀더 자세하게 말하자면, 해파리는, 활성화를 위해 필요한 에너지에 노출된 후에 마그네슘을 급속히 산화시켜 밝은 빛을 발산하게 되는 거지. 그게 그 과정의 요지란다.

S: 그러니까 해파리는 빛을 방사하는 과정에 필요한 화학물질을 자신의 몸에서 만들어낸다는 말씀인가요?

P: 바로 그거야. 네가 본 해파리는 아마 Aequorea Victoria였을 꺼야. [Q3] 이 종류는 다른 해파리들과는 다르게 파란색 빛을 발산하지.

S: 네 맞아요. 그것은 파란색의 빛을 발산했었어요.

P: 그렇다면 그 종류가 확실할거야. 넌 학기말 리포트로 생물 발광하는 해파리에 대해 쓰려고 생각중이니?

S: 음, 그것에 대해 교수님이 어떻게 생각하시는지 알고 싶었어요. 그러니까 주제가 충분히 흥미로운가요?

TEST 1 — Set 1-1 — Conversation: Implications od Bioluminescence

P: [Q4]It's definitely interesting, but it's going to require a lot of work. Jellyfish aren't easy to understand because they are a relatively new field of study and scientists find them radical in the field of marine biology. [Q5]Are you still up for it?

S: I am. I think it will be very fun.

P: Well, I'm also a big fan of jellyfish. I'm excited to see how you're going to organize the scientific data that may be… rather complicated. Feel free to ask me for guidance at any time.

P: [Q4]확실히 흥미롭긴 하지만, 그걸 쓰려면 해야 될게 많을거야. 해파리를 이해하기는 쉽지 않거든. 왜냐하면 해파리는 상대적으로 새로운 연구 분야로 과학자들은 해파리를 해양생물학의 급진적인 주제로 여기고 있어. [Q5] 그래도 할 수 있겠니?

S: 네. 아주 재미있을 것 같아요.

P: 음, 나도 해파리를 무지 좋아해. 내가 다소 복잡할 수도 있는 과학데이터를 어떤 식으로 풀어나갈지 기대되는 구나. 내 도움이 필요하면 언제든지 물어보렴.

01 What is the conversation mainly about?

(A) ~~The student's thoughts about the conference~~ in South Florida *
(B) ~~A new field of molecular biology~~ that the student learned about during a conference from which he has just returned
(C) **The topic of the student's research paper**
(D) The professor's research project on the bioluminescence of jellyfish

대화는 주로 무엇에 관한 내용인가?

(A) ~~South Florida에서 열린 학회에서 얻은 학생의 생각~~ *
(B) ~~방금 돌아온 학회로부터 학생이 배운 분자 생물학의 새로운 분야~~
(C) **학생의 연구 리포트의 주제**
(D) 해파리의 생물 발광에 대한 교수의 연구 프로젝트

Main Idea And… I was wondering if you could explain the mechanism a little bit. I have interest in using it as a topic for my term paper (그래서… 그것의 원리를 약간 설명해주실 수 있나 해서요. 제 학기말 리포트 주제로 삼으면 흥미로울 것 같아요.).라고 학생이 한 말을 보면 이 대화는 학생의 과제물 주제와 관련된 것이 주된 내용임을 알 수 있다. 따라서 정답은 (C)이다. 학생이 학회에서 얻은 생각이나 분자 생물학 분야에 대한 내용은 주가 아니므로 (A), (B)는 오답이며, (D)는 언급된 적이 없으므로 오답이다.

02 What can be inferred about the student?

(A) He met a lot of interesting people who ~~research organisms that emit light.~~
(B) He is ~~hardly surprised~~ that some squid, shrimp, and fungi are bioluminescent.
(C) He attended a lecture about the molecular biological aspect of ~~bioluminescence~~ at the conference. *
(D) **He basically had no idea how organisms produce light within themselves.**

학생에 대해 추론할 수 있는 바는 무엇인가?

(A) 그는 ~~빛을 발산하는 생물체들을 조사하는~~ 흥미로운 사람들을 많이 만났다.
(B) 그는 몇몇 오징어, 새우, 곰팡이류들이 발광 생물이라는 것에 ~~거의 놀라지 않았다~~.
(C) 그는 학회에서 ~~발광 생물~~의 분자 생물학적인 측면에 대한 강의를 들었다. *
(D) **그는 생물체들이 어떻게 자체적으로 빛을 발산하는지 기본적으로 몰랐다.**

Inference (Infer) As mysterious as this is, do you know why certain animals produce light? I mean, is it just a random emission of energy? (이게 참 신비로운데요, 교수님은 혹시 특정 동물들이 왜 빛을 발산하는지 아세요? 그러니까, 그냥 무작위로 에너지를 방출하는 건가요?)에서 학생은 메커니즘을 모른다는 것을 알 수 있으므로 정답은 (D)이다. (A)는 학회에서 빛을 발산하는 생물체를 조사하는 사람들을 만났다는 언급이 없으므로 (B)는 교수가 언급하는 발광 생물들에 대해 학생이 놀랍다는 반응을 보이므로 각각 오답이다. (C)는 학회에서 들은 강의는 발광 생물과 관련이 없으므로 정답이 될 수 없다.

TEST 1 — Set 1-1 Conversation: Implications od Bioluminescence

03 According to the conversation, what points were mentioned about the bioluminescence of organisms?

Click on 2 answers

(A) Some of them produce light in order to attract prey when they choose to.
(B) They utilize magnesium and other internal chemicals to produce light only when avoiding predators. *
(C) The emission of light is an intermittent process with no specific purpose.
(D) The color of light emitted varies by organism.

대화에 따르면, 생물체의 자체 발광에 대해 언급된 사항은 무엇인가?

두 개의 답을 고르시오.

(A) 일부 생물들은 선택한 먹이를 유인하기 위해 빛을 발산한다.
(B) 그들은 오로지 포식자를 피하기 위해 마그네슘과 다른 내부 화학 물질을 활용해 빛을 발산한다. *
(C) 빛을 발산하는 것은 특정한 목적이 없는 간헐적인 과정이다.
(D) 발산된 빛의 색깔은 생물체에 따라 다양하다.

Detail (Characteristic)   They only produce lights at certain time periods, so the purpose differs from animal to animal, but generally it can be categorized into three reasons: communicating amongst themselves, predator avoidance, or to attract their own prey. (그것 들은 오직 특정한 시간대에만 빛을 발산한단다. 그래서 동물마다 목적이 다르지만 일반적으로 3가지로 분류될 수 있지: 동물들 간의 의사소통을 위한 것, 포식자를 피하기 위한 것, 혹은 먹이를 유인하기 위한 것이야.)… 중략 … It produces a blue-colored light, which may be different from others.(이 종류는 다른 해파리들과는 다르게 파란색 빛을 발산하지.)에서 언급된 것처럼, 자체 발광에 대한 것은 (A), (D)가 옳다는 것을 알 수 있고,(B)에서 오로지 포식만을 위한 것과, (C)에서 목적이 없다는 것은 틀리므로 각각 오답이다.

04 What is the professor's attitude toward jellyfish as a topic of research for the student's paper?

(A) They are a radical topic that she has always expected students to write about. *
(B) They can be an adequate topic of research only if the student manages to do it adeptly.
(C) They lack the scientific interest of other complex creatures.
(D) There has not been sufficient research in the field because getting into the details would take too much time.

학생이 해파리를 리포트의 조사 주제로 삼는 것에 대한 교수의 태도는 무엇인가?

(A) 해파리는 급진적인 주제로서 그녀는 학생들이 그것에 대해 쓰길 항상 바래왔다. *
(B) 해파리는 학생이 뛰어나게 해냈을 때만 적절한 조사 주제가 될 수 있다.
(C) 해파리는 다른 복잡한 생물들에 대한 과학적인 흥미를 떨어뜨린다.
(D) 그 분야에 대한 조사가 충분히 이루어지지 않았는데, 왜냐하면 구체적으로 깊게 조사하는 것은 시간이 너무 오래 걸리기 때문이다.

Inference (Attitude) It's definitely interesting, but it's going to require a lot of work. Jellyfish aren't easy to understand because they are a relatively new field of study, and scientists find them radical in the field of marine biolgy. (확실히 흥미롭긴 하지만, 그걸 쓰려면 해야 될게 많을 거야. 해파리를 이해하기는 쉽지 않거든. 왜냐하면 해파리는 우리에게 상대적으로 새로운 연구 분야로 과학자들은 해파리를 해양생물학의 급진적인 주제로 여기고 있어)에서 교수는 학생의 주제에 대해 (B)와 같은 태도를 지닌 것을 알 수 있다. (A)는 급진적 주제인 것은 맞으나 교수가 그것에 대해 학생들이 리포트를 써주길 바래왔다는 언급은 없으므로 오답,이다. (B)에서 해파리가 다른 생물들에 대한 과학적인 흥미를 떨어뜨린다는 것은 언급된 적 없으므로 오답이며, (D)는 해파리가 새로운 분야라는 언급이 있을 뿐, 조사하는데 시간이 오래 걸려서 충분한 조사가 이루어지지 않았다는 내용은 없으므로 정답이 될 수 없다.

05 Listen again to part of the conversation. Then answer the question.

"It's definitely interesting, but it's going to require a lot of work. Jellyfish aren't easy to understand because they are a relatively new field of study, and scientists find them radical in the field of marine biology. Are you still up for it?"

What does the professor mean when she says this : 🎧

Are you still up for it?

(A) She is asking the student if he ~~understands what she is saying~~. *
(B) She is asking the student to ~~work harder than usual~~.
(C) She is asking the student if he thinks he can pull off this topic with success.
(D) She is asking the student if he ~~agrees with everything she has just said~~.

대화의 일부분을 다시 듣고, 질문에 답하시오.

" 확실히 흥미롭긴 하지만, 해야 될게 많을 거야. 해파리를 이해하기는 쉽지 않거든. 왜냐하면 해파리는 상 대적으로 새로운 연구 분야로 과학자들은 해파리를 해양생물학의 급진적인 주제로 여기고 있어. 그래도 할 수 있겠니?"

다음과 같이 말할때, 교수가 의미하는 바는 무엇인가?

그래도 할 수 있겠니?

(A) 그녀는 학생에게 자신이 하는 말을 이해하는지 물어보고 있다. *
(B) 그녀는 학생에게 평소보다 더 열심히 노력할 것을 요구하고 있다.
(C) 그녀는 학생이 이 주제를 성공적으로 해낼 수 있다고 생각하는지 물어보고 있다.
(D) 그녀는 학생에게 자신이 방금 말한 모든 것에 동의하는지 물어보고 있다.

Inference (Headset) Are you still up for it? (그래도 할 수 있겠니?)라고 물은 것은 해파리가 어려운 주제라는 것을 알고서도 할 준비가 되어있는지 학생의 의사를 물어보는 것이므로 (C)가 정답이다. (A)에서 교수는 학생의 이해 여부를 묻는 것이 아니며, (B)는 교수가 다른 때보다 더 열심히 해야 한다고 요구하는 것이 아니므로 각각 오답이다. (D)는 교수가 학생에게 자신이 한 말에 동의하는지 묻는 것이 아니므로 답이 될 수 없다.

TEST 1 Set 1-2 Lecture 1: Types of Renaissance Gardens

문단주제	본문내용	해석
	Listen to part of a lecture in an art history class. The professor is discussing Renaissance gardens.	예술사 강의의 일부를 들으시오. 교수는 르네상스 정원에 대해 논의하고 있습니다.
르네상스의 의미와 르네상스 정원 소개	P: Okay, I introduced the concept of the Renaissance in last week's lecture. This was the period when new ideas swept across Europe after the Middle Ages. If you'll remember, the term Renaissance means rebirth in French. This cultural movement aspired to popularize the forgotten classic concepts of the ancient Romans across Europe. Countless artistic works were produced during this period, [Q6]**but today we are going to focus on Renaissance gardens.** Is anyone familiar with the gardens constructed during the Renaissance? S: [Q10]**I believe that Renaissance gardens were built to emulate those popular during ancient Roman times.**	P: 좋아요, 제가 지난주 강의에서 르네상스의 개념에 대해 소개했는데요. 이때는 중세 이후 새로운 아이디어가 유럽을 휩쓴 시기였어요. 여러분이 기억한다면, 르네상스라는 용어는 프랑스어로 재탄생을 의미해요. 이것은 잊혀졌던 고대 로마의 고전 개념을 유럽 전역에 대중화하고자 열망했던 문화운동이에요. 수많은 예술 작품들이 이 시기 동안에 제작되었는데요, [Q6]하지만 오늘 우리는 르네상스 정원에 초점을 맞춰볼게요. 르네상스 시기에 건설된 정원에 대해 아는 사람이 있나요? S: [Q10] 제가 알기로는 르네상스 정원은 고대 로마 시대에 유행했던 정원을 모방하기 위해 지어졌어요.
르네상스 정원의 일반적인 특징과 발전 단계별 특징	P: **Yes, that is the most important characteristic of the Renaissance gardens. In other words, they were pretty much built as the ancient Romans 'would' have built them, using assumptions of what Roman gardens were actually like.** As the idea of emulating the beauty of lost classical artwork became popular, wealthy people, such as merchants and political figures, craved to recreate the magnificent gardens of ancient Rome, so they started to hire prestigious architects to build them. Let's take a look at some of the features that Renaissance gardens shared. The most noticeable features were walkways lined with marble statues and fountains like those featured in ancient Roman gardens. They were also filled with allegorical statues of animals, giants and fantastic creatures, as well as bushes trimmed into specific shapes to further emulate ancient Roman architecture. Renaissance gardens brought the gardens of ancient Rome back to life in every possible way. S: Professor, what were the ancient Roman gardens actually like? P: That's a good question. Well, they were pretty much the prototypes of the Renaissance gardens. There were different designs, but Roman gardeners adhered to certain styles that developed in three main stages. The first garden of ancient Rome were built near homes to	P: 네, 그것이 르네상스 정원의 가장 중요한 특징이에요. 다시 말하면, 이 정원들은 마치 고대 로마인들이 지었을 법한 정원처럼 만들어졌죠. 로마 정원이 실제로 어떻게 생겼을지에 대한 가정 하에서요. 잊혀진 고전 예술작품의 아름다움을 모방하고자 하는 생각이 인기를 얻으면서, 상인이나 정치 거물과 같은 부자들은 고대 로마의 웅장한 정원을 재건하고자 열성적이었죠, 그래서 그들은 유명한 건축가를 고용해 정원을 건설하기 시작했어요. 르네상스 정원들이 공통적으로 갖고 있는 몇몇 특징들을 살펴봅시다. 가장 눈에 띄는 특징은 고대 로마 정원에서 보여지는 것처럼 대리석 조각상들이 줄지어 서있는 통로들과 분수대에요. 고대 로마 건축을 더욱 모방하기 위해 특정 모양으로 다듬어진 관목뿐만 아니라 동물, 거인, 환상적인 존재 같은 우화적인 조각품들로 정원이 가득 찼죠. 르네상스 정원은 가능한 모든 방식을 동원하여 고대 로마 정원을 되살려낸 것이지요. S: 교수님, 그럼 고대 로마 정원은 실제로 어떻게 생겼나요? P: 좋은 질문이에요. 음, 그것들은 르네상스 정원의 원형과 꽤 비슷했는데요. 여러가지 다른 스타일이 있었지만, 로마 정원사들은 특정 스타일을 고집했는데 이것은 3단계로 발달했어요. 첫 번째 고대 로마 정원은 집 근처에 만들어졌는데 먹기

르네상스 시대에 정원을 건설한 이유

grow vegetables and herbs for consumption. This type of garden, known as a hortus, was usually built in the backyard of a house. They served as the primary source of vegetables and herbs for the Romans. At the time, these gardens served more of a practical need than an ornamental one. The second type of Roman garden developed as the quality of life in ancient Rome improved and they enlarged their living spaces. This expansion gave birth to the peristyle, or columned porch and colonnade, in Roman architecture. During this period, the garden moved to the front yard and was decorated with walkways bordered by statues. Further, flowers and shrubs were planted for ornamental purposes rather than the practical vegetables and herbs. The final stage in the evolution of Roman gardens was the villa garden. This was the most luxurious style of Roman garden in which ornamental plants and artwork were arranged for the pleasure of visitors strolling through the peristyles of the gardens. [Q7]**The major difference was that this style of garden contained buildings other than the house itself and more complex ornaments, such as fountains.** In some of the larger ones, they even built exercise facilities such as swimming pools! This was the style that drew the greatest praise from Renaissance garden builders.

S: Professor, why did the people build gardens during the Renaissance?

르네상스 시대에 정원을 건설한 이유

P: I'm glad you asked that question. There are several assumptions regarding why people built these gardens. The most important role of these gardens was to symbolize the status of their owners. Umm… To be straightforward, there are no other significant reasons behind the garden construction at the time. It is fair to say that these gardens were a manifestation of the pursuit of the beauty of ancient Roman architecture. However, [Q8]**research into the purpose of these gardens shows that they were, in fact, mainly displays of wealth and power to the world.** These formal gardens served as a medium to impress visitors. People such as writers, poets and philosophers would gather and praise the beauty of the garden. [Q8]**The owners of the gardens would have been able to derive a great deal of satisfaction and pride from the profuse attention and wonder people displayed regarding them.**

위해 채소나 허브를 키우기 위함이었어요. 이런 종류의 정원은 hortus라고 알려져 있고, 보통 집 뒷마당에 지어졌죠. 그곳은 로마인들에게 채소와 허브의 중요한 공급원 역할을 했어요. 그 당시에는 이러한 정원들이 장식적인 것보다는 실용적인 필요를 위해 더 많이 사용되었죠. 두 번째 타입의 로마 정원은 고대 로마 사회에서 삶의 질이 향상되고 주거 공간 또한 확장되면서 발달했어요. 이러한 확장은 로마 건축에 회랑, 즉, 기둥이 있는 현관과 주랑을 탄생시켰죠. 이 시기에 정원은 앞 뜰로 옮겨졌고, 조각상에 의해 경계가 구별되는 복도로 꾸며졌어요. 게다가, 실용적인 채소나 허브보다는 장식적인 목적을 위해 꽃과 관목이 심어졌죠. 로마 정원 발달의 마지막 단계는 빌라 정원인데요. 이것은 가장 호화스러운 스타일의 정원으로, 많은 관상용 식물들과 예술품들이 회랑 정원을 산책하는 관람객에게 즐거움을 주기 위해 놓여졌어요. [Q7]**주요 차이점은 이런 종류의 정원은 집 자체와는 다른 별도의 건물들과, 분수대와 같은 좀 더 복잡한 장식물들을 포함하고 있었다는 것이죠.** 일부 커다란 정원에는, 심지어 수영장과 같은 운동 시설도 지어졌어요! 이것은 르네상스 정원 건축가들에게 최고의 찬사를 받는 스타일이었죠.

S: 교수님, 르네상스 시대의 사람들은 왜 정원을 만든거죠?

P: 좋은 질문이에요. 사람들이 왜 이러한 정원을 지었는가에 대해서는 몇 가지 추측들이 있는데요. 이 정원들의 가장 중요한 역할은 소유주의 지위를 상징하는 것이었어요. 음… 단도직입적으로 말하면 그 당시에는 정원을 건설하는데 다른 중요한 이유는 없었어요. 이 정원들은 고대 로마 건축의 아름다움을 추구하는 열망이 표출된 것이라고 말하는 게 맞긴 해요. [Q8]**하지만 이런 정원들이 지어진 목적에 대한 연구를 통해 사실상 그것들이 주로 부와 권력을 세상에 과시하는 역할을 했다는 것이 드러났죠.** 이러한 공적인 정원들은 방문객을 감명시키는 매개물로서의 역할을 했는데요. 작가, 시인, 철학자와 같은 사람들이 모여서 정원의 아름다움을 칭송했어요. [Q8]**정원의 소유주들은 사람들이 보여주는 풍부한 관심과 감탄을 보면서 많은 만족감과 자긍심을 가질 수 있었을거에요.**

TEST 1　Set 1-2　Lecture 1　Types of Renaissance Gardens

이탈리아 르네상스 정원의 특징1: 동전 조작식 분수

S: [Q11] Professor, were there any other unique features of these gardens, besides their beauty?

P: Hmm... Were there any other features? Umm... well, I do remember one thing that might interest you... Oh yes, there was another major interesting feature of the gardens: coin operated fountains. The idea behind these came from the Greek mathematician "Heron of Alexandria". He came up with a device that dispensed water when a coin was inserted. The fountains were set up to release water in the same way as a coin operated vending machine. The official term for these was "giochi d'aqua", which literally means "water jokes," since they were concealed to drench unsuspecting visitors. These were one of the most famous features added to Italian Renaissance Gardens for the purpose of entertaining visitors.

이탈리아 르네상스 정원의 특징2: 미로

S: Professor, I recall there being another interesting feature of Renaissance gardens. I believe that they contained labyrinths to emulate those of ancient Rome, right?

P: Well, ironically, they did build labyrinths for this reason, but there is no evidence of ancient Roman gardens containing labyrinths. The fact that Renaissance gardeners included them has led many to the misconception that they existed in ancient Rome. Why, then, did labyrinths become a common feature of Renaissance gardens? Well, according to Roman mythology, the labyrinth was an impossible maze where the Minotaur was imprisoned. [Q9] Later, Italians built labyrinths in their gardens to imitate the mythical maze, so the legendary labyrinth came to life as an entertainment venue. The Italians redefined the meaning of the word to mean an outdoor playground for guests. Whenever there was a large group of guests, labyrinths were not only used as multipurpose grounds for dancing and games, but they also offered a pleasant atmosphere for visitors, as their walls were comprised of herbs and shrub plants. People loved to take walks and enjoy nature within the labyrinths.

S: [Q11] 교수님, 그럼 아름다움 외에, 이 정원들이 가진 다른 독특한 특징들이 있나요?

P: 음… 다른 특징들이 있냐구요? 음… 여러분의 관심을 끌만한 것이 하나 생각날 듯 한데요… 오, 그래요, 정원에는 또 다른 흥미로운 주요 특징이 있었어요.: 바로 동전으로 조작되는 분수에요. 그 아이디어는 그리스의 수학자인 "Heron of Alexandria"로부터 나온 것인데요. 그는 동전을 넣으면 물이 나오는 장치를 생각해 냈어요. 그 분수대는 동전으로 조작되는 자판기와 똑같은 방식으로 물이 분출되게끔 한 것이죠. 이것의 공식 용어는 "giochi d'aqua"로, 물장난'이라는 뜻인데, 왜냐하면 그것이 숨겨져 있어서 예상하지 못한 방문객들을 물에 젖게 하기 때문이었어요. 이것은 방문객들을 즐겁게 하기 위한 목적으로 이탈리아 르네상스 정원에 더해진 가장 유명한 특징 중의 하나입니다.

S: 교수님, 제가 기억하기로는 르네상스 정원의 또 흥미로운 특징이 하나 더 있었어요. 거기에는 고대 로마 시대의 정원을 모방하기 위해 미로가 포함됐던 걸로 아는데, 맞나요?

P: 음, 아이러니하게도, 그들이 그런 이유로 미로를 지었지만, 고대 로마 정원에 미로가 있었다는 증거는 없어요. 르네상스 정원을 지은 건축가들이 미로를 포함했다는 사실은 고대 로마 시대에 미로가 존재했었다는 오해를 하게 만들었죠. 그럼 왜 미로가 르네상스 정원의 공통적인 특징이 되었을까요? 음, 로마 신화에 따르면, 미로는 Minotaur가 갇혀있는 탈출이 불가능한 미궁이었어요. [Q9] 나중에, 이탈리아인들은 신화 속 미궁을 모방하기 위해 자신의 정원에 미로를 건설했는데요, 그래서 전설적인 미로가 오락의 장소로 다시 부활하게 되었던 거죠. 이탈리아인들은 손님을 위한 실외 놀이터를 뜻하는 것으로 그 단어의 의미를 재정의했어요. 큰 규모의 단체 손님들이 있을 때면, 미로는 춤이나 게임을 위한 다목적 장소로 사용되었을 뿐만 아니라, 또한 벽이 허브와 관목으로 이루어져서 관람객에게 기쁨을 주는 분위기를 연출했죠. 사람들은 미로 안에서 산책하고 자연을 즐기는 것을 좋아했어요.

06 What is the lecture mainly about?

(A) Reasons that ~~people in Fran~~ce built Italian Renaissance gardens
(B) Pointing out the differences between the gardens of the Italian Renaissance and ancient Roman gardens *
(C) Analysis of the types of gardens built during the Renaissance era
(D) Similarities between the gardens of the ancient Roman and Renaissance ages

강의는 주로 무엇을 말하는가?

(A) 프랑스 사람들어 이탈리아 르네상스 정원을 건설한 이유
(B) 이탈리아 르네상스 정원과 고대 로마 정원사이의 차이점들을 지적 *
(C) 르네상스 시대의 지어진 정원의 종류에 대한 분석
(D) 고대 로마 시대와 르네상스 시대의 정원들에서 나타나는 유사점

Main Idea 교수는 강의의 도입부에서 but today we are going to focus on Renaissance gardens.(하지만 오늘 우리는 르네상스 정원에 초점을 맞춰 볼께요.)라고 말하며 앞으로의 강의 주제가 르네상스의 정원에 대한 것임을 미리 밝히고 있으므로 정답은 (C)가 된다. 본문에 언급하는 르네상스 정원은 이탈리아인들이 만든 것이므로 (A)는 오답이다. (B)는 고대 로마 정원과 르네상스 정원의 차이점을 밝힌 부분이 있으나 주제로 삼기에는 부족하므로 오답이며, (D)는 고대 로마의 정원이 르네상스에 영향을 끼친 것에 대한 것이지 둘 사이의 유사점만을 언급하여 주제로 삼기에는 지엽적인내용이므로 답이 되기 힘들다.

07 According to the professor, what was the difference between the peristyle and the villa in the Romans gardens?

(A) Practicality
(B) Ornamental purpose
(C) Social symbolism
(D) Separate structures

교수에 따르면, 로마 정원에서 회랑과 빌라의 차이점은 무엇이었는가?

(A) 실용성
(B) 장식적 목적
(C) 사회적, 상징
(D) 분리된 구조

Detail (Difference) 차이점이 언급된 부분을 살펴보면 The major difference was that this style of garden housed separate buildings from the house itself and more complex ornaments such as the fountains were built.(주요 차이점은 이런 종류의 정원은 집 자체와는 다른 별도의 건물들과, 분수대와 같은 좀 더 복잡한 장식물들을 포함하고 있었다는 것이죠.)에서 분리된 구조가 특징임을 말하고 있음으로 (D)가 정답이다.

TEST 1 Set 1-2 Lecture 1 Types of Renaissance Gardens

08 What was the common reason for building gardens during the Renaissance era?

르네상스 시대에 정원을 지은 공통적인 이유는 무엇인가?

(A) They wanted to ~~mimic the beauty of nature~~ and the classic artwork of ancient Rome. *
(B) **They wanted to emphasize and display their social status and power.**
(C) They ~~wanted to possess~~ a structure with a lavish exterior.
(D) They wanted to have a villa where ~~they could relax~~ and entertain visitors.

(A) 그들은 ~~자연의 아름다움과~~ 고대 로마의 고전 예술 작품을 모방하길 원했다. *
(B) **그들은 자신의 사회적 지위와 권력을 강조하고 드러내길 원했다.**
(C) 그들은 사치스러운 외관을 가진 구조물을 ~~소유하길 원했다~~.
(D) 그들은 ~~자신이 쉴 수 있고~~ 방문객들을 즐겁게 하는 빌라를 가지길 원했다.

Detail (Reason)   정원을 건설한 목적이 언급되어 있는 부분인 However, research into the purpose of these gardens shows that they were, in fact, displays of wealth and power to the world.(하지만 이런 정원들이 지어진 목적에 대한 연구를 통해 사실상 그것들이 주로 부와 권력을 세상에 과시하는 역할을 했다는 것이 드러났죠), 또한 The owners of the gardens would have been able to derive a great deal of satisfaction and pride from the profuse attention and wonder people displayed regarding them.(정원의 소유주들은 사람들이 보여주는 풍부한 관심과 감탄을 보면서 많은 만족감과 자긍심을 가질 수 있었을 거에요.)에서 정답이 (B)임을 알 수 있다. (A)는 자연을 모방했다는 내용은 없으며, 그 당시 인기 있었던 로마풍을 따른 이유는 단순한 모방을 원했던 것이 아니라 자신의 지위를 드러내기 위함이므로 오답이다. (C)는 사치스러운 건축 물을 소유하고자 한 것은 맞으나 공통적인 건설 이유로 보기에는 어려움이 있으므로 오답이 된다. (D)는 소유주가 쉬기 위한 목적은 언급되어 있지 않고, 방문객들을 즐겁게 하는 것은 르네상스 정원의 특징 중 하나이므로 각각 오답이다.

09 Why did the professor mention ancient Roman mythology?

왜 교수는 고대 로마 신화를 언급했는가?

(A) ~~To emphasize~~ that the labyrinth was an impossible maze from which the Minotaur could not escape
(B) To describe ~~the origin of the artwork and statues~~ depicted in the Renaissance gardens *
(C) To illustrate ~~the origin of the Roman gardens~~
(D) **To explain how gardeners derived the idea for mazes**

(A) ~~미로는 Minotaur가 탈출하기 불가능한 미궁임을 강조하기 위해~~
(B) 르네상스 정원에 묘사된 ~~예술 작품과 조각상의 기원을 묘사하기 위해~~ *
(C) ~~로마 정원의 기원을 설명하기 위해~~
(D) **어떻게 정원 건축가들이 미궁에 대한 아이디어를 얻었는지 설명하기 위해**

Inference (Purpose)   로마 신화가 언급된 부분을 살펴보면 Later, Italians built labyrinths in their gardens to imitate the mythical maze; so the legendary labyrinth came back to life as an entertainment object.(나중에, 이탈리아인들은 신화 속 미궁을 모방하기 위해 자신의 정원 에 미로를 건설했는데요; 그래서 전설적인 미로가 오락의 장소로 다시 부활하게 되었던 거죠.)에서 이탈리아인들이 미로에 대한 아이디어를 신화 속에서 얻은 것임으로 정답은 (D)가 된다. (A)는 교수는 미로가 빠져나가기 힘든 미궁이라는 것을 강조하기 위해 로마 신화를 언급한 것은 아니며, (B)는 작품과 조각상의 기원이 아닌 미로 자체의 기원을 설명하기 위한 것이므로 각각 오답이다. (C) 또한 르네상스 정원 안에 있는 미로의 기원을 찾고자 하는 것이지 로마정원 자체의 기원은 아니므로 오답이다.

10 Listen again to a part of the lecture. Then answer the question.

S: I believe that Renaissance gardens were built to emulate those popular during ancient Roman times.
P: Yes, that is the most important characteristic of the Renaissance garden. In other words, they were pretty much built as 'would' have built them, using sumptions of what Roman gardens were actually like

What does the professor imply when he says this: 🎧

> In other words, they were pretty much built as the ancient Romans 'would' have built them, using assumptions of what Roman gardens were actually like.

(A) There were no ancient Roman gardens left behind.
(B) The ancient Romans wished for even greater gardens than they had originally built. *
(C) The ancient Romans would have built the gardens to fit Italian homes of the Renaissance era.
(D) There were no descriptions of ancient Roman gardens for the Renaissance gardeners to copy.

강의의 일부를 다시 듣고, 질문에 답하시오.

S: 제가 알기로는 르네상스 정원은 고대 로마 시대에 유행했던 정원을 모방하기 위해 지어졌어요.
P: 네, 그것이 르네상스 정원의 가장 중요한 특징이에요. 다시 말하면, 이 정원들은 마치 고대 로마인들이 지었을 법한 정원처럼 만들어졌죠. 로마 정원이 실제로 어떻게 생겼을 지에 대한 가정하에서요.

이 말을 할 때 교수는 무엇을 암시하는가?

> 다시 말하면, 이 정원들은 마치 고대 로마인들이 지었을 법한 정원처럼 만들어졌죠. 로마 정원이 실제로 어떻게 생겼을 지에 대한 가정하에서요.

(A) 남아있는 고대 로마 정원이 없었다.
(B) 고대 로마인들은 자신들이 원래 지었던 정원보다 훨씬 큰 정원을 갖길 원했다. *
(C) 고대 로마인들은 르네상스 시대의 이탈리아인들의 집에 어울리는 정원을 지었을 것이다.
(D) 르네상스 정원이 복제할 수 있는 로마시대의 정원에 대한 묘사가 견혀 없었다.

Inference (Headset) 고대 로마 정원의 모습을 르네상스 시대에 추정하여 건설했다는 것은, 실제로 남아 있는 고대 로마 정원이 없었다는 것을 의미하므로 (A)가 정답이 된다. (B), (C)의 내용은 언급이 없으므로 각각 오답이다. (D)는 실제로 남아있는 실물은 없어도 기록 등에 있는 정원에 대한 묘사 부분을 보고 이를 통해 추정했을 것이므로 묘사가 없었다는 말은 맞지 않는다. 따라서 오답이다.

---

11 Listen again to part of the lecture. Then answer the question.

S: Professor, were there any other unique features of these gardens, besides their beauty?
P: Hmm... Were there any other features? Umm... well, I do remember one thing that might interest you... Oh yes, there was another major interesting feature of the gardens: coin operated fountains.

Why does the professor say this? 🎧

> P: Hmm... Were there any other features? Umm... well, I do remember one thing that might interest you....

(A) He needs a moment to reconsider the statement mentioned previously. *
(B) He has forgotten what he intended to tell the students.
(C) He has something in his mind to respond with.
(D) He is about to tell the students that the class is finished.

강의의 일부를 다시 듣고, 질문에 답하시오.

S: 교수님, 그럼 아름다움 외에, 이 정원들이 가진 다른 독특한 특징들이 있나요?
P: 음… 다른 특징들이 있냐구요? 음… 여러분의 관심을 끌만한 것이 하나 생각날 듯 한데요… 오 그래요, 정원에는 또 다른 흥미로운 주요 특징이 있었어요.: 바로 동전으로 조작되는 분수에요.

교수는 왜 이런 말을 하는가

> P: 음… 다른 특징들이 있냐구요? 음… 여러분의 관심을 끌만한 것이 하나 생각날 듯 한데요.

(A) 그는 이전에 언급한 말을 다시 생각하는데 약간의 시간이 필요하다. *
(B) 그는 학생들에게 말하려고 의도했던 내용을 잊어버렸다.
(C) 그는 대답할 어떤 것을 마음속에 가지고 있다.
(D) 학생들에게 수업이 끝날 것임을 말하려고 한다.

Inference (Headset) 이미 마음 속에 대답할 예를 가지고 있고 그것을 말하려고 잠시 시간을 가지는 것이므로 (C)가 정답이 된다. (A)는 교수가 이전에 언급한 내용이 아니므로, (B)는 학생의 질문에 대답하는 것이지 교수가 원래 말하려고 마음먹었다가 잊은 것이 아니므로, (C)는 수업이 끝나는 것을 말하려는 것이 아니므로 각각 오답이다.

TEST 1 — Set 1-3 — Lecture 2: Einstein's Theory of Relativity

문단주제	본문내용	해석
들어가기	**Listen to part of a lecture in a physics class. The professor is discussing Relativity.** P: I'm sure you have all heard of Albert Einstein, one of the most influential figures of the past century and the greatest physicist of the modern era. You may wonder what he did to become so famous. Well, he came up with the most significant discovery of modern physics: the Theory of Relativity. This theory gave us new insight into what light is and how it works, changing the way physicists think and reshaping modern physics. Ironically, however, the greatness of this work wasn't fully recognized at the time and he was never awarded a Nobel Prize for his Theory of Relativity. This is because his work's legitimacy and his unorthodox methods were questioned by his contemporaries. [Q12] **The debate over whether Einstein received proper recognition for his signature work continues to this day.**	물리학 강의의 일부를 들으시오. 교수는 상대성 이론에 대해 논의하고 있습니다. P: 여러분 모두는 지난 세기의 가장 영향력있는 인물 중 한 명이자, 현대의 최고 물리학자 중 하나인, 앨버트 아인슈타인에 대해 들어봤을 거라 전 확신해요. 여러분은 아마 그가 무엇때문에 그렇게 유명했는지 궁금할 거예요. 음, 그는 현대 물리학의 가장 중요한 발견을 생각해냈어요: 바로 상대성 이론이죠. 이 이론은 우리에게 빛이 무엇이고 그것이 어떻게 작동하는지에 대해 새로운 통찰력을 가져다 주었고, 물리학자들의 사고방식을 바꾸며 현대물리학을 재정비했죠. 하지만, 아이러니하게도, 이 위대한 업적은 그 당시에 온전히 인정받지 못했고, 그는 상대성 이론으로 노벨상을 받은 적이 없어요. 이것은 왜냐하면 그의 연구의 타당성과 비정통적인 연구방식에 대해 그 당시의 과학자들이 의문을 제기했기 때문이죠. [Q12] 아인슈타인이 자신의 위대한 연구에 대해 제대로 인정을 받았는지에 대한 논쟁은 오늘날까지 계속 되고 있어요.
상대성 이론의 성장배경	P: Before I get into his work's impact, we should understand where Einstein came from. He was born in Germany in 1879, and although he loved academics, he hated the formal education system so much that he eventually dropped out, resulting in his failure to enter university on his first attempt. He returned to formal schooling and eventually graduated from Zurich's Federal Polytechnic in 1900. After graduation, he was unable to find employment in academia, so he became a patent office clerk in Switzerland in 1902. Although many have argued that he wasted his time there, Einstein disagreed, citing this as the most productive time of his life and crediting it with his later creativity and productivity. [Q13] **How, then, did examining patent applications help reshape modern physics? Well, it was clearly a combination of genius and experience. In order for him to approve a patent, Einstein had to work backwards, meaning he had to breakdown an invention or an idea himself in order to determine the patent claim's validity. He studied innumerable ideas and inventions during those years. All the information, ideas, and experience he gained became the foundations of his most famous work, the Theory of Relativity.**	P: 아인슈타인의 연구가 가져온 영향력에 대해 다루기 전에, 우리는 먼저 그가 어디서 왔는지 이해해야만 해요. 그는 1879년 독일에서 태어났어요. 공부하는 것을 좋아했지만, 정규 교육 제도는 무척 싫어해서 결국 자퇴를 했는데, 이로 인해 대학에 입학하려는 그의 첫 번째 시도가 좌절되었죠. 그는 정규 학교로 되돌아갔고 결국엔 1900년에 취리히 국립기술학교를 졸업했죠. 졸업 후에 그는 학교에서 일자리를 찾을 수 없어서, 1902년 스위스특허국의 사무원이 되었어요. 많은 사람들이 그가 그곳에서 시간을 낭비했다고 주장했지만, 아인슈타인은 그 말에 동의하지 않았는데 이 기간이 자신의 인생에서 가장 생산성있는 시간이었으며 훗날에 나타난 창의성과 생산성은 이 시절 덕분이었다고 말했죠. [Q13] 그렇다면, 어떻게 해서 특허 출원신청서를 검토하는 일이 현대물리학을 재정비하는데 도움을 주었을까요? 음, 바로 천재성과 경험의 조합을 통해서였죠. 각각의 특허를 허가해주기 위해서 아인슈타인은 귀납적인 추론을 해야만 했는데, 이는 그가 특허권 청구의 타당성을 결정하기 위해선 발명품이나 아이디어를 스스로 하나씩 분해해서 살펴봐야 했다는 의미예요. 그는 그 당시 수년 동안 무수한 아이디어들과 발명품들을 검토했어요. 그가 습득한 모든 정보와 아이디어, 그리고 경험들은 그의 가장 유명한 업적인 상대성 이론의 기초가 되었죠.

상대성 이론은 무엇인가?

So, let's get in to what the theory actually is. First off, the Theory of Relativity can be divided into two parts: the Theory of Special Relativity and the Theory of General Relativity. The Theory of Special Relativity states that everything has its own time. In other words, each object or person has its own clock. Einstein claims that this is due to a phenomenon called time dilation, under which time is affected by very fast velocities, like the speed of light. Ever heard of the twin paradox? The twin paradox is a good example of how time is affected by speed. Imagine that there are twins; let's call them Jeff and John. Say Jeff takes off in a spaceship travelling at the speed of light to a distant planet and John stays home. When Jeff returns, he will be much younger than his brother. This happens because he travels faster than time has passed for John. When speed exceeds time, time is slowed for quickly travelling objects. [Q14]This revolutionary idea contradicted the traditional view that time flows for everyone at the same rate.

아인슈타인의 라이벌 데이톤 밀러

[Q15] In 1915, Einstein shocked the world again with his follow-up theory, known as General Relativity, which combined the previous theory with gravity. He theorized that light usually travels straight, but when it hits heavy masses, such as planets and stars, it bends around them. We can't see the bending light, but the phenomenon clearly exists throughout nature. One example of this is light bending around the sun. This is how we see the light of stars that are positioned behind the sun. Validation of these theories only became possible after Einstein's time, due to the lack of equipment and technology. Due to this lack of empirical data, physicists such as Dayton Miller spent decades attempting to discredit Einstein's theory. In opposition to Einstein's belief that light travelled independently, regardless of its source's speed, Miller believed that light's speed was determined by an invisible matter surrounding it called ether. Unlike Einstein, he was able to produce numerous measurements and data sets to support his argument. [Q17]Even though Miller's data was less than convincing, his ability to experimentally measure ether over a course of decades and his established position in the physics community allowed his theory to gain widespread support. Eventually, review of other experiments such as the Michelson-Morley

그럼 실제로 이 이론이 무엇인지 살펴봅시다. 첫째, 상대성 이론은 두 가지 부분으로 나뉠 수 있어요: 특수상대성 이론과 일반상대성 이론이죠. 특수상대성 이론은 모든 것이 고유의 시간을 가지고 있다고 주장하는 이론이에요. 다른 말로 하면, 각각의 물체나 사람은 자신만의 시계를 가지고 있죠. 아인슈타인은 이것이 시간 팽창이라 불리는 현상때문이라고 주장했는데, 시간이 빛의 속도와 같은 아주 빠른 속도에 의해 영향을 받게 된다는 거에요. 쌍둥이 패러독스에 대해 들어본적 있나요? 쌍둥이 패러독스는 시간이 어떻게 속도에 의해 영향을 받는지에 대한 좋은 예에요. 한 쌍둥이가 있다고 가정해 봅시다; 그들을 각각 Jeff와 John이라고 부르기로 해요. Jeff가 우주선을 타고 이륙하여 먼 행성을 향해 빛의 속도로 여행을 하고, John은 지구에 머물러 있다고 치죠. Jeff가 돌아왔을 때, 그는 그의 형제보다 훨씬 어려져 있을 거에요. 이런 일이 발생하는 이유는 그는 John에게 흐르는 시간보다 더 빠른 속도로 여행을 하기 때문이에요. 속도가 시간을 넘어서면, 시간은 빠르게 움직이는 물체들에게는 느리게 진행되는 것이죠. [Q14] 이런 혁신적인 아이디어는 시간이 모든 사람들에게 똑같은 속도로 흘러간다는 전통적인 관점과 상반되는 것이었어요.

[Q15]1915년에, 아인슈타인은 일반 상대성이라 알려진 후속 이론으로 세상을 또 한번 놀라게 했는데, 이는 이전의 이론을 중력과 결합시킨 것이었어요. 그는 빛이 보통 직선으로 이동하는데, 행성이나 별과 같은 무거운 질량에 부딪히게 되면, 그 주위로 구부러지게 된다는 이론을 제시했어요. 우리는 빛이 구부러지는 것을 볼 수는 없지만, 이 현상은 자연 곳곳에서 명백히 존재하고 있죠. 한 예는 태양 주위로 구부러지는 빛이에요. 이로인해 우리가 태양 뒤에 위치하고 있는 별들의 빛을 보게 되는 것이죠. 이 이론들을 입증하는 것은 아인슈타인 시대 이후에나 가능해졌는데, 기술과 장비가 부족했기 때문이에요. 실증적인 데이터가 부족했기 때문에, Dayton Miller같은 물리학자들은 아인슈타인의 이론을 부정하기 위해 수 십년을 보냈어요. 빛은 공급원의 속도와 상관없이 독립적으로 이동한다는 아인슈타인의 믿음에 반하여, Miller는 빛의 속도가 에테르라고 불리는 빛 주변의 보이지 않는 물질에 의해 결정된다고 믿었어요. 아인슈타인과 달리, 그는 자신의 주장을 뒷받침하는 수많은 측정과 데이터를 만들어낼 수 있었죠. [Q17]비록 Miller의 데이터가 타당성이 조금 약했음에도 불구하고, 수 십년에 걸쳐 에테르를 실험적으로 측정할 수 있었던 능력과 물리학계에서 기반이 확고했던 그의 지위로 인해 그의 이론은 폭넓은 지지를 얻을 수 있었어요.

experiment showed that Miller's numerical measurements of ether fell within the margin of error and had most likely occurred due to the lack of laboratory equipment needed to perform the experiment in a vacuum, or an area without pressure and gravity. These variables could have easily altered his results.

Even the Nobel Prize Committee didn't initially recognize the brilliance of Einstein's theory at the time. This may seem ridiculous now, but at the time they had the same issues with it as Miller. The theory was based on Einstein's ingenuity and creative mind, but lacked any conclusive data or experimental results to support it; he had simply thought it up one day! The idea that a 26-year-old patent office clerk had simply used reason to come up with ideas that reformulated the equations of physics was too shocking. While we can recognize the tremendous discovery he made today, Einstein's contemporaries and the Nobel Prize Committee could not accept concepts with such shaky foundations. They needed to be able to evaluate the source and methodology of a contribution in order to recognize it, but due to Einstein's disregard of the traditional scientific method, the lack of empirical evidence and the physics community's opposition to his ideas, the Nobel Committee could not award the prize for the theory. [Q16]**While hindsight shows us that Einstein's theory was deserving of recognition, the committee acted fairly. Even Einstein accepted the limits of his theories and once said that they were just his imaginings and could be proven wrong by future experiments.**

After all this talk of the greatness of Einstein's theory, you may be wondering how it affects your daily life. Well, the GPS system in your car or mobile phone can be traced back to Einstein's theory. His work also opened up new fields in physics, such as quantum physics, which has yielded numerous inventions like microchips, electron microscopes, and MRI. Einstein's work has not just changed physics, but created new previously unimaginable areas of science.

12 What is the lecture mainly about?

(A) The ~~debate~~ between Einstein and his opponents on the existence of relativity
(B) The ~~struggles~~ Einstein faced and validity of his bold theory *
(C) The impact of the Theory of Relativity on modern physics
(D) Discussion of Einstein's Theory of Relativity and his recognition for it

강의는 주로 무엇을 말하는가?

(A) 상대성 이론의 존재에 대한 아인슈타인과 그 반대자들 사이의 ~~논쟁~~
(B) 아인슈타인이 ~~직면한 어려움과~~ 그의 대담한 이론의 타당성 *
(C) 상대성 이론이 현대 물리학에 끼친 영향
(D) 아인슈타인의 상대성 이론과 인정여부에 대한 토론

Main Idea 교수는 강의 전반에 걸쳐서 아인슈타인의 상대성 이론에 대한 설명과 그가 자신의 업적에 대해 타당한 인정을 받았는지에 대해 이야기하고 있다. 따라서 답은 (D)가 된다. 아인슈타인과 반대자들 사이에 있었던 논쟁, 아인슈타인이 직면한 어려움은 본문에 언급되지 않았으므로 (A)와 (B)는 각각 오답이다. (C)는 본문에 나온 내용이나 너무 지엽적이므로 주제가 되기 힘들다.

---

13 According to the professor, what contributed to the foundation of Einstein's theory during his time at the patent office?

(A) The reverse engineering process of new inventions and ideas for patent approval
(B) Incorporation of various ideas and invention he ~~designed~~ *
(C) ~~Sources and methods~~ of new discoveries and inventions
(D) ~~His creativity assisted him~~ in examining patent applications.

교수에 따르면, 특허국에서 보낸 시간 동안에 무엇이 아인슈타인 이론의 토대를 쌓는데 공헌하였는가?

(A) 특허허가를 위한 새로운 발명품과 아이디어들의 역공학 과정
(B) 그가 ~~디자인한~~ 다양한 아이디어와 발명들의 결합 *
(C) 새로운 발견들과 발명품들의 ~~근원과 방법~~
(D) 특허신청을 조사하는데 ~~도움이 된 그의 창의성~~

Detail (Cause) How, then, did examining patent applications help reshape modern physics? Well, it was clearly a combination of genius and experience. In order for him to approve a patent, he had to work backwards, meaning he had to breakdown an invention or an idea himself in order to determine the patent claim's validity. He studied innumerable ideas and inventions during those years. All the information, ideas, and experience he gained from those years became the foundations of his most famous work, the Theory of Relativity. (그렇다면, 어떻게 해서 특허출원 신청서를 검토하는 일이 현대물리학을 재정비하는데 도움을 주었을까요? 음, 바로 천재성과 경험의 조합을 통해서였죠. 각각의 특허를 허가해 주기 위해서 아인슈타인은 귀납적인 추론을 해야만 했는데, 이는 그가 특허권 청구의 타당성을 결정하기 위해선 발명품이나 아이디어를 스스로 하나씩 분해해서 살펴봐야 했다는 의미예요. 그는 그 당시 수 년 동안 무수한 아이디어들과 발명 품들을 검토했어요. 그가 습득한 모든 정보와 아이디어, 그리고 경험들은 그의 가장 유명한 업적인 상대성이론의 기초가 되었죠.)에서 보면 특허를 허가하기 위해 발명품과 아이디어들을 역으로 추론하고 분해해서 살펴보는 과정이 추후 아인슈타인 이론에 도움이 되었다는 사실을 알 수 있어 정답은 (A)가 된다. 나중에 이론을 형성하는데 도움이 되는 것은 정보와 경험들이지 그가 디자인한 발명품들은 아니며, (C), (D)는 강의내용에 나와 있지 않으므로 각각 오답이다.

TEST 1   Set 1-3   Lecture 2 Einstein's Theory of Relativity

14 According to the professor, what is true about the Theory of Special Relativity?

(A) The theory ~~used scientific evidence~~ to explain the natural phenomenon of time dilation
(B) The theory explained how time is affected by gravity. *
(C) **The theory challenged the long established concept of time's progression being fixed.**
(D) The theory ~~supported~~ the traditional idea that time flows at the same speed

교수에 따르면, 특수상대성이론에 대해 맞는 내용은 무엇인가?

(A) 그 이론은 ~~과학적인 증거를 사용해서~~ 시간팽창의 자연적 현상을 설명했다.
(B) 그 이론은 어떻게 시간이 중력에 의해 영향을 받는지 설명했다. *
(C) **그 이론은 시간진행이 고정되어 있다는 오랫동안 확립된 개념에 도전했다.**
(D) 그 이론은 시간이 똑같은 속도에 따라 흐른다는 전통적 생각을 ~~지지했다~~.

Detail (Characteristic)   특수상대성이론을 설명한 부분 중에서 This revolutionary idea contradicted the traditional view that time flows for everyone at the same rate (이런 혁신적인 아이디어는 시간이 모든 사람들에게 똑같은 속도로 흘러간다는 전통적인 관점과 상반되는 것이었어요.) 를 보면 정답이 (C)임을 알 수 있다. 아인슈타인의 이론은 천재성과 창의적 사고에 기초한 것이나 과학적인 증거는 부족하므로 (A)는 오답이며 (B)는 특수상대성이론이 아닌 일반 상대성 이론을 설명하고 있는 것이므로 오답이다. (D)는 시간이 똑같은 속도로 진행한다는 전통적인 개념을 지지하는 것이 아니라 그것에 상반되는 것이므로 답이 될 수 없다.

15 Why did the professor mention light bending around the sun?

(A) To give an example of ~~the speed of light~~ *
(B) To prove that the sun was the ~~source of the light's speed~~
(C) To bolster a point about ~~gravitational forces~~ around the sun
(D) **To demonstrate a real life example of General Relativity**

왜 교수는 태양 주변에서 빛이 휘는 것을 언급하였는가?

(A) ~~빛의 속도~~에 대한 예시를 들기 위해 *
(B) 태양이 ~~빛의 속도의 근원~~이라는 것을 증명하기 위해
(C) 태양 주위의 ~~중력에 대한~~ 주장을 지지하기 위해
(D) **일반상대성이론의 실제 예를 증명하기 위해**

Inference (Purpose)   In 1915, Einstein shocked the world again with his follow-up theory, known as General Relativity, which combined the previous theory with gravity. He theorized that light usually travels straight, but when it hits heavy masses, such as planets and stars, it bends around them. We can't see the bending light, but the phenomenon clearly exists throughout nature. One example of this is light bending around the sun.(1915년에, 아인슈타인은 일반 상대성이라 알려진 후속 이론으로 세상을 또 한 번 놀라게 했는데, 이는 이전의 이론을 중력과 결합시킨 것이었어요. 그는 빛이 보통 직선으로 이동하는데, 행성이나 별과 같은 무거운 질량에 부딪히게 되면, 그 주위로 휘게 된다는 이론을 제시했어요. 우리는 빛이 휘는 것을 볼 수는 없지만 이 현상은 자연 곳곳에서 명백히 존재하고 있죠. 한 예는 태양 주위로 구부러지는 빛이에요.)에서 보면 빛이 휘는 것은 일반상대성이론이 실생활에서 적용되는 예임을 알 수 있으므로 정답은 (D)이다. (A)는 빛의 속도는 태양과 무관하고, (B)와 (C)는 빛의 속도의 근원이나 태양주위의 중력에 대해 본문에 언급된 내용이 없으므로 각각 오답이다.

16 According to the professor, what can be inferred about Einstein's attitude towards his own theory?

(A) He ~~had unwavering faith~~ in his theory and ~~provided hard evidence~~ for it.
(B) **He thought that he could share Miller's fate and be proven wrong in the future**
(C) He ~~had a strong belief~~ that no one could disprove his theory.
(D) He thought that his theory was not yet conclusive ~~but he had enough evidence to prove his theory~~.

교수에 따르면, 자신의 이론에 대한 아인슈타인의 태도에서 유추할 수 있는 것은 무엇인가?

(A) 그는 자신의 이론에 대한 ~~확고한 신념을 가지고 확실한 증거를 제시했다~~.
(B) 그는 미래에 Miller와 같은 운명을 가지게 되어 자신이 틀렸음이 증명될 수도 있다고 생각했다.
(C) 그는 아무도 자신의 이론을 반증할 수 없을거라는 ~~강한 믿음을 가지고 있었다~~.
(D) 그는 자신의 이론이 아직 결정적이진 않지만 이론을 증명할 충분한 증거를 가졌다고 생각했다. *

Inference (Attitude)　자신의 이론에 대한 아인슈타인의 태도를 나타내는 부분을 보면, while hind sight shows us that Einstein's theory was deserving of recognition, the committee acted fairly Even Einstein accepted the limits his theories and once said that they were just his imaginings and could be proven wrong by future experiments. (나중에 와서야 아인슈타인의 이론은 인정을 받을만했고, 상위위원회도 타당하게 행동했다는 사실을 알게 되었죠. 심지어, 아인슈타인 스스로도 자신의 이론들이 가진 한계를 인정해서 그것들은 단순히 그의 상상일 뿐이고 미래의 실험에 의해 반증될 수도 있다고 말한 적이 있었으니까요.)에서 아인슈타인은 스스로의 이론에 절대적인 확신이 없었음을 알 수 있다. 따라서 정답은 (B)이다. 아인슈타인은 증거도 없었고 자신의 이론에 확신도 없었으므로 (A), (C)는 각각 오답이다. (D)는 앞부분의 내용은 맞지만, 자신의 이론을 증명할 충분한 증거를 가졌다는 말은 내용과 다르므로 정답이 될 수 없다.

17 Listen again to part of the lecture. Then answer the question.

P: Even though Miller's data was less than convincing, his ability to experimentally measure ether over a course of decades, and his established position in the physics community, allowed his theory to gain widespread support.

Why does the professor mention this? 🎧

P: ...his established position in the physics community...

(A) To indicate why Einstein's theory was ~~wrong~~
(B) To prove that ~~Einstein's theory~~ was more satisfactory to the world
(C) To give additional information regarding the ~~inferiority~~ of Miller's theory
(D) **To explain one reason Miller gained support from the physics community**

강의의 일부분을 다시 듣고, 질문에 답하시오.

P: 비록 Miller의 데이터가 타당성이 조금 약했음에도 불구하고, 수 십 년에 걸쳐 에테르를 실험적으로 측정할 수 있었던 능력과 물리학계에서 기반이 확고했던 그의 위치로 인해, 그의 이론은 폭넓은 지지를 얻을 수 있었어요.

교수는 왜 이 말을 하는가?

P: 물리학계에서 기반이 확고했던 그의 위치로 인해.

(A) ~~아인슈타인의 이론이 틀렸음을 알리기 위해~~
(B) ~~아인슈타인의 이론이 세상에 더욱 만족감을 주었다는 것을 증명하기 위해~~
(C) ~~Miller의 이론이 열등하다는 것과 관련된 부가적인 정보를 주기 위해~~
(D) Miller가 물리학계에서 지지를 얻은 하나의 이유를 설명하기 위해

Inference (Headset)　Miller가 물리학계에서 가지고 있던 확고했던 지위를 교수가 언급한 것은, 당시 그의 이론이 아인슈타인의 이론에 비해 지지를 많이 얻었음을 설명하기 위해서이다. 따라서 답은 (D)가 된다. (A)는 교수가 말하고자 하는 내용은 아인슈타인의 이론이 틀렸다는 것이 아니므로 오답이다. (B)는 아인슈타인의 이론이 아닌 Miller의 이론에 대한 내용이므로, (C)는 당시에는 Miller의 이론이 더 우월하다는 인식이 우세했으므로 각각 오답이다.

TEST 1

Set 2-1 Conversation: Student's Opposition to Renovation

문단주제	본문내용	해 석
	Listen to a conversation between a student and an office clerk.	학생과 사무실 직원의 대화를 들으시오.
	S: Excuse me, sir.	S: 실례합니다.
	O: Yes, ma'am.	O: 네
	S: Well, I don't know if you heard, but they're going to rebuild the science library... and well, [Q1]I'm here because I'm against it, and... long story short, I need a signature from the board so I can officially start a protest against it.	S: 음, 들으셨는지 모르겠는데, 과학 도서관을 다시 짓는다고 하더라고요… 그러니까… 음, [Q1]제가 여기온 이유는 그것에 반대를 하거든요. 그리고 음… 간략하게 말씀 드리면, 제가 공식적으로 반대하는 항의 시위를 시작할 수 있도록 이사회의 허가가 필요해요.
	O: Well... I'm not officially authorized to give out any names, but if I could get your name and contact information, I would be happy to deliver a message.	O: 음… 제가 담당자의 이름을 드릴 수 있는 권한을 공식적으로 갖고 있는 것이 아니라서요. 하지만 만약 제가 학생의 이름과 연락처를 받는다면, 기꺼이 메시지를 전해줄 수 있어요.
	S: My name is Meghan Young, and my student ID number is 110509.	S: 제 이름은 Meghan Young이고, 제 학생 ID 번호는 110509에요.
	O: Got it. Do you mind me asking why you have a problem with the renovations? I just want to deliver my message to the higher authorities as accurately as possible.	O: 알겠어요. 왜 학생이 수리하는 것을 맘에 들어 하지 않는지 물어봐도 될까요? 더 높은 관리자에게 메시지를 가능한 한 정확하게 전달하고 싶어서요.
	S: Not at all... To be honest, I really like the way it is right now. I don't even think it needs to be renovated at all! [Q2]I think the glass walls are all still intact. Wasn't it recently renovated anyway?	S: 괜찮아요… 솔직히 말하자면, 전 지금 그대로가 정말 좋아요. 그 건물이 수리가 필요하다는 생각조차 전혀 안 드는걸요. [Q2]제 생각엔 그 유리 벽들은 아직도 멀쩡해요. 최근에 수리하지 않았나요?
	O: I guess I see your point. It hasn't been that long.	O: 학생이 뭘 말하고 싶은지 알 것 같아요. 그렇게 오래되진 않았죠.
	S: [Q2]Also... I mean... A lot of students rely on the library to study... Some people may even lose their scholarships.	S: [Q2]또한… 제 말은… 많은 학생들이 공부하기 위해서 도서관에 의지하잖아요… 몇몇 사람들은 심지어 장학금을 잃을 수도 있다구요.
	O: Uh-huh. Anything else?	O: 그렇군요. 다른 사항은요?
	S: [Q2]Well, the source materials and reference materials that we require for our studies... [Q5]need I say more?	S: [Q2]음, 우리가 공부할 때 필요한 자료나 참고서 들이요… [Q5]더 말할 필요가 있나요?
	O: I understand... I'm pretty sure that the board won't just cut out the reference sources; they'll probably place the materials in another location, and even provide an alternative study area. But then again... there have been rumors that the school failed to raise enough funds and that there may not be any renovations at all.	O: 알겠어요… 이사회가 그냥 참고 자료들을 없애 진 않을 거라고 확신해요. 아마도 책들을 다른 장소에 옮겨 놓겠죠, 그리고 심지어 공부할 수 있는 다른 장소도 제공할 거에요. 그런데… 학교가 충분한 기금을 마련하는데 실패해서 아예 수리가 없을 지도 모른다는 소문이 있긴 해요.
	S: Really?	S: 정말요?
	O: Yeah... I mean... at first I thought it was just a rumor too. But false rumors don't last this long... You know what I mean?	O: 네… 저도 처음엔 그것이 그저 소문일 뿐이라고 생각했어요. 하지만 거짓 루머는 이렇게 오래가지 않죠… 무슨 말인지 알겠죠?
	S: I guess so...	S: 그런 것 같아요…

O: [Q3] How many signatures opposing the renovations do you have so far? Do you mind me asking?

S: Not at all. There are currently about 250 people and the number is growing as we speak.

O: I can sympathize; we office workers were actually appalled as well.

S: [Q4] Yeah... I mean, why not just add a new wing to the library? They released a possible blueprint to the students, and it looked ridiculous to close the whole place. I just want to deliver our new ideas, and maybe even possibly shut down the whole project.

O: Even if the rumors aren't true, I bet you have enough people to make a difference. I mean 250 and growing... that's not a number the school can ignore.

S: I'm just glad there are others that feel the same way that I do...

O: You know... If I were you... I would wait to find out if the rumors are true or not. I mean... I wouldn't want to get people excited over something that isn't even happening... you know how rough these things can get, don't you?

S: You're right... I thought everything was set. I was in such a foul mood because of this... Thank you for the helpful information.

O: No problem.

S: Do you know when the decision is final though? I'm eager to find out.

O: Well, there's a hearing sometime this week between the faculty and the board members.

S: That's great. Should I come back when it's over? Do you know when it starts?

O: Tell you what. If you leave me your number, I'll get back to you as soon as I can.

S: OK. Sounds great. Thank you!

O: [Q3] 보수공사에 빈대하는 서명은 지금까지 얼마나 받았나요? 물어보는게 실례가 될까요?

S: 전혀요. 현재 대략 250명인데 우리가 얘기를 전하면서 수가 점점 증가하고 있어요.

O: 저도 공감해요. 우리 사무실 직원들도 여러분과 마찬가지로 놀랐거든요.

S: [Q4] 그래요… 그러니까, 왜 도서관에 그냥 신축 동을 추가하지 않는거죠? 학생들에게 예상 청사진을 공개했는데, 전체공간을 닫는 건 말도 안돼 보였어요. 전 그저 저희의 새로운 의견을 전달하고 싶어요. 그리고 가능하면 그 프로젝트 전체를 멈추게 하면 더 좋겠죠.

O: 비록 소문이 사실이 아니더라도, 학생은 변화를 이루어 낼 만큼 충분한 수의 사람을 모았다고 장담해요. 그러니까 250명의 인원에다 더 늘고 있잖아요… 그건 학교가 무시할수 있는 숫자가 아니죠.

S: 전 그저 나와 똑같은 생각을 지닌 다른 사람들이 있다는 게 기쁠 뿐이에요.

O: 있죠… 제가 만약 학생이라면… 기다렸다가 그 소문이 사실인지 아닌지 알아내겠어요. 그러니까… 지금 일어나고 있지 않은 일때문에 사람들을 흥분하게 만들고 싶진 않잖아요… 이런 일들 이 얼마나 거칠어질 수 있는지 알죠, 그렇죠?

S: 맞아요…. 전 모든 것이 준비되었다고 생각했어요. 이것 때문에 정말 불쾌한 기분이었거든요… 도움되는 정보에 감사드려요.

O: 천만에요.

S: 그런데 그 결정이 언제 나는지 아시나요? 전 정말 알고 싶거든요.

O: 음, 직원측과 이사회 간의 공청회가 이번 주에 있을 거에요.

S: 좋아요. 공청회가 끝날 때 제가 다시 와야 할까요? 그게 언제쯤 시작되는지 아세요?

O: 이렇게 하죠. 만약 학생이 제게 번호를 남겨주면, 가능한 빨리 연락해줄게요.

S: 네. 좋아요. 감사해요!

TEST 1 — Set 2-1 — Conversation: Student's Opposition to Renovation

01 Why does the student go to talk to the office clerk?

왜 학생은 사무실 직원에게 얘기하러 갔는가?

(A) To ask for proper approval for a protest she has been planning
(B) To ask for ~~funding~~ regarding a protest
(C) To ~~make sure that she has taken the right steps~~ in organizing a protest
(D) To make sure that a protest is ~~not against school regulations~~

(A) 그녀가 계획하고 있는 항의시위에 대한 적절한 허가를 요청하기 위해
(B) 항의시위와 관련된 ~~자금마련~~을 요청하기 위해
(C) 그녀가 항의시위를 조직하는 데 ~~올바른 단계를 밟고 있는지~~를 확인하기 위해
(D) 항의시위가 ~~학교 규정에 위반되지 않는지~~ 확인하기 위해

Main Purpose I'm here because I'm against it' and well… long story short' I need a signature from the board so I can officially start a protest against it.(제가 여기에 온 이유는 그것에 반대를 하거든요' 그리고 음· 간략하게 말씀드리면' 제가 공식적으로 그에 반대하는 항의 시위를 시작할 수 있도록 이사회의 허가가 필요해요.)라고 처음에 학생이 온 이유를 밝혔으므로 정답은 (A)이다.

02 According to the student, what are the problems with the renovation?

학생에 의하면, 수리와 관련된 문제점들은 무엇인가?

Click on 3 answers   3개의 답을 고르시오

(A) The construction would cost way too much for the school to handle.
(B) The library seems to be in a condition that does not require renovation.
(C) The construction would lead to academic difficulties for students in terms of space.
(D) The information that the students need may not be accessible for a certain period of time.
(E) The school ~~may not be able to provide~~ scholarships to students.

(A) 학교가 감당할 수 없을 만큼 건설하는데 너무 많은 비용이 든다
(B) 도서관은 수리가 필요없는 상태처럼 보인다
(C) 그 건설은 공간과 관련해서 학생들에게 학업적인 불편함을 야기할 것이다
(D) 일정 기간 동안 학생들이 필요한 정보에 접근하지 못할 수도 있다
(E) 학교는 아마 학생들에게 장학금을 ~~제공하지 못할 지도 모른다~~ *

Detail (Problem)   학생들이 생각하는 수리와 관련된 문제점들을 I think the glass walls are all still intact…. Also I mean…. A lot of students rely on the library to study… well, the source materials and reference materials that we require for our studies. (제 생각엔 그 유리벽들은 아직도 멀쩡하거든요…… 또한... 제말은... 많은 학생들이 공부하기 위해서 도서관에 의지하잖아요. 그리고 우리가 필요한 자료나 참고서들 이요…)라고 말했으므로 정답은 (B), (C), (D)이다. (A)는 학생이 주장하는 문제점이 아니므로, (E)는 학생이 장학금을 잃을 수도 있다는 것이지, 학교가 장학금을 제공할 수 없게 되는 것이 아니므로 각각 오답이다.

03 According to the speakers, what can be inferred about the current views on the renovation project?

화자에 의하면, 보수공사를 바라보는 현재 관점에 대해 추론할 수 있는 것은 무엇인가?

(A) Rumors about the construction have just begun to spread and may or may not be valid. *
(B) Some students of the school are against the possible reconstruction.
(C) The school has decided to ~~push for the renovation after considering~~ their monetary situation.
(D) The reasons why students are against it are ~~nearly all academic.~~

(A) 건설공사에 대한 소문이 막 퍼지기 시작했는데 그 내용 이 사실일 수도 그렇지 않을 수도 있다. *
(B) 학교의 일부 학생들은 재건축에 반대한다.
(C) 학교는 금전적인 상황을 ~~고려한 후 보수공사를 밀어붙이기로~~ 결정했다.
(D) 학생들이 그것에 반대하는 이유는 ~~거의 모두 학업적인~~ 것이다.

Inference (Infer) 학생들이 생각하는 수리와 관련된 문제점들을 I think the glass walls are all still intact…. Also I mean…. A lot of students rely on the library to study… well, the source materials and reference materials that we require for our studies. (제 생각엔 그 유리벽들은 아직도 멀쩡하거든요…… 또한… 제말은… 많은 학생들이 공부하기 위해서 도서관에 의지하잖아요. 그리고 우리가 필요한 자료나 참고서들 이요…)라고 말했으므로 정답은 (B), (C), (D)이다. (A)는 학생이 주장하는 문제점이 아니므로, (E)는 학생이 장학금을 잃을 수도 있다는 것이지, 학교가 장학금을 제공할 수 없게 되는 것이 아니므로 각각 오답이다.

04 Why does the student mention a new wing on the library building?

학생이 도서관 건물의 신축 동을 언급한 이유는 무엇인가?

(A) To ~~specify which~~ area of the library is intact enough to avoid construction
(B) To show her concern about a new wing ~~jeopardizing~~ the current library
(C) **To suggest an alternative plan to the renovation**
(D) To show that ~~there is a flaw~~ in the blueprints that the school released

(A) 도서관의 ~~어느 부분이~~ 수리를 안해도 될만큼 멀쩡한지 ~~구체적으로 말하기 위해~~
(B) 현재 도서관을 ~~위태롭게 하는~~ 새로운 동에 대해 걱정하고 있음을 보여주기 위해
(C) **보수공사에 대한 대안책을 제안하기 위해**
(D) 학교가 발표한 건설 계획의 청사진에서 ~~오류가 있음을~~ 알려주기 위해

Inference (Purpose) 학생이 신축동을 언급한 부분을 살펴보면 Yeah… I mean, why not just add a new wing to the library? They released a possible blueprint to the students, and it looked ridiculous to close the whole place(그래요… 그러니까 왜 도서관에 그냥 신축동을 추가하지 않는거죠? 학생들에게 예상 청사진을 공개했는데, 전체 공간을 닫는다는 것은 말도 안돼 보였어요)에서 학생은 새로운 동을 언급한 것은 보수공사의 대안책을 제안하는 것이므로 (C)가 정답이다. (A)는 수리가 필요없는 도서관의 구역을 구체적으로 알려주는 것이 아니라 건축공사 대안책을 언급하는 것이므로 오답이다. (B)는 현재 도서관을 위태롭게 하는 내용은 나오지 않으므로, (D)는 청사진에 오류가 있음을 말하는 내용은 언급이 없으므로 각각 오답이다.

05 Listen again to part of the conversation. Then answer the question

대화의 일부분을 다시 듣고, 질문에 답하시오.

"well, the source materials and the reference materials that we require for our studies… need I say more?"

Why does the student say this? : 🎧

"음, 우리가 공부할 때 필요한 자료나 참고서들이요… 더 말할 필요가 있나요?"

왜 학생은 이 말을 하는가?

need I say more?

더 말할 필요가 있나요?

(A) She ~~doesn't want to talk~~ about other problems the students may possibly face
(B) She ~~finds it too painful to even imagine~~ the hardships that the students may go through
(C) **She believes the clerk has already been given enough information to understand**
(D) She is ~~asking~~ the clerk if he needs additional reasons for the protest

(A) 그녀는 학생들이 아마도 겪게 될지도 모르는 다른 문제점들에 대해 ~~말하길 원치 않는다.~~
(B) 그녀는 학생들이 경험하게 될 어려움을 ~~상상하는 것조차 너무 고통스럽다고 생각한다.~~
(C) **그녀는 직원이 이해할 수 있도록 정보를 충분히 주었다고 생각한다.**
(D) 그녀는 항의시위를 위해 부가적인 이유들이 더 필요한지 직원에게 ~~묻고 있다.~~

Inference (Purpose) S: need I say more? O: I understand(더 말해야 하나요? 알겠어요)라고 서로 이야기하는 부분에서 알 수 있듯이 (C)가 정답이다. (A)는 이야기를 하고 싶지 않은 것이 아니라 지금까지 한 얘기들로 충분하기 때문에 더 얘기할 필요가 없다는 의미이므로 오답이다. (B)는 대화에 언급되지 않은 내용이며, (D)는 비록 학생이 질문 형태로 말을 하지만, 직원에게 묻는 것이 아니라 이해여부를 확인하는 것이므로 각각 오답이다.

Lecture 1 — The Space Elevator Technology

문단주제

우주 여행에 대한 소개

잘못된 인식

본문내용

Listen to part of a lecture in an engineering class.

P: In our globalized world, barriers between nations are breaking down, as is the barrier between Earth and the universe. Since its first foray into space, mankind has achieved remarkable things. However, due to the energy and resource inefficiencies of the current methods of space travel, even a short trip into space remains an expensive proposition. This is because an enormous amount of fuel is required to reach Earth's escape velocity of 11 kilometers per second. The inefficiency of this method is evident when you look at the external fuel tanks of the space shuttle. They are the biggest, and heaviest, parts of the shuttles.

[Q7] Oddly, however, a lot of people still seem to have misconceptions about going to space. Um, let me give you an example. The idea that the only way to escape Earth's atmosphere is by travelling at Earth's escape velocity is not absolutely true. Um... before I go any further, let's make sure we're on the same page about the concept of escape velocity. Escape velocity is the speed at which an object must move to overcome Earth's gravitational pull. Objects that reach their escape velocity are fast enough that they won't lose their velocity before leaving Earth's gravitational influence. Theoretically though, all one really needs to enter space is a constant force pushing upwards or holding one firmly in place. Scientists are, therefore, trying to build that force: a sturdy human construction on which passengers or payloads could travel up and down.

S: So... what you are saying is that if we could somehow build something like a huge ladder, then we could slowly climb our way up into space, right?

P: Exactly. You understand that a person climbing a ladder wouldn't reach speeds that are anywhere near the escape velocity, but that person wouldn't be pulled down by gravity, because they would be holding on to the ladder, right? [Q11] There is a problem, however... although the ladder idea makes sense mathematically and conceptually, it is very improbable. Nobody could climb ometers before being exhausted. Let's not forget that you would also need to be carrying a heavy oxygen tank and space suit.

해석

공학 강의의 일부를 들으시오.

P: 글로벌화된 세계에서는, 국가간의 장벽이 허물어 지고 지구와 우주간의 벽도 무너지고 있죠. 우주에 처음 진출한 이후로 인류는 놀라운 일들을 성취해왔어요. 하지만, 현재 우주를 여행하는 방법이 에너지와 자원이 소모되는 면에서 너무 비효율적이기 때문에 우주로 짧은 여행을 하는 것도 비용이 비싼 문제로 남아있죠. 이것은 1초당 11km인 지구 탈출 속도에 도달하기 위해 엄청난 양의 연료가 필요하기 때문인데요. 우주선에 장착되어 있는 거대한 외부 연료탱크를 생각해보면 이 방법이 얼마나 비효율적인지 분명해지죠. 그것들은 우주선의 가장 큰 부분이자 가장 무거운 부분이니까요.

[Q7] 그러나, 이상하게도, 많은 사람들이 우주로 가는 것에 대해 여전히 잘못 이해하고 있는것 같아요. 음.. 예를 하나 들어보죠. 지구대기권을 탈출할수 있는 유일한 방법이 지구 탈출 속도로 가는 것이라는 생각은 절대적으로 옳은건 아니에요. 음...이 내용을 더 깊이 들어가기 전에, 우리가 탈출속도라는 개념에 대해 정확히 알고 있는지 확인해봅시다. 탈출속도란 지구가 끌어당기는 힘인 중력을 넘기 위해 물체가 필요한 속도에요. 탈출속도에 도달한 물체들은 충분히 속도가 빠르기 때문에 지구 중력의 영향을 벗어나기 전까지 자신의 속도를 잃지 않게 되죠. 그러나 이 론적으로는, 우주에 들어가기 위해 필요한 건 위로 밀거나 우주선을 제자리에 단단히 고정시킬 수 있는 지속적인 힘이에요. 그래서 과학자들은 그러한 힘을 만들려고 시도 중인데요.: 바로 승객이나 화물이 우주와 지구 사이를 올라갔다 내려갔다 할 수 있는 인간이 만든 견고한 건축물이죠.

S: 그러니까.. 교수님 말씀은, 만약 우리가 어떤식으로든 거대한 사다리 같은 것을 만들 수 있다면, 그 때 우주로 천천히 올라갈수 있다는 거네요, 맞죠?

P: 바로 그거에요. 사다리를 타고 올라가는 사람은 탈출 속도에 근접하는 어떤 속도도 내지 못하지만, 그 사람은 중력에 의해 지구로 당겨지지 않게 되는데, 왜냐하면 사다리에 꼭 붙어있게 되기 때문이라는걸 여러분은 이해할 수 있을 거예요, 맞죠? [Q11] 하지만, 문제가 하나 있어요. 비록 사다리 이론이 수학적으로나 말이 되지만, 실현되기가 무척 어려워요. 그 누구도 수천 킬로미터 높이를 오르다 보면 누구라도 완전히 지치게 될테니까요. 또한 무거운 산소탱크와 우주복을 지니고 가야한다는걸 잊으면 안되요.

우주 엘리베이터에 대한 소개	The ladder example is not as outrageous as it sounds, though. Research is being done on the construction of a very similar concept: a space elevator. The space elevator is a proposed structure designed to transport material from Earth to space. [Q8-D] A Russian rocket scientist, Konstantin Tsiolkovsky, who was inspired by the Eiffel Tower, first proposed this idea in 1895. His theory was immediately ridiculed and his fellow scientists told him that it would never be possible. His idea wasn't totally forgotten though. One of the early, and most enthusiastic, proponents of the idea of a space elevator was the science-fiction author Arthur C. Clark, and it appears repeatedly in his works. One example was the 1979 novel 'The Fountains of Paradise'. In this novel, a 22nd century engineer is charged with creating a means of moving people and supplies to a 'terraforming' project in outer space. To do this, he develops a space elevator linking Earth to the 'circumterran' (Earth encircling) space station.	그렇지만 사다리 예시는 들리는것 만큼 터무니 없게 들리지 않아요. 매우 비슷한 개념을 가진 건설에 대한 연구가 현재 진행되고 있는데요. 바로 우주 엘리베이터에요. 우주엘리베이터는 물체를 지구 에서 우주로 운반할 수 있게 디자인된 구조물로 제안된 거에요. [Q8-D] 러시아의 로켓 과학자인 Konstantin Tsiolkovsky가 에펠탑에서 영감을 얻어 1895년에 처음으로 제안했죠. 그의 이론은 곧바로 비웃음을 샀는데 심지어 동료 과학자들 조차도 절대 가능하지 않을 거라고 말했어요. 하지만 그의 아이디어가 완전히 잊혀진건 아니었어요. 우주엘리베이터에 대한 초기의 가장 열성적인 지지자는 공상과학소설가인 Arthur C. Clark 이라는 사람으로, 우주엘리베이터는 그의 작품들 에 여러 번 동장 했죠. 한 예가 바로 1979년에 쓰 여진 소설인 파라다이스의 분수들"이에요. 이 소설에는 22세기에 사는 한 공학자가 우주에서 진행되고 있는 지구행성화 프로젝트로 사람들과 공급품을 운반할 수 있는 수단을 발명하는 임무 를 맡았죠. 이것을 위해, 그는 지구와 지구를 도는 우주정거장을 연결하는 우주엘리베이터를 개발합니다.
우주 엘리베이터 건설	So… Let's talk about how a space elevator would work. Hmm… The first part of the project would be a base station on Earth that would be attached to a pillar upon which an elevator car could travel. This structure would be flexible, and would be called the cable. You may be wondering how we could construct a cable that is strong enough to stand up straight, yet tall enough to reach space. Well… Remember when you were kids, you would tie a rope to a bucket full of water, and swing it over your head? How did the water stay inside the bucket while gravity pulled it downwards? A natural force, known as centrifugal force, pushed the water into the bucket, away from the center of the circular motion, which was the hand holding the rope. The same principle would apply to the space elevator: when the cable is long enough, the spinning of the Earth will create a centrifugal force on the space elevator. To accomplish this, the space elevator would need a heavy weight, called a counterweight, at its highest point to make it more stable.	그럼… 우주엘리베이터가 어떻게 작동하는지 이야기해 보죠. 흠… 프로젝트의 첫 번째 파트는 지구에 있는 정거장으로 거기에 고정된 기둥이 붙어있어 그 위로 엘리베이터 몸체가 움직이는 거 예요. 이런 구조는 유연해서 케이블이라고 불려질 거예요. 여러분은 어떻게 똑바로 서있을 수 있을 만큼 충분히 강하지만 우주까지 닿을만큼 키가 큰 케이블을 건설할 수 있을까 궁금할지 몰라요. 음… 여러분이 아이였을 때, 물이 가득 담긴 양동이에 밧줄을 매달아 머리위로 돌렸던 것을 기억 하나요? 중력이 양동이를 아래로 끌어당기는데 어떻게 물이 안에 머물 수 있었을까요? 원심력이라 불리는 자연적으로 발생하는 힘이 밧줄을 잡고 있는 손 즉, 원 움직임의 중심으로부터 멀리 있는 양동이 안으로 물을 밀어냈던 것이죠. 똑같은 원리가 우주엘리베이터에 적용될 수 있어요. 케이블이 충분히 길어서 지구의 자전이 우주엘리베이터에 원심력을 만들어 낼 것이니까요. 이것이 가능하기 위해선, 우주엘리베이터 꼭대기에 균형추라 불리는 무거운 중량이 필요한데, 이것은 우주엘리베이터를 좀 더 안정적으로 만들죠.

Lecture 1
The Space Elevator Technology

나노 튜브 케이블

P: The cable itself is probably the biggest hindrance to a space elevator's construction, as it would need to be made of an extremely light, durable material, but as long as people have been dreaming of building a space elevator, no material strong enough has existed...until the recent discovery of a new material made purely of carbon, that is. Due to the extremely strong chemical bonds that carbon atoms form with one another, scientists have discovered a way to form tiny tubes called 'carbon nanotubes,' which are stronger and lighter than steel, and able to conduct electricity. [Q8-A] These tubes of pure carbon have shown great promise: they can be used in everything, from electronics to airplanes, as well as space elevator cables.

지구 정지궤도

P: The next question about a space elevator is 'how long would the cable have to be'? Well, there are several factors that must be considered when determining this length. If you think about satellites orbiting Earth you'll recognize that their speed is actually determined by how high above Earth their orbits are. [Q9] As the space elevator would be attached to the Earth's surface, its mass would have to be centered at 36,000 km, which is the height at which it would achieve geosynchronous orbit. That leads us to the question 'What is geosynchronous orbit'? This is when an object's orbital period is synchronized with the Earth's rotation. In other words, the orbiting object will always appear at the same spot in the sky to an observer on Earth.

방해물

P: Despite these high hopes and technological advances, there are still many hurdles to actualizing this dream. [Q10] For one, as a space elevator cable, carbon nanotubes, have a major problem. The longest nanotubes ever created were only a few centimeters long, and linking them together to a length of 36,000 km would be impractical. In addition, some feel that a space elevator would present a navigational hazard, both to aircraft and spacecraft, as well as space objects. Further, it would be exposed to the radiation belts orbiting the Earth, and the passengers would need to be shielded from them. You can see that a lot more work is necessary before construction of a space elevator is feasible. If technology advances enough, though, it may be built in your lifetimes.

P: 케이블 자체가 아마도 엘리베이터 건설에 있어 가장 큰 장애일거에요. 그래서 그것은 정말 가볍고 내구성이 뛰어난 물질로 만들어질 필요가 있죠. 하지만 사람들이 오랫동안 우주엘리베이터를 만드는 것을 꿈꿔오는 기간 동안, 충분히 튼튼한 재료가 존재하지 않았어요. 최근에 순전히 탄소로만 만들어진 새로운 타입의 물질이 발견될 때까지는요. 탄소원자는 서로 매우 강한 화학적 결합을 하고 있기 때문에, 과학자들은 탄소 나노튜브라고 일컬어지는 아주 작은 튜브들을 만들 수 있는 방법을 발견하게 되었는데, 이것은 강철보다 훨씬 강하고 가벼우며 전기를 전도 시킬 수 있죠. [Q8-A] 이러한 단일 탄소 튜브들은 앞으로 전망이 무척 밝아요: 우주엘리베이터 뿐만 아니라 전자기기부터 항공분야에 이르기까지 모든 부문에서 사용되어 질 수 있거든요.

P: 우주 엘리베이터에 관한 다음 질문은 케이블이 얼마나 길어야 하는가?"에요. 이 길이를 결정하는 데에는 몇 가지 염두해야할 사항들이 있어요. 지구를 돌고 있는 인공위성들을 생각해 보면, 그것의 궤도가 지구위로 얼마나 높게 도느냐에 따라 실제로 속도가 결정된다는 걸 알게 될 거에요. [Q9] 우주 엘리베이터는 지구의 표면에 고정되어질 것이기 때문에, 그것은 지구 정지궤도에 도달할 수 있는 높이인 36,000km에 질량의 중심이 있어야만 해요. 그럼 '지구 정지궤도란 무엇인가?' 라는 다음 질문으로 이어지네요. 이것은 물체의 공전주기가 지구의 자전과 일치하는 때를 말해요. 다른 말로 하면, 돌고 있는 물체가 지구 위에 서있는 사람에게는 항상 하늘의 같은 지점에서 보이게 되는 거죠.

P: 큰 희망과 기술발달에도 불구하고, 꿈을 현실시키는 데는 넘어야 할 산이 여전히 많이 있어요. [Q10] 그중 한 가지는 우주 엘리베이터에 사용되는 줄인 탄소 나노튜브가 큰 문제점을 안고있죠. 지금까지 만들어진 가장 긴 나노튜브는 겨우 몇 cm 이어서 그것들을 하나씩 연결해서 36,000km를 만든다는건 그다지 실용적이지 못해요. 게다가 어떤 사람은 우주 엘리베이터가 우주에 있는 물체 뿐만 아니라 항공기와 우주선 둘 다의 항해에 위험을 가할 수 있다고 생각해요. 더욱이, 그것은 지구 주변을 공전하는 방사능대에 노출될 수가 있는데, 그러면 승객들은 보호를 받아야할 필요가 있게 되는 것이죠. 우주엘리베이터 건설이 실현 가능해지려면 좀 더 많은 작업이 이루어질 필요가 있다는 걸 알 수 있네요. 하지만 만약 기술이 충분히 발전한다면, 아마 여러분이 살아있는 동안 만들어질 수 있을지도 몰라요.

06 What is the author mainly discussing?

(A) How the invention of a space elevator ~~would bring~~ innovations in technology
(B) **The innovations and setbacks involved in space elevator technology**
(C) The opinions of scientists and other ~~famous figures~~ on the idea of a space elevator
(D) How the concept of a space elevator has affected ~~popular culture~~

교수는 주로 무엇을 논의하고 있는가?

(A) 우주엘리베이터의 발명이 어떻게 기술 혁신을 ~~가져올것인가~~
(B) **우주 엘리베이터 기술에 포함된 혁신과 장애**
(C) 우주 엘리베이터에 대한 과학자와 ~~유명인사들~~의 의견들
(D) 우주 엘리베이터라는 개념이 ~~대중문화에~~ 어떻게 영향을주어왔는가

Main Idea 글의 내용이 전체적으로 우주 엘리베이터에 대한 소개 및 특성, 앞으로 넘어야 할 장애를 설명하는 글이므로 (B)가 답이다. (A)는 기술혁신이 미래에 우주엘리베이터 건설을 가능하게 하는 것이지 그 반대는 아니므로 오답이다. (C)는 유명인사의 의견이, (D)는 우주 엘리베이터에 대한 아이디어가 대중문화에 끼친 영향에 대해서 본문 내용에 언급이 없으므로 각각 오답이다.

07 Why does the professor mention escape velocity?

(A) To give an example of ~~natural phenomena~~ caused by gravity
(B) ~~To show~~ that a rocket needs a lot of energy to leave Earth's gravitational pull *
(C) To explain that building a ladder into space is ~~impossible~~
(D) **To correct an idea that is misunderstood by many people**

왜 교수는 탈출 속도를 언급하는가?

(A) ~~중력에 의해 발생된 자연현상의~~ 예를 주려고
(B) 로켓이 지구 중력을 벗어나기 위해서는 많은 에너지가 필요하다는 것을 ~~보여주려고~~ *
(C) 우주로 가는 사다리를 만드는 것이 ~~불가능하다~~는 것을 설명하려고
(D) **많은 사람들이 잘못 이해하는 개념을 고쳐주려고**

Inference (Purpose) 교수가 탈출 속도를 언급한 부분을 살펴보면, Oddly, however, a lot of people still seem to have misconceptions about going to space. Um, let me give you an example. The idea that the only way to escape Earth's atmosphere is by travelling at Earth's escape velocity is not absolutely true.(그러나, 이상하게도, 많은 사람들이 우주로 가는 것에 대해 여전히 잘못 이해하고 있는 것 같아요. 음... 예를 하나 들어보죠. 지구 대기권을 탈출할 수 있는 유일한 방법이 지구 탈출 속도로 가는 것이라는 생각은 절대적으로 옳은 건 아니에요)에 서 (D)가 정답임을 알 수 있다. (A)는 지구 탈출속도가 중력을 벗어나기 위해 필요한 속도이기 때문에 중력에 의해 발생되었다는 것은 틀리므로 오답이다. (B)는 본문에 나와있는 내용이나 교수가 탈출 속도를 언급한 목적이 아니므로, (C)는 본문의 내용과 틀리므로 각각 오답이다.

TEST 1 Set 2-2   Lecture 1
The Space Elevator Technology

08 What does the professor say about space elevators?

Click on 2 answers

(A) Carbon nanotubes are the best candidate for space elevator cables.
(B) The space elevator can ~~only~~ be built on Earth. *
(C) The space elevator cannot function without ~~a rocket~~.
(D) The idea of building space elevators was inspired by the Eiffel Tower.

우주 엘리베이터에 관해 교수는 무엇을 말하는가?

2개의 답을 고르시오.

(A) 탄소 나노튜브는 우주엘리베이터 케이블을 만드는 데 가장 적합한 물질이다.
(B) 우주 엘리베이터는 오직 지구 위에서만 건설될 수 있다. *
(C) 우주 엘리베이터는 ~~로켓 없이는~~ 작동할 수 없다.
(D) 우주 엘리베이터는 에펠탑에서 영감을 받았다.

Detail (Characterisitc) 교수가 우주엘리베이터에 관해 말한 내용중에, These tubes of pure carbon have shown great promise: they can be used in everything, from electronics to airplanes, as well as space elevator cables.(이러한 단일 탄소 튜브들은 앞으로 전망이 무척 밝아요. 우주엘리베이터 뿐만 아니라 전자기기부터 항공분야에 이르기까지 모든 부문에서 사용되어 질 수 있거든요.)에서 (A)가 답임을 알 수 있고, A Russian rocket scientist, Konstantin Tsiolkovsky, who was inspired by the Eiffel Tower, first proposed this idea in 1895.(러시아의 로켓 과학자인 Konstantin Tsiolkovsky가 에펠탑에서 영감을 얻어 1895년에 처음으로 제안했죠.)를 보면 (D)가 정답이다. (B)는 우주엘리베이터가 오직 지구에서만 건설된다는 말은 없으므로, (C)는 우주 엘리베이터와 관련하여 로켓이 언급이 되지 않아 답이 될 수 없으므로 각각 오답이다.

09 Why does the professor mention geosynchronous orbit at the height of 36,000 km?

(A) ~~To describe the model~~ of a space elevator that was proposed by a science fiction author
(B) Because current technology allows the elevator to be built ~~only up to~~ 36,000 km *
(C) Because the space elevator will remain in one location relative to earth if its center of mass is at that height
(D) ~~To illustrate that more research is required~~ before the construction of the space elevator becomes plausible

왜 교수는 36,000km의 높이에 있는 지구정지궤도를 언급하는가?

(A) 한 공상과학 작가에 의해 제안된 우주엘리베이터 모형을 묘사하려고.
(B) 왜냐하면 현재의 기술로는 ~~최대~~ 36,000Km높이 ~~까지만~~ 올라갈 수 있는 엘리베이터를 만들 수 있다. *
(C) 왜냐하면 무게중심이 그 높이에 있다면 지구에 대하여 상대적으로 한 자리에 남아있을 것이기 때문이다.
(D) 우주엘리베이터 건설이 가능하게 되기 전에 ~~더 많은~~ 연구가 필요하다는 것을 설명하려고.

Inference (Purpose)   지구 정지궤도에 관해 언급된 내용을 보면, As the space elevator would be attached to the Earth's surface, its mass would have to be centered at 36,000 km, which is the height at which it would achieve geosynchronous orbit. That leads us to the question"What is geosynchronous orbit"? This is when an object's orbital period is synchronized with the Earth's rotation. In other words, the orbiting object will always appear at the same spot in the sky to an observer on Earth.(우주 엘리베이터는 지구의 표면에 고정되어질 것이기 때문에, 그것은 지구 정지궤도에 도달할 수 있는 높이인 36,000km에 질량의 중심이 있어야만 해요. 그럼"지구 정지궤도란 무엇인가?"라는 다음 질문으로 이어지네요. 이것은 물체의 공전주기가 지구의 자전과 일치하는 때를 말해요. 다른 말로 하면, 돌고 있는 물체가 지구 위에 서있는 사람에게는 항상 하늘의 같은 지점에서 보이게 되는 거죠.)에서 정답은 (C)임을 알 수 있다. (A)는 우주엘리베이터 모형은 본문에서 언급되지 않았고, (B)는 현재의 기술이 우주엘리베이터가 얼마만큼의 높이까지 올라가게 건설할 수 있는지 언급되지 않아 둘 다 오답이다. (D)는 우주엘리베이터가 건설되기까지 연구가 더 필요하다는 말은 맞지만, 이것은 정지궤도와 상관이 없는 내용이므로 정답으로 보기 어렵다

10 According to the professor, what is the disadvantage of using carbon nanotubes to construct the space elevator cable?

(A) It is too light to be used as a construction material for a space elevator
(B) It is difficult to make long carbon nanotube structures
(C) It will be hard to find enough carbon deposits to build a space elevator
(D) Nanotubes are undesired because carbon is more valuable when used in other products

교수의 말에 따르면, 우주 엘리베이터의 케이블을 건설하는데 탄소 나노튜브를 사용할 때의 단점은 무엇인가?

(A) 우주 엘리베이터 건설 자재로 사용되기에는 너무 가볍다.
(B) 긴 나노튜브 구조물을 만들기가 어렵다.
(C) 우주 엘리베이터를 짓는데 필요한 충분한 탄소층을 찾기가 힘들것이다.
(D) 탄소가 다른 제품에 사용될 때 가치가 더 크기 때문에 나노튜브에 대한 수요가 없다.

Detail (Disadvantage) 탄소 나노튜브의 단점에 대해 설명한 부분을 보면, For one, as a space elevator cable, carbon nanotubes, have a major problem. The longest nanotubes ever created were only a few centimeters long, and linking them together to a length of 36,000km would be impractical.(그 중 한가지는 우주 엘리베이터에 사용되는 줄인 탄소 나노튜브가 큰 문제점을 안고 있죠. 지금까지 만들어진 가장 긴 나노튜브는 겨우 몇 cm이어서 그것들을 하나씩 연결해서 36,000km를 만든다는 것은 그다지 실용적이지 못해요.)에서 나노튜브들이 짧아서 하나씩 연결하는 것은 실용적이지 않다고 했으므로 (B)가 정답이다. (A)는 나노튜브가 가벼운 것은 단점이 아니라 장점이며, (C)는 본문에 언급된 내용이 없으므로 각각 오답이다. (D)는 나노튜브에 여러 가지 분야에서 쓰일 수 있기 때문에 앞으로의 전망이 밝다고 했으므로 틀린 답이다.

11 Listen again to part of the lecture. Then answer the question.

P: There is a problem, however... although the ladder idea makes sense mathematically and conceptually, it is very improbable. Nobody could climb thousands of kilometers before being exhausted. Let's not forget that you would also need to be carrying a heavy oxygen tank and space suit.

What does the professor mean when he says this :

P: Let's not forget that you would also need to be carrying a heavy oxygen tank and space suit.

(A) He wants to emphasize that it would be impossible to climb such a ladder.
(B) He realizes that the student overlooked an important detail.
(C) He wants to clarify that the climber will get quite far up the ladder.
(D) He wants to illustrate his explanation using another example.

강의의 일부를 다시 듣고 질문에 답하시오.

P: 하지만, 문제가 하나 있어요… 비록 사다리 이론이 수학적으로나 개념적으로는 말이 되지만, 실현되기 가 무척 어려워요. 수천 킬로미터 높이를 오르다 보면 누구라도 완전히 지치게 될테니까요. 또한 무거운 산소탱크와 우주복을 지니고 가야한다는 걸 잊으면 안되요.

이렇게 말하며 교수는 어떤 것을 암시하는가?

p: 또한 무거운 산소탱크와 우주복을 지니고 가야한다는 걸 잊으면 안되요.

(A) 그는 이러한 사다리를 오르는 것이 불가능하다는 것을 강조하고자 한다.
(B) 그는 학생들이 중요한 세부사항을 간과하고 있다는 것을 알고 있다.
(C) 그는 사다리를 오르는 사람이 꽤 높이까지 올라갈 거라는 점을 분명히 하고 싶어한다.
(D) 그는 다른 예를 사용하여 자신의 설명을 자세히 전달하고 싶어한다.

Inference (Intention) 교수는 사람이 수 천 km를 사다리를 오르는 것은 실행되기 어려운데, 거기에 산소탱크와 우주복까지 더해진다면 더 힘들어질 거라고 말하고 있는 것이다. 따라서 (A)가 정답이 된다. (B)는 산소탱크와 우주복은 자신이 전달하고자 하는 의미를 강조하기 위해 든 예로써 학생들이 간과하면 안되는 세부사항이 아니고, (C)는 사다리를 오르면 금방 지치게 된다는 점을 말하고 싶어하는 것이므로 각각 오답이다. (D)는 산소탱크와 우주복은 사다리이론에 포함된 부분일 뿐 다른 예는 아니므로 오답이다

TEST 1 Set 2-3 — Lecture 2: Investigation of Ester Island

문단 주제	본문내용	해석
소개	Listen to part of a lecture in an archaeology class. The professor is discussing Easter Island. P: Let's continue researching lost civilizations with Easter Island; the mysterious island discovered by Dutchman Jacob Roggeveen in 1722. Roggeveen discovered an island filled with cannibalistic savages, but later found evidence suggesting that it was once occupied by an advanced, orderly civilization. If this was true, what happened to it? [Q12] What could have caused the demise and destruction of this prominent civilization? Archaeologists and scientists are working together to unravel this mystery. And today, we'll look into this obscurity in detail.	고고학 강의를 들으시오. 교수는 이스터섬에 관해 논의하고 있습니다. P: 계속해서 이스터섬의 사라진 문명에 관해 살펴볼 께요. 그 기이한 섬은 1722년 네덜란드인 Jacob Roggeveen 에 의해 발견되었죠. Roggeveen은 미개한 식인종으로 가득한 섬을 발견했는데요, 하지만 나중에 발견된 증거들은 이 섬이 한때 발전되고 질서있는 문명이 존재했음을 알려주고 있어요. 만약 이것이 사실이라면, 그곳에는 무슨 일이 있었던 걸까요? [Q12] 무엇이 이 뛰어난 문명의 종말과 파괴를 가져왔을까요? 고고학자 들과 과학자들은 이러한 미스터리를 밝혀내려고 함께 작업하고 있어요. 그래서 오늘 우리는 이러한 미스터리에 대해 좀 더 자세히 알아볼꺼에요.
이스터섬에 대한 소개	P: Does anyone know anything about Easter Island? S: Isn't it famous for gigantic statues? P: Ah, yes, Jonathan, Those are the island's most renowned features, but let's get some background information. Easter Island, measuring only 64 square miles, is located in the southern Pacific about 2,000 miles west of Chile, with its closest inhabited island neighbor being 1,400 miles away. Despite its isolation, the humid, subtropical climates with its mild winters and hot, rainstorm-filled summers make it ideal for inhabitation. When Roggeveen landed, however, there were no signs of outside connections. He found approximately 2,000 barbarians on an island wasteland devoid of trees and animals. On an island-wide search for usable resources, however, he discovered the astonishing moai. S: What are the moai? P: They're the gigantic statues that Jonathan mentioned. Anyway, this shocking discovery drew a lot of worldwide attention. These 887 giant faces were carved into giant stones, which averaged 14.5 feet tall and 14 tons, with some reaching 33 feet and weighing 165 tons! [Q13] Roggeveen found these strange because 2,000 people couldn't have possibly carved and hauled these statues, especially without the tools to perform such tasks! They didn't even have trees which are a basic component of construction tools.	P: 이스터 섬에 대해 아는 사람있나요? S: 거대 석상으로 유명하지 않나요? P: 아, 맞아요, Jonathan. 그것들이 가장 잘 알려진 섬의 명물이긴 하지만, 배경 정보에 대해 좀 더 알아보죠. 크기가 겨우 64제곱평방 미터밖에 되지 않는 이스터섬은, 칠레 서부로부터 2000마일 밖에 있는 남태평양에 위치하고 있는데, 사람이 사는 가장 가까운 섬은 1400마일이나 떨어져 있어요. 이렇게 고립돼있음에도 불구하고, 온난한 겨울과 덥고 비가 많이 오는 여름을 만드는 습한 아열대 기후는 그 섬을 사람이 거주하기에 이상적인곳으로 만들었죠. 그러나 Roggeveen이 도착했을 때는 외부와 접촉한 흔적이 전혀 없었어요. 대략 2000명의 야만인들이 나무와 동물이 없는 황무지에 살고 있는 것을 발견했죠. 그런데 그는 쓸만한 자원을 찾으려고 섬을 수색하다가 놀라운 모아이를 발견했어요. S: 모아이가 뭐에요? P: 그건 Jonathan이 말한 거대 석상이에요. 어쨌든, 이 놀라운 발견은 전 세계의 이목을 집중시켰어요. 887개의 거대 두상들은 큰 바위에 조각돼 있는데, 평균 14.5피트의 높이와 14톤의 무게를 가지고 있으며 어떤 석상은 높이가 33피트, 무게는 165톤에 이르기도 하죠. [Q13] Roggeveen는 이것이 이상하다고 생각했는데 왜냐하면 2000명의 사람들이 이 기이한 석상을 조각하고 끌어오는 것이 불가능했기 때문이에요. 특히 그러한 작업에 적합한 도구도 없이 말이죠! 그들은 심지어 건설도구의 기본 재료가 되는 나무조차 가지고 있지 않았어요.

과거의 이스터섬

S: Professor, who would have chosen to live in such a remote, barren place...and why?

P: [Q14] There's no definitive proof of where the people came from, only competing theories. Norwegian explorer Thor Heyerdahl originally proposed that they were from Chile, the closest continental land. He also claimed that the moai resembled Incan statues found throughout present-day Chile. His theory was widely accepted until modern science proposed another explanation.

Modern scientists performed a series of DNA tests on skeletons found on the island and discovered that they were from Polynesia, the area of islands near Australia in the southern Pacific Ocean inhabited by a population of seafarers who migrated over great oceanic routes in canoes. It is likely that they sailed from Marquesas or the Society islands, Easter Island's closest island neighbors, but got lost and settled on Easter Island. Strangely though, not all islanders are of Polynesian origin.

P: It's now believed that until a couple centuries ago, the island housed a lot more people: probably around 11,000 to 15,000, based on estimates of the labor required to build the moai, and the habitable areas of the island. The dispersion of the moai around the island also leads archaeologists to assume that the conditions on the island in the past were quite different. This was proven true by a test called pollen analysis. [Q17] The process involves a column of sediment collected from a swamp or pond, showing the different layers of sediment over time. Each of these layers is then dated through radiocarbon dating.

S: Professor, I'm confused about the procedure. What exactly is radiocarbon dating?

P: It's a process used to measure the age of dead organisms by measuring the remaining carbon levels. [Q15] These two tests proved that the island once supported flourishing gigantic palm trees, which were ideal for making canoes, logs, and ropes to transport the moai.

S: 교수님, 누가 그렇게 멀고 황량한 곳을 거주지로 택했을까요. 그리고 왜 그랬을까요?

P: [Q14] 서로 경쟁하는 이론들만 있을뿐 사람들이 어디에서 왔는지에 대한 정확한 증거는 없어요. 노르웨이 탐험가 Thor Heyerdahl은 최초로 그들이 가장 가까운 대륙인 칠레에서 왔을 거라고 제안했죠. 그는 또한 모아이석상이 오늘날 칠레 전역에서 발견되는 잉카 조각상과 닮았다고 주장 했어요. 그의 이론은 현대 과학이 또다른 설명을 내놓을 때까지 널리 받아들여졌죠.

P: 현대 과학자들은 섬에서 발견된 유골을 가지고 DNA 테스트를 했는데, 그들이 남태평양의 오스트레일리아 근처에 있는 섬들인, 카누로 거대한 바다를 항해하며 이동하는 사람들이 살았던 폴리 네시아 섬에서 왔다는 것을 알아냈어요. 그들은 이스터섬의 가장 가까운 이웃 섬들인 마르키즈 제도나 소사이어티 제도로부터 항해해 오다가 방향을 잃고 이스트섬에 정착했을 가능성이 크다는 것이죠. 그러나 이상한 점은, 모든 주민들이 폴리 네시아에서 유래한 것은 아니라는 거에요.

P: 지금은 2세기 정도 전까지는 그 섬에 더 많은 사람들이 거주했을 거라고 믿어지고 있죠: 모아이 석상을 세우는데 필요한 노동력과 섬에서 사람이 살 수 있는 지역을 추정하여 계산하면 아마도 대략 11,000명에서 15,000명 정도의 인구였을거예요. 섬 주변에 모아이 석상이 흩어져있는 것은 또한 고고학자들로 하여금 과거에는 이 섬의 상태가 지금과 꽤 많이 달랐다는 것을 가정하게 해 주었어요. 이것은 꽃가루 분석이라고 불리는 테스트에 의해 증명되었는데요. [Q17] 그 과정은 습지나 연못에서 하나의 퇴적층 기둥을 수집하는 것을 포함하는데, 이것은 시간이 지나면서 쌓인 각각 다른 퇴적층을 보여주죠. 그런 다음에 각각의 이 층들은 방사성탄소연대측정법에 의해 연대가 추정되죠.

S: 교수님, 저는 그 과정이 혼란스러운데요. 정확히 방사성탄소연대측정법이 뭔가요?

P: 그것은 남아있는 탄소의 수치를 측정해서 죽은 유기체의 나이를 측정하는데 사용되는 과정이에요. [Q15] 이러한 두개의 테스트는 그 섬에 한 때 거 대한 야자나무가 번성했었다는 것을 증명했는데, 이 나무들은 모아이석상을 운반하는데 사용되는

They were also required for everyday things such as building houses and fires. According to scientists, the natives cut down these palm trees and rolled them horizontally to transport the moai.

Anyway, long story short, the palm trees and animals went extinct for some reason, spelling doom for the islanders. This led to a dramatic population decrease; falling as low as 111 in 1877.

Let's look at possible explanations behind the downfall of the civilization. The traditional theory, suggested by American scientist Jared Diamond, was that the civilization destroyed itself through overconsumption and deforestation. He claimed that native people cut down all of the trees to transport the moai. The lack of trees then halted the production of the moai. Soon, necessities such as fire and housing became luxuries. Eventually, the island descended into a self-inflicted chaos. This is, however, only a theory and there is no corroborating data.

Archaeologist Terry Hunt has come up with a theory that points to rats as the main culprits behind the demise. He found a plethora of rat bones when sampling the soil from Anakena beach, the most likely landing spot for the first settlers. [Q16]**He deduced that the Polynesians brought rats with them for food, but there were no natural predators to keep the rat population in check. This combined with the tons of rat-chewed palm seeds strewn across the island led him to this new theory. He theorized that the rat population exploded and consumed all the palm seeds on the island. With no seeds to germinate and the natives still cutting down trees, deforestation occurred.** It was as if they were adding insult to injury. Soon, all of the trees were extinct and the islanders could no longer produce the canoes needed for fishing, so they started to consume the terrestrial animals. After these died out, they turned to warfare and cannibalism. By 1722, he says, no trace of the great civilization that once ruled the island existed.

12 What is the lecture mainly about?

(A) The gap between the past and present day conditions of Easter Island *
(B) ~~How to solve~~ the puzzle of the demise of an island.
(C) **Investigation of the disaster and chaos behind an island's modern conditions**
(D) Two possible theories about what could have caused Easter Island's disaster

강의는 주로 무엇에 대해 말하고 있는가?

(A) 과거와 현재의 이스터섬 환경 차이 *
(B) 섬 몰락에 대한 수수께끼를 ~~푸는 방법~~
(C) **어떤 섬의 현재 상태 뒤에 감춰진 재난과 혼란에 대한 조사**
(D) 이스터섬 재난을 야기시킨 두 가지 가능성 있는 이론

Main Idea 도입부분을 보면, 교수는 이스터섬의 사라진 문명에 대해 살펴보겠다고 말하여 강의 주제를 미리 밝히고 있음으로 정답은 (C)가 된다. (A), (D)는 주제가 되기에는 너무 지엽적인 내용이고, (B)는 본문에 언급되지 않았으므로 각각 오답이다.

13 According to the professor, what did the Dutch explorer Roggeeveen find mysterious about Easter Island?

(A) The fact that the moai statues ~~looked like animals~~ *
(B) **The absence of the devices and labor force required for the construction of the impressive moai**
(C) The low grade craftsmanship and knowledge of the sea displayed in the ~~poorly built canoes~~
(D) ~~A lack of evidence~~ of civil leadership and ongoing warfare

교수에 따르면, 네덜란드 탐험가 Roggeeveen가 이스터섬에 대해 기이하게 여긴 것은 무엇인가?

(A) 모아이 조각상들이 동물을 ~~닮았다는~~ 사실 *
(B) **놀라운 모아이를 건설하기 위해 필요한 도구와 노동력의 부재**
(C) 엉성하게 만들어진 카누들에서 보여지는 수준 낮은 기술들과 항해지식
(D) 사회지도력과 끊임없는 전쟁에 대한 ~~증거 부족~~

Detail (Finding) 탐험가 Roggeeveen가 언급된 부분을 살펴보면, Roggeveen found these strange because 2,000 people couldn't possibly carve and haul these statues, especially without the tools to perform such tasks! They didn't even have trees which are a basic component of construction tools.(Roggeveen는 이 점이 이상하다고 생각했는데, 왜냐하면 2,000명의 사람들이 이 기이한 석상을 조각하고 끌어오는 것이 불가능했기 때문이에요. 특히 그러한 작업에 적합한 도구도 없이 말이죠! 그들은 심지어 건설도구의 기본 재료가 되는 나무조차 가지고 있지 않았어요.)에서 모아이 석상 건설에 필요한 도구와 노동력의 부족에 대해 의아해 하고 있음을 알 수 있다. 따라서 정답은 (B)가 된다. (A)는 조각상이 동물을 닮았다는 언급은 없고 (C) 는 본문에 언급되지 않은 내용이며, (D)는 일부분이 후반부의 내용과 관련될 뿐 Roggeveen과는 상관이없으므로 각각 오답이다.

TEST 1   Set 2-3   *부록 Lecture 2   Investigation of Ester Island

14 What can be inferred about the native people who once lived on Easter Island?

(A) They were most likely Polynesian seafarers ~~from Europe~~.
(B) They are probably a mixed group of people who ~~travelled from place to place.~~ *
(C) A series of DNA tests ~~on the inhabitants confirmed~~ that Polynesian sailors had settled on the island.
(D) **Their origin is uncertain but theories suggest that they were either from Chile or Polynesia.**

이스트섬에 살았던 원주민에 대해 추론할 수 있는 점은 무엇인가?

(A) 그들은 거의 ~~유럽에서 온~~ 폴리네시안 항해자들일 가능성이 크다.
(B) 그들은 아마도 ~~이곳 저곳을 돌아다니는~~ 여러 사람들이 섞여 있는 그룹일 것이다. *
(C) ~~섬주민에 대한~~ 일련의 DNA 검사는 폴리네시아 선원들이 섬에 정착했었다는 사실을 ~~확인시켜 주었다~~.
(D) **그들의 기원은 불확실하지만 그들이 칠레 혹은 폴리네시아로부터 왔다는 이론들이 있다.**

Inference (Infer)   원주민에 관해 언급된 부분을 보면, There's no definitive proof of where the people came from, only competing theories. (서로 경쟁하는 이론들만 있을 뿐, 사람들이 어디에서 왔는지에 대한 정확한 근거는 없어요.)에서 이론은 있지만 확실한 기원은 불분명하다고 설명하고 있다. 따라서 (D)가 정답임을 알 수 있다. (A), (B), (C)는 일부 사실에 관해 언급한 내용을 일반화시켜 잘못된 결론을 도출했기 때문에 각각 오답이다.

15 What is revealed about palm trees through pollen analysis?

(A) Palm trees ~~could be used~~ to measure the age of dead organisms in the sediment.
(B) The palm trees were necessary ~~to supply food~~ for the islanders.
(C) **The palm trees were required to supply the basic necessities and tools for daily life once existed on the island.**
(D) Palm trees were the ~~raw ingredients~~ necessary for the ~~production~~ and transportation of moai.

꽃가루 분석을 통해서 야자나무에 대해 무엇이 밝혀졌는가?

(A) 야자나무는 퇴적물에 있는 죽은 유기체의 나이를 측정 하는데 ~~쓰여질 수 있다~~.
(B) 야자나무는 섬주민들이 ~~음식을 공급받는데~~ 필요했다.
(C) **야자나무는 섬에 한 때 존재했던 일상생활을 위한 필수품과 도구들을 공급하는데 필요했다.**
(D) 야자나무는 모아이 석상의 ~~생산과~~ 운반을 위해 필요한 ~~원재료였다~~. *

Detail (Finding)   꽃가루 분석에 대해 언급된 부분을 살펴보면, which were ideal for making canoes, logs, and ropes to transport the moai. They were also required for everyday things such as building houses and fires.(이 나무들은 모아이석상을 운반하는데 사용되는 카누, 원목 그리고 밧줄을 만드는데 적합했죠. 그들은 또한 집을 짓기 위해서나 불을 피우는 것 같은 일상생활에도 필요했어요.)에서 일상생활을 위한 필수품을 만드는데 있어서 야자나무가 필요했음을 알 수 있다. 따라서 정답은 (C)이다. (A)와 (B)는 본문에 언급되지 않은 내용이므로 각각 오답이다. (D)는 야자나무는 석상의 생산재료가 아니라 운반을 위한 재료이고 꽃가루 분석과는 관련이 없어 답이 될 수 없다.

16 According to the professor, what is the main piece of evidence that suggests that rats were the main reason for deforestation?

교수에 따르면 쥐가 숲을 황폐화 시킨 주요 원인이라는 중점적인 증거는 무엇인가?

Click on 2 answers	2개의 답을 고르시오.

(A) There was an excessive use of palm trees for fire and housing.
(B) Chewed premature palm trees were discovered on the island. *
(C) There were no natural predators to control the growth of the rat population.
(D) Rat-gnawed palm seeds were found throughout the island.

(A) 장작과 집을 짓기 위해 야자나무가 과도하게 사용되었다.
(B) 씹은 자국이 있는 덜 성숙한 야자나무가 섬에서 발견되었다. *
(C) 쥐 개체수의 번식을 조절할 어떠한 자연 천적도 없었다.
(D) 쥐에 의해 갉아 먹힌 야자나무 씨들이 섬 전체에서 발견되었다.

Detail (Evidence) 쥐에 의해 숲이 황폐화된 것을 언급한 부분을 살펴보면, He deduced that the Polynesians brought rats with them for food, but there were no natural predators to keep the rat population in check. This combined with the tons of rat-chewed palm seeds strewn across the island led him to a new theory… (중략) … deforestation occurred. (그는 폴리네시아인들이 식용으로 쥐들을 섬에 가져왔지만, 쥐의 개체수를 조절할만한 어떠한 천적도 없었다고 추론했어요. 이것은 섬전반에 걸쳐 쥐가 씹고 버린 수톤에 이르는 야자수 씨앗이 발견 됨으로써 더욱 힘을 얻어 그의 세로운 이론으로 이어졌는데요… (중략) … 산림파괴가 일어났죠.)에서 쥐의 개체수를 조절할 어떠한 천적도 없었다는 것 과 쥐에 의해 씹힌 야자나무 씨앗들이 언급되어 (C)와 (D)가 답임을 알 수 있다. (A)는 쥐와 상관없는 내용이고, (B)는 섬에서 발견된 씹은 자국이 있는 것은 야자수 씨앗이지 어린 나무가 아니므로 각각 오답이다.

17 Listen again to part of the lecture. Then answer the question.

강의 일부분을 다시 듣고, 질문에 대답하시오.

P: The process involves a column of sediment collected from a swamp or pond, showing the different layers of sediment over time. Each of these layers is then dated through radiocarbon dating.
S: Professor, I'm confused about the procedure. What exactly is radiocarbon dating?

P: 그 과정은 습지나 연못에서 하나의 최적층 기둥을 수집하는 것을 포함하는데, 이것은 시간이 지나면 서 쌓인 각각 다른 퇴적층들을 보여주죠. 그런 다음에 각각의 이 층들은 방사성탄소연대측정법에 의해 연대가 추정되죠.
S: 교수님, 저는 그 과정이 혼란스러운데요. 방사성탄소 연대측정법이 정확히 뭔가요?

Why does the student say this? :🎧

왜 학생은 이렇게 말하는가?

S: Professor, I'm confused about the procedure. What exactly is radiocarbon dating?

S: 교수님, 저는 그 과정이 혼란스러운데요. 방사성탄소연대측정법이 정확히 뭔가요?

(A) He needs more information on ~~the details of pollen analysis~~ to understand the radiocarbon dating method. *
(B) He thinks that pollen analysis and radiocarbon dating are the ~~same~~.
(C) He is curious about the accuracy and ~~validity~~ of radiocarbon dating method.
(D) He needs clarification about the procedures used to determine the materials once found on the island.

(A) 그는 방사성탄소연대측정법을 이해하기 위해 ~~꽃가루 분석에 대한 더 많은~~ 정보를 필요로 하고 있다. *
(B) 그는 꽃가루 분석과 방사성탄소연대측정법을 ~~같다고~~ 생각하고 있다.
(C) 그는 방사성탄소연대측정법의 정확성과 ~~타당성에~~ 대해 궁금해 하고 있다.
(D) 그는 한때 섬에서 발견된 물질의 연대를 측정하기 위해 사용되는 과정들에 대해 분명히 아는 것을 필요로 한다.

Inference (Purpose) 묻는 내용으로 미루어 학생은 꽃가루 분석과 방사능탄소연대측정법을 혼동하고 있으며 이것들에 대해 명확히 하고 싶어 하는것을 알 수 있다. 따라서 정답은 (D)가 된다. (A)는 꽃가루분석을 자세히 알고 싶어 질문한 것은 아니고, (B)는 둘을 혼동하는 것이지 같다고 생각하는 것이 아니므로 각각 오답이다. (C)는 타당성에 관해 질문한 것이 아니므로 답이 될 수 없다.

usherin.usher.co.kr

USHER iBT TOFLE
FINAL TEST LISTENING
TEST 2/해설

TEST 2

Set 1-1

Conversation
Biology Research Plan

문단주제	본문내용	해 석
	Listen to part of a conversation between a graduate Student and her biology professor.	대학원 학생과 생물학 교수의 대화의 일부를 들으시오.
	S: Hi, professor. What brings you by the lab today?	S: 안녕하세요, 교수님, 실험실엔 무슨 일로 오셨어요?
	P: Hi Janet. I just wanted to check on how the experiments were coming along. I heard you've put in a lot of hours in the lab recently.	P: 안녕 Janet. 실험이 어떻게 되어가는지 확인하고 싶어서 말야. 최근에 네가 실험실에서 많은 시간을 보낸다고 들었어.
	S: Well, to be honest, I have been putting in more time at the lab because things haven't been going all that... smoothly.	S: 음, 솔직히 예전보다 더 많은 시간을 실험실에서 보내긴 해요. 왜냐하면 일들이 그다지… 순조롭게 되어가지 않거든요.
	P: May I ask why?	P: 왜 그런지 물어봐도 되니?
	S: [Q1] Well, the task that you assigned me. The... uh... purification of protein RP73 from human tissue? Well, the experiment was going really well... until... a problem in the cooling process occurred.	S: [Q1] 그러니까, 교수님이 제게 내주신 과제 있잖아요? 그 음… 인체 조직에서 단백질 RP73을 정제하는 거요. 음, 그 실험이 굉장히 잘 되고 있었어요… 냉각과정에 문제가 생기기 전까지는요…
	P: Oh. Did you forget to fully heat it before you lowered the temperature? If we're going to determine if the problem is still reversible, we have to know the exact process that you followed.	P: 오. 온도를 낮추기 전에 열을 완전히 가하는 걸 잊었니? 만약 우리가 그 문제를 아직 되돌릴 수 있는지 결정하려면, 난 네가 행한 과정을 정확히 알아야만 해.
	S: Not quite. Everything up to the heating process was perfect, [Q2] I actually set an alarm on Friday night to come back the next morning and cool it to room temperature... and then do the precipitation process, hopefully. Well, anyway, I overslept and forgot to come back to the lab.	S: 꼭 그런건 아니에요. 가열과정까진 모든 것이 완벽했어요. [Q2] 사실 제가 금요일 밤에 알람을 맞춰놨거든요. 다음날 아침에 다시 와서 실온이 될때까지 식히고… 그 후에 침전과정을 하려고요. 음, 어쨌든, 제가 늦잠을 자는 바람에 실험실에 되돌아오는 걸 깜빡했어요.
	P: I've been there. Back when I was a graduate student like you, I wasn't used to going to a boring laboratory on a Saturday, either. Well, if it was heated all weekend, there's no way we can still purify the protein.	P: 나도 그런 적이 있단다. 너처럼 대학원생이었을때, 토요일에 지루한 실험실에 오는 것이 익숙하지 않았거든. 음, 만약 그것이 주말 내내 가열되었으면, 우리가 그 단백질을 정제할 수 있는 방법은 없겠구나.
	S: I'm so sorry, professor. I know you were hoping to submit a paper to the journal about its possible uses.	S: 너무 죄송해요, 교수님. 이것의 가능한 사용법에 대해서 얼마나 학술지에 논문을 기고하고 싶어하셨는지 알고 있어요.
	P: [Q5] It can wait for a couple of weeks. I mean... it's not like the function of the protein is going to change anytime soon. So, no harm, no foul. Now the important question is "When can I expect to see the results that I'm looking for?"	P: [Q5] 그건 한 2주 정도 더 기다릴 수 있단다. 내 말은… 단백질의 기능이 당장 변하거나 그런 건 아니잖니. 그러니까, 아무런 해가 없으면, 아무 잘못도 없는거지. 좋아, 이제 중요한건, "언제쯤 이면 내가 원하던 결과를 볼 수 있는가?" 인데 말야.
	S: Well, I've been working on it, even right before you arrived. So it shouldn't take much longer than a couple days.	S: 음, 교수님이 도착하시기 바로 전까지도 연구하고 있었어요. 그러니 2일 이상은 걸리지 않을거에요.
	P: [Q3] Well, the problem is, I leave town for a week tomorrow... and...	P: [Q3] 음, 문제는 내가 내일 일주일동안 도시를 떠난다는 거야… 그리고…

S: Oh, you're worried that the protein won't be in tiptop condition when you come back in a week.

P: Yes, I would like to work with the material as soon as it's successfully purified.

S: Okay... then I should probably get rid of what I've been working on and start again sometime this week?

P: Oh, that would make me feel like one of those professors who asks too much of their graduate students.

S: Don't worry. I think it's better if I keep practicing the process. You know... to reduce the margin of error. Plus, it was my fault that you're not getting the results right now.

P: Well, I'm glad to see you have taken a rather professional attitude about your job. [Q4] You know, reducing the margin of error is quite critical in designing and implementing an experiment as a scientist. You know the story about spinach and its supposed effects on strengthening muscles, don't you?

S: No, but I'm guessing it's not true because you used the word 'supposed'... hahaha.

P: Hahaha... True. People believe that spinach is rich in iron, a muscle supplement, but, in fact, a German chemist, in 1870, made an error in his experiments, making people think that spinach has 10 times more iron than it actually does! He did everything else right in his experiments, but a simple misplaced decimal provided the public with inaccurate information that continues to fool a lot of people.

S: Wow, I did not know that. I guess I get what you're trying to say. I'll have the protein ready and in perfect condition for your research when you return. And... place all my decimal points in the right place!

P: Thanks, Janet. I'll be back in a week and we'll talk more then.

S: 오, 교수님이 일주일 후에 돌아오셨을 때 단백질이 최상의 상태가 아닐까봐 걱정하시는 거죠?

P: 그래, 나는 그게 가능한 한 성공적으로 정제되자마자 그걸로 연구하고 싶거든.

S: 알겠어요. 그럼 제가 현재 연구하고 있던 것을 중단하고 이번주쯤 다시 시작해야만 하겠네요.

P: 오, 그러면 내가 마치 내 대학원생에게 너무 많은걸 요구하는 교수처럼 느껴지는데.

S: 걱정하지 마세요. 그 과정을 계속 연습하는 게 저한테는 더 나은 것 같아요. 그러니까.. 오차범위를 줄이려면요. 게다가, 교수님께서 지금 바로 결과를 얻지 못하는건 제 잘못이잖아요.

P: 음, 난 네가 일에 대해 훨씬 전문적인 태도로 임하는걸 보게 되어 정말 기쁘구나. [Q4] 있지, 오차범위를 줄이는건 과학자로써 실험을 구상하고 실행할 때 매우 중요한 거야. 시금치와 근육을 강화시키는 기대효과에 대한 이야기를 알거야, 그렇지?

S: 아뇨, 하지만 교수님이 '기대' 라는 단어를 쓰셨으니 사실이 아닐 것 같은데요... 하하하.

P: 하하하... 맞아. 사람들은 시금치가 근육을 보충해주는 철분이 풍부하다고 믿어. 하지만, 사실은 독일의 한 화학자가 1870년에 자신의 실험에서 실수를 해서 시금치가 실제보다 10배나 더 많은 철을 가지고 있다고 사람들이 생각하게 만들었어! 그는 실험에서 다른 모든 것을 옳게 했지만, 단순하게 잘못 놓은 소수점 하나가 대중에게 정확하지 않은 정보를 줬고, 이는 많은 사람들을 아직까지도 속이고 있지.

S: 와우, 그건 몰랐어요. 교수님이 제게 하려는 말씀이 뭔지 알것 같아요. 교수님이 돌아오실 땐 단백질을 준비해서 연구를 할 수 있는 완벽한 상태로 해 놓을께요. 그리고... 소수점 하나하나 정확한 위치에 놓을께요.

P: 고마워, Janet. 일주일 뒤에 돌아올테니까 그때 더 얘기하자꾸나.

TEST 2 Set 1-1 Conversation
Biology Research Plan

01 What is the conversation mainly about?

(A) The ~~difficulties~~ of purifying a certain protein from human tissue *
(B) **A step a student missed in a research project and a plan to make it up**
(C) An experiment the professor performed during the ~~biology lecture~~
(D) ~~A topic in a research paper~~ that the ~~student~~ will submit to the journal

대화의 주된 내용은 무엇인가?

(A) 인체조직으로부터 특정 단백질을 정제하는 것의 ~~어려움~~ *
(B) **연구프로젝트에서 학생이 놓친 절차와 그것을 보충하기 위한 계획**
(C) ~~생물학 강의에서~~ 교수가 행한 실험
(D) 학생이 학술지에 기고할 ~~연구논문의 주제~~

Main Idea Well, the task that you assigned me. The…uh….purification of protein RP73 from human tissue? Well, the experiment was going really well…until….there was a problem in the cooling process.(그러니까, 교수님이 제게 내주신 과제 있잖아요? 그 음… 인체조직에서 단백질 RP73를 정제하는 거요. 음, 그 실험이 굉장히 잘 되고 있었어요… 냉각과정에 문제가 있기 전까지는요.)의 주요 대화 내용은 단백질 정제 과정 중 학생이 실수를한 절차와 그것을 보충하려는 계획이므로 정답은 (B)이다. (A)의 정제 과정에서의 어려움과 (C)는 생물학 강의에서 한 교수의 실험에 대한 내용은 언급이 없으므로 각각 오답이다. (D)는 논문을 기고하는 사람은 학생이 아닌 교수이고 또한 이 논문의 주제가 대화의 주된 내용은 아니므로 답이 될 수 없다.

02 What can be inferred about the student from the conversation?

(A) ~~She had high hopes~~ for her research on the protein. *
(B) She ~~has completed~~ this experiment successfully before.
(C) She ~~does not know exactly~~ what she is supposed to do at each step of the experiment.
(D) **She is not accustomed to working in the laboratory on the weekends.**

대화에서 학생에 대해 추론할 수 있는 점은 무엇인가?

(A) 여자는 자신의 단백질 연구에 대한 ~~기대가 높다~~. *
(B) 여자는 이전에 이 실험을 성공적으로 ~~끝낸 적이 있다~~.
(C) 여자는 실험의 각 단계에서 무엇을 해야할지 ~~정확히 알지 못한다~~.
(D) **여자는 주말에 실험실에서 연구하는 것이 익숙하지 않다.**

Inference (Infer) 학생이 말한 내용 중에서, S: I actually set an alarm on Friday night to come back the next morning and cool it to room temperature….and then do the precipitation process, hopefully. Well, anyway, I overslept and forgot to come back to the lab. (S: 사실 제가 금요일 밤에 알람을 맞춰놨거든요. 다음날 아침에 다시 와서 실온이 될 때까지 식히고… 그 후에 침전과정을 하려고요. 음, 어쨌든, 제가 늦잠을 자는 바람에 실험실에 되돌아오는 걸 깜빡했어요.)을 보면, 학생은 주말에 연구실에 나오는 것이 익숙하지 않음을 알 수 있다. 따라서 (D)가 정답이다. (A)는 여자가 아니라 교수가 기대가 높은 것이며, (B)는 대화의 전반적인 내용을 보면 여자는 이 실험에 대한 경험이 없음을 알 수 있으므로 각각 오답이다. (C)는 학생이 교수가 돌아올 때까지 연습해서 최고의 상태로 준비해 놓겠다고 말한 것으로 보아 실험의 각 단계를 잘 알고 있으므로 정답이 될 수 없다.

03 Why is the professor worried about leaving town for a week?

(A) **He does not want to work with the proteins unless they are freshly purified.**
(B) He thinks that the proteins ~~will return to their original state~~ if they are left for a week.
(C) He is concerned that ~~the temperature will fluctuate too much, affecting~~ the functions of the proteins.
(D) He is afraid that the graduate student will ~~not practice enough~~ to reduce the margin of error while he is away.

왜 교수는 일주일 동안 마을을 떠나는 것에 대해 걱정하는가?

(A) **그는 금방 정제되지 않은 단백질로 작업하고 싶어하지 않는다.**
(B) 그는 단백질을 일주일 동안 내버려두면 ~~원래 상태로 되돌아갈 것이라고 생각한다~~.
(C) 그는 기온의 변동이 너무 심해서 단백질의 기능에 영향을 미칠까봐 걱정한다.
(D) 그는 자신이 떠나있을 동안 대학원생이 오차범위를 줄이기 위한 ~~연습을 충분히 하지 않을까봐 두려워하고~~ 있다. *

Detail (Reason)   교수가 걱정하는 부분을 살펴보면, P: Well, the problem is, I leave town for a week tomorrow…and…. S: Oh, you're worried that the protein won't be in tiptop condition when you come back in a week. P: Yes, I would like to work with the material as soon as it's successfully purified.(P: 음, 문제는 내가 내일 일주일 동안 도시를 떠난다는 거야… 그리고… S: 오, 교수님이 일주일 후에 돌아오셨을 때 단백질이 최상의 상태가 아닐까봐 걱정하시는 거죠? P: 그래, 나는 그게 가능한 한 성공적으로 정제되자마자 그걸로 연구하고 싶거든.)에서 교수는 단백질이 정제되자 마자 그걸로 연구하고 싶어하므로 정답은 (A)이다. (B)는 본문에 언급이 없고, (C)는 단백질의 기능이 당장 변하지는 않는다고 했으므로 각각 오답이다. (D)는 학생이 교수가 돌아올 때까지 실험연습을 열심히 하겠다고 했으므로 맞는 내용이 아니다.

04 Why does the professor mention spinach?

(A) To explain specifically ~~what he was going to research~~ with his protein
(B) To explain ~~a breakthrough~~ in a field regarding proteins *
(C) To explain how unnoticed errors can go a long way in science
(D) To explain that ~~some plants can be utilized~~ in scientific experiments

왜 교수가 시금치를 언급하는가?
(A) 단백질로 ~~무엇을 연구하려 했는지~~ 세부적으로 설명해주기 위해
(B) 단백질과 관련된 분야의 ~~획기적인 성과~~를 설명하기 위해 *
(C) 과학에서 알아차리지 못한 실수 때문에 얼마나 멀리 우회할 수 있는지 설명하기 위해
(D) 몇몇 식물들은 과학적 실험에서 ~~사용될 수 있다~~는 것을 설명하기 위해

Inference (Purpose)   교수가 시금치를 언급한 부분에서, You know, reducing the margin of error is quite critical in designing and implementing an experiment as a scientist. You know the story about spinach and its supposed effects on strengthening muscles?(있지, 오차범위를 줄이는 건 과학자로써 실험을 구상하고 실행할 때 매우 중요한 거야. 시금치와 근육을 강화시키는 기대효과에 대한 이야기를 알거야, 그렇지?) 부분에서 교수는 실험 오차에 관한 내용을 말하기 위해 시금치를 예로 드는 것임을 알 수 있다. 따라서 답은 (C)이다. (A), (B),(D)는 본문에 언급되어 있지 않으므로 각각 오답이다.

05 Listen again to part of the conversation. Then answer the question. What does the professor imply when he says this : 🎧

P: It can wait for a couple of weeks. I mean… it's not like the function of the protein is going to change anytime soon. So, no harm, no foul.

(A) To ~~encourage~~ the student to make fewer mistakes in the future *
(B) To imply that the student's mistake did not cause permanent damage
(C) To imply that the ~~foul odor~~ of the protein means ~~damage has been done~~ to it
(D) To ~~show his frustration~~ with the current situation regarding his project

대화의 일부분을 다시 듣고, 질문에 답하시오. 교수가 이 말을 할 때 무엇을 암시하는가?
P: 그건 한 2주 정도 더 기다릴 수 있단다. 내 말은… 단백질의 기능이 당장 변하거나 그런 건 아니잖니. 그러니까, 아무런 해가 없으면, 아무 잘못도 없는 거지.

(A) 나중에 실수를 덜 하도록 학생을 ~~격려하기 위해~~ *
(B) 학생의 실수가 영구적인 해를 끼치지는 않았다는 것을 말해주기 위해
(C) 단백질의 독한 ~~악취~~가 그것에 ~~해가 입혀졌음~~을 의미한다는 것을 말해주기 위해
(D) 그의 프로젝트와 관련해 현재의 상황에 대한 그의 ~~불만을 나타내기 위해~~

Inference (Headset)   교수는 학생의 실수가 영구적으로 단백질의 기능을 변하게 한 것이 아니므로, 아무런 잘못이 없다고 안심시키기 위해 말한 것이므로 (B)가 정답임을 알 수 있다. (A)는 다음에 실수하지 말라고 격려를 한 것이 아니고, (C)와 (D)는 대화 내용에 없으므로 각각 오답이다.

TEST 2 Set 1-2 Lecture 1 — Mysteries of the Egyptian Pyramid

문단주제	본문내용	해석
서문	Listen to part of a lecture in a history class. The professor is discussing pyramids. P: Today we're going to switch to manmade wonders and talk about the Great Pyramid at Giza! At 756 feet wide and 450 feet high, this massive ancient structure is composed of 2,300,000 stone blocks. The mere sight of this giant, ancient structure causes many people to wonder, 'How on Earth did the ancient Egyptians build this 4,500 years ago?' Due to the lack of direct evidence, though, no one knows exactly how the Great Pyramid was constructed. Scientists and archaeologists aren't clueless though; they have come up with theories explaining the construction process. [Q6] **Let's look at how the pyramid might have been built.**	역사학 강의의 일부를 들으시오. 교수는 피라미드에 관해 논의하고 있습니다. P: 오늘 우리는 인류가 만들어낸 불가사의들로 주제를 옮겨서 기자에 있는 대 피라미드에 대해 얘기해 볼께요. 넓이가 756피트, 높이가 450피트인, 이 거대한 고대 건축물은 230만개의 석조 블록 들로 이루어져 있어요. 이 거대한 구조물을 단순히 바라보기만 해도 많은 사람들에게 궁금증을 불러 일으켰죠. "도대체 고대 이집트인들은 어떻 게 이걸 4500년 전에 지었을까?" 하지만, 불충 분한 증거로 인해 피라미드가 어떻게 건설되었는지는 아무도 알지 못해요. 그러나 과학자들과 고 고학자들이 전혀 짐작을 못하는 것은 아닌데요; 그들은 피라미드의 건축과정을 설명하는 몇 가지 이론들을 생각해 내었죠. [Q6] **피라미드 건설을 가능하게 했을지도 모르는 방법을 살펴봅시다.**
피라미드에 대한 소개	P: Before we get to the construction methods used to build the Great Pyramid, does anyone know why the pyramids were constructed? S: Didn't they build pyramids for the afterlife? P: Exactly. Pharaohs commissioned pyramids to serve as tombs for them to rest in during the afterlife. All of the labor and construction materials consumed were for just one man! Anyhow, pyramids had multiple chambers and passages within them, but only one was the true resting place of the pharaoh. The others were made to fool grave robbers who may try to steal the pharaoh's precious treasures. S: [Q11] **Why would there be treasures in the pharaohs' tombs? Wouldn't that be kind of a waste?** P: **Well, yes, but the ancient Egyptians considered the afterlife to be eternal, so they wanted to be prepared for it. To do this, they took their most precious belongings with them. After living a life of luxury, they were the icing on the cake.** Unfortunately, their trickery didn't work that well. Over time, most of the pyramids were robbed and looted. Luckily for us, though, the advanced architecture and craftsmanship of the ancient Egyptians allowed the overall structures to remain intact.	P: 자, 피라미드를 짓는데 사용된 건축술에 대해 본격적으로 들어가기 전에, 그것들이 왜 지어졌는지 아는 사람 있나요? S: 사후세계를 위해 만들어진 것이 아닌가요? P: 맞아요. 파라오들은 피라미드가 자신들이 내세에서 편히 쉴 수 있는 무덤의 역할을 할 수 있게 만들라고 명령했어요. 수많은 노동력과 건축자재들이 오직 한 사람만을 위한 거였지요! 어쨌든, 피라미드 안에는 여러 개의 방과 통로들이 있었는데, 오직 한 장소만이 파라오가 진정으로 쉴 수 있는 곳이었어요. 다른 곳들은 파라오의 값진 보물들을 훔치려는 도굴꾼들을 속이려고 만든 것이죠. S: [Q11] **왜 파라오들은 자신의 무덤 안에 보물을 두었던거죠? 그건 일종의 낭비 아닌가요?** P: **네, 맞아요. 하지만 고대 이집트인들은 사후세계가 영원하다고 생각했어요. 그래서 그들은 그것에 대한 준비를 하고 싶어했죠. 이를 위해, 자신의 가장 귀중한 소지품들을 함께 가지고 간거예요. 사치스러운 삶을 산 이후에, 그건 금상첨화였지요.** 안타깝게도, 그들의 속임수는 그다지 효과가 없었어요. 시간이 흐르면서, 대부분의 피라미드들은 도굴되고 약탈당했죠. 그렇지만, 우리에게는 다행히도, 고대 이집트인들의 훌륭한 건축술과 기술 덕분에 전체적인 무덤의 구조는 손상을 입지 않고 남게 되었어요.
과거 이론들: 직선 경사로 이론과 나선형 경사로 이론	P: Let's move on to theories explaining how the Great Pyramid was built. According to the ancient Greek historian Herodotus, the ancient Egyptians used wooden cranes located on every level of the pyramid to lift the	P: 피라미드가 어떻게 지어졌는지에 대한 이론들을 살펴봅시다. 고대 그리스 역사학인 Herodotus에 따르면, 고대 이집트인들은 나무로 된 기중기를 피라미드의 각 층에 올려놓아 돌을 들어올렸다고 해요.

stones. There is a major problem with this theory though, because Giza is located in a desert they wouldn't have had access to enough wood to construct cranes. Further, they would have also lacked space for the cranes. [Q7] Using Herodotus' records, and other sources, Egyptologists came up with the theory that the ancient Egyptians used ramps to transport the massive stone blocks, as they were the main devices for lifting heavy materials at the time. There have been many theories about possible ramp shapes, but I'm just going to concentrate on the most common ones. Egyptologist Jean-Philippe Lauer suggested that straight ramps, reaching the top of the pyramid, were used. These simplest of ramps would have been massive! They would require a slope of about a half mile to reach the top of the Great Pyramid.

S: But professor, you said the ramp would have to be about a half mile. Wouldn't this task be too much for the laborers? I mean, didn't they already have enough work?

P: Exactly! Constructing a ramp of that size would have been a massive waste of labor and materials. This brings us to another style of ramp, the spiral ramp, which was suggested by tomb excavator Mark Lehner. A spiral ramp is a more complex design that would have wrapped around the pyramid until it reached the top. Compared to other ramps, it would've required much less material and labor. However, this type of ramp also has problems. [Q8] First, it would have ruined the builders' external sightlines. Because they used ropes to measure, the ancient Egyptians needed clear lines of vision to check how precisely the blocks were layered. Another design problem is the ramp's corner... Imagine turning a corner high in the air with a 2.5 ton stone block! Both ramp theories also share the problem of needing to destroy the ramps to ensure a clean, smooth exterior surface for the pyramid.

Jean-Pierre Houdin의 이론

P: Recently, a French architect who specializes in 3D designs, Jean-Pierre Houdin, suggested a new theory. He surveyed the pyramid with infrared cameras and developed a 3-D model of the Great Pyramid to support his new theory that the Great Pyramid was built using internal ramps. He felt that the Egyptians built external ramps to reach about 141 feet in the beginning, and then switched to using internal ramps. These ramps would wrap around the i side of the pyramid and reach the apex like spiral ramps.

S: But professor, wouldn't corners still be problematic?

P: [Q9] I was just about to explain that. Spiral ramps can be compared to the winding roads built on the sides of mountains. You know that cars driving along these roads risk falling off. In much the same way, workers could have easily stumbled off the side of an external spiral ramp. Internal ramps, on the other hand, have space around the corners thus making it easier, and safer, for laborers to haul stones up the ramps.

S: [Q10-B] Ah, so the internal ramps provided safety for the workers!

P: Exactly.

S: But, didn't you say that ramps require too much labor and material?

P: [Q10-D] Yes, they do indeed, but internal ramps are different. They would basically become a part of the pyramid. Since they weren't going to be taken down after construction, they could simply be sealed off after use, significantly conserving materials and labor.

S: It sounds like Houdin's theory is the best explanation.

P: Yes, his theory is a revolutionary explanation regarding the construction of the pyramids and is likely to be accepted by the Egyptologist community since it alimates the problems associated with the previous theories.

06 What is the lecture mainly about?

(A) In-depth analysis of the structure and ~~composition~~ of the Great Pyramid of Giza
(B) A revolutionary idea suggested by Jean-Pierre Houdin using modern 3D modeling
(C) Explanations behind the enigmatic construction techniques used for the Egyptian Pyramid.
(D) Theories regarding the ~~mysterious development~~ of pyramid architecture

강의는 주로 무엇에 대한 것인가?

(A) 기자의 대 피라미드 건축과 ~~구조~~에 대한 면밀한 분석
(B) 현대식 3D모델링을 이용한 Jean-Pierre Houdin 이 제시한 혁신적인 아이디어
(C) 이집트 피라미드에 사용된 불가사의한 건축기술 뒤에 감춰진 설명들
(D) 피라미드 건축이 ~~미스터리하게 발견된~~ 것에 대한 이론들*

Main Idea 교수는 강의 도입부에서 'Let's look at how the pyramid might have been built.(피라미드 건설을 가능하게 했을지도 모르는 방법을 살펴봅시다)'라고 말하며 앞으로의 주제가 이집트 피라미드의 불가사의한 건축기술에 대해 살펴볼 것임을 밝히고 있으므로 정답은 (C)가 된다. (A)는 피라미드 구조를 분석하는 것이 아니라 건축과정을 설명하는 이론들을 살펴보는 것이므로 오답이다. (B)는 내용은 맞으나 너무 지엽적인 사실을 다룸으로써 전체 주제로 보기엔 어려움이 있고 (D)는 피라미드 건축술이 발달된 것에 대한 언급이 본문에 없으므로 각각 오답이다.

07 Why was the theory of ramps so popular amongst Egyptologists?

(A) In the ancient times, ramps were able to transport heavy objects ~~efficiently~~.
(B) Ramps were the most common devices used to haul overwhelmingly large objects at the time.
(C) Evidence that pointed towards ramps was ~~provided by renowned Egyptologists~~.
(D) Ramps were the ~~only device~~ of the ancient times for transportation of stone.

왜 경사로 이론이 이집트학자들 사이에서 무척 인기가 있었는가?

(A) 고대에는 경사로들이 무거운 물체들을 ~~효율적으로~~ 운반할 수 있었다
(B) 경사로는 그 당시 부담스럽게 큰 물체들을 운반하는데 가장 흔하게 사용된 도구이다.
(C) 경사로에 대한 증거들이 ~~저명한 이집트학자들에 의해 제공되었다~~.
(D) 경사로는 고대에 돌을 운반하는데 사용되었던 ~~유일한 도구이다~~. *

Detail (Reason) 이집트학자들이 경사로 이론을 지지한 이유를 보면 Using Herodotus' records, and other sources, Egyptologists came up with the theory that the ancient Egyptians used ramps to transport the massive stone blocks, as they were the main devices for lifting heavy materials at the time.(Herodotus가 남긴 기록들과 다른 정보들을 보면, 이집트학자들은 고대 이집트인들이 경사로를 사용해서 거대한 석조 덩어리들을 운반했다고 생각했는데, 그것이 당시에 무거운 물체를 들어올리는데 주로 사용된 장치였거든요.)에서 경사로가 무거운 물건을 운반하는데 그 당시 가장 주요하게 쓰인 장치였기 때문이므로 (B)가 정답이다. (A)는 효율적이라는 말은 언급이 없었으므로, (C)는 경사로에 기록을 남긴 사람은 그리스 역사학자이므로 각각 오답이다. (D) 또한 경사로가 무거운 물체를 운반하는데 사용된 유일한 도구라는 말은 본문에 나와있지 않으므로 정답이 될 수 없다.

TEST 2   Set 1-2   Lecture 1
Mysteries of the Egyptian Pyramid

08 According to the lecture, why was the suggestion of spiral ramps flawed?

(A) Because they took longer to build and ruined the aesthetic aspect of the pyramids.
(B) Because they lacked sturdiness and made it too challenging for the workers to transport stone.
(C) Because they ruined the viewing angles and potentially risked brittle composition. *
(D) Because they ruined the builders' ability to utilize their measuring tools and made it too difficult to convey stone blocks.

강의에 의하면, 왜 나선형 경사로 이론 제안이 문제가 되었는가?

(A) 왜냐하면 그것들은 피라미드를 건설하는데 더 오랜 시간이 들게 했고 미적인 부분을 망쳤기 때문이다.
(B) 왜냐하면 그것들은 견고성이 부족해서 건설 노동자들이 돌을 운반할 때 어렵게 만들었기 때문이다.
(C) 왜냐하면 그것들은 바라보는 각도를 방해해서 건물이 잠정적으로 불안정한 구조를 가지게 했다. *
(D) 왜냐하면 그것들은 건축자들이 측정도구를 사용하는데 방해를 해서 돌 블럭들을 운반하기 어렵게 만들었기 때문이다.

Detail (Problem)   나선형 경사로 이론은, First, it would have ruined the builders' external sightlines. Because, they used ropes to measure, the ancient Egyptians needed clear lines of vision to check how precisely the blocks were layered.(첫째, 건축자들의 외부 시야를 방해했을 거에요. 왜냐하면, 고대 이집트인들은 밧줄을 사용해서 측정을 했기 때문에, 석조 블록들이 얼마나 정확하게 놓여져 있는지 확인하기 위해서는 시야가 잘 보여야 했죠.)이 문제점이므로 (D)가 정답이다. (A)는 피라미드의 미적인 부분을 망쳤다는 말은 언급되어 있지 않고, (B)는 견고성이 부적한 것이 아니라 코너를 돌 때 떨어질 위험이 있어 돌 운반을 어렵게 한다고 했으므로 잘못 기술되어 각각 오답이다. (C)는 나선형 경사로가 바라보는 각도를 방해하는 것은 맞지만 그로 인해 피라미드의 구조가 불안정해진다는 말은 언급이 없으므로 오답이다.

09 Why does the professor mention mountain roads in the lecture?

(A) To explain the vulnerability of using mountain roads
(B) To emphasize the great height of the external ramps used to construct the pyramids *
(C) To correlate the similarity of mountain roads and spiral ramps
(D) To describe the differences between spiral ramps and roads

왜 강의에서 교수는 산 도로에 대해 언급하는가?

(A) 산 도로들을 이용하는 것에 대한 취약성을 설명하려고
(B) 피라미드를 건설하는데 사용되는 외부 경사로의 높이를 강조하려고 *
(C) 산 도로와 나선형 경사로의 유사점을 연관시키려고
(D) 나선형 경사로와 도로의 차이점을 묘사하려고

Inference (Purpose)   교수가 산 도로를 설명하는 부분을 보면, I was just about to explain that. Spiral ramps can be compared to the winding roads built on the sides of mountains. You know that cars driving along these roads risk falling off. In much the same way, workers could have easily stumbled off the side of an external spiral ramp.(그 점에 대해 막 설명하려고 했어요. 나선형 경사로는 마치 산의 모서리에 도로를 돌아서 내는 것에 비교될 수 있어요. 여러분도 알듯이 이런 길을 달리는 차는 추락할 위험이 있죠. 이와 거의 비슷하게 건설하는 사람들이 외부 나선형 경사로에서 떨어질 수 있었을 거에요.)에서 나선형 경사로가 산 주변에 도로들을 건설하는 과정과 비슷하다는 것을 언급함으로써 둘 사이의 상관관계를 설명하는 것으로 (C)가 정답이다. (A)는 산 도로를 이용하는 것에 대한 취약점이 언급되어 있지만 질문에 대한 답은 아니며, (B)는 외부 경사로의 높이가 아니라 단점을 설명하는 것이므로 각각 오답이다. (D)는 또한 경사로와 도로의 차이점이 아닌 공통점을 보여주기 위한 것이므로 오답이다.

10 According to the lecture, what were the conveniences of internal ramps?

강의에 의하면, 내부 경사로의 편리한 점은 무엇인가?

Click on 2 answers

2개의 답을 고르시오.

(A) They did ~~not require as much time~~ to be built as straight ramps.
(B) **They provided safety for the workers around the corners when transporting stone blocks.**
(C) They could also ~~serve as routes~~ for the laborers when they were building pyramids from within. *
(D) **Their construction was more efficient because they eventually became a part of the pyramid.**

(A) 직선 경사로에 비해 건설하는데 ~~많은 시간이 걸리지 않는다.~~
(B) **그것들은 석조 블록을 운반할 때 코너 주변에 있는 노동자들에게 안전을 제공한다.**
(C) 그것들은 또한 피라미드를 내부에서 지을 때 노동자들에게 ~~길로써의 역할도~~ 할 수 있다. *
(D) 그것들은 피라미드의 일부가 되었기 때문에 건설이 효율적이었다.

Detail (Advantage) 내부경사로의 편리한 점에 대해 언급한 부분을 보면, S: Ah, so the internal ramps provided safety for the workers! P: Exactly.(S:아, 그러니까 내부 경사로가 건설자들에게 안전을 제공하게 되는 거군요. P: 바로 그거예요)와 P: Yes, they do indeed, but internal ramps are different. They would basically become a part of the pyramid. Since they weren't going to be taken down after construction, they could simply be sealed off after use, significantly conserving materials and labor.(네, 사실이에요, 하지만 내부경사로는 달라요. 그것들은 기본적 으로 피라미드의 일부가 되는 거에요. 건설이 끝난 후에 없어지지 않기 때문에, 사용 후에 그냥 봉인될 수 있어서, 훨씬 더 많은 노동력과 자원을 보존할 수 있는 것이죠.)에서 노동자의 안전을 위해서라고 말한 (B)와 피라미드의 일부로 포함되기 때문에 건설이 효율적이라고 말한 (D)가 정답이다. (A)와 (C)는 본문에 언급되지 않은 내용이므로 각각 오답이다.

11 Listen again to part of the lecture. Then answer the question.

강의의 일부를 다시 듣고, 질문에 답하시오.

S: Why would there be treasures in the pharaohs' tombs? Wouldn't that be kind of a waste?
P: Well, yes, but the ancient Egyptians considered the afterlife to be eternal, so they wanted to be prepared for it. To do this, they took their most precious belongings with them. After living a life of luxury, they were the icing on the cake.

S: 왜 파라오들은 자신의 무덤 안에 보물을 두었던거죠? 그건 일종의 낭비 아닌가요?
P: 네, 맞아요. 하지만 고대 이집트인들은 사후세계가 영원하다고 생각했어요. 그래서 그들은 그것에 대한 준비를 하고 싶어했죠. 이를 위해, 자신들의 가장 귀중한 소지품들 함께 가지고 간 거예요. 사치스러운 삶을 산 이후에, 그건 금상첨화였지요.

What does the professor imply when he says this? 🎧

이 말을 할 때 교수는 무엇을 암시하는가?

P: After living a life of luxury, they were the icing on the cake.

P: 사치스러운 삶을 산 이후에, 그건 금상첨화였지요.

(A) **He implies that a pharaoh's belongings were meant to make the afterlife even better.**
(B) It was their belief that a pharaoh's belongings were to be reserved for him only.
(C) He is explaining that a pharaoh's treasures were sacred and they were to be used after death.
(D) It was ~~only natural~~ for a pharaoh's goods to be buried with him ~~due to tradition~~.

(A) **그는 파라오의 소지품들이 내세를 더욱 풍족하게 하기 위한 목적을 가지고 있음을 암시한다.**
(B) 파라오의 소지품들은 오직 그만을 위해 보관되는 것이라는 것이 이집트인들의 믿음이었다.
(C) 그는 파라오의 보물들을 ~~신성해서~~ 사후에 사용되기 위함 이었다고 설명하고 있다.
(D) 파라오의 물건들이 그와 함께 묻히는 것은 ~~전통으로써 무척 자연스러운 일이었다.~~ *

Inference (Headset) 교수가 말한 icing on the cake은 케익에 꼭 필요한 건 아니지만 보충적으로 장식해서 케익을 돋보이게 해주는 크림을 나타내는 말로, 파라오의 무덤에 부장된 귀중한 보물들이 사후세계로 가는데 필수적이진 않지만 그곳에서도 쓸 수 있는 보조적인 사치품들을 빗대어 말한 것이다. 따라서 이런 의미를 전달하는 (A)가 정답이다. (B)는 맞는 내용이나 질문에 대한 답이 아니므로, (C)와 (D)는 파라오의 보물들이 신성하다는 것이나 물건들이 파라오와 함께 묻히는 것이 전통이라는 말은 본문에 언급되지 않아 각각 오답이다.

TEST 2 Set 1-3   Lecture 2: Coral Reef Destruction

문단 주제	본문 내용	해 석
	Listen to part of a lecture in a marine biology class. The professor is discussing coral reef destruction by crown-of-thorns starfish.	해양생물학 강의의 일부를 들으시오. 교수는 악마불가사리에 의한 산호초의 파괴에 대해 논의하고 있습니다.
산호와 악마불가사리에 대한 정보	The Great Barrier Reef, the world's largest reef system, is home to more than 400 coral, 1,500 fish, and 200 bird species. The reefs are made of living things called coral polyps... which are organisms that attach themselves to the ocean floor in large colonies. [Q17] **Before it was fully researched, scientists thought that coral was, uh, strangely shaped rock, and I don't blame them. Coral doesn't move and, therefore, provides homes for the local fish species among their tough calcium-carbonate skeletons.** Recently, the coral population of the Great Barrier Reef has been decreasing at an alarming rate. It turns out that a species of starfish, the crown-of-thorns, has had a sudden population increase and is preying upon the coral, threatening the reef population. This species got its name from the poisonous spines that cover its body. As the second largest starfish in the world, they can grow up to a meter across, and eat coral by climbing atop the polyps and releasing digestive enzymes. These break down and liquefy the coral, which the starfish can then absorb into its stomach. Scientists have come up with several theories to explain the sudden explosion of the starfish population.	세상에서 가장 큰 산호초 지대인 그레이트배리어 리프(The Great Barrier Reef)는 400종 이상의 산호, 1,500종 이상의 물고기, 200종 이상의 새들의 서식지에요. 암초들은 산호폴립이라고 불리는 살아 있는 것들에 의해 만들어지는데… 이들은 무리를 지어 해양 바닥에 자신을 붙이고 사는 생물체들이에요. [Q17] **완벽하게 연구되기 전에는, 과학자들은 산호들이… 음, 이상한 모양의 바위라고 생각했는데요, 전 그들을 탓하지 않아요. 산호들은 움직이지 않기 때문에, 그로 인해, 탄산칼슘으로된 그들의 단단한 뼈대 사이에 그 지역에 사는 물고기를 위한 서식지를 제공하죠.** 최근에, 그레이트배리어리프의 산호 개체수는 급속도로 줄어들고 있어요. 이는 악마불가사리라는 어떤 한 불가사리 종의 가시관불가사리의 개체수가 급격히 증가해서 산호를 먹어치우며 산호 초의 개체수에 위협을 가해 왔다는 사실이 밝혀졌죠. 이 종은 몸을 덮고 있는 독성의 가시로부터 이름을 얻었는데요. 세계에서 두 번째로 큰 불가사리로, 1미터 크기까지 자랄 수 있고, 폴립 꼭대기에 올라가서 소화 효소를 분비해 산호를 먹을 수 있어요. 이 효소들은 산호를 파괴하고 액화시키는데, 불가사리는 이것을 자신의 위로 흡수하죠. 과학자들은 불가사리의 개체 수가 갑자기 증가한 이유를 설명하기 위해 몇 가지 이론들을 제시했어요.
자연적인 원인	Their first explanation is that the increase in the starfish population doesn't really have a specific reason, but is a natural phenomenon. Like many species' populations and the cyclical variations in the Earth's temperature, the increase in the starfish population and decrease in the coral population may simply be part of a natural cycle that occurs in the ecosystem. [Q13] **Um... Due to the lack of scuba technology before the 1960s, studying organisms on the ocean floor was difficult, but in the last few decades we've already seen three major outbreaks of the crown-of-thorns starfish.** This is one of the reasons why scientists are inclined to think that coral destruction is mostly natural... This claim also has more scientific grounds. We know that a crown-of-thorns starfish produces around a billion eggs in its lifetime. So let's say there is an extremely slight change in the conditions, such as water temperature or	첫번째 설명은 불가사리의 개체수 증가가 실제로 특정한 이유가 있어서가 아닌 자연현상인거에요. 다른 종들의 개체수와 지구 온도의 주기적인 자연 변화처럼, 불가사리의 개체수 증가와 산호 개체수의 감소는 아마 단순히 생태계에서 발생하는 자연 순환의 일부일지도 모른다는 거죠. [Q13] **음… 1960대 이전에는 잠수기술의 부족으로, 해저의 생물들을 연구하는 것이 어려웠어요. 하지만 지난 몇십 년 동안 벌써 우리는 악마불가사리가 세 번이나 급증하는 것을 보았죠.** 바로 이것때문에 과학자들이 산호 파괴가 대부분 자연적이라고 생각하는 경향이 있어요… 이런 주장은 또한 더 많은 과학적 근거를 가지고 있는데요. 우리는 악마불가사리가 일생동안 약 10억개의 알을 낳는다는 걸 알고 있어요. 자, 여기 물의 온도나 혹은 염분처럼 극히 미세한 변화가 일어났다고 칩시다. 이는 불가사리가 생존할 수 있는 확률을 1% 증가시키죠…

salinity, which results in a 1% increase in the survival chances of the starfish... That yields 10 million more starfish! With 10 million more individuals than the previous generation, the starfish will mate and reproduce even more, causing a domino effect, with the population increasing in each successive generation. As you can see, even the slightest change can theoretically bring about a huge increase in starfish population, so natural fluctuations seem a pretty believable cause.

The second hypothesis cites predator decline. Due to their thorns, crown-of-thorns starfish actually don't have many predators. One of the few is the giant triton. When these snails smell a starfish, they chase after it and attach themselves to the starfish, stabbing it with their radula. Um... this is kind of like a tongue, but is actually made of chitin, and is toothed, like a saw. So once the triton has made an opening in the starfish, it produces saliva that paralyzes the starfish, and it slowly feeds on its victim. [Q14] **Fortunately for the starfish, these snails were hunted for their ornamental shells so greatly that their population decreased to unsustainable levels around 1969.** Even after 40 years of government protection, the population hasn't bounced back enough to pose a threat to the crown-of-thorns starfish.

Okay, that brings us to the final hypothesis. This one may seem strange, but it suggests that human activities on land, such as deforestation, are affecting starfish populations. Deforestation for farmland, which occurs on 80% of the land adjacent to the Great Barrier Reef, makes the land vulnerable to sediment runoff and flooding, so during the rainy season fertilizers and organic materials get washed into rivers and make their way to the Great Barrier Reef. When rivers flood the land, even more sediment-filled freshwater is discharged into the sea. This affects the starfish population in a number of ways. [Q15] **First, fertilizers contain nitrogen and phosphorous, which cause massive algae and plankton blooms, providing copious nourishment for the crown-of-thorns starfish larvae. It also dilutes the coastal water, lowering its salinity.** Since starfish larvae cannot osmoregulate, ummm... regulate their salinity with regards to the environment, sea water is normally too salty for many of them to survive. When river water dilutes the ocean water, however, their chances of survival increase. Scientists believe that the combination of these two effects

Set 1-3 Lecture 2 Coral Reef Destruction

may explain the starfish population explosions.

So... today we've talked about how crown-of-thorns starfish affect the Great Barrier Reef negatively, but I should also mention that they have useful functions, too. First, they tend to feed on rapidly growing coral species. **[Q16] These coral species are kept in check by the starfish, which allows slower-growing coral a better chance of survival. This helps maintain species diversity on the reef.** Further, we also know that the starfish is a natural part of the ecosystem, and is preyed upon by other species, such as the giant triton. Knowing that some species have unpredictable effects on their ecosystems, perhaps it's better that we take care not to have too great an influence over the starfish populations.

서 불가사리 개체수의 폭증을 설명하는 것이라고 믿고 있어요.

그래서.... 오늘 우리는 어떻게 악마불가사리가 그 레이트배리어리프에 안좋은 영향을 끼치는지에 대해 얘기했는데요, 하지만 그들은 쓸모있는 역할도 가지고 있다는걸 언급하고 싶네요. 우선, 그들은 상대적으로 빠르게 자라는 산호를 먹는 경향이 있어요. **[Q16]이 산호종들은 불가사리에 의해 끊임없이 견제를 당하고, 이로 인해 느리게 자라는 산호들은 자신의 생존율을 높이게 되는 거죠. 이것은 산호초의 다양성을 유지하는데 도움이 되구요.** 이 외에도, 우리는 불가사리가 생태계의 자연적 부분이고, 앞서 말했던 거대트리톤고둥같은 다른 종들에게 먹힌다는걸 알고 있죠. 특정 종들이 우리가 예측할 수 없는 방법으로 생태계에 영향을 준다는걸 알고 있기 때문에, 인간이 불가사리 개체 수에 너무 많은 영향을 주지 않으려고 노력하는 것이 아마 더 나을거에요.

12
What is the main topic of the lecture?

(A) Suggested causes of crown-of-thorns starfish outbreaks
(B) ~~Problems caused~~ by the increasing number of crown-of-thorns starfish *
(C) Hypotheses on ~~how to protect~~ coral on the Great Barrier Reef
(D) Human influence on the ecosystems of the Great Barrier Reef

강의의 주제는 무엇인가?

(A) 악마불가사리의 급증에 대해 제시된 원인들
(B) 악마불가사리의 개체수 증가에 의해 발생한 문제점들*
(C) 그레이트배리어리프에 있는 산호를 보호할 방법에 관한 가설들
(D) 그레이트배리어리프의 생태계에 끼친 인간의 영향

Main Idea 이 강의는 악마불가사리의 개체수가 급증한 원인에 관한 가설들을 하나씩 나열하면서 설명하고 있으므로 정답은 (A)이다. (B)와 (C)는 강의에 언급된 내용이 아니며, (D)는 제시한 가설 중 하나일 뿐 주제가 아니므로 각각 오답이다.

13
What does the professor imply about crown-of-thorns starfish outbreaks?

(A) The outbreaks are ~~triggered by~~ increases in the coral population.*
(B) Researchers believe that outbreaks occurred even before the 1960s due to their occurrence recently.
(C) Their reproduction rate is ~~solely responsible~~ for the starfish outbreaks.
(D) The coral population has been threatened ~~even without a starfish outbreak~~.

악마불가사리의 급증에 대해 교수는 무엇을 암시하는가?

(A) 개체수의 급증은 산호 개체수의 증가에 의해 ~~야기되었다~~. *
(B) 연구자들은 최근에 있었던 급증으로 보아 1960년대 이전에 불가사리의 급증이 있어왔다고 믿고 있다.
(C) 그들의 번식 속도는 오로지 불가사리의 급증과 ~~관련이 있다~~.
(D) 산호의 개체수는 ~~불가사리의 급증이 없어도~~ 위협을 받아왔다.

Interference (Imply) Um... Due to lack of scuba technology before the 1960s, studying organisms on the ocean floor was difficult, but in the last few decades we've already seen three major outbreaks of the crown-of-thorns starfish.(음· 1960년대 이전에는 잠수 기술의 부족으로, 해저의 생물들을 연구하는 것이 어려웠어요, 하지만 지난 몇십 년 동안 벌써 우리는 악마불가사리가 세번이나 급증하는 것을 보았죠.)에서 보면, 1960년대 이전에도 불가사리 급증이 있었지만 스쿠버 장비의 부족으로 연구하는 것이 어려웠고, 최근에 세번 급증하는 것을 보았다고 했으므로 정답은 (B)임을 유추할 수 있다. (A)는 불가사리의 급증은 산호 개체수의 감소를 야기하는 것이며, (C)는 번식속도가 오로지 불가사리 급증과 관련이 있다는 것은 본문 내용과 다르므로 각각 오답이다. (D)는 또한 강의내용에 언급된 적이 없으므로 오답이다.

TEST 2　　Set 1-3　　Lecture 2
Coral Reef Destruction

14 According to the lecture, why is the giant triton no longer a threat?

(A) Because most of them ~~get stung~~ by the starfish's venomous spines
(B) Because they were caught for aesthetic purposes
(C) Because they are ~~slow and cannot catch up~~ with the crown-of-thorns starfish *
(D) Because ~~a species of fish that preys on the starfish was introduced~~ to the Great Barrier Reef

강의에 따르면, 왜 거대트리톤고둥이 더 이상 위협이 되지 않는가?

(A) 그들 대부분은 불가사리의 독성이 있는 가시에 ~~찔리기 때문에~~
(B) 그들이 미적인 목적으로 잡혔기 때문에
(C) 그들이 ~~느려서 악마불가사리를 따라잡지 못하기 때문에~~ *
(D) 불가사리를 잡아먹는 한 종의 물고기가 그레이트 배리어리프에 ~~유입되었기 때문에~~

Detail (Reason)　본문에서 거대트리톤고둥이 나오는 내용을 보면, Fortunately for the starfish, these snails were hunted for their ornamental shells so greatly that their population decreased to unsustainable levels around 1969.(불가사리에겐 다행히도, 이런 고둥들은 장식용 껍질을 노린 사냥을 꽤 많이 당해서, 1969년경엔 정부의 보호가 필요할 정도로 그 개체수가 줄어들었어요.)에서 트리톤고둥은 미적인 목적으로 많이 잡혀서 개체수가 급격히 줄어들었음을 알 수 있으므로 (B)가 정답이다. (A), (C), (D)는 본문에 언급된 내용이 아니므로 각각 오답이다.

---

15 Why does the professor mention fertilizers with nitrogen and phosphorous?

(A) To explain that starfish larvae feed on ~~nutrients in the runoff sediment~~ *
(B) To provide examples of ~~chemicals that maintain ocean water salinity~~
(C) To imply that human influence was a factor in starfish population increase
(D) To suggest a ~~possible solution to water contamination~~

왜 교수는 질소와 인을 함유한 비료를 언급하는가?

(A) 불가사리의 유충이 ~~빗물에 쓸려온 침전물의 영양분을 섭취한다는 것을~~ 설명하기 위해 *
(B) ~~바닷물의 염분을 유지하는 화학물질의~~ 예를 들기 위해
(C) 인간의 영향이 불가사리 개체 수 증가의 요인임을 암시하기 위해
(D) ~~수질오염에 대한 가능한 해결책을~~ 제시하기 위해

Inference (Purpose)　교수가 비료를 언급한 부분을 보면, First, fertilizers contain nitrogen and phosphorous, which cause massive algae and plankton blooms, providing copious nourishment for the crown-of-thorns starfish larvae.(우선, 비료는 질소와 인을 포함하고 있는데, 대량의 조류와 플랑크톤을 증가시켜서 악마불가사리 유충에게 영양분을 제공해요.)에서 알 수 있듯이 인간이 사용하는 비료가 악마불가사리의 개체 수에 영향을 미친다는 말이므로 정답은 (C)이다. (A)는 침전물 안에 있는 영양분이 아닌 침전물에 의해 쓸려 온 비료에 있는 질소와 인이 대량의 해조류와 플랑크톤을 증가시켜 이것이 불가사리 유충에게 영양분을 제공하는 것이므로, (B)와 (D)는 언급된 적이 없으므로 각각 오답이다.

16

What is one way the crown-of-thorns starfish benefit the coral?

(A) They keep the coral from occupying too much of the ocean floor. *
(B) They release nutrients when they die which helps coral grow.
(C) They protect uninfested coral patches from other coral predators.
(D) They allow certain coral types to compete more effectively.

악마불가사리가 산호에게 이득이 되는 한 가지 방법은 무엇인가?

(A) 산호가 해저를 너무 많이 점령하는 것을 막는다. *
(B) 불가사리가 죽을 때 나오는 영양분이 산호가 자라는데 도움을 준다.
(C) 산호무리들이 다른 산호 천적으로부터 점령당하지 않게 보호한다.
(D) 특정 산호들을 더 효율적으로 경쟁하도록 도와준다.

Detail (Advantage) These coral species are kept in check by the starfish, which allows slower-growing coral a better chance of survival. This helps maintain species diversity on the reef.(이 산호 종들은 불가사리에 의해 끊임없이 견제를 당하고, 이로 인해 느리게 자라는 산호들은 자신의 생존율을 높이게 되는 거죠. 이것은 산호의 다양성을 유지하는데 도움이 되구요.)에서 보면 불가사리는 산호 종들간의 경쟁력을 높여주는 것이므로 정답은 (D)이다. (A), (C), (B)는 강의내용에 언급된 적이 없으므로 각각 오답이다.

17

Listen again to part of the lecture. Then answer the question.

P: Before it was fully researched, scientists thought that coral was... uh, strangely shaped rock, and I don't blame them. Coral doesn't move and, therefore, provides homes for the local fish species among their tough calcium-carbonate skeletons.

What does the professor mean when she says this :🎧

강의의 일부를 다시 듣고, 질문에 답하시오.

P: 그들이 완전히 연구되기 전에는, 과학자들은 산호들이… 음, 이상한 모양의 바위라고 생각했는데요, 전 그들을 탓하지 않아요. 산호들은 움직이지 않기 때문에, 그로 인해, 탄산칼슘으로 된 그들의 단단한 뼈대 사이 에 그 지역에 사는 물고기를 위한 서식지를 제공하죠.

교수가 이 말을 할 때 무엇을 의미하는가?:

and I don't blame them.

전 그들을 탓하지 않아요.

(A) The early misconception of coral was easy to understand.
(B) Scientists were responsible for people thinking that coral is a form of rock. *
(C) Coral's strange appearance causes confusion for the professor.
(D) Scientists proved that coral was made of living organisms.

(A) 산호에 대한 초기의 오해는 쉽게 수긍할 수 있다.
(B) 산호가 암석의 한 종류라고 사람들이 생각하는 것에 대해 과학자들에게 책임이 있다. *
(C) 산호의 기이한 생김새가 교수에게 혼란을 주고 있다.
(D) 과학자들은 산호들이 살아있는 유기체임을 증명했다.

Inference (Headset) 교수는 연구 초기에는 과학자들도 오해할 정도로 산호의 겉모양이 바위를 닮았다는 말을 하고 싶은 것이므로 (A)가 정답임을 알 수 있다. (B)는 교수가 과학자들의 책임을 말하기 위한 것이 아니고, (C)는 산호의 겉모양이 혼란을 준 사람은 교수가 아닌 과학자이며, (D)는 본문에 언급되지 않은 내용이므로 각각 오답이다.

TEST 2

Set 2-1 Conversation: Whale Breathing Patterns

문단주제	본문내용	해 석
	Listen to a conversation between a student and a professor.	교수와 학생의 대화를 들으시오.
	S: Hello, Professor McGee.	S: McGee교수님 안녕하세요.
	P: Oh. Hello, Kevin. Come on in and have a seat. What's on your mind?	P: 오, 안녕, Kevin. 어서 와서 앉아. 무슨 일이니?
	S: [Q1] Well, I was looking for your insight into a problem I've been having... I mean... academically.	S: [Q1] 그게… 제가 갖고 있는 문제에 대한 교수님의 의견을 듣고 싶어서요… 그러니까… 학술적인 건데요.
	P: Oh, Okay. Shoot.	P: 그래. 뭔지 말해보렴.
	S: Well, I was researching whale breathing patterns during migration... and...	S: 음, 전 고래가 이동하는 동안의 호흡패턴에 대해 조사하고 있었는데요… 그리고…
	P: Let me stop you right there. You do know that different whales have different breathing patterns, right?	P: 잠깐만. 고래들마다 각기 다른 호흡패턴을 가지고 있다는 건 알거야, 그렇지?
	S: [Q3] I know that baleen whales have two blowholes while toothed whales only have one.	S: [Q3] 수염고래들은 두 개의 숨구멍을 가진 반면 이빨고래들은 하나만 갖고 있다는 걸 알긴 하죠…
	P: Even though all whales are mammals and have the fundamental characteristics of mammals, certain attributes differ completely according to their specific species.	P: 비록 모든 고래들이 포유류이고, 포유류의 기본적인 특징을 갖고 있다해도, 특정한 세부 특징들은 종에 따라 완전히 달라진단다.
	S: Uh... I'm not following.	S: 어…이해가 잘 안가요.
	P: [Q2] Let me put it this way. Although humans are all mammals, we can be biologically differentiated by ethnicity, gender, and even age. What I'm trying to say is... you should pick a specific type of whale.	P: [Q2] 이렇게 설명해볼게. 우리 인간들은 포유류에 속하지만 민족성, 성별, 그리고 혹은 심지어 나이에 따라 생물학적으로 서로 다르지. 내가 하고자 하는 말은… 특정한 하나의 고래종을 고르라는 거야.
	S: I've already done that. I started my report on the bowhead whale.	S: 벌써 그렇게 했는걸요. 북극고래에 대해 리포트를 쓰기 시작했어요.
	P: Ah, the bowhead whale. I believe they're baleen whales. Correct?	P: 아, 북극고래 말이구나. 그것들은 수염고래에 속하는 걸로 알고 있는데, 맞니?
	S: Of course. Well... I was wondering what about the anatomy and breathing patterns of whales allows them to migrate over such great distances without taking short breaths.	S: 맞아요. 음… 저는 고래들이 그렇게 먼 거리를 이동하는 중에도 숨을 쉬지 않고 움직이는 것을 가능케 하는 신체구조와 호흡패턴에 대해서 궁금해 하고 있어요.
	P: Well... what's interesting about bowhead whales is that unlike other whales, they can only stay submerged for up to 40 minutes per dive.	P: 음… 북극고래에 대한 흥미로운 사실은… 다른 고래들과는 달리, 한 번 물에 들어가있는 동안 최대 40분 동안만 잠수할 수 있다는 거야.
	S: [Q3] 40 minutes? Isn't that a really long time? What about other whales?	S: [Q3] 40분이요? 엄청 긴 시간 아닌가요? 다른 고래들은 어떤데요?
	P: Well... again, it depends on the whale species, and their reason for submerging. How long whales remain underwater when they are feeding or when they have no other choice but to remain underwater differs completely.species can stay a kilometer underwater for 90 to inutes.	P: 음… 또 그건 고래종에 따라 그리고 잠수 목적에 따라 다르단다. 얼마나 오래 잠수하냐는 먹이를 구할 때와 다른 선택의 여지없이 물속에만 있어야 할 때 완전히 다르지. 어떤 종들은 1킬로미터 아래의 수중에서 90분에서 120분 가량 잠수할수 있거든.

S: [Q5] That is so fascinating. Well... I think we got sidetracked... What I was originally wondering was, biologically speaking, what enables whales to stay underwater for such a long time?

P: Well... There are a few things that enable them to stay underwater for so long, but some of them are highly theoretical. The first is the most obvious. Can you guess what it is?

S: Uh... their size?

P: Close. It's actually their ability to physically hold large amounts of oxygen, in their bloodstreams.

S: [Q3] Aha, I see. What's another factor?

P: Well, another factor is a very unique ability that whales possess. They actually have the ability to reduce the amount of oxygen they need while they are submerged. They can reduce the amount of oxygen delivered to the body parts they aren't using during their dives in order to use it more efficiently.

S: Wow, I wasn't aware of that.

P: Actually a few years ago, a group of biologists at a university fitted cameras to whales, including a 100 ton blue whale. [Q4-1] According to them, whales expel air from their lungs shortly after diving so they can stop floating. The rest is squeezed out by increasing water pressure. [Q4-2] Although they lose oxygen, they are able to remain underwater by releasing more oxygen from their blood and their muscles. The secret is in the relaxation of their muscles by simply thrusting themselves down with a few powerful strokes, and then continuing to glide down...

S: Ok. I think that's the kind of information that can help me along with my research...

P: I'm glad to hear that. I'm always happy to help.

S: [Q5] 정말 흥미롭네요. 음… 잠깐 얘기가 다른 데로 샌 것 같은데요… 제가 원래 궁금했던 건, 생물학적으로 봤을때, 무엇이 고래들을 그렇게 오랫동안 잠수할 수 있게 하는 거죠?

P: 그건… 오랫동안 잠수를 가능케 하는 것들이 몇 가지 있는데, 그 중 일부는 매우 이론적이야. 첫 번째 것은 가장 당연한 건데. 뭔지 한번 맞춰볼래?

S: 어… 크기인가요?

P: 거의 맞췄어. 사실은 아주 많은 양의 산소를 지닐 수 있는 고래의 신체적인 능력이야, 그들의 혈류에 보관하는 거지.

S: [Q3] 아하, 알겠어요… 다른 요인은 뭐죠?

P: 음, 다른 요인은 고래들이 가진 매우 독특한 능력이야. 그들은 실제로 잠수하는 동안 필요한 산소의 양을 줄이는 능력을 갖고 있지. 고래들은 산소를 더욱 능률적으로 사용할 수 있도록 신체부분으로 전달되는 산소의 양 중에서 잠수하는 동안에는 필요하지 않은 양을 줄일 수 있어.

S: 와우, 전 그건 몰랐어요.

P: 사실 몇 년 전에, 어떤 대학에서 한 그룹의 생물학자들이 무게가 100톤인 흰긴수염고래를 포함해서 고래들에게 카메라를 설치한 적이 있었지. [Q4-1] 그들에 의하면, 고래들은 물속에 들어간 후 부력을 없애기 위해 허파로부터 공기를 내뿜는다고 하더구나. 나머지는 증가하는 수압에 의해 짜내어지고 말야. [Q4-2] 고래들은 산소를 잃더라도, 자신의 피와 근육으로부터 산소를 더 방출해 물속에 있을 수 있는 거지. 잠수의 비밀은 단지 몇 번의 힘찬 일격과 함께 아래로 이동한 후 근육을 이완시켜 아래로 계속 하강하는 거야.

S: 오케이. 그게 바로 제 연구에 도움을 줄 수 있는 정보인거 같아요.

P: 그 말을 들으니 기쁘구나. 필요하면 언제든지 도와줄게.

TEST 2

Set 2 - 1 | Conversation
Whale Breathing Patterns

01 Why does the student go to talk to his professor?

(A) To ask about ~~different diving patterns~~ of whales during migration *
(B) **To clear up some of the difficulties he was having regarding whales.**
(C) To ask for ~~definitions of some of the names~~ of different whale species
(D) To talk about why he got a ~~low grade on the midterm exam~~ about whales

왜 학생은 교수에게 얘기하러 갔는가?

(A) 이동 중 고래의 ~~각기 다른 잠수 패턴~~ 에 대해 묻기 위해*
(B) 고래에 관한 그의 궁금증들을 해결하기 위해
(C) 여러 종의 고래의 ~~명칭에 대한 정의~~를 물어보기 위해
(D) 고래에 대한 ~~중간고사의 점수가 왜 낮게 나왔는 지~~에 대해 이야기 하기 위해

Main Purpose Well, I was looking for your insight into a problem I've been having…. I mean…academically.(그게… 제가 갖고 있는 문제에 대한 교수님의 의견을 듣고 싶어서요… 그러니까… 학술적인 건데요.)에서 학생은 고래에 관해 궁금한 점들을 물어보기 위해 온 것임을 알 수 있으므로 정답은 (B)이다. (A), (C), (D)는 대화 내용에 언급되어 있지 않거나 사실과 다르므로 오답이다.

02 Why does the professor mention differences in ethnicity, gender and age?

(A) To discuss that ethnicity, gender and age ~~matter~~ in deciding the diving time of whales. *
(B) To show that gender and age ~~play vital roles in determining~~ the capacity of whale lungs.
(C) To show that even within a species there are various subtypes.
(D) To tell the student to pick whales of ~~a specific age and gender to research further~~.

왜 교수는 민족성, 성별 그리고 나이에 대해 있어서의 차이를 언급하는가?

(A) 고래의 잠수시간을 결정하는데 있어 민족성, 성별, 그리 고 나이가 ~~상관이 있음~~을 말하기 위해 *
(B) 고래의 성별과 나이가 ~~허파의 용량에 중요한 역할~~을 한 다는 것을 설명하기 위해
(C) 같은 종 내에서도 다양한 하위 부류가 있다는 것을 설 명하기 위해
(D) 학생에게 ~~특정한 나이와 성별~~의 고래를 정해서 ~~더 자세히 조사~~하라고 말하기 위해

Inference (Purpose) 교수가 언급한 부분을 살펴보면, Let me put it this way. Although humans are all mammals, we can be biologically differentiated by ethnicity, gender, and even age. What I'm trying to say is·you should pick a specific type of whale. (이렇게 설명해볼게. 우리 인간들은 포유류에 속하지만 민족성, 성별, 그리고 혹은 심지어 나이에 따라 생물학적으로 서로 다르지. 내가 하고자 하는 말은… 특정한 하나의 고래 종을 고르라는 거야)에서 교수는 같은 고래 종이더라도 그 안에서의 부류에 따라 각기 다르다는 것을 말하고자 함을 알 수 있으므로 정답은 (C)이다. (A)에서 잠수시간을 결정하는 요인과, (B)는 허파의 용량을 결정짓는 요소와, (D)에서 특정한 성별과 나이가 아닌 종류를 고르라는 것이므로 오답이다.

03 What can be inferred about the student?

(A) He already knows quite a bit about whales, but is still eager to learn more.
(B) He ~~already knows~~ that whales adjust their oxygen usage when they dive below the water. *
(C) He ~~already knows~~ that whales ~~take intermittent short breaths~~ during their migrations.
(D) He ~~already knows~~ whales travel ~~with other mammals of the opposite sex~~ during their migrations.

학생에 대해 무엇을 추론할 수 있는가?

(A) 그는 이미 고래에 대해 상당히 알고 있지만, 좀 더 배우길 원하고 있다.
(B) 그는 고래들이 잠수할 때 산소의 사용을 조정한다 는 것을 ~~아마 알고있다~~. *
(C) 그는 고래들이 물 속에서 이동 중에 ~~간헐적인 짧 은 숨을 쉰다는 것을~~ 아마 알고 있다.
(D) 그는 고래들이 이동 중에 ~~다른 성별의 포유류~~와 움직인다는 것을 ~~아마 알고 있다~~.

Inference (Infer) 대화 내용을 전반적으로 살펴보면, 학생이 고래에 대해 꽤 많이 알고 있으며, 교수에게 질문하는 것을 보면 더 많은 내용을 궁금해 한다는 사실을 알 수 있으므로 (A)가 정답이다. (B)는 학생이 교수에게 들어 알게된 사실로 이미 아는 내용이 아니고, (C)는 본문의 내용과 반대의 사실을 나타내며, (D)는 대화에 언급된 내용이 아니므로 각각 오답이다.

04 According to the professor, how do whales effectively use oxygen during their dives?

교수에 의하면, 어떻게 고래는 잠수하는 동안 산소를 효율적으로 사용하는가?

Click on 2 answers | 2개의 답을 고르시오.

(A) They intentionally release air from their lungs in order to allow themselves to dive deeper into the water.
(B) They make little use of the reserved oxygen in their muscles and blood to survive once they are in the water. *
(C) They keep their muscles loosened to ensure sufficient oxygen.
(D) They keep their oxygen distributed evenly throughout their bodies.

(A) 그들은 의도적으로 허파에서 산소를 방출해 더 깊게 물속으로 잠수할 수 있다.
(B) 그들은 물에 들어가면 생존을 위해 근육과 피에 저장해둔 산소를 ~~거의 사용하지 않는다.~~ *
(C) 그들은 충분한 양의 산소를 확보하기 위해 근육을 느슨하게 한다.
(D) 그들은 ~~신체 내부 곳곳에 산소를 고르게 분배한다.~~

Detail (Characterisitc) 교수가 고래의 산소 이용에 대해 언급한 부분을 살펴 보면, According to them, whales expel air from their lungs shortly after diving so they can stop floating. …(중략)… Although they lose oxygen, they are able to remain underwater by releasing more oxygen from their blood and their muscles. The secret is in the relaxation of their muscles by simply thrusting themselves down with a few powerful strokes, and then continuing to glide down.(그들에 의하면, 고래들은 물속에 들어간 후 부력을 없애기 위해 허파로부터 공기를 내뿜는다고 하더구나… (중략)… 고래들은 산소를 잃더라도, 자신의 피와 근육으로부터 산소를 더 방출해 물에 있을 수 있는 거지. 잠수의 비밀은 단지 몇 번의 힘찬 일격과 함께 아래로 이동한 후 아래로 계속 하강하는 거야.)에서 고래들은 의도적으로 허파로부터 산소를 더 많이 방출해서, 그리고 산소 보관을 위해 근육을 이완시키므로 정답은 (A), (C)이다. (B)는 사실과 반대이며, (D)는 언급된 내용이 아니므로 각각 오답이다.

05 Listen again to part of the conversation. Then answer the question.

S: That is so fascinating. Well… I think we got sidetracked. What I was originally wondering was, biologically speaking, what enables whales to stay underwater for such a long time?

What does the student mean when he says this : 🎧

대화의 일부를 다시 듣고, 물음에 답하시오.

S: 정말 흥미롭네요. 음… 잠깐 얘기가 다른 데로 샌거 같은데요… 제가 원래 궁금했던 건, 생물학적으로 봤을 때, 무엇이 고래들을 그렇게 오랫동안 잠수 할수 있게 하는 거죠?

학생이 다음의 말을 할 때 무엇을 의미하는가?

'I think we got to sidetracked …' | "잠깐 얘기가 다른 데로 샌거 같은데요.."

(A) To imply that the professor ~~may have misunderstood~~ the student's question *
(B) To ask ~~another~~ question that ~~wasn't~~ his initial purpose
(C) To imply that the professor may have digressed a bit
(D) To ~~show his amazement~~ at the professor's knowledge

(A) 교수가 그의 질문을 오해했을 수도 있음을 넌지시 말하기 위해*
(B) 그의 원래 목적이 ~~아닌 다른~~ 질문을 하기 위해
(C) 교수가 주제를 약간 벗어났을 수도 있음을 넌지시 말하기 위해
(D) 교수의 지식에 대한 ~~그의 놀라움을 표현하기 위해~~

Inference (Headset) sidetrack이라고 말한 것을 보아 학생이 대화의 주제가 약간 빗나갔음을 지적하는 것이므로 정답은 (C)이다.

TEST 2 Set 2-2
Lecture 1
Horse Domestication of Botai People

문단주제	본문내용	해 석
도입	**Listen to part of a lecture in an anthropology class.**	인류학 강의의 일부를 들으시오.
	P: For decades anthropologists speculated that horses were domesticated during the Bronze Age in the Eurasian steppes. However, new evidence found in Northern Kazakhstan suggests that the Botai people began to domesticate horses there nearly 1,000 years earlier than previously thought. Because this idea is so groundbreaking, there is some controversy surrounding its veracity. The fact that the Botai people had a close relationship with horses is undeniable; the question is whether these animals were domesticated. [Q6] **Today I'd like to examine some of the evidence put forth by the proponents of this theory.**	P: 지난 수 십년 동안, 인류학자들은 말이 청동기 시대에 유라시아 스텝지역에서 길들여졌다고 생각 했어요. 그러나, 북카자흐스탄에서 발견된 새로운 증거는 보타이 민족이 이전의 견해보다 거의 천년 정도 일찍 앞서 사육하기 시작 했다는걸 나타 내고 있죠. 이 견해는 너무 획기적이어서, 그것의 정확성을 둘러싸고 어느 정도의 논쟁이 있기도 해요. 보타이 민족이 말과 친밀한 관계였다는 사실은 의심할 여지가 없어요; 문제는 이 동물이 과연 길들여졌느냐 아니냐에 있죠. [Q6] 오늘 저는 이 이론의 지지자들이 제시하는 증거들을 검토해 보려고 해요.
보타이 민족은 누구인가?	P: Now before I jump right in, does anyone know who the Botai people were?	P: 본격적으로 시작하기 전에, 보타이 민족이 누구 인지 아는 사람 있나요?
	S: Well, you mentioned they originated in central Asia. Umm... weren't they also hunters?	S: 음, 그들이 중앙아시아에 기원을 뒀다고 교수님이 말씀하신 적이 있어요. 음 또한 사냥꾼이지 않았나요?
	P: Yes, the Botai were nomads who hunted game like red deer, moose, and Equus Ferus, an early cousin of the modern horse, in the steppes of modern day Kazakhstan. Horse meat was such an important food source that 90% of the remains found in excavation sites were from horses. For shelter, the Botai would build shallow campsites with one or two small mobile houses suited to their nomadic ways. This implies that they traveled in small bands and did not stay in a single area for long. This whole way of life changed drastically with the domestication of the horse. Does anyone know how?	P: 네, 보타이족은 오늘날 카자흐스탄의 스텝지역에서 붉은 사슴, 무스, 현대 말의 초기 사촌 뻘인 에쿠스 패러스 같은 먹이감을 사냥하던 유목민이었어요. 말고기는 너무나 귀중한 식량이어서 발굴지에서 발견되는 유물들의 90%가 말과 관련된 것이죠. 주거지는, 보타이족이 야트막한 야영지에 자신들의 유목방식에 적합한 한 두 개의 작고 유동성 있는 집을 세웠어요. 이것은 그들이 작은 무리로 여행하며 한 곳에 오래 머무르지 않았다는 것을 보여주죠. 이러한 삶의 방식이 말의 사육과 함께 급격하게 변했어요. 어떻게 변화했는지 아는 사람?
	S: If they bred horses as livestock, then wouldn't that provide food for more people?	S: 만약 그들이 말을 가축으로 키웠다면, 더 많은 사람들에게 식량을 공급할 수 있지 않았을까요?
	P: Exactly. The Botai domesticated horses around 6,000 years ago and gained access to a stable source of meat year-round. This led to explosive population growth and a shift from a nomadic lifestyle to a more permanent, settled one. After eliminating the need to follow the wild horses, the Botai started to build pit houses sunk into the ground to provide insulation against the cold. [Q7] **You see... what I didn't mention is the weather in Northern Kazakhstan is frigidly cold, with subzero temperatures throughout the nine-month winter. Horses proved exceptionally useful since they could survive snowstorms and forage through snow unlike most animals domesticated later, such as sheep and cattle.** The domestication of horses eventually revolutionized	P: 맞아요. 보타이족은 대략 6000년 전부터 말들을 길들여서 일년 내내 안정되게 고기를 먹을 수 있었어요. 이것은 급속한 인구 성장을 가져왔고 유목 생활을 더 지속적이고 정착된 생활방식으로 바꾸었죠. 더 이상 야생말을 쫓아다닐 필요가 없게 되자, 보타이족은 추위를 막기 위해 반 지하식 온실집을 짓기 시작했어요. [Q7] 그러니까... 제가 언급을 안했던 사실이 있는데, 북카자흐스탄의 기후는 엄청 추워서 무려 아홉 달 동안 지속되는 겨울 내내 기온이 영하로 내려가죠. 말은 특히 유용한 것으로 밝혀졌는데, 왜냐하면 양이나 소처럼 나중에 길들여지는 대부분의 동물과는 달리 눈보라 속에서도 살 수 있었고, 눈을 헤치고 먹이를 찾을 수 있었

many aspects of people's lives worldwide.

P: The effects of the so called 'equine revolution' affected everything from agriculture to warfare. In the early stages, these animals provided a stable and reliable source of both meat and milk. As time progressed, humans began using horses for other tasks, such as transportation. [Q8] This allowed societies to greatly increase their ranges and brought an early form of globalization due to cultural interaction and the spread of ideas. The domestication of horses even revolutionized warfare. War shifted from ground troops to mounted soldiers who represented a greater value in battle since they could cover much more ground and, thereby, quicken the pace of military campaigns.

S: Umm… But how can we prove the Botai people were the first to domesticate horses?

P: Well, archeologist Sandra Olsen, one of the leading proponents of the theory, has been gathering evidence to corroborate these claims. The three most credible and positively reviewed of her claims are from soil samples gathered in the Botai region, the presence of 'bit wear,' or markings caused by the use of man-made bits or harnesses, on the horses' teeth, and compounds of fat molecules found on pottery shards.

S: Umm.. what do soil samples have to do with evidence of horse domestication?

P: That's a very good question. Scientists examining sites in Northern Kazakhstan took soil samples from the ground around ancient vertical posts where horses would have been tied, and found a phosphorus concentration that was ten times greater than that of soil from outside of them. How is this all related? Well, horse manure has higher phosphorus and nitrogen concentrations than normal soil, so high levels of phosphorus inside the large confinements would imply the presence of horses…Additionally, the soil samples had low nitrogen levels. Nitrogen, as we all know, is very volatile and is easily washed away or released into the atmosphere. [Q9] **The minute nitrogen traces eliminate the possibility that the phosphorus came from more recent manure.**

There's also proof to be found in the horses' remains. Examining the skulls from horse remains found in the region, researchers found a peculiarity in their teeth.

Horse Domestication of Botai People

Careful observation revealed indentations in the large hind teeth which could have only been caused by a bridle, or a man made bit, used to mount and ride a horse.

And finally, by utilizing a method of lipid, or fat analysis, scientists found traces of fats from mare's milk on shards of Botai pottery. While the first two points were circumstantial evidence that relied heavily on inferences, this information was the first piece of direct evidence that proved the Botai domesticated horses. [Q11] By proving they milked mares and preserved the milk in their pottery, researchers were able to provide the 'smoking gun.' I mean, unless you're suggesting the Botai were milking wild horses.

S: Umm... why didn't the researchers just examine the skeletal structures of the remains?

P: Well, I think you're assuming that all animals change physically due to domestication. This is only partly true. Certain animals, such as dogs, cattle or pigs, do develop different physical structures as they undergo morphological changes over generations of domestication and selective breeding. [Q10] This does not hold true for horses, though. It is nearly impossible to discern whether a horse was tame or wild or even the precise era it lived in judging solely by the skeletal evidence.

P: Judging by the evidence presented by the researchers, I think it's safe to say the theory is probable. In fact, with the constant flow of new evidence and the persistence of archeologist Sandra Olsen, more and more people have finally started to accept that the Botai people domesticated horses almost 1000 years earlier than previously thought.

06 What is the lecture mainly about?

(A) ~~The ways~~ that the domestication of horses influenced the Botai people
(B) Evidence that the Botai people had a cultural and economic relationship with horses *
(C) A theory about horse domestication by the Botai people that is ~~proven~~ through skeletal structures
(D) **The signs pointing to the domestication of horses that have been uncovered in the Botai region**

(A) 보타이 사람들에게 영향을 미친 말을 길들이는 ~~방법~~
(B) 보타이 사람들이 문화적, 경제적으로 말과 관계가 있다는 증거*
(C) 골격 구조를 통해 ~~증명된~~ 보타이 사람들에 의한 말의 가축화에 대한 이론
(D) **보타이 지역에서 모습을 드러낸 말 사육을 나타내는 흔적들**

Main Idea 본문 내용의 도입 부분에서 보면, Today I'd like to examine some of the evidence put forth by the proponents of this theory.(오늘 저는 이 이론의 지지자들이 제시하는 증거들을 검토해 보려고 해요.)에서 교수는 앞으로의 강의 주제가 보타이 주민들이 말을 가축화했다는 증거들을 검토하는 것임을 말하고 있으므로 정답은 (D)가 된다. (A)는 말을 길들이는 방법은 언급되지 않는 내용이며, (B)는 너무 세부적 사실이라 전체 주제로 보기에 어려움이 있으므로 각각 오답이다. (C)는 골격구조를 통해서는 말이 가축화 된 것을 증명하기 힘들다고 했으므로 정답이 될 수 없다.

07 What can be inferred about horses as livestock?

(A) Horses ~~were not~~ well suited as livestock since they grazed well year round. *
(B) **The Botai were able to use them for sustenance through the harsh weather conditions.**
(C) The Botai constructed pit houses that ~~provided insulation~~ to accommodate these animals.
(D) ~~They were not stronger~~ than sheep and cattle to survive year-round.

(A) 말은 일년 내내 풀을 잘 먹기 때문에 가축으로 적합하지 ~~않다.~~*
(B) **보타이 인들은 혹독한 기후 환경에 있어 그들을 주요한 생계수단으로 활용했다.**
(C) 보타이족들은 이 동물들을 ~~키우기 위해~~ 반지하식 온돌집을 지었다.
(D) 그들은 일년 내내 살아가기에 양과 소보다 ~~강하지 않았다.~~

Inference (Infer) 가축으로서 말에 관해 언급된 부분을 살펴보면, You see... what I didn't mention is the weather in Northern Kazakhstan is frigidly cold, with subzero temperatures throughout the nine-month winter. Horses proved exceptionally useful since they could survive snowstorms and forage through snow unlike most animals domesticated later, such as sheep and cattle.(그러니까... 제가 언급을 안했던 사실이 있는데 북카자흐스탄의 기후가 엄청 추워서 무려 아홉 달 동안 지속되는 겨울 내내 기온이 영하로 내려가죠. 말은 예외적으로 유용한 것으로 밝혀졌는데, 왜냐하면 양이나 소처럼 나중에 길들여지는 대부분의 동물들과는 달리 눈보라 속에서도 살아남을 수 있었고, 눈을 헤치고 먹이를 찾을 수 있었기 때문이에요.)에서 척박한 환경에서도 말이 적응할 수 있었으므로 보타이족에게 중요하게 사용되었다는 내용이므로 (B)가 정답이다. (A)와 (D)는 말의 유용한 부분에 대해 본문의 내용과 반대로 설명했으므로 각각 오답이다. (C)는 말의 거처에 관한 얘기는 언급되지 않았으므로 정답이 될 수 없다.

TEST 2 Set 2-2   Lecture 1
Horse Domestication of Botai People

08 According to the professor, what are two effects of the 'equine revolution'?

교수말에 따르면, '말의 혁명'이 끼친 두 가지 영향은 무엇인가?

| Click on 2 answers | 2개의 답을 고르시오. |

(A) By providing a stable source of food, it ~~lowered the people's dependence on agriculture~~.

(B) It broadened the limits of the area people could cover due to the previous lack of an efficient means of travel.

(C) It brought about the advent of mounted troops which greatly changed the way wars were fought.

(D) It ~~helped prove~~ that the Botai people were the first to domesticate horses.

(A) 안정적인 음식 공급원을 제공함으로써, 사람들의 농업에 대한 의존도를 낮추었다.

(B) 그것은 효과적인 여행 수단의 결핍으로 인해 이전에 존재했던 지역의 경계를 넓혔다.

(C) 그것은 전쟁 방식을 엄청나게 변화시킨 기병의 출현을 가져왔다.

(D) 그것은 보타이 사람들이 제일 먼저 말을 길들였다는 것을 증명하게 해주었다. *

Detail (Influence) 교수가 말의 혁명에 대해 언급한 부분을 보면, This allowed societies to greatly increase their ranges and brought an early form of globalization due to cultural interaction and the spread of ideas. The domestication of horses even revolutionized warfare.(이것은 사회의 범주를 넓혔고, 상호적인 문화교류와 생각의 확장으로 인해 세계화의 초기 형태를 가져오게 되었죠. 말을 길들이기 시작함으로써 심지어 전쟁에도 대변혁이 일어났어요.)를 설명한 (B)와 (C)가 정답임을 알 수 있다. (A)는 농업에 관한 언급이 없으므로, (D)는 보타이족의 삶에끼친 영향이지, 처음으로 말을 길들였는지에 대한 증거가 될 수 없으므로 각각 오답이다.

09 Why does the professor mention the presence of nitrogen in the soil samples?

왜 교수는 토양 샘플에 있는 질소의 존재를 언급했는가?

(A) To further support the theory by proving that the phosphorus in the soil had ancient origins

(B) To explain the ~~high~~ concentration of nitrogen in soil containing horse manure

(C) To explain ~~why the presence of nitrogen is not a possible cause~~ of the high levels of the phosphorus in question *

(D) To point out that ~~the markings left in the horses' teeth~~ were caused by consuming nitrogen from the soil ~~while wearing a harness~~

(A) 인이 고대에 기원을 가진다는 것을 증명하는 이론을 더욱 뒷받침하려고

(B) 말의 배설물이 포함되어 있는 토양안에 있는 높은 질소 함량을 설명하려고

(C) 왜 질소의 존재가 인의 높은 함유량에 대해 의문을 가질 수 있는 원인이 되지 않는지 설명하기 위해 *

(D) 말의 이빨에 남겨진 흔적들이 마구를 매고 있는 동안 토양에서 나오는 질소를 사용함으로써 생겼다는 것을 지적하기 위해

Inference (Purpose) 본문에서 질소가 언급된 부분을 보면, The minute nitrogen traces eliminate the possibility that the phosphorus came from more recent manure.(아주 미세한 질소 흔적은 인이 최근의 배설물에서 왔을지도 모르는 가능성을 배제시켜 줘요.)에서 교수는 인의 기원이 최근이 아니라 오래되었음을 확실히 하려고 질소를 언급했다는 것을 알 수 있다. 따라서 (A)가 정답이다. (B)는 본문과 반대로 설명했으므로, (C)는 질소와 인의 상관관계를 말하고 있어 교수의 의도와는 맞지 않으므로 각각 오답이다. (D)는 말의 이빨에 난 자국을 설명하는 것으로 질소와는 관계가 없어 질문에 대한 답이 될 수 없다.

10 What does the professor say about the skeletal structures of the remains?

교수는 유물들의 골격 구조에 대해 무엇을 말하는가?

(A) ~~All animals~~ undergo an alteration of physical traits.
(B) Bone shape is a good ~~indicator~~ of the time period the horse originated from. *
(C) ~~Milking mares may cause a change~~ in the skeletal structure.
(D) Horses have not physically changed over time as a result of domestication.

(A) 모든 동물들은 신체적인 특징의 변화를 겪는다.
(B) 뼈의 모양은 말이 기원한 시대에 대한 좋은 ~~지표이다.~~ *
(C) ~~말젖을 짜는 것은 골격구조에~~ 변화를 일으킬 수 ~~도있다.~~
(D) 말은 가축화의 결과로써 시간에 걸쳐 신체적으로 변화하지 않았다.

> **Detail** (Characteristic) 골격에 관해 언급된 부분을 살펴보면, This does not hold true for horses, though. It is nearly impossible to discern whether a horse was tame or wild or even the precise era it lived in judging solely by the shape of the skeletal evidence.(그러나 이것은 말에게는 해당되지 않아요. 말이 길들여졌는지 혹은 야생상태인지 아니면 심지어 말이 살았던 정확한 시대조차, 골격의 증거만 가지고 판단하여 구분하는 것은 거의 불가능해요.)에서 신체적 변화가 말에는 일어나지 않았다는 것을 알 수 있다. 따라서 (D)가 정답이 된다. (A)는 말에 해당하는 사실이 아니라고 했는데 성급한 일반화를 했고 (B)는 본문 내용과 반대로 기술했으며, (C)는 말젖을 짜는 것과 골격 구조는 전혀 상관없는 내용이므로 각각 오답이다.

11 Listen again to part of the lecture. Then answer the question.

강의의 일부를 다시 듣고, 질문에 답하시오.

P: By proving they milked mares and preserved the milk in their pottery, researchers were able to provide the 'smoking gun.' I mean, unless you're suggesting the Botai were milking wild horses.

What does the professor imply when he says this : 🎧

P: 그들이 말젖을 짜내고, 항아리에 보관했다는 것을 증명함으로써, 연구자들은 "결정적인 증거"를 제시 할 수 있었던 거에요. 제 말은, 여러분들이 보타이 족이 야생 말의 젖을 마셨을 거라는 터무니없는 주 장을 하지 않는다면 말이에요

이 말을 할 때 교수는 무엇을 암시하는가?

> I mean, unless you're suggestimg the Botai were, milking wild horse

제 말은, 여러분들이 보타이족이 야생말의 젖을 마셨을 거라는 터무니없는 주장을 하지 않는다면 말이에요

(A) He believes milking wild horses is ~~a valid alternative theory~~.
(B) **He is skeptical about the possibility of milking a wild horse.**
(C) He is ~~unsure~~ of whether the Botai took part in milking wild horses.
(D) He is ~~opening up the possibility of another possible theory~~.

(A) 그는 야생 말젖을 먹는 것이 ~~타당한 대안 이론~~이라고 믿는다.
(B) **그는 야생말의 젖을 먹는 것에 대한 가능성에는 회의적이다.**
(C) 그는 보타이족이 야생말젖을 먹었는지에 대해 ~~확신이 없다.~~
(D) 그는 또 다른 이론의 가능성을 열어놓고 있다. *

> **Inference** (Headset) 교수는 가능성이 희박한 사실에 대해 학생들이 하는 황당한 제의만 아니라면 앞에 언급한 내용은 사실이라고 말하고 싶은 것이다. 따라서 정답은 (B)가 된다. (A)는 야생말 젖을 먹는 것을 타당한 대안으로 제시한 것이 아니고, (C)는 교수가 보타이족이 야생말 젖을 먹었는지 여부에 대해 집중하고 있는 것이 아니므로, (D)는 또 다른 이론에 대한 얘기가 아니므로 각각 오답이다

TEST 2   Set 2-3   *부록 Lecture 2 Biofuel Production Process

문단주제	본문내용	해석
	Listen to part of a lecture in a biology class. The professor is discussing alternative energy.	생물학 강의의 일부를 들으시오. 교수는 대체에너지에 대해 논의하고 있습니다.
애탄올설명, 셀룰로오스 에탄올 생산에 대한 소개	P: So, last time we talked about producing ethanol from corn. If you'll remember, ethanol is the same type of alcohol found in alcoholic beverages, and one of the main candidates to substitute for fossil fuels, such as crude oil and coal. The most important difference between biofuels, like ethanol, and fossil fuels is that biofuels are renewable. They are derived directly from living organisms, while fossil fuels can only be formed after long periods of time under specific conditions, like high temperature and pressure. But, guess what? Scientists have found a new process of making ethanol, which many believe is a more efficient way of making biofuel! [Q12] **It's called cellulosic ethanol production... which is what we're going to talk about today.** It's actually very similar to corn ethanol production because both convert carbohydrate compounds into ethanol. First, let's talk about what cellulose is. Does anyone remember? John?	P: 자, 지난 시간에 우리는 옥수수로부터 에탄올을 만드는 것에 대해 얘기했었는데요. 여러분이 기억한다면, 에탄올은 알코올 음료에서 찾을 수 있는 것과 같은 종류의 알코올이며 원유나 석탄 같은 화석 연료를 대체할 수 있는 주요 후보 중 하나예요. 에탄올 같은 바이오연료와 화석연료 사이의 가장 중요한 차이점은 바이오 연료는 재생 가능하다는 것이에요. 그것은 살아있는 유기물로 부터 바로 얻어질 수 있으며, 반면에 화석 연료는 높은 온도와 압력 같은 특수한 조건하에서 오랜 시간이 있어야 생성되죠. 하지만, 놀랍게도, 과학자들은 에탄올을 만드는 새로운 과정을 발견했는데, 많은 이들은 이것이 바이오연료를 만들어내는데 더 효율적인 방법으로 여기고 있어요. [Q12] **그것은 셀룰로오스 에탄올 생산이라 불리는데요… 이게 바로 오늘 우리가 얘기할 주제입니다.** 그것은 옥수수 에탄올 생산과 매우 비슷한데 왜냐하면 둘 다 탄수화물 복합체를 에탄올로 전환시키기 때문이죠. 먼저, 셀룰로오스가 무엇인지 얘기해봅시다. 누구 기억하는 사람 있나요? John?
	S: Isn't cellulose a type of carbohydrate that makes up the rigid support structures of plant cells?	S: 셀룰로오스는 식물세포를 지탱하는 단단한 조직을 구성하고 있는 일종의 탄수화물 아닌가요?
	P: Very good! [Q17] **Cellulose is a polymer of simple sugar molecules called glucose. Uh… let's try that again. Hmm… In other words, cellulose is a long sugar unit made up of smaller units called glucose.** It is the most abundant organic compound on Earth, and makes up about 33 percent of a typical plant. This huge abundance is probably the biggest reason that biofuel companies are switching from corn to cellulosic ethanol, but there are also other advantages.	P: 아주 좋아요! [Q17] **셀룰로오스는 포도당이라 불리는 단순 설탕분자들의 중합체에요. 어… 다시 설명해 볼게요. 흠…다른 말로 하면, 셀룰로오스는 포도당이라 불리는 작은 단위들로 구성된 긴 설탕입자예요.** 그것은 지구에서 가장 풍부한 유기물 복합체로써 일반 식물의 약 33%를 구성하 고 있어요. 이러한 풍부함이 바이오 연료 회사들이 옥수수에서 셀룰로오스 에탄올로 눈을 돌리는 가장 큰 이유일 거예요. 하지만 다른 이점들도 있어요.
셀룰로오스 에탄올 생산의 역사	P: For one, corn ethanol conversion uses plant starch. Starch is a carbohydrate, just like cellulose, but it is an essential nutrient for humans, so using it cuts into our food supply. However, cellulose, is not digestible by humans, which makes its use more beneficial. [Q13-C] **Another reason why cellulosic ethanol is better is an supply cellulose for the process. This mean that there are**	P: 그 중 하나는, 옥수수 에탄올은 변환할 때 식물 전분을 사용하는 거예요. 전분은 셀룰로오스처럼 탄수화물이지만, 그것은 인간에게는 필수영양소이기 때문에, 그것을 사용하면 식량공급 지장을 받을 수 있어요. 하지만, 셀룰로오스는 인간이 소화시킬 수 없기 때문에 유용성이 더 크죠. [Q13-C] **셀룰로오스 에탄올이 더 좋은 또 다른 이**

means that there are increased options and supplies of feedstock, which is the raw material that supplies or fuels machines or industrial processes. Feedstock leads us to another advantage. [Q13-A] **The main feedstock for cellulosic ethanol, woody plants, has much higher density than corn, which makes transporting it more efficient.** Hmmm... let me explain with an analogy. Um... say you're trying to fill two boxes, one with stacks of paper and the other with bubble wrap. Obviously, the box filled with paper will be heavier, meaning you're carrying more... substance... whereas the box filled with bubble wrap will be mostly air, which is useless in this process. Although density doesn't seem like a big deal, transportation of raw material plays a huge role in business. Other than that, plants used to produce cellulosic ethanol are cheaper to grow and more eco-friendly than corn, which could reduce greenhouse gas production by 85 percent! So... if we efficiently produce energy from this source, the future of alternative energy sources will be much brighter. This is why there have been so many attempts to increase the efficiency of cellulosic ethanol production.

P: As technology has progressed, a new process known as celluloysis, or the 'biological approach' has been developed. In this method, the cellulose is um... loosened. [Q15-D] **After it's loosened, enzymes break it down into glucose, its smallest units.** [Q15-A] **The glucose is then fermented. The fermentation process produces a... uh... thick soup composed of ethanol and other chemicals.** A process called distillation, which is boiling the soup so that the compounds evaporate separately from each other, isolates the ethanol.

[Q14] **This approach normally uses baker's yeast in the fermenting process, which is a good choice since it's abundant and can withstand extreme temperature and pH levels.** Recently, scientists have engineered special resilient yeasts that can convert cellulose directly into ethanol. This means that the process of breaking down cellulose into glucose can be entirely forgone, whichproduction process and reduces costs furtuer

TEST 2 Set 2-3 *부록 Lecture 2 Biofuel Production Process

셀룰로오스 에탄올 생산방법 2: 열화학적 접근

P: Okay... So... The second major method used today is called gasification, or the thermo-chemical approach. In this process, instead of fermenting glucose, [Q15-C] selected cellulose particles are... combusted, or blown up, to separate their carbon atoms. [Q15-B] These atoms are then converted into compounds and fed to microorganisms called Clostridium ljungdahlii. The organisms eat the carbon compounds and release ethanol and water. This ethanol is then distilled in the same way as in the biological approach.

P: Even with recent progress, [Q16] there are some difficulties in making the switch to cellulosic ethanol for a few reasons. A major one is that even with high efficiency, cellulosic ethanol costs an additional 120 dollars to convert per barrel. Moreover, alternative energy projects are not well-funded, so companies that make biofuel can't carry out as much research as they need. They also suffer from a lack of commercial plants in which to execute conversion. The interesting part is that all of these problems could be, to some extent, resolved through government support. Once cellulosic ethanol production gains more public attention and interest, hopefully the industry will acquire more financial support.

P: 오케이.. 자.. 오늘날 사용되는 두 번째 주요 방법은 기화, 또는 열 화학 접근 이라고 알려진 방법이에요. 이 과정에서는 포도당을 발효하는 대신, [Q15-C] 선택된 셀룰로오스 입자들은... 연소하거나 혹은 폭발시켜 그 안의 탄소 원자들을 분리하게 돼요. [Q15-B] 그리고 난 후에는 이 탄소 원자들이 복합물로 변환되고 Clostridium ljungdahlii 이라 불리는 미생물 유기체에게 먹이로 제공되죠. 이 유기체들은 탄소화합물을 먹고 에탄올과 물을 방출해요. 그리고 나서 이 에탄올은 생물학적 접근법에서와 같은 방법으로 증류되는 거죠.

P: 심지어 최근 연구 과정에서도, [Q16] 셀룰로오스 에탄올로 변환하는데 몇몇의 어려움이 있어요. 가장 큰 문제점은 높은 효율성을 가진 과정에서도 셀룰로오스 에탄올은 1배럴 당 약 120달러의 추가비용이 든다는 것이에요. 더군다나, 대체에너지 프로젝트는 자금이 충분히 확보되지 않기 때문에, 바이오연료를 만드는 회사들은 원하는 만큼 충분히 많은 연구를 할 수가 없어요. 그들은 또한 생산을 위해 상업적으로 재배한 식물들도 부족하기 때문에 어려움을 겪고 있죠. 흥미로운 부분은 이 모든 문제들이 어느 정도까지는 정부 지원을 통해 해결될 수 있다는 것이에요. 일단 셀룰로오스 에탄올 생산이 대중의 관심과 흥미를 더욱 얻게 되면, 더 많은 재정 지원을 얻게 될꺼에요.

12 What is the lecture mainly about?

(A) The characteristics of one particular biofuel production process
(B) The differences between cellulosic ethanol and corn ethanol *
(C) ~~The history~~ of alternative energy source development
(D) ~~The multiple aspects of cellulose in plant structures~~

강의는 주로 무엇에 관한 것인가?

(A) 하나의 특정 바이오연료 생산과정의 특징들
(B) 셀룰로오스 에탄올과 옥수수 에탄올의 차이점*
(C) 대체에너지 원료의 발달 ~~역사~~
(D) ~~식물 구조 내의 셀룰로오스의 다양한 양상들~~

Main Idea 강의의 도입부에서 보면, It's called cellulosic ethanol production…which is what we're going to talk about today.(그것은 셀룰로오스 에탄올 생산이라 불리는데요…이게 바로 오늘 우리가 얘기할 주제입니다)에서 교수는 앞으로 셀룰로오스 에탄올 생산이라 불리는 특정한 바이오연료 생산 과정에 대해 얘기할 것을 언급하고 있다. 따라서 정답은 (A)가 된다. (B)는 본문에 나와있는 내용이나 주제가 되기엔 너무 지엽적이며, (C)는 대체에너지 원료의 발달 역사를 말하는 것이 아니기 때문에 각각 오답이다. (D)는 강의내용에 언급 되어 있지 않아 답이 될 수 없다.

13 According to the lecture, what are the advantages of cellulosic ethanol over corn ethanol?

Click on 2 answers

(A) It mainly uses resources that are denser than corn ethanol.
(B) Its production process releases no pollution into the environment
(C) It can be converted from a wider variety of feedstock
(D) It is drawn from an ingredient which is essential to humans

강의에 따르면, 옥수수 에탄올과 비해 셀룰로오스 에탄올이 가지는 장점은 무엇인가?

2개의 답을 고르시오.

(A) 그것은 옥수수 에탄올보다 밀도가 높은 원료를 주로 사용한다.
(B) 그것의 생산과정은 환경오염을 전혀 일으키지 않는다.
(C) 그것은 더 다양한 공급 원료로부터 변환될 수 있다.
(D) 그것은 인간에게 필수적인 구성성분으로부터 추출되어진다. *

Detail (Advantage)   셀룰로오스 에탄올의 장점이 언급된 부분을 살펴보면, Another reason why cellulosic ethanol is better is that all plants can supply cellulose for the process· (중략)· The main feedstock for cellulosic ethanol, woody plants, has much higher density than corn, which makes transporting it more efficient.(셀룰로오스 에탄올이 더 좋은 또 다른 이유는 모든 종류의 식물이 생산에 필요한 셀룰로오스를 공급할 수 있다는 것이에요· 중략 · 셀룰로오스 에탄올의 주요 공급원료인 목질 식물은 옥수수보다 훨씬 높은 밀도를 가지고 있는 데, 그렇게 때문에 운반면에서 더 효율적이지요.)에서 높은 밀도와 다양한 식물로부터의 변환이 용이함을 알 수 있다. 따라서 정답은 (A)와 (C)가 된다. (B)는 이 과정이 좀더 친환경적이라고는 했으나 환경오염을 전혀 일으키지 않는다고는 하지 않았으므로, (D)는 인체에 필수구성성분에 관한 내용이 본문에 언급되지 않았으므로 각각 오답이다.

14 Why does the professor mention baker's yeast?

(A) To point out that the biological approach ~~costs more~~ than the thermo-chemical approach
(B) ~~To explain the need~~ for suitable temperatures and pH levels in ethanol production *
(C) To introduce the catalyst used in the fermentation process
(D) ~~To give an example of one of the products~~ of the ethanol production process

왜 교수는 제빵사의 효모를 언급하는가?

(A) 열화학적 접근보다 생물학적 접근이 ~~비용이 더 든다는~~ 것을 지적하려고
(B) 에탄올 생산시 적절한 기온과 pH 레벨이 ~~필요함을 설명하려고~~ *
(C) 발효과정에서 사용되는 하나의 촉매제를 소개해주려고
(D) 에탄올 생산의 ~~산물들에 대한 하나의 예를 언급하려고~~

Inference (Purpose)   교수가 제빵사의 효모를 언급한 부분을 살펴보면, This distillation approach normally uses baker's yeast in the fermenting process, which is a good choice since it's abundant and can withstand extreme temperature and pH levels.(이런 증류 처리방법은 보통 제빵사가 발효과정에 사용하는 효모를 이용하게 되는데, 이것은 좋은 선택이에요. 왜냐하면 양이 풍부하고 무척 높은 온도와 pH 레벨을 견뎌낼 수 있기 때문이죠)에서 이 부분은 촉매제를 사용해서 효과적으로 발효하는 과정을 소개하고 있다. 따라서 (C)가 정답이다. (A)는 생물학적 접근법의 과정에 속하는 증류처리방법에 관한 질문이지 비용에 관한 얘기가 아니기 때문에 오답이며, (B)는 온도와 pH 레벨에 관한 내용은 맞으나 교수가 효모를 언급한 목적이 아니며, (D)는 에탄올 생산물이 아닌 셀룰로오스 에탄올 생산과정에 대한 내용이므로 각각 오답이다.

TEST2 — Set 2-3 *부록 Lecture 2 Biofuel Production Process

15 In the lecture, the professor explains two ethanol production methods. Indicate whether each of the following was a feature of celluloysis or gasification

	Celluloysis	Gasification
(A) Fermentation is needed to produce ethanol	O	
(B) Gas compounds are fed to microorganisms		O
(C) Cellulose molecules are combusted		O
(D) Enzymes break down cellulose molecules	O	

강의에서, 교수는 두 가지 에탄올 생산방법을 설명하고 있다. 다음의 내용이 각각 celluloysis 인지 아니면 gasification인지 구분하시오.

	Celluloysis	Gasification
에탄올을 생산하기 위해서 발효과정이 필요하다	O	
가스 화합물이 미생물 유기체의 먹이다		O
셀룰로오스 분자가 연소된다		O
효소가 셀룰로오스 분자를 분해한다	O	

Category (Matching) 본문에서 두 가지 에탄올 생산 방법인 celluloysis와 gasification을 설명한 부분을 각각 살펴보면, (A)는 The glucose is then fermented. The fermentation process produces a… uh… thick soup composed of ethanol and other chemicals.(그 다음엔 포도당이 발효되구요. 그 발효과정으로… 어… 에탄올과 다른 화학물질로 구성된 걸쭉한 액체가 만들어지는데요.) (C)는 Selected cellulose particles are… combusted, or blown up, to separate their carbon atoms. (B)는 These atoms are then converted into compounds and fed to microorganisms called Clostridium ljungdahlii.(선택된 셀룰로오스 그안의 입자들을 연소하거나 혹은 폭발시켜 그안의 탄소 원자들을 분리하게 되요. 그리고 난 후에는 이 탄소 원자들이 복합물로 변환되고 Clostridium ljungdahlii이라 불리는 미생물 유기체에게 먹이로 제공되죠.)…. (D)는 After it's loosened, enzymes break it down into glucose, its smallest units.(느슨해진 이후에는, 효소가 그것을 가장 작은 조각인 포도당으로 분해하죠.)에서 특성들을 비교할 수 있다.

16 Which of the following is NOT a drawback of cellulosic ethanol production?

(A) The conversion process is much more expensive.
(B) Very little financial support is directed towards alternative energy research.
(C) The public is against the idea of alternative energy.
(D) Few production plants exist where the production can be implemented.

다음 보기 중 셀룰로오스 에탄올 생산의 결점이 아닌 것은 무엇인가?

(A) 변환 과정이 훨씬 더 비싸다.
(B) 대체에너지 연구에 대한 지원을 거의 받지 못하고 있다.
(C) 대중은 대체에너지에 대해 반대한다.
(D) 제조가 시행될 수 있는 곳에 생산공장이 거의 없다.

Detail (Difficulty) 셀룰로오스 에탄올 생산의 어려운 점에 대해 언급한 부분을 보면, ...there are some difficulties in making the switch to cellulosic ethanol for a few reasons. A major one is that even with high efficiency, cellulosic ethanol costs an additional 120 dollars to convert per barrel. Moreover, alternative energy projects are not well-funded, so companies that make biofuel can't carry out as much research as they need. They also suffer from a lack of commercial plants in which to execute conversion. The interesting part is that all of these problems could be, to some extent, resolved through government support. Once cellulosic ethanol production gains more public attention and interest, hopefully the industry will acquire more financial support(셀룰로오스 에탄올로 변환 하는데 몇 가지 어려움이 있어요. 가장 큰 문제점은 높은 효율성을 가진 과정에서도 셀룰로오스 에탄올은 1배럴 당 약 120달러의 추가비용이 든다는 것이에요. 더군다나, 대체에너지 프로젝트는 자금이 충분히 확보되지 않기 때문에, 바이오연료를 만드는 회사들은 원하는 만큼 충분히 많은 연구를 할 수가 없어요. 그들은 또한 생산을위해 상업적으로 재배하는 식물들도 부족하기 때문에 어려움을 겪고 있죠. 흥미로운 부분은 이 모든 문제들이 어느 정도까지는 정부 지원을 통해 해결될 수 있다는 것이에요. 일단 셀룰로오스 에탄올 생산물이 대중의 관심과 흥미를 더욱 얻게 되면, 그 산업은 더 많은 재정 지원을 얻게 될 거에요.)에서 (A), (B), (D)가 단점으로 언급되어 있음을 알 수 있다. (C)는 본문과 내용이 다르므로 질문에 대한 정답이다.

---

17 Listen again to part of the lecture. Then answer the question.

P: Cellulose is a polymer of simple sugar molecules called glucose. Uh... let's try that again. Hmm... In other words, cellulose is a long sugar unit made up of smaller units called glucose.

Why does the professor say this :

강의의 일부를 다시 듣고, 질문에 답하시오

P: 셀룰로오스는 포도당이라 불리는 단순 설탕분자들의 중합체에요. 어… 다시 설명해 볼께요. 흠…다른 말로 하면, 셀룰로오스는 포도당이라 불리는 작은 단위들로 구성된 긴 설탕입자에요.

왜 교수는 이런 말을 하는가?

P: Uh... let's try that again.	P: 어.. 다시 설명해 볼께요

(A) She ~~does not think~~ the students are paying attention
(B) She wants to ~~emphasize an important concept~~ *
(C) She wants to ~~correct the student's answer to her question~~
(D) She thinks that the students didn't understand her explanation

(A)그녀는 학생들이 집중하지 ~~않는다고 생각한다.~~
(B)그녀는 ~~중요한 개념을 강조하기 원한다.~~ *
(C)그녀는 ~~자신이 한 질문에 대한 학생들의 대답을 고쳐주길 원한다.~~
(D)그녀는 학생들이 자신의 설명을 이해하지 못했다고 생각한다.

Inference (Headset) 교수는 자신이 말한 전문적인 내용에 대한 설명을 학생들이 이해하기 어려울 것 같아서 좀 더 부연설명을 덧붙이려는 것이므로 (D)가 정답이다. 학생들이 집중하지 못하고 있다는 (A)는 오답이며, (B)는 개념을 강조하고자 하는 것이 아니므로 답이 될 수 없다. (C)는 학생들의 대답을 바로잡아 주기 위해서가 아니므로 오답이다.

usherin.usher.co.kr

USHER iBT TOFLE
FINAL TEST LISTENING
TEST 3/해설

정답 및 Self-check List

문제유형과 Signals

오답정리표

TEST 3

Set 1-1 Conversation: Community Service at Museum

문단주제	본문내용	해 석
	Listen to a conversation between a student and a museum officer.	학생과 박물관 직원간의 대화를 들으시오.
	S: Excuse me, sir.	S: 실례하겠습니다.
	M: Yes, ma'am. How may I help you?	M: 네. 무엇을 도와드릴까요?
	S: I have some questions regarding community service.	S: 사회 봉사에 대해서 몇 가지 물어볼 게 있어서요.
	M: Uh huh? Go ahead.	M: 네, 계속 말씀하시죠.
	S: [Q1] Well, I already checked with the Downtown Museum, and I can't submit the hours I worked there as community service... so I was wondering how community service works here.	S: [Q1] 음, 제가 다운타운 박물관은 이미 확인했는데요, 그곳에서 사회 봉사로 일한 시간을 학교에 제출할 수가 없어요… 그래서 이곳에서는 사회 봉사가 어떻게 운영되는지에 대해 궁금해요.
	M: You can submit your hours here as community service. We don't mind completing all of the necessary forms. Anything else you'd like to know?	M: 이곳에서 봉사한 시간은 제출할 수 있어요. 우리 는 필요한 모든 서류를 작성해 주거든요. 더 알고 싶은 것이 있나요?
	S: Well, I am a history major, and I do have a great deal of background knowledge of world history, but I was just curious if there was anything... I... uh... should prepare for.	S: 음, 전 역사를 전공하고 있구요, 세계사에 대한 폭 넓은 배경지식을 갖고 있는데요, 근데 궁금한 건 제가 더 준비해야 할 것들이… 어… 더 있나 해서요.
	M: Well... I don't know if you already know or not, but younger children are our main customers. We mostly get visitors that are 6 or 7 years old.	M: 음… 이미 알고 계신지는 모르겠지만, 저희의 주요 고객은 어린 아이들이죠. 대부분 6세나 7세의 방문객들을 주로 맞이하고요.
	S: I wasn't aware of that... anyway, go on	S: 그건 몰랐네요… 아무튼, 계속하세요.
	M: So knowing a lot about history isn't as important as being familiar with dealing with children.	M: 그래서 역사를 많이 아는 건 아이들을 잘 다루는 것만큼은 중요하지 않아요.
	S: I see... Is there anything else I should know?	S: 그렇군요… 제가 알아야 할 것이 더 있나요?
	M: Well the job is basically supervising kids.	M: 음, 하는 일은 기본적으로 아이들을 감독하는 일이에요.
	S: [Q5] (laughs) OK. What kinds of, uh... activities can children do around here? Can you walk me through a typical day in the museum?	S: [Q5] (웃음) 알겠어요. 어떤 종류의… 음… 활동을 아이들이 여기서 하나요? 이 박물관에서의 일상적인 하루를 보여주실 수 있나요?
	M: Well, right now, we have an exhibition of Picasso's paintings. With children, rather than explaining the hidden meanings in the paintings, community service workers, such as you, would explain the shapes, colors and sizes and how they suit each other. The children seem more interested in stuff like that than the actual... artistic technicalities.	M: 음, 지금은, 피카소 그림을 전시하고 있어요. 아이들한테는 그림에 담긴 숨은 의미를 설명하기 보다는, 학생과 같은 사회 봉사자들이 모양, 색, 그리고 크기와 이것들이 어떻게 서로 어울리는지에 대해 설명해주는 거죠. 아이들은 그런 것들에 더 관심 있어 하거든요, 실제… 예술 기법보다는요.
	S: I see. I guess Picasso's paintings would be perfect for children since they consist of a lot of different colors, shapes and sizes.	S: 그렇군요. 그렇다면 피카소의 그림들이 아이들한테는 완벽하겠네요, 왜냐하면 그것들은 다양한 색깔, 모양, 그리고 크기로 구성되어 있으니까요.
	M: Exactly. It's a big hit right now, which reminds me, the Egyptian Room is also popular with children, especially the mummies. Children are awfully interested in mummies.	M: 바로 그거에요. 이 전시전은 지금 큰 성공을 거두고 있죠. 그러니까 생각나는데, 이집트방 또한 아이들 사이에서 매우 인기 있어요, 특히 미라들이요. 아이들은 미라들에 몹시 흥미있어 하거든요.
	S: I can totally see children being interested in mummies.	S: 아이들이 미라에 관심이 많다는 걸 저도 잘 알고 있어요.

M: Since you're a history major you probably know a lot about Egyptian history, right?

S: I have a good grasp of most of the concepts, although I would have to review.

M: You probably don't need to do that. Children usually have only simple questions about different Egyptian pharaohs and mummies and pyramids. All you have to do is walk around with the children, and briefly explain some of the pieces to them, and answer any questions they might have.

S: That seems pretty easy. I mean, according to everything I've heard so far, it seems like a lot of fun.

M: Don't underestimate how hard taking care of children is. I mean, looking after children is a lot harder than it sounds.

S: [Q3] I know... I had a part time job before in a daycare center... and it was... hectic.

M: I'm glad that you have some experience. It'll definitely be a lot of help later on when you actually start.

S: [Q3] I can't say that I'm not excited; since I want to get into education once I graduate.

M: If you would just fill out this application, and let me know when you can start, I will let you know how the process goes as soon as possible.

S: OK.

M: Do you have any questions?

S: I was just wondering about the working hours?

M: Well, since you're just going to be a community service worker, hours will be flexible. We can work out some kind of schedule and figure something out that will suit both you and the museum. [Q4] Would you like for me to just go ahead and select an appropriate time?

S: Yeah, that shouldn't be a problem, I have a pretty open schedule.

M: Let me know when you're done filling out the application.

M: 학생은 역사를 전공하니까 아마 이집트 역사에 대해 많이 알고 계시겠군요, 그렇죠?

S: 내용의 대부분을 잘 알고 있긴 하죠, 비록 다시 살펴봐야겠지만요.

M: 아마 그럴 필요는 없을 거에요. 아이들은 서로 다른 이집트 파라오들과 미라, 그리고 피라미드들에 대한 단순한 질문들만 물어볼 테니까요. 학생이 그저 해야할 일은 아이들과 함께 걸으며, 그들에게 전시물들 중 몇몇에 대해 간략하게 설명해 주는 거에요, 그리고 질문이 있다면 대답해 주면 되구요.

S: 꽤 쉬워 보이네요. 제 말은, 지금까지 들은 대로라면, 아주 재미있을 것 같아요.

M: 아이들을 관리하는것이 얼마나 힘든지에 대해 과소평가하지 마세요. 제 말은, 아이들을 챙기는건 보기보다 아주 힘들어요.

S: [Q3] 잘 알죠... 어린이집에서 파트타임으로 일해본 적이 있는데요... 그땐 정말... 정신 없었죠.

M: 그런 경험이 있다니 다행이네요. 나중에 일을 실제로 시작할 때 분명 많은 도움이 될 거에요.

S: [Q3] 전 흥분하지 않았다고 말할 수 없겠어요; 왜냐하면 졸업하고 나서 교육 쪽으로 나가고 싶었거든요.

M: 이 지원서를 작성해 주시구요, 언제부터 시작할 수 있는지 알려주시면, 가능한 빨리 결과를 통보해 드릴께요.

S: 네.

M: 질문이 있으신가요?

S: 근무 시간이 어떻게 되는지 궁금한데요?

M: 음, 사회 봉사자로 일할거니까, 시간은 자율적으로 조정 가능할 거에요. 학생과 박물관 양쪽에게 맞도록 스케줄을 조정할 수 있어요. [Q4] 혹시 제가 그냥 적당한 시간을 정해줘도 될까요?

S: 네, 문제될게 없어요. 제 스케줄은 꽤 여유가 있거든요.

M: 지원서 다 작성하시면 알려주세요.

TEST 3 Set 1-1 Conversation: Community Service at Museum

01 Why does the student go to see the museum officer?　　학생은 왜 박물관 직원을 만나러 갔는가?

(A) To ~~ask~~ the officer whether her background knowledge of history may help in getting a job at the museum　　(A) 직원에게 역사에 대한 그녀의 배경 지식이 그 박물관에서 일자리를 얻는데 유용한지 ~~문의~~하기 위해

(B) To ~~decide how many working hours~~ at the museum ~~can be counted~~ as community service hours *　　(B) 박물관의 근무시간 중 몇 시간이 사회봉사 시간으로 ~~계산될 수 있는지 결정~~하기 위해 *

(C) To ask if her experiences at the museum will be of help in getting into graduate school to study education　　(C) 그 박물관에서의 경험이 그녀가 교육학을 공부하기 위해 대학원에 진학할 때 도움이 되는지 물어보기 위해

(D) To inquire about the possibility of volunteering at the museum for community service hours　　**(D) 사회 봉사 시간을 위해 박물관에서 자원 봉사하는 것이 가능한지 문의하기 위해**

Main Purpose Well, I already checked with the Downtown Museum' and I can t submit the hours I worked there as community service· so I was wondering how community service works here.(음 제가 다운타운 박물관은 이미 확인했는데요 그곳에서 사회 봉사로 일한 시간을 학교에 제출할 수가 없어요. 그래서 이곳에서는 사회 봉사가 어떻게 운영되는지에 대해 궁금해요.)에서 학생은 박물관에서의 근무시간이 사회봉사시간으로 인정되는지를 물어보기 위해 왔음을 알 수 있으므로 정답은 (D)이다. (A)와 (C)는 대화에 나오는 내용이나 학생이 온 이유가 아니므로 각각 오답이다. (B)는 구체적으로 몇 시간이 사회봉사로 인정되는지는 대화에 언급되지 않으므로 답이 될 수 없다.

02 What can be inferred about the museum?　　박물관에 대해 무엇을 추론할 수 있는가?

(A) It offers different types of art that interest children.　　**(A) 아이들의 관심을 끌만한 다양한 종류의 예술작품을 제공한다.**

(B) The Egyptian room is ~~off-limits due to problems with mummy preservation.~~　　(B) 이집트 방은 ~~미라의 보존에 문제가 생겨서 출입이 금지~~된 상태이다.

(C) It has ~~a special course~~ that involves a room of Picasso's works in it. *　　(C) 피카소의 작품들이 있는 방을 포함하는 ~~특별한 과정을~~ 제공한다. *

(D) The museum offers artwork that is too ~~confusing for children~~.　　(D) 박물관에서 ~~아이들에게 너무 많은 혼란을 주는~~ 미술품을 제공한다.

Inference (Infer) 대화 내용에서 박물관은 아이들의 흥미를 끌만한 피카소의 전시회 등의 다양한 예술 종류를 제공하는 것을 추론할 수 있으므로 정답은 (A)이다. (B)는 이집트 방이 현재 출입이 금지되었다는 언급은 없고, (C)에서 피카소의 작품을 전시한다는 것은 맞지만 특별한 과정을 제공한다는 내용은 언급된 적이 없으며, (D)는 대화에 전혀 나와 있지 않은 내용이므로 각각 오답이다

03 What is the student's attitude towards the job at the museum?　　박물관 일자리에 대한 학생의 태도는 무엇인가?

(A) She ~~doesn't necessarily~~ need the community service hours.　　(A) 그녀는 사회 봉사 시간이 ~~꼭 필요한건 아니다.~~

(B) She is worried that she ~~may not have~~ enough background in the field.　　(B) 그녀는 그 분야에 대한 충분한 배경이 ~~없을까봐 걱정하고 있다.~~

(C) She has experience in dealing with children and is confident enough to do it well.　　**(C) 그녀는 학생들을 다루어 본적이 있기 때문에 잘 할 수 있다는 자신감을 갖고 있다.**

(D) She ~~has her own set of rules~~ that she would like to apply.　　(D) 그녀는 적용하고 싶은 ~~자신만의 규칙을 가지고 있다.~~

Inference (Attitude) 일에 대한 학생의 태도가 드러난 부분을 보면, I know… I had a part time job before in a daycare center… and it was…hectic.(잘 알죠… 어린이집에서 파트타임으로 일해본 적이 있는데요… 그땐 정말… 정신 없었죠.)… I can't say that I'm not excited; since I want to get into education once I graduate.(전 흥분하지 않았다고 말할 수 없겠어요; 왜냐하면 전 졸업하고 나서 교육 쪽으로 나가고 싶었거든요.)에서 학생은 아이들을 다뤄본 경험이 있고, 일에 대한 기대감을 가지고 있음을 알 수 있으므로 정답은 (C)가 된다. (A)는 학생이 사회 봉사 시간이 필요해서 박물관에서 일하려고 하는 것이며, (B)는 자신의 배경지식이 불충분하다고 느끼지 않으므로, (D)는 대화에 언급되지 않은 내용이므로 각각 오답이다.

04 What will the museum officer do for the student?

(A) ~~Provide a list of questions~~ that the children may ask the student.
(B) ~~Help the student fill out~~ the parts of the application that the student ~~finds confusing~~.
(C) ~~Work together~~ with the student to find the most appropriate work hours. *
(D) **Just pick a specific time for the student and notify her later.**

학생을 위해 박물관 직원이 무엇을 할 것인가?

(A) 아이들이 그 학생에게 물어볼 수도 있는 ~~질문목록을 제공한다.~~
(B) ~~지원서에서 학생이 헷갈려 하는 부분을 작성하는 것을 도와 준다.~~
(C) 가장 적절한 근무 시간을 찾기 위해 학생과 ~~함께 짜본다.~~ *
(D) **학생을 위한 특정한 시간대를 골라서 나중에 통보해 준다.**

Detail (Future action)   Would you like for me to just go ahead and select an appropriate time? S: Yeah, that shouldn't be a problem, I have a pretty open schedule. (혹시 제가 그냥 적당한 시간을 정해줘도 될까요? S: 네, 문제될게 없어요. 제 스케줄은 꽤 여유가 있거든요)에서 정답은 (D)임을 알 수 있다. (A)는 대화 내용에 언급되지 않고, (B)는 학생에게 지원서 작성이 다 끝나면 알려달라고 했지 도와준다는 내용은 없으므로 각각 오답이다. (C)는 직원이 학생에게 스케줄을 조정하는 것이 가능하다고 말한 것은 맞으나 그 다음에 시간은 직원이 정해서 알려준다고 했으므로 답이 될 수 없다.

05 Listen again to part of the conversation. Then answer the question.

S: OK. What kinds of, uh... activities can children do around here? Can you walk me through a typical day in the museum?

Why does the student say this? : 🎧

Can you walk me through a typical day in the museum?

(A) **To learn more about the museum and what it offer its visitors**
(B) To ask the officer the ~~exact times that the museum opens and closes~~
(C) Because she has not yet understood what ~~she would be asked to do~~ *
(D) Because she wants to explore the museum ~~for her own interests~~

대화의 일부를 다시 듣고, 질문에 답하시오.

S: 알겠어요. 어떤 종류의… 음… 활동을 아이들이 여기서 하나요? 이 박물관에서의 일상적인 하루를 보여주실 수 있나요?

왜 학생은 이 말을 하는가?

이 박물관에서의 일상적인하루를 보여주실 수 있나요?

(A) **박물관에 대해 배우고 그곳이 방문객들에게 무엇을 제공하는지 알아보기 위해**
(B) ~~박물관이 열고 닫는 정확한 시간대를 직원에게 물어보기 위해~~
(C) 왜냐하면 그녀가 ~~어떤 일을 하게 될지 아직 이해하지 못하기 때문에~~ *
(D) 그녀의 ~~개인적인 관심을 위해 박물관을 둘러보기 위해서~~

Inference (Headset)   학생은 아이들이 박물관에서 무슨 활동을 하는지 물어본 후에 박물관의 일상에 대해 얘기해 달라고 요청하는 것이므로 박물관에 대해 알기 위해서 질문했음을 알 수 있다. 따라서 정답은 (A)이다. (B),(D)는 대화 내용에 언급된 적이 없으므로, (C)는 자신이 앞으로 할 일이 이해가 안가서 물어본 것이 아니므로 각각 오답이다.

TEST 3 Set 1-2 Lecture 1 Architectural Acoustics

문단주제	본문내용	해석
건축음향의 중요성 증가	Listen to part of a lecture in an architecture class. The professor is discussing architectural acoustics. P: We've been focusing on the architectural features of opera houses and concert halls that make them so unique and aesthetically appealing. Today, we'll look at the science involved in these designs and why sound related buildings are built the way they are. This correlation between architecture and sound has not been thoroughly researched until recently, but with the rising importance of acoustics when building concert halls or theatres, the field of architectural acoustics has been gaining much attention. [Q6] Let's explore some of the integral factors that play a role in defining structural acoustics.	건축학 강의의 일부를 들으시오. 교수는 건축 음향에 대해 논의하고 있습니다. P: 우리는 오페라 하우스나 콘서트 홀을 매우 독특 하고 미적으로 매력있게 만드는 건축의 특징들에 주목해 왔는데요. 오늘은 이러한 디자인들 속에 숨어있는 과학과 왜 음향과 관련된 건물들이 그렇게 건설되었는지를 살펴볼게요. 건축과 소리와의 이러한 상관관계는 최근까지 자세하게 연구되지 않았어요, 하지만 콘서트 홀이나 극장을 지을 때 음향의 중요성이 증가하면서, 건축 음향 분야가 많은 주목을 받고 있죠. [Q6] 건축 음향을 규정 짓는 역할을 하는 몇 개의 필수 요소들에 대해 알아봅시다.
잔향 시간의 정의와 그 길이에 따른 방향	P: One of the most important concepts in architectural acoustics is called 'reverberation time.' When a sound wave is created in a confined space, the listener not only hears the sound wave directly from the source but also its reflections from the surrounding walls, floor, and ceiling. These reflected waves are called reverberant sound, and the time required for them to drop by 60 decibels, when they can no longer be heard by humans after the original sound ceases, is defined as reverberation time. This interval is the most important quantitative indicator in determining a room's acoustic suitability. S: Does longer reverberation time mean better acoustics? P: Not necessarily. The optimum reverberation time of a space depends largely on its use. A space with a long reverberation time is called 'live,' whereas an acoustically 'dead' environment is one that causes sound to fade quickly. Typically speaking, facilities such as lecture halls require a shorter reverberation time in order to maximize the clarity and intelligibility of the words spoken. If the reverberation time is too long, the reflected sound from one syllable will still be audible while the next is spoken resulting in poor perceptibility and may end up sounding mumbled. On the other hand, if the reverberation time is too short, then the speaker or the performers will struggle to be loud enough to fill the room. [Q7] In music, solos or piano recitals are often performed in a 'dead' environment because there is only one instrument playing and thus clarity and precision are the most important factors. Conversely, symphony orchestras require a 'live' space because the longer reverberation time blends the notes for a more harmonious sound that	P: 건축 음향에서 가장 중요한 개념 중의 하나는 '잔향 시간'이라고 불리는 것인데요. 음파가 제한 된 공간에서 만들어질 때, 청자는 음원으로부터 직접 음파를 들을 뿐 아니라, 주위의 벽들, 바닥, 그리고 천장으로부터 반사되는 음도 듣게 되죠. 이렇게 반사된 음파는 잔향음이라 불리며, 원래의 소리가 멈춘 후에 반사된 음파가 사람이 더 이상 들을 수 없는 소리크기인 60 데시벨로 떨어질 때까지 시간을 잔향시간이라고 정의해요. 이 간격은 방의 음향적인 지속성을 결정하는데 가장 중요한 수량적 지표이죠. S: 잔향 시간이 더 길다는건 음향이 더 좋은 것을 의미하나요? P: 꼭 그렇지만은 않아요. 한 공간의 최적 잔향시간은 대부분 그것의 용도에 달려있어요. 긴 잔향시간을 갖고 있는 공간은 '살아있다'라고 일컬어지는 반면, 음향학적으로 '죽은'환경은 소리를 빠르게 사라지게 하는 곳이죠. 일반적으로 말하자면, 강의실과 같은 시설들은 소리로 전달되는 말의 명확성과 명료성을 극대화하기 위해 더 짧은 잔향 시간을 필요로 해요. 만약 잔향시간이 너무 길면, 반사된 한 음절의 소리가 그 다음 음절을 말하는 중에도 여전히 들려서 다음 소리를 인식하기 어렵게 되고 결국에는 웅얼거리는 소리로 들리게 될 수도 있죠. 반면에, 만약 잔향시간이 너무 짧으면, 화자나 말을 하는 사람들은 방을 채울 만큼 충분히 큰 소리를 내려고 애써야 할 거에요. [Q7] 음악에서는, 독주나 피아노 연주회가 '죽은 환경'에서 종종 수행되는데 왜냐하면 단지 하나의 악기를 연주하기 때문에 명확성과 정확성이 가장 중요한 요소인거죠. 반면에, 교향악단은 '살아있는'공간이 필요

gives the music 'body'.

Wallace Clement Sabine의 건축 음향장치 개선과 활용

P: Now, let's take a look at the history of the field beginning with Harvard physics professor Wallace Sabine, one of the first to study the science behind acoustics and widely considered to be the father of modern architectural acoustics. Sabine had no acoustics training when Charles William Eliot, the president of Harvard, asked him to improve the acoustics of a lecture hall in the university's newly built Fogg Art Museum. Sabine tackled this seemingly impossible problem with great persistence. For several years, he conducted experiments utilizing different materials, such as cushions, oriental rugs and even different numbers of people, to see how they affected the acoustics of a space. After years of hard work, Sabine discovered that the materials present in a room could affect the reverberation time. Since various materials absorb different sounds at unique rates, depending on the absorbency of the material, they can either increase or decrease the reverberation time. Foam insulation, for example, almost completely absorbs sound and reflects little to none, while a thick, smooth painted concrete wall would be the acoustic equivalent of a mirror.

P: Wallace Sabine used his findings to convert the Fogg Art Museum space into an acoustically acceptable lecture hall by using thick drapes and sound absorbent cushions to shorten the room's reverberation time. [Q8] After the success of this project, switching up interior features to change reverberation time became widely used and proved to be particularly effective in adjusting the acoustics of preexisting and older buildings.

S: Umm… why do older structures have such poor acoustics? I mean, what were some of the problems?

음향 문제의 원인

P: Well, a lot of the times acoustic problems result from improper design or construction limitations. [Q9] Before the field of architectural acoustics was widely studied and applied to real life designs, architects often only emphasized the grandeur of the structure without thinking about the acoustics. In some extreme cases, these non-acoustically engineered buildings suffered from sound being focused on only one section of the audience, especially in domes or structures with smooth curved walls.

TEST 3 Set 1-2 Lecture 1 Architectural Acoustics

잔향시간에 영향을 주는 측면들

S: You've mentioned materials, but what other factors determine the reverberation time of a room?

P: There are two other important ones: the room's size and the shape of the room. The size of a room is an important dictating factor in reverberation times. In general, larger rooms have longer reverberation times because there is more uninterrupted space for the sound waves to travel across and reverberate. On the other hand, smaller rooms have shorter reverberation times since sound waves are reflected, but quickly die out due to the small size of the space. Shape also plays a critical role. Since reverberation time measures the reflected sound waves, the number of reflecting surfaces available directly correlates to the reverberation time. Therefore, more walls mean more reflection, which ultimately means longer reverberation times. Domes increase the reverberation time because their high ceilings increase the overall size of the space.

사람의 인원수와 음향과의 관계

P: Even with these factors in mind, it is nearly impossible to construct an acoustically perfect structure, as even the audience will affect the acoustics. The average human, as Sabine roughly calculated, absorbs the same amount of sound as six seat cushions. As you can see, this is one of the biggest acoustical dilemmas faced by architects when designing such structures. I mean... How do you know how many people will show up? No one can accurately predict the effect of the attendees since this is an uncontrollable variable. Even if attendance is confirmed beforehand, there is no way of knowing the audience members' exact weight, height, or clothing type, all of which would affect the space's reverberation time.

S: Really? How do engineers solve this problem? Do they just guess?

P: Well, they make educated estimates. [Q10] **One way engineers and architects handle this problem is by designing the room to produce optimum reverberation at full occupancy, but this still leaves room for imperfections.** The many factors involved make acoustics a difficult and imperfect craft. Even the most precise engineering and calculations cannot create a perfect acoustical environment. [Q11] **This is also why adjusting the acoustics of a concert hall or a theater is a continuous task that doesn't end with construction completion.**

S: 교수님이 재료를 말씀하셨는데요, 방의 잔향시간을 결정하는 다른 중요한 요소에는 어떤 것이 있나요?

P: 두 가지 중요한 요소가 있는데요: 방의 크기와 모양이에요. 방의 크기는 잔향시간에 중요한 영향을 미치는 요소에요. 일반적으로, 크기가 큰 방들은 더 긴 잔향시간을 가지는데 이것은 소리 파장이 움직이고 울려 퍼지는데 방해를 받지 않는 공간이 더 많기 때문이에요. 반면에, 작은 방들은 짧은 잔향시간을 가지는데 이것은 소리 파장이 반사는 되지만 작은 공간 크기 때문에 재빨리 사라지기 때문이죠. 모양 또한 중요한 역할을 해요. 반사된 소리 파장으로 측정되기 때문에, 반사 가능한 표면의 수는 잔향 시간과 직접적으로 관련돼요. 따라서, 벽이 더 많다는 것은 더 많은 반사를 의미하며, 이것은 결국 더 긴 잔향시간을 의미하게 되는 거죠. 돔에서는 높은 천장이 공간의 전체적인 크기를 증가시켜 잔향 시간을 증가시켜요.

P: 이러한 요소들을 고려한다 해도, 음향적으로 완벽한 구조물을 건설하는 것은 거의 불가능한데, 심지어 청중도 음향에 영향을 주기 때문이에요. sabine이 대략 계산한 바에 의하면, 일반인은 6개의 의자 쿠션에 해당하는 소리의 양을 흡수해요. 여러분도 알 수 있듯이, 이게 바로 건축가들이 구조물을 지을 때 직면하는 가장 큰 음향학적 난관이에요. 제 말은……얼마나 많은 사람들이 올지 어떻게 알 수 있겠어요? 이것은 통제 불가능한 변수이기 때문에 누구도 정확하게 참석자의 영향에 대한 부분을 측정할 수 없어요. 비록 사전에 참석 여부가 확인되더라도, 청중의 정확한 몸무게, 키, 또는 의복 종류를 알 길이 없는데, 이 모든 것들이 공간의 잔향 시간에 영향을 주게 되죠.

S: 정말요? 공학자들은 어떻게 이 문제를 해결하나요? 그냥 추측하나요?

P: 음, 그들은 지식에 기반한 추정을 해요. [Q10] **공학자와 건축가가 이 문제를 다루는 방법은 좌석이 완전히 찬 상태에서 최적의 잔향 시간을 만들어내는 방을 설계하는 것이에요. 하지만 이것은 여전히 불완전한 여지를 남기게 돼요.** 관련된 많은 요소들 때문에 음향이 어렵고 불완전한 작업이 되는거죠. 심지어 가장 정확한 기술이나 계산도 완벽한 음향 환경을 만들어 내지는 못해요. [Q11] **이것은 또한 콘서트홀이나 극장의 음향을 조절하는 일이 건물이 완성되어도 끝나지 않는 지속적인 작업인 이유에요.**

06 What is the lecture mainly about?

(A) The acoustical problems that some older structures had
(B) The importance of reverberation time in the field of architectural acoustics
(C) The scientific explanation behind how reverberation time ~~affects~~ the acoustics of a structure *
(D) **The factors that determine the acoustics of a sound related structure and how they can be adjusted**

강의는 주로 무엇에 관한 것인가?

(A) 몇몇의 오래된 건물이 가지고 있는 음향 문제
(B) 건축 음향 분야에서 잔향시간의 중요성
(C) 어떻게 잔향 시간이 구조물의 음향에 ~~영향을 끼치~~ 는지 에 대한 과학적인 설명 *
(D) **구조물에 관련된 소리의 음향과 그것들이 조절될 수 있는 방법을 결정짓는 요소들**

Main Idea 교수는 강의 도입부에서 Let's explore some of the integral factors that play a role in defining structural acoustics.(건축 음향을 규정짓는 역할을 하는 몇 개의 필수 요소들에 대해 알아봅시다.)라고 말하며 앞으로의 강의 주제가 건축 음향의 요소들에 대한 것임을 미리 밝히 고 있으므로 정답은 (D)가 된다. (A), (B)의 경우에는 본문에 언급된 내용이나 강의의 전체 주제로 보기에는 어려움이 있고, (C)는 음향 구조에 따라 잔향 시간이 변하는 것임으로 사실을 잘못 기술한 것이 되어 각각 오답이다.

07 Why does the professor mention piano recitals?

(A) ~~To further establish the relationship~~ between acoustically live and dead environments
(B) **To explain that the optimum reverberation time of a structure varies with its usage**
(C) To ~~point out the significance~~ of reverberation time in the field of architectural acoustics *
(D) To describe ~~how correct acoustics can further enhance~~ the quality of music

왜 교수는 피아노 연주회를 언급하는가?

(A) 음향적으로 살아있는 환경과 죽은 환경 사이의 ~~관계를 더 확립하기 위해~~
(B) **한 건축물의 최적 잔향시간이 용도에 따라 변한다 는 것을 설명하기 위해**
(C) 건축 음향 분야에서 잔향시간의 중요성을 ~~지적하 기 위해~~ *
(D) ~~어떻게 정확한 음향이 음악의 질을 더 강화시키~~ 는지를 묘사하기 위해

Inference (Purpose) 교수가 피아노 연주회를 언급한 부분을 살펴보면, In music, solos or piano recitals are often performed in a "dead" environment because there is only one instrument playing and thus clarity and precision are the most important factors.(음 악에서는, 독주나 피아노 연주회가 "죽은 환경"에서 종종 수행되는데 왜냐하면 단지 하나의 악기를 연주하기 때문에 명확성과 정확성이 가장 중요 한 요소인거죠.)에서 공간의 사용 목적에 따라 건물의 최적 잔향 시간은 달라져야 한다는 것을 말하고 있음을 알 수 있다. 따라서 정답은 (B)가 된 다. (A)는 언급되지 않은 내용이며, (C)는 음향 잔향 시간이 중요하기는 하지만 교수가 연주회를 언급한 이유와는 관련성이 부족하고, (D)는 음향이 음악의 질에 있어 중요하나 그 방법적인 측면을 언급하는 것은 아님으로 각각 오답이다.

TEST 3 Set 1-2 Lecture 1 Architectural Acoustics

08 What can be inferred about Sabine's method being used mainly with older buildings? | 오래된 건물에 주로 사용된 Sabine의 방법에 대해 무엇을 추론할 수 있는가?

(A) It did not require altering the fundamental dimensions of a structure.
(B) It was the most structurally dependent means of adjusting the acoustics of a building.
(C) It had already proved its effectiveness with the Fogg Art Museum at Harvard. *
(D) It also helped improve the stability of the building.

(A) 그것은 건축물 구조의 기본적인 면들을 바꿀 필요가 없게 했다.
(B) 건물의 음향을 조정하는데 가장 구조적으로 의존한 수단이었다.
(C) 그것은 하버드 대학의 Fogg Art Museum에서 그 효율성이 이미 증명되었다. *
(D) 그것은 또한 건물의 안정성을 증가시키는데 도움을 주었다.

Inference (Infer) Sabine의 방법이 언급된 부분을 살펴보면, After the success of this project, switching up interior features to change reverberation time became widely used and prove to be particularly effective in adjusting the acoustics of preexisting and older buildings.(이 프로젝트가 성공한 후에, 잔향시간을 변화시키기 위해 건물 내부의 특징을 바꾸는 방식이 폭넓게 사용되었는데, 이미 존재하는 오래된 건물의 음향을 조정하는 데 특히 효과적이라는 사실이 증명되었죠.)에서 내부적인 특징들만 조정하기 때문에 건물의 기본 구조를 바꿀 필요가 없다는 (A)가 정답임을 알 수 있다. (B)는 구조적으로 의존도가 가장 컸다는 것은 본문 내용과 다르며, (C)는 Fogg Art Museum에서 만족스런 결과가 나왔지만 그것은 Sabine이 성공한 이후부터 이미 예전에 증명되었다는 것은 틀린 말이므로 각각 오답이다. (D)는 본문에 언급되지 않으므로 답이 될 수 없다.

09 What does the professor say about the acoustic problems that often occur in older structures? | 교수는 오래된 건축물에서 종종 발생하는 음향 문제에 관해 무엇을 말하는가?

(A) Acoustic echoes were created when the focus of the sound was confined to a limited portion of the audience.
(B) The diffraction of sound waves would consequently increase its intensity.
(C) Older materials in the structures would make the acoustics inaudible to certain sections of the audience. *
(D) Acoustic flaws were created when the sole design emphasis was placed on constructing aesthetically pleasing structures.

(A) 소리의 집중이 관객석의 제한된 부분으로 한정될 때 음향의 메아리가 만들어졌다.
(B) 소리파장의 회절이 결국 그 강도를 증가시킬 것이다.
(C) 구조물 안의 낡은 재료들은 특정 구역에 있는 청중이 소리를 들을 수 없게 만들 것이다. *
(D) 미적으로 즐거움을 주는 구조물을 건설할 때 오직 디자인만 강조되었기 때문에 음향 결점들이 생겨났다.

Detail (Problem) 교수가 오래된 건축물의 음향문제에 대해 언급한 부분을 살펴보면, Before the field of architectural acoustics was widely studied and applied to real life designs, architects often only emphasized the grandeur of the structure without thinking about the acoustics.(건축 음향 분야가 폭 넓게 연구되고 실용디자인에 응용되기 전에는, 건축가들이 종종 음향에 대한 고려없이 단지 구조물의 웅장함만을 강조했어요.)에서 건축가들이 구조물의 웅장함, 즉 미적인 면에서만 중점을 두어 문제가 생겼다는 것을 알 수 있다. 따라서 (D)가 정답이된다. (A)와 (B)는 본문과 관련없는 내용이며, (C)는 특정 구역에 있는 청중이 소리를 들을 수 없게 만드는 것은 재료가 아닌 건물 구조이므로 각각 오답이다.

10 What can be inferred about the problems presented by the varying number of people present in a structure?

구조물에 있는 존재하는 다양한 사람의 수와 관련된 문제점에 대해 무엇을 추론할 수 있는가?

(A) The total level of absorption caused by the audience ~~can be accurately calculated prior to construction~~.
(B) Architects ~~need to calculate~~ not only the size of the audience but also the absorbency of their clothes. *
(C) **By designing spaces with optimal reverberation times at full occupancy, engineers make it easier for adjustments to be made after the space has been completed.**
(D) Sabine's calculation of human to cushion absorption is ~~one way engineers avoid the problem~~.

(A) 청중에 의해 야기된 전체 흡수 레벨은 ~~건설 이전에 정확하게 측정될 수 있다~~.
(B) 건축가들은 청중의 수뿐만 아니라 그들이 입은 의복의 흡수성도 계산할 필요가 있다. *
(C) **기술자들은 사람들로 가득 차 있는 상태에서 최적의 잔향시간을 설계함으로써 공간이 완성된 후에도 조절하기 더 쉽게 만든다.**
(D) Sabine이 사람을 쿠션의 흡수성으로 계산한 것은 공학자들이 문제점을 ~~피하는 하나의 방법~~이 된다.

Detail (Problem) 교수가 오래된 건축물의 음향문제에 대해 언급한 부분을 살펴보면, Before the field of architectural acoustics was widely studied and applied to real life designs, architects often only emphasized the grandeur of the structure without thinking about the acoustics.(건축 음향 분야가 폭 넓게 연구되고 실용디자인에 응용되기 전에는, 건축가들이 종종 음향에 대한 고려없이 단지 구조물의 웅장함만을 강 조했어요.)에서 건축가들이 구조물의 웅장함, 즉 미적인 면에서만 중점을 두어 문제가 생겼다는 것을 알 수 있다. 따라서 (D)가 정답이된다. (A)와 (B)는 본문과 관련없는 내용이며, (C)는 특정 구역에 있는 청중이 소리를 들을 수 없게 만드는 것은 재료가 아닌 건물 구조이므로 각각 오답이다.

11 Listen again to part of the lecture. Then answer the question.
What does the professor imply when he says this:

강의의 일부를 다시 듣고, 질문에 대답하시오
이 말을 할 때 교수는 무엇을 암시하는가:

P: This is also why adjusting the acoustics of a concert hall or a theater is a continuous task that doesn't end with construction completion.

P: 이것은 또한 콘서트 홀이나 극장의 음향을 조절하는 일이 건물이 완성되어도 끝나지 않는 지속적인 작업인 이유에요.

(A) Acoustics ~~cannot be changed~~ to fit a concert hall or a theatre. *
(B) **Ensuring optimal acoustics is an ongoing process that must be performed throughout the life of a venue.**
(C) The number of people in a structure is a variable that cannot be controlled.
(D) Engineers need to continue to ~~calculate the number of audience members~~ even after construction is finished.

(A) 콘서트 홀이나 극장에 맞추기 위해 음향을 바꿀 수 없다. *
(B) **최적의 음향을 확보하는 것은 그 장소의 일생 동안 수행되어야만 하는 지속적인 과정이다.**
(C) 구조물에 있는 사람의 수는 통제할 수 없는 변수이다.
(D) 공학자들은 심지어 건설이 끝난 후에도 청중의 수를 지속적으로 계산할 필요가 있다.

Inference (Headset) 교수가 말하고자 하는 바는 완벽한 음향 환경을 만들어 내지는 못하므로 최적의 음향을 위해서는 지속적인 수정작업이 필요하다는 것이다. 따라서 (B)가 정답이다. (A)는 교수의 의도와는 반대되는 내용이고, (C)는 내용은 맞으나 문제와의 연관성이 부족하며, (D)는 청중의 수를 계산하는 것이 아니라 음향을 조절하는 일이 계속되어야 한다는 말이므로 각각 오답이다.

TEST 3 Set 1-3 Lecture 2: Disapprearance of Anasazi People

문단주제	본문내용	해 석
컴퓨터 모형	Listen to part of a lecture in an anthropology class. The professor is discussing Has anyone here ever heard of computer models? Not models of computers, but rather, simulation models for would-be situations. Today's advanced technology allows researchers to find data about families, populations, or even entire societies using computer simulations they basically create on their own. Fortunately, the development of these virtual situations, has allowed us to look deeper into ancient civilizations. By entering data about the environment and societal rules and patterns, researchers can find answers regarding what happened to historical human civilizations over a certain amount of time and even point out patterns in specific families from the past. For instance... they might use a model to see how population density is affected if life expectancy increases... or... what happens if people start spreading out from a densely populated area. [Q13] **It's important, however, to remember that these models only give theoretical answers about the results of changes in a population.** Real life situations are obviously a little different since the population is made of unique individuals, and, well, unexpected events can occur. Still, these computer models give us relatively correct answers when researching large patterns in a population.	인류학 수업의 일부를 들으시오. 교수는 아나사지에 대해 논의하고 있습니다. 컴퓨터 모형에 대해 들어본 사람 있나요? 이것은 컴퓨터의 종류가 아니라, 있을 법한 상황에 대한 시뮬레이션 모형을 말해요. 오늘날의 진보된 기술은 연구자들이 직접 창조해낸 컴퓨터 모의실험을 사용해 가계들, 인구, 혹은 심지어 사회 전체에 대한 정보를 찾을 수 있게 해주죠. 다행히도, 이런 가상의 상황들의 발들은 우리가 고대문명을 더욱 면밀히 살펴보게 하였어요. 환경과 사회 규칙과 그리고 인구패턴에 대한 데이터를 입력함으로써, 연구자들은 특정 시간 동안 인간 문명의 역사에서 무슨 일이 일어났는지에 대한 답을 찾을 수 있고, 심지어는 과거의 특정한 가계의 패턴을 볼 수도 있어요. 예를 들어…. 그들은 기대 수명이 증가하면 어떻게 인구 밀도가 영향을 받는지… 또는… 사람들이 인구가 밀집된 지역에서 다른 곳으로 퍼져나가기 시작하면 무슨 일이 생기는지 알아보기 위해서 모형을 사용할 수도 있어요. [Q13] **하지만, 이런 모형들은 인구 변화의 최종 결과에 대해 단지 이론적인 해답만 줄 수 있다는 것을 기억하는게 중요해요.** 실제 삶의 상황들은 확실히 조금 다른데, 왜냐하면 인구는 독특한 개인들로 구성되어 있고, 음, 예상하지 못한 사건들이 발생할 수 있기 때문이죠. 그래도, 이 컴퓨터 모형들은, 인구의 전반적인 패턴을 연구할 때 상대적으로 정확한 해답을 우리에게 주고 있어요.
아나사지 건물들	These computer simulations have been used to find the likely causes of the declines of past societies, such as the Anasazi. As we discussed last week, the Anasazi lived around seven hundred years ago in the area of the southwestern United States now known as the Four Corners, present day Arizona, Utah, Colorado, and New Mexico. The Anasazi are probably most well-known for their mud villages that look like gatherings of boxes strategically placed above cliffs and along rivers. [Q14] **These villages consist of buildings that could house about a hundred people each. You would think they would have been spread out over the land, like ranches; however, they more closely resemble apartment buildings, but lack stairs to enter the higher levels, so you couldn't even enter most of them without climbing a ladder.** Their most common building material appears to have been bricks which they made using a mixture of straw, natural clay, and stones. Because entire Anasazi villages are still standing intact	이러한 컴퓨터 시뮬레이션은 Anasazi처럼 과거 사회들이 쇠퇴한 원인들을 찾는 데 사용되어 왔어요. 우리가 지난주에 논의했듯이, Anasazi 사람들은 700년 전 지금의 애리조나, 유타, 콜로라도 그리고 뉴멕시코로 알려진 미국 남서부지역에 있는 Four Corners에 거주했던 사람들이에요. Anasazi인들은 절벽 위와 강을 따라 위치해 있는 전략적으로 모여 있는 상자처럼 보이는 진흙으로 지어진 마을들로 아마 가장 잘 알려져 있을 거에요. [Q14] **이 마을들은 각각 약 100명의 사람들을 수용할 수 있는 건물들로 구성되어 있어요. 여러분은 집들이 목장처럼, 땅에 흩어져 있을 거라고 생각할지도 모르지만, 그 집들은 아파트 건물처럼 지어졌는데 위층으로 올라갈 계단이 없어서, 사다리로 올라가지 않고서는 대부분의 건물에 들어갈 수조차 없죠.** 가장 흔한 건축 재료는 벽돌로 보이는데, 짚, 자연 진흙, 그리고 돌들을 혼합해서 만들었어요. 아나사지 마을 전체의 건축물이 손상되지

in the region today, we know for sure that they were excellent builders. By simply looking at the complexity of these buildings, we are able to see the intricate techniques that these people used. One of the unique buildings found there is the kiva, a separate circular underground room where they asked for assistance in agriculture and health from the serpents, fire, and sun. We know this because they also left behind petroglyphs, engravings in stone, that give us a peek inside their culture and beliefs. These historical sites have provided abundant historical artifacts and knowledge, but they haven't been able to explain exactly why the Anasazi suddenly disappeared after thriving for a thousand years.

Most people assumed that it was because of changes in the climate during the period. By studying their environment, we can see that there was a 50 year period with very little rain during the 1200s. Such a prolonged decrease in water availability seems like clear evidence that the farming Anasazi culture couldn't have continued to produce harvests sufficient for sustaining the population of the region.

[Q15] **After more in-depth research, however, some scientists began to question this theory. One of them was archaeologist Jeffrey Dean.** He studied the rings in the logs used in the Anasazi buildings which are still standing today. Tree rings, as you know, are the circles found when you cut down a tree. Because they are developed through a trees growth pattern, they can be seen as signs of the climate and nutrients available during the time. Dean discovered possible inaccuracies in the drought theory by studying these rings from the 14th century. He found that instead of undergoing a true drought, the area may have experienced a shift in the typical precipitation patterns in which the heavy summer rains that helped bring late spring crops to harvest did not occur as expected. This may have caused the Anasazi to became unsure of their gods and religious practices. Other research opposing the theory was conducted by Carla Van West who studied the harvest and nutrition consumption of individuals during normal circumstances. Her data led her to believe that a drought wouldn't have caused the entire population to leave the land or leave them unable to grow enough harvest to sustain themselves.

Set 1-3 Lecture 2: Disappearence of Anasazi People

Based on the data these two scientists began to look like drought couldn't have been the only reason the Anasazi civilization disappeared.

This is where computer simulations became useful. We already knew the location of their settlements, what they ate... even what the environment was like every year. So, to figure out what happened to the Anasazi, we put in all the data we knew about them and the valley in which they lived. We also entered facts about the water supply and gave people characteristics that corresponded to the environment. Say, like, they might have had fewer children if the harvest wasn't good enough that year, since not all of the families could survive, or... perhaps they left the area to find a place with better weather.

Basically we used the program to recreate a period of time from, uh... about the 800s to like, 1300, which is when they disappeared. Then do you know what happened? The program gave us results that correlated with the historical information that we already have. [Q16] **The first fact that the simulation supported was that the population grew in size, then declined over time,** which probably means that the population increased when the harvest was plentiful, then shrunk when the harvest wasn't as good. [Q16] **The results also confirmed where the people lived within the valley.** The biggest inaccuracy in the conclusions was that the computer simulation showed that by 1300, the population had decreased to only a few families, but in reality the population had disappeared completely.

So what are some of the final conclusions that the computer simulation gave about the Anasazi people? Well, first, it shows that the environment really affects every aspect of a population, its size, where they lived... [Q17] **However, it still doesn't answer all of the questions about their disappearance.** It shows us that a small population could have kept living there. We're still left to wonder why they all disappeared from the area if the land could still support some people.

12 What is the lecture mainly about?

(A) **Figuring out the reason for the disappearance of the Anasazi people using computer simulations**
(B) Understanding the reasons ~~for the failure of harvest~~ in the Four Corners region
(C) ~~How mistakes were found~~ in previous research regarding the climate in the 1300s
(D) The reasons for ~~fluctuation~~ in the population of the Anasazi society

강의는 주로 무엇에 대한 것인가?

(A) **컴퓨터 시뮬레이션을 이용해서 아나사지 사람들이 사라진 이유를 알아내는 것.**
(B) Four Corners에서의 ~~추수 실패~~에 대한 이유들을 이해하는 것.
(C) 1300년대의 기후에 관련된 이전 연구에서 한 ~~실수가 어떻게 발견되었나.~~
(D) 아나사지 사회의 ~~인구 변동~~에 대한 이유들. *

Main Idea 교수는 처음 도입부에서 computer model에 대한 설명을 한 후에, 아나사지 사람들이 사라진 이유에 대한 이론에 이를 적용시키면서 강의를 전개하고 있다. 그러므로 강의 주제는 (A)가 된다. Four Corners의 추수 실패에 대한 이유나, 이전 연구의 실수 그리고 아나사지 사회의 인구변동은 본문에 언급된 내용이 아니므로 (B), (C), (D)는 각각 오답이다.

---

13 What does the professor imply about computer simulations?

(A) **They offer speculative answers, not necessarily precise ones.**
(B) Scientists have used them to ~~accurately map~~ the rise and fall of civilizations. *
(C) They can ~~always predict unexpected events~~.
(D) They ~~are not accurate enough~~ to support theories about the past.

컴퓨터 시뮬레이션에 대해 교수는 무엇을 암시하는가?

(A) **그들은 꼭 정확한 것은 아닌 추측에 근거한 답을 제공한다.**
(B) 과학자들은 그것을 사용하여 문명의 흥망성쇠를 ~~정확히 그려낼 수 있었다.~~ *
(C) 그것은 ~~항상 예상치못한 사건들을~~ 예측할 수 있다.
(D) 그것은 과거에 대한 이론들을 지지할 정도로 ~~충분히 정확하지는 않다.~~

Interference (Imply) 본문 내용의 도입부에서, It's important, however, to remember that these models only give theoretical answers about the results of changes in a population.(하지만, 이런 모형들은 인구 변화의 최종 결과에 대해 단지 이론적인 해답만 줄 수 있다는 것을 기억하는게 중요해요.)을 보면 교수는 컴퓨터 시뮬레이션이 이론적인 답을 줄뿐이며 그것이 완전히 정확하다고 생각하지 않는다는 것을 알 수 있다. 따라서 정답은 (A)이다. (B), (C)는 본문의 내용과 어긋나게 기술되었으며, (D)는 교수가 예를 든 사례를 통해서 컴퓨터 시뮬레이션이 과거에 대한 이론을 지지할 정도의 정확성은 보이고 있음을 알 수 있으므로 오답이다.

TEST 3 Set 1-3 Lecture 2 Disappearence of Anasazi People

14 According to the professor, which of the following is one of the characteristics of the Anasazi villages?

교수에 따르면, 다음 중 어떤 것이 아나사지 마을의 특징인가?

(A) They ~~were built~~ like ranches.
(B) **Their structures resembled apartment complexes.**
(C) The ladder was considered an important tool ~~due to its use in hunting~~.
(D) They ~~did not form a community since they were nomads who travelled often~~.

(A) 그것은 목장처럼 ~~지어졌다~~.
(B) **그들의 구조는 아파트 건물을 닮았다.**
(C) ~~사냥에서의 용도때문에~~ 사다리는 중요한 도구로 여겨졌다.
(D) ~~자주 여행을 하던 유목민이었기 때문에 그들은 공동체를 형성하지 않았다~~.

> **Detail** (Characteristic) 교수가 아나사지 마을의 특징에 대해 언급한 부분을 보면, The villages consist of buildings that could house about a hundred people each. You would think they would have been spread out over land, like ranches; however, they more closely resemble apartment buildings, but lack stairs to enter the higher levels, so you couldn't even enter most of them without climbing a ladder.(이 마을들은 각각 약 100명의 사람들을 각각 수용할 수 있는 건물들로 구성되어 있어요. 여러분은 집들이 목장처럼, 땅에 흩어져 있을거라고 생각할지도 모르지만, 그 집들은 아파트 건물처럼 지어졌는데 위층으로 올라갈 수 있는 계단이 없어서, 사다리로 올라가지 않고서는 대부분의 건물에 들어갈 수조차 없죠.)에서 아나사지 마을의 건물들은 목장처럼 흩어져있지 않고 아파트처럼 가까이 붙어 지어졌기 때문에 구조적으로 비슷한 모양임을 알 수 있다. 따라서 (B)가 정답이고 (A)는 오답이다. 또한 (C)는 사다리는 사냥 도구가 아니므로, (D)는 아나사지 사람들이 마을을 이루어 건물들을 짓고 살았다는 것은 유목민이 아니라 정착민이고 공동체를 이뤘다는 의미이므로 각각 오답이다.

15 Why does the professor mention Jeffrey Dean?

왜 교수는 Jeffrey Dean을 언급하는가?

(A) **Dean was one of the people who challenged the idea that the Anasazi disappeared due to climate change.**
(B) He ~~supported Carla Van West's conclusion~~ that a drought caused the Anasazi society to move away from the valley.
(C) Jeffrey Dean ~~analyzed the rainfall~~ that occurred during the 1300s that led to poor harvests.
(D) He pointed out that ~~poor nutrition~~ led to the disappearance of the Anasazi population.

(A) **Dean은 아나사지 사람들이 기후 변화 때문에 사라졌다는 생각에 도전한 사람 중 한 명이었다.**
(B) 그는 아나사지 사회가 가뭄때문에 골짜기에서 이동했다는 ~~Carla Van West의 결론을 지지했다~~.
(C) Jeffrey Dean은 적은 수확을 야기한 1300년대에 발생한 ~~강수량을 분석했다~~.
(D) 그는 ~~부족한 영양분이~~ 아나사지 인구가 사라지는 것으로 연결되었다고 지적했다.

> **Inference** (Purpose) 교수가 Jeffrey Dean에 대해 언급한 부분을 보면, After more in-depth research, however, some scientists began to question this theory. One of them was an archaeologist Jeffrey Dean.(하지만 더 깊은 연구가 이루어지자, 몇몇 과학자들이 이 이론에 의문을 제기하기 시작했어요. 그들 중 한 명이 고고학자인 Jeffrey Dean이에요.)이후의 내용에서 Dean은 기후 변화가 아나사지 사람들이 사라진 원인 이라는 이론에 도전을 한 사람 중 하나임을 알 수 있으므로 (A)가 정답이다. (B), (C)는 강의 내용과 다르므로 각각 오답이다. (D)는 Dean이 제시한 내용과 다르며 교수가 언급한 이유가 아니므로 오답이다.

16 According to the professor, which two of the following were the results of the computer model?

Click on 2 answers

(A) The population increased then decreased.
(B) It confirmed the location of settlements.
(C) The ~~amount of harvest~~ should have been enough to support a large population.
(D) The results illustrated ~~the current locations of the descendants~~.

교수님에 따르면, 다음 중 어떤 것이 컴퓨터 모델의 두 개의 결과인가?

2개의 답을 고르시오.

(A) 이 인구가 증가했다가 그 다음에 감소했다.
(B) 정착지의 위치를 확인시켜 주었다.
(C) ~~수확량~~이 많은 인구를 지탱할 수 있을 만큼 충분했을 것이다.
(D) 그 결과는 후손들의 현재 위치를 설명했다.

Detail (Result) The first fact that the simulation supported was that the population grew in size, then declined over time, ……(중략)…. The results also confirmed where the people lived within the valley.(모의실험이 지지한 첫번째 사실은 인구의 규모가 커지고 나서 시간에 걸쳐서 쇠퇴했다는 것인데, …… 그 결과는 또한, 사람들이 골짜기 내에서 거주했던 사실을 확인시켜 주었어요.)에서 모델의 결과 두 가지는, 인구의 변동 추이와 거주 지역임을 알 수 있으므로 (A), (B)가 각각 정답이다. (C)의 수확의 양과 (D)의 후손들이 현재 사는 위치는 본문에 언급되지 않으므로 오답이다.

17 What does the professor conclude about the disappearance of the Anasazi?

(A) He states that the model does not give an exact answer.
(B) He thinks climate ~~did not have any impact~~.
(C) He implies that using computer simulations was ~~a waste of time and energy~~.
(D) He explains that some Anasazi people ~~are still alive today~~.

교수님은 아나사지 사람들이 사라진 것에 대해 어떤 결론을 내리는가?

(A) 그는 이 모델이 정확한 해답을 주지 않는다고 말한다.
(B) 그는 기후가 ~~어떤 영향도 미치지 않았다~~고 생각한다.
(C) 그는 컴퓨터 시뮬레이션을 사용하는 것은 ~~시간과 에너지 낭비라고~~ 생각한다.
(D) 그는 일부 아나사지 사람들이 ~~오늘날에도 여전히 살아있다고~~ 설명한다.

Inference (Opinion) 본문의 결론 부분에서 교수의 의견을 살펴보면, However, it still doesn't answer all of the question about their disappearance.(하지만, 이것은 여전히 그들이 사라진 것에 대한 의문을 모두 해결해 주지는 못해요.)에서 이 모델이 의문에 대한 명확한 답을 주지 않는다고 말하고 있다. 그러므로 정답은 (A)가 된다. (B)는 앞부분에서 기후가 영향을 주었다고 말했으므로, (C)는 교수가 도입부분에서 말한 것과 반대되는 내용이고 결론으로써 부적절하므로 각각 오답이다. 그리고 (D)는 본문에 언급되지 않은 내용이므로 답이 될 수 없다.

TEST 3 — Set 2-1

Conversation: Psychological Impact of Music

문단주제	본문내용	해석

Listen to a Conversation between a student and a professor.

S: [Q5] Hi, Professor Wilkins. I'm in your music appreciation class... [Q1] I'm here about the project...

P: Well, I assume you've chosen the genre and topic of the music, by now. What are you having trouble with?

S: I've just been so caught up with other classes...and frankly, [Q1] I haven't even decided on the genre, let alone the topic.

P: Oh, not even the genre? Wow, you must have been either really busy or procrastinating.

S: I've been swamped lately, and plus, I've had no good ideas regarding the genre of music.

P: Oh, why don't you try to think about it differently... think backwards? I mean, instead of worrying that you haven't chosen the genre yet.

S: I don't follow.

P: Make a... a rough-draft in your head; how you're feeling at a certain time of day, this could be your topic. And then find a genre that best fits those feelings. Are you into hip-hop?

S: Huh? Are you saying that I should match a random feeling to a specific genre?

P: [Q2] I sure am, but it sure would be helpful if you could actually capture the moment when you're feeling the need to listen to a genre like hip-hop. Take, for example, when you feel the need for something with a rapid beat, tempo, and fast wording.

S: Oh, I certainly know that feeling.

P: The hip-hop genre is one that I'm personally eager to read about. Its relatively short history and rapid spread and development have fascinated me for quite a while.

S: Anything else I should keep in mind?

P: Technicality. The usage of slang, I believe some words in hip-hop are related to the concept of oxymorons.

학생과 교수의 대화를 들으시오.

S: [Q5] 안녕하세요, Wilkins교수님. 저는 교수님의 음악감상 수업을 듣고 있는데요… [Q1] 제가 여기 온건 프로젝트 때문이에요…

P: 음, 내 생각엔 지금쯤이면 음악 장르나 주제는 골랐을 것 같은데. 무슨 문제가 있는 거니?

S: 저는 다른 강의들 때문에 무척 바빴거든요… 그래서 솔직히 말씀드리면… [Q1] 전 아직 장르조차 정하지 못했어요, 주제는 말할 것도 없고요.

P: 오, 심지어 장르도? 와우, 넌 정말 바빴거나 아님 꾸물거리거나 둘 중 하나겠구나.

S: 최근에 할 일이 너무 많았어요. 그리고 거기에다, 음악 장르와 관련된 좋은 아이디어도 없었구요.

P: 오, 다르게 생각해보는건 어떨까… 반대로 생각해 볼래? 그러니까, 아직 장르를 정하지 못했다고 걱정하는 대신에 말이야.

S: 이해가 안 되는데요.

P: 네 머리 속에 초안을 만들어 보렴; 하루의 특정 시간에 네가 어떻게 느끼는지를 말이야, 이것이 주제가 될 수 있는거지. 그런 다음 그런 느낌에 가장 잘 들어맞는 장르를 찾는거야. 넌 힙합을 좋아하니?

S: 네? 제가 무작정 고른 느낌을 특정 장르와 연결시켜야 한다고 말씀하시는 거에요?

P: [Q2] 맞아, 하지만 만약 네가 힙합같은 어떤 장르를 들을 필요가 있다고 느끼는 그런 순간을 잡아 낼 수 있다면 확실히 도움이 될꺼야. 예를 들면 빠른 박자, 템포 그리고 빠른 가사가 필요한 때를 생각해봐.

S: 오, 그 느낌은 확실히 알겠네요.

P: 힙합은 내가 개인적으로 읽어보고 싶어하는 장르란다. 상대적으로 짧은 역사를 가졌는데도 빠르게 전파되고 발전한 부분이 한동안 나를 매혹시켰거든.

S: 제가 염두에 둬야할 다른 사항이 있나요?

P: 전문적인 표현이야. 속어의 사용 말인데, 나는 힙합에서 쓰이는 몇몇 단어들이 모순어법의 개념과 관련이 있다고 생각해.

S: What was that?

P: An oxymoron... It's when two contradictory words make up a phrase, such as 'dark sun', or 'mandatory charity'. I'm sure you've heard some of them in hip-hop. You can note them and write about how they came into being.

S: I think I get it. Well, can I also incorporate some psychology into it; since it's my major?

P: Sure, whatever you can do. Say... if you're a psychology major, would you mind helping me out with something? There's not much glory in it, but if you're up for it.

S: Sure! What is it?

P: [Q3] Well, I'm attending a symposium about certain types of music and their effect on infants. I'm okay with all the musical aspects, but the psychology part... I need someone to help me out. I'm sure you've heard of the research on music during pregnancy...

S: Oh! I've actually wanted to be a part of that. I've read about it. They mentioned the psychological change of mothers and... surprisingly it affects the fetus. Many pregnant women listen to calm, classical music, which they feel leads to happier childhoods for their children. I'll have to review it to remember the specifics, though, the research was quite old... maybe the symposium will cover new details that I haven't read about yet.

P: How about you gather a couple of your friends from your department and bring them along? The school will cover expenses for accommodations.

S: I'll have to talk to them, [Q4] I don't know if we can be of much help with this sort of information... and plus, our department is conducting a huge research project and most of the students are being used as the control group. I don't know if we will be able to leave town during the project.

P: Well, I will contact the head of the psychology department and see what I can do.

S: That'd be great. We've all been wanting to leave town for ice break.

TEST 3　Set 2 - 1　Conversation: Psychological Impact of Music

01 Why does the student go to see her professor?

(A) To ask for guidance so she can get a proper start on his class assignment
(B) To ask if she can incorporate her major into the assignment
(C) To ~~get approval for her choice~~ of genres for her music project *
(D) To get further information on a ~~psychology symposium~~ she needs for her report

왜 학생은 교수를 찾아갔는가?

(A) 강의 과제를 올바르게 시작할 수 있게 지도를 부탁하기 위해
(B) 교수에게 그녀의 전공을 과제에 접목시켜도 되는지 묻기위해
(C) 음악프로젝트를 위해 자신이 ~~선택한 장르에 대한 허락을 받기~~ 위해*
(D) 레포트를 위해 필요한 ~~심리학 심포지엄에~~ 대해 더 많은 정보를 얻기 위해

Main Purpose　본문 내용의 도입 부분에서, I'm here about the project …(중략)…I haven't even decided on the genre, let alone the topic(제가 여기 온 건 프로젝트 때문인데요.…(중략)…. 전 아직 장르조차 정하지 못했어요, 주제는 말할 것도 없고요.)을 보면 학생은 강의의 프로젝트 과제를 시작하는 것에 대해 물어보려고 온 것임을 알 수 있으므로 (A)가 정답이다. (B)는 학생이 질문한 내용은 맞지만 교수를 찾아온 이유는 아니며, (C)는 학생은 장르를 이미 선택해서 교수에게 허락을 받으러 온 것이 아니므로, 또한 (D)는 학생이 찾아온 이유와 심포지엄은 관계가 없으므로 각각 오답이다.

02 What does the professor suggest the student do regarding the assignment?

(A) ~~Use~~ information from a psychology symposium and ~~write on~~ how classical music affects infants.
(B) Wait until the student feels an emotion that she feels comfortable enough with to link it to her favorite genre.
(C) Elaborate on the ~~history~~ of hip-hop and focus on how ~~it succeeded in captivating the public~~.
(D) ~~Utilize psychology~~ in order to further study a certain type of music and its ~~effect~~ on infants.

과제와 관련해서 교수가 학생에게 제안한 것은 무엇인가?

(A) 심리학 심포지엄으로부터 얻은 정보를 ~~사용하여~~ 고전음악이 어떻게 유아에게 영향을 미치는 지에 ~~대해 써라~~.
(B) 학생이 가장 좋아하는 장르와 연결시킬 만큼 충분히 안정적인 감정을 느낄 때까지 기다려라.
(C) 힙합의 역사를 깊게 다루고 그것이 어떻게 ~~대중을 사로잡는데~~ 성공했는지에 초점을 맞춰라.
(D) 특정 종류의 음악과 그것이 아이에게 끼치는 ~~영향~~에 대해 더 깊이 공부하기 위해 ~~심리학을 적용해라~~.

Detail (Suggestion)　과제와 관련해서 교수가 제안한 것은, I sure am, but it sure would be helpful if you could actually capture the moment when you're feeling the need to listen a genre like hip-hop.(맞아, 하지만 만약 네가 힙합같은 어떤 장르를 들을 필요가 있다고 느끼는 그런 순간을 잡아낼 수 있다면 확실히 도움이 될꺼야)이므로 정답은 (B)이다. (A), (B), (D)는 본문에 언급된 적은 있으나 질문과 관계는 내용이므로 각각 오답이다.

03 Why does the professor mention music and its effect on infants?

(A) To let the student know about a symposium that can ~~help her finish the assignment~~
(B) To indicate that ~~behavioral psychology~~ of infants is an area of study that ~~will be covered in the professor's class~~
(C) To encourage the student to ~~study a new topic~~ that the professor is not familiar with
(D) To indicate that the professor is new to the field and would like some assistance

왜 교수는 음악과 그것이 태아에 끼치는 영향에 대해 언급하는가?

(A) ~~학생이 과제를 끝내는 데 도움이 되는 학술회를 알려주기 위해~~
(B) 유아 ~~행동심리학은 교수의 강의에서 다루게 될 분 야~~라는 것을 알려주기 위해
(C) 교수가 친숙하지 않은 새로운 주제를 ~~학생에게 공 부하라고 격려하기 위해~~
(D) 교수가 그 분야에서 초보자이고 도움이 필요하다 는 것을 말하기 위해

Inference (Purpose)   교수가 음악이 유아에게 미치는 영향에 대해 언급한 부분을 살펴보면, Well, I'm attending a symposium about certain types of music and their effect on infants. I'm okay with all the musical aspects, but the psychology part…I need someone to help me out, I'm sure you've heard of the research on music during pregnancy…(음, 내가 특정 종류의 음악이 유아에게 미치는 영향 에 관한 심포지엄에 참석하게 되었거든. 난 음악적 측면은 전혀 문제가 없는데, 심리학 부분은… 누군가의 도움이 좀 필요해. 넌 임신기간 동안 에 듣는 음악 에 관한 연구를 들어봤을 거야.)에서 교수가 앞으로 참석하게 되는 심포지엄에서 다루는 주제에 대해 잘 모르는 부분이 있고 다른 사 람의 도움이 필요 하다는 것이므로 정답은 (D)가 된다. (A)는 학술회에 대한 언급은 맞으나 학생의 과제와는 관계가 없고, (B)는 언급된 내용이 아니며, (C)는 교수가 친숙하지 않은 주제인건 맞지만, 학생에게 그것에 대해 공부하라고 격려하는 건 아니므로 각각 오답이다.

TEST 3 — Set 2-1 | Conversation: Psychological Impact of Music

04 What can be inferred about the students of the psychology department?

심리학과 학생들에 대해 추론할 수 있는 것은 무엇인가?

(A) The accommodations may be ~~too expensive for the students to handle.~~

(B) The students may be able to attend the symposium if the professor can get them excused from the project.

(C) The topic covered at the symposium may be too difficult for the students to fully understand.

(D) The students are not an important part of the psychology experiment, but are still reluctant to attend the symposium.

(A) 참석 비용은 학생들이 감당하기에는 너무 비쌀지도 모른다.

(B) 만약 교수가 학생들을 프로젝트에서 빼내어 줄 수 있다면 학생들은 심포지엄에 참여하게 될지도 모른다.

(C) 학술회에서 다루는 내용은 아마도 학생들이 완전히 이해하기에는 너무 어려울지도 모른다.

(D) 학생들은 심리학과 실험의 중요한 부분을 차지하지는 않지만, 학술회에 참여하기를 여전히 꺼려하고 있다.

Inference (Infer) 심리학과 학생들에 대해 언급된 부분을 살펴보면, S: I don't know if we can be of much help with this sort of information… and plus, our department is conducting a huge research project and most of the students are being used as the control group. I don't know if we will be able to leave town during the project. P: Well, I will contact the head of the psychology department and see what I can do. (이런 종류의 정보에 저희가 얼마나 도움이 될지 몰라서요… 그리고 또, 저희 과에 거대한 연구프로젝트가 진 행 중인데 대부분의 학생들이 대조군이거든요. 그래서 프로젝트를 하는 동안 저희가 마을을 떠날 수 있을지 모르겠어요. P: 음, 내가 심리학과 학과장 님께 연락해서 알아볼께.)에서 아마 학생들은 교수님의 도움을 받아 학술회에 참석할 수 있을지도 모른다는 것을 짐작할 수 있으므로 정답은 (B)이다. (A)는 참석비용은 학교에서 부담한다고 했으므로, (C)는 사실과 다르므로 각각 오답이다. (D)는 학생들은 실험에서 대조군으로 중요한 역할을 하고 있으며, 심포지엄 참여 희망 여부는 언급되지 않아 답이 될 수 없다.

05

Listen again to part of the conversation. Then answer the question.

S: Hi, Professor Wilkins. I'm in your music appreciation class... I'm here about the project.
P: Well, I assume you've chosen the genre and topic of the music, by now. What are you having trouble with?

What does the professor imply when he says this? : 🎧

> Well, I assume you've chosen the genre and topic of the music, by now.

(A) His assignment ~~included a specific set of instructions~~ that stated the genre and topic.
(B) He ~~assumes~~ that the student hasn't even decided on a topic yet.
(C) It has been long enough since the assignment was given out for the students to choose a genre and topic.
(D) He ~~is asking~~ if the student has chosen a proper genre and topic. *

대화의 일부를 다시 듣고, 물음에 답하시오.

S: 안녕하세요, Wilkins교수님. 저는 교수님의 음악감상 수업을 듣고 있는데요… 제가 여기 온 건 프로젝트 때문이에요…
P: 음, 내 생각엔 지금쯤이면 음악 장르나 주제는 골랐을 것 같은데. 무슨 문제가 있는 거니?

교수가 이 말을 할 때 무엇을 암시하는가?

> 음, 내 생각엔 지금쯤이면 음악 장르나 주제는 골랐을것 같은데

(A) 그의 과제는 장르와 주제를 언급하는 ~~특정한 일련의 지시를 포함하고있다.~~
(B) 그는 학생이 주제를 아직 정하지 않았음을 ~~가정하고 있다.~~
(C) 과제가 주어진 이후 학생이 장르와 주제를 선택할 만큼의 충분한 시간이 흘렀다.
(D) 그는 학생이 올바른 장르와 주제를 선택했는지 ~~묻고 있다.~~ *

Inference (Headset) 교수가 말한 의미는 과제의 장르와 주제를 선택할 시간은 이미 충분히 주어졌다는 것이므로 정답은 (C)이다. (A)는 언급되지 않는 내용이고, (B)는 교수는 그 반대인 상황을 가정하고 있으며, (D)는 학생에게 묻는 것이 아니라 자신의 짐작을 말하는 것이므로 각각 오답이다.

TEST 3 Set 2-2 — Lecture 1: Invention of Electric Guitar

문단주제	본문내용	해석
전자기타에 대한 소개	Listen to part of a lecture on music history. The professor is discussing electric guitar. P: We've been studying the development of 18th and 19th century musical instruments, but today we'll move on to the 20th century... Okay... so what do jazz, rock 'n' roll, country, and blues have in common? Well, one major connection is the important role of the electric guitar in these genres. Of all the musical instruments used during the 1900s, the electric guitar is probably the most versatile and influential. It can be played in harmony with almost any other instrument or hold the spotlight on its own. [Q6] **Let's look at the changes the electric guitar went through to become the instrument that we know today.**	음악에 관한 강의 일부를 들으시오. 교수는 전자기타에 관해 논의하고 있습니다. P: 우리는 18-19세기 악기의 발달에 대해서 공부를 해왔는데요, 오늘은 20세기로 넘어갈께요... 자... 그럼 재즈와 로큰롤, 컨트리 음악과 블루스가 가지는 공통점은 뭘까요? 음, 한가지 중요한 연결점은 이들 장르에서 전자 기타가 가지는 중요한 역할이에요. 1900년대에 사용된 모든 악기들 중에서, 전자기타는 아마 가장 용도가 다양하고 영향력이 큰 악기일거에요. 그것은 거의 모든 다른 악기들과 하모니를 이룰 수 있었고 또한 그 자체로도 각광을 받았죠. [Q6] **그럼 오늘날 우리가 알고 있는 악기가 되기까지 전자 기타가 겪었던 변화들을 살펴보기로 해요.**
전자기타의 필요성	P: Can anyone tell me what motivated the development of electric guitars? S: Um... They can make a lot of strange noises... Was it to give the acoustic guitar a wider range of sounds? P: Close. An electric guitar does have a wider range of sounds, or effects, but they were not considered when designing the electric guitar. Effects were developed by guitarists experimenting with fully constructed guitars, after the design was finished. One of the biggest incentives for developing an electric guitar was amplifying the guitar's sound. Already beloved by both artists and audiences alike, guitars couldn't be used in concerts or ensembles because they were buried and lost amidst the louder brass and horn instruments. [Q10-C] **Also, if you remember, phonograph recordings and commercial radio became popular music media in the 1920s. Along with big band music popularity, this meant that guitars needed to change, or live guitar performances would disappear. This is why louder guitars became even more necessary,** and guitar makers experimented with many innovative changes such as the curved archtop shape and larger bodies.	P: 여러분 중에서 무엇이 전자기타를 발전시켰는지 말해 볼 사람 있나요? S: 음. 그건 특이한 소리를 많이 낼 수 있잖아요.. 클래식 기타에 좀 더 넓은 영역을 소리를 제공한점인가요? P: 근접해요. 전자기타는 폭넓은 소리와 효과를 가지고 있지만, 처음 설계할 때는 그 점이 고려되지 않았어요. 음악효과는 설계가 다 끝난 후에 연주자들이 시험해 보면서 발달하게 되었죠. 전자 기타가 발달하게 된 가장 큰 이유 중 하나는 기타 소리를 증폭시켜야 하기 때문이에요. 기타는 이미 예술가들과 청중들에게 사랑을 받고 있었으나, 콘서트나 앙상블에서는 사용될 수가 없었는데 왜냐하면 이것은 소리가 큰 금관악기나 혹은 호른 악기 속에 묻히고 사라졌기 때문이죠. [Q10-C] **또한, 만약 여러분이 기억한다면, 축음기나 상업 라디오가 1920년대에 인기 있는 음악 매체가 되었잖아요. 큰 악단의 밴드 음악이 인기를 얻게 되면서, 기타에도 변화가 필요하게 되었고 그렇지 않으면 라이브 기타 연주는 사라질 수 밖에 없었죠. 이것이 바로 소리가 큰 기타가 더욱 더 필요한 이유였어요.** 그래서 기타 제작자들은 아치형 모양이나 더 큰 몸체와 같은 많은 혁신적인 변화들을 실험하게 되었죠.

|전자 기타의 발명| P: Around this time, engineers and inventors began tinkering with electricity and the guitar as well; one of them was George Beauchamp. Beauchamp, co-founder of the biggest guitar maker of the time, figured that a magnet could capture the motion of a steel string within its magnetic field and convert it to electrical energy. The electrical energy created by the strings' vibrations' strength depended on a combination of factors, such as the string's thickness, the rate of vibration, and the strings' distance from the magnet. Since the motion could be captured as electrical energy, each unique sound from the string could be digitized and amplified through a speaker or a similar device. [Q7/Q10-A] **In 1931, Beauchamp and his partner used horseshoe magnets to design a device called a 'pickup', that did exactly that. They incorporated it into a Hawaiian lap steel guitar creating the first electric guitar in history, the 'Frying Pan'.** If you think that name is funny, you should see its shape; you'd understand.

P: Beauchamp believed that the future of guitars was electric and started selling electric guitars like the 'Frying Pan.' They were an instant success, getting praise from the most popular guitarists of the time. [Q8] **Unfortunately, for Beauchamp, other manufacturers had copied his technology and began producing electric guitars before he could stop them six years later.**

|스페인풍 전자 기타| P: Lap steel guitars like Beauchamp's are not really widely used today. We're more used to the larger, curved bodies of Spanish-style guitars, which are held sideways and finger-strummed. A company called Gibson Guitars was the first to successfully implement and commercialize Beauchamp's technology in Spanish guitars. [Q10-B] **By 1933, they'd produced their first electric guitar, the extremely popular ES-150. Country and blues guitarists, as well as skilled jazz guitarists switched over to this electric guitar and produced innovative sounds that were never before heard in guitars, or in any other instrument for that matter.**

TEST 3 Set 2-2 — Lecture 1: Invention of Electric Guitar

ES-150의 문제점

P: [Q9-D] The ES-150 was, however, far from perfect. Since the pickups at the time were not very advanced, rather than isolating the vibrations from the strings, they acted as sort of a microphone, amplifying everything, like the vibration of the guitar body. This caused a lot of fuzzy background noises, not the clean, crisp sound guitarists sought. Another problem was audio feedback. [Q9-B] This occurs when a guitarist strums a guitar and the sound gets amplified by a loudspeaker. If this amplified sound reaches the guitar strings, it causes them to vibrate more. These vibrations are picked up and amplified again and again; creating a loop of loud, digitized noise.

P: [Q9-D] ES-150은 완벽함과는 거리가 멀었어요. 당시의 픽업들이 그리 발달되지는 않았기 때문에, 기타 줄로부터 진동을 분리하기보다는 일종의 마이크 같은 역할을 하게 되어 기타 몸체의 진동과 같은 모든 것들을 증폭시켰죠. 이것은 명료하지 않는 많은 잡음을 야기했는데 기타연주자들이 추구했던 깨끗하고 산뜻했던 소리가 아니었어요. [Q9-B] 또 다른 문제는 오디오 피드백이에요. 이것은 기타연주자들이 기타를 치고 소리가 스피커에 의해 증폭될 때 발생해요. 만약 이런 증폭된 소리가 기타 줄에 닿으면, 그것은 줄을 좀 더 진동시키게 되죠. 이러한 진동들이 다시 잡혀서 계속 증폭되는 거에요; 그래서 크고 디지털화된 잡음이 반복적으로 만들어 지는 것이지요.

The Log의 발달

P: To fix those problems, a prominent jazz musician went to work at a local guitar workshop. In 1940, he produced 'The Log,' a guitar whose body was constructed of a long piece of solid wood instead of a hollow body. 'The Log' had two major advantages over hollow bodies. The first is that feedback was diminished because the body was more resistant to vibrations. Second, its notes lasted longer because the strings maintained vibrations, rather than dissipating them to the rest of the guitar.

P: 이러한 문제점들을 고치기 위해, 한 저명한 재즈 음악가가 주변에 있는 기타작업실에서 연구했어요. 1940년에, 그는 몸체가 텅 비어있지 않고 길고 단단한 원목으로 된"The Log"라는 기타를 만들었어요. "The Log"는 텅 빈 몸체에 비해 두 개의 중요한 장점을 가지고 있었는데요. 첫째는 몸체가 진동에 좀 더 저항력이 있기 때문에 오디오 피드백이 사라지는 것이었죠. 둘째는 음이 좀 더 길게 지속된다는 것인데 이것은 기타의 줄이 진동을 다른 부분으로 분산시키기보다는 유지하기 때문이었어요.

S: [Q17] Hmm… It seems like all the guitar makers were trying to reduce the electric guitar's effects. I always thought they sounded really cool, and actually prefer the effects, like in Jimi Hendrix's music.

S: [Q17] 흠….마치 모든 기타 제작자들이 전자 기타의 소리 효과를 줄이려고 노력한 것 같네요. 저는 늘 전자 기타 소리가 멋있다고 생각했는데요, 사실 Jimi Hendrix의 음악에서와 같은 소리 효과를 더 좋아해요.

결론

P: You're not alone, but musicians didn't open up to the idea of incorporating electric effects into their music until after the 1950s, and largely due to Jimi Hendrix. [Q10-D] Hendrix is considered one of the greatest guitarists ever, due to his innovative style. Rather than avoiding feedback and distortion, he took advantage of them. For example, his Fender Stratocaster, had three pickups and a switch for selecting which to use, but Hendrix wasn't satisfied with only three choices, so he jammed the pickup selector on his guitar so that he could play using two pickups at the same time and create some strange new sounds. This techinque has become extremely popular since then.

P: 학생만 그런게 아니에요. 하지만 음악가들은 1950년대 이후가 될 때까지는 자신들의 음악에 전자음의 효과를 통합할 생각을 하지 못했는데, 그 이유는 대부분 Jimi Hendrix 때문이에요. [Q10-D] Hendrix는 그의 혁신적인 스타일로 인해 역사상 가장 위대한 기타연주자로 여겨지고 있죠. 그는 소리의 피드백과 왜곡현상을 피하기 보다는, 그것들을 장점으로 이용했어요. 예를 들면, 그의 Fender tratocaster는 3개의 픽업과 그 중에서 뭘 사용할지 고르는 스위치를 가지고 있었지만, Hendrix는 단지 3개의 선택만으로는 만족하지 않았죠. 그래서 그는 픽업 선택기를 기타에 끼워넣고 2개의 픽업을 동시

P: Now you can see that the electric guitar's evolution is tied very closely with that of music itself. As guitars improve, they introduce new musical styles and as musicians experiment with new guitars, they lead to adaptation by manufacturers.

에 사용함으로써 낯설고 새로운 소리를 만들어 낼 수 있었어요. **이 기법은 이후에 매우 큰 인기를 끌게 되었죠.**

P: 이제 여러분은 전자 기타의 발달이 음악 자체와 매우 밀접하게 연관되어 있다는 걸 알 수 있을 꺼에요. 기타가 개선되면서, 그것은 새로운 음악스타일을 소개하게 되었고, 음악가들이 새로운 기타로 연주를 시도하게 되면 이것이 제작자들에게 받아들여진 것이죠.

TEST 3　Set 2-2　Lecture 1　Invention of Electric Guitar

06 What is the lecture mainly discussing?

(A) The ~~differences~~ between a Hawaiian lap steel guitar and an electric Spanish guitar
(B) **The series of events that occurred in the invention of the electric guitar**
(C) The evolution and development of the ~~guitar throughout history~~ *
(D) The ways popular guitarists influenced the designs of electric guitars

강의는 주로 무엇에 관해 논의하는가?

(A) 하와이 랩스틸기타와 스페인풍 전자기타의 ~~차이점~~
(B) 전자기타의 발명과정에서 발생한 일련의 사건들
(C) ~~역사 속의 기타~~의 진화와 발달 *
(D) 인기 있는 기타리스트들이 전자 기타 설계에 영향을 준 방법들

Main Idea　강의의 도입부에서 교수는, Let's look at the changes the electric guitar went through to become the instrument that we know today(그럼 오늘날 우리가 알고 있는 악기가 되기까지 전자기타가 겪었던 변화들을 살펴보기로 해요.)라고 말하므로 (B)가 정답임을 알 수 있다. (A)는 두 종류의 기타의 차이점은 언급되지 않았고, (C)는 기타 전체의 진화와 발달을 말하는 것이 아닌 전자기타에 관한 것이므로 각각 오답이다. (D)는 물론 기타연주자들이 전자기타에 어느 정도 영향을 주었지만 설계 부분과는 관련이 없으므로 정답이 될 수 없다.

07 What does the professor say about the pickup that Beauchamp invented in 1931?

(A) **The first pickup in history was mounted on 'the Frying Pan'.**
(B) It ~~was based on an electrical device~~ in a Hawaiian lap steel guitar.
(C) It was invented ~~by engineers who worked for a guitar company~~.
(D) It was invented to allow guitarists to ~~produce more sounds~~ with their instruments.

교수는 1931년에 Beauchamp가 발명했던 픽업에 관해 무엇을 말하는가?

(A) 역사상 첫 번째 픽업이 "the Frying Pan"에 장착되었다.
(B) 하와이 랩스틸기타 내부에 있는 ~~전자 장치를 기반~~ ~~으로했다~~.
(C) ~~기타 제조 회사에서 일하는 엔지니어들에 의해 발~~ ~~명되었다~~.
(D) 기타 연주자들이 악기로 ~~더 다양한 소리를 낼 수~~ ~~있게하기~~ 위해 개발되었다. *

Detail (Characteristic)　교수가 Beauchamp에 관해 언급한 부분을 살펴보면, In 1931, Beauchamp and his partner used horseshoe magnets to design a device called a "pick up," that did exactly that. They incorporated it into a Hawaiian lap steel guitar creating the first electric guitar in history, the "Frying Pan,".(1931년에 Beauchamp와 그의 동료는 말굽자석을 사용해서 "pick up"이라 불리는 장치를 개발했는데, 말 그대로 소리를 잡아냈어요. 그들은 그것을 하와이 랩스틸기타에 결합시켜 "Frying Pan"이라는 역사상 최초의 전자기타를 만들었어요.) 에서 역사상 첫 번째 픽업은 "the Frying Pan"에 장착된 사실을 알 수 있으므로 (A)가 정답이다. (B)는 픽업을 하와이 랩스틸기타에 결합시킨 것이지 그 안에 있는 전자장치를 기반으로 한 것은 아니며, (C)는 픽업을 발명한 사람은 Beauchamp과 그의 동료이므로 각각 오답이다. (D)는 전자 기타의 효과에 대한 설명으로 픽업과는 관계없으므로 오답이다.

08 What can be inferred about the 'Frying Pan' from the lecture?

(A) It was not awarded a patent until several years later.
(B) It incited the invention of many new types of guitars. *
(C) It could not entice Spanish-style guitarists to switch over to Hawaiian-style guitars.
(D) It was more popular than the guitars made by Beauchamp's rivals.

강의에서 'Frying Pan'에 관해 무엇을 추론할 수 있는가?

(A) 몇 년이 지날 때까지 특허를 받지 못했다.
(B) 많은 새로운 종류의 기타가 발명되도록 자극을 주었다. *
(C) 스페인 풍의 기타연주자들을 하와이 풍의 기타로 전환시킬 수 없었다.
(D) Beauchamp의 라이벌 회사에 의해 제작된 기타보다 더 인기가 있었다.

Inference (Infer)   Frying Pan"이 언급된 부분 중에서, Unfortunately for Beauchamp, other manufacturers had copied his technology and began producing electric guitars before he could stop them six years later.(Beauchamp에게는 불행히도, 다른 제조업자들이 그의 기술을 모방해서 전자 기타를 생산하기 시작했는데, 그가 그들을 막을 수 있었던 것은 6년이나 지난 후였어요.)을 보면 다른 제조업자들이 모방하는 것을 몇 년 뒤에 막았다는건 특허를 받는데 시간이 걸렸다는 말이므로 (A)가 정답이다. (B)는 바로 뒤 부분에서 Beauchamp가 만든 기타는 오늘날에는 널리 쓰이지 않고 있으며 다른 종류의 기타가 개발되는 과정을 언급하고 있으므로 오답이다, (C)와 (D)는 본문에 언급되지 않은 내용이므로 각각 오답이다.

09 According to the lecture, what were two problems of ES-150?

Click on 2 answers

(A) The guitar could not digitize certain unique sound ranges. *
(B) The guitar's amplifier reboosted the sounds it had already produced.
(C) It could not play higher notes without a pickup selector.
(D) It picked up any vibrations around it.

강의에 따르면, ES-150의 2가지 문제점은 무엇인가?

2개의 답을 고르시오.

(A) 그 기타는 특정 음역대의 독특한 소리를 디지털화 할수 없었다. *
(B) 그 기타의 증폭기는 이미 발생한 소리를 다시 증가시켰다.
(C) 그것은 픽업 선택기 없이는 고음을 낼 수 없었다.
(D) 그것은 주변에 있는 어떤 진동도 잡아냈다.

Detail (Problem)   ES-150의 문제점을 언급한 부분을 보면, (중략)… they acted as sort of a microphone, amplifying everything, like the vibration of the guitar body….(중략)… and the sound gets amplified by a loudspeaker. If this amplified sound reaches the guitar strings, it causes them to vibrate more. These vibrations are picked up and amplified again and again; creating a loop of loud, digitized noise(…일종의 마이크 같은 역할을 하게 되어 기타 몸체의 진동과 같은 모든 것들을 증폭시켰죠…. 소리가 스피커에 의해 증폭될 때 발생 해요. 만약 이런 증폭된 소리가 기타 줄에 닿으면, 그것은 줄을 좀 더 진동시키게 되죠. 이러한 진동들이 다시 잡혀서 계속 증폭되는 거에요; 그래서 크고 디지털화된 잡음이 반복적으로 만들어 지는 것이죠.)에서 보면 (B)와 (D)가 각각 정답임을 알 수 있다. (A)는 모든 소리를 디지털화 한다고 했으므로, (C)는 픽업 선택기는 추후 개선된 기타에서 나오는 장치이므로 각각 오답이다.

TEST 3　Set 2-2　Lecture 1　Invention of Electric Guitar

10 In the lecture, the professor identifies key events regarding the electric guitar. Arrange them in order from earliest to latest.

강의에서, 교수는 전자 기타에 관련된 주요 사건들을 밝히고 있다. 초기부터 가장 최근까지의 순서로 나열하시오.

Step1	(C) Phonographs and radios created a need for louder guitars.	Step1	(C) 측음기와 라디오가 더 큰 소리를 가진 기타에 대한 수요를 만들었다.
Step2	(A) Pickups were invented by Beauchamp and his partner.	Step2	(A) 픽업은 Beauchamp과 그의 동료에 의해 발명되었다.
Step3	(B) Popular musicians started using ES-150 guitars.	Step3	(B) 인기있는 음악가들이 ES-150 기타를 사용하기 시작했다.
Step4	(D) Jimi Hendrix introduced a popular technique of guitar playing.	Step4	(D) Jimi Hendrix는 인기있는 기타 연주법을 소개했다.

Category (Ordering) 본문에서 각 사건이 설명된 부분을 보면,

(C)는 Also, if you remember, phonograph recordings and commercial radio became popular music media in the 1920s. Along with big band music popularity, this meant that guitars needed to change, or live guitar performances would disappear. This is why louder guitars became even more necessary.(또한, 만약 여러분이 기억한다면, 축음기나 상업 라디오가 1920년대에 인기 있는 음악 매체가 되었잖아요. 큰 악단의 밴드 음악이 인기를 얻게 되면서, 기타에도 변화가 필요하게 되었고 그렇지 않으면 라이브 기타 연주는 사라질 수 밖에 없었죠. 이것이 바로 소리가 큰 기타가 더욱 더 필요한 이유였어요)

(A)는 In 1931, Beauchamp and his partner used horseshoe magnets to design a device called a "pickup," that did exactly that. (1931년에 Beauchamp와 그의 동료는 말굽자석을 사용해서"pickup"이라 불리는 장치를 개발했는데, 말 그대로 소리를 잡아냈어요.)

(B)는 By 1933, they'd produced their first electric guitar, the extremely popular ES-150. Country and blues guitarists, as well as skilled jazz guitarists switched over to this electric guitar and produced innovative sounds that were never before heard in guitars, or in any other instrument for that matter.(1933년이 되자, 그들은 자신들이 만든 최초의 전자기타를 생산했는데 그것이 바로 엄청난 인기를 얻었 던 ES-150이죠. 연주솜씨가 뛰어난 재즈 기타연주자들 뿐만 아니라 컨트리나 블루스 기타연주자들도 이 전자기타로 바꾸었고 이전에는 기타나 다른 악기를 통해서 들어본 적이 없는 혁신적인 소리를 만들어 냈어요.)

(D)는 Hendrix is considered one of the greatest guitarists ever, due to his innovative style. Rather than avoiding feedback and distortion, he took advantage of them. …… This technique has become extremely popular since then.(Hendrix는 그의 혁신적인 스타일 로 인해 역사상 가장 위대한 기타연주자로 여겨지고 있죠. 그는 소리의 피드백과 왜곡현상을 피하기 보다는, 그것들을 장점으로 이용했어요….이 기법 은 이후에 매우 큰 인기를 끌게 되었죠.)

에서 각각의 순서를 확인할 수 있다.

11 Listen again to part of the lecture. Then answer the question.

> S: Hmm… It seems like all the guitar makers were trying to reduce the electric guitar's effects. I always thought they sounded really cool, and actually prefer the effects, like in Jimi Hendrix's music.
> P: You're not alone

Why does the professor say this: 🎧

> P: You're not alone.

(A) To note that other musicians experimented with guitar effects
(B) To indicate that the student's remark is a matter of personal taste
(C) To imply that others share the student's opinion
(D) To acknowledge that other students have also listened to Jimi Hendrix

---

강의의 일부를 다시 듣고, 질문에 답하시오.

> S: 흠…. 마치 모든 기타 제작자들이 전자 기타의 소리 효과를 줄이려고 노력한 것 같네요. 저는 늘 전자 기타 소리가 멋있다고 생각했는데요, 사실 Jimi Hendrix의 음악에서와 같은 소리 효과를 더 좋아해요.
> P: 학생만 그런 게 아니에요

왜 교수는 이 말을 하는가?

> P: 학생만 그런 게 아니에요

(A) 다른 음악가들이 기타의 효과를 실험했다는 사실에 주목하기 위해
(B) 학생이 언급한 것이 개인적인 취향 문제라는 것을 말하기 위해
(C) 다른 사람들도 학생의 의견에 함께한다는 것을 암시하기 위해
(D) 다른 학생들도 Jimi Hendrix의 음악을 들은 적이 있다는 것을 알려주기 위해 *

Inference (Headset)   교수는 학생의 언급에 대해 혼자만의 생각이 아니며 다른 사람들도 비슷한 의견을 가지고 있다는 것을 말하는 것이므로 정답은 (C)가 된다.

문단주제	본문내용	해석
	Listen to part of a lecture in a physics class. The professor is discussing lightning.	물리학 강의의 일부를 들으시오. 교수는 번개에 관해 논의하고 있습니다.
번개에 대한 사람들의 잘못된 이해	P: We all think we know what lightning is, right? Well, scientists will tell you that you actually don't. Because it's extremely dangerous and short-lived, it's a phenomenon that isn't understood very well, even by the most renowned scientists. Scientists have currently identified eight different types of lightning, with cloud-to-ground lightning being the best known and most common type. However, there's another atypically long-lasting type of lightning that doesn't even involve clouds at all. This type, called ball lightning, may not even be true lightning at all, because there is no evidence of its existence except for eyewitness accounts. What's more is that descriptions from those who claim to have seen ball lightning are wildly different from one another, meaning they're not very credible. If there's one thing scientists know, it is that people can't be trusted to accurately retell facts. [Q13] Scientists don't even trust their own intuition, only hard, reproducible, experimental data. The lack of a verifiable cause for ball lightning - it's been blamed on black holes and even extra terrestrials - means it is considered little more than an urban legend and scientists consider it only a hypothetical phenomenon.	P: 우린 모두 번개가 무엇인지 잘 알고 있다고 생각 해요, 그렇죠? 글쎄요, 과학자들에 따르면 여러분은 사실 잘 모르고 있어요. 왜냐하면 번개는 극히 위험하고 짧은 순간에 일어나기 때문에, 심지어 저명한 과학자들조차도 아주 잘 이해하지는 못해요. 과학자들은 현재 8가지 종류의 번개에 대해 확인했는데요, 구름으로부터 지면에 닿는 번개가 가장 잘 알려져있죠. 하지만, 다른 타입으로 비정상적으로 오래 지속되는 번개가 있는데 이것은 구름을 전혀 포함하지 않아요. 구상번개라고 불리는 이러한 타입의 번개는 진짜 번개라고 말할 수도 없는데, 왜냐하면 목격자들의 증언을 제외 하고는 이 번개의 존재에 대한 증거가 없기때문 이에요. 더군다나 구상번개를 목격했다고 주장하는 사람들의 증언이 서로 다르기 때문에, 그들의 말을 신뢰하기도 힘들죠. 과학자들이 한가지 확신하는 것이 있다면, 사람들이 어떤 사실에 대해 다시 말할때 정확성을 신뢰하기 힘들다는 거에요. [Q13] 과학자들은 자신들의 직관도 믿지 않고, 오직 명백하고 재생가능한 실험 데이터만을 믿죠. 구상번개의 원인을 입증하는 것이 부족하기 때문에, 그것은 블랙홀 현상이나 심지어 외계인에 의한 것일지도 모른다는 근거없는 소문으로 여겨졌고 과학자들은 그것을 단지 가설적인 현상으로 생각하고 있죠.
구상번개	P: [Q12] Before we go any further, let's define ball lightning. OK... well... According to witnesses, ball lightning is a luminous, spherical, and electrical object. It is around the size of a golf ball, and is usually observed during thunderstorms. It's most often red, orange, or yellow, and moves horizontally. It has also been reported to pass through walls and approach people without harming them, and, usually explodes leaving a sulfurous smell at the end of its life. [Q17] The properties of ball lightning are not as clear-cut as those of other lightning forms, though. For example, despite the tiny size usually reported, a church in Widencombe-in-the-Moor, England was reported to have been hit by a ball lightning of 2.4 meters in diameter, knocking down the walls, killing four people and injuring 60. Despite these difficulties in defining ball lightning, recent experiments	P: [Q12] 우리가 내용을 좀 더 깊이 들어가기 전에, 구상번개가 무엇인지 알아보도록 하죠. 오케이... 음... 목격자들에 의하면, 구상번개는 환하게 빛을 발하는 구형의 전기를 띤 물체에요. 그건 골프공 만한 크기이고, 보통 천둥이 칠 때 관찰되죠. 대부분 빨강색, 주황색 또는 노란색을 띠고 있으며, 보통 수평으로 움직여요. 이 번개는 벽을 통과하고 아무 해를 입히지 않고 사람에게 도달 하는데, 보통 소멸될 때 유황 냄새를 남긴다고 해요. [Q17] 구상번개의 특성들은 다른 형태의 번개들처럼 명확히 밝혀진 바가 없어요. 예를 들면, 보통 작은 크기라고 보고되곤 하지만, 영국의 Windencombe-in-the-Moor란 곳에서 지름2.4미터의 구상번개가 쳐서 벽들이 무너지고 4명 의 사망자와 60명의 부상자가 발생했다는 보고가 있었어요. 구상번개를 정의하

have shown very promising results in trying to recreate it.

플라스마 가설

P: One of the first of those experiments was carried out in 2006 by a team led by Professor Gerd Fussmann. His team produced clouds of plasma 10-20 centimeters in diameter that resembled ball lightning. For those of you who don't know what plasma is, I'll explain. You're all familiar with the three states of matter: solid, liquid, and gas, and that matter is most stable during its solid state, and most active as a gas. Well... there is actually a fourth state of matter, called plasma that comes after gas and is even more energetic. Now back to Fussmann's experiment... it worked by passing a huge electrical current through a beaker filled with salt water using electrodes. The water was electrically heated until it gained enough energy to become plasma. This plasma bubble evaporated and left the beaker, burning brightly in an oval shape above the water for about 300 milliseconds. What's interesting is that this cloud couldn't even ignite a piece of paper. It was a great discovery because the plasmic cloud created in the labs was different from our previous understanding of plasma. Plasma is actually a highly energetic form of matter that characteristically rises into the sky, but does not have a defined shape. **[Q14] If scientists want to contain plasma in a specific shape, lots of equipment and power are required to keep it in that shape for even a fraction of a second.**

실리콘 가설

P: **[Q12] So instead of trying to figure out the issues with the plasma hypothesis, scientists came up with a more plausible theory.** Professor John Abrahamson at the University of Canterbury introduced a theory which suggested that ball lightning was a result of a chemical reaction of silicon particles that burn in the air. Uh... silicon is a chemical element that is found naturally in the ground, and is widely used for making electronics and mirrors. When a lightning bolt hits the ground, the heat and current cause a chemical reaction where silicon in the soil turns into vapor and rises into the air.

The pure silicon particles in the air are attracted to each other by the electrical charge created by the lightning strike, binding together into a ball shape. [Q15] **The silicon reacts with atmospheric oxygen and glows brightly.** This chemical reaction between silicon and oxygen takes place from the outside in, burning for as long as there is unreacted silicon left.

P: There is a problem with this theory as well. During World War II, Allied pilots often noticed 'balls of fire' which seemed to trail fighter jets at night. These balls were later called 'foo fighters' and pilots assumed that they were secret weapons developed by Germany and Japan, but the Axis forces also reported them. Interestingly, the descriptions of foo fighters and ball lightning, like their color and speed, were almost identical, leading to the conclusion that they were the same thing. [Q16] **But this conclusion gives rise to another problem:** the silicon molecules hypothesized to create ball lightning cannot reach the altitudes where the foo fighters were spotted.

P: So... there is still no theory that can fully explain what ball lightning is, or what causes it. You can see that it is hard to study these phenomena too, because they are so unpredictable and infrequent. The only way I can think of studying them is to find a location famous for ball lightning sightings and basically wait for something to happen.

12 What is the lecture mainly discussing?

(A) The different types of lightning and ~~their characteristics~~
(B) **Various scientists' explanations of a particular type of lightning**
(C) A hypothesis ~~on lightning that has replaced older ones~~
(D) The ~~cause~~ of the creation and ~~destruction~~ of ball lightning

강의는 주로 무엇에 관해 논의하는가?

(A) 여러 가지 종류의 번개와 ~~그것의 특징들~~
(B) **특정한 종류의 번개에 대한 과학자들의 다양한 설명들**
(C) 번개에 대한 ~~이전의 가설을 대체한 새로운~~ 가설
(D) 구상번개의 생성과 ~~파괴의~~ 원인 *

Main Idea 교수는 도입부에서 Before we go any further, let's define ball lightning.(우리가 내용을 좀 더 깊이 들어가기 전에, 구상번개가 무엇인지 알아보도록 하죠)라고 말하며 구상번개라는 특정 종류의 번개가 무엇인지 설명하며 그것에 대한 과학자들의 이론들을 함께 소개하고 있으므로 (B)가 정답이다. (A),(D)는 다양한 번개의 종류는 도입부분에 살짝 언급되었지만 각각의 특징들은 전혀 언급되지 않았고, 구상번개의 파괴 원인도 본문에 없는 내용이라 오답이다. (C)는 번개의 일반적인 가설이 아닌 하나의 특정 번개에 대한 이론들을 다루고 있으므로 정답이 될 수 없다.

13 According to the lecture, why does the professor mention black holes and extra-terrestrials?

(A) To ~~describe the differences~~ between ball lightning and the urban legends
(B) To ~~compare~~ ball lightning with other types of urban legends *
(C) **To show how unreliable the proof of ball lightning's existence is**
(D) To explain ~~the causes of some of types of lightning~~

강의에 따르면, 왜 교수는 블랙홀과 외계인을 언급하는가?

(A) 구상번개와 근거 없는 전설의 ~~차이점을 설명하기 위해~~
(B) 구상번개를 다른 종류의 근거 없는 전설과 ~~비교하기 위해~~ *
(C) **구상번개의 존재에 대한 증거가 얼마나 믿을 수 없는지를 보여주기 위해**
(D) 몇 가지 종류의 ~~번개의 발생원인들~~에 대해 설명하려고

Inference (Purpose) 교수가 블랙홀과 외계인을 언급한 부분을 살펴보면, Scientists don't even trust their own intuition, only hard, reproducible, experimental data. The lack of a verifiable cause for ball lightning, it's been blamed on black holes and even extra terrestrials, means it is considered little more than an urban legend and scientists consider it only a hypothetical phenomenon.(과학자들은 자신들의 직관력도 믿지 않고, 오직 명백하고 재생가능한 실험 데이터만 믿죠. 구상번개의 원인을 입증하는 것이 부족하기 때문에, 그것은 블랙홀 현상이나 심지어 외계인에 의한 것일지도 모른다는 근거없는 소문으로 여겨졌고 과학자들은 그것을 단지 가설적인 현상으로 생각하고 있죠.)에서 교수가 블랙홀과 외계인을 언급한 목적은 구상번개에 대한 증거가 신뢰할 수 없는 자료임을 보여주기 위한 것이다. 그러므로 (C)가 정답이다. (A)는 구상번개를 블랙홀과 외계인이 만들어낸 근거없는 소문이라고 생각하는 것이지 둘 사이의 차이점을 언급하는 것이 아니므로, (B)는 구상번개와 여러 근거없는 소문들을 비교하기 위함이 아니므로 각각 오답이다. (D)는 번개의 발생원인은 전혀 관계없는 내용이므로 답이 될 수 없다.

TEST 3 Set 2-3 *부록 Lecture 2 Examination on Ball Lightning

14 What does the professor say about plasma and the plasmic cloud hypothesis?

(A) It is costly and difficult to contain and control plasmic clouds.
(B) The plasmic cloud hypothesis was ~~disproved~~ by the silicon hypothesis. *
(C) The substance created by Fussmann ~~was mistaken~~ for plasma.
(D) Water is the ~~only compound~~ that can be used to create plasma.

교수는 플라스마와 플라스마 구름 가설에 관해 무엇이라고 말하는가?

(A) 플라스마 구름을 만드는 것과 통제하는 것은 어렵고 비용이 많이 든다.
(B) 플라스마 구름 가설은 실리콘 가설에 의해 ~~오류임이 입증되었다~~. *
(C) Fussmann 교수 팀에 의해 창조된 물질이 플라스마라고 ~~잘못 받아들여졌다~~.
(D) 물은 플라스마를 만드는데 사용되는 ~~유일한 화합물~~이다.

Detail (Characteristic) 교수는 플라스마와 플라스마 구름 가설에 관해 설명한 부분을 보면, If scientists want to contain plasma in a specific shape, lots of equipment and power are required to keep it in that shape for even a fraction of a second.(만약 과학자들이 플라스마를 특정한 모양으로 얻고 싶다면, 찰나의 순간 동안 모양을 유지하는 데에도 많은 장비와 에너지가 필요해요.)라고 했으므로 (A)가 정답이다. (B)는 플라스마 가설은 실리콘 가설에 의해 오류가 입증된 것이 아니므로, (C)는 Fussmann교수팀이 플라스마를 성공적으로 만들었으므로 잘못 받아들여졌다는 말은 틀리다. 따라서 각각 오답이다. 또한 (D)는 플라스마를 만드는데 다른 요소들도 필요하고 물이 유일하게 사용되는 물질은 아니므로 오답이다.

15 According to the silicon hypothesis, why does ball lightning glow?

(A) ~~Small lightning strikes are constantly created~~ inside the silicon ball.
(B) Electrical attractions between the pure silicon molecules ~~cause them to shine~~. *
(C) ~~Atmospheric water vapor becomes energized and burns brightly.~~
(D) Silicon and oxygen in the air react to produce light.

실리콘 가설에 따르면, 왜 구상번개는 빛을 내는가?

(A) 실리콘 공 안에서 ~~지속적으로 작은 번개들이 만들어진다~~.
(B) 순수 실리콘 분자들 사이에서 일어나는 전기 인력이 ~~빛을 내게 한다~~. *
(C) ~~대기중의 수증기가 활성화되어 밝게 연소된다~~.
(D) 실리콘과 공기에 있는 산소가 서로 반응하여 빛을 만들어낸다.

Detail (Cause) 구상번개가 빛을 내는 이유에 대해 교수가 설명한 부분을 보면, The silicon reacts with atmospheric oxygen and glows brightly.(실리콘은 대기중의 산소와 반응하여 밝게 빛이 나요)에서 (D)가 정답임을 알 수 있다. (A)는 실리콘 공안에서 번개가 지속적으로 만들어지는 것에 대해 본문내용에 언급되지 않았고, (B)는 실리콘 분자들 사이에서의 전기인력은 실리콘이 뭉쳐져서 구 모양이 되게 하는 원인이지 빛을 내는 원인은 아니므로 잘못 기술되어 각각 오답이다. (C)는 플라스마에 관한 내용이므로 답이 될 수 없다.

16 What does the professor imply about foo fighters?

(A) They prove that the silicon hypothesis is not very reliable.
(B) They ~~helped~~ fighter jets navigate to their bases at night. *
(C) They were ~~developed by nations that were not involved in the~~ war.
(D) ~~Ball lightning can be created~~ at the same altitudes at which foo ~~fighters~~ were reported.

빛 덩어리에 관해 교수는 무엇을 암시하는가?

(A) 그것들은 실리콘 가설이 그다지 신뢰할만한 것이 아님을 증명한다.
(B) 그것들은 야간에 전투기들이 기지로 돌아갈 때 항해하는데 도움을 준다. *
(C) 그것들은 전쟁에 참여하지 않은 국가들에 의해 개발되었다.
(D) 구상번개는 빛 덩어리가 보고된 높은 고도에서 발생될 수 있다.

Inference (Imply) 교수가 foo fighters에 관해 언급한 부분을 보면, But this conclusion gives rise to another problem.(하지만 이러한 결론은 또 다른 문제점을 야기시키는데요.)라고 말함으로써 가설이 완전히 신뢰할 만한 것은 아니라는 암시를 주고 있으므로 (A)가 정답이다. (B)는 전투기를 따라다닌다고 했지만 도움을 주는지 여부에 대한 언급은 없고, (C)는 foo fighters가 인위적으로 개발된 것이 아닌 실리콘이 자연적으로 뭉쳐서 빛이 나는 현상이므로 잘못 기술되어 각각 오답이 된다. (D)는 구상번개가 아닌 실리콘 분자에 대한 내용으로 볼덩어리가 발견된 높이까지 올라올 수 없다고 했으므로 오답이다.

17 Listen again to part of the lecture. Then answer the question.

P: The properties of ball lightning are not as clear-cut as those of other lightning forms, though. For example, despite the tiny size usually reported, a church in Widencombe-in-the-Moor, England was reported to have been hit by a ball lightning of 2.4 meters in diameter, knocking down the walls, killing four people and injuring 60.

Why does the professor say this : 🎧

> The properties of ball lightning are not as clear-cut as those of other lightning forms, though.

(A) To provide an example of the inconclusiveness of ball lightning's ~~existence~~ *
(B) ~~To introduce~~ one of the most devastating disasters of ball lightning
(C) To show that there are exceptions to the normal characteristics of ball lightning
(D) To explain the ~~need to study and understand~~ ball lightning more learly

강의의 일부를 다시 듣고, 질문에 답하시오.

P: 구상번개의 특성들은 다른 형태의 번개들처럼 명확히 밝혀진 바가 없어요. 예를 들면, 보통 작은 크기라고 보고되곤 하지만, 영국의 Windencombe-in-the-Moor란 곳에서 지름 2.4미터의 구상번개가 쳐서 벽들이 무너지고 4명의 사망자와 60명의 부상자가 발생했다는 보고가 있었어요

왜 교수는 이 말을 하는가?

> 구상번개의 특징들은 다른 형태의 번개들처럼 명확히 밝혀진 바가 없어요.

(A) 구상번개의 존재가 명확히 결론지어지지 않았다는 것에 관한 예를 제공하려고 *
(B) 구상번개로 인해 발생한 가장 참혹한 재앙 중의 하나를 소개하려고
(C) 구상번개의 일반적인 특징들 중 예외가 있다는 점을 보여주려고
(D) 구상번개에 대한 이해와 연구를 좀 더 명확하게 할 필요가 있음을 설명하려고

Inference (Headset) 교수는 not as clear-cut as those of other lightning forms.(다른 번개 형태의 특징들처럼 명확하지 않다)라고 말함으로써 구상번개는 분류되지 않은 예외적인 특징을 지니고 있음을 암시하는 것이므로 (C)가 정답이다. (A)는 구상번개의 존재가 아니라 특징에 관해서 설명하는 것이고, (B)는 구상번개로 인해 발생한 사고에 대해 언급한 것은 사실이나 교수가 의도한 바가 아니며, (D)는 구상번개에 대한 이해와 연구를 더 할 필요가 있다는 말은 본문 내용에 나와있지 않으므로 각각 오답이다.

usherin.usher.co.kr

USHER iBT TOFLE
FINAL TEST LISTENING
TEST 4/해설

정답 및 Self-check List

문제유형과 Signals

오답정리표

TEST 4

Set 1-1 Conversation Tutoring

문단주제	본문내용	해석
단락 1 과외 프로그램 소개	Listen to a conversation between a student and an English professor S: Good afternoon, Dr. Lawlor. The, um…, calculus professor told me that you were looking for me earlier this morning. P: Yes, Sarah, how have you been? Please come in and take a seat. S: I've been great…just swamped with all these assignments and papers… I haven't seen you since I was in your literature class. P: Yes, it has been quite a while, hasn't it? Well, when I was going through my old files, you know, just to organize them, [Q1-D] I remembered how impressed I was by the papers you wrote for my class last year. And… You see, our school has a tutoring program set up for students who need help with writing. [Q2] But since about half of our tutors are quitting soon or graduating this July, we need to recruit more tutors as quickly as possible.	학생과 영어교수의 대화를 들으시오. S: 안녕하세요, Lawlor 교수님. 음…… 오늘 아침에 저를 찾으셨다고 수학과 교수님이 말씀하셔서요. P: 그래, Sarah. 어떻게 지냈니? 와서 자리에 앉거라. S: 잘 지냈어요. 과제들과 레포트들 때문에 바빴죠… 문학 수업 이후로 교수님을 한동안 뵙지 못했네요. P: 그래, 꽤 오래 되었네, 그렇지? 음, 내가 예전 파일들을 살펴보다가, 그러니까 그냥 정리하려구 말야, [Q1-D] 네가 작년에 내 수업을 위해 썼던 레포트들이 얼마나 인상 깊었는지 생각이 났어. 그래서…… 있지, 우리 학교에 과외 프로그램이 있는데, 글쓰기에 도움이 필요한 학생들을 위해 준비되어 있거든. [Q2] 그런데 지금 지도 교사들의 약 반 정도가 곧 그만두거나 이번 7월에 졸업을 하기 때문에, 우린 가능한 빨리 교사들을 모집을 해야 돼서 말이야.
단락 2 교사직 제안 및 협의	S: [Q1] And, you want me to take one of their spots? P: Exactly! S: Hmm… What would I be doing? P: It's as simple as it sounds! You'd just need to teach the students how to improve their writing skills and help them with their papers. S: [Q3] But… I only took your class to meet the graduation requirement. I'm a chemistry major. What I want to pursue is completely different from what I would be doing as a writing tutor… You know, someday I want to be a biomedical engineer [and work in a lab to save people's lives. P: I understand that. I figured [Q2-D] you could work with the students who need help with their chemistry or science-related papers.	S: [Q1] 그래서, 제가 그들 자리 중 하나를 맡았으면 좋겠다는 말씀이신가요? P: 정확해! S: 흠…… 제가 무슨 일을 하게 되는 건가요? P: 들리는 것만큼 단순해! 그냥 학생들에게 어떻게 하면 글 쓰는 실력을 향상시킬 수 있는지 가르쳐주고, 레포트 쓰는 걸 도와주면 돼. S: [Q3] 하지만…… 전 단지 졸업 요건을 채우기 위해 교수님 수업을 들은 건데요. 전 화학 전공이에요. 제가 추구하는 것과 작문교사로서 하는 일들이 완전히 달라요…… 그러니까, 전 언젠가 생체의학 공학자가 되어서, 연구소에서 일하며 사람들의 생명을 구하고 싶어요. P: 이해해. [Q2-D] 난 네가 화학이나, 과학과 관련된 레포트를 쓰는데 도움이 필요한 학생들을 가르칠 수 있다고 생각했어.

단락 3 교사 자격 취득 관련 세부 소개	S: Oh, Okay. That sounds like a reasonable plan, but wouldn't I need formal training before I start tutoring since I'm not an English major? I mean, I don't want to do too much strenuous work just to tutor people in writing… P: Well, not exactly. I mean, it's true you would be taking one of our weekly training courses and work with a mentor who has been tutoring for a while, but once you complete the training sessions, you will be good to go and can start tutoring on your own. It's not just about tutoring people, though. [Q5] You will also get class credits and community service hours, [Q3] which will count towards your graduation requirements. S: Oh, that certainly grabs my attention! Also, would I be observed by anyone? P: Just for your first session! The professor whose course you'd be taking for tutoring will be present and give you feedback and advice for your next sessions.
단락 4 충고	S: [Q1-A]Hmm… before I accept this offer, do you have any tips, professor? P: (laughs) Of course, Sarah. When it comes to tutoring someone, it sometimes takes a lot of perseverance. You should keep in mind that there are two ways to teach students how to enhance their papers. Most of the time, their papers are unorganized, yet they don't see it. [Q4] So, what do you do? The simplest thing to do would be to directly tell them the flaws they need to fix to organize their papers. And… S: [Q4-C]…And the other way would be asking them questions that would ultimately guide them and help them organize their papers on their own, right? P: Excellent! S: Well, I think you should put me down on the list. I'm pretty much convinced to take the job. P: That's perfect. Thank you for coming in today, Sarah. I really appreciate it!

S: 아, 그렇구나. 합리적인 계획처럼 들리네요. 하지만, 전 영어를 전공하지 않았으니까 학생들을 가르치기 전에 훈련을 받아야 하지 않을까요? 제 말은, 단지 학생들을 가르치기 위해서 너무 많은 힘든 일들을 하고싶지 않거든요.

P: 음, 꼭 그렇지만은 않아. 내 말은, 넌 매주 교육 과정 중 하나를 받아야 하는 게 사실이고, 지도 교사를 해온 멘토와 함께 한동안 작업해야 할거야. 하지만 일단 훈련들을 마치면, 너 혼자서 사람들을 순조롭게 가르칠 수 있을거야. 하지만, 이건 단지 사람들을 가르치는 것만이 아니야. [Q5] 학점과 사회 봉사 시간도 얻을 수 있는데, [Q3] 이건 졸업 요건으로 인정될꺼야.

S: 오, 확실히 관심이 생기는데요! 또한, 다른 사람이 저를 지켜보게 되나요?

P: 첫 번째 수업에서만 그럴꺼야! 있잖아, 네가 들어야 할 강의의 담당 교수님이 계셔서 너에게 피드백을 주고, 다음 수업들을 위한 조언을 해 주실 거야

S: [Q1-A] 흠…… 제가 이 제의를 받아들이기 전에, 주실 수 있는 충고가 있나요, 교수님?

P: (웃음)당연하지, Sarah. 누군가를 가르치려면, 가끔 인내심이 많이 필요해. 학생들에게 글쓰기를 향상시키는 법을 가르칠 때는 두가지 방법이 있다는 걸 명심했으면 해. 대부분의 경우, 레포트는 정리되어있지 않은데, 학생들은 그것을 보지 못해. [Q4] 그럼 넌 무엇을 해야 할까? 가장 간단한 방법은, 그들에게 고쳐야 할 잘못들을 직접 말해서 레포트를 정리하게 하는거야. 그리고……

S: [Q4-C] 그리고 다른 방법은 질문들을 해서 그들 스스로 레포트를 정리하게끔 안내하고 도와주는 것이죠. 맞나요?

P: 훌륭해!

S: 음, 제 생각에 교수님께서 제 이름을 명단에 적어 넣으셔도 될 것 같아요. 일을 할 거라는 확신이 드네요.

P: 좋아. 오늘 와줘서 고마워, Sarah. 정말 고맙게 생각해!

TEST 4 Set 1-1 Conversation: Tutoring

01 [Main Idea-Main Purpose] What does the professor want to discuss with the student?
교수가 학생과 의논하고 싶은 무엇인가?

(A) He wants to give the student some advice about her ~~term paper~~ in his ~~Chemistry class~~. *(wrong fact)*
(A) 그는 학생의 화학 수업의 학기말 레포트에 대해 조언을 주길 원한다.

(B) He wants to know if the student is willing to take a job as a tutor.
(B) 그는 학생이 지도 교사로서의 일을 택할 의향이 있는지 알고 싶어한다.

(C) He wants to introduce the tutoring system to the student and ask her to ~~spread the word~~ about it. *(partial error)*
(C) 그는 학생에게 과외 제도를 소개해주고, 이것에 대한 소문을 퍼뜨릴 수 있도록 부탁하고 싶어한다. ★

(D) He wants to get the student's ~~permission~~ to use her papers as examples in his class. *(not mentioned)*
(D) 그는 학생의 레포트들을 자신의 수업에서 예로 쓸 수 있도록 허락을 받길 원한다.

> 해설 | (A)는 학생의 major인 chemistry를 왜곡하여 써놓은 것이고, (C) 와 (D)는 언급된 적이 없으므로 오답이다.
> 교수는 처음부터 학생에게 tutor을 해달라고 부탁을한다.

02 [Detail-Cause/Reason] Why does the professor need to recruit more people urgently?
왜 교수는 급히 사람들을 더 모집해야 할 필요가 있는가?

(A) Because he needs help with ~~organizing~~ the tutoring system that has ~~yet to be established~~. *(wrong fact)* ★
(A) 그는 아직 정착되지 않은 과외 제도를 정비 하는데 도움이 필요하기 때문이다. ★

(B) Because the student body is ~~getting bigger~~, and he's expecting that more students will wish to be tutored. *(not mentioned)*
(B) 학생들의 수가 증가하고 있고, 앞으로 더 많은 학생들이 과외를 받고 싶어할 거라고 예상하기 때문이다.

(C) Because the number of tutors will decrease in the near future.
(C) 가까운 미래에 교사들의 수가 감소하기 때문이다.

(D) Because he needs more people to tutor his ~~literature-class~~ students. *(partial error)*
(D) 그는 자신의 문학 수업을 듣는 학생들을 가르치는 사람들을 더 많이 필요로 하기 때문이다.

> 해설 | (A) tutoring system에 관련되어 organize를 해달라 부탁하는 것이 아니라 학생들을 가르쳐 달라는게 맞으므로 오답이다.
> (B) 는 일하는 사람의 숫자가 급격히 하락 함으로서 학생의 도움이 필요필요한 것이므로 오답. (D) literature-class student 뿐만 아니라 모든 field의 학생들을 도와주는게 목적이므로 이것 또한 오답.

03 [Detail-Similarity/Compare] What do the literature class the student took last year and the training course have in common?
학생이 작년에 들었던 문학 수업과, 훈련과정의 공통점은 무엇인가?

(A) Both of them offer students an opportunity to fulfill their graduation requirements.
(A) 둘 다 학생의 졸업 요건을 충족시킬 수 있는 기회를 제공한다.

(B) ~~Both~~ of them guarantee a certain number of community ~~service hours~~. *(partial error)* ★
(B) 둘 다 사회 봉사의 일정시간을 보장한다. ★

(C) Both of them are ~~prerequisites~~ for the tutoring job. *(wrong fact)*
(C) 둘 다 과외를 하기 위한 선수과목들이다.

(D) Both of them ~~are required~~ for a degree in the ~~English field~~. *(not mentioned)*
(D) 둘 다 영어 분야에서의 학위를 따기 위해 필요하다.

> 해설 | (B)는 graduation requirement 포인트를 쌓아가는 것이 공통점이고 community service hours는 (C)에만 관련되있다.
> 똑같은 이유에서, (C)는 오직 training course만이 필수 조건 이기 때문에 오답. (D)는 언급된 내용이 아니므로 오답.

04 [Detail-Suggestion] Which of the following is the first method the professor suggests for helping students who need to correct their unorganized papers?

다음 중 정리되지 않은 레포트들을 수정하기 위해, 교수가 제안한 첫 번째 방법은 무엇인가?

(A) To directly tell the students how to revise their papers.

(B) To help the students ~~research~~ the information they lack in their papers. *(not mentioned)*

(C) To encourage the students to fix what they think is wrong by ~~asking questions~~. *(opposite fact)* ★

(D) To suggest ~~alternative sources~~ that may help them improve their papers on their own. *(not mentioned)*

(A) 학생들에게 레포트를 어떻게 수정해야할지 직접적으로 말하는 것.

(B) 학생들이 레포트에서 부족한 정보들을 ~~조사하는~~ 것을 도와주는 것.

(C) 학생들에게 ~~질문을 함으로써~~ 틀렸다고 생각되는 것을 고칠 수 있게 격려하는 것.

(D) 레포트들을 자신들 스스로 향상시킬 수 있게 도와줄 ~~대안들을 제안하는~~ 것

> 해설 | (B)와 (D)는 언급된 내용이 아니므로 오답이다. (C)는 첫번째 suggestion이 아니고 두번째 suggestion이기 때문에 오답이다.

Listen again to part of the conversation. Then answer the question.

It's not just about tutoring people, though. You will also get class credits and community service hours, which will count towards your graduation requirements.

대화의 일부를 다시 듣고, 질문에 답하시오.

"하지만, 여기, 사람들을 가르치는 것만이 너를 위한 게 아니야. 학점을 받을 수 있고, 사회 봉사 시간도 받을 수 있고 한 개의 졸업 요건을 채울 수도 있어."

05 [Inference-Headset] Why does the professor say this: 🎧

왜 교수는 이 말을 하는가: 🎧

> "You will also get class credits and community service hours, which will count towards your graduation requirements."

> "학점을 받을 수 있고, 사회 봉사 시간도 받을 수 있고 한 개의 졸업 요건을 채울 수도 있어."

(A) To ~~distinguish~~ the training course from other regular classes the student has taken. *(not mentioned)* ★

(B) To let the student know about the potential non-monetary compensation that the job provides.

(C) To tell the student that the training course is a way of ~~giving back to the community~~. *(not mentioned)*

(D) To inform the student that she will be receiving ~~homework assignments~~ in the training course, just like any other class. *(not mentioned)*

(A) 학생이 들었던 정규 수업들과 훈련과정을 ~~구별~~하기 위해

(B) 그 일이 잠재적으로 가지고 있는 비금전적인 보상을 학생에게 알려주기 위해

(C) 학생에게 훈련과정이 ~~사회에 환원하는~~ 하나의 방법임을 말하기 위해

(D) 학생에게 다른 수업들과 마찬가지로 훈련과정에서 ~~과제들을 받을 것임을~~ 알려주기 위해

> 해설 | 학생은 지난번 교수의 literature class를 들은게 graduation requirement를 충족시키기 위해서라 말한다. 따라서, 교수는 학생에게 부가적으로 따라오는 혜택을 주면서 설득하려 한다. 따라서 (A), (B), (C) 모두 오답이다.

TEST 4 — Set 1-2 — Lecture 1: Global Temperatures

문단주제	본문내용	해석
단락 1 지난 수업 복습	**Listen to part of a lecture in an earth science class** P: Continuing our discussion on global climate change, I'd like to address a remarkable and feasible technology that's been recently developed. Last time, we talked about the current level of carbon dioxide, CO_2 emission, and its detrimental effect on the global climate. I've mentioned that the rate at which global temperatures are rising has gone beyond the 2 degree centigrade limit that scientists consider to be the allowable maximum. At the current rate of increase, catastrophic events could occur within around 10 years. S1: Yes, and… Last class, the bell rang right when you were about to introduce some kind of solution, right?	기후학에 관한 강의를 들으시오. P: 지구기후변화에 대한 논의를 계속하면서, 저는 최근에 개발된 실현 가능한 놀라운 기술을 언급하고 싶어요. 지난 시간에, 우리는 이산화탄소의 현재 방출 상태와 그것이 지구 기후에 미치는 해로운 영향에 대해 이야기 했죠. 지구 기온이 상승하는 비율이 과학자들이 허용치로 여기고 있는 섭씨 2도를 초과했다는 걸 제가 언급했구요. 현재의 속도로는 10년 안에 재앙으로 여겨지는 사건이 발생할 수 있어요. S1: 네, 그리고… 지난 시간에, 교수님이 어떤 종류의 해결책을 소개하려고 하셨는데 바로 종이 울렸잖아요. 맞죠?
단락 2 지구 온난화 해결책	P: [Q1] **Yes, that's exactly what we'll be talking about today: solutions to the rising global temperatures.** So, how can we prevent the temperatures from continually increasing past the limit and keep our CO_2 emissions under control? Well, there has been an enormous amount of research to find a suitable solution to the problem and numerous strides have been made. S2: I think I remember something about oxy-fuel combustion in yesterday's reading. Is that one of the solutions?	P: [Q1] 맞아요, 그게 바로 우리가 오늘 얘기할 거에요. 지구의 기온 상승에 대한 해결책이요. 그럼, 어떻게 우리는 온도가 한계점을 지나 계속 증가하는 것을 막고 이산화탄소 배출량을 통제할 수 있을까요? 음, 이 문제에 대한 적합한 해결책을 찾기 위한 거대한 양의 연구가 있었고 많은 진전이 있었죠… S2: 제가 어제 순 산소 연소에 대해 읽은 게 있는데요. 이것이 하나의 해결책이 되나요?
단락 3 탄소 수집과 저장	P: That is certainly one of the solutions, yes. Instead of using air in the combustion process, it uses pure oxygen. By doing so, nitrogen, which is the main component of air, is not heated, and therefore, nitrous oxide production is reduced. [Q2] **Remember, nitrous oxide is also a major greenhouse gas that contributes to the global increase in temperatures, just like carbon dioxide.** Today we will focus on an advanced form of oxyfuel combustion: Carbon capture and storage! As the name implies, it is a process that collects, isolates, and safely stores the emissions generated during fossil fuel combustion in power plants. There are two types: post-combustion and pre-combustion capture.	P: 네, 그건 분명 하나의 해결책이 될 수 있죠. 연소과정에서 공기를 사용하는 대신, 순수한 산소를 사용하는 거에요. 그렇게 함으로써, 공기의 주요 구성요소인 질소는 가열되지 않고 따라서 이산화질소가 덜 발생하게 되요. [Q2] 기억하세요, 이산화 질소 또한 주요 온실가스로써 이산화탄소처럼 지구 기후 상승에 영향을 끼쳐요. 오늘 우리는 진화된 산소 연소 형태에 초점을 맞출 건데요. 바로 탄소 수집과 저장이에요! 이름이 암시하듯이, 이것은 발전소에서 화석연료가 연소되는 동안 발생하는 배기가스를 모으고 분리시켜 안전하게 저장하는 과정이에요. 여기에는 2가지 종류가 있는데 여기에는 연소 후 포집과 연소 전 포집이에요.

Even though they're highly technical, both processes have advantages and drawbacks. I'd like to have a class discussion with you guys regarding these.

As you may already be speculating, post-combustion capture comes into play after fossil fuels are burned and CO_2 is separated from the gas stream in the 'flue.' While the emitted CO_2 is passing through the flue, it goes through a chemical solution that binds with and saturates the gas, like smoke coming out of the chimney. Well, the chemical itself is not very important for this lecture, so let's not go too deep into that.

As the saturated solution leaves the flue, it releases the gas. Subsequently, the gas is collected, transported and trapped underground along with the chemicals used in the process, and… that's where the problem with post-combustion capture emerges. Not only are really, really [Q3] **huge amounts of these absorbent materials and chemicals required, they are also an economic burden.** Additionally, the equipment and machinery necessary for the process are extremely large, and of course, expensive. However, there are some positive aspects of post combustion capture. First of all, when compared to other solutions, it's a far more developed form of technology and [Q3-C] **ready to be put into use**, which means it can be implemented right away. Also, working power plants that have already been built can be easily retrofitted, so [Q3-A] **it does not require the construction of new plants.** Okay, now let's take a look at pre-combustion capture.

S: Let me guess. It [Q4-A] **captures CO_2 emissions before the fossil fuels are burned, right?**

P: (a little laugh) Yes, you're right. Unlike post-combustion capture, [Q4] **pre-combustion capture takes place before CO_2 is released.** It is considered a very efficient method because… it first converts the fuels into hydrogen and CO_2. By isolating CO_2, it only allows hydrogen to be combusted to produce power, effectively preventing any release of CO_2 into the air.

비록 최신식 기술이지만, 둘 다 모두 장점과 함께 단점도 가지고 있죠. 전 여러분과 함께 이것들에 관해 토의해 보려고 해요.

여러분이 이미 짐작했겠지만, 연소 후 포집 방식은 화석연료가 연소된 후에 이산화탄소가 연통 안에서 흐르는 가스로부터 분리되면서 실행돼요. 마치 굴뚝에서 나오는 연기처럼, 방출된 이산화탄소가 연통을 통과해 빠져나가면서 화학 용액을 통과하는데 그것이 가스와 결합하여 그것을 빨아들이게 되죠. 음, 화학 물질 그 자체는 이 강의에서 별로 중요치 않으니까, 그 부분으로는 너무 깊이 들어가지는 맙시다.

포화된 용액이 연통을 빠져나가면서 가스를 배출하는데요. 여기에 이어서, 배출된 가스는 수집되어 운반되고 처리과정에서 사용된 화학 물질과 함께 땅속에 저장되는 거죠. 그리고… 여기에서 바로 연소 후 포집 방식에 문제점이 발생하게 돼요. [Q3] **정말 어마어마한 양의 흡수물질과 화학물질이 요구될 뿐만 아니라, 이것들은 경제적으로도 부담 돼요.** 추가적으로, 처리과정에 필요한 장치와 기계들은 매우 큰데다가 당연히 값이 비싸죠. 하지만 연소 후 포집 방식에 긍정적인 부분이 있어요. 첫째로, 다른 해결책과 비교했을 때, 이것은 훨씬 발전된 형태의 기술이고 [Q3-C] **실제 이용할 수 있게 준비되어있죠.** 이 말은 즉시 실행될 수 있음을 의미해요. 또한 이것은 이미 설립되어 가동 중인 발전소들을 쉽게 개조할 수 있기 때문에 [Q3-A] **새로운 공장 설립이 필요치 않죠.**
좋아요, 이제 연소 전 포집 방식에 대해 살펴보죠.

S: 제가 맞춰볼게요. 그건 [Q4-A] **화석연료가 연소되기 전에 이산화탄소 배출을 수집하는 거에요, 맞지요?**

P: (약간 웃으며) 그래요, 학생 말이 맞아요. 연소 후 포집 방식과 달리 [Q4] **연소 전 수집 방식은 이산화탄소가 대기로 방출되기 전에 일어나요.** 이것은 아주 효율적인 방법으로 여겨지는데요. 왜냐하면… 첫째로, 이것은 연료를 수소와 이산화탄소로 전환시키죠. 이산화탄소를 분리해냄으로써 오직 수소만을 연소시켜 에너지를 생산하고 이산화탄소가 대기로 배출되는것을 효율적으로 막는 거죠.

TEST 4 — Set 1-2 — Lecture 1: Global Temperatures

The storage process of CO_2 works the same way as in post-combustion capture; CO_2 is securely transported to underground storage sites, where it will remain for thousands of years without any leakage problems.

Anyway… Although some people believe that it is a better fit for the future, at present it suffers from numerous drawbacks, which make me believe that it needs to be improved in many ways before it can be considered the ideal method. [Q4-B] **The first is that it's a far less developed form of technology than postcombustion capture**, so it will take another 15 to 20 years until it's ready to be implemented. Another drawback is that it requires an enormous amount of construction work. I mean, unlike post-combustion capture, [Q4-D] **new power plants need to be built** so that the equipment and machinery necessary can be installed prior to completion.

S: So, Professor, which is a better method in your opinion?

P: Well, I can't really say one is better than the other. Many scientists and researchers prefer postcombustion capture to pre-combustion because they believe that speed is the key factor. [Q5] **We are currently living in a generation where the so-called 'climate deadline' is approaching, and we need to make a move as quickly as possible**. The longer we wait, the worse the situation gets, so speed is the key here. Like I said, pre-combustion capture still needs to be developed and enhanced in many ways. Regardless of its effectiveness, it's an irrefutable fact that it cannot be employed as of now, and maybe not for another 15 to 20 years. Post-combustion capture methods, on the other hand, can be added to working power plants globally right now and immediately start reducing CO_2 emissions, right? If we focus on both of them, [Q5-C] **it's only going to split our resources and risk making us miss the deadline that we have set**, so that won't do any good. [Q6] **So my point is… Instead of wasting our time debating which to use, we should primarily focus on encouraging people to start looking into using post-combustion capture**,

---

단락 6

결론 : 급해서 Post가 낫다.

P: 이산화탄소를 저장하는 과정은 연소 후 포집과 같은 방식으로 적용 돼요. 이산화탄소는 안전하게 지하 저장소로 운반되고, 거기서 누출 위험에 대한 문제없이 수천 년 동안 남아있게 될 거에요.

어쨌든, 비록 나와 같은 몇몇 사람들은 이것이 미래에 더 적합하다고 믿고 있지만, 현재는 수많은 단점들을 갖고 있는데, 이것은 이상적인 방법으로 여겨지기 전에 많은 국면에서 보완될 필요가 있다고 생각되네요. [Q4-B] 첫째로, 이것은 연소 후 포집 기술에 비해 훨씬 발달되지 않은 형태의 기술이에요. 그래서 시행될 준비가 될 때까지 15년에서 20년이 더 걸릴 거에요. 또 다른 단점은 엄청난 양의 건설 작업을 필요로 해요. 제 말은, 연소 후 포집 방식과는 달리, [Q4-D] 새로운 공장이 지어져서 필요한 장비와 장치들이 이미 그곳에 설치되어 있어야 한다는 말이에요.

S: 그러면, 교수님, 어떤 것이 더 좋은 방법이라고 생각하시나요?

P: 음, 저는 뭐가 더 나은 거라고 말씀드릴 수 없겠네요. 많은 과학자들과 연구자들은 연소 후 포집을 연소 전 포집보다 선호하는데, 왜냐하면 그들은 속도가 주요 요인이라고 생각하기 때문이죠. [Q5] 우리는 현재 이른바 '기후 마감일' 라고 불리는 것이 다가오는 세대에 살고 있는데요, 그래서 가능한 한 빨리 행동을 취해야 할 필요가 있어요. 더 오래 기다릴 수록 상황은 더 악화되죠. 그래서 여기에서는 속도가 중요해요. 제가 말했듯이, 연소 전 포집은 아직도 많은 면에서 개발되고 향상될 필요가 있어요. 그것의 효율성과 상관없이, 이것은 현재 이용될 수 없고, 아마도 앞으로 15년에서 20년동안 이용될 수 없을지도 모른다는 것이 반박할 수 없는 사실이죠. 반면에 연소 후 포집 방식은, 지구 전체에 가동 중인 발전소에 지금 당장 투입할 수 있고 이산화탄소 배출량을 줄일 수 있잖아요, 그렇죠? 만약 우리가 둘 다에 초점을 맞춘다면, [Q5-C] 이는 그저 자원을 분산 시키고 우리가 세워놓은 마감일을 놓칠 수 있는 위험이 있어요. 그래서 아무것도 좋을 게 없죠. [Q6] 그래서 제 요점은…어떤 것을 사용할지 논쟁하는데 시간을 낭비하는 대신, 우리는 주로 사람들이 연소 후 포집 방식을 이용하는데 관심을 갖도록 장려하는데 집중해야 해요.

| [Q5-A] because if this trend continues, the next generations won't exist. [Q5-B] It's a very urgent matter, and [Q6-A] awareness of it should be spread as quickly and as widely as possible. | [Q5-A] 왜냐하면 만약 이런 상태가 지속되면 우리의 다음 세대는 존재조차 못 할 것이기 때문이죠. [Q5-B] 이것은 매우 긴급한 문제에요. 그리고 [Q6-A] 이에 대한 인식은 가능한 한 빨리 퍼져나가야 해요. |

06 [Main Idea] What is the main topic of the lecture?

(A) Solutions to the increase in global temperatures
(B) Detrimental effects of carbon dioxide and ~~nitrous dioxide~~
   (not mentioned) ★
(C) The ~~factors~~ contributing to the rise in global temperatures
   (fact, but not related to the question)
(D) ~~Comparison~~ of oxy-fuel combustion and pre- and post-combustion capture *(partial error)*

강의의 주제는 무엇인가?

(A) 지구 온도 상승에 대한 해결책
(B) 이산화탄소와 ~~이산화질소의 해로운 영향~~
(C) 지구 기후 상승에 작용하는 요인들
(D) 순산소 연소와 연소 전 포집 및 연소 후 포집과의 ~~비교~~ ★

해설 | 근래에 문제가 되고 있는 global warming에 대한 3가지의 해결책을 다루는 내용.
(B)는 introduction에 global warming의 심각점을 emphasize하기위해 말한 내용이고, (C)는 lecture의 main idea가 되기위해서는 너무 일부분의 내용이다. (D)는 pre combustion 하고 post combustion의 compare 하는 건 어느 정도 맞는데, 말했듯이 전체적인 내용은 global warming에 대한 해결책을 다루는 것이다.

07 [Detail-Characteristic] Which of the following is true about nitrous oxide?

(A) It plays a ~~major role~~ in pre- and post-combustion capture.
   (wrong fact)
(B) It is a great ~~solution~~ to the increase in global temperatures.
   (wrong fact)
(C) Along with other factors, it ~~contributes to~~ CO₂ emission. *(wrong fact)*
(D) **It is a greenhouse gas and contributes to the increase in global temperatures.**

다음 중 이산화 질소에 대한 설명으로 바른 것은?

(A) 이 것은 예비와 후기 연소 수집에 있어 ~~중요한 역할을 한다.~~ ★
(B) 이것은 세계 기후 변화에 대한 훌륭한 ~~해결책이다.~~
(C) 다른 요인들과 함께, 이것은 이산화탄소 배출에 ~~작용한다.~~
(D) 이는 온실가스이며 지구 기후 상승에 작용한다.

해설 | (A) nitrous oxide는 oxy-fuel combustion에 해당되는 내용.
(B) solution이 아니라 contributor가 맞는 것.
(C) CO₂ 와 nitrous oxide는 두개의 다른 greenhouse gas이다 관련이 없음.

TEST 4　　Set 1-2　Lecture 1　Global Temperatures

08 **[Detail-Advantage/Disadvantage]** What are the disadvantages of post-combustion capture?

후기 연소 수집의 단점들에는 무엇이 있는가?

Click on 2 answers　　　　　　　　　　　2개의 정답을 고르시오

(A) Construction of new power plants is required.*(wrong fact)*
(B) **Excessive amounts of absorbent materials and chemicals are required**
(C) It is not ready to be used right now and can't be implemented right away.*(wrong fact)*
(D) **It is economically demanding and burdensome**

(A) 새로운 공장의 설립이 요구된다.
(B) **엄청난 양의 흡착물질과 화학물질이 요구된다.**
(C) 즉시 사용 될 준비가 안되어 있으며 바로 실현 가능하지 않다.
(D) **경제적으로 힘들고 부담이 크다.**

해설 | (A)는 pose combustion capture의 advantage의 정 반대되는 내용.
(C)는 pre combustion capture의 disadvantage를 나타낸다.

---

09 **[Detail-Difference/Contrast]** How is pre-combustion capture different from post-combustion capture?

예비 연소 수집은 후기 연소 수집과 어떻게 다른가?

(A) After fossil fuels are burned, pre-combustion capture comes into play. *(wrong fact)*
(B) Pre-combustion capture is much more sophisticated and a more advanced form of technology.*(wrong fact)* ★
(C) **Pre-combustion capture takes place before the fossil fuels are burned and CO_2 is released into the air**
(D) Pre-combustion capture can be easily implemented to already existing power plants.*(wrong fact)*

(A) 화석연료 연소 후, 예비 연소 수집이 이루어진다.
(B) 예비 연소 수집은 훨씬 더 섬세하고 보다 발전된 기술이다. ★
(C) **예비 연소 수집은 이산화탄소가 대기에 방출되기 이전에 이루어진다.**
(D) 예비 연소 수집은 이미 존재하는 발전소에 쉽게 실행 가능하다.

해설 | (A)는 pre-combustion capture이 아니라 post combustion capture이 맞는 답.
(B)는 pre combustion capture가 단지 new plants를 건설해야 한다고 해서 more advanced라 하기엔 무리가 있다. (D)는 없는 내용.

10 [Inference-Purpose/Intention] Why does the professor mention the 'climate deadline'

(A) To imply that the issue of global climate change ~~has been settled~~ *(wrong fact)*
(B) To emphasize that there is ~~a plenty of time~~ to decide which solution to focus on. *(wrong fact)*
(C) ~~To give an opportunity~~ for students to guess when the climate deadline is *(wrong fact)*
(D) **To alert the students to the urgency and danger of global climate change**

교수가 왜 기후의 최후를 언급했는가?

(A) 지구 기후 변화의 문제가 ~~안정적이게 되었다는~~ 것을 암시하기 위해
(B) 어떤 해결책에 집중할지 결정하는데 ~~충분한 시간이 있다는~~ 것을 강조하기 위해
(C) 학생들에게 기후의 최후가 언제 올지 ~~맞춰볼 수 있는~~ 기회를 주기 위해
(D) **지구 기후 변화의 긴급성과 위험성을 알리기 위해**

해설 | 여기서 말하는 climate deadline는 global warming의 심각성과 대비책이 한시 급히 필요로 한다는 교수의 주장을 뒷받침하기 위한 term 이다. (A)는 근거 없는 말이고, (B)는 교수의 주장과 정 반대되는 내용. (C)는 없는 말이다.

11 [Inference-Opinion/Attitude] What is the professor's opinion regarding pre- and post-combustion capture?

(A) She believes that awareness of the solutions is ~~widespread~~. *(wrong fact)*
(B) **She thinks that employing one of the methods now and trying to handle the global climate issue immediately is an urgent matter.**
(C) She believes both of them are insufficient, and ~~other solutions~~ are required. *(wrong fact)*
(D) She feels that ~~more research on both~~ of the methods should be done before using either of them. *(partial error)* ★

교수가 왜 기후의 최후를 언급했는가?

(A) 해결책에 대한 인식이 ~~잘 알려져 있다고~~ 생각한다.
(B) **하나의 방법을 도입하고 지구 기후 문제를 다루기 위한 노력이 시급하다고 생각한다.**
(C) 두 방법 모두 부적합하고 ~~추가적인 해결책들이~~ 필요하다고 생각한다.
(D) 어떤 것을 도입하던지 두 방법에 대한 더 많은 연구가 되어야 진행되어야 한다고 생각한다. ★

해설 | (A)는 교수가 더 많은 사람들에게 awareness를 spread해야 한다는 주장과 반대되는 말. (C) 교수는 post-combustion capture에 집중해야 한다고 생각하므로 오답이다. (D) pre-combustion capture를 뜻하는 거지 post combustion capture는 해당하지 않는다.

문단주제	본문내용	해석
	Listen to part of a lecture in an art history class	예술사 강의의 일부를 들으시오.

단락 1
그리스와 로마 예술품 소개

Okay… in the last chapter, we looked at the fundamental roots of Greek and Roman mythology and their historical backgrounds. Even though they are mistakenly regarded as mere myths by some, we've learned that there were once political and social parallels in the stories, correct? Um, the most convincing tangible evidence of such a belief is, perhaps, the art made during these eras… sculptures, to be specific. I'm sure you've all seen a variety of statues, whether vibrantly colored or plain white. Our understanding of Greek and Roman statues is usually most compatible with the latter case, though, right? Everything is usually white from the head to the toes…

좋아요… 저번 장에서는, 우리가 그리스와 로마 신화의 근본적인 뿌리와 그것의 역사적인 배경들에 대해 살펴보았는데요. 비록 어떤 사람들은 그것을 단순히 신화로 잘못 생각하고 있지만, 그 이야기에는 정치적이고 사회적인 유사점이 있다고 배웠었죠, 맞나요? 음, 그런 믿음에 대한 가장 확실한 명백한 증거는, 아마도 이 시기에 만들어진 예술품일 거예요… 구체적으로 동상이죠. 여러분들은 다양한 동상을 보았을 텐데요, 선명하게 색깔이 들어가 있거나 단순히 흰색이거나요. 그런데 그리스와 로마 동상에 대한 우리의 이해 수준은 보통 후자의 경우와 가장 부합할 거예요, 맞죠? 보통 머리부터 발끝까지 모든 것이 흰색이죠.

단락 2
단색 조각상의 유래

Now, the history of these monochromatic sculptures dates back to 15th century Europe… especially Italy, where the impact of the Renaissance was greatest. During this era, some ancient Greek and Roman sculptures were rediscovered in many parts of the world. Umm… If you guys refer back to the previous chapter, the Apollo Belvedere was one of the sculptures that was rediscovered during this period. It depicts the Greek god, Apollo, in one color - white… a symbol of aesthetic perfection. Anyway, [Q2-B, C, D] **what the Renaissance artists did when they rediscovered such ancient statues was that they strove to emulate their most distinctive characteristic - the monochromatic coloration.** This "trend," so to speak, influenced the society in a significant way… I mean, think about it this way. Let's just say that you were one of the people living at the time, and all of the statues you saw were uniformly white. They were certainly beautiful, but they had no color.

[Q2] **Contravening the earlier perspectives on sculpture, Renaissance era white marble statues, created in accordance with these ancient sculptures, instilled a new set of standards in contemporary artists that suggested that form was more important than color.** It was not until the early 19th century that the art historians realized that their belief that the ancient marble statues were originally white was inaccurate.

자, 이런 단색의 조각상들은 15세기 유럽, 르네상스의 영향을 가장 많이 받았던 이탈리아로 시기가 거슬러 올라가요. 이 시기 동안에, 일부 그리스와 로마 조각상들이 세계의 많은 지역에서 재발견되었는데요. 음…. 만약 여러분이 이전에 배웠던 장 중의 하나를 참고 한다면, Apollo Belvedere는 이 기간에 발견된 조각상들 중에 하나였어요.

그것은 그리스의 신인 아폴로를 흰색 한가지로 표현했는데… 이건 미적인 완벽함의 상징이죠. 어쨌든, [Q2-B, C, D] **그런 고대 동상들이 재발견되었을 때 르네상스 예술가들이 한 일은 그 동상들의 두드러진 특징-단색 채색법을 모방하고자 애쓴 거예요.** 말하자면 이러한 트렌드는 사회에 중요한 영향을 끼쳤죠… 제 말은, 이런 식으로 생각해보세요. 여러분이 그 당시에 살고 있는 사람들 중 하나이고, 여러분이 보는 동상들이 모두 똑같이 흰색이라고 해보죠. 그것들은 확실히 아름답지만, 색깔이 전혀 없어요.

[Q2] **조각상에 대한 이전의 관점에 반대하여, 르네상스 시대의 조각상들은 이러한 고대의 조각상과 일치하게 만들어졌고, 동시대의 예술가들에게 형태가 색보다 더 중요하다는 새로운 일련의 기준을 주입했죠.** 19세기 초가 되어서야 미술가들이 고대 대리석 동상들이 원래 흰색이라는 자신들의 믿음이 틀렸다는 걸 깨달았죠.

단락 3
다색 조각상의 증거 및 흔적

In the early 19th century, archaeologists found subtle traces of visible paint on the statue and, after further research, arrived at the conclusion that the statues that were once believed to be monochromatic were originally polychromatic. You see, the current absence of visible coloration doesn't necessarily mean that it never existed. [Q6] **The color could have either simply deteriorated due to the effect of wind, water, and other such factors over thousands of years… or someone could have vigorously scrubbed the paint off while trying to clean the statues … (laughs).** Anyway, today, with the advent of new technology, archaeologists are able to execute more in-depth research into these sculptures. [Q3-8] **For instance, they can use ultraviolet light on the statues and distinguish formerly colored parts from the non-colored ones.** Umm… [Q3] **UV light is very useful and efficient for this particular task because it causes organic compounds to, sort of, fluoresce.** You see, unlike modern paints, the paints that the Greek and Roman artists used were mainly composed of organic compounds… Anyway, we'll be re-visiting this matter in the next lesson, so let's get back on topic.

단락 4
예술가의 의도에 따른 예술품의 해석

We were talking about… Oh, yeah. Right. The evidence they found proved that the statues were originally polychromatic. Today, it's generally accepted by art historians and researchers that the Greek and Roman sculptures from the 7th century B.C.E through 4th century C.E were all polychromatic. Some believe that it's unfortunate that Renaissance art standards were established based on the "supposed" Roman and Greek principle that has now been proven wrong. I agree to a certain extent, but I don't think that the principle was entirely wrong. I mean, there can certainly be multiple interpretations of one piece of art. As I mentioned previously, monochromatic sculptures were interpreted with a heavy emphasis on the form. [Q4] **In this sense, we must first take a careful approach to understanding the artists' intentions, particularly when it comes to interpreting polychromatic sculptures.**

19세기 초에는, 고고학자들이 동상에서 눈에 띄는 페인트의 미세한 흔적을 찾아냈는데, 좀 더 연구를 한 뒤에, 한때 단색이라고 믿어졌던 동상들이 원래는 다색이었다는 결론에 도달하게 되었죠. 그러니까, 현재 눈에 보이는 채색이 없다고 해서 꼭 그것이 전혀 존재한 적이 없다는 걸 의미하지는 않는다는 거예요. [Q6] **단순히 색깔이 수천 년에 걸쳐 바람, 물 그리고 다른 요인들의 영향 때문에 퇴색되었을 수도 있고요… 또는 누군가가 동상을 청소할 때 너무 열심히 닦았을 수도 있죠. (웃음)** 어쨌든, 오늘날에는 새로운 기술의 도래와 함께, 고고학자들이 이러한 조각상들에 대해 심도 있는 조사를 더 많이 실행할 수 있어요. [Q3-8] **예를 들어, 그들은 동상들에 자외선을 사용해서 예전에 색이 칠해졌던 부분을 색이 없는 부분과 구별할 수 있어요.** 음… [Q3] **자외선은 이런 특수한 작업에 매우 유용하고 효과적인데, 왜냐하면 그것이 유기 혼합물이, 일종의 형광색을 발하게끔 만들기 때문이에요.** 그러니까 현대 페인트와는 달리, 그리스와 로마 시대의 예술가들이 사용했던 페인트는 주로 유기 화합물로 구성되어 있었어요. 어쨌든, 우리는 다음 시간에 이 부분에 대해 다시 살펴볼 테니, 다시 주제로 돌아가도록 하죠.

우리가 얘기하고 있던게… 아 맞아요. 그들이 발견했던 증거들은 동상이 원래 다색이었다는 걸 증명했어요. 오늘날에는, 기원전 7세기부터 4세기에 만들어진 그리스와 로마의 조각상들이 모두 다색이라는 것이 미술사에 의해 일반적으로 인정되고 있어요. 어떤 사람들은 이제는 틀린 것으로 증명된 로마와 그리스의 것으로 가정한 원리에 바탕을 두고 르네상스 시대의 예술 기준이 정립되었다는 것은 유감스러운 일이라고 믿고 있죠. 전 이 말에 어느 정도까지는 동의하지만, 그 원리가 완전히 틀렸다고는 생각하지 않아요. 제 말은, 하나의 예술품에 대해 여러 개의 해석이 확실히 있을 수 있다는 것이죠. 제가 앞서 언급했듯이, 다색의 조각상들은 형태에 상당히 중점을 두고 해석되어 왔어요. [Q4] **이 경우에는, 우리는 일단 예술가의 의도를 이해하는데 조심스럽게 접근해야 하는데, 특히 다색의 조각상을 해석할 때 그렇죠.**

Lecture 2 — Monochromatic Sculptures

단락 5 — 예술품의 해석: 색깔의 역할

The first thing to consider is the role of the colors. Some parts or features of the statues were accentuated with different colors. How, you may wonder, could that be related to the artists' intentions? Well, one compelling explanation is that a color may have symbolized many facets… things such as invincibility, patriotism, honor, heroism, and so on. Let's take the statue of Augustus, the founder and first emperor of the Roman Empire, into consideration to clarify the point. It was discovered on April 20, 1863 in the Villa of Livia at Prima Porta. In addition to founding the Roman Empire, Augustus was also the imperator, or commander, of the great Roman army. Observing his statue, we can see that he's in military clothing, holding a baton and posing as if he'd been victorious in battle. When the statue was examined thoroughly, it was revealed that its most abundant color was red, which is generally associated with energy, war, passion, and strength. You see the connection now, right? The sculptures weren't just randomly polychromatic; the colors actually played a symbolic role in highlighting certain features or characteristics of the subjects.

단락 6 — 단색 조각상의 유래

The next aspect we should study is the kind of pigments used to produce the colors. As you may already know, the quality of paint color is dependent upon the quality of the pigments used. Keeping that in mind, let's take a look at the statue of Augustus once again. The pigments used for his statue weren't just normal pigments. They were very expensive at the time. [Q4-A] **The use of these particular pigments shows his importance and authority as the emperor, in addition to his importance as the imperator.**

단락 7 — 연구의 중요성과 긴급함

Okay. I think that was enough explanation of these statues, right? I'm sure you can see how the colors of the sculptures were associated with social, economic, and political values. You see, there're still a great number of sculptures that have yet to be deciphered the way that the statue of Augustus has been. [Q5] **We have the technology required to pursue further investigation, and it's urgent that we carry out more research and studies immediately, because the paint pigments deteriorate very rapidly.** Through this, I'm certain that our knowledge of the art of the Greek and Roman empires will be greatly enhanced, along with our understanding of the culture that created the statues.

첫 번째로 고려해야 할 것은 색깔의 역할이에요. 조각상들의 일부나 특징들이 다른 색들로 강조되었어요. 그것이 어떻게 예술가의 의도와 관련이 있을까 여러분은 궁금해할지도 몰라요. 음, 설득력 있는 한 가지 설명은 하나의 색이 많은 면들을 상징한다는 것인데요, 무적, 애국심, 명예, 영웅심 등이죠. 그 점을 명확히 하기 위해 로마제국의 창시자이자 초대 황제인 Augustus 동상을 생각해 보도록 하죠. 그것은 1863년 4월 20일에 Villa of Livia at Prima Porta에서 발견되었어요. Augustus는 로마제국을 창시한 것과 함께, 위대한 로마 군대의 개선장군 혹은 총사령관이었어요. 그의 동상을 관찰해보면, 군복을 입고 지휘봉을 들고서 마치 전투에서 승리한 것처럼 포즈를 취하고 있어요. 동상을 세세히 검사해보면, 가장 풍부한 색깔이 빨간색으로 드러났는데, 이것은 에너지, 전쟁, 열정, 그리고 강인함과 관련이 있죠. 이제 연결고리가 보이나요? 조각상들은 단순히 무작위로 단색으로 되어 있는 게 아니에요; 색들은 실제로 대상의 특정한 특성이나 특징들을 강조하는데 상징적인 역할을 했죠.

우리가 다음으로 살펴볼 면은 색을 만들어내는데 사용한 안료의 종류에요. 여러분이 이미 알고 있을지도 모르겠지만, 페인트 색의 품질은 사용되는 안료의 품질에 달려있죠. 이 점을 유의하면서, Augustus 동상을 다시 한번 보도록 하죠. 동상에 사용된 안료들은 단순히… 평범한 안료가 아니었어요. 그것들은 당시에 매우 비싼 것이었죠. [Q4-A] 이런 특별한 안료를 사용했다는 것은 개선장군으로서의 중요성에 더해 황제로서의 중요성과 권위를 나타내죠.

네. 제 생각엔 이 동상에 대한 설명은 이 정도로 충분한 것 같아요, 그렇지 않나요? 여러분이 조각상의 색들이 사회적, 경제적, 그리고 정치적인 가치와 어떻게 연결되어 있는지 알 수 있을 거에요. 그러니까, Augustus 동상처럼 해독 되지 않은 조각상들이 아직 많이 있어요.

[Q5] 조사를 더 하려면 기술이 필요하고, 우리는 더 많은 리서치와 연구를 당장 시행하는 것이 급선무에요, 왜냐하면 페인트의 안료가 매우 빨리 퇴색되기 때문이에요. 이 과정을 통하여, 그리스와 로마 제국의 동상들을 탄생시킨 문화에 대한 이해와 더불어, 예술품에 대한 지식이 무척 향상될 거라 전 확신해요.

12 [Main Idea] What is the lecture mainly about?

(A) The ~~historical backgrounds~~ of the Greek and Roman empires *(fact, but not related to the question)* ★

(B) A ~~general exploration~~ of the ~~notable characteristics~~ of Emperor Augustus' statue *(fact, but not related to the question)*

~~(C) Technological advances~~ that help archaeologists interpret ancient sculptures *(fact, but not related to the question)*

(D) The evolution of our understanding of Greek and Roman sculptures

강의는 주로 무엇에 관한 것인가?

(A) 그리스와 로마 제국에 대한 역사적인 배경들 ★

(B) Augustus황제의 동상이 지닌 눈에 띄는 특징들에 대한 일반적인 탐사

(C) 고고학자들이 고대 조각상들을 해석하는 도움을 주는 기술의 진보

(D) 그리스와 로마 조각상들에 대한 우리의 이해의 진화

해설 | (A) 역사적 배경은 지난 시간 복습 차원에서 간략히 언급했기 때문에 오답.
(B) Augustus 황제는 예술품 해석의 예시로 든 것이기 때문에 오답.
(C) UV light 등의 technological advances는 다음시간 주제이므로 오답.

13 [Category-Introduce] How did the Greek and Roman sculptures influence the Renaissance artists?

(A) They helped the artists to establish that form was the primary principle.

(B) They caused the artists ~~to use color~~ as a mechanism to highlight certain features of their sculptures. *(opposite fact)* ★

(C) They helped artists ~~abandon~~ the practice of sculpture and employ ~~other methods~~ of representation, such as painting. *(wrong fact)*

(D) They motivated the artists to solely focus on applying ~~various forms of paint~~ to their sculptures. *(wrong fact)*

그리스와 로마 조각상은 어떻게 르네상스 예술가들에게 영향을 끼쳤는가?

(A) 예술가들이 형태가 주요한 원리라고 확립하도록 도와주었다.

(B) 예술가들이 조각상의 특징들을 강조하기 위한 방법으로 색을 사용하도록 만들었다. ★

(C) 그들은 예술가들이 조각을 포기하고 회화와 같은 다른 표현 방법들을 사용하도록 도왔다.

(D) 예술가들이 다양한 형태와 페인트를 조각상에 적용하는 데에만 집중하도록 동기를 부여했다.

해설 | (B) 그리스와 로마 동상이 단색이라고 생각했던 르네상스 예술가들은 색깔을 쓰지 않음.
(C) 르네상스 예술가들은 계속해서 조각상을 만들었기 때문에 오답.
(D) 논점은 페인트 형태의 다양성이 아닌 제한된 색상 표현이었으므로 오답.

TEST 4 Set 1-3 Lecture 2 Monochromatic Sculptures

14 [Detail-Characteristic] According to the professor, how does ultraviolet light aid archaeologists studying polychromatic sculptures?

(A) **It helps them discern the colored parts of statues by illuminating organic compounds.**
(B) It enables them to figure out the ~~time period~~ in which they were made. *(not mentioned)*
(C) It distinguishes the parts of sculptures with a ~~dense concentration~~ of organic compounds from those without. *(partial error)* ★
(D) It works like an ~~x-ray machine~~ and ~~locates sculptures~~ during excavation. *(wrong fact)*

교수에 따르면, 어떻게 자외선이 고고학자들이 다색의 조각상들을 연구하도록 도움을 주었는가?

(A) 유기 화합물이 빛을 나게 함으로써 조각상의 색이 있는 부분을 구별하게 도와준다.
(B) 조각상들이 언제 만들어졌는지 파악하는 데 도움을 준다.
(C) 조각상에 유기 화합물이 집중적으로 몰려있는 부분과 그렇지 않은 부분을 구별해낸다. ★
(D) 엑스레이 기계처럼 작동하여 발굴할 때 조각상의 위치를 추적해낸다.

해설 | (B) 자외선의 사용은 만들어진 시기를 식별하는 일과 무관하므로 오답.
(C) 자외선을 사용한 고고학자들의 연구는 유기화합물의 집중도가 아닌 유무의 판별이 주된 목적이므로 오답.
(D) 색 판별과 발굴과는 무관하므로 오답

---

15 [Inference-Purpose/Intention] Why does the professor mention the Roman Emperor Augustus?

(A) To illustrate that ~~his sculpture~~ represents his great authority
(B) ~~To clarify~~ the ~~common misconception~~ that his sculpture was originally monochromatic
(C) **To explain how polychromatic sculptures are interpreted in regard to the artists' motive**
(D) ~~To begin a new discussion~~ of the various pigments used in painting sculptures during the Roman era

교수는 왜 로마의 Augustus 황제를 언급했는가?

(A) 그의 조각상이 위대한 권력을 대표한다는 것을 알려주기 위해 ★
(B) 조각상이 원래는 단색이었다는 널리 알려진 잘못된 오해를 명확히 하기 위해
(C) 다색의 조각상이 예술가의 동기와 관련하여 어떻게 해석되는지 설명하기 위해
(D) 로마 시대에 조각상을 칠할 때 사용된 다양한 안료에 관한 새로운 토론을 시작하기 위해

해설 | (A) 권력을 표현하는 것은 조각상이 아닌 특정 안료의 사용이므로 오답.
(B) 조각상이 단색이었다는 오해는 언급되지 않음.
(D) 토론을 시작하기 위함이 아닌 안료의 대한 설명 및 예시의 일부이므로 오답.

16 [Detail-Characteristic] What property or characteristic of the pigments in paints calls for an immediate investigation of the Greek and Roman sculptures?

(A) ~~The value~~ of the paint pigments used during Greek and Roman time was extremely high. *(not mentioned)*
(B) ~~Certain colors~~, such as red and blue, ~~decompose~~ due to factors, such as the wind. *(not mentioned)*
(C) The pigments ~~gradually change~~ color depending on the amount of ~~sunlight absorption~~. *(not mentioned)*
(D) **The pigments used on the sculptures deteriorate at quite a rapid rate.**

페인트에 있는 안료의 어떤 특성과 특징이 그리스와 로마 조각상들을 즉시 조사하도록 요구하는가?

(A) 그리스와 로마시대에 사용된 페인트의 안료의 가치가 매우 높다.
(B) 빨간색이나 푸른색 같은 특정한 색들은 바람과 같은 요인 때문에 분해된다. ★
(C) 안료는 흡수되는 태양빛의 양에 따라 점차적으로 색을 변화시킨다.
(D) **조각상에 사용된 안료는 꽤 빠른 속도로 퇴색된다.**

> 해설 | (A) 가치에 대한 언급은 본문에 없으므로 오답.
> (B) 분해되는 것은 특정한 색에 한한 것이 아닌 조각상에 쓰인 안료의 보편적인 특징이므로 오답.
> (C) 색의 변화가 아닌 안료의 퇴화가 즉시적인 조사를 요하기 때문에 오답.

Listen to part of the lecture again, then answer the question

"The color could have either simply decomposed due to thousands of years of wind, water, and such or…or someone could have vigorously scrubbed the paint off while trying to clean the statues…"

강의의 일부를 다시 듣고, 질문에 답하시오.

"단순히 색깔이 수천년에 걸쳐 바람, 물 그리고 다른 요인들의 영향 때문에 퇴색되었을 수도 있구요… 또는 누군가가 동상을 청소할 때 너무 열심히 닦았을 수도 있죠…"

17 [Inference-Imply] What does the professor imply when he says this : 🎧

"someone could have vigorously scrubbed the paint off while trying to clean the statues"

(A) That scrubbing is ~~very damaging~~ to paints, especially those used on sculptures *(not mentioned)* ★
(B) That the latter case is also ~~one of the most compelling theories~~ to explain the disappearance of the paints *(not mentioned)*
(C) That ~~keeping sculptures clean~~ required strenuous work in the ancient times *(not mentioned)*
(D) **That there are many possible reasons that the pigments disappeared from the statues**

교수가 이 말을 할 때 무엇을 암시하는가 : 🎧

"누군가가 동상을 청소할 때 너무 열심히 닦았을 수도 있죠."

(A) 문지름이 페인트를 많이 손상시키는데 특히 조각상에 사용되는 페인트가 그렇다. ★
(B) 후자의 경우가 또한 페인트가 사라진 것을 설명하는 가장 설득력 있는 이론들 중의 하나이다.
(C) 조각상을 깨끗하게 유지하는 것은 고대에 힘든 일을 요구했다
(D) **안료가 조각상에서 사라지는 데에는 가능성 있는 이유들이 많다**

> 해설 | 헤드셋 문제는 노트테이킹을 하면서 어느 부분에서 언급되었는지 반드시 잡아 내야 한다. 노트테이킹에서 언급된 내용을 잡아낸다면 그 말을 왜 했는지와 그 말이 함축하고 있는 의미를 쉽게 알아낼 수 있다. 이 문제에서는 "눈에 보이지 않는다고 없었던 것은 아니다"라고 말하면서 든 예시 중 한가지가 청소하면서 문질렀던 것 때문에 페인트가 벗겨진 것을 예로 든 것이다. 그러므로, 주목해야 할 문장은 "the current absence of visible coloration doesn't necessarily mean that it never existed." 이고 해석대로, 눈에 보이지 않는다고 존재하지 않았다는 사실을 얘기하기 위해서 예를 든 것뿐임을 알아야 한다.

TEST 4 Set2-1 — conversation: 19th century Female artist

문단주제	본문내용	해석
단락 1 레포트 주제 선정 고민	**Listen to part of a conversation between a student and a professor** S: Professor? Um… about the paper you asked us to turn in next week? P: Ah… [Q5-D] yes, the paper on a 19th century female artist. S: Yes, while I was looking for a good example from the feminist era, I came across an artist named Rosa Bonheur. P: Yes, [Q2] the French proto-feminist. How's your research coming along? S: [Q1] Um… I'm having a hard time choosing what to write about. [Q2] I mean, should I just write about her legacy as one of the pivotal figures in the initiation of the feminist movement? Or should I focus more on her life as an artist? P: I can definitely see that you've been doing some research. Well, of course, you can't write a single paper on all of the topics, right? (laughs) S: [Q5] There is so much information about her that it made me think about choosing someone else to write about, but I'm a really big fan of her work personally… I'm of two minds on this… P: When researching the personal aspects of Rosa Bonheur's early life, [Q2] there isn't really much to write about other than the fact that she had a hard time adapting to school, I guess, and maybe her family's background. S: So I should probably rule out writing about her early life? P: Exactly. There isn't much to write about. That is, if you decide to stick with Bonheur… S: Then I should choose between [Q2-B] the role she played in the beginning of the feminist movement by wearing men's clothes and her artwork?	학생과 교수의 대화를 들으시오 S: 교수님? 음…… 다음주까지 제출하라고 하셨던 레포트 말인데요? P: 아.. [Q5-D] 그래. 19세기 여성 예술가에 대한 레포트지. S: 네, 제가 페미니스트 시대의 좋은 본보기를 찾던 중에, Rosa Bonheur라는 예술가를 알게 되었거든요 P: 맞아, [Q2] 프랑스 최초의 페미니스트지. 조사는 어떻게 되고 있니? S: [Q1] 음…… 무엇에 대해서 써야 할지 고민돼요. [Q2] 제 말은, 페미니스트 운동의 시초에서 그녀가 중추적인 역할 중 한명으로서의 업적에 대해 써야 하나요? 아니면 예술가로서의 삶에 대해서 초점을 더 맞춰야 할까요? P: 네가 조사를 좀 했다는 걸 확실히 알겠어. 음, 확실히, 그 모든 주제들을 한 레포트에 다룰 수는 없잖아, 그렇지? (웃음) S: [Q5] 그녀에 대한 정보가 너무 많아서, 다른 사람에 대해서 써볼까도 생각을 했지만, 개인적으로 그녀의 작품을 정말 좋아하거든요… 이 문제에 대해 정말 고민돼요… P: Rosa Bonheur의 유년기에 대한 개인적인 면들을 조사해보면, [Q2] 그녀가 학교에 적응하는 것에 힘들어했다는 사실과, 그리고 아마 그녀의 가족 배경 말고는 쓸 게 그다지 많지 않아 S: 그러면 그녀의 유년기에 대해서 쓰는 건 제외시킬까요? P: 바로 그 말이야. 쓸게 별로 없잖아. 그 말은, 만약 네가 Bonheur에 대해서 쓰겠다고 결심한다면… S: 그럼 전 [Q2-B] 그녀가 남자 옷을 입음으로써 여성운동 초기에 했던 역할과 그녀의 예술 작품 사이에서 선택을 해야 되는 거군요.

단락 2 여성운동에서의 본허의 역할 관련 논란	**P:** Yes. But I have to tell you that her role in the feminist movement is highly controversial. She insisted that the only reason she wore men's clothing was because they were more comfortable and better suited for her type of work, which involved a lot of traveling to farms for research. Nobody has been able to validate this theory, however. **S:** I see. I should probably write about her work then, huh? **P:** I would recommend that you do, unless you're willing to push yourself to go deeper into the controversy I just mentioned. **S:** It would certainly be a challenge.
단락 3 추가점수 제안	**P:** [Q3-D] **I actually have some books on the topic, but the ones that debate the controversy go on for nearly a thousand pages.** I'll tell you what. [Q3] **If you decide to go for it, I'm willing to give you extra credit**, if, and only if, you pull it off in a manner that I approve of. **S:** Any hints about the criterion on which I'll be graded? **P:** Hmm… [Q4] **If you can prove whether or not Bonheur's statement was true, using conclusive proof and statements, I will approve it.** You don't have to worry about whether I agree with your stance or not. **S:** Isn't that… a bit abstract? I mean, "conclusive" is a rather objective term. **P:** Yes, what I meant was, find information that can be used to support your opinion on Bonheur's statement, sort of like a persuasive essay. I think this assignment would be a great opportunity for you to expand your knowledge on the feminist era and your understanding of the artist. **S:** Wow, as tempting as it sounds, it doesn't sound easy. **P:** That's true. That's why I will give you extra points if you manage to do it. Well, I hope you make the right decision… Remember, this topic will be as difficult as it is intriguing.

P: 맞아. 하지만 여성운동에 있어서의 그녀의 역할은 논쟁의 여지가 많아. 그녀는 자기가 남자 옷을 입었던 단 하나의 이유는 옷이 편하고 조사를 위해 농장으로 자주 여행해야 하는 자신의 일에 더 잘 맞기 때문이라고 주장했었지. 하지만 아무도 그녀의 주장을 분명하게 증명하지 못하고 있어.

S: 그렇군요. 그럼 전 그녀의 예술 작품에 대해서 써야겠네요, 맞죠?

P: 그렇게 하는 걸 권하겠어, 단지 내가 방금 전에 언급한 논쟁에 대해 더 깊이 들어가려고 자기자신을 몰아세울 의지가 없다면 말이야.

S: 확실히 도전 과제이겠는데요.

P: [Q3-D] **사실은 내가 그 주제에 관한 책들을 몇 권 가지고 있어, 그런데 그 논쟁에 대해 토론하는 책들은 거의 천 장이나 된단다.** 이렇게 하자. [Q3] **만약 네가 이 주제에 대해서 쓴다고 하면, 네게 추가 학점을 줄 의향이 있어**, 하지만 오직, 내가 인정할 수 있을 만한 방식으로 써야 해.

S: 제가 점수를 받는 기준에 대한 힌트가 있나요?

P: 음…… [Q4] **만약 네가 결정적인 증거와 진술들을 사용해서 Bonheur의 주장이 맞는지 아닌지를 증명할 수 있다면, 인정해 줄게.** 내가 너의 주장에 대해 동의하는지 안 하는지는 걱정하지 않아도 돼.

S: 그건 조금 추상적이지 않나요? 제 말은 "결정적인"이라는 말은 좀 객관적이라고 생각하는데요.

P: 그래, 내가 의미했던 건, Bonheur의 진술에 대한 너의 의견을 지지하는데 사용되는 정보를 찾으라는 거야, 일종의 설득력 있는 논문 같은 거 말야, 내 생각엔 이 과제는 페미니스트 시대에 대한 지식과 예술가에 대한 이해력을 넓힐 수 있는 좋은 기회라고 생각해.

S: 와우, 매력적으로 들리는 만큼 쉽게 들리지도 않네요.

P: 그래 맞아. 그래서 네가 해내면 추가 점수를 주겠다고 한 거야. 음, 올바른 결정을 하길 바래. 기억해, 이 주제는 너한테 흥미롭게 들릴 수도 있겠지만, 어려운 주제라는 걸 말야.

TEST 4 Set 2-1 conversation 19th century Female artist

01 [Detail-Cause/Reason] Why does the student go to see her professor?

(A) To get guidance on what ~~references~~ would be of help to her *(wrong fact)*
(B) To get the professor's ~~approval~~ for her paper *(wrong fact)*
(C) To get advice from the professor on how to approach her paper
(D) To ask her professor if ~~extra points~~ are available for the paper *(partial error)* ★

학생이 교수를 찾아간 이유는 무엇인가?

(A) 도움이 될 ~~참고 자료들~~에 대한 안내를 받기 위해
(B) 그녀의 레포트에 대한 ~~승인~~을 받기 위해서
(C) 그녀의 레포트를 어떤 식으로 접근해야 할지 조언을 얻기 위해
(D) 레포트에 대한 ~~추가 점수~~를 받을 수 있는지 물어보기 위해 ★

해설 | 학생은 교수를 찾아가기 전에 이미 topic을 가지고 있었다. 단지 그 artist의 어떤 부분을 주제로 삼을까 고민했던 것뿐.
(A) 참고 자료에 대한 도움이 필요했던 게 아니라 오답.
(B) 학생은 approval이 아닌 advice를 구하러 간 것이다. (D) 나중에 교수의 권유사항이지 학생이 교수를 찾아간 이유는 아니다.

02 [Detail-Characteristic] What do the speakers say about Rosa Bonheur?

Click on 2 answers

(A) It has been argued that she was a pioneer in the feminist movement.
(B) Her artistic work ~~portrayed~~ women that wore men's clothing. *(partial error)* ★
(C) She ~~formed an organization~~ of people who shared her artistic views. *(not mentioned)*
(D) Her early life is not very significant when compared to other aspects of it.

왜 교수는 급히 사람들을 더 모집해야 할 필요가 있는가?

2개의 정답을 고르시오

(A) 그녀는 여성운동의 선구자였다고 주장되어진다.
(B) 그녀의 예술 작품은 남자 옷을 입는 여자들을 ~~묘사했다.~~ ★
(C) 그녀는 자신의 예술적 견해를 공유하는 사람들을 모아 ~~단체를 만들었다.~~
(D) 그녀의 유년기는 다른 부분들과 비교했을 때 아주 중요하지는 않다.

해설 | (B) 는 로사 본허가 평소에 남자의 옷을 즐겨 입었다는 걸 왜곡 시켜놓은 내용.
(C) 그녀가 movement의 선구자였다고는 하지만 그렇다고 그녀가 단체를 형성했다는 내용은 언급된 적이 없다.

03 [Inference-Attitude] What is the professor's attitude towards the student's completing her assignment?

(A) The professor thinks the student should ~~disregard~~ her personal preferences and view Rosa Bonheur ~~objectively~~ *(opposite fact)*
(B) The professor suggests that the student can choose a harder approach to the assignment if she wants to
(C) The professor encourages the student to do ~~what she has always been interested in~~. *(wrong fact)*
(D) The professor believes the student ~~should include~~ some parts from the ~~professor's book~~ in her research paper. *(wrong fact)*

학생이 과제를 완성하는 데에 대한 교수의 태도는 무엇인가?

(A) 교수는 학생이 자신의 개인적인 선호를 ~~무시하고~~ Rosa Bonheur를 ~~객관적으로~~ 바라봐야 한다고 생각한다.
(B) 교수는 학생이 원한다면 과제에 좀 더 어려운 접근을 선택할 수 있도록 제안하고 있다.
(C) 교수는 학생에게 ~~항상 흥미로워 했던걸~~ 하도록 격려하고 있다.
(D) 교수는 학생이 레포트의 일부분으로 ~~자신의 책을 사용해야 한다고~~ 믿고 있다. ★

해설 | (A) 교수는 객관성이 아닌 학생의 의견을 지지할 수 있는 근거를 바탕으로 설득력 있는 논문을 쓸 것을 요구했다.
(C) 흥미를 따를 것이 아닌 어려운 주제에 도전해 볼 것을 권유함.
(D) 본인에게 관련된 책이 있다고 언급했을 뿐, 사용 및 참고를 강요하지는 않았으므로 오답.

04 [Detail-Requirement] According to the professor, what should be included in the student's paper in order to receive extra points?

(A) ~~Abstract~~ information that is presented in an organized manner
   (opposite fact)
(B) Indisputable information which proves ~~that Bonheur was an actual feminist~~ (wrong fact)
(C) **Persuasive information that argues for or against the validation of Bonheur's statement**
(D) Insightful analysis of Bonheur's ~~standing~~ in the history of feminism
   (wrong fact)★

교수에 따르면, 추가 점수를 받기 위해서는 학생의 레포트에 무엇이 포함되어야 하는가?

(A) 정리되어 있는 ~~추상적인~~ 정보
(B) ~~Bonheur가 실제로 페미니스트였다는 걸 증명하는~~ 반박할 수 없는 정보
(C) **Bonheur의 진술이 사실인지 아닌지 주장하는 설득력 있는 정보**
(D) 페미니즘의 역사에서 자리하는 Bonheur의 ~~지위~~에 대한 통찰력 있는 분석 ★

해설 | (A)의 abstract란 단어는 학생이 "Conclusive proof and statements"를 이해 하지 못해서 쓴 단어를 왜곡해서 써놓은 것이다.
(B) Bonheur가 feminist였는지에 대한 논란은 애초에 제기 되지 않았다.
(D) 교수는 Bonheur의 역사적 지위가 아닌 그녀가 했던 발언을 둘러싼 논란에 대해 글을 써보라 권유했다.

Listen again to part of the conversation then answer the question.

"There is so much information about her that it made me think about choosing someone else to write about, but I'm a really big fan of her work personally… I'm of two minds on this…"

대화의 일부를 다시 듣고 질문에 답하시오.

"그녀에 대한 정보가 너무 많아서, 다른 사람에 대해서 써볼까도 생각을 했지만, 개인적으로 그녀의 작품을 정말 좋아하거든요…… 이 문제에 대해 정말 고민돼요."

05 [Inference-Imply] Why does the student mean when she says this? : 🎧

"I'm of two minds on this…"

(A) She is being ~~pressured~~ by two people that have different views.
   (wrong fact)
(B) She's is having a hard time deciding between ~~Bonheur's legacy as a feminist~~ and ~~her life as an artist.~~ (wrong fact)★
(C) **She is considering choosing a different 19th century artist to write about.**
(D) She's uncertain about whether she should focus on the 19th century ~~or the 20th century~~. (wrong fact)

왜 교수는 이 말을 하는가: 🎧

"이 문제에 대해 정말 고민돼요."

(A) 그녀는 다른 의견을 가진 두 사람에게서 ~~압박~~을 받고 있다.
(B) 그녀는 ~~본허의 페미니스트로써의 업적과 예술가로써의 삶~~ 중에서 고민하고 있다. ★
(C) **그녀는 19세기의 다른 예술가에 대해 쓰는 것을 고려 중이다.**
(D) 그녀는 19세기에 초점을 맞춰야 할지, ~~20세기에~~ 초점을 맞춰야 할지 확신이 없다.

해설 | (A) (B) 학생이 교수를 찾아갔을 때 언급한 첫 번째 고민으로, 학생이 이 말을 한 것과는 무관하다.
(D)과 제는 초반에 교수가 얘기 했듯이 '19세기 여성 예술가'로 정해져 있다. 초점을 20세기에 맞출지는 적절한 고민대상도, 언급된 고민대상도 아니다.

TEST 4 — Set2-2 — Lecture 1: Light Energy

문단주제	본문내용	해석
	Listen to part of a lecture in a physics class	물리학 강의의 일부를 들으시오.
단락 1 전자기 에너지 및 에너지 전환의 과정	P: We witness and encounter many different forms of energy, such as heat, light, and electricity, on a dailybasis. Whenyou turn on the lights in your room, what do you think you have just done? Well, you have simply transformed electrical energy into light energy. The same phenomenon occurs everywhere in our daily lives. So, how does the transformation of energy work exactly? Well, the way it works is a little complicated, so listen carefully. You guys rememberelectrons in atoms, right? They play a very vital role in the process. When stimulated, the electrons collide and change orbital levels, they release energy that we experience as light or heat. We collectively call these forms of energy emitted electromagnetic energy. Is anybody aware of this? S: Of course, light, heat, x-rays, microwaves, and electricity are great examples of it. P: Perfect! [Q1] **Today, we'll be focusing primarily on exploring various aspects of the technology that enable us to generate light energy.**	P: 우리는 날마다 열, 빛 그리고 전기와 같은 매우 다른 형태의 에너지를 보고 접하고 있어요. 여러분이 방에 불을 켤 때, 방금 무엇을 했다고 생각하나요? 음, 간단하게 전기에너지를 빛 에너지로 바꾼 거죠. 우리의 일상생활 어디에서 나 같은 현상이 발생해요. 그럼 정확히 어떻게 에너지 전환이 이루어지는 걸까요? 음, 이것이 작용하는 방법은 다소 복잡해요, 그러니까 잘 들어보세요. 여러분은 원자 안에 전자가 있는걸 기억하고 있죠, 그렇죠? 이것들은 그 과정에서 매우 중요한 역할을 해요. 자극을 받으면, 전자들은 충돌하고 도는 궤도를 바꾸게 되어, 에너지를 방출하는데 우리는 빛이나 열로 느끼게 되죠. 우리는 방출되는 이런 형태의 에너지를 통틀어서 전자기 에너지라고 부릅니다. 이에 대해 알고 있는 사람 있나요? S: 물론이죠. 빛, 열, 방사선, 전자파 그리고 전기들이 좋은 예들이죠. P: 훌륭해요! [Q1] 오늘 우리는 주로 빛 에너지를 만들어내는 기술의 다양한 국면을 탐구하는데 초점을 맞출 거에요.
단락 2 빛 에너지 생성 기술	Hmm… Imagine what it would have been like back in our ancestors' times. There was almost total darkness because no electricity existed. Their solution was to use a campfire. Very simple, right? In today's society, where people demand more advanced forms of technology, a fire is not efficient enough. Why? Well… while fires are capable of generating light energy, they also produce tremendous thermal energy, which is the heat that results from the potential and kinetic energy of the burning materials. The problem with fires is that the amount of heat being produced is much higher than the amount of light they produce. A similar phenomenon happens with incandescent light bulbs… the light bulbs you probably have in your homes. Well… to give you a clearer vision of it, think about umm… your house! Has your mom ever asked you to replace a light bulb in the house? I'm sure some of you have accidently tried to unscrew a light bulb not long after it was turned off. You probably quickly pulled your fingers off of it because the light bulb was still hot.	흠… 우리 선조들이 살았던 시대에는 어땠을지 상상해보세요. 전기가 전혀 존재하지 않았기 때문에 거의 완전히 깜깜했어요. 그들이 발견한 해결책은 모닥불을 사용하는 거였죠. 아주 간단하죠, 그죠? 하지만 요즘 사회에서는, 사람들이 고도의 기술을 더 많이 요구하는데요, 불은 충분히 효율적이지 못해요. 왜 그럴까요? 음… 불이 빛 에너지를 만들어 낼 수 있는 동안 에, 엄청난 열에너지 또한 생성되는데, 이것은 타는 물체로부터 나오는 잠재적 운동 에너지로부터 결과입니다. 불이 가진 문제점은 생산되는 열의 양이 생산되는 빛의 양보다 훨씬 높다는 거에요. 비슷한 현상이 백열전구에서 발생하는데요… 여러분들이 집에서 보는 전구 말이에요. 음…더 명쾌한 설명을 위해, 음… 여러분의 집을 생각해보세요. 여러분의 어머니가 집에서 전구를 교체해달라고 부탁한 적이 있지 않았나요? 여러분들 중 몇몇은 불을 끈 지 오래 지나지 않아 백열전구의 분명 전구의 나사를 풀려고 한 적이 있을 거에요. 그리고는 분명 손가락을 빠르게 떼었겠죠 왜냐하면 전구가 여전히 뜨거웠을 테니까요.

S: Yes! I almost burned my finger when I was very young.. Why is it still hot even when it's turned off?

P: (laughs) Yes, we've all had that kind of painful experience… Although they utilize electrical energy to generate light energy, the process of creating light itself creates a major practical drawback. Going a little deeper into the process, light is produced when electricity goes through a filament and becomes converted to heat. So, simply, electricity results in both heat and light. [Q2] **The problem with the process is that the amount of heat energy generated is much greater than the amount of light energy produced - about 90% of the output is heat, so a great deal of electricity is wasted.** It's the same problem as the campfire… It's not effective enough, right? I mean, it's also quite inconvenient, because when heat is released from the bulbs it simultaneously increases the room temperature. Consumers demand better and more effective technologies. So, to satisfy their desires, fluorescent light tubes filled with mercury gas were developed.

Now, keep in mind that this light generating device works quite a bit differently than incandescent bulbs. Okay, stay with me. [Q3] **First, when the electrons in the gaseous mercury are stimulated, they start bouncing off of a special coating on the inside of the tube.** [Q3-C] **The coating glows, and that's how we get light energy using fluorescent light bulbs.** They're a little more sophisticated and harder to understand than incandescent bulbs, but their production of heat is substantially lower, so they sure are a better option at this time. Unfortunately, however, this method has detrimental effects on the environment as well. [Q3-A, B] **Since the gaseous mercury used in the tube is highly toxic, safe disposal of the tubes is nearly impossible.** [Q6] **As far as we are concerned, we are living in a generation where solving environmental problems is a priority. Therefore, this method isn't seen as very effective.** So, now, we can conclude that neither incandescent nor fluorescent light bulbs are good solutions because the former do not significantly reduce the amount of heat production, whereas the latter contaminate the environment. Although there are other light generating devices that have been developed, similar drawbacks to those of incandescent and fluorescent bulbs have made them less than ideal.

S: Then, there's no way we can generate light energy without producing a lot of heat energy or contaminating the environment?

TEST 4 — Set 2-2 — Lecture 1: Light Energy

화학발광의 원리

P: Well… for now at least, we don't have any other fully developed lighting devices, but scientists and researchers have recently proposed a new form of technology, and they're currently working on making it feasible for everyone to utilize in the near future. It's called chemiluminescence.

S: Chemiluminescence… I think I've heard of it before. Its mechanism is a little different from the other two methods, right?

P: You bet! The way it works is a little different from the other two methods we've discussed! Okay, uh, I've mentioned that the other two methods require some kind of transformation of energy, right? Like… converting electrical energy to light energy and so on. [Q4] **Well, this case is an exception.** Instead of providing some source of energy to generate another, chemiluminescence is a result of an exothermic chemical reaction, and thus, does not require any energy input, such as electricity or heat energy. When electrons are stimulated, they cause the breakdown of reactants, which go through a series of chemical reactions that ultimately result in a light emission, which is what chemiluminescence is.

화학발광의 장점

[Q5-D] **Furthermore, it does not produce significant quantities of heat, so that it doesn't suffer from the same drawbacks as incandescent light bulbs.** Further, unlike fluorescent light bulbs, it's composed of all natural non-toxic chemical energy sources, so safe disposal of chemiluminescent bulbs would certainly not be a big concern. No unnecessary production of heat and no environmental contamination… It sure sounds like a great idea, doesn't it?

화학발광의 실용성

[Q5] **Well… with respect to its pragmatic use, chemiluminescence is not a perfected technology yet, because it remains in the developmental stage.** Let me give you a little background knowledge about the mechanism to help you understand how it occurs. [Q5-B] **Okay, the source of energy for chemiluminescence is found in nature.** [Q4-A] **It's what allows fireflies and marine animals to glow and light up in the darkness.** Scientists have successfully extracted the genes responsible for the production of chemiluminescence, and they're now striving to enhance the brightness of the light generated by the chemical and to apply it to existing technologies. Although it does have a few aspects that need improvement at this point, it might be the most promising method we have come up with, so far.

P: 음… 적어도 지금으로서는, 완전히 개발된 다른 장치가 없어요. 하지만 과학자들과 연구자들은 최근에 새로운 형태의 기술을 제안했고, 그들은 현대 이것을 실현 가능하게 만들어 가까운 미래에 활용하도록 하려고 하고 있어요. 이것은 화학발광이라고 불리죠.

S: 화학발광… 예전에 들어본 것 같아요. 그것의 체계는 다른 두 방법과 약간 달라요. 그렇죠?

P: 그렇죠! 그것이 작용하는 방법은 우리가 토의해온 다른 두 방법과 약간 달라요! 좋아요, 어, 다른 두 방법은 에너지 전환 같은 것을 필요로 한다고 제가 말했었죠, 그죠? 마치… 전기 에너지를 빛 에너지 따위로 바꾸는 것과 같은 거예요. [Q4] 음, 이 경우는 예외인데요. 다른 에너지를 만들기 위해 약간의 에너지 자원을 제공하는 대신, 화학발광은 발열성의 화학 반응의 결과이고, 따라서 전기나 열에너지 같은 다른 에너지 투입을 필요로 하지 않아요. 전자가 자극을 받으면, 반응물의 파괴를 야기시키는데, 이는 일련의 화학반응의 과정을 겪고 궁극적으로 빛을 방출하게 되는데, 이것이 화학발광이죠. [Q5-D] 더욱이, 이것은 많은 양의 열을 만들어내지 않아요. 그래서 백열등과 같은 문제점으로 고생하지 않죠. 더군다나, 형광등과 다르게, 이것은 모두 무독성인 자연적인 화학 에너지원으로 구성되어 있는데,. 그래서 화학발광 전구를 안전하게 처리하는 것은 분명 큰 문제가 아닐 거예요. 불필요한 열 생성도 없고 환경 오염도 없어요. 이것은 분명 훌륭한 아이디어처럼 들려요, 그렇지 않나요? [Q5] 음… 하지만, 실용적인 사용과 관련해서는 화학발광은 아직 완벽한 기술이 아닌데요, 왜냐하면 개발 단계에 머물러 있기 때문이죠. 이것이 어떻게 발생하는지에 대한 이해를 돕기 위해 메커니즘에 대한 배경지식을 약간 드릴께요. [Q5-B] 좋아요. 화학발광의 에너지 자원은 자연에서 발견돼요. [Q4-A] 이것은 반딧불이나 해양 생물들이 빛나고 어둠 속에서 환하게 해주는 것이에요. 과학자들은 화학발광 생성에 관련이 있는 유전자를 성공적으로 추출했는데, 이들은 지금 화학 물질에 의해 생성되는 빛의 밝기를 강화시키는 것과 현존하는 기술에 이것을 적용하는 데 노력을 기울이고 있죠. 비록 현재로서는 개선되어야 할 점이 몇 가지 있지만, 아마도 우리가 지금까지 생각해낸 방법 중 가장 유망할 거예요.

06 [Main Idea] What is the main topic of the lecture?

(A) Technologies that generate ~~electrical energy~~ using other forms of energy *(partial error)* ★
(B) Electromagnetic energy and its use in generating heat energy *(fact, but unrelated to the question)*
(C) **The evolutionary developments in light-generating technology**
(D) ~~Chemical reactions~~ that significantly reduce the amount of heat generation *(fact, but unrelated to the question)*

강의의 주제는 무엇인가?

(A) 다른 형태의 에너지를 사용하여 전기 에너지를 생성하는 기술들 ★
(B) 전자기에너지와 열에너지를 발생시키는데 이용
(C) **빛 생성 장치들의 최신 기술과 개발**
(D) 열 생성의 양을 상당히 줄이는 화학 반응

해설 | (A) electrical energy가 아니라 light energy.
(B) electromagnetic은 light, heat, x-rays, microwaves, and electricity를 통합 적으로 부르는 term. Lecture의 main topic과 큰 연관이 없음.
(D) fluorescent bulbs와 chemiluminescence를 다루는 내용이지만 incandescent light bulbs는 해당 되지 않는다. 또, 전체적인 내용에 지극히 일부 분이다.

07 [Detail-Problem] What is the major drawback of incandescent light bulbs?

(A) ~~Toxic chemicals~~ that are hard to dispose of *(wrong fact)*
(B) Their ~~heaviness~~ makes them difficult to ~~carry around~~ *(not mentioned)*
(C) ~~Short duration~~ of usefulness caused by the filament used in the process *(not mentioned)*
(D) **The excessive production of unwanted heat energy**

백열등이 갖고 있는 주요한 단점은 무엇인가?

(A) 처리하기 어려운 유독성의 화학물 ★
(B) 휴대하기 어렵게 만드는 무거움
(C) 과정에서 사용되는 필라멘트에 의해 야기되는 짧은 수명주기
(D) **불필요한 열에너지의 과도한 생성**

해설 | (A)는 fluorescent bulbs에 관련된 내용. (B), (C) 휴대성과 지속성을 다루는 내용은 없음.

08 [Detail-Solution] How were scientists able to reduce the amount of heat production in fluorescent light bulbs?

(A) By using ~~natural chemicals~~ that prevent the reactions that create heat *(wrong fact)*
(B) By filling light bulbs with a ~~non-toxic~~ gas *(opposite fact)*
(C) By using ~~mercury gas that glows~~ when stimulated *(partial error)*
(D) **By inserting a gas into a bulb that has a special inner coating**

과학자들은 어떻게 형광등에서 생성되는 열의 양을 줄일 수 있었는가?

(A) 열을 생성하는 반응을 방해하는 자연 화학물질을 이용함으로써
(B) 전구를 무독성 가스로 채움으로써
(C) 자극 받으면 빛나는 수은 가스를 이용함으로써 ★
(D) **내부에 특수한 코팅이 있는 전구에 가스를 주입함으로써**

해설 | (A)는 chemiluminescence에 해당하는 내용. (B) 이 method에 쓰이는 mercury란 gas는 highly toxic하므로 틀린 말이다.
(C) mercury gas 자체가 빛을 발사하는 게 아니라 그 tube의 special coating으로 인해 발생되는 현상이다.

TEST 4 — Set 2-2 — Lecture 1: Light Energy

09 **[Detail-Difference/Contrast]** How is chemiluminescence different from incandescent or fluorescent light bulbs?

화학발광은 백열등이나 형광등과 어떻게 다른가?

(A) Genes for chemiluminescence extracted from ~~human beings~~ play a vital role in it. *(partial error)*

(B) It ~~uses a chemical~~ to minimize the amount of heat production. *(partial error)* ★

(C) **A chemical reaction replaces the input of energy sources such as heat or electricity.**

(D) It generates very low quantities of heat and ~~high quantities of light~~. *(not mentioned)*

(A) 인체에서 추출되는 화학발광 유전자는 중대한 역할을 한다.

(B) 열 생산 양을 최소화시키기 위해 화학물질을 ~~이용한다~~. ★

(C) **화학반응은 열이나 전기 같은 에너지의 투입을 대체한다.**

(D) 아주 적은 양의 열을 생성하고 ~~많은 양의 빛을~~ 생성한다.

해설 | (A)는 human beings가 아니라 fireflies나 marine animals에서 발견된다. (B) 열 생산 양이 줄어드는 건 맞는 말이지만, 화학물질을 사용하는 게 틀리다. 화학물질을 사용하는 건 fluorescent bulbs에 해당되는 말.
(D)의 일부분인 low quantities of heat은 맞는 말이지만 high quantities of light는 언급된 내용이 아니다.

---

10 **[Inference-Imply/Infer]** According to the professor, what can be inferred about the chemiluminescent technology?

교수에 따르면, 화학발광 기술에 관해 추론할 수 있는 것은 무엇인가?

(A) ~~Since~~ the input of energy is not required, the brightness of the light is dim. *(partial error)* ★

(B) The genes for chemiluminescence ~~cannot be~~ found in modern organisms. *(opposite fact)*

(C) **The technology has yet to become accessible to consumers.**

(D) Chemiluminescence causes an ~~increase~~ in room temperature. *(wrong fact)*

(A) 에너지의 투입이 필요하지 않기 ~~때문에~~ 빛의 밝기는 어둡다. ★

(B) 화학발광의 유전자는 현대에 사는 유기체에서는 ~~발견되지 않는다~~.

(C) **기술이 아직 소비자에게 적용 가능하지 못하다.**

(D) 화학발광은 방의 온도를 ~~높인다~~.

해설 | (A) 잘못된 인과관. (B)는 교수의 chemiluminescence는 동물에게서 발견된다는 주장과 정 반대 되는 말.
(D)는 incandescent light bulb에 해당되는 내용이다.

11 [Inference-Headset] What does the professor imply when he says this: 🎧

> "As far as we are concerned, we are living in a generation where solving environmental problems is a priority, therefore, this method isn't seen as very effective."

교수가 이 말을 할 때 암시하는 것은 무엇인가: 🎧

> "우리가 알고 있는 한, 우린 현재 환경 문제의 해결이 최우선인 세대에 살고 있어요. 그래서 이 방법은 그다지 효과적으로 보이진 않죠."

(A) That the method has a critical disadvantage.
(B) That today's environment needs to be improved as quickly as possible *(fact, but unrelated to the question)* ★
(C) That developing a light-generating device is ~~not a priority~~
(not mentioned)
(D) That ~~all~~ light generating devices are harmful to the environment
(partial error)

(A) 그 방법이 중대한 단점을 갖고 있다
(B) 오늘날 환경은 가능한 한 빨리 개선되어야 함을 암시하기 위해 ★
(C) 빛을 내는 장치의 개발이 ~~우선 순위가 아니라는 것을~~ 암시하기 위해
(D) ~~모든~~ 빛을 내는 장치가 환경에 나쁘다는 것을 설명하기 위해

해설 | 위에 내용은 fluorescent bulbs의 disadvantage를 강조하기 위한 교수의 부가적인 내용이다.
(B)는 교수가 주장하는 light-producing technology에 관련 없는 내용이다.
(C) solving environmental problems가 우선 순위인건 맞지만 빛 생성 기술의 개발이 우선순위가 아니라고 주장하는 바는 아니다.
(D) 오직 fluorescent bulbs만 가지고 있는 문제이다.

TEST 4 Set 2-3 *부록 Lecture 2 Human Personality

문단주제	본문내용	해 석
	Listen to part of a lecture in a psychology class	심리학 수업의 일부를 들으시오
단락 1 성격심리학에 대한 소개 및 정부의 재정지원	If I remember correctly, I briefly introduced the concept of personality psychology in the last class, right? For those who were absent, personality psychology is basically a branch of psychology devoted to studying the human personality. It's very closely related to neuroscience, you know, the study of the nervous system and the brain in particular. Umm… I also mentioned that ever since the advent of the Human Genome Project, or the HGP, a tremendous amount of research has been done to identify the fundamental roots of personality and whether or not personality is static. [Q6] **President Barack Obama has even recently announced his plan to fund a $100 million project to unlock the incredibly intricate mysteries of the brain and to enhance our understanding of its functions. Why so much money?** Well… one of the most apparent reasons is that [Q1-B] **the discovery process is not only very complicated but also involves the use of highly technical tools.**	내 기억이 맞다면, 지난 시간에 성격심리학의 개념을 간략히 소개했었지, 그치? 결석했던 학생들을 위해 말하자면, 성격심리학은 기본적으로 인간의 성격을 공부하는데 전념하는 심리학의 한 분야에요. 이것은 신경과학과 매우 밀접하게 관련되어 있는데요, 그러니까, 구체적으로 신경계와 뇌를 연구하는 학문 말이죠. 음… 그리고 저는 또한 인간게놈프로젝트 또는 HGP의 출현 이후, 성격의 근본 뿌리와 성격이 안정적인지 아닌지에 대해서 확인하는 수많은 연구가 행해졌어요. [Q6] Barack Obama 대통령은 최근에 믿을 수 없을 만큼 복잡한 뇌의 신비를 풀고 그것의 기능에 대한 우리의 이해도를 향상시키기 위해 1억 달러짜리 프로젝트에 자금을 지원하겠다는 계획을 공표했어요. 왜 그렇게 많은 돈을 쓰냐구요? 음… 가장 명확한 이유 중 하나는 [Q1-B] 발견 과정이 매우 복잡할 뿐만 아니라, 첨단 기술 사용을 포함하기 때문이죠.
단락 2 EEG 기계의 기능 및 한계점	If we look back to the beginning of the study of the human personality back in the 1990's, which is not that long ago, we will find that researchers and neuroscientists began to use Electroencephalography, or EEG… Umm… If you refer back to the beginning of our textbook, you will see that EEG machines detect brain activity by directly measuring the oscillations caused by the neurons in the brain. Well, it was a fairly good start for neuroscientists in that they were able to carry out a series of tests on their subjects…you know, the people on whom experiments are performed, and figure out what changes their brains were experiencing over time. Umm… It was once praised as one of the most effective methods of promoting the enlightenment of the personality, [Q2] **but now it's a bit obsolete in the field of personality psychology. It seems that with the shift in focus to a new topic, the stability of personality, a new form of technology, called Functional Magnetic Resonance Imaging or FMRI, seems to have taken over as the new revolutionary invention in the field.**	1990년대에 인간의 성격에 대한 연구가 시작되었던때-그다지 오래되지 않았죠-를 되돌아보면, 연구자들과 신경과학자들이 뇌파도 혹은 EEG를 사용하기 시작했어요. 음, 우리 교재의 첫 부분으로 돌아가보면, EEG 기계가 뇌의 신경 세포에 의해 발생하는 진동을 직접적으로 측정함으로써 뇌의 활동을 감지하는걸 알 수 있죠. 음, 신경 과학자들이 대상자… 그러니까 실험이 행해지는 사람들에게 일련의 테스트를 할 수 있었고, 그들의 뇌가 시간이 지나면서 무슨 변화를 겪었는지를 알 수 있었다는 점에서 좋은 출발이었죠. 음… 이것은 한때 성격의 계발을 촉진하는 가장 효과적인 방법의 하나로 칭송을 받았는데요, [Q2] 하지만 지금은 성격심리학 세계에서 약간 구식이 되어버렸어요. 성격의 안정성이라는 새로운 주제로 초점이 바뀜에 따라, 기능성 자기 공명 영상 혹은 FMRI라고 불리는 새로운 형태의 기술이 이 분야에서 새로운 혁명적인 발명술로 자리를 잡은 것 같네요.

단락 3
MRI와 FMRI의 기능, 원리, 및 특징 비교

It sure sounds familiar, doesn't it? Right! Our previous chapter dealt with MRI and its medical uses. Try not to get the similar names mixed up, though. The new technology is used almost exclusively as a laboratory research tool. Umm… To help you draw a clear distinction between the two, MRI is almost like a camera; it takes pictures of the brain structures for scientists to use for diagnostic purposes, [Q3] **while FMRI, as the name suggests, depicts the functions of the brain in addition to the structures**… In other words… Umm… Okay. Let's say you're under stress because of homework assignments and whatnot, and you feel the sudden urge to express your anger. Well, your emotions originate from your brain's activities. In response to stimuli, your brain activates its different parts and sort of works as a command control center and tells your body which action to take. [Q2-C, Q3-D] **During this process, neuroscientists can detect changes in blood flow and oxygen levels in the brain that occur in response to external stimuli using FMRI.**

Okay… Now that's a lot of information for you to take in all at once, so let me help you with it. I've mentioned that your emotions are the output of the brain activities that occur when your brain processes certain stimuli in the environment, correct? Whether you let yourself express those emotions or restrain yourself from doing so is your particular personality. Because of this property of the brain, or I should say nature, whether or not personality is static has been questioned numerous times over the years. [Q3-C] **FMRI has become a very useful tool for scientists who argue that it is in fact a stable aspect of the brain.**

단락 4
편도체 연구의 과정, 결과, 및 의의

Those scientists, who theorize that personality does not change, have done some case studies, and one of them involved the amygdala, the section of the temporal lobe responsible for processing external stimuli, such as emotional reactions. To stimulate this part of the brain, the scientists had all of the subjects sit in a straight line and showed them photographs taken during wartime… angry, scared, horrified, and fearful faces.

Using the FMRIs, the scientists were able to detect that the amygdala was activated in some of the subjects when the pictures were displayed in front of them. To ensure the validity of the experiment, the subjects, whose amygdalae were stimulated in the experiment, were brought back two years later and underwent the same process. The significance of this study was that when they were brought back, their brains responded to the photos in the same way as they had in the initial experiment. The scientists, therefore, claimed that since the response to such stimuli didn't change over the course of two years, it partially proved that personality was also stable… Well, a contradictory argument does exist, but it involves another long, boring experiment, so we won't go into it in this class.

You should also try to keep in mind that FMRI studies aren't perfect yet… a lot of controversies concerning them still exist, and neuroscientists in the field tend to exaggerate the significance of their findings. I mean, the brain is, after all, comprised of the most perplexing elements… Although some scientists say we have come to the final stage of solving the brain's mysteries, truthfully, our knowledge of the brain is still rudimentary… You see, FMRI is certainly one of the most practical and efficient tools we have as of now, [Q4-C] but it still doesn't account for why we behave the way we do. [Q4] Yes, it tells us which part of the brain is activated when certain stimuli are applied, [Q4-D] but that's not enough to determine that personality of human beings never changes.

For this reason, we shouldn't overlook our good, old traditional research methods. I'm sure most of you are familiar with this concept. You know, using questionnaires… such as "Do you enjoy meeting new people and socializing with them?" or "Are you the type of person who gets disappointed or sad easily?" [Q5] Although using questionnaires has some drawbacks, like the respondents manipulating their answers to portray themselves differently, it's perhaps the most reliable way we have to inquire about people's behavioral preferences and personalities at the present time.

12 [Main Idea] What is the topic of the lecture?

(A) ~~Criticism~~ of the theories that support the stability of personality
  (partial error) ★
(B) General exploration of the functions of various highly technical tools.
(C) **Current progress in personality psychology with supporting details**
(D) The ~~advantages~~ that traditional research methods have ~~over the new~~ highly technical tools *(fact, but unrelated to the question)*

강의의 주제는 무엇인가?

(A) 성격의 안정성을 지지하는 이론들에 대한 ~~비판~~ ★
(B) 다양한 첨단 기술을 가진 도구의 기능들에 대한 전반적인 탐사
(C) 성격 심리학의 최근 발전과 지지하는 세부사항
(D) 전통적인 연구 방법이 새로운 첨단 기술 도구들을 뛰어넘는 장점들

해설 | (A) 교수는 비난 또는 비판이 아닌 객관적인 입장에서 바라본 성격의 안정성을 주장하는 이론들의 한계점들을 제시하므로 오답.
(B)는 highly technical tools의 사람의 성격에 관한 기능이라 해야 맞는 답인데 성격이란 내용이 없어 오답.
(D) 첨단기술 도구를 보충 할 수 있는 도구의 예로 전통적인 연구 방법이 제시된 것이므로 이게 main idea가 되기엔 너무 narrow하다.

13 [Detail-Problem/Difficulty] According to the professor, for what is Electroencephalography or EEG insufficient?

(A) **Substantiating the stability of the nature of personality**
(B) Elucidating ~~why~~ human beings ~~behave~~ the way they do *(wrong fact)*
(C) Analyzing the ~~brain's activities and waves~~ when stimuli are applied
  (not mentioned) ★
(D) Enhancing our understanding of the ~~nature of human personality~~
  (wrong fact)

교수님에 따르면, 뇌파도 혹은 EGG는 무엇을 하기에 불충분한가?

(A) 성격 특성의 안정성을 입증하는 것
(B) 인간이 왜 그런 방식으로 행동하는지 밝히는 것
(C) 자극이 주어질 때 뇌의 활동과 뇌파를 분석하는 것 ★
(D) 인간 성격의 본질에 대한 우리의 이해를 향상시키는 것

해설 | 교수는 personality 자체를 measure하는건 EEG가 좋다 하지만, stability를 measure하기 위해선 FMRI가 더 적합하다고 주장한다.
(B), (D)는 personality만 가지고 내용을 다루기 때문에 오답. (C)는 FMRI의 actual use이고, 이에 EEG가 insufficient하다고는 주장이 안되어 오답이다.

TEST 4 Set 2-3 *부록 Lecture 2 Human Personality

14 [Detail-Difference/Contrast] What makes FMRI more suitable for research purposes than MRI?

강의의 주제는 무엇인가?

(A) FMRI captures the activities of the brain as well as its structures.
(B) FMRI enables researchers and scientists to detect ~~tumorous cells~~ in the body. *(not mentioned)*
(C) FMRI helps scientists prove that the personality ~~goes through a series of changes~~ over time *(opposite fact)*
(D) FMRI can detect changes in blood flow and oxygen levels ~~throughout the body~~ *(partial error)* ★

(A) FMRI는 뇌의 구조와 함께 뇌의 활동을 잡아낸다.
(B) FMRI는 연구자들과 과학자들에게 몸 속에 있는 ~~종양 세포~~를 감지하게 해준다
(C) FMRI는 과학자들이 성격이 시간이 지남에 따라 ~~변화를 겪는다는~~ 사실을 증명할 수 있게 도와준다
(D) FMRI는 몸 속에 흐르는 혈류와 산소 농도의 변화를 감지 할 수 있다. ★

> 해설 | (B)는 언급된 내용이 아니므로 오답.
> (C) FMRI를 근거로 과학자들은 stability of personality를 주장했으므로 정 반대된 내용이다.
> (D)는 throughout the body가 아니라 in the brain이기 때문에 오답이다.

15 [Detail-Imply/Infer] What does the professor insinuate about the validity of the amygdala case study?

교수는 편도체 사례 연구의 유효성에 대해서 무엇을 암시하는가?

(A) That it is ~~revolutionary~~ and ~~refutes~~ other conventional beliefs and theories *(not mentioned)*
(B) That though it may seem credible to a certain degree, it's not a reliable means for proving the stability of the personality
(C) That it also ~~accounts for~~ the behavior of human beings *(opposite fact)*
(D) That its results prove that human personality ~~does not change at all~~ *(opposite fact)* ★

(A) 그것은 획기적이며 다른 기존의 믿음과 이론을 ~~반박한다~~.
(B) 어느 정도까지는 신뢰할 수 있지만, 성격의 안정성을 증명할 수 있는 믿을만한 도구가 아니다.
(C) 그것은 또한 인간의 행동에 대해 ~~설명하고 있다~~.
(D) 그것의 결과는 인간의 성격이 ~~전혀 변하지 않는다는~~ 것을 증명한다. ★

> 해설 | 교수는 personality 자체를 measure하는건 EEG가 좋다 하지만, stability를 measure하기 위해선 FMRI가 더 적합하다고 주장한다.
> (B), (D)는 personality만 가지고 내용을 다루기 때문에 오답.
> (C)는 FMRI의 actual use이고, 이에 EEG가 insufficient하다고는 주장이 안되어 오답이다.

16 [Inference - Intention] Why does the professor mention traditional research methods?

(A) ~~To start a new class discussion~~ on how people behave when responding to lists of questions

(B) To give an example of a tool that can supplement the highly technical tools

(C) ~~To criticize~~ the people who question the validity of the results of tests performed with highly technical tools. *(too extreme)*

(D) To point out the ~~incapability~~ of highly technical tools *(too extreme)* ★

교수는 왜 전통적인 연구 방법을 언급 하는가?

(A) 사람들이 질문들에 응답할 때 어떤 반응을 보이는지에 대한 ~~새로운 수업 토론을 시작하기 위해서~~

(B) 첨단 기술 도구들을 보충 할 수 있는 한 도구의 예를 보여주기 위해서

(C) 첨단 기술 도구를 가지고 행한 테스트의 결과의 타당성에 의문을 제기하는 사람들을 ~~비판하기 위해서~~

(D) 첨단 기술 도구들의 무능력함을 지적하기 위해서 ★

해설 | (A) 부가적인 설명이지 new discussion으로 시작하는 것은 아니다.
(C), (D) 첨단 기술 도구의 한계를 보충하기 위해 전통적인 연구방법을 쓰는 것도 나쁘지 않다고 주장하는 교수의 입장을 too extreme 하게 끌고 간다.

---

17 [Inference-Imply] What does the professor imply when she says this : 🎧

"President Barack Obama has even recently announced his plan to fund a $100 million project to unlock the incredibly intricate mysteries of the brain and to enhance our understanding of its functions. Why so much money?"

(A) That, in her belief, it's ~~unnecessary~~ to spend so much money on fields in which it is difficult to conduct research *(opposite fact)*

(B) That the government ~~should pay~~ for the highly technical tools and labor required for the study of personality change *(wrong fact)* ★

(C) That other areas of scientific study are ~~unfairly treated~~ compared to neuroscience and psychology *(not mentioned)*

(D) That understanding the human personality is so important today that vast sums are being spent to further research in the field.

교수님이 이 말을 할 때 무엇을 암시하는가 : 🎧

"Barack Obama 대통령은 최근에 믿을 수 없을 만큼 복잡한 뇌의 신비를 풀고 그것의 기능에 대한 우리의 이해도를 향상시키기 위해 1억 달러짜리 프로젝트에 자금을 지원하겠다는 계획을 공표했어요. 왜 그렇게 많은 돈을 쓰느냐구요?"

(A) 그녀가 믿기에는, 연구를 수행하기에 너무 어려운 분야에 많은 돈을 지출하는 것은 불필요하다는 것.

(B) 성격 변화 연구에 요구되는 첨단 기술과 노동력에 대해 정부가 지원해야 한다는 것. ★

(C) 다른 과학 연구 분야는 신경 과학 및 심리학과 비교해 볼 때 부당한 취급을 받고 있다는 것

(D) 인간 성격을 이해하는 것은 오늘날 무척 중요해서 이 분야에 더 많은 연구를 하기 위해 많은 양의 돈이 쓰여지고 있다는 것

해설 | 오늘날의 미국의 대통령까지 적지 않은 금액으로 서포트 하는 study를 설명하면서 교수가 주장하고 싶은 건 personality psychology의 상승세이다.
(A) 연구를 수행하기에 어려운 분야이기에 많은 돈을 지출하는 것이 필요하다고 주장하므로 정반대의 내용이다.
(B) 정부 지원 계획이 공표되었으므로 정부에서 자금 지원을 해야 한다고 주장하는 것은 문맥 상 맞지 않는다.
(C) 다른 과학 연구 분야의 재정 지원과의 비교는 언급된 바 없다.

별도 구매 서비스 소개

usherin.usher.co.kr

1. USHER **단어암기** 프로그램 소개
2. **첨삭권** 소개
3. **인강**
4. **모의토플**
5. 토플 Reading 공부방법
6. 토플 Listening 공부방법
7. 수강 후기

1 USHER 단어암기 프로그램 소개

usherin.usher.co.kr

1. **듣고** - 아직도 눈으로만 외우나요?
   어셔단어 프로그램에서는 듣고, 쓰고, 품사외우고, 동의어까지 한번에 진행합니다.
2. **말하고** - 아직도 발음을 못하나요?
   발음 연습을 정확하게 프로그램이 읽어, 단어 외우면서 발음까지 한번에 준비할 수 있습니다.
3. **집중 암기**하고 - 천천히 성장 VS 고성장
   90일 동안 외울 단어를 13일 안에 끝내므로 반복효과 및 고성장을 이루어 낼수있습니다.
4. **internet based test** - 즉시채점+틀린것만 계속 테스트
   틀린 단어들만 다시 시험보기가 가능합니다.
5. **기분좋은 성취 확인** - 향상 기록 personal trainer
   본인이 본 시험 기록 내용이 누적 확인되어 본인에 성취를 확인 할수있습니다.

1. 어셔 책으로 공부하는 법

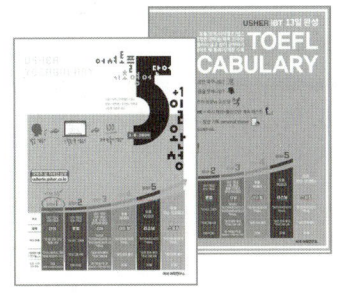

1. 타사 책으로 공부하는 법

2. 발음을 먼저 듣고

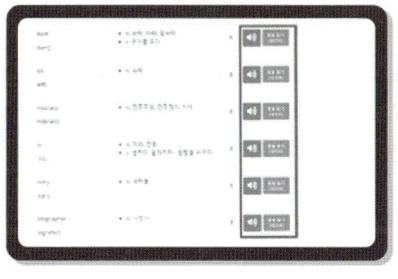

2. 읽지도 못하는 발음기호 주고

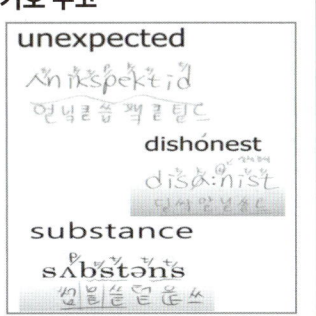

3. 들어본 발음 시켜보고

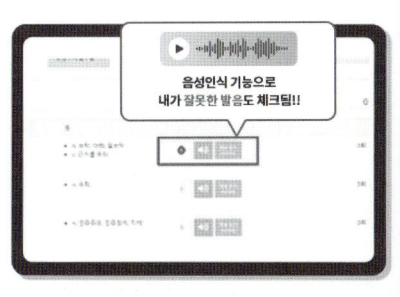

3. 내가 읽은 발음이 맞는지 모르고

4. 인터벌

4. 빽빽이 써가면서 단어 외워야하는데

5. 분량을 나눠서 모의시험

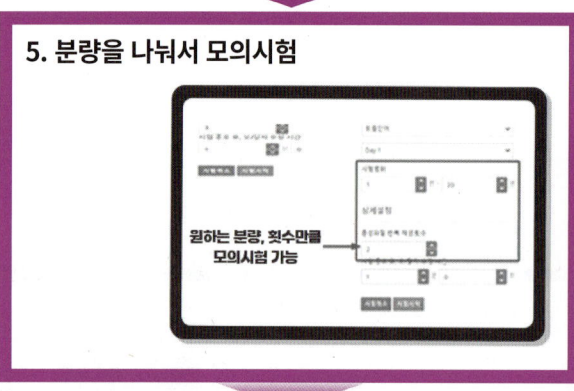

5. 빽빽이 써가면서 단어 외워야하는데

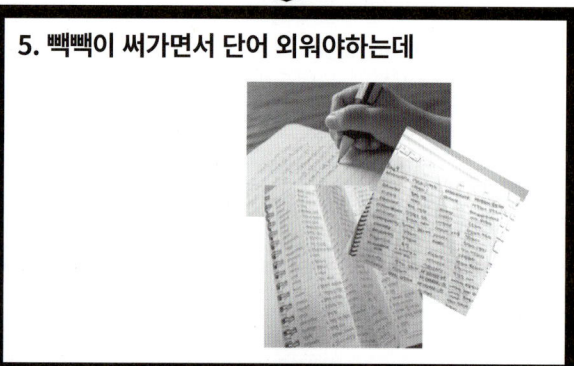

6. 준비되면 시전시험!
듣고 → 스펠링 → 품사 → 뜻 순으로 적기

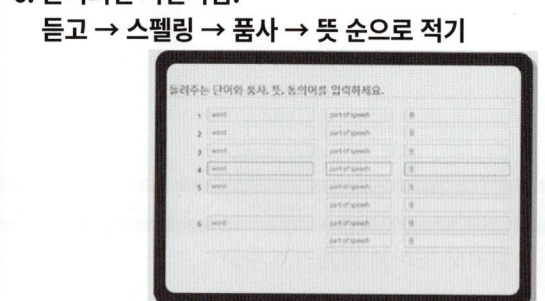

6. 학교 or 학원가서 종이에
한글 또는 스펠링 중 하나만 시험

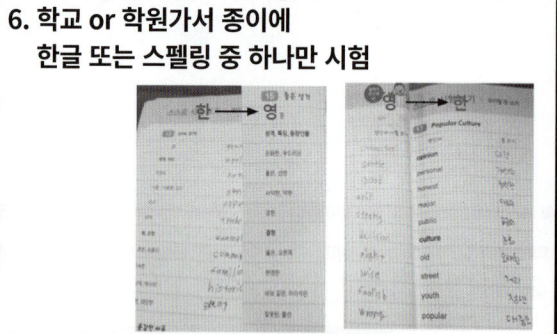

7. 하나라도 틀리면 오답처리
시험결과 자동체크

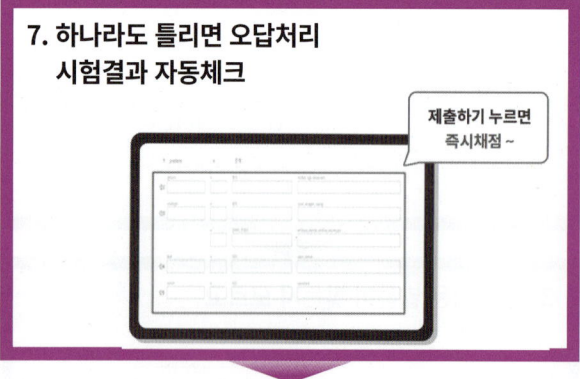

7. 채점을 내가 하면 잘못 외운 스펠링체크 못해주고
친구가 해주면 우정으로 틀린 것도 맞다고 해주고

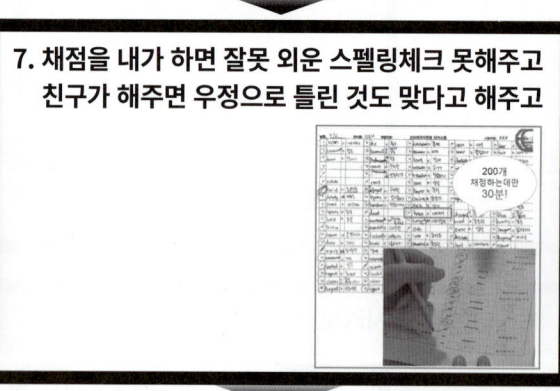

8. 틀린 단어 묶음으로 즉시 **오답노트** 만들어줌

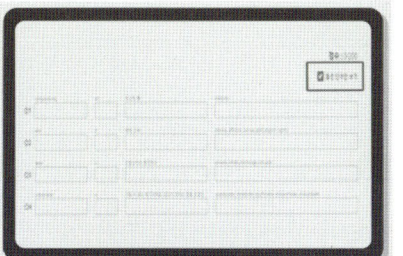

8. 내가 뭘 틀렸는지 일일히 추려내야 하지만... 보통은 보지도 않고 그냥 버리게 됨

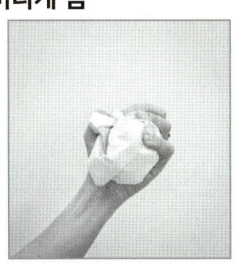

9. 틀린 개수 0으로 만들기 틀린 단어만 **재시험**

9. 틀린 단어가 뭔지 보지도 않고

10. 한달 동안 시험 본 모든 기록 체크해주며 자극주는 시스템

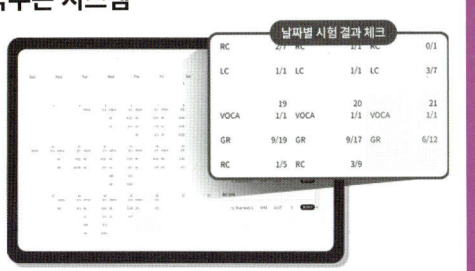

10. 종이가 너덜너덜해지면 그냥 버림

단어 프로그램 가격 소개

💬 카카오톡으로 문의하기

	1개월 사용	3개월 사용	6개월 사용
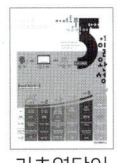 기초영단어	25,000원	~~75,000원~~ 60,000원 (1개월당 20,000원 20% DC)	~~150,000원~~ 84,000원 (1개월당 7,000원 44% DC)
 토플단어	25,000원	~~75,000원~~ 60,000원 (1개월당 20,000원 20% DC)	~~150,000원~~ 84,000원 (1개월당 7,000원 44% DC)
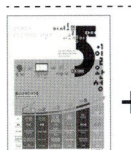 기초영단어 + 토플단어	40,000원	~~120,000원~~ 90,000원 (1개월당 30,000원 25% DC)	~~240,000원~~ 108,000원 (1개월당 9,000원 55% DC)

2 첨삭권 소개
usherin.usher.co.kr

01 스피킹/라이팅 첨삭이 필요한 이유?

대체로 독학을 할 수 있다고 생각하는 리딩, 리스닝과는 달리 스피킹 라이팅은 독학이 힘듭니다.

이유는? "내가 뭘 틀렸는지 모르니까!!!"

대안은?? 독학이라고 했으니, 과외나, 학원은 빼고, 남는 건 첨삭이나, 그냥 혼자 틀린 걸 계속 보거나….

그런데, 첨삭을 받으러 검색을 해보면 가격이 라이팅 한편 당 23,000…원…?

한편만 첨삭 받으면 끝날 것 같진 않은 내 실력을 봐서는…

비용 감당 안됨. 어쩌지?

02 학원까지 다니고 싶진 않은데 스피킹/라이팅 첨삭만 받을 순 없나요?

▼라이팅 첨삭 *10회권은 어셔수강생에게만 제공됩니다* (2024.08. 현재)

1회권	어셔	1회 첨삭권 25,000원	최저가 1회당 25,000원
	해**	1회권 없음 / 2회 첨삭권 54,000원	1회당 27,000원
	영**	1회 첨삭(1일 소요)권 28,000원	1회당(1일 소요)권 28,000원
5회권	어셔	5회 첨삭권 100,000원	최저가 1회당 20,000원
	해**	5회권 없음	5회권 없음
	영**	5회 첨삭(1일 소요)권 119,000원	1회당(1일 소요)권 23,800원
10회권 *어셔 수강생 한정	어셔	10회 첨삭권 150,000원	최저가 1회당 15,000원
	해**	10회권 없음	10회권 없음
	영**	10회권 없음	10회권 없음

▼스피킹 첨삭 (2024.08. 현재)

1회권	어셔	1회 첨삭권 15,000원	최저가 1회당 15,000원
	해**	1회권 없음 / 2회 첨삭권 54,000원	1회당 27,000원
	영**	1회 첨삭(1일 소요)권 16,000원	1회당(1일 소요)권 16,000원
5회권	어셔	5회 첨삭권 60,000원	최저가 1회당 12,000원
	해**	5회권 없음	5회권 없음
	영**	5회 첨삭(1일 소요)권 68,000원	1회당(1일소요)권 13,600원
10회권 *어셔 수강생 한정	어셔	10회 첨삭권 110,000원	최저가 1회당 11,000원
	해**	10회권 없음	10회권 없음
	영**	10회권 없음	10회권 없음

구매처 및 자세한 설명 usherin.usher.co.kr

03 첨삭 구성은 어떻게 되나요?

▼ 스피킹 첨삭

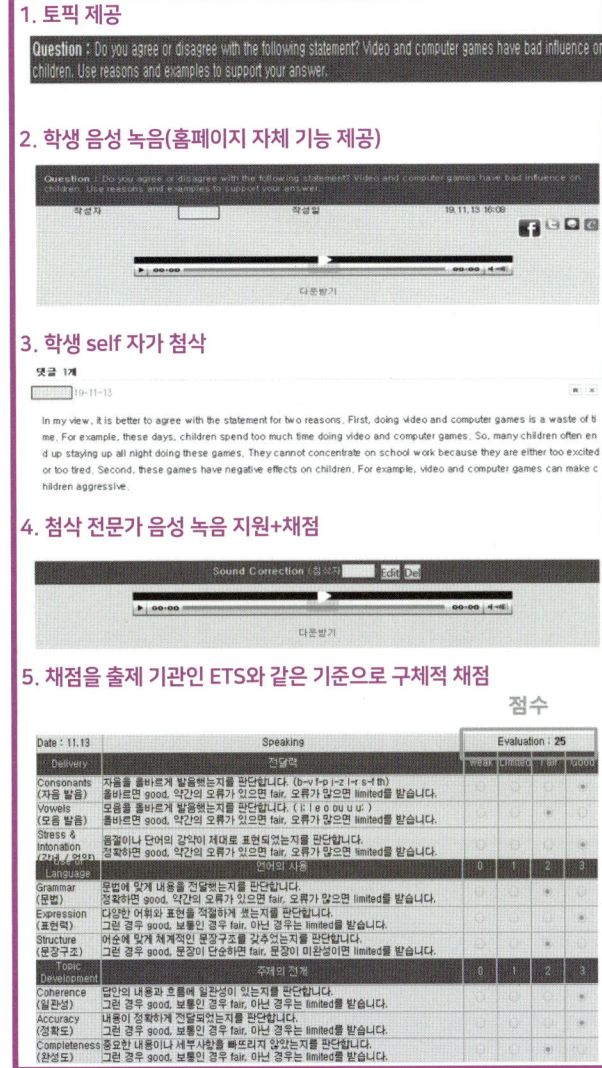

▼ 라이팅 첨삭

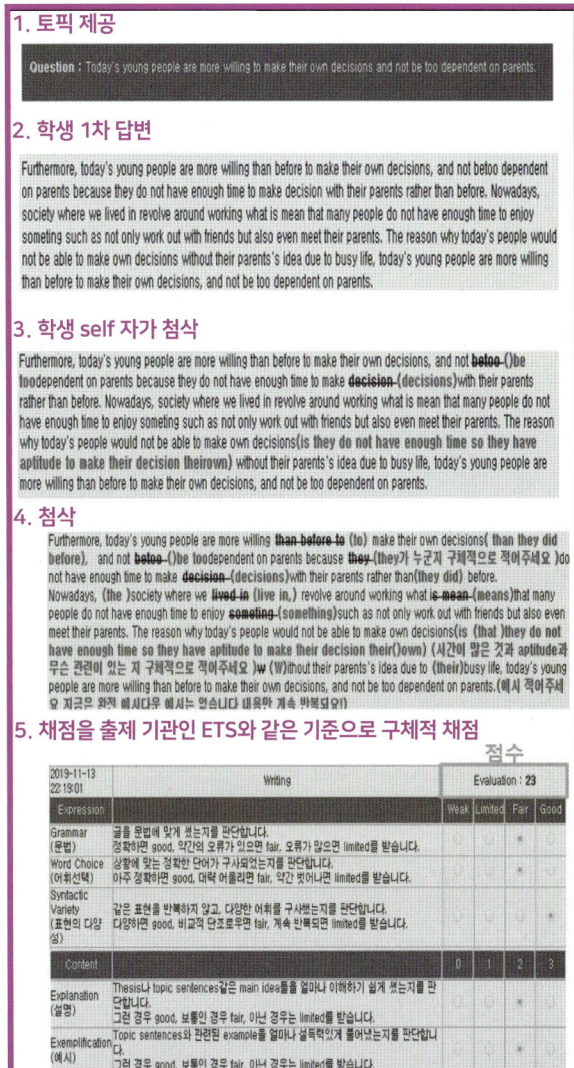

04 첨삭 신청하기

라이팅 첨삭권

10회권은 어셔수강생에게만 제공됩니다

1회 첨삭권	5회 첨삭권	10회 첨삭권
사용기간 15일	사용기간 30일	사용기간 60일
25,000원	~~125,000원~~ ➤ 100,000원	~~250,000원~~ ➤ 150,000원

스피킹 첨삭권

10회권은 어셔수강생에게만 제공됩니다

1회 첨삭권	5회 첨삭권	10회 첨삭권
사용기간 15일	사용기간 30일	사용기간 60일
15,000원	~~75,000원~~ ➤ 60,000원	~~150,000원~~ ➤ 110,000원

첨삭은 근무일 기준(평일)으로 진행되며, 주말 또는 휴일은 익일 평일에 진행됩니다.

3 인강-리스닝

usherin.usher.co.kr

나의 성격 PERSONALITY
ENTP
저는 유연성과 적응력을 가진 사람입니다.
성공의 길과 개인적 성장은 순식간에 이루어지는 것이 아닙니다.
하지만 저는 작은 발전의 단계를 거듭하면서
성장하고자 합니다. 저는 변화하는 세상에 꾸준히 적응하고,
그것을 통해 계속해서 성장하려고 합니다.

핵심 가치 CORE VALUE
저의 주된 가치는 꾸준함입니다. 어떤 일이든지 지속성이
있으면 결국 목표를 달성할 수 있다고 믿습니다.

나의 강점 STRENGTH
저는 변화하는 환경에 잘 적응하고,
다양한 상황에서 필요한
해결책을 발견하는 것을 잘합니다.

This Too Shall Pass
이 또한 지나가리라

VISION BIG5
건강한 삶 저는 몸과 마음이 건강한 삶을 추구합니다.
항상 배우기 저는 세상이 계속 변하고 발전하는 것처럼,
자신도 항상 새로운 것을 배우며 성장하고자 합니다.
긍정적인 삶 저는 긍정의 힘을 믿습니다. 긍정적인 태도를 가지고 삶을 대하고자 합니다.
인내심 저는 어려움을 겪을 때에도 인내심을 잃지 않고 목표를 향해 나아갑니다.
감사함 저는 삶의 모든 것에 감사의 마음을 가지고 그 감사의 마음을 통해
더 많은 긍정적인 에너지를 발산하고자 합니다.

USHER
김채운 부원장

USHER
김석균

나의 성격 PERSONALITY
ISTJ 현실주의자. 모든 일을 꾸준히 체계적으로

핵심 가치 CORE VALUE
#희망 #긍정 #재미

나의 강점 STRENGTH
#성실함 #솔직함 #원칙적 #긍정적 #체계적

하루아침에
되는것은 없다

VISION BIG5
1. 발전하는 하루 2. 건강한 신체 3. 활기찬 분위기
4. 겸손한 마음 5. 간결한 수업

4 모의토플
usherin.usher.co.kr

01 모의토플? 왜 봐야 하지?

Q1. 토플 시험 초보자
난 토플이 뭔지, 이름도 겨우 들었거나, 토플 공부를 해야한다는걸 겨우 알았는데, 일단, 내 실력이나 좀 보고, 대충 시험 구성부터 잡아 보고 싶다면?

A. 27만원짜리 진짜 토플 덜컥 잡고, 돈 날리지 말고, 일단 5만원짜리 모의 토플로, 어찌 생겼는지 파악하는 기회로 사용 바랍니다.

Q2. 영어 실력 충분히 있는 분?
A. 나는 영어 실력은 충분히 있는데, 그냥 시험 유형정도나 파악하고, 바로 시험 보면 되지 않을까? 라는 자신감이 있을 때, 실제 시험 전 몸풀기로 활용 바랍니다.

Q3. 토플 공부를 하면서, 본인의 실력 향상이 궁금하신 분
A. 이제 한달 공부 했는데, 내 공부 한 것이 얼마나 나아졌을지 궁금하다면, 실력 점검용으로 활용 바랍니다.

Q4. 실제 시험전에 최종 확인을 원하시는 분
A. 실제 시험장을 가야 하는데, 계속 종이로만 공부해서, 실제 토플시험장에서 모니터 적응과, 라이팅에서의 타이핑 적응등이 부족하다는걸 안다면, 미리 시험장 분위기를 확인용이 활용 바랍니다.

02 왜 모의토플? 을 봐야 하는가?
▼상세설명

📖 Reading
가. 종이로 보는것과 컴퓨터로 보는 것 만으로도 심한경우 리딩 점수 30점 만점중, 5점 차이까지 나므로, 별도로 준비 해야합니다.
나. 밑줄치면 시험 보는거나, 연필로 위치를 가리키며 시험을 보는것과, 마우스를 움직여 가며 보는 것을 다르게 느끼는 경우, 시험장 환경에 적응하기 위해
다. 시험장의 엄격한 시간 관리를 미리 준비해야 하므로
라. 내가 많이 틀린 문제 분석을 통해 어느 유형이 약한지 파악하기 위해
마. (선택: 내가 어느유형이 약한지 파악후, 추가 관련 문제의 인강을 통해 미진한 부분에 대한 설명을 듣기 위해)

🎧 Listening
가. 스피커를 통해 시험을 보는게 아닌, 헤드셋을 통해 나오는 소리에서의 차이를 어색해 하는 경우가 있다.
나. 시험장 화면에서, 가장 조심 해야 하는 것은, 리딩은 한번 본 화면도 다시 되돌아 와서 체크 할수있지만, 리스닝의 경우, 한번 진행한 문제는 되돌아 가서 수정이 안되는데, 연습 없는 학생들이 가장 어이없게 많이 하는 실수이므로, 실수를 방지하기 위해
다. 시험장의 엄격한 시간 관리를 미리 준비해야 하므로
라. 내가 많이 틀린 문제 분석을 통해 어느 유형이 약한지 파악하기 위해
마. (선택: 내가 어느유형이 약한지 파악후, 추가 관련 문제의 인강을 통해 미진한 부분에 대한 설명을 듣기 위해)

🎤 Speaking
가. 시험장에서 마이크에 대고 말하는 것은, 무조건 소리를 크게 내야하는데, 학생들의 경우, 옆에 잘 하는 학생들이 있을 경우, 기가 죽어 목소리를 작게 내서, 본인 실력보다 낮은 점수를 받는 경우가 있으므로, 미리 연습해서 본인의 목소리가 얼마나 작게 녹음 되는지 확인 해볼 기회
나. 1번부터 4번까지 네 개의 문제 순서에 적응하여, 실제 시험당일 문제 순서에 당황할일 없게 하기 위해
다. 내가 어느 유형이 약한지 파악하기 위해
라. (선택: 시험 본 것을 "첨삭"으로 이어져, 내 실력의 문제를 점검하기 위해) - **별도서비스**
마. (선택: 내가 어느유형이 약한지 파악후, 추가 관련 문제의 인강을 통해 미진한 부분에 대한 설명을 듣기 위해)

✍ Writing
가. 시험장에서 라이팅 시험은 모두 타이핑 시험인데, 시험장 갈때까지도 독수리 타자를 쳐야 할만큼 준비 없는 것을 막기 위해
나. (선택: 시험 본 것을 "첨삭"으로 이어져, 내 실력의 문제를 점검하기 위해) - **별도서비스**
다. (선택: 내가 어느유형이 약한지 파악후, 추가 관련 문제의 인강을 통해 미진한 부분에 대한 설명을 듣기 위해)

03 토플의 평가 영역(리딩, 리스닝, 스피킹, 라이팅) 및 어셔 모의토플 소개

	실제토플	모의토플
응시료	280,000원 (220$ ×1,227원 2023년 2월 현재)	50,000원
성적확인	시험종료 후 업무일 기준 15일 후 온라인으로 확인가능	시험 후 3일 내 Section 모두 확인가능

실제 시험 그대로, 가격은 1/5 저렴하게

어셔 모의 토플 시험은, TOEFL iBT와 동일한 방식의 온라인 모의고사로, 실제 시험과 똑같은 환경을 경제적이고 합리적인 가격에 부담 없이 이용하실 수 있습니다.

시험 구성

평가영역	구성	시간	세부사항	만점
Reading	Passage 2개(700단어 X 2개)	35분	Passage 당 17분 30초 10문제	30점
Listening	Conversation 1개/Lecture 1개	36분	문제풀이시간 7분	30점
Speaking	Independent 1개/Intergrated 3개	16분 내외	-	30점
Writing	Intergrated 1개/Discussion 1개	29분	-	30점
총 약 2시간 (116분)				총점 120점

시험 화면: Reading, Listening, Speaking, Writing

04 구매하기 (개별 과목 별도)

시험명	사용기간	가격
USHER 공식 토플모의고사 Full TEST	1년	50,000원
USHER 공식 토플모의고사 Half(R/L) TEST	1년	27,000원
USHER 공식 토플모의고사 Half(S/W) TEST	1년	27,000원
개별 과목	1년	15,000원

5 토플 Reading 공부방법
usherin.usher.co.kr

리딩 점수에 따라서

- 20점 미만이라면, 리스닝에는 너무 많은 힘을 쓰지 말고, 단어와 리딩에 집중 바랍니다.
  둘 다 하려다 하나도 못 할 수 있습니다.
- 20점 이상이라면, 1. 단어 2. 구문 3. 묶기 4. 열번읽기 까지 꼼꼼히 처리 바랍니다.
- 25점 이상이면, 단어, 구문은 거의 알 겁니다.
  대략 틀린 것 정도 간단히 마무리 하고 **묶기 및 오답 패턴 확인**에 집중하면 됩니다.

각각의 과정을 적으면 다음과 같습니다.

Step 1. 문제풀이
Step 2. TAGGING
Step 3. 구문 / 단어시험
Step 4. 묶기
Step 5. 타이핑
Step 6. 별지
Step 7. 접속사 암기

과정 순서대로 공부를 해야하는 구체적인 이유와 방법을 적어보겠습니다.

Step 1. 문제 풀이

- 문제 풀이는 실전 화면처럼 컴퓨터로 직접 풀면서 익숙해지는게 좋습니다.

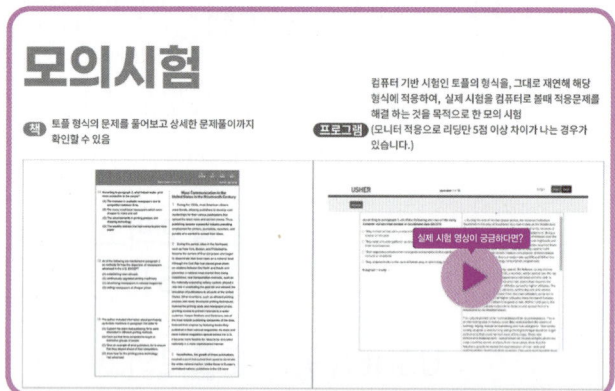

Step 2. TAGGING

- 문제 풀이 직후, 잊기 전에, 문제 풀면서 가장 짜증 났던 부분 = 즉, 이해하기 힘들었던 부분을 체크해 둬야 합니다.

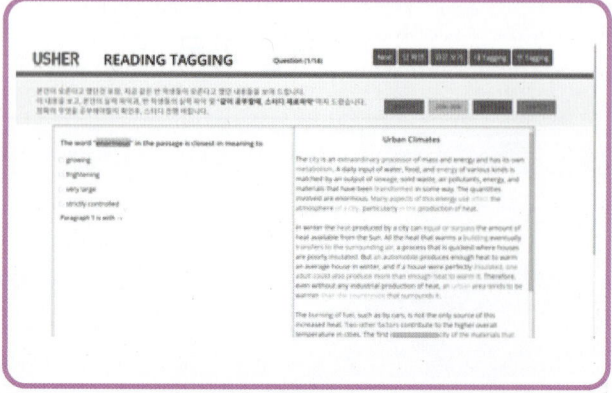

Step 3. 구문 / 단어 시험

- 귀찮은 거 압니다. 그래도 해두시기 바랍니다. 리딩 20점 미만은 실력 없어서 하기 싫어도 해야 하고, 리딩 25점 넘는 분들은 별로 할 것도 없겠지만, 그래도 다 챙겨 두시기 바랍니다.

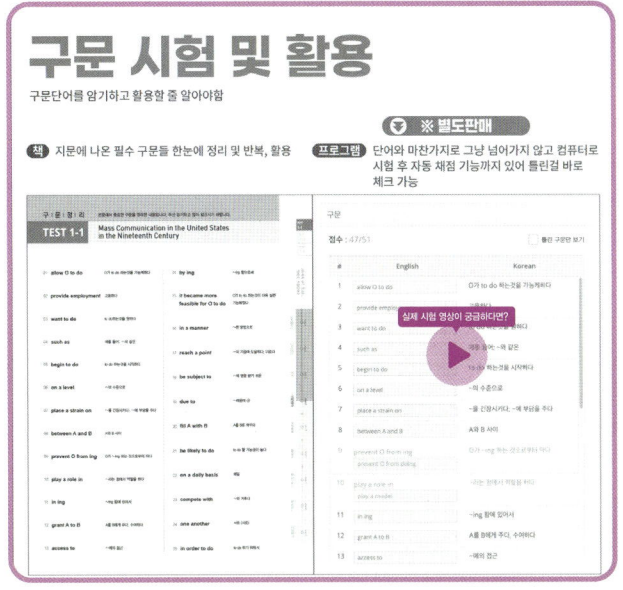

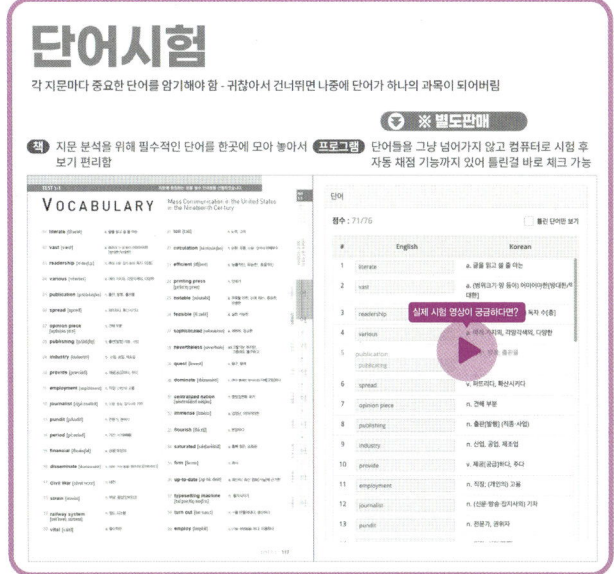

Step 4. 묶기

- 리딩 20점 미만은 실력이 없으니, 파악+ 실력 자체를 늘리기 위해 필요합니다.
- 리딩 25점 이상은 만점 받기 위해서, 본인이 어느 부분이 약한지 "샅샅이 훑어야 할 때", 가장 강력한 툴입니다.
 "30점의 절박함과 귀찮음 중", 더 강한 것이 여러분의 행동을 바꿀겁니다.

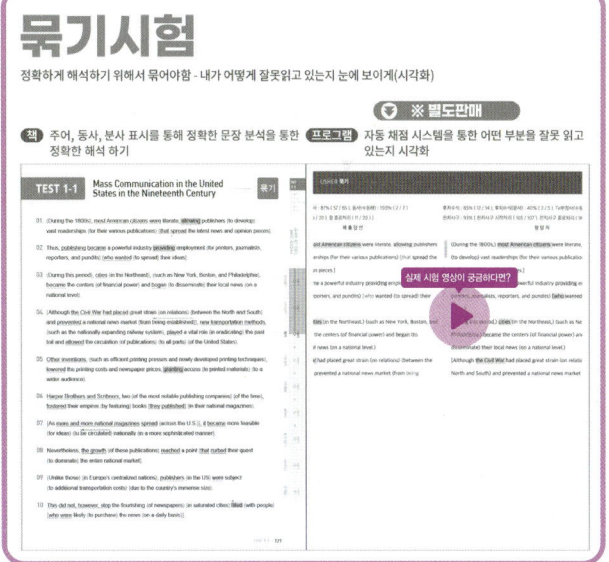

Step 5. 열번읽기(내 발음 체크 = 말 할 수 있으면 들린다)

- 리딩 20점 미만의 학생들에게 가장 중요한 점은 "말 할 수 없으면, 들을 수 없다!!!" 입니다.
- 본인만 아는 이상한 발음으로 기억하면, 절대 못듣습니다.
 이그제그래이션? Exaggeration을 이렇게 읽는 학생. 답 없습니다.
- 말 할 수 있는지는, 학원 프로그램이 모두 파악해 줍니다. 채점까지.
 여러분은 성실함만 있으면 됩니다.

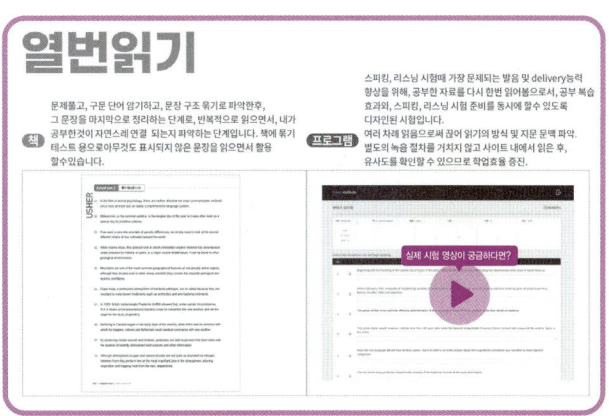

Step 6. 타이핑

- 라이팅 시험은 영타가 기본인데, 이를 따로 준비하는것이 아닌, 공부한 자료를 반복 연습함을서, 영타와 복습을 동시에 진행 가능케 하는 시험
- 주어진 문장을 따라 써 보며 정확도와 속도를 올려, 문맥 파악과 더불어 컴퓨터 기반 시험인 토플에서 고득점 하기 위한 필수 역량을 증진

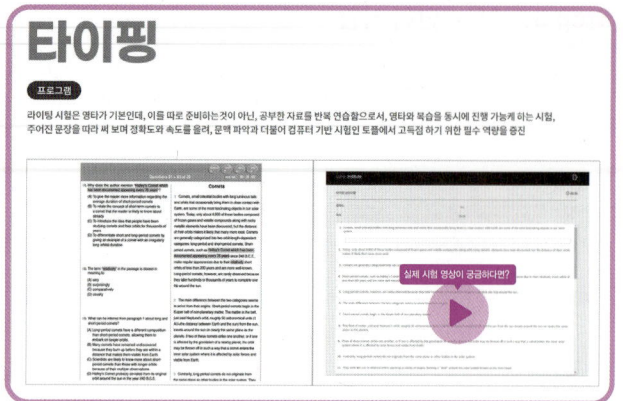

Step 7. 별지

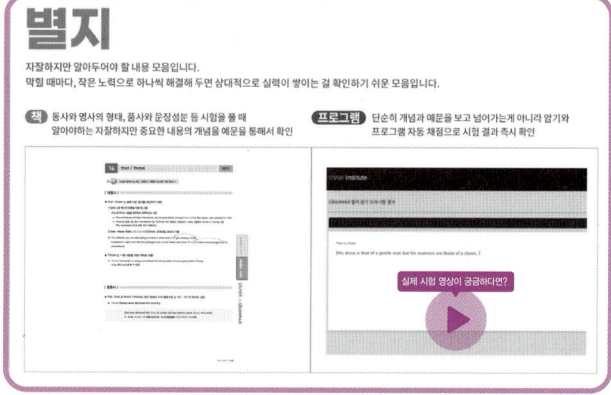

Step 8. 접속사 암기

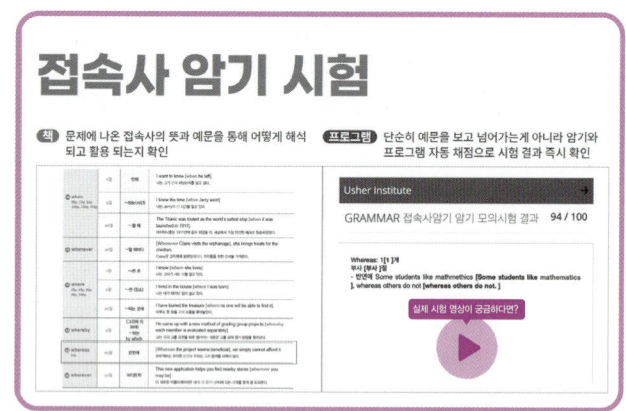

어셔어학원을 다니면,

어셔어학원을 다니면, 이 과정을 모두 스터디 시간에 **무료**로 합니다.

하지만, 사정이 있어서 **인강을 듣거나 프로그램만 구매하시는 분들은**

반드시, 위 내용들을 기억하고, 실행하면, 실력 향상에 큰 도움 되실겁니다.

6. 토플 Listening 공부방법

usherin.usher.co.kr

리스닝 점수에 따라서

- 20점 미만이라면, 리스닝에는 너무 많은 힘을 쓰지 말고, 단어와 리딩에 집중 바랍니다.
  둘 다 하려다 하나도 못 할 수 있습니다.
- 20점 이상이라면, **1.** 단어 **2.** 구문 **3.** 딕테이션 **4.** 열번읽기 까지 꼼꼼히 처리 바랍니다.
- 25점 이상이면, 단어, 구문은 거의 알 겁니다.
  대략 틀린 것 정도 간단히 마무리 하고 **딕테이션 및 오답 패턴 확인**에 집중하면 됩니다.

각각의 과정을 적으면 다음과 같습니다.

Step 1. 문제풀이
Step 2. TAGGING
Step 3. 구문 / 단어시험
Step 4. 딕테이션
Step 5. 열번읽기 (내 발음 체크 = 말 할 수 있으면 들린다)
Step 6. 타이핑

과정 순서대로 공부를 해야하는 구체적인 이유와 방법을 적어보겠습니다.

Step 1. 문제 풀이

- 문제 풀이는 실전 화면처럼 컴퓨터로 직접 풀면서 익숙해지는게 좋습니다.

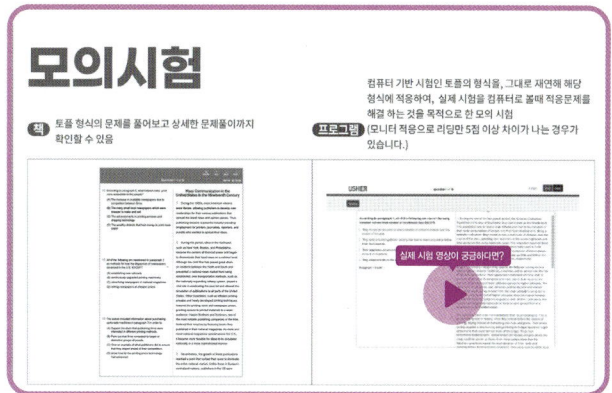

Step 2. TAGGING

- 문제 풀이 직후, 잊기 전에, 문제 풀면서 가장 짜증 났던 부분 = 즉, 이해하기 힘들었던 부분을 체크해 둬야 합니다.

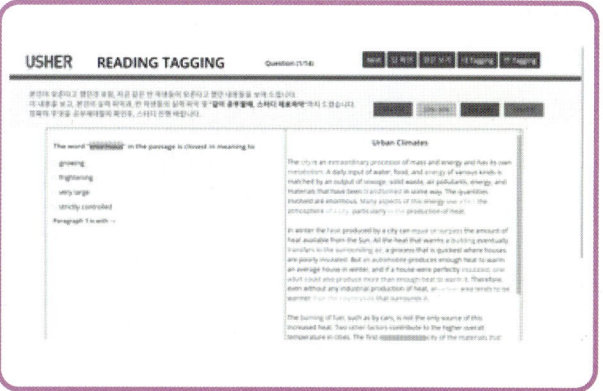

Step 3. 구문 / 단어 시험

- 귀찮은 거 압니다. 그래도 해두시기 바랍니다.

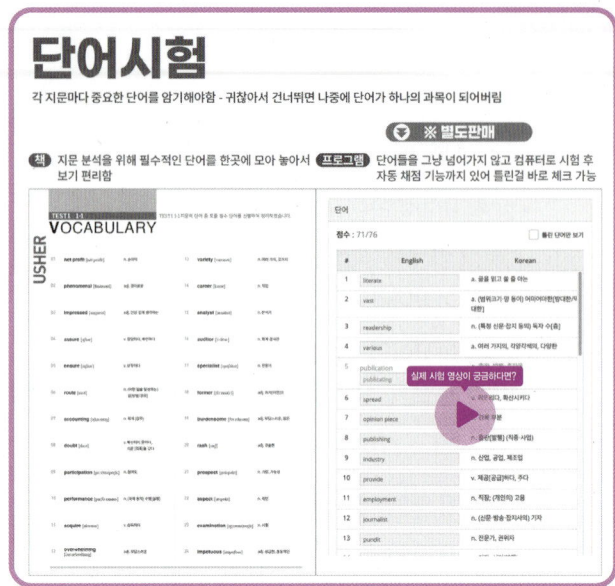

Step 4. 딕테이션

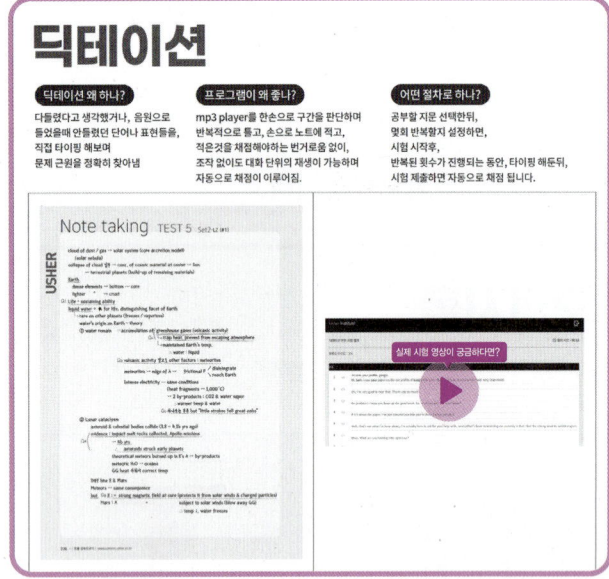

Step 5. 열번읽기(내 발음 체크 = 말 할 수 있으면 들린다)

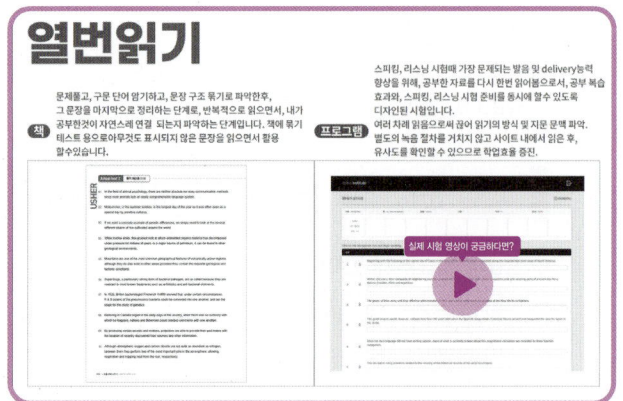

Step 6. 타이핑

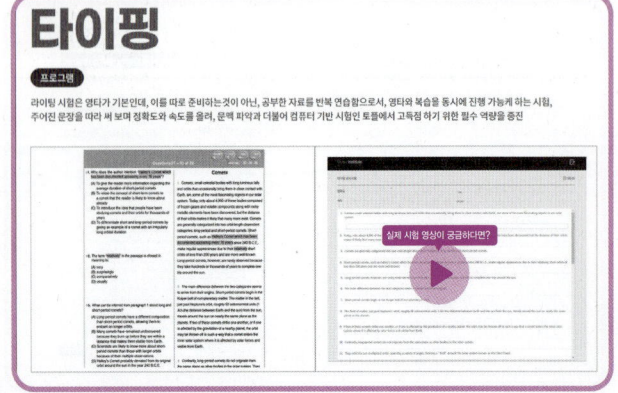

7 수강 후기
usherin.usher.co.kr

김유석
97점 두달간 토플 시험에서의 승리: 훌륭한 교사진, 함께 노력한 학원 동료들에게 감사를

반배치고사

일자	반	GR			RC	LC
		SW1	SW2	SW1+SW2		
2024-03-29	성인 정규 Intermediate반	10	18	28	32	23
2024-02-29	성인 정규 Intermediate반	11	11	22	28	22
2024-01-23	신규	9	13	22	25	

모의토플

일자	RC	LC	SP	WR	합계
2024-03-15	17	25	19	20	81
2024-02-16	22	19	0	0	41

2024.03 성인교육중급반 김유석 성취표

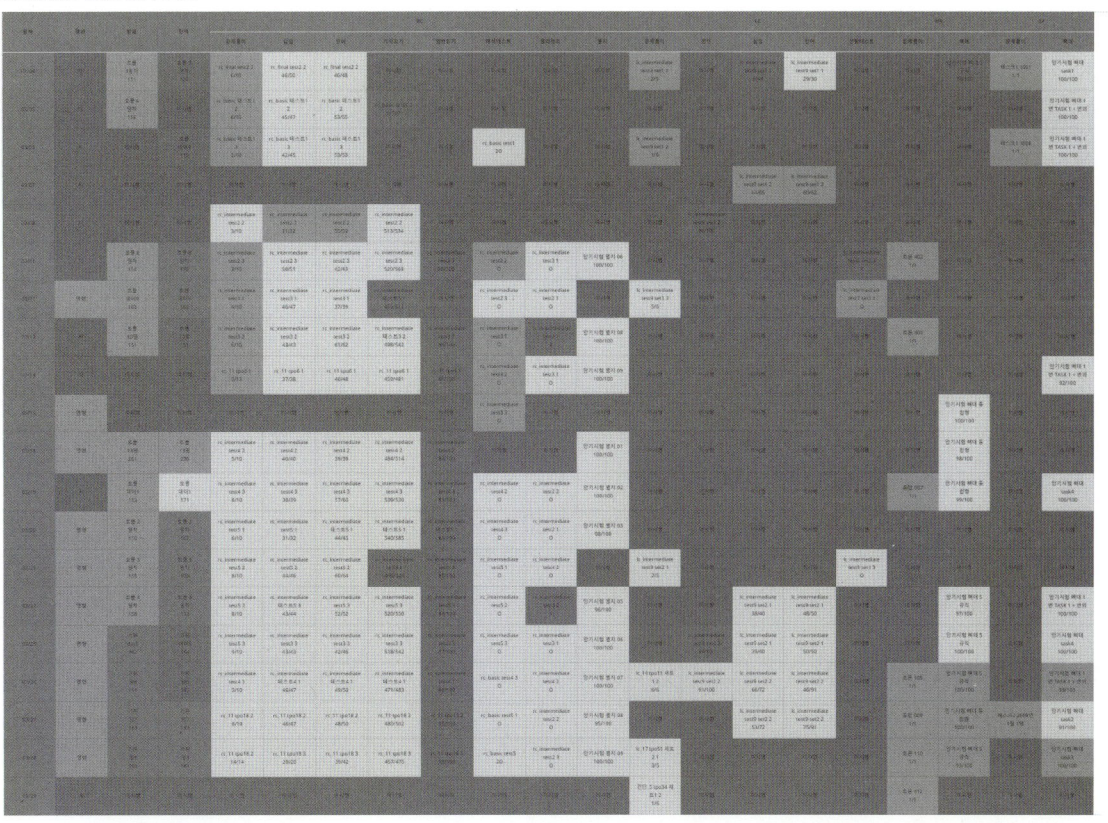

마이페이지 MYPAGE

배치고사 신청/결과확인	예습공지 게시판	수강증 확인	교재 확인하기	증명서 발급
사물함 안내	무료교재 mp3/부록	토익특강 성적표	쿠폰함	사물함 신청

김유석님 반갑습니다 회원정보수정

수강중인 강의 / 반별게시판	결제 진행중인 강의	결제내역	장바구니	교재확인 / 배송조회
0건	0건	20건	0건	0건
자세히 보기	자세히 보기	자세히 보기	자세히 보기	자세히 보기

▌처음 학원에 들어올 때 시작 했던 반
2024년 02월 성인 정규 Intermediate반

▌수강 했던반 / 총 개월수
2024년 02월 성인 정규 Intermediate반
2024년 03월 성인 정규 Intermediate반
2024년 04월 성인 정규 K1반

▌학원에 오기전에 가지고 있었던 점수 (파트별)
- 토익점수_ 합계 : 0 RC : 0 LC : 0
- 토플점수_ 합계 : 70 RC : 19 LC : 18 SP : 13 WR : 20

▌목표했던 토플 점수
100점

▌취득한 토플 점수
RC: 28 LC: 22 SP: 20 WR: 27

▌최초/중간/ 최종
- 최초_ 합계 : 70 RC : 19 LC : 18 SP : 13 WR : 20
- 중간_ 2024-01-23 배치고사 SW:22, RC:25, LC:0
  2024-02-16 모의고사 RC:22, LC:19, SP:0, WR:0
  2024-02-29 배치고사 SW:22, RC:28, LC:22
  2024-03-15 모의고사 RC:17, LC:25, SP:19, WR:20
  2024-03-29 배치고사 SW:28, RC:32, LC:23
- 최종_ RC: 0 LC: 0 SP: 0 WR: 0

▌토플 공부한 이유(학업 이유)
일본유학(EJU)

파트별 상세 설명

• Reading

제가 가장 나댈수 있는 영역입니다.
저는 한 달동안 삼지문 -> 인터 -> K반 까지 승반했었던 유일한 사람이기에, 현재 인터반 학생들이 주의깊게 봤으면 합니다. 다만 한가지 전제조건은, 저는 원래 문해력으로 승부보는 사람이었다는 점입니다. 즉 지문 이해력은 높으나, 영어해석능력이 부족해서 RC영역에서 고생했다는 점을 말해두고 싶습니다.

우선 첫 달은, 영어를 읽고 푸는데에 대한 '자신감', 그리고 긴 문장을 만났을때 '익숙함' 에 중요성에 대해서 배웠습니다. 혜성쌤 께서 강조하신 '오늘 푼 지문 10번 읽기' 과제를 다 하진 못했었으나, 세번씩이라도 읽다보니, 모르는 단어가 나오거나, 긴 문장을 봤을때 느끼는 자신감이 상당히 올라갔고, 정답률 또한 올라갔습니다. 그러나, 아직 이 시기에서는, 문장 직독직해의 수준이 낮은상태였으며, 주어진 시간안에 한 지문을 읽는것이 불안했습니다.

두 번째 달에는, 사실상 제 RC영역에 가장 큰 영향을 주신 김석균 선생님의 수업을 들었습니다.
선생님의 가르침 하에서 선생님이 강조하시는, 그리고 제가 느끼는 중요성의 순서는 다음과 같습니다.

1.수업시간에 선생님께서 워드에 정리하고, 수업 후에 올려주시는 메모를 빠르게 기억하고 넘어가기 입니다.
>> 각 지문 테마 별, 자주 나오는 단어나 표현들이 익숙해지기 때문에, 다음 번, 비슷한 지문을 만났을 때, 읽는 속도와 정확성, 자신감이 매우 다릅니다.

2. 묶기 빠르게 할 것***
묶기를 연구해가며 하지마세요. 묶기는 하나의 시험입니다. 문장 내에서, 본인이 약한 문법의 영역을 파악할 수 있는 부분이기 때문에, 빠르게 풀 되, 묶기의 결과를 잘 살펴보고, 메모를 남겨둡시다. 특히 토플 RC에서 등위접속사 and, or 과 같은 문법을 다르게 읽는다면, 해석이 전혀 다른 내용이 되기 때문에 지문 이해에 큰 방해가 될 것 입니다.

3. 해석테스트
토플의 RC는 사실 이해를 하지 못한다고 해도, 70프로의 정답률을 보장할 수 있는 시험이라고 생각합니다.
그 이유로는, 어차피 문제에서 물어보는것은 지문의 특정 부분에 관해서 이고, 지문을 한번 읽었을때 기억을 살려, 빠르게 문제에서 요구하는 부분을 지문에서 찾기만 한다면, 정답률 또한 상당히 올라갈 것 입니다.
다만, 지문을 읽고 기억하는데에 있어서, 중요한 능력이 직독직해라고 생각합니다. 토플은 영어단어 바꿔넣기의 시험. 즉 영어를 잘한다는 느낌보다, 유의어 단어나 표현을 얼마나 알고있는지를 묻기에, 기계적인 암기능력을 요구한다고 생각합니다.
그렇기 때문에, 직독직해가 된다면, 유의어가 페러프라이징 된 선지를 고를수 있기때문에, 정답률이 올라갑니다.
또한, 결정적으로 직독직해를 잘 하게 된다면, 영어문장을 빠르게 읽게 되기 때문에, 시간안에 문제를 다 읽고 푸는것이 가능해 진다고 생각합니다. 이런 직독직해능력을 기를 수 있고, 내 상태를 점검할 수 있는 해석테스트를 열심히 준비합시다.

4. 네 번째로 제가 생각하는 석균쌤의 RC포인트 + 어셔에서 가장 중요하게 강요하는 부분인 단어 입니다.
어셔를 다니면서 단어시험은 가장 큰 스트레스중 하나라고 생각합니다. 우선 학원측에서 단어암기를 하라고 과제를 내주면, 암기조차 안하는 학생들이 있기 때문에, 인터반 기준 200개중 180개의 빡센 목표를 요구하는 것 같습니다.
다만 제 생각으로, 단어를 암기하는데에 있어 가장 중요한것은 200개중 180개로 통과해서 초록불을 띄우는 것이 아니라, 내가 한번 본 단어의 뉘앙스를 얼마나 파악했는지 입니다.
아마 저와 수업을 들어보신 분들은 공감하시겠지만, 석균쌤이 수업중에 나온 단어에 대해 동의어를 물어보실 때, 가장 대답을 잘하는 학생이 저 였을 것입니다. 하지만, 반면에 3월달 VOCA 성취율이 가장 낮은 학생도 저라고 생각합니다. 매번 160~170개로 180개를 통과하지 못한적이 허다했거든요.
하지만 그렇다고해서 저는 단어공부의 시간을 줄인적이 없습니다. 대신 낯선 단어가 갖고있는 의미, 그리고 동의어, 이 단어가 어떤 주제의 지문에서 나오는가 에 초점을 맞췄습니다.
그와 반대로, 단어시험 통과율이 엄청 높으신 분들 혹은, 학원을 오랫동안 다니신 분들에게 있어, RC의 점수를 큰 폭으로 향상시키는 대에 방해되는것이 바로 180개 제한 통과방식인것 같습니다. 160개에서 180개로 단어시험 정답률을 높이기 위해선, 한글뜻에 초점을 맞추게 되고, 그러다보면, RC지문에서 만난 낯선 단어를 빠르게 의미를 떠올리는데에 딜레이가 생길 것 입니다. 물론 우선 단어의 익숙함을 줄이고, RC지문에서 만났을 때, 자신감 있게 한글로 해석할 수 있다면, RC의 한 지문을 읽는데에 유의미한 정답률 상승이 있다고 생각합니다. 그렇기 때문에, 단어를 열심히 외우시고, 통과를 잘하는 분들이라면, 지문에서 모르는 단어가 나왔을때는, 남들도 모르는 단어라고 생각하고 일단 자신감 있게 읽고 넘어가셔야 한 지문을 넘어 RC, RC를 넘어 LC, SPK, WRT까지,, 나머지 영역에도 전반적인 영향을 주는 자신감을 잃지 않을 수 있습니다. 그렇기에 본인의 자신감을 유지하는데에 가장 중요한 단어를 소홀히 하시지 마시길 바랍니다.

마지막으로 제 어셔에서의 토플 기간동안 가장 중요했던 3월달 첫 주 "삼지문 반" 입니다.
삼지문반을 수강함으로써, RC에서의 제 단점을 확실히 파악하는것이 가능했습니다.
수강후기 Reading 영역 첫 문두 에서도 말했다시피, 저는 상대적으로 감각적인 문해력을 가진 반면에, 영어를 한국말로 옮기는 부분에 대해서 많이 부족했습니다. 그러다보니 제가 이해를 할 수 있는 지문들에 대해서는 70% 까지의 정답률을 보장했으나, 이해가 되지않는 주제에 관해서는 그야말로 처참했었죠..
그러다 원장님이 삼지문반 승반테스트를 진행하시고, RC영역에 대해서 설명해주실때, 그야말로 광명을 찾았습니다.
RC = R+C, 즉, Reading +comprehension 이라는 말, Reading 이 7, Comprehension이 3의 비율을 갖는다는 것을 듣고 나서야 비로소, 그때야 제 단점이 Reading (직독직해) 라는 점에 대해 확신할 수 있었습니다.

그 이후로는, 인터반 -> 삼지문반으로 하반당했다는 압박을 머금고 친한 동료들 경선이와 건우형과 함께 세가지 지문 부수기에 목숨 걸었습니다. 저의 지문 이해과 설명 + 경선, 건우의 직독직해 설명이 서로에게 큰 시너지를 주었습니다. 3월의 첫 주에 삼지문 반을 경험한 것이, 지속적인 제 RC점수의 상승에 포문을 열었다고 생각합니다.

그렇게 터프하게 학원 불 꺼져도 11시 반까지 공부하다가 보니 한 가지 재미있는 일화도 남겼던것이 기억에 남네요 ㅋㅋㅋ
원장님이 퇴근하시다가 어둠속에서 공부하던 저와 소연, 경선의 공부하는 동영상을 찍어가신것, 채운쌤께서도 퇴근 하시다가 저희를 발견하시고 기분좋아하셨던 그런것들이 저희에게도 큰 원동력이 되었던 것 같습니다.

다시 궤도로 돌아와서 정리하자면, 삼지문 반을 거쳐, 3월 모의토플 이전까지 문제풀이및 석균쌤의 수업에 익숙해졌고, 3월 셋째 주부터 RC점수가 팍 뛰더니 변동기에 들어오기 시작한 것 같습니다. 그리고 3월 이후 어셔에서의 생활을 마무리 하려던 찰나, 석균쌤과 채운쌤의 설득과 조언에 못이겨 4/2, 4/3의 수업도 듣게 되었고, 이 기간에 RC 고득점 평탄화가 이뤄져, 저를 하여금 어셔에서 졸업을 하도록 만들어 준 것 같습니다.

마무리로, 쌤들 말 안듣는 친구들에게도 한마디 하자면, 자기 멋대로 공부를 하려면 우선 쌤들이 시킨것부터 끝내고 하는것은 어떨까요? 석균쌤의 말씀대로, 제 RC점수가 상승하고 안정된 시기는, 어셔의 syllabus를 다 채우는데 성공한 시점부터라는 점을 알아주셨음 합니다.

- **Listening**

저에게 있어서, 시험 한번한번의 변동이 가장 큰 과목입니다.
모의토플 에서는 25점도 맞아보았고, 수업시간에 풀었던 문제는 컨버 렉쳐 렉쳐 다 맞은 적도 있었던것을 비추어 볼 때,
듣기의 고점 자체를 한번 끌어올리는데에는 성공했다고 생각됩니다.
먼저 그렇게 끌어올리는데 성공했던 이유를 생각해 보면

첫째. 채운쌤의 세뇌.
질문과 답변 위주로 들어라, 고유명사 연도 는 꼭 적어라, 동사위주로 들어라, 예시는 예시가 나온이유, 그것에 대한 결과를 들어야 한다,, 노트테이킹은 왼쪽에서 오른쪽으로 해라.
사실 더 많은데,, 신입분들은 수업료 내고 들으시라고 여기까지만 !! / 기존 학생들은 본인들이 메모했던 내용들을 한번 정리한다음, WRT통합형의 파이브룰즈 처럼 달달 외우는 것을 추천합니다.

둘째. 디스커버리 유튜브채널의 영상 "마지막 알레스카인" 반복 청취.
1시간 46분짜리 몰아보기 영상을 매 대중교통에서, 집안일 할때, 밥먹을때 반복해서 들었을 시기가 LC점수가 가장 잘 나왔던 시기입니다. 저는 시골출신에, 서바이벌에 관심이 많아 재밌게 봤던 영상인데, 토플 bio지문에 나오는 단어들을 귀로 반복해서 들었던것이 상당히 고무적 이었습니다. 시각을 이용해서 공부하지 않는 시간에는 꼭 귀라도 영어로 채워두길 바랍니다.

셋째. 딕테이션을 단어 단어 단어 적고, 중간에 비었던 부분을 다시 매꾸는 것이 아니라, 영어를 한 뭉탱이 단위로 듣고 적었을 때, 내용이 가장 잘 들렸고, 그러다 보니 노트의 위에도 적어야 하는 내용만 적을 수 있어서, 정답률이 높았던 것 같습니다. 채운쌤이 말하시는 딕테이션의 방식 1단계 2단계 3단계를 잘 수행하시길 바랍니다.

다만, 더 높은 점수를 내지 못한 이유에는

첫째. 어셔에 있는 도중, 리스닝 자습에 시간을 많이 쓰지 못한것.
RC와 LC는 몇번 고점을 찍는것이 가능하다면, 그 이후에는 점수의 변동을 잡아주는것이 중요하다고 생각하는데, 이 변동을 잡는것에 시간을 투자하지 못한것 같아서 아쉽습니다.

둘째. 노트테이킹을 점점 많이 적게 된 것.
노트테이킹의 양에 대해서도, 선생님들마다 다르지만, 저는 적게 적었을때가 오히려 더 정답률이 높았습니다.
단순하게 내용을 많이 적은것은, 디테일을 놓칠 확률이 큽니다.

셋째. 단기기억 기르는 연습을 게을리 함.
영어는 한국말처럼 단어만 투욱 툭 던져서는 의미가 만들어지지 않는다고 선생님들이 많이 말씀하십니다.
그렇다면 영어를 잘 듣기위해선, 언어 하나의 덩어리가 어디부터 어디까지인지 인식을 하고, 기억을 하고있어야 합니다.
청취테스트 연습을 부지런히 한다면, 본인이 들은 한 덩어리 덩어리가, 잘 기억에 남고, LC정답률 상향에 크게 기여할 것 같습니다.
LC영역에서 저의 결론은 "문제풀이 방식에 시간을 쏟지 맙시다" 라는 것입니다. 토플 리스닝 특성 상, 내용이 잘 들리고, 디테일을 기억하거나 노트에 옮겨적는다면 문제는 어지간히 다 맞을 것 이라 생각합니다.

- **Speaking**

4과목 중 가장 낮은 점수를 맞아서 가장 할말이 적습니다. 뼈대 잘 외우고, 12간지 잘 외우고, 리스닝영역 문장단위로 적고!! 이 삼박자가 맞지 않고서는 의미있는 점수를 낼 수 없다고 생각합니다. 토플이 단과시험이 아니고, 여러 영역을 요구하는 만큼, 전체의 성적을 끌어올리기 위해선, 무리를 해서라도 하루에 스피킹 하나정도 녹음하는것을 추천드립니다.

두번째로 스피킹 1번과 같은경우 암기가 끝이 아니고, 주어진 주제문에 대해 뼈대와 12간지를 변형시키는 유연함 도 길러야한다는 점 잊지 말아주세요.

저 같은 경우, 솔직히 유연하게 대처하는 연습이 소홀했기 때문에, 걍 논리 안맞는 문장나와도 자신있게 어거지로 밀고 들어갔습니다. 그래서 20점이라도 나오지 않았나 싶어요..
자신있게 어거지로 밀고가서 20점이라도 확보하려면 뼈대 + 12간지를 반드시 외워야 할 것입니다.

- **Writing**

4과목중 가장 의외인 점수를 가져다준 고마운 과목입니다. 사실 WRT이 고맙기보단 당연히 채운쌤께 너무 감사드립니다..
스피킹과 더불어 공부량이 적었던 과목인데, 왜 27점이 나왔을까요??...
바로 제 WRT점수가 12간지와 파이브룰즈에 위대함을 다시금 증명했다고 생각합니다.
물론 저도 작전을 세우긴 했는데,, 그게 12간지의 위대함과 더불어 잘 들어맞았네요.
제 작전은, 제가 많은 내용을 생산할 수록, 문법과 스펠링 미스가 많아져서, WRT의 총점을 깎을것이라 예상해서, 안전빵 문장들만 가져다 적었습니다. 절때 어렵게 쓰려고 하지 마시고, 본인만의 예시 뼈대를 만들고, 12간지에 기대어 최대한 문장을 간단하게 쓰는것을 추천드립니다.

- **어셔의 관리 프로그램 (asap프로그램) 관련 사용 팁**

점수 취득 후 얻게된 결과
1) 한번 실패를 맛 보았던 토플에서 성공을 거둔것.
매번 꿈에 나오던 학창시절 담당일진을 길에서 만나 뚜드려 팬것과 동일한 기분이지 않을까요??
2) 자신감
내 인생에 있어서 가장 높았던 벽 '토플'을 넘었기 때문에,, 앞으로 못할건 하나도 없을것 같다는 근자감
저는 ○○스에서 1년 이상의 시간과 돈을 써가며 영어의 5형식부터 공부했었습니다. ○○스의 기본문법 교실은 to부정사가 뭔지 모르는 저에게는 꽤나 재미있고 이해가 잘 갔던 수업이었죠.
그러나 문제는 ○○스 토플 커리큘럼에 들어가면서 시작입니다. 제가 생각한 ○○스 토플의 문제를 순서대로 나열하자면,
1) 영어 기초반에서 토플 기초반으로 넘어갈 때, 간극이 꽤 크다.
>> 단어 요구량이 너무 차이나기 때문에, 영어 기초반에서 공부한 뒤 바로 토플 기초반수업 못따라갑니다.
2) 영어실력의 "근본"을 경시한다.
>> 이게 가장 큰 문제라고 생각합니다. 특히, 만약 이글을 보는 본인의 목표가 80점 이상이라면.
제 생각으론, ○○스의 '입문+인터미디엇' 반의 수준이, 어셔의 '완초 1~2반' 이랑 비슷합니다.
근데 차이점이 있다면, ○○스에서는 딱 그정도의 영어수준을 지닌 학생들이 그 상태에서 점수를 잘 내도록 교과과정이 맞춰져 있습니다. 그말은 즉, 더 높은 점수대로 도전하는 "근본"을 쌓는데에 아 무 런 도움이 되지 않는 다는 점입니다.
본인이 영어가 안읽히고, 안들려도.. 그 상태에서 점수를 내게 알려주는 방법이 ○○스식 입니다.
이 방식으로는 저같이 영어의 "근본"이 없는 학생들에게 있어서 90점대의 아성에 도전할수가 없습니다.
3)각 과목 선생님들이 다르고, 같은 과목의 선생님들도 너무 많다.
>> 템플릿 다 난리납니다. 같은 과목의 선생님들 마다 말이 아 다르고 어 다릅니다.
각 과목 선생님들의 목소리가 너무 큽니다. 수업시간 40~50분의 짧은 시간에 수업을 듣기 위해서, 하루 과목당 4~5시간 정도의 자습량을 요구합니다. 즉, 토플 4과목의 과제를 마치지 않는다면, 수업을 듣는 의미가 없습니다.
○○스 다녀보신 분들 수업 1주차 부터 같은 교실에 사람들이 적어지는것을 경험했거나, 혹은 본인이 점점 수업에 참여를 못하게 되는 학생이셨죠?
그~러~니, 어셔를 토플 학원에 안중을 넣고 계신 분이라면, 혹은 지금 다니고 계신 분이라면 영어의 "근본" 을 쌓기위해서 어떻게 해야하나 열심히 고민해보세요. 공부법에 최첨단 방식은 없습니다.
암기, 반복, 직독직해 이런 무식 하다고 여겨지는 공부가 아직도 사용 되는 이유는 '전통적' 이기 때문입니다. 전통이 전통으로 이어져 온 것에는 그것이 최선책 이어왔기 때문입니다.
학생분들의 뇌는 그저, 때려 넣는것만 생각하시고, 학원에서 시키는것에 대해 의문을 가지지좀 마세요.
그렇게 본인이 학원보다 좋은방법을 알고 있었다면, 지금 이 후기를 볼 일도 없을 테니까요.
뇌의 사용량을 다른데 투자할 것 없이, 내용을 집어넣는 것에만 집중한다는것이 얼마나 효율적입니까?
대신, 학원이 이걸 왜 시키는걸까? 에 대해서만 '고민' 수준에서 머물도록 하는것을 추천합니다..
어셔 어학원에서의 시간들을 돌이켜보며...

어셔에서의 두 달은 제 수명 1~2년을 끌어쓴다는 느낌으로 지냈습니다.
1) 수면은 두달동안 평균 5시간 안넘을거라 생각하구요,,
2) 점심또한 편의점 삼각김밥만 먹어서 소화장애 심각했었죠..
같이 공부했던 친구들은 알겠지만 제 말버릇 중 하나가 소화안되서 죽을것같다..
위생천/까스활명수 마셔야겠다 아마 지겹도록 들었을 것입니다

근데 할만했습니다.. 어셔에서 토플은 공부라기 보단, 하나의 팀 스포츠라고 생각합니다. 매일같이 남아서 동료들과 훈련을 하고, 스스로의 한계를 극복하고, 결과로써 증명한다. 이렇게 생각했기 때문에 어셔에서 상당히 즐거운 시간을 보낼 수 있었습니다.
인생에서 무언가를 위해 몰두하는 경험을 쌓기위해 최적의 환경을 잘 조성해주신 원장님, 그리고 채운쌤과 석균쌤, 해성쌤과 같이 교사진들의 엄청난 하드워킹.. 어셔에서의 두 달은 진정한 낙수효과에 대해서도 느끼게 해준 것 같습니다.
저는 두 달하고 빠질생각으로 다녔기 때문에 제가 열심히 해야하는건 당연했구요..
그런데도 불구하고 나를 가르치는 선생님들은 몇년씩 이 생활을 반복하고 있다는 사실을 생각해 본다면,, 적어도 본인이 어셔에 있는 동안은 그들보다 열심히 해야한다는걸 잊지마세요.

▌어셔생활백서

[1] 밥집:
1) 먹고싶은것 없으면 "감미옥" - 시간은 금입니다. 가장 가까운 복합 한식 분식집이며, 맛 또한 일대에서 상위권입니다. 만약 사장님께 아양을 잘 떤다면, 공짜 밥 무한리필도 가능합니다.
2) 먹고싶은것 없고, 감미옥이 질린다면 "KFC" (도보 왕복 약 8분)
3) 학원 MZ세대들이 아마,, 제일 좋아할 김치볶음밥&돈까스 "하트타임" (KFC 근처)
4) 든든한 국밥 "장터순대국" (KFC 아랫층)
5) "뉴코아 킴스클럽" 푸드코드: 가지마세요 시간 다 뺏깁니다. (도보 왕복 약 16분)
>> 참고로 점심은 빠르게 편의점에서 드시고 구문/단어, 묶기 하세요.. 시간은 금입니다.

[2] 자습실 (=학원 오픈시간)
1) 평일: 매일 아침 7시 30분 안에 열리고, 오후 11시 ~ 11시 30분에 닫힙니다.
2) 주말: 주 마다 쌤들께 여쭤보세요. 열릴때도, 안 열릴때도 있습니다.
>> 토플 학원의 학원비는 결코 싸지 않습니다. 최대한 학원의 전기, 수도, 난방 비용을 털어간다는 생각으로 남으세요.

[3] 대인관계:
제 생각으로 어셔에서 공부 다음으로 중요한 영역같습니다. 얼굴을 본 기억이 있는 사람과 마주친다면 정중히 인사부터 나눕시다. 특히, 열심히 하는 학생이 있다면, 혹은 점수를 잘 내는 친구가 있다면 잘 보고 배웁시다.

▌Thanks to

1) 경선.. 어셔가 나에게 선물한 가장 친한 친구.. 덕분에 어셔 너무 재미있게 다녔다... 나도 가끔 너무힘들고 맨탈 흔들릴때 있었는데, 그때마다 경선이의 활기랑 에너지가 나아갈 힘을 계속해서 준것같아.. 진짜 너 없었으면 쉽게 졸업하기 힘들었을것같아 너무고맙다 경선아. 빠르게 졸업하고 서로 남은 한국에서의 목표한 바를 완수한 다음에 또 신나게 놀아보자

2) 소연.. 아마 본인은 모르실 것 같은데, 소연님이 제 점수가 오르는데 1등 공신이십니다.. 소연님 분석을 꽤 했거든요 ㅋㅋㅋ 소연님 같은 분이랑 수업을 들을수 있었던것이 진짜 엄청난 행운이었습니다. 그리고 왜 또 공부는 그렇게 열심히 하시는지.. 서로 각자의 위치로 돌아간다음에도 잊지말고 자주 연락해요. (콩고물 얻어먹으려니까)

3) 환준.. 같은 일유생의 키즈나.. 인터에서 K반으로 넘어간 동료이자 산책 나카마... 뭐 우리는 일본에서 끈덕지게 볼것같으니 짧게 씀

4) 건우.. 건우햄 행동력 하나는 진짜 끝내줍니다.. 사실 저도 제 친구들 사이에서 미친행동력으로 비난과 감탄 둘다 받는데 형은 그 이상인 것 같아요.. F-k ng 트래블러 건우형. 저도 여행 좋아하니까 아프리카 정도 아니면 한번 같이 가는것도 좋을지도 ..?

5) 혜성.. 경선, 건우와 더불어 삼지문 -> 인터반의 동료.. 혜성님 힘들어 하시다가 저랑 경선이가 혜성님 웃게 만들었을때 상당히 성취감 있었습니다. 그리고 제가 생각하는 가장 빨리 졸업할 것 같은 맴버 3명중 한 분이십니다. 자신감 잃지마시고 토플 부수기 기원합니다.

6) 인터반 친구들
졸업하고 하느라 교실의 분위기도 많이 달라졌지만,, 다들 함께 할 수 있었기 때문에 토플이라는 거대한 압박 안에서 나름 즐겁게 보냈던것 같습니다.. 2월달에 인터반의 화목하고 재미난 분위기를 만들어두고 가신 하륜이형, 동훈이형도 너무 감사드리고,, 수업시간에 저랑 경선이가 어떻게보면 수업을 방해할 수도 있을 수준에 헛소리를 해도 다들 웃고 넘어가주셔서 감사합니다. 모두 목표한 바를 이루시길 기원합니다.

김유석 어셔졸업 일등공신 채운쌤:
처음에 상담할 시기부터 제 토플공부에 가장 크게 기여해주셨다는 점 알아주셨음 합니다 ㅋㅋㅋ
선생님만 믿고 다른생각 안한 덕에, 기대하지 않은 좋은 점수를 만들 수 있었던 것 같아요.. 비록 처음 반 배치가 완초 2반으로 떨어졌지만, 쌤 께서 2달안에 졸업하려면, 힘들더라도 인터반이 좋을수 있다고 조언해주신 덕에, 인터반에서 기분좋은 시작을 할 수 있었습니다. 그리고 또 가끔 제 기강이 해이해질 타이밍에 완벽히, 교실 전체에 기강 다져주신것도 큰 도움이 되었습니다 ㅋㅋㅋㅋㅋ
12간지야 뭐 말하는거 입아프구요.. 저는 선생님께서 단순히 '선생님'이라는 직책을 빼고도 '김채운'이라는 훌륭한 사람을 만난것에 대해 좋은 경험한 것 같습니다. 하지만 건강도 잘 챙기셔서 롱런하셨음 좋겠어요 ㅋㅋ 채운쌤 너무 감사합니다 !!

석균쌤:
가끔 편한길 찾고싶어서 쌤한테 시도할때마다 본전도 못찾고 깨진 기억들이 떠오르네요.. 덕분에 정신차리고 공부했습니다 쌤. ㅋㅋㅋ 어셔 한달 더 다니고 싶었던 가장 큰 이유가 바로 석균쌤의 수업이었는데,, 다행히도 금방 졸업을 했네요...
그리고 리딩 테마별로 지문 별 문제풀이 순서를 직접 고안하셨는지는 모르겠지만,, 테마별 리딩 문제풀이 순서가 너무 도움됐습니다.. 딱 우주에 대해 잊어먹었을 즈음에 복습시키고,, 슬슬 적응되던 테마에서 벗어나서 낯선거 풀게시키고.. 그 외에도 쌤께 고마운거 많지만 이만 줄이겠습니다. 쌤은 쿨하시니까요 ~

조교쌤들도 너무 감사했습니다 !! 특히 예림쌤, 유하쌤, 명준쌤,, 매번 해태할때마다 답답하셨을텐데,, 저였으면 좀 화났을수도 있엇을 것 같은데, 친절하게 질문받아주시고 너무 감사했습니다 !!!